Arab Politics,
Palestinian Nationalism and
the Six Day War

To my wife Rachel

Arab Politics, Palestinian Nationalism and the Six Day War

The Crystallization of Arab Strategy and Nasir's Descent to War, 1957–1967

Moshe Shemesh

sussex
ACADEMIC
PRESS

BRIGHTON • PORTLAND

2 4 6 8 10 9 7 5 3 1

First published 2008 in Great Britain by
SUSSEX ACADEMIC PRESS
PO Box 139
Eastbourne BN24 9BP

and in the United States of America by
SUSSEX ACADEMIC PRESS
920 NE 58th Ave   Suite 300
Portland, Oregon 97213-3786

British Library Cataloguing in Publication Data
A CIP catalogue record for this book is available from the British Library.

Library of Congress Cataloging-in-Publication Data
Shemesh, Moshe.
   Arab politics, Palestinian nationalism, and the Six Day War :
the crystallization of Arab strategy and Nasir's descent to war,
1957–1967 / Moshe Shemesh.
      p. cm.
   Includes bibliographical references and index.
   ISBN 978-1-84519-188-7 (h/c : alk. paper)
   1. Israel–Arab War, 1967. 2. Arab–Israeli conflict. 3. Palestine—
Politics and government—1948– 4. Arab countries—Politics and
government—1945– I. Title.

DS127.S485 2008
956.04′6—dc22
                                                          2007022751

Typeset and designed by SAP, Brighton & Eastbourne
Printed by TJ International, Padstow, Cornwall
This book is printed on acid-free paper.

Contents

Preface and Outline of the Book   viii
Acknowledgments   xix
List of Abbreviations   xx

CHAPTER 1
The Arab–Israeli Conflict Escalates, 1957–1963: A Turning Point   1
in the Arab States' Attitudes towards the Palestinian Problem
    The Egyptian Strategy   7
    Qasim's Strategy   13
    Jordan's Strategy   17
    The Syrian Ba'th Strategy   22

CHAPTER 2
Formulation of Arab Strategy in the Israeli–Arab Conflict,   27
1964–1965: Prelude to the Six Day War
    Part I   The Intensification of Arab Activity, 1959–1963   27
      The Arab–Israeli Struggle Over Water   32
    Part II   The Crystallization of Arab Strategy: Decisions of   41
    the First and Second Arab Summit Conferences, 1964

CHAPTER 3
Failure of the Arab Plan for Diverting the River Jordan's   49
Tributaries
    Partial Implementation of the Diversion Plan in Lebanon   51
    Syria's Dilemma in Implementing the Diversion Plan   55
    Conference of the Heads of Arab Delegations to the Mixed   58
      Armistice Commissions
    Failure of the Arab Strategy   67

CHAPTER 4
The Rise of the Palestinians as a Factor in the Arab–Israeli Conflict

                                                          70

    Part I   Establishment of the PLO – The Jerusalem Congress,
    May 1964   70
    The Egyptian Attitude   73

The Jordanian Stand   73
Syria's Antithesis   75
Fatah's Reaction   77
Palestinian Organizations' Alignment   77
Part II   Jordan's Confrontation with the PLO – National   78
Awakening in the West Bank
Shuqayri's Goals   79
The Jordanian Conception   81
The Confrontation   82
The Palestinians' National Awakening in the West Bank: In the   85
    Aftermath of the Samu' Raid
Conclusion: The Struggle for Control of the West Bank and   89
    the Fate of the Hashemite Regime

CHAPTER 5
The Fida'iyyun Organizations' Contribution to the Descent to   91
the Six Day War
The Emergence of Fatah   92
The Egyptian Position   94
The Change in Egypt's Policy toward Fida'iyyun Activity   99
Syria's Position
Jordan's Dilemma: Between an Israeli Invasion of the West Bank   106
    and the Campaign against Fatah
The Impact of the Samu' Raid on Jordan's Participation in the   116
    War: A Turning Point

CHAPTER 6
The Arab Military Build-Up   119
The Authority and Status of the UAC and its Commander   121
Continuing Discussions on the Dispatch of Arab Forces to Jordan   128
Egypt and the UNEF on the Israeli Border (1965–1966)   131
The Convening of the ADC in March 1967: Jordan is Again the   133
    Center of Discussion
The UAC's Contribution to the Build-up of the Arab Armies   135
The UAC at the Operational Level   142
The Failure to Establish a Northern Air Theater   146
The Arab (UAC) Position on Israel's Nuclear Project   147
Changes in Jordan's Position on the Eve of War   151
Conclusion: The Failure to Establish an Arab
    "Power Center"   153

CHAPTER 7
Nasir's Steps toward the Six Day War: May 13 to June 5, 1967   157
Assessing Israel's Intentions   157
Part I   Basic Factors in Syria's Estimation   159
Deep Fears of an Israeli Attack   159
The Soviet Factor   167

Contents

The Syrian Attempt to Drag Egypt into a Military Operation –   170
    The Cairo Agreement, November 4, 1966
The April 7, 1967 Incident and its Repercussions   172
The Formulation of Syria's May 12, 1967 Assessment   175
Part II   Nasir and the Arab World March toward War   177
Strengthening of the Egyptian Commitment to Syria After   177
    the April 7, 1967 Incident
In the Wake of Soviet and Syrian Warnings   180
The First Stage, May 15–17, 1967: Deterrence and the   183
    Evacuation of UN Forces
The Second Stage, May 18–22, 1967: The Egyptian Front and   188
    the Closing of the Straits
The Third Stage, May 23–28, 1967: Crystallization of the   197
    Second-Strike Strategy
The Fourth Stage, May 29–June 5, 1967: Waiting for the First Strike   213
Part III   The Arab Propaganda Campaign   226
Part IV   Conclusion and Evaluation   231

CHAPTER 8
In the Wake of the Six Day War   **241**
The Khartoum Summit, August 29–1 September, 1967: A New   241
    Arab Strategy

Conclusion: The Arab–Israeli Conflict between the *Nakba* and   **249**
the *Naksa* – The Emergence of the New Palestinian National
Movement

Appendixes: Fatah, Jordanian, Egyptian and Syrian Documents,   **265**
Letters and Operational Orders in Arabic

Notes   290
Bibliography   334
Index   340

Preface and Outline of the Book

The Six Day War was the climax in the deterioration of the Arab–Israeli conflict. The downturn started in 1957 when Nasir began preaching and promoting the idea of Arab nationalism, while placing the Palestinian problem, including the liberation of Filastin, at its center. The decade between the Sinai War and Six Day War was marked by preparations by the Arabs and Israelis for an all-out military confrontation, which both sides viewed as inevitable. During this period, as the Arab states formulated their positions on all aspects of the conflict's goals and the ways of attaining them, differences of opinion erupted between Egypt and Syria on their path to war.

Nasir aspired to determine the time and place for the war that would "liberate Filastin." He wanted to meet Israel on the battlefield only when he was ready, thereby being certain that the outcome would mean a decisive Arab victory. Until the crisis of May 13, 1967, neither side had determined nor predicted the timing of the war. But when the crisis erupted and the Egyptian army moved into Sinai, Nasir calculated his moves. Eventually, he allowed Israel to determine the date for the war, even though he foretold it with astonishing accuracy. This volume's re-examination of historical events leading to the 1967 War, is based almost exclusively on Arab primary sources, most of which were either not available or not used before, allows a number of conclusions to be reached that contribute to a better understanding of the Arab–Israeli conflict, and to the outbreak and results of the Six Day War.

1 The outcome of the Sinai War–Suez Campaign (October 1956) exacerbated the Arab–Israeli conflict that had developed after the 1948 War. The outcome runs counter to the accepted assessment – especially among Israeli statesmen and scholars – that the years after the Sinai War were tranquil. One scholar went so far as to state that "the struggle over the Baghdad Pact had pushed. . . the Filastin question . . . into the corner and reduced its importance, [while] the main discussion on the issue related to the refugee question and cross-border infiltration into Israel. Nor did the Suez War revive the Filastin problem – which remained dormant at least until 1959 when the issue of the Palestinian entity was raised within the framework of the rivalry between Iraq and Egypt and the establishment of the Fatah organization."[1] This book sets out to demonstrate that the importance of the Filastin problem did not diminish. On the contrary, it became the main issue in intra-Arab policy and pan-Arab policy for the Arab–Israeli conflict. Already in 1957 Nasir launched a campaign to promote the idea of Arab nationalism and the Palestinian problem, thus placing the latter at the center of discourse and political debate in the Arab world. In March 1959, the Egyptians raised the issue of reviving the Palestinian entity – the Palestinians' goal of statehood

– and Colonel Qasim responded to this initiative in December 1959. During the second Arab summit (September 1964) a long-range Arab strategy for destroying Israel was ratified for the first time. Among the factors in the worsening of the Arab–Israeli conflict were the deterioration in the security situation on Israel's borders because of the water struggle which began in 1959; the Arabs' response to Israel's opening of the National Water Carrier (NWC); Israel's military reaction to the Arab plan for diverting the river Jordan's tributaries; sabotage operations against Israel by Fatah and other fida'iyyun organizations beginning in January 1965; and as a result, increased hostilities on Israel's border with Syria and Jordan throughout most of the period. The border situation peaked twice: first on November 13, 1966 with the IDF raid on the Jordanian village of Samu', and again on April 7, 1967 with the Syrian border incident.

2 The Six Day War was the result of political–military processes that developed after the Sinai War and were part of the Arab–Israeli conflict in general, and the Palestinian problem in particular, and not because of factors or related events that began on May 13, 1967: the day the Syrians informed the Egyptians that IDF forces had allegedly concentrated on the Syrian border. The Syrian warning was merely the catalyst. Any attempt to explain Nasir's moves during the crisis after May 13 by other factors in the conflict, or by complementary political–military moves, is only a partial explanation. Thus, this study rejects the assessment that the war erupted because Nasir's recklessness and loss of control catapulted him toward a confrontation that neither he nor any other party in the conflict wanted. The main event that hastened confrontational processes in the prewar period was the convocation of the first Arab summit (January 1964) and its decisions. In this light, the water struggle may be seen as the key motivating factor. Nasir indeed planned for war. The problem, as he saw it, was one of timing.

3 Nasir consciously led Egypt and the Arab world to the Six Day War, carefully weighing the implications of each step from May 14, 1967 onward; nevertheless, he blundered. He estimated the chances of an outbreak of war at each stage of the crisis. He marched to war open-eyed, believing what Mushir (Field Marshal) Abd al-Hakim Amer, the deputy supreme commander of the Egyptian armed forces and in this capacity the commander of the Egyptian army, had promised him (Nasir), the Egyptian command, and the entire Arab world: near-certain victory over Israel. Not only was the Egyptian army capable of repulsing an Israeli attack, it would transfer war to the enemy's territory. It is unrealistic, therefore, to claim that Nasir embarked upon a war he did not want. The assertion that war erupted without either side wanting it is unwarranted [2] since both sides planned for confrontation and expected it.

4 From the start of the crisis, when Nasir decided to concentrate his forces in Sinai (May 14, 1967), he was prescient enough to realize that this move that was designed to deter Israel, completely nullified the role of the UN Emergency Force (UNEF). The UNEF's presence, according to Nasir's opponents, testified to Egypt's unwillingness to fight. Nasir therefore felt he had to oust the Force. His goal was to prove to Israel and the Arab world that he was ready for a military clash. A major conclusion is then that from the start of the crisis, Nasir's intention was to remove the UNEF from the Sinai border (including Sharm e-Sheikh and the Gaza Strip). Moreover, I believe that Nasir's march to the Six Day War was done consciously and rationally. Although he was impulsive and unpredictable when he moved against foreign opponents – including the West – he was also a clever and adamant statesman in his basic positions; he had previously demonstrated his masterly abilities as a tactician, practical and skilled in the art of maneuvering. The research presented in this book shows that Amer, who stood at the top of the military pyramid and directed military operations from the beginning of the crisis, bears the brunt of responsibility for the ensuing Egyptian military fiasco.

5 Between May 23 and 25, Nasir's strategic security perception underwent a momentous change. The cornerstone of his new strategy was the principle that Egypt had to absorb the first Israeli strike which would be followed by Egypt's delivery of a second, decisive strike. This revolutionary change in Nasir's assessment developed after the closure of the Straits of Tiran (May 22, 1967) and after he realized that a full war with Israel was inevitable. The question he faced was how to guarantee the greatest success and accomplishment in the approaching clash. On the one hand, he wanted to assure himself of international support – especially from the United States; on the other hand, he wanted to prevent Israel from reaping the same support. The adoption of the second-strike strategy stemmed from an exaggerated estimate of Egypt's military power and the belief that the Egyptian army could not only initiate a war but also absorb the first blow, incur the loss of 20 percent of its air force, and still emerge victorious by responding with a second strike. If Israel did not initiate hostilities, then Egypt was prepared to settle with the status quo, which it considered a great political achievement in itself.

The Egyptian high command determined, however, because of its political and military deployment after the closure of the straits to Israeli shipping, that although Egypt was ready for a full-scale clash with Israel, for strategic and international reasons it was preferable if Israel initiated the first attack. This was the first time, since the 1948 war, that an Arab country – and not by chance Egypt – had taken the initiative: namely, a preparedness to engage in a war with Israel. As a result, both Egypt's stature and Nasir's skyrocketed. Egypt had amassed nearly all the high cards in its hands, forcing Israel to face the toughest security-strategic challenge since the establishment of Israel.

6 The Arab commitment, in general, and Egypt's in particular, to the Palestinian problem – and especially the obligation to Palestinian self-determination – was thereby bolstered. Against the background of this obligation and its strengthening, it is possible to better understand the achievements of the New Palestinian National Movement – which had stepped onto the political stage in the early 1960s. Both the Egyptian and the Arab commitment to solving the Palestinian problem – that is, the Arab–Israeli conflict – is key to understanding the Arab position. Throughout this period, experts – including those in the Israeli establishment responsible for political–military assessments – failed to evaluate the degree of Nasir's and the Arab world's commitment to the Palestinians and to a solution to the Palestinian problem. Some experts referred to Nasir's declarations on the Palestinian question and the liberation of Filastin as mere "ritual" or "lip service" to the Palestinians. In hindsight, forty years later, nothing could be further from the truth.

What, then is the meaning of the term "commitment to the Palestinians and the Palestinian problem?" Nasir defined the term widely to encompass different circumstances: an action that employs all the means at his and the Arab world's disposal for the liberation of Filastin, the Palestinian people's self-determination, and the establishment of Palestinian national institutions, that is, the rise of a Palestinian state on Palestinian lands.

This study questions the view of Arab and western scholars – including Israelis – that the Arab states exploited the Palestinian issue in order to promote their interests in the Arab arena. These scholars tend to see Nasir's policy on the Palestinian question and the Palestinian entity as a "tool" or "means" to magnify his popularity in the Arab world and attain credibility for his strategy in relation to the Arab–Israeli conflict. Some scholars even claim that Nasir's approach is characterized by "cynicism." In his book *The Arab Cold War: Jamal Abd Al-Nasir and his Rivals* (1971), Malcolm Kerr claims that "the PLO was widely regarded, with considerable cynicism, as a device to enable the Arab governments to pass the responsibility of confronting Israel to the Palestinians and thereby avoid shouldering it themselves. The choice of Ahmad Shuqairi as leader of the PLO seemed to suggest an intention to ensure that the organization would remain ineffectual; for Shuqairi, an ageing Palestinian lawyer . . . enjoyed the reputation of an opportunist and charlatan."[3]

Avraham Sela writes in *The Decline of the Arab–Israeli Conflict* (1998), "The reason for the proposal (of establishing a Palestinian entity) was apparently the intensive criticism of his inaction on behalf of the Palestine cause by Arab adversaries, primarily Qasim." In Sela's opinion, "in hindsight, the Palestinian entity idea was Nasir's first step toward limiting his role in the liberation of Palestine . . .Thus, while Nasir paid lip service to the idea of the liberation of Palestine, he was in fact bent on full subordination of the PLO's military activity to the JAC (Joint Arab Command)." Or, "On the whole, Arab regimes – with varying degrees of cynicism – treated the PLO and its cause as pawns in their ongoing struggle for legitimacy and power, summit resolutions and Arab nationalist principles notwithstanding."[4]

Naji Alush, a Palestinian writer and scholar, in his book *al-Masira ila Filastin* (1964) opined: "The goal of the league's discussions on the Palestinian entity is more for political argument than for the benefit of Filastin." [5] In his work *al-'Amal al-'Arabi al-Mushtarak wa Isra'il* (1989), Faysal Hourani, another Palestinian writer and scholar, wrote: "The call to highlight the Palestinian entity [also] stems from the Arab states' desire to suppress the growing Palestinian will [for an independent entity], so as to enable the Arab states to oversee it before [it] slips between their fingers."[6]

7 The rise of the Palestinians as a key player in the Arab–Israeli conflict was an important factor in the deterioration of the conflict. After the Egyptian initiative to revive the Palestinian entity in March 1959, the Palestinian problem was presented in its widest possible context not as a humanitarian problem of refugees and their resettlement, but as a national problem of a people with nationalist aspirations and the right to their own representative institutions. Historically the establishment of the PLO in June 1964 was a milestone in the history of the Palestinian National Movement in general, and the future of Jordan in particular. Ahmad al-Shuqayri is credited with having made an important contribution to the New Palestinian National Movement – the founding of the PLO. Thus, a process began in which the Palestinians became the main party to the conflict, and the Palestinian problem – in its national-territorial sense – the heart of the Arab–Israeli conflict. The West Bank Palestinians went through an accelerated process of Palestinian national awakening whose outstanding expression culminated in the West Bank riots following the IDF's Samu' raid on November 13,

1966. This awakening forced the Jordanian leadership to consider granting some degree of autonomy to the West Bank inhabitants.

8 With the appearance of the fida'iyyun organizations – headed by Fatah – another historical turnabout occurred in the Palestinian problem and the elements of the Arab–Israeli conflict: the Palestinians themselves began to take an active role in the armed struggle against Israel. The conclusion drawn here is that the beginning of sabotage operations in January 1965 by the fida'iyyun organizations – headed by Fatah – contributed to the deterioration in the security situation on Israel's borders with Jordan and Syria, and led directly to the Six Day War. And this even though prior to the war, Palestinian active contribution to the struggle for the "liberation of Filastin" had not been appreciable. After the Samu' raid, which was carried out in retaliation to Fatah sabotage in Israel, Husayn realized that if war erupted, Israel would seize the West Bank whether or not Jordan joined in the hostilities.

9 The Arab summit in Khartoum (late August 1967) endorsed resolutions that were a turning-point on the Arabs' path to attempting to solve the Arab–Israeli conflict: a new Arab strategy was decided on following the outcome of the war. With the perspective of almost forty years and after closely studying the protocols of the debates, this book reappraises the influence and consequences of the Arabs' path to resolving the conflict. Without discarding the military option, the summit conference added "political process" to the modus operandi. The summit gave Nasir and Husayn the authority to hold political negotiations as a means of achieving the first stage of the Arab strategy, the "elimination of the traces of aggression", that is, getting Israel to withdraw to the lines of June 5, 1967. The protocols of these discussions reveal that Khartoum's three "nays" (no – to the recognition of Israel; no – to negotiations with Israel; and no – to peace with Israel) were not the product of Nasir's or any other Arab leader's demands, but of the head of the PLO, Shuqayri, who wanted to impede Husayn's search for a political solution to the West Bank issue. On Nasir's initiative and backing, the summit authorized Husayn to take any political step necessary to gain the return the West Bank and East Jerusalem to his kingdom (as long as he stayed within the bounds of Khartoum's three "nays"). Nasir's agreement to a political solution brought about his acceptance of Security Council Resolution 242 which, in his opinion, served as the basis for Israel's withdrawal from the territories captured in the war. Nevertheless, he felt that the UN resolution was insufficient to solve the Palestinian problem, that is, the "1948 problem." His decision made possible the Jarring mission – designed to realize the UN resolution – and American mediation whose high-point was the June 1970 initiative of William Rogers, the American secretary of state. Nasir's and the Arab summit's decision to adopt a political track undoubtedly paved the way for Sadat's political initiative in February 1971 and his peace initiative in 1977.

10 The enlistment of all the Arab states to Nasir's moves in May 1967 a few days after the outbreak of the crisis testifies not only to the president's charismatic leadership, but also to the depth of the 1948 defeat (*al-nakba*) trauma and the powerful urge to atone for it. This explains the extent to which the 1967 defeat (*al-naksa*) and the trauma of 1948 penetrated the Arab public's consciousness. In light of the Arabs' war fervor, the humiliation they suffered from Israel in the Six Day War became a personal blow to every individual and the antithesis of the glorious victories of the past that every Arab had been weaned on. Unsurprisingly, a new Salah al-Din was awaited after the war, and the expectation of an Arab victory was felt stronger than in the prewar period. In this light, it is possible to understand more clearly the historical importance of Sadat's strategic victory in the Yom Kippur War.

11 In retrospect, Israel's capture of the West Bank in the Six Day War seems to have saved Husayn's regime. Israeli occupation freed him of the turbulent Palestinian factor in his kingdom that had gone through a rapid process of *Palestinization* before the war, and was expressed in opposition to the Hashemite regime as demonstrated by the Palestinian *intifada* after the Samu' operation. If the West Bank had remained part of kingdom, then the Palestinians' heightened national awakening would have eventually endangered the Hashemite regime and continued the *Palestinization* of the kingdom with the aim of making Jordan a provisional "alternative homeland" for the Palestinians (*al-watan al-badil*).

The research method adopted in this book is historical discipline based on various types of documentation, most particularly Arab primary sources. Since the official Arab archives are closed to the general community of scholars, wide use has been made of official and non-official declassified material that is of great importance in the study of the Arab world. The available material, despite the extreme care needed in handling it, is a treasure chest for anyone wishing to follow and understand political and social processes in the Arab world.

Another valuable primary source has been a private collection of documents captured by the IDF in the Six Day War in the Jordanian, Egyptian, and Syrian theaters of operation. First and foremost are Jordanian administration, security, and intelligence files that were captured on the West Bank. The material sheds light on Jordan's policy in the conflict, in general, and on the Palestinian question and the PLO, in particular. The material furnishes the most solid proof of the national awakening among the Palestinians in the West Bank that, it turns out, took place earlier than the writer of these lines had assumed in his previous works.[7] The documentation also provides important information on Jordan's daily security policy on the Israeli border. It includes the protocols of meetings of the heads of the Arab delegations to the Armistice Commissions with Israel; and files from the Jordanian GHQ – Western Front (West Bank) which contain information on Jordanian army and intelligence operations and Jordanian security services' handling of Fatah in Jordan, including instructions and UAC orders for dealing with the organization. The private collection also includes Egyptian administration documents from the Gaza Strip and files from PLO offices in Gaza which contain, *inter alia*, protocols of the debates and decisions of the first, second, and third Palestinian National Congress; files connected with the status of Palestinian military units in the Egyptian army to whom they were subordinate; and instructions from the Egyptian administration on all aspects of daily security matters on the Israeli border. The documentation also includes Syrian army files from the Golan Heights which provide information on the deployment and activity of the Syrian army up to the eve of the Six Day War.

Regarding the position of the Syrian and Iraqi Ba'th parties on the conflict in general and the Palestinian problem in particular, we should note two series of books that were published by the Ba'th party: the *Nidal Hizb al-Ba'th* series and the *al-Ba'th Waqadiyat Filastin* series. Both provide details on the discussions of the Ba'th party's regional and national congresses in Syria and Iraq, the party's branch in Lebanon and their decisions, and the party's official announcements and internal publications, including secret ones. In addition to this material, of course, are Syrian newspaper publications and the Ba'th organ in Lebanon *al-Sahafa*.

The source of information on the fida'iyyun organizations – first and foremost the Fatah organization – and their positions and operations was the official and internal publications that circulated among members of the fida'iyyun organizations, including Fatah. This included the Fatah organ – the monthly *Filastinuna* – that was published in Beirut between 1959 and 1965.

The memoirs of leading figures in the Arab politics in the period being discussed were also a valuable research aid. These included the works of King Husayn; Ahmad al-Shuqayri (four volumes); Abd al-Latif al-Baghdadi (vice president of Egypt); Anwar al-Sadat; Mahmud Riyad (an advisor to Nasir and Egyptian foreign minister); Muhammad Hasanayn Haykal (an advisor to and close associate of Nasir and editor of the newspaper *al-Ahram*) who was well known for his weekly articles entitled *Bisraha*; Abd al-Ghani al-Jamasi (the Egyptian chief-of-staff); Muhammad Fawzi (the Egyptian chief-of-staff and minister of war); and Sayid Mar'i (deputy prime minister of Egypt). In addition there are the important works of Amin Huwaydi (an advisor to Nasir, minister of war, and head of Egypt's general intelligence services) on "Nasir's wars" and Egyptian policy before and after the Six Day War; the memoirs of Jozef Abu Khatir (the Lebanese ambassador to Cairo); Shafiq al-Hut (PLO representative in Beirut and editor of the Lebanese weekly *al-Hawadith*, and a leader of the Arab Nationalists); Salah Khalaf (Abu Iyyad – one of the founders and leaders of Fatah); Dr. Gerorge Habash (a founder of the Arab Nationalists Movement and the leader of the Popular Front for the Liberation of Filastin); Nayif Hawatma (the leader and founder of the Democratic Front for the Liberation of Palestine); and the collections of speeches of Nasir, Sadat, and King Husayn.

Other primary sources were the secret and published decisions from Arab forums such as the first, second, and third Arab summit conferences; the discussions, debates and decisions of the Arab League's institutions: The Arab chiefs-of-staff conferences; the Arab Defense Council; the Arab League Council and its Political Committee. Mention should be made, naturally, to nearly all of the minutes and decisions of the Khartoum summit (August–September 1967); the internal debates of Egypt's ruling party prior to and after the Six Day War as they appear in the works of Ahmad al-Shuqayri, Shafiq al-Hut, and Abd al-Majid Farid (Nasir's political advisor and the Egyptian minister of presidential affairs); sections from inter-Arab discussions in the memoirs of King Husayn and Jordanian Prime Minister Sa'ad Jum'a and Dr. Haytham al-Kaylani's book.

The Arab press has also been an important source in this study. Despite the benefits of this material, its use requires special caution and awareness of the political tendencies, financial sources, and political elements behind each newspaper. Nearly all of the papers in Arab countries have been used in this study: Egyptian, Jordanian, Syrian, Iraqi, Saudi, and especially Lebanese papers that regularly publish reports of internal Arab discussions based on reliable sources. Another source is material intentionally leaked by Arab states, including the pro-Egyptian Lebanese press that reflects Egypt's positions. Press reports also contain commentaries and editorials that cast light on the important events. For example, Hasanayn Haykal's articles in *al-Aharam* and his books elucidate Egyptian policy and its motivations, as well as occasionally detailing the Arab position. Haykal's weekly articles, which he claimed were written after talks with Nasir, reliably express Nasir's positions. We should also note the Arabic radio broadcasts from Arab states that recorded the speeches and declarations of Arab leaders, and the decisions of Arab meetings and conferences, and the regular reportage of events in the Arab world. Like the press, the radio commentaries generally reflect the official position of a particular state, and contribute to an understanding of that state's policy in the Arab arena or toward Israel. In this context, the author attributes great importance to the spoken and written word of Arab leaders, especially the central figures, or those who spoke or wrote in their name. This is particularly true of spoken statements or decisions made in closed Arab forums. I felt it essential to provide the reader with the details of secret decisions made in Arab forums attended by Arab leaders. In order to illustrate this, I have included in the Appendix documents in the original Arabic (the English wording or synopsis of the material appears in the text or notes).

I have also used academic studies on the Arab–Israeli conflict and Palestinian problem – especially material written by Arabs (including Palestinians) in Arabic; and professional monthlies and quarterlies published in Arabic, English, and Hebrew, including material published by Arab and Palestinian research institutes, such as the PLO Research Center. Of special importance has been the monthly *Shuun Filastiniya* that was published by the PLO Research Center.

The picture that finally comes into focus from the vast amount of material on decision-making, the crystallization of general Arab policy, the policymaking and considerations of each individual state, and the survey of main events and changes in the Arab states involved in the conflict – including the Six Day War – is, in my opinion, generally reliable.

Outline of the Book

Chapter 1 – The Arab–Israeli Conflict Escalates, 1957–1963: A Turning Point in the Arab States' Attitudes towards the Palestinian Problem – surveys the factors that aggravated the conflict after the Sinai War and Suez Campaign when Nasir became the undisputed leader of Egypt and the Arab world. In early 1957 Nasir began promoting Arab nationalism in whose center was the Arab–Israeli conflict and whose stated objective was the liberation of Filastin. He strove to inculcate the Palestinian problem into the Arab public's conscious. The Arab response to Israel's plan for a national water carrier (NWC) for conveying water from the Sea of Galilee to the Negev contributed to the exacerbation of the conflict and launched the Arab–Israeli struggle over water sources. In late 1959 the Egyptian leadership estimated that 1963 would be the year of decision – when Israel completed its water plan. The chapter also deals with the Arabs' military strengthening – especially Egypt's – and the start of the Egyptian initiative that led to the Palestinians becoming a central player in the conflict through the revival of the Palestinian entity and establishment of Palestinian representative institutions. Egypt's strategy in the Arab–Israeli conflict and Colonel Qasim's concept that centered on the establishment of an "Eternal Filastin Republic," and Jordan's opposition to the idea of reviving the Palestinian entity, are also addressed. Chapter 1 concludes with a summary of the Syrian Ba'th party's strategy.

The first part of Chapter 2 – Formulating the Arab Strategy in the Arab–Israeli Conflict 1964–1965: Prelude to the Six Day War – discusses the increase of Arab activity between 1959 and 1963 on two issues that contributed to a deterioration in the Arab–Israeli conflict: the first issue was the proposal to revive the Palestinian entity and solve the Palestinian problem; the second was the Arab–Israeli water struggle. The second part of the chapter inquires into the formulation of Arab strategy during the first and second summit conferences (January and September 1964 respectively). Nasir called the first summit conference because his strategy of 1959 had been stuck in a dead-lock over a solution to Israel's opening of the NWC. The first summit's decisions discussed three areas: the diversion of the Jordan's tributaries; the creation of a United Arab Command for defending Arab diversion operations and preparing the Arab armies for a confrontation with Israel; and assigning Ahmad al-Shuqayri the role of organizing the Palestinian people, a decision that paved the way for his founding of the PLO. The second summit decided on a two-stage program for implementing Arab strategy in the conflict: in the short term – strengthening Arab defense in order to provide the Arab states with freedom of action; the second stage – the long–term – called for the "liberation of Filastin from Zionist imperialism" and handing the United Arab Command the task of preparing a plan for the destruction of Israel.

Chapter 3 – The Failure of the Arab Plan for Diverting the River Jordan's Tributaries – reviews the Arab plan for diverting the Jordan's tributaries in Lebanon, Syria, and Jordan after the second Arab summit had given the green light for beginning diversion operations. Syria was the first Arab state to begin implementing the plan on its soil in November 1964. The plan went "bankrupt" after a few months mainly because of the IDF's immediate military response which caused extensive damage to the operations and nearly shut them down. In the third summit meeting (September 1965), the Arab states came to the conclusion that Israel was determined to halt the implementation of the Arabs' water plan even if it meant using air force and embarking on an all-out war that the Arab states and Egypt in particular were not ready for. My research draws the conclusion that all aspects of the Arabs' water struggle against Israel – political, technical, and military – contributed to the exacerbation of the Arab–Israeli conflict and was the main factor in the Arab world's descent, especially Egypt's, to the Six Day War. The Arabs states' frustration over the failure of their water plan only strengthened their determination to free themselves from the trauma of the 1948 *nakba* by a comprehensive solution to the conflict by use of force. The only remaining question was one of timing.

The first part of Chapter 4 – The Rise of the Palestinians as a Factor in the Arab–Israeli Conflict – looks at Shuqayri's convening of the first Palestinian National Congress (PNC May 1964) in East Jerusalem. At the end of the meeting, the establishment of the Palestinian Liberation Organization (PLO) was announced. The composition of the Palestinian National Congress and Shuqayri's considerations in determining its make-up are discussed, as well as Egypt's positions on the PLO, the Syrian position (which was cool toward the establishment of the organization and its leadership), and the Fatah's and other Palestinian organizations' view of the PLO. Special emphasis is placed on King Husayn's reasons for agreeing to the convening of the Palestinian National Congress in Jerusalem and the establishment of the PLO. The second part of the chapter examines the tense relations between Jordan and the PLO in view of the fact that the establishment of the organization was an historical turning-point in Jordan's relations with the Palestinians. This study concludes that due to the large gap between Husayn and Shuqayri on PLO activity inside Jordan and the organization's goals, and the distrust between the two men, every potential agreement became a case of "mission impossible." The clash between Jordan and the PLO erupted in mid-1966, and worsened until the outbreak of the Six Day War. The creation of the PLO, the rise of Fatah, Arab activity over the revival of the Palestinian entity, and the struggle between Husayn and Shuqayri – all these factors strengthened the awareness of Palestinian identity among the West Bank's inhabitants and led to a renewal of the Palestinian nationalist awakening. This nationalist awakening was an important element in the ascent of the Palestinians as a major player in the Arab–Israeli conflict. This was conspicuous following the IDF's Samu' operation. The result was that for the first time the Jordanian leadership appraised the degree of autonomy to be given to the inhabitants of the West Bank.

Chapter 5 – The Fida'iyyun Organizations' Contribution to the Descent to the Six Day War – observes the sabotage activities carried out by the fida'iyyun organizations and especially Fatah's role in the deterioration of border security leading to the Six Day War. The focus is on the following areas: the continuation of sabotage operations despite Israel's warnings that Arab states on whose soil fida'iyyun activity was permitted would be held responsible; Syria as the home base for the fida'iyyun organizations, especially Fatah, and its full backing of them which included a logistical base, training camps, equipment and weapons; IDF retaliatory acts that forced the Jordanians, Syrians, and Egyptians to realize that Israel intended to seize the West Bank and topple the Ba'th regime in Damascus; and the change beginning in mid-1966 in the Egyptian and PLO position on support of fida'iyyun activity. The increasing border tension, because of sabotage activity against Israel, reached its climax in the IDF raid on the village of Samu' after saboteurs coming from Syria via Jordan struck in the Arad region. The Israeli raid sparked riots in the West Bank that lasted several weeks. The Jordanian leadership's analysis of the background and results of the operation was a decisive factor in Jordan's entry into the Six Day War in conjunction with Nasir. Jordan estimated that Israel planned to conquer the West Bank whether or not Jordan joined Nasir's war initiative.

Chapter 6 – The Arab Military Build-Up – examines the functioning of the United Arab Command (UAC) that was established by the first summit. On the one hand, the UAC accomplished matters at the staff level, including the preparation of a comprehensive Arab defense plan; on the other hand, the UAC demonstrated failure on the operational–logistical level, failing to transform into an authoritative GHQ that could move forces or take command of local units. This failure was also the result of mutual distrust among the Arab countries. The UAC's main contribution was to strengthen the Arab armies – including those of the confrontation states with Israel. The chapter surveys this plan and its implementation, and also discusses Egypt's position on the UNEF issue prior to the war and the Arab position on Israel's nuclear research. The Arab states entered the war lacking basic military coordination among them. Military coordination between Egypt and Syria was also weak. Thus, in the end Nasir failed to achieve the main element of his conflict strategy – the creation of an Arab power center capable of meeting Israel on the battlefield.

Chapter 7 – Nasir's Steps toward the Six Day War – May 13 to June 5, 1967 – analyzes the political and military developments between the start of the crisis on May 13, 1967, which began with the Syrian warning to the Egyptians based on information supplied by the Soviet Union that the IDF had allegedly concentrated its forces on the Syrian border with the intention of attacking within two weeks. At the same time, Egypt received similar information from the Soviet Union. In line with its commitment to Syria and in order to deter Israel from attacking, the Egyptian leadership decided that it would openly deploy Egyptian forces in Sinai beginning on May 15. As the military flow into Sinai increased, the gravity of the crisis transferred from the Syrian border to the Egyptian border within a few days. On May 16, in order to prove it "meant business," Egypt asked the UN forces to evacuate the border – including Sharm al-Sheikh. On May 22, after Egyptian forces took control of Sharm al-Sheikh, Nasir declared the closure of the Straits of Tiran to Israeli vessels sailing to and from Eilat. It was clear to both Nasir and Israel that war was inevitable. The question was who would fire the first shot. The Arab world was elated over the long-awaited Arab military victory over Israel that Nasir and other Arab leaders were promising. Based on Amer's and Egyptian general staff's estimate that the Egyptian army was capable not only of repelling an Israeli attack but of carrying the war onto Israel's soil, and given Egypt's political achievements, Nasir decided to forfeit the offensive initiative and opt for the second-strike strategy if Israel initiated the first strike. On June 2 he predicted that Israel would open the war with an air attack within three days at the most. Chapter 7 concludes with a conclusion and evaluation of Nasir's moves from the start of the crisis to the outbreak of war.

Chapter 8 – In the Wake of the Six Day War – relates how, despite the defeat, Nasir managed to preserve his leadership position in the Arab world and dictate a new Arab strategy to the Khartoum summit (August–September 1967) for solving the conflict in two stages. The first stage would be "the eradication of the results of aggression," that is, Israel's withdrawal from the occupied territories to the June 5, 1967 borders. The second stage called for "safeguarding the rights of the Palestinian people on their land," that is, solving the 1948 problem. It was the first time that Arab leaders agreed on a political action designed to achieve the first stage. Husayn appeared at the summit and was greeted as a national hero. Shuqayri's status, however, reached its nadir. The Palestinians and the Arab states regarded the fida'iyyun organizations as the leaders of the New Palestinian National Movement, and would eventually see them as the main party in the conflict. With the rise of the fida'iyyun organizations and the bitter criticism directed against him, it became clear to Shuqayri that he had lost Nasir's support (after Nasir had shifted his bets to the new fida'iyyun organizations), and he resigned on December 24, 1967. In light of these events, a new era opened in the history of the Palestinian problem and the Arab–Israeli conflict in general.

Acknowledgments

I would like to thank the Ben-Gurion Research Institute for the Study of Israel and Zionism at Sede-Boker, Ben-Gurion University of the Negev, and its Director Professor Yehuda Gradus. The Institute has been my "home" for research and writing.

Special thanks to Professors Avi Shlaim of St. Antony's College, Oxford and Yezid Sayigh of King's College, London, for their valuable comments on the manscript; also to Professor Carl Brown of Princeton University for his remarks on chapter 7.

I am most grateful to the Chaim Herzog Center for Middle East Studies & Diplomacy, Ben-Gurion University of the Negev and its former Director Dr. Nimrod Hurvitz for the generous financial assistance and to Aryeh Shur, former Vice-President of Ben-Gurion University of the Negev. Special thanks to Dr. Natan Aridan.

I am indebted to the Israel Science Foundation, The Israel Academy of Sciences and Humanities, for the financial assistance bestowed to my project *The Palestinian National Re-awakening, 1949–1965*, some of its conclusions are encompassed in this study. My thanks also to Yad Ben-Gurion.

The collegial atmosphere afforded me at the Department of Near Eastern Studies, Princeton University during my sojourn as a Visiting Fellow provided me with the opportunity to crystallize and complete chapter 7.

My thanks to the staffs of the Israel Defense Forces Archives, the Israel State Archives, Jerusalem, and the the Ben-Gurion Archives Sede Boker, Israel (especially to Hana Pinshow), for their professional guidance.

I would like to thank Anthony Grahame, Editorial Director at Sussex Academic Press, for his editorial work and his staff for their work in producing this book. I also thank Moshe Tlamim for his translation work and Inna Osadchy for preparing the index. Thanks go also to my graphic artist Sefi Sinay.

MOSHE SHEMESH
June 2007

Abbreviations

ADC	Arab Defense Council (Joint Arab Defense Council)
AL	Arab League
ALC	Arab League Council
ANM	Arab Nationalists Movement
ASC	Arab Science Council
CAPM	Conference of Arab Prime Ministers (mini summit)
CENTO	Central Treaty Organization
EC	Executive Committee (PLO EC)
EGD	Egyptian Government Documents
FO	Foreign Office
FRUS	Foreign Relations of the United States
GHQ	General Headquaters
GD	Gaza (PLO offices) Documents
IAF	Israeli Air Force
IDF	Israel Defense Forces
JAA	Jordanian Arab Army
JAC	Joint Arab Command
JACARPP	Joint Arab Council for Atomic Research for Peaceful Purposes
JASCUAPP	Joint Arab Science Council for the Use of the Atom for Peaceful Purposes
JADC (JDC)	Joint Arab Defense Council, Arab Defense Council
JGD	Jordanian Government Documents
MAC	Mixed Armistice Commission
MER	Middle East Record
MP	Member of Parliament (Jordan)
NC	National Congress
NWC	National Water Carrier
NYT	*New York Times*
PA	Palestinian Army
PEC	Palestine Experts Committee
PLA	Palestinian Liberation Army
PLO	Palestinian Liberation Organization
PNC	Palestinian National Congress
PNU	Palestinian National Union
PRO	Public Record Office
SGD	Syrian Government Documents

UAC	United Arab Command
UAR	United Arab Republic
UNEF	United Nations Emergency Force
UNRWA	United Nations Relief and Works Agency
UNSC	United Nations Security Council

The Arab–Israeli Conflict Escalates, 1957–1963

A Turning Point in the Arab States' Attitude toward the Palestinian Problem

A new period began in both the Middle East and the Arab–Israeli conflict following the Sinai War and Suez Campaign in October–November 1956. The political victory of Jamal Abd al-Nasir in the wake of the Suez–Sinai War was apparent to all the Arabs, and there is no better proof than the facts themselves: the evacuation of the British and French forces by December 23, 1956 without achieving any tangible result, the resignation of Eden (and Guy Mollet), and the withdrawal of the IDF from Sinai and the Gaza Strip with conditions not affecting the sovereignty of Egypt. For Nasir the crisis was a test of the legitimacy of his leadership and his decision to nationalize the Suez Canal Company.

Nasir emerged from the crisis as the charismatic leader of Egypt and the Arab world. He subsequently decided to exploit his political success to make a sweeping turn to the Arab domain in order to establish his position as the leader of the Arab World after having emerged as the undisputed leader of Egypt. He captured the Arab world politically by instilling the notion of the Arab nationalism (*al-qawmiya al-'Arabiya*), which became the main pillar of Arab politics in this period and thereafter. His idea of Arab nationalism appeared on several occasions in his speeches in 1955 but without any explanation of its significance. In his speech of November 7, 1956, he initiated his drive for this idea.[1]

The years 1957–1961 were the glorious period of Arab nationalism, whose peak was the unification between Syria and Egypt in February 1958 (The United Arab Republic – UAR). The tenets of Nasir's Arab nationalism were the essence of Nasirism. Nasir preached a militant and active Arab nationalism, using all means, including force, to achieve its goals. He believed that in so doing he, more than any other Arab leader of his time, expressed the aspirations of the Arab nation. Nasir defined a number of aims of Arab nationalism: the political, social and economic liberation of the Arab world, and the elimination of imperialism and Arab reactionarism. Arab nationalism was designed to fill the vacuum that had been created in the Arab world following the demise of Western influence. It would be a powerful weapon for guaranteeing the security of the Arab world. Arab nationalism meant Arab solidarity (later he added "Arab unity") based on the Arab states' independence. As time passed he added further content such as "positive neutrality," "non-alignment," "social justice," and "true democratic life." In one of his speeches he defined Arab nationalism as a "spiritual movement" and "historic movement" (without clarifying the meaning of these terms).[2] He threatened to use military force to defend Arab nationalism, and he carried out this threat in Yemen between 1962 and 1967. Nasir divided the Arab world into allies and enemies, nationalists and agents of imperialism, and progressives and reactionaries. On this basis he undermined regimes that refused to take up the banner of his path. The dissolution of the Egyptian–Syrian unity in September 1961 symbolized the beginning of the decline of Arab nationalism à la Nasirism. A serious blow to Nasirism was the Arabs' military defeat in June 1967. But prior to this, at the pinnacle of Nasir's glory in October 1960, the Egyptian daily *al-Ahram* wrote about Arab nationalism and its realization:

> Arab nationalism is spreading day by day among the Arab masses in a vast area stretching from the Atlantic Ocean to the Persian Gulf. Every Arab feels this nationalism and believes himself a member of the Arab nation . . . Arabs have started moving from the stage of believing in the idea of Arab nationalism to the stage of acting toward the realization of nationalistic goals. Many obstacles stood in the way of the dissemination of this idea. Many elements fought against it, but failed. The vast majority of Arabs believe in the idea of Arab nationalism, and perceive that Arab unity is beneficial and conducive to building Arab strength, and therefore they [the Arabs] must unite. Every Arab state naturally tries to convince Arab public opinion of the need to realize this idea.[3]

During this period Nasir was the acknowledged leader of the Arab world, as "Arab nationalism marches from victory to victory."[4] "Arab public opinion outside the UAR, and especially in the Arab East (*mashriq*), was enthralled by Nasir and the unity that he symbolized. This reality did not change even after the breakup of the UAR."[5] Facing the stability of the Egyptian regime was the unrest and instability in the Arab world. Political events in the Arab world and Arab states – such as Iraq, Syria, and Jordan – revolved around, or resulted from, Nasir's decisions and moves in the Arab arena even during the "low tide" of his leadership after the UAR's disintegration.

However, in the period being discussed, unprecedentedly acute inter-Arab conflicts erupted in the Arab world – the worst it had experienced since the founding of the Arab League in 1945. One cannot describe the Arab world in this period as one engaged in a "cold war"[6] since armed conflicts between Arab states were being fought with the most massive military involvement the Arab world had known in the twentieth century. Seventy thousand Egyptian troops took part in a five-year war in Yemen. The period also witnessed violent political intrigues in attempts to bring down regimes, assassinate leaders, and wage extremely venomous propaganda war.

Against this background, opposing trends emerged in the Arab world. On the one hand, this period was the culmination of the realization of the Arab nationalist vision – the unification of Egypt and Syria (February 1958) and establishment of the UAR; at the same time it was also the nadir – the dissolution of the UAR (September 1961), which created the "crisis of unity" and "unity trauma" that put the lid on the chances for realizing unification for many years. Both of these historical events exacerbated the conflict between the concept of pan-Arab nationalism (*qawmiya*) and that of regionalism (*wataniya, iqlimiya*). Both created a polarity in the Arab nationalist view between the Nasir-led "national revolutionary" trend and the "moderate" trend (then led by Abd al-Karim Qasim – the leader of Iraq's July 1958 revolution) that favored a federated unification (*itihad*) of Arab states that would preserve their sovereignty and independence. In the middle stood a third group of Arab states, mostly kingdoms struggling for their territorial integrity; they vacillated between the two concepts of Arab nationalism – either crossing swords with them or coexisting with them.

The disputes over Arab nationalism and the threat of communism in Syria (then united with Egypt in the UAR), especially after the strengthening of communist activity there, forced Nasir, in the first half of 1959, to launch an open ideological attack against communism, which he utterly rejected, and the internal regime in the Soviet Union, his sometime friend. Communism in the Arab countries, specially in Iraq and Syria, was portrayed as a betrayal of Arab nationalism and a heresy against Islam whose proponents were considered agents of Moscow and imperialism, and as Zionist collaborators who wanted to destroy Arab nationalism. On the other hand, emphasis was stressed on Arab nationalism's special social message, as expounded by Nasir. Eventually the Soviet Union managed to come to terms with Nasir in order to halt the erosion of the position it had gained in the Arab states and to restrain Egypt from resuming its ties with the West. This brief period of ideological struggle gave the "moderate" Arab states a breathing spell since it enabled them to enjoy a greater degree of maneuverability in both their inter-Arab and foreign relations.

In April 1963, during talks on the Egyptian–Syrian–Iraqi tripartite unification, Nasir described the political trends in the Arab world:

> The struggle now being waged in the Arab homeland is a struggle between two trends: the nationalist trend and non-nationalist trend. The first comprises all of the true progressive nationalist forces, while the second [comprises] the enemies of Arab nationalism and unification, including pan-Arabism's deniers, reactionaries, sectarians, and imperialists, with Israel and capitalism linked to reactionarism and imperialism. The struggle between the two trends is cruel and far from simple, since this is a fateful struggle.[7]

Despite his leadership and overwhelming influence in the Arab world, Nasir failed to implement part of his policy in the Arab arena: The realization of Arab unity, the overthrow of Qasim's and Husayn's regimes, and undermining of the Syrian regime that came to power after the break-up of the UAR. The two Ba'th revolutions – Iraq (February 1963) and Syria (March 1963) – surprised Egypt. The tripartite Egyptian–Syrian–Iraqi unification that was signed on April 17, 1963 lasted merely two weeks, dissolving before the ink was dry. Nasir declared it officially null and void in July 1963. In the wake of these setbacks, the Egyptian policy underwent a change. After the Sinai War, Egypt had favored a policy based on "unity of the ranks" (*wahdat al-saff*); after the disbandment of the UAR (September 1961), the slogan "unity of aim" (*wahdat al-hadaf*) was heard; and when he called for an Arab summit conference (December 23, 1963) the catch phrase "unity of action" (*wahdat al-'amal*) was coined.[8]

The second result of Nasir's political victory after the Sinai war and Suez campaign, and following his drive for Arab nationalism, was a serious deterioration in the

Arab–Israeli conflict; or as the Arab states termed it – the "problem of Filastin"; or as it was popularly referred to at the time, the "1948 problem." Although quiet seemed to prevail on Israel's borders, in reality only the Egyptian border was quiet (while the Jordanian and especially the Syrian borders were not). It was in this period that Nasir elevated the "problem of Filastin" or "liberation of Filastin" to the forefront of the agenda in the Arab world. He laid out his position on the solution to the Arab–Israeli conflict. It would entail: the implementation of the UN Assembly resolutions on the Palestinian issue, including the November 1947 (181) Partition Plan, the refugees' right to return to their homes, and compensation for property damages to those who preferred not to return (UN Assembly Resolution 194, December 11, 1948). He claimed that, "the pan-Arab national obligation (*qawmiya*) to achieve these goals is [the responsibility] of the UAR," and that "the rights of the Palestinian people are Arab rights before they are Palestinian rights . . . Peace will not come to the region as long as the rights of the Palestinian people are ignored."[9]

The escalation in the conflict was expressed in the following ways:

1 Nasir made a concentrated effort to cement the Palestinian problem into the Arab consciousness. He regarded the problem as an integral part of his Arab nationalist outlook. The struggle against Zionism, as he saw it, was the second of Arab nationalism's objectives, along with the war against imperialism. He stressed that the call for Arab nationalism meant the Arab nation's non-recognition of Israel's existence. He tried to imbue in the Arabs an awareness that Israel's existence and its expansionist ambitions from the Nile to the Euphrates were, in his opinion, a threat to Arab nationalism. After the Sinai War he began speaking more passionately about the "liberation of Filastin," impressing upon his listeners that his views on this issue expressed the heart-felt feelings of Arabs everywhere. He claimed that the liberation of Filastin was the goal behind all of his conduct in Egypt and in the Arab arena, including Egypt's involvement in Yemen. He once stated: "After the 1956 aggression, the Arabs' position on Arab rights in Filastin was the major driving force in the events taking place in the Arab East . . . From our point of view Israel is a basic problem, it is a question of life or death . . . It is a cancer in the body of the Arab people."[10] In this way Nasir gave the Palestinian problem a new political dimension.

2 The conflict was exacerbated by the Arab response to Israel's project to establish the National Water Carrier (NWC) (a major excavation/construction project designed to carry water from the north of Israel to the south) and to Israeli leaders' declarations of determination to carry out the project. From September 1959 until the Six Day War the Arab struggle against Israel's plan to build the NWC and utilize the water of the Jordan River became the main issue in Arab political discourse, in inter-Arab forums, and in the Arab media. Arab debates revolved around the question of how to tackle the challenge. Thus the "water struggle" led to a heightening of the conflict that culminated in the Six Day War. It catalyzed discussion in all aspects of the Arab–Israeli conflict, following which the Arabs determined for the first time their long-range strategic goal and prepared a military plan for annihilating Israel. The entire Arab world regarded the question of the Jordan's water as a key factor in the Palestinian problem, the Arab–Israeli conflict, and the Arab struggle against Israel's very existence. In other words, the way that the problem should be resolved became an integral part of the Arab, Egyptian or Syrian, strategy. Just as Egypt's position determined Arab strategy in the conflict with Israel, it also determined the way to deal with Israel's plan to build the NWC. And just as the Syrian position was the antithesis of the Egyptian's, so too on the water issue. Egypt's dilemma was highlighted during the Egyptian–Syrian union when Nasir became responsible for what took place on Syria's border with Israel.

In late 1959 and early 1960 the UAR leadership estimated that 1963 would be the year of decision in the Arab–Israeli conflict – after Israel completed its project to divert the Jordan's water. The UAR (Egypt) believed that it was in its vital interests to thwart the diversion project lest Israel increase its strength and jeopardize the future of the Palestinian problem.[11] The way to block Israel became an inter-Arab problem since blocking Israel was liable to entangle the Arab world in a war. The Arab states began to compete over the best way to meet the Israeli "threat." A sharp and all-encompassing propaganda struggle ensued where the image of the Arab leaders in Arab public opinion played an important but disturbing part. Each Arab state tried to prove to the masses that it championed the more radical line on the way the struggle against Israel should be waged. It sometimes seemed that radicalism towards Israel became more of a weapon in inter-Arab rivalry than against the Zionist state.

3 The Arabs' military strengthening (or the arms race between the Arab states and Israel) paved the way for the next military confrontation. Arab military preparations for the next war – which, according to assessments of the Arab states, especially Egypt's, was unavoidable – began already in 1957 and peaked between 1964 and 1967 with the fulfillment of the rearmament plan that the Joint Arab Command (hereafter: JAC) had approved. (The United Arab Command – UAC – was established by the First Arab Summit Conference in January 1964.) For Egypt, 1957 was a year of transition in the development of its military forces, when the army began to undergo a vigorous reorganization according to the Soviet doctrine of warfare. This process was completed in 1960. Three stages are discernible in the process up to 1967:

(A) The reorganization stage (1957–1961) saw the Egyptian army adopt Soviet structural and organizational patterns. The main formations of the land forces in 1961 included: two infantry divisions and two independent infantry brigades; an armored division; a paratroop brigade along with two or three commando battalions; a GHQ artillery brigade; total: approximately five hundred tanks.

(B) The first stage of military strengthening (up to 1965) took place when Egypt was involved in military operations in Yemen, after which the build-up was speeded up.

(C) The second stage in the build-up (up to the Six Day War) basically involved qualitative strengthening through the absorption of new and improved weapons.

Nasir publicly heralded the new build-up program in a speech at Port Sa'id on December 23, 1961, after the dissolution of the UAR. He announced that the addition of two infantry divisions and another armored division would double Egypt's military strength. Indeed, in early May 1967 Egyptian land forces numbered four infantry divisions and eight independent brigades; an armored division, corps headquarters, and four independent armor brigades; a paratroop brigade, ten commando battalions, and six GHQ artillery brigades. Altogether the army had one thousand serviceable tanks. Thus, when the Six Day War broke out, Egyptian land forces were going through an intense military build-up that had begun in 1965.[12]

4 A process began in which the Palestinians would become a party to the

5

Arab–Israeli conflict through the revival of the Palestinian entity. The Egyptian initiative in March 1959 regarding the revival of the Palestinian entity was the direct result of Nasir's intense preoccupation in the Palestinian problem. This initiative triggered a process in which the Palestinian problem was presented in its widest sense not as a humanitarian problem of refugees and their settlement but as a political problem of a people with nationalist aspirations that was entitled to representative institutions. In June 1964, in the wake of the Egyptian initiative and inter-Arab discussions, Ahmad al-Shuqayri founded the PLO. This was the start of a process in which the Palestinians would become the main party in the Arab–Israeli conflict, and the Palestinian problem, in its national-territorial meaning, would become the heart of the conflict.

The term "Palestinian entity" (*kiyan filastini*) was relatively new in Arab-Palestinian politics and in the lexicon of the Arab–Israeli conflict. *Kiyan*, in its political sense, means entity or existence. Therefore, the coupling of *al-kiyan* to Palestinian had a special political meaning in the history of the New Palestinian National Movement: the political organization of the Palestinian people that granted the Palestinian people independent political status or the establishment of representative institutions. At a later stage the Arab states and the Palestinians added institutional elements to the term, such as elected bodies, Palestinian republic, or Palestinian government in exile. The establishment of these institutions was considered an expression of the Palestinian entity's rebirth. Today the Arab world understands this term as meaning the establishment of a Palestinian state in the West Bank and Gaza Strip.[13]

On March 29, 1959, the 31st session the Arab League Council discussed for the first time, as an inter-Arab forum, the UAR (that is, Egyptian) initiative for reviving the Palestinian entity. The council decided to convene "a high level Arab conference to review the stages in the Palestinian problem's development in light of current developments and circumstances, and to outline a joint Arab policy that each Arab member state in the League would be committed to implementing." It was also decided "to reorganize the Palestinian people and highlight its entity as a unified people, rather than mere refugees, whose voice would be heard in the Arab national arena [*al-majal al-qawmi*] and international arena through representatives to be elected by the Palestinian people."[14] This revival of the Palestinian entity was intended to establish independent political institutions that would represent the Palestinians as a people. For tactical reasons the Egyptians avoided official mention at this stage of "self-determination" or the creation of "a Palestinian state." Instead, the existence of a Palestinian people and their political representation as such were emphasized.

As the Arab–Israeli conflict escalated and the Palestinian problem became the central issue in the Arab political discourse and in discussions on all aspects of the conflict, especially the pan-Arab dispute over the method of solving the Palestinian problem, each Arab state, for its own reasons, found it necessary to define its strategy in the conflict. Polar differences appeared in the Egyptian (UAR) position on the one hand, and the Syrian Ba'th and Iraqi positions on the other. Only at a later stage, and upon Egypt's initiative, were pan-Arab short-range and long-range strategies formulated for the first time. Naturally the point of departure and the basis of the agreed-upon strategy that was formulated at the First Arab Summit (January 1964) and Second Arab Summit (September 1964) were the strategy of the Arab states that preceded the First Arab Summit.

Therefore, it is important to outline the general strategy in the conflict of the main Arab states (Egypt, Iraq, Jordan, and Syria) in the period prior to the First Arab Summit.

The Egyptian Strategy

The lessons from the 1948 defeat served as the starting point for Egyptian strategy in the Arab–Israeli conflict. During the 1948 War Nasir had been an operations officer with the 6th Egyptian Battalion that became trapped in the Faluja Pocket (fifty-five kilometers southeast of Tel Aviv, present-day Kiryat Gat). This traumatic experience engraved itself on his view of the solution to the Arab–Israeli conflict.[15]

One important lesson that he learned from the Sinai War was the need to prepare for the next round of fighting that he saw as inevitable. He claimed that he had to plan not only for war with Israel but also against "whoever supports Israel." Following the Sinai War Nasir realized that the Arab world would have to be mobilized on more than one front in a war against Israel. The war, he perceived, would be easier to wage if both the Egyptian and Syrian armies came under one command.[16]

For these reasons he decided, in June 1959, to set up a Supreme Planning Committee for working out UAR policy on the Palestinian problem. The committee would include representatives from all the Egyptian institutions linked to the Palestinian issue and would be headed by Mushir (Field Marshal) Abd al-Hakim Amer, who bore the title of Deputy Supreme Commander of the Egyptian Forces (the supreme commander was Nasir): Ali Sabri, minister for the republic's presidential affairs; his deputy, Abd al-Qader Hatim; Dr. Husayn Dhu al-Fiqar Sabri, deputy foreign minister; Salah al-Bitar (one of the leaders of the Syrian Ba'th party), minister of culture and guidance; Kamal Rif'at, acting minister of Awqaf; and two representatives of the military government in Gaza. Two sub-committees would also be set up: one, for Palestinian affairs, would be headed by Aqid (Colonel) Salah Jawhar; the second, for war against Zionist activities, would be chaired by Ibrahim Baghdadi (a senior officer in charge of the Israeli desk in the Egyptian General Intelligence).[17]

Official Egyptian circles explained the establishment of the Supreme Committee for Planning the Palestinian Problem in the following manner:

> The Palestinian problem demands extensive political planning from all its aspects in order to present it to the UN and world public opinion. According to the new planning, a policy will be drawn up that takes into consideration all Arab and foreign elements that have a stake in the Palestinian problem. The planning will be based on the idea that the Palestinian problem is a permanent Arab problem closely tied to the rest of the Arab problems. The Committee will discuss the steps to stop Zionist penetrations in Asia and Africa. The Arabs are currently united and joined together in their war against Zionist activity.[18]

The following is a survey of the main components of Egyptian strategy in the period being discussed and, to a great extent, afterwards:

1 The military inability of the UAR and the Arab world to impose an Arab solution for the Palestinian problem or prevent Israel from implementing its water diversion plan. The basic line that guided Nasir in formulating his strategy in 1959 was that a war with Israel must be avoided at all costs until an Arab victory could be guaranteed. Nasir believed that "Israel is not alone, there are those who support it." In late 1959, in a UAR government meeting on the Israeli plan to divert the Jordan's water, and in answer to Akram al-Hourani, deputy president of the UAR and a leader in the Syrian Ba'th Party, who demanded "carrying out limited operations" in order to obstruct the Israel's NWC project, Nasir stated:

> I think that 1963 or 1964 will be the decisive year of decision . . . I do not know what 'limited operations' are. When the time comes, and we're ready to go to war, it must be [a] full-scale [war]; it's inconceivable that I would agree to 'a limited war.' And [what would happen] if we launch a limited war that develops into a full-scale one when we're not prepared for a decisive victory . . . There's only one possible outcome that I want to achieve – decisive victory . . . We must not go to war if we haven't determined its time and place and [if] preparations have not been completed."[19]

Nasir's policy of not getting dragged into a war with Israel strengthened following the demise of the UAR. He admitted to having no plan to liberate Filastin, and that the first thing to be done was "to liquidate the reactionary fifth column in the Arab world and carefully prepare for the [coming] war with all the material and moral forces [available]." In a meeting with the members of the legislative council of the Gaza Strip on June 26, 1962, Nasir admitted:

> The most vexing problem in the Arab world today is your problem. Whoever wants to fight must be prepared and not gamble at the expense of the fate of his and other countries . . . I admit that I have no plans. I cannot tell you that I have plans to liberate Filastin. If I said that I had plans to liberate Filastin I'd be lying and mocking you, and then I'd be a statesman who barters in policy. Anyone who tells you that he has a plan today for liberating Filastin mocks you. What I am telling you is that we face a difficult complex problem . . . [and] I want to prepare for it with all the material and moral strength [possible].[20]

After the collapse of the UAR (September 1961), Nasir had to reassess the changed situation in the inter-Arab alignment, mainly because the brunt of a confrontation with Israel would fall on the Egyptian army, and the balance of forces between the two countries was very much to Egypt's disadvantage. In order to redress this imbalance the Egyptian army prepared a plan to double its strength. And indeed, the plan was implemented by the time of the Six Day War. The massive Egyptian involvement in Yemen that commenced in 1962 reinforced Egypt's basic estimate that its army was unprepared for war with Israel. Furthermore, Egypt realized that it could not rely on any Arab army whose leadership was "in the reactionary camp" and feared the possibility that if it became entangled in such a war, the rest of the Arab states would leave it alone and see this as "a golden opportunity to stab Egypt in the back."[21]

The UAR understood that it had to take political steps that would prove to the Arab world that despite its military limitations, it was taking steps toward solving the problem. The Egyptian plan to revive the Palestinian entity was one way for Nasir to overcome the dilemma of keeping his promise to the Arab world – that the Egyptian–Syrian unity being a power in itself "is the path to obtain the rights of the

Palestinian people" on the one hand, and Nasir's inability to make good on this promise since the Palestinian problem was growing more acute on the other.[22]

2 Nasir's assessment or belief that Israel, with Western aid, was working to liquidate the Palestinian problem. Israel's aim was to prove that the conflict was with the Arab states, rather than between Israel and the Palestinians, and that it revolved around the question of borders. Nasir stated specifically that:

> The goal in establishing the Palestinian entity is to thwart Israel's efforts to eradicate the Palestinian problem and to prevent the loss of the Palestinian people's rights . . . Israel is using every means in its power to have the world forget the question of Arab Palestinian rights . . . The Palestinian entity must be preserved since its destruction means the elimination of the Palestinian problem forever.[23]

Two major events roused the Egyptians' fear of a "conspiracy to eliminate the Palestinian problem." The first was the assessment that a large wave of Jewish immigration could be expected from the Eastern bloc. On February 14, 1959 the Cairo daily *al-Ahram*, according to instructions from "above," launched a weeks-long campaign warning of "the great danger" menacing Arab nationalism in the form of a wave of immigration of three million Jews from the Eastern bloc, which would "double Israel's population, strengthen its military power, and enhance its motivation for territorial expansion." The UAR succeeded in drawing the entire Arab world into political and propaganda activity on this issue.[24]

The second event was the report of the UN secretary-general, Dag Hammarskjöld, to the UN General Assembly (June 1959) recommending that the Middle East states absorb the Palestinian refugees.[25] President Kennedy's official dispatch to the heads of the Arab states on May 11, 1961, which underscored US willingness to help solve the Palestinian refugee problem, only added fuel to fire.[26]

According to Nasir, the blockage of Israel's use of the Suez Canal was also "part of the Palestinian problem and Palestinian people."[27] Regarding Israel's attempt to have the Danish vessel *Inge-Tofet* traverse the Suez Canal, he stated (June 30, 1959):

> We should not see Israel's failed attempt to pass through the Suez Canal as a chance event or a common international problem. The truth of the matter is that this incident is a new link in the chain of aggressive acts intended to destroy the Palestinian people, grab its land, usurp its rights, and in the end completely wipe out its existence so that Filastin itself will serve as the basis for similar operations against other Arab peoples, until world Zionism fulfills its dream of expansion from the Nile to the Euphrates. Israel's primary goal in this plot is to destroy the vestiges of the Palestinian problem. The ban on Israeli shipping in the Suez Canal is definitely one of the cards left in the hands of the Palestinian people . . . In my opinion, the real problem that we face is not navigation freedom in the Suez Canal, but [a question of] the Palestinian Arabs' right and Israel's aggressive ambitions.[28]

In the last quarter of 1959, especially during the month of November, Israel's plan to divert the Jordan River became a major issue on the Arab agenda and an integral part of the debates on the entire Palestinian problem. The issue became embedded in the assessment and fears of Egypt and the Arab states regarding Israel's moves to eliminate the refugee problem and the entire Palestinian problem.

In December 1959 UAR media launched an unprecedentedly hostile propaganda campaign against Israel that focused on the NWC, the Palestinian refugee issue, and immigration to Israel from the Eastern bloc. The main issue in the discussions of the refugee issue was the Arab demand to return the refugees to their lands and reimburse them for property loss – "Any other solution means the liquidation of the problem at the refugees' expense, the deletion of the name Filastin from the map, and guarantee of Israel's existence."[29]

3 Nasir's commitment to the Palestinians and Palestinian problem. Nasir's efforts for a solution to the Palestinian problem or the Arab–Israeli conflict stemmed from his deep awareness of Egypt's pan-Arab nationalist mission and the revolution that he was leading. He did his utmost to convince the Arab world and Palestinian people that even if he postponed the military solution, he was taking political steps designed to realize the goal in the long run. His vigorous moves to set up Palestinian representative institutions were also intended to shift Arab and Palestinian public opinion to his advantage. These efforts, and especially the struggle for the "Palestinian soul," increased when he was compelled to respond in defense of his opponents' accusation that he was shirking on the Palestinian issue. Nasir believed that his policy expressed "the will of all the Arabs," and that herein lay his strength. Therefore he had to meet the expectations of the Arab masses and their heart-felt yearnings, the masses "who went into a frenzy when he spoke about the 'Palestinian problem'." For example, when he catered to the enthusiastic crowd in his speech at a public assembly in Damascus on October 18, 1960:

> As for the Palestinian problem, wherever I have traveled to in this region [the Syrian region of the UAR], and wherever I go in the southern region [Egypt], I hear the continuous call, the continuous cry for Filastin and the liberation of Filastin. I like to say that everything we are doing today is a step in the struggle for Filastin. If we free ourselves from imperialism, then we move closer to the liberation of Filastin, and if we liberate ourselves from those who support imperialism, then we take another step on the path to the liberation of Filastin.[30]

During his speech (July 22, 1963) in honor of the Revolution Day in Egypt the masses cried "Filastin, ya Jamal." During his speech in Bizerte on December 13, 1963 the crowds screamed "Filastin, Filastin." He answered them, "When I hear you, O brothers, calling Filastin, Filastin, I am filled with the same feeling that I feel in every visit in the Arab world." This was the proof of his deep sensitivity toward the positive image of his attempts to solve the Palestinian problem. "All that we are doing is a step in the campaign for Filastin," he promised his listeners. It should come as no surprise then that even Egypt's military involvement in Yemen was presented as a step destined "to get rid of Zionism" on the way to liberating Filastin.[31]

The dissolution of the UAR was received with great disappointment in the Arab world, especially among the Palestinians. But the result was to further encourage Nasir to instill in the Arabs the idea, with justification, that despite this setback Egypt was "the only Arab country that possessed influential political, economic, and military strength that other parts of the Arab world lacked." Egypt preached to the Palestinians that "unity was the path to return to Filastin [and restore the Palestinian people's rights] and this is why the Palestinians, wherever they were situated, had a great role to play in the realization of unity."[32]

The Egyptian plan that was broached at the end of March 1959 for reviving the Palestinian entity, and Egypt's vigorous efforts to realize this goal, were an historical turning point in Egypt's path to solving the Palestinian problem. This problem in its widest and most comprehensive sense was one of the main foundations on Nasir's political outlook.

Egypt tried to prove the existence of an independent Palestinian political element with nationalist aspirations that symbolized the existence of a Palestinian problem and granted legitimacy to the continuation of the Arab struggle against Israel. It also tried to substantiate the claim that the problem was basically between Zionism (or the Zionist Movement) and the Palestinian people. The plan to revive the Palestinian entity (or identity) was intended to have the Palestinians become a party in the Arab–Israeli conflict, therefore Nasir stressed that the Palestinians had "to take the initiative and make an effort to realize the Palestinian entity."[33]

Egypt endeavored to establish independent Palestinian representative bodies that would be elected by the entire Palestinian population living in the Arab world. The Egyptian plan envisaged the election of a "national assembly" by Palestinians of the UAR, Jordan, and Lebanon. The assembly would draw up a "national charter for the liberation of Filastin" that would be binding on the Arab states. The assembly would also vote for an executive committee or, alternatively, a Palestinian government that would represent the Palestinians and speak in their name in the Arab and international arenas. For tactical reasons Egypt proposed that this organization would be set up under the supervision of the Arab League. The organization would preserve the Palestinians' existence by granting them citizenship. Filastin, in its new organization, would join the Arab League. In the middle of 1960 the Egyptians raised the idea – not as an official proposal – "to secure the Palestinian people's right to self-determination and national sovereignty."[34] A similar proposal appeared in the Cairo weekly *al-Musawar* on July 10, 1959:

> The creation of a strong Palestinian government along the lines of the Algerian government. This government must be established on the basis of a referendum by the Palestinians themselves in their various [dwelling] places so that they will elect the people responsible for restoring Filastin . . ."

The Gaza Strip served as a testing ground for implementing the Egyptian view. The regime's starting point was the Gaza Strip's legal position in 1949 that defined it as "a region under the control of the Egyptian forces in Filastin."[35] As such, Gaza was administered by the Egyptian War ministry. On March 29, 1962 Nasir signed a new constitution for the Gaza Strip.[36] Egypt determined that, *inter alia*, "Filastin is a revered and integral part of the glorious Arab homeland . . ." The constitution has been described as " temporary until the promulgation of the permanent constitution for the state of Filastin." "The Gaza Strip is an inseparable part of Filastin land and is destined to be part of the Filastin state that will be established in the future." The executive authority is under the auspices of both the governor-general and the executive council. The governor-general will be appointed by the Egyptian president's order. The legislative authority comes under the auspices of both the governor-general and legislative council.

Although according to the constitution three authorities (judicial, legislative, and executive) were established, as an expression of the autonomous nature of the

Palestinian rule, in practice the constitution enabled Egypt to maintain its hegemony in the Gaza Strip as being an (occupied) Egyptian region, while the inhabitants' participation in government was only a sham since it came without any real authority. Gaza's 1962 constitution was an Egyptian attempt to prove it was fulfilling its idea for the revival of the Palestinian entity.

The constitution was the first "Palestinian" document that defined the Palestinians' rights and duties as citizens of a "state." The Egyptian media referred to it as "the beginning of the Filastin state and the declaration of the Palestinian government on the Gaza Strip's soil, . . . a revolution in the life of Filastin, and a new stage in the history of the struggle for the liberation of Filastin." The Egyptian media also proclaimed that the constitution was an expression of Egypt's concern for the Palestinian problem and the Palestinian people: "This constitution restores to the Palestinians their faith in the power of their special entity, and Gaza was the core of the state of Filastin and a symbol of its existence and future mission. From this point on, the laws will be published in the Gaza Strip in the name of the Arab people in Filastin, and the people themselves will rule this region of Filastin and enjoy their legal rights." When referring to the Palestinians' conditions in Jordan, it was emphasized that "the Gaza Strip represents the only Palestinian land in which a people dwells that still preserves its Palestinian name."[37]

The UAR (or Egypt after its dissolution) was the only Arab state during the period being discussed, that implemented the representative element of the Palestinian entity, namely "the establishment of independent representative institutions." But the implementation was not carried out democratically, and the system corresponded more with UAR pattern of elections. An expression of this was the establishment of "the Palestinian National Union" (that paralleled the government party in the UAR).

Egypt viewed the founding of a Palestinian army as an important element in the independent Palestinian entity. The establishment of this army would complement the entity's political organizations and be under their authority. The Egyptians aspired to set up Palestinian military units (hereafter: the Palestinian Army or PA) that would be recruited from the Palestinian population in every Arab state. Most of the decisions in Egyptian or Palestinian forums in Gaza regarding the right to revive the Palestinian entity were accompanied by the demand to establish the PA. But in light of the experience with Gaza's 8th Palestinian Division that was decimated in the 1956 War, little value was attributed to the PA's ability to alter the balance of forces between Egypt, in particular, or the Arab states, in general, and Israel. "Relying on this kind of army meant that the solution to the Palestinian issue would take hundreds of years."[38] Therefore, Nasir's declaration that "the PA's goal is basically to defend the rights of the Palestinian people," seems quite overstated. Egypt regarded the establishment of the PA merely as a symbol expressing the Palestinians' desire to contribute their part to the Arab military effort and join in the Arab preparations for the liberation of Filastin. Despite the Egyptians' call to set up a Palestinian army and the demands for such an army by Gaza's populace, the Egyptians avoided mandatory enlistment to the Palestinian army out of deep concern that armed units in the Gaza Strip would instigate security incidents. During the 1950s the Egyptian government suffered considerably from the undisciplined fida'iyyun units and National Guard that were formed in the Gaza Strip, and which acted independently along the border with Israel. The Egyptians were also worried over the possibility that these units would take part in future riots against the Egyptian administration, as they had in late 1958 and late 1961.[39]

Egypt never recognized Jordan's formal annexation of the West Bank in 1950.[40] Egypt's revolutionary regime claimed in this period that co-existence was impossible between Egypt's nationalist regime and the Hashemite Kingdom's conservative or reactionary regime. Nasir believed that the differences between the two regimes over the Palestinian problem had to be revealed. In his opinion, "much of the discord [between Egypt and Jordan] on political matters was over Filastin." He also accused Husayn of being "a fifth column who stands as an obstacle before the liberation of Filastin."[41]

Egypt relentlessly carried out subversive activity, using all the means at its disposal, to undermine Husayn's regime. Nasir cast doubt on the Jordanian kingdom's legitimacy. He saw Jordan as an artificial creation, the product of British policy after World War I that divided up its occupied areas in the Arab East that had come under the administration of the British colonial minister, Winston Churchill. It was Britain that had effectively wrenched from Syria the area that became the principality of Jordan. Haykal went so far as to term Husayn's throne "a paper carton."[42] During this period the Egyptians frequently called for the toppling of Husayn's regime and incited the inhabitants of Jordan, especially the Palestinians, to rebel against the government and bring it down. Egypt also clamed that the unity of the two banks, under the protection of King Husayn's government, was not only illegal but also nullified the essence of the Palestinian entity.[43]

Egypt stressed that Jordan's annexation of the West Bank was an illegal act. It claimed that since the West Bank was "part of Filastin land" its status was that of "a deposit in Jordan's hands just as the Gaza Strip is a deposit in Egypt's hands that will be immediately returned to its inhabitants once the Palestinian entity is realized." Thus, "the annexation of the West Bank meant the liquidation of the Palestinian entity and the problem of Filastin." Egypt not only declared its position but it also acted in accordance with it. Secret official internal documents and correspondence with other Arab states pointed to the fact that the West Bank was not an integral part of the Jordanian kingdom.[44] The letter of appointment of the new UAR consul in Jerusalem (January 16, 1960) explicitly stated that he was appointed "general consul in all the territories of Filastin west of the Jordan River that had been seized by the Jordanian army." [This terminology corresponded with Egypt's legal view of the status of the Gaza Strip.] The Jordanian government responded sharply by refusing to accept the letter of appointment, claiming that it undermined the kingdom's sovereignty.[45]

Qasim's Strategy

Colonel Abd al-Karim Qasim, who came to power in Iraq following the July 14, 1958 revolution, lacked a clearly defined strategy for the Arab–Israeli conflict. His approach was characterized by impulsiveness and overweening self-confidence. The major factors that determined Qasim's solution to the conflict were Iraqi isolationism in the Arab arena, Iraq's distance from Israel's border, and the absence of a large Palestinian population in Iraq.[46] According to Qasim "[Iraq] was still in a state of war with the Zionists because it had not signed an armistice agreement with them." In his opinion,

"The Palestinian problem would never be resolved until aid was given to its inhabitants and a state was established in the areas that were the plundered parts of Filastin." Unlike Nasir, he recalled his experiences in the 1948 war in a favorable light and called attention to the fact that the "the Iraqi army had not faltered in the Filastin war. It had taught [Israel] a lesson and inflicted heavy blows on the [Zionist] gangs at Jenin, Kafr Qasim, Qalqiliya, Tulkarm, Majdal, and other places where it had fought for Allah, the Palestinian nation, and the Arab peoples."[47] Qasim had been the commander of an infantry battalion in the Iraqi expeditionary force in Filastin (1948). After Iraq's July 1958 revolution, he adopted the slogan, "We shall return" (*innana 'a'idun*), which had a central place on his office desk. He believed that the Palestinian problem would be solved only by war. He spoke in general terms of his intention to annihilate Israel. In July 1959 he boasted to an Arab diplomat that, "regarding Filastin, I understand it better than [everyone] because I fought there and know how to destroy Israel quickly. The Arabs must decide on war, and we will serve as the spearhead . . . It will take me five days to exterminate Israel." In one of his speeches he claimed that "Iraq is the most powerful state in the Near East and possesses the most advanced army and weapons" and that "Iraqi army officers will liberate the plundered parts of the homeland." He advocated "preparing for a historical leap so that the heroic Iraqi army, with the help of the Arab and Islamic peoples, will restore Filastin to the Arab nation." The Iraqi regime, too, was convinced that "there was no turning back from an armed confrontation between the Arabs and Israel over the problem of allocating the Jordan's waters."[48]

Nevertheless, the Arab–Israeli conflict remained on the regime's sidelines, and discussion over it in Iraq was mainly against the background of Qasim's struggle with Nasir in the Arab arena. In effect, Qasim and the Iraqi media raised the elements of the Arab–Israeli conflict – such as Israeli shipping in the Suez Canal and Gulf of Eilat and the UN forces on the Egyptian–Israeli border – primarily in order to attack Nasir in the Arab arena.

Qasim hoped that the Palestinians would act as the Algerians had done in the struggle against the French. In his opinion, the Algerian resistance movement had fulfilled his political view on "national liberation by the people themselves." His military and financial support of the Algerian movement represented his promise to assist in the "liberation of Arab peoples." The militant aspect of this movement interested him more than its political framework (a provisional government). He praised his support of the Algerian movement by supplying it with weapons and money that, as he announced disparagingly though justifiably, came to more than all the material support rendered it by Egypt. Qasim figured that after "a Palestinian republic" was established, then the West Bank, like the territory from which the Algerians had launched strikes against the French, would serve as an operations base for attacks against Israel. He reiterated that, "The Palestinians, like the Algerians, had to carry the heavy burden for [attaining] selfhood and declare their existence." He called on the Palestinians "to follow in Algeria's footsteps and proclaim to the entire world their [right to] exist on all the land of Filastin." When Algeria declared independence in February 1962, Qasim saw it as reinforcing and substantiating his view of the correct path for "liberating Filastin."[49]

In the mid December 1959 he broached, for the first time, the idea of the "Eternal Palestinian Republic" (*khalida*).[50] Although the plan was better defined than Nasir's in its final goal and territorial framework, it was still vague and lacking practical details for its realization. Qasim formulated the plan concurrently with the deterioration of his relations with Nasir.

Qasim raised the idea of establishing a "Palestinian republic" on December 15, 1959 in a speech at the First Conference of Iraqi Physicians:

> Arab Filastin should not be revived unless an Arab state is established that contains all the pillaged parts of the homeland and unless its [original Palestinian] inhabitants have control over it . . . Who attacked Filastin? Three gangs did: The children of Israel who grabbed the bulk of it, and Jordan that expropriated another part and annexed it to its territory, and Egypt that tore off another section of Filastin during Farouq's reign. It would have been better if the merchants had called, in the name of Filastin, to set up a Palestinian state whose inhabitants rule it.[51]

In a speech on December 21, 1959, Qasim reiterated his earlier statements, adding, "Imperialism and the gluttons must be ousted from Filastin soil so that the Eternal Palestinian Republic can be established." Qasim presented his plan to set up an "Eternal Palestinian Republic" as a solution to the Palestinian problem and as part of "Filastin's self-determination." "A Palestinian republic must be set up on all of Filastin soil. We disagree with our Arab brothers on partition or asking the UN to renew the partition resolutions. We believe that all Filastin is Arab [land] and must be returned to its owners. The Arab Palestinian people rejects the Jews' right to Filastin land, and we will never agree to the existence of an Israeli state in an Arab country."[52]

In this vein he tried to prove that he could outdo everything that Nasir did. But, despite the similarities between his and the Egyptians' plans, Iraq emphasized their basic differences in the practical political and territorial spheres. Unlike the Egyptians, the Iraqis claimed that the Palestinian state would rise in stages and that it held a central role for the Palestinians in the liberation of Filastin.[53] Qasim's plan was concrete and defined the general political and territorial frameworks. He left no room for doubt as to where the Palestinian state had to be established and the stages needed in the process, but the institutional features of the future state were ambiguous and his thinking on all aspects of statehood was impractical.

His summons to establish a Palestinian republic was the first of its kind by the head of an Arab state. He regarded it as an expression of the idea of a Palestinian entity and used the term "eternal," borrowing it from the "Eternal Iraqi Republic." Qasim believed that the Palestinian republic would have to be established on "all the lands of Filastin" in two stages. In the first stage, a state would be created in the West Bank and Gaza Strip. In the second stage, the state would be established "on all of Filastin territory after its liberation . . . The Palestinian state will be a separate regional unit." It would have to be set up "on the lands that were stolen by three thieves. The one hostile toward Arab nationalism is Zionism; the other two thieves come from the Arabs themselves – Egypt and Jordan." He also stated, "It will have to encompass all three parts of Filastin – the eastern [West Bank], western [Gaza Strip], and central [Israel]; that is, all the territory extending to the Jordan River and Dead Sea." The first stage of the plan would see the Palestinian republic comprising "all the territories, excluding those held by Israel;" the second stage would include "the territories that Israel, Jordan, and the UAR had conquered." Like Nasir, Qasim also claimed that Jordan's annexation of the West Bank was illegal. He repeatedly accused Jordan "of having stolen part of Filastin and appending it to its territory [and] grabbing part of Filastin after the Iraqi army withdrew [in 1949]." He spoke in the same vein about the Gaza Strip's status, which, he felt, "Egypt had stolen, plundered, and forcefully annexed."[54]

Qasim continuously promised to help the Palestinians establish a Palestinian republic by providing them "with weapons, money, and manpower" just as he had assisted the Algerians. He backed up his words by creating the "Palestinian liberation battalion" (fawj al-tahrir al-filastini) that was designed to be the nucleus of the Palestinian army. In this way he also gave practical expression to his assessment that the Palestinian problem would be solved solely by war. On March 26, 1960, the Iraqi government decided "to prepare armed forces for the Palestinian republic,"[55] but only on August 29 did the official Iraqi newspaper publish the law establishing "the Palestinian liberation army." The law went into effect retroactively from April 15, 1960, the date of the opening of the first officers' course for Palestinians. According to the law "a Palestinian Liberation Army" (jaysh al-tahrir al-filastini) would be set up subordinate to the Iraqi Defense Ministry and under the command of the Iraqi chief-of-staff. Also, the "Palestinian Liberation Army" would be built on a voluntary basis, and graduates of the officers' course would receive the rank of lieutenant.[56]

Qasim stressed that Iraq wanted "to establish a Palestinian army and a Palestinian state for the liberation of Filastin" and that this step was designed "to prepare the Palestinian republic's armed forces."[57]

On April 7, 1960 the Iraqi press published a defense ministry announcement "To the Sons of the Eternal Palestinian Republic" calling on volunteers "for the Palestinian republic's army." The defense ministry offered the Palestinian volunteers two tracks: one, an officers' course for graduates of high schools and colleges. The four-month course would be held at an Iraqi reservists' college starting on April 16, 1960. The second course was an NCO-enlisted man's course for Palestinian recruits who did not complete their high school studies. This course, too, would begin on April 16.[58]

The first officers' course opened on April 15, 1960 at the reserve officers' college, and finished in August. Sixty officer candidates took part. During the first four months almost three hundred Palestinian soldiers and fifty officer candidates (mostly from the Gaza Strip) joined the Palestinian battalion. After their training in Mosul, mainly in guerilla warfare, and their return to Baghdad in November 1960, the establishment of the Palestinian Liberation Battalion was announced – to be made up of graduates of the officers' course and the NCO-enlisted men's course. The second officers' course for Palestinians began in November 1960. By the end of Qasim's regime, four groups of Palestinian officers had completed the reservist military course, and by 1963 one hundred and fifty Palestinians were graduates of the officers program, even though the required number of officers for a battalion was only thirty-two. The battalion commander was an Iraqi officer, Colonel Abd al-Razaq Ahmad al-Sheikh, and the senior officers, such as the deputy battalion commander and company commanders, were also Iraqis. The Palestinian officers served in subordinate positions, usually as deputy company commanders.[59] In establishing the Palestinian Liberation Army, Qasim had tried to prove to the Arab world and the Palestinians that he "fulfilled his promises with action, not with words."

Unlike the Egyptians, Qasim actually established something new. though, it was not a real military force. Its main role was limited to showcase presentations, propaganda, and endless training exercises at the al-Rashid military camp outside Baghdad.

In February 1963, after the revolution that toppled Qasim's regime, the Iraqi Defense Ministry offered the battalion's officers three options: discharge, transfer and integration into Iraqi units, or remaining in the battalion. In 1964 the battalion was annexed to Iraqi units that were fighting the Kurds in Northern Iraq. The battalion's name was changed to the "First Battalion – 65th Independent Brigade." After this, many of the first "Liberation Battalion's" soldiers requested to be discharged. The battalion's officers continued to serve in Iraqi units until the Palestinian Liberation Army was established upon the PLO's founding in 1964. The battalion's units, officers, and other volunteers, were then assigned to Iraqi PA units called the "al-Qadisiya Forces."[60]

Qasim perceived Jordan as a starting point for realizing his vision – the establishment of a Palestinian republic – and materializing his concept of the key elements of the Palestinian state. His basic approach to Jordan was similar to Nasir's. He too rejected the Hashemite Kingdom's legitimacy, claiming that "the Lausanne Agreement recognizes the independence of Filastin that was torn from the Ottoman Empire" and that "the bogus Hashemite Kingdom, the godchild of imperialism, had been founded on the ruins of Filastin." Qasim also stated that "Husayn, the son of a traitorous dynasty . . . had annexed half of Filastin to his fraudulent crown." Naturally, then, Qasim refuted the legitimacy of the unification of West and East Banks (1950) since the "Palestinians, who settled in Jordan, were not asked how they felt about unification with Jordan."[61] Qasim realized that his plan to create a Palestinian republic meant the dissolution of the Jordanian kingdom.

To conclude: Qasim's plan was characterized by the discrepancy between his vaunting ambitions and his promises – that "the Filastin flag would soon be flying over Filastin soil";[62] or, his statement at the opening of the Iraqi students' conference that he "sees an independent Filastin even before your studies are over."[63] and his practical steps for realizing his plan in the near future were unrealistic, considering the political and military conditions of the period. It would take another fifteen years and an additional two Arab–Israeli wars before the PLO and the Arab states adopted Qasim's "stages concept" whereby a Palestinian state would be established in the West Bank and Gaza Strip as part of their political plan for solving the Palestinian problem.

Jordan's Strategy

Husayn believed, justifiably so, that his opposition to the plan for establishing a Palestinian entity was part of the struggle for the survival of his kingdom. He correctly perceived the goals of the Egyptian and Iraqi plans: not only to grant the Palestinians representation but also to threaten the integrity of his kingdom.[64] Jordan had to prove that it was, in effect, the sole representative and spokesman of the Palestinians, so that he could justify his determined opposition to all aspects of the plan for creating a Palestinian entity. Since the plan to revive the Palestinian entity was only one side of the plan for solving the Palestinian problem, Jordan too had to present its own counter-plan for solving the problem, a plan that would encompass the principle of Palestinian representation and at the same time guarantee the integrity of the Hashemite Kingdom. The following are Jordan's main arguments for opposing the plans for establishing a Palestinian entity:

17

1 Jordan is the *de facto* representative of the Palestinians. "The Jordanian government is the sole legal representative of the Palestinians living in Jordan who have the legal right to decide on all aspects of their rights in Filastin," Majali, the prime minister of Jordan, declared. The king rejected the proposals to establish a Palestinian army, asserting that, "The national guard troops are the army of Filastin. Our armed forces [stationed] along the ceasefire lines are the army of Filastin, they serve, not by rhetoric, as the real army of Filastin." In order to prove that the Jordanian government represented the Palestinians, Majali summed up the Jordanian position:

> We are the government of Filastin, the army of Filastin, and the refugees of Filastin, and our leader is King Husayn. These words are not only a verbal challenge, but a fact based on the legal documentation that expresses: (a) Jordan's unification that was approved by the majority of Palestinian Arabs [living] in Jordan; (b) the Palestinian Arabs' agreement to fully participate in the Jordanian government, its legislative, executive, and judicial authorities – and in all state mechanisms, including the army. The establishment of a showcase Palestinian government contributes nothing to the Arab effort. On the contrary such a government is likely to hamper the effort . . . when the vast majority of the Palestinians are Jordanian citizens . . . We are Filastin and its fate is our fate.[65]

The Jordanian government emphasized that since it "speaks in the name of Jordan's citizenry [and represents] the majority of Palestinian Arabs" then it cannot, for legal and constitutional reasons, recognize the right of "a body speaking in their name outside Jordan that wishes to represent it or part of its population."[66]

2 Unity of the two banks. Correctly assessing that the elements in the proposed Palestinian entity meant the break-up of the kingdom after the West Bank was detached from it, the Jordanian rulers claimed that Jordan's annexation of the West Bank in 1950 stemmed from the freely made decision of the West Bank's inhabitants to unite with Jordan "under one crown." Therefore, Jordanian officials asserted that "Jordan on both banks is a single unit." Husayn too stressed that "unity between the two banks was more vital than unity between any other two Arab countries [read: the UAR]." Prime Minister Majali avowed that

> over two-thirds of the Palestinian Arabs dwell on Jordan's two banks and make up two-thirds of Jordan's population. They freely chose to join their brethren in Jordan under one crown on the basis of full equal rights and obligations . . . [Unification] is the best example of realizing the unity of the people of one county and one nation through equality and responsibility . . . Every plan for solving the Palestinian problem must first acknowledge the present situation in Jordan and the legal and constitutional unity of the two banks. The Jordanian unity has safeguarded the remnants of Filastin and has enabled the Arabs to work with their brethren in Jordan for [a solution to] the Palestinian problem.[67]

In order to justify these claims and prove that the West Bank Palestinians rejected a separate Palestinian entity that would change their status, Husayn summed up this point:

> Unity was created following the *nakba* of 1948, and it is the necessary step for the national interest, self-defense, and preservation of the holy places. This means that unity between the two banks was more important than unity between any two other Arab

18

states . . . If I was convinced that [our] guests, my brothers from Filastin, wanted to exchange this unity for a different status, then I would not have hesitated for a moment to help them realize their ambition. To those who doubt this position and claim that our [Jordan's] presence in Filastin is our greediness for profit, I say, permit neutral representatives of Arab League states to come, make contact with each of the sides in Jordan, learn the truth of the situation, and supervise, if necessary, any form of national plebiscite that can clarify the real situation. I am not worried about the results, just as I am certain of the nation's consciousness, and am prepared to accept the results of this national referendum, whatever they may be. [68]

3 A solution to the Palestinian problem must be found within a general Arab framework and not a separate solution. Jordan claimed that "the problem of Palestinian representation must not be discussed separately, but as part of a comprehensive [Arab] plan." Unlike Nasir's view, Jordan claimed that the Arab–Israeli conflict "is not a struggle between the Palestinian people and Zionism, but between the Arab world and Zionism. Therefore, [its solution] is the responsibility of all the Arabs . . . [and] no [single] Arab state is allowed to take a partial or separate step in solving the Palestinian problem." The establishment of the Palestinian entity is only a partial step and insufficient to solve the problem. Jordan understood that an all-Arab solution meant Jordan's active participation in the Arab planning and the status of the representative of the Palestinian in its country. On the other hand, if the Palestinians are a party in the conflict, then they will ask for separate representative institutions. Therefore Jordan rigorously opposed Nasir's and Qasim's plans to make the Palestinians a party in solving their problem.

Jordan considered both Egypt's proposal to establish the Palestinian entity's institutions and Qasim's "Eternal Palestinian Republic" plan as dangerous and unrealistic. They were, in effect, the Arabs' "evasion of responsibility" by placing responsibility on the shoulders of the Palestinians:

> It would be madness if the Arabs of Filastin accept this grave responsibility in its disguise as the establishment of the organization [the Palestinian entity]. Attempts in the past, such as the installment of the All-Palestine Government [the Gaza government] and the appointment of a representative of the refugees to the Arab League have proven the futility of this method . . . Mobilization of the Palestinians must be carried out within the framework of the general Arab mobilization for Filastin . . . [because] . . . the problem will not be solved by handing out rifles to a few hundred Palestinians.

In order to fulfill Jordanian obligations and curb Arab pressure, Jordan suggested postponing the solution to the problem of Palestinian representation until the distant future, and recommended that, "the Palestinians determine their political future only after the liberation of Filastin."[69]

On January 19, 1960, the Jordanian House of Representatives convened an "historic meeting" in the Old City of Jerusalem, in the presence of members of government and public figures from the West Bank. In the course of the meeting Majali declared:

> The Old City is the capital of Filastin . . . Every plan dealing with the Filastin problem must conform to the following principles: (a) The removal of the Filastin problem from the field of internal bartering and need for commerce in pain and emotions among the

Arabs in general and the Palestinians in particular. (b) Placing the plan on a realistic foundation of understanding and awareness, while evaluating all our options and overall preparedness in human and material resources. (c) Every plan for Filastin must be carried out with full Arab cooperation. (d) Realizing that every attempt to shift the responsibility for Filastin from joint Arab responsibility to narrow regional responsibility, and every attempt to shirk responsibility and call for what has been termed the Palestinians' status will hurt the effort to help Filastin. (e) It is of primary importance that the current Jordanian position and the legal and constitutional unification of the two banks of the Jordan River are recognized. Jordanian unity has preserved what is left of Filastin . . . In our opinion, this is the practical plan that will enable the return of Palestinian rights and attainment of the goal; when this goal is realized, the Jordanian government will be the last party to oppose the aspirations of the entire Palestinian people to determine its future and destiny.[70]

4 The Jordanian plan for a comprehensive solution to the Palestinian problem (The White Paper): Following the dissolution of the UAR and the improvement of Jordan's position in the Arab arena, the Hashemite Kingdom initiated its own plan for a comprehensive solution to the Palestinian problem, and presented it to the Arab world. The godfather of the plan was Wasfi al-Tal, who was prime minister at the time. This plan, too, stressed the Palestinian nature of the Jordanian kingdom, and Jordan's position as "the Palestinian springboard for the liberation of Filastin." The plan was officially published in July 1962 in the form of a White Paper (*al-Kitab al-Abyad*) (on July 2, 1962 Wasfi al-Tal presented it to the press). The plan's main point was that Jordan would become the center of a military power that would serve as the basis of an Arab security belt surrounding Israel. It was decided that Jordan, "the first target of Israel's expansion," would be the natural center of this power that would have to be reinforced for a number of reasons: the human reservoir; military, geographical, and psychological factors; the one million Palestinians living in Jordan as citizens and making up two-thirds of the population; Jordan controlled the longest border with Israel (650 kilometers); East Jerusalem was situated only a few hundred meters from Israel; the West Bank was the heart of Palestinian territory; and finally, considering the manpower under its disposal with the support of the Arab states, Jordan would be able to become the center of the military power and assimilate it within its full defense framework in a short time. The plan called for mobilizing a pan-Arab, political–military, organizational, and propaganda effort in order to give preference to the Palestinian problem, while avoiding Arab disputes. The plan also envisaged political and financial aid being channeled to the countries where the refugees lived, including Jordan. The Arab states would be asked to assist Jordan, just as they had helped Algeria, because Jordan would be the first base of the power center, in other words, Jordan would become Filastin.[71]

Additional principles in the plan:

1 Jordan believes in absolute faith that it belongs to the Arab nation and that its primary national role is to work for Arab unity. This belief stems (*inter alia*) from the will to survive. A state where the majority of its inhabitants have tasted the catastrophe of expulsion from their homeland, in the wake of the Filastin War, understands better than any other state the feelings of a people disenfranchised from its rights and homeland, a result of improvised policy and lack of unified meticulous Arab planning.

2 Arab unity must be based on free will and choice. Jordan believes that the Arab League is essential, for nationalist reasons, since it is the only institution [engaged] in inter-Arab work and cooperation and the only instrument currently assigned the task for coordinating this policy and [that has] the potential to channel it to the common good. Therefore Jordan favors strengthening the League and helping it carry out its mission.

3 If the Filastin problem is an important issue for all Arabs, then Jordan regards it as an issue of its very survival. The merging of Palestinians and their Jordanian brothers at school, in the streets and fields, is the living mirror of the longed-for dream of unity. From Jordan's point of view Filastin is not only a question of policy, principles, or rights, but a question that fills the reality and thinking of every [Jordanian] citizen.

4 Jordan sees the Filastin problem summed up by two major points:

A The Filastin problem contains the use of armed aggression against Arab existence, an attempt to expunge the history and heritage of a people that has been dwelling in this part of the world for generations, and [an attempt] to transform the geographic reality.

B The nature of Zionist aggression is expressed in the desire for unlimited expansion.

5 In order to halt this danger, a power center has to be created that can meet the challenge of the threat and restore the rights of the Arabs in Filastin. For this reason the Jordanian government believes that the first major step [in solving] the Filastin problem is [to take] immediate action for uniting the Arab political, organizational, military, and propaganda effort by rising above all present political differences and refraining from using the problem as a political weapon.

6 Once an independent Palestinian front is established, the Arab governments will be able to coordinate their efforts on new revolutionary foundations.[72]

The Egyptian and Iraqi response to the Jordanian plan for a comprehensive solution to the Palestinian problem was naturally negative. The plan was depicted as "the plan for eliminating the Filastin problem." The Iraqi press bitterly criticized the Hashemite dynasty and claimed that "only one possibility was to be expected [from the plan], that the Kingdom of Jordan would become a Palestinian kingdom so that Husayn could demand the annexation of the Gaza Strip to the Palestinian kingdom."[73]

Against the background of Jordan's isolation in the Arab arena and its opposition to the Palestinian entity's plan, and in order to improve its image and prove its national position on the question of the conflict, the Jordanian position, in a number of inter-Arab conferences, especially in 1961 (the Arab Chiefs-of-Staff meeting, April 22–26, 1961; the Conference of Experts on Filastin Affairs, June 1961; the Arab Defense Council, June 10–18, 1961), was exceptionally belligerent and extremist (compared to Egypt's "moderate" and reserved approach). Jordan adopted this radical position in order to defend itself from Egyptian criticism, and pointed to its commitment to the Filastin problem despite its opposition to the Palestinian entity's plan. During discussions at the Arab chiefs-of-staff meeting on Israel's plan to divert the Jordan's waters, Jordan broached a plan that was even more radical than the UAR's. Jordan proposed a joint Arab military plan to forcibly prevent Israel from implementing its plan to divert the Jordan's riverbed facing the Syrian front. According to the plan, the Arab forces would initiate provocative acts compelling Israel to attack, which the world would interpret as Israeli aggression. Jordan suggested integrating artillery harassment into the military plan and fida'iyyun actions in the Syrian sector to be carried out by Palestinians especially trained for this goal. The Egyptians rejected this proposal because they estimated that it would lead to war with Israel.[74]

Jordan brought up the proposal again in the Arab Defense Council in June 1961, and called for the convening of an Arab summit conference in order to formulate Arab strategy "in light of the danger of Israel's water plan." But this action did not succeed and the Defense Council approved the Egyptian position that included the establishment of a joint Arab command.[75] Thus, Jordan's extreme position came to naught.

The Syrian Ba'th Strategy [76]

In the Arab arena the Ba'th party faced a dilemma – which was in fact Syria's dilemma too – between the pan-Arab national (*qawmiya*) aspiration, the ideological basis of the party, and the tendency to regionalism (*iqlimiya, wataniya*) of the regional Ba'th leaderships (*qutriya*), especially the Iraqi branch, and at a later stage also of the Syrian branch, which had control over the pan-Arab national command (leadership) (*qawmiya*).

The Ba'th leaders, who had been partners in the UAR government (1958–1959), took great pains in dealing with this dilemma, ironically, even after they realized the "one Arab nation" (*umma 'rabiya wahida*) or "unity" (*wahda*) principle, which was one of main tenets of the party's doctrine – "unity, freedom, socialism" (*wahda, huriya, ishtirakiya*). This dilemma was the background to the Ba'th ministers' resignation from the UAR government (in December 1959), and also led to the UAR's final dissolution in September 1961. Hence, the solution to the dilemma lay, precisely, in strengthening the regional–separatist trend, at the expense of the pan-Arab principle. This was clearly manifested when the party ascended to power – in Iraq in February 1963 and in March 1963 in Syria – and was able to fulfill the principle of Arab unity or, as Michel Aflaq has stated, "to realize its slogans and pave a new and daring path for the Arab revolution whose goals are unity, freedom, and socialism."[77]

The Arab socialist Ba'th party, unlike the Arab Nationalists Movement (ANM) (*harakat al-qawmiyin al-arab*), was the only pan-Arab political movement that succeeded in coming to power either as a main partner in the UAR period or as the government party in Iraq (February 1963) and Syria (March 1963).[78] But, instead of having the sense to take advantage of these opportunities and bringing about its political ideas especially in the Arab–Israeli conflict, it caved in to inner party wrangling at the pinnacle of its achievement, and failed to properly consider one of the main problems occupying the Arab world in this period – the Palestinian entity or the Palestinian problem. From 1958 to 1963 the party was overcome by organizational crises, personal intrigues, and disciplinary problems that sapped its energy and prevented it from concentrating on carrying out its political–social program. At a later stage, however, and against the backdrop of vigorous Arab activity on the Palestinian entity issue, the Ba'th party proposed a plan that included the establishment of Palestinian representative institutions. This was an ideological program that was more of a view of the nature of a solution to the Palestinian problem, rather than an achievable operative program based on current conditions.

In April 1965, an official document of the 8th (Pan-Arab) National Ba'th Congress (NC) harshly criticized the party's blunders in dealing with the Palestinian problem, noting that the national command (leadership) had not only been "ostentatiously absent from the Palestinian arena of activity . . . [but] had [also] flagrantly abandoned the Palestinian problem." Furthermore, "the party has failed to reach the Palestinian masses in order to sufficiently explain its positions, motivate the Palestinian people, and spur it into action."[79]

The Ba'th strategy on the question and solution of the Arab–Israeli conflict (the Palestinian problem) in this period was based on three main issues:

1 Solving the Palestinian problem by "annihilating the Israeli state and restoring the lands that had been plundered from their owners."
2 Applying all means necessary to prevent Israel from making any new gains, especially by blocking it from diverting the flow of the Jordan River and hampering Israeli shipping through Arab waterways.
3 Establishing a "popular front" of all the Palestinian popular groups in Arab countries in order to form an organization that would be independent in its activity.

These three areas formed a single bloc in Syrian strategy up until the Six Day War.

The Ba'th party's decisions were marked by success in the theoretical realm and failure in their practical implementation.[80] This evaluation of the Ba'th Sixth Congress's accomplishments (October 1963), according to a senior party member, was also applicable to the party's decisions regarding the Palestinian problem. The party practically ignored the issue. There were no differences between the pan-Arab national command's position and that of the regional (*qutri*ya) Ba'th commands. The party's position on the Palestinian problem developed in two main stages:

The first stage – until July 1960

The party was mainly characterized by internal crises during this stage. The Third National Ba'th Congress (August 1959) avoided a specific statement on the Palestinian issue, except for emphasizing that "the party had presented the Palestinian problem to the public as a pan-Arab national problem."[81] The Ba'th national command's announcement on February 16, 1960 was devoted to "preventing Israel from diverting the Jordan's waters."[82] At this stage the party refrained from serious discussion on the Palestinian entity; however, at the same time it stressed that expressions of a Palestinian entity must be rooted in the party's ideological (pan-Arab) principles, and that the Palestinians must work within the party's framework, and not within that of a separate entity.

The Ba'th party strongly opposed Qasim's position on the Palestinian problem and his proposal to establish an "Eternal Palestinian Republic." On December 18, 1959 *al-Sahafa*, the party's newspaper in Beirut, responded to Qasim's December 15 speech at the Doctors' Conference. It claimed that: "(1) These declarations revealed to the Arab public again the truth about Qasim and the dangerous role that he filled for the benefit of Zionist and imperialist interests. (2) Qasim accused the UAR of aggression toward Filastin and demanded the establishment of a Palestinian government in order to shift Arab public opinion from the Israeli imperialist plot [to divert the Jordan River] on the one hand, and justify his non-participation in the Arab campaign against it, on the other hand. They [the declarations] were also designed to turn the Iraqi people's attention away from the numerous domestic problems it was convulsed by because of Qasim's black regime." Furthermore, "The sons of Filastin believe that the correct pan-Arab national solution is through liberated Arab unity."[83]

During the Lebanese Ba'th party's regional congress (December 1959), the leadership's political report on the branch came under criticism because "it made no mention of the Filastin problem." Against this background, the congress demanded that the Lebanese party regional command "pay greater attention to the Palestinians' problems as it did to the inhabitants of Lebanon because of the Palestinians' influence in Lebanon, in general, and in the party apparatus, in particular." The congress demanded that the party's newspaper, *al-Sahafa*, "show an interest in the Filastin problem, in general, and the Palestinians' problems and the information [on their situation] in particular, and also allocate a special place for the voice of the (Palestinian refugee) returnees ['a' idun]." It should be noted that from 1959, the Lebanese branch of the Ba'th party paid more attention to the Palestinian problem than any other branch of the party in the Arab world, and sometimes even criticized the national leadership's activity and position on the Palestinian issue."[84]

In a May 15, 1960 announcement, the national command criticized the Egyptian and Iraqi proposals regarding the Palestinian entity, stating that the Ba'th position toward these plans would depend on the amount of seriousness and loyalty of those who proposing them. "According to the noble pan-Arab nationalist view of the Palestinian problem, since this is a great pan-Arab national problem and not merely a local national [one] . . . The Arab states' activity must be serious and loyal about organizing the struggle of the uprooted people (*nazihun*) since they are the vanguard of the campaign (against Israel), and developing their revolutionary strength far from local policy and its complications." The Ba'th saw that "the Palestinian problem would be resolved only through revolutionary, pan-Arab national (*qawmi*) struggle." The national command urged "determined opposition to all Zionist-imperialist plans that were designed to destroy the Filastin problem," and argued for "stubbornly demanding a pan-Arab national struggle for the return of the uprooted people to their homes and [the] annihilation of the State of Israel.[85]

Second Stage: August 1960–October 1963

A major shift in the Ba'th position on the Palestinian issue took place at the 4th National Ba'th Congress in late August 1960. This was the first congress since the Ba'th party had bolted from the UAR government, and a time when the Palestinian problem in general and the Palestinian entity in particular had become the main issues in inter-Arab discussions and propaganda. Because the approaching Arab Foreign Ministers' Conference in January 1961 would be discussing the Palestinian entity, the Ba'th national command could no longer avoid taking a position on this issue or ignore the criticism directed against it for having shunned the matter. The starting point was the "adoption of the Algerian revolution as the national leadership's first political task."[86] However Algeria's declaration of independence in 1962 annulled this priority.

The party's position on the Arab–Israeli conflict in this stage was defined in two documents: the decisions of the Fourth National Congress and the "memorandum of the Ba'th Party to the Arab Foreign Ministers' Conference regarding the problems of Filastin and Algeria" (January 31, 1961).[87] Both documents stated that:

1. "The solution to the Palestinian problem, destruction of the Israeli entity, and return of the plundered lands to their owners depend on a basic revolution in the life of the Arab people at the all-Arab-national level. The [Fourth National] Congress adopts the stages path for [its] political activity. The economic and political blockade of Israel must be intensified."
2. The Arab League Council must "draw up a realistic plan for dealing with the danger of Israel's increasingly aggressive military strength and manpower, a plan that will serve as a first step in the strategy for liberating the plundered land and restoring the rights of the Arabs of Filastin." This being the goal, Israel "has to be forcefully obstructed from diverting the Jordan's tributaries."
3. "Establishing an entity for the struggle that unites the sons of Filastin and organizes their struggle for the liberation of Filastin. [This entity] will organize and lead the various efforts of the Arab governments and popular organizations for the liberation of the plundered land."
4. The right way to establish "this entity of a struggle for the Palestinian people" is by establishing "a popular front for the liberation of Filastin" that will be like the "Algerian Popular Front." It must represent all of the Palestinian people. This front "has to unite all of the Palestinian revolutionary elements, including the popular organizations, and rely on the support of the legal trade unions of workers, professionals, and intelligentsia."

Following the resolutions of the Ba'th Fourth National Congress, in September 1960 the Iraqi Ba'th party came out against Qasim's plan to establish a Palestinian republic. However, the Iraqi Ba'th party announced that "the establishment of a Palestinian republic is the goal of the Arabs everywhere," but its establishment should be "closely tied to the Arab Liberation Movement" and "it would not be realized in Qasim's improvisatory manner." The republic's establishment "is an act that demands enormous material resources so that the new state can meet the challenge of a state [Israel] that is supported by imperialism and world Zionism . . . None of this will be realized unless it is based on a unified Arab plan."[88]

The Sixth National Ba'th Congress met on October 23–25, 1963 with the rise of the Ba'th regimes in Iraq and Syria in the background. The congress retained its basic position on the Palestinian issue, excluding a slight change from the Fourth National Congress's position, following discussions in the Arab League Council in September 1963. The part of the political announcement at the end of the congress that was devoted to the Palestinian problem was entitled "The Filastin Liberation Front." This section stated:

> The congress focused its discussion on the current Arab problem in Filastin and its likely future developments. [The congress] came to the conclusion that the Arabs of Filastin

must be seen as a first means for liberating Filastin. [The congress] decided to follow through with the idea [of establishing] a 'Filastin Liberation Front.' It calls on the Arab states in general, and the revolutionary governments in Syria and Iraq in particular, to help by all [available] means in the creation and organization of this front, and also to supply it with the tools and loyal revolutionary leaderships [that are] beyond Arab differences of opinion.[89]

In conclusion, this is the period in which the Arab–Israeli conflict began to escalate, the Arab states' political positions on the conflict were formulated, and the guidelines for its solution drawn up. These positions were the basis of viewing the Palestinian issue as a major factor in the conflict. The year 1959 may be considered the tuning point in the Arab–Israeli conflict, when the focus was concentrated on the Palestinian problem in its inter-Arab and Palestinian aspects. The events of this year opened a new page in the history of the Palestinian entity. Thus, 1959 may be termed "the year of Filastin," when all the elements of the Palestinian problem came under discussion, and following this, the question of the Palestinian entity, were now seen in a new light. A new political process was set in motion when Egypt raised the Palestinian problem, with all its new components, and introduced its initiative on the Palestinian entity, with all its implications, to the center of the Arab arena. Several years and two Arab–Israeli wars (1967 and 1973) later, the foundations of the Palestinian problem altered completely. This process added a new independent dimension to the Arab–Israeli conflict – the "Palestinian dimension" that "had disappeared" from the region's political arena and the Arab–Israeli conflict after the 1948 War. From this point on the Palestinians became a central factor in the Arab–Israeli conflict and the Palestinian problem, and at a later stage they became the heart of the conflict.

Formulation of the Arab Strategy in the Israeli– Arab Conflict, 1964–1965

Prelude to the Six Day War

Part I   *The Intensification of Arab Activity, 1959–1963*

The exacerbation of the conflict also came to expression in the discussions that were held in Arab forums (the Arab League Council that occasionally met at the level of Arab foreign ministers), the Arab Defense Council (which included Arab foreign ministers), the Arab chiefs-of-staff meetings, and in the decisions on matters related to the conflict. The decisions in these forums served as the basis for the formulation of the Arab strategy in the conflict in the first and second Arab summits (January and September 1964). The debates in these meetings also served as a catalyst for the Arab states to formulate their positions in the Arab–Israeli conflict. Discussions centered on two main issues.

1   The establishment of Palestinian representative institutions that would be recognized by the Arab states and that would express the national problem of a people that aspires to self-determination under the banner of "the revival of Palestinian entity." Thus, the Arab states, led by Egypt, tried to transform the Palestinians into a separate party in the Arab–Israeli conflict and the solution to the Palestinian problem. Naturally the aim was to perpetuate the Palestinian problem until the Palestinians obtained the right to self-determination; in other words, to add a new dimension to the Palestinian problem, one that had been absent from the Middle East political arena since the 1948 war.

2   The Arabs' struggle with Israel over the water issue, that is, against Israel's intention to realize its water carrier plan. This struggle had military and political implications that exacerbated the conflict, especially the deterioration in the

security situation on the Syrian border, and the events culminating in the Six Day War. The struggle contributed to the formulation of the Arabs' conflict strategy in the first and second Arab summits.

Inter-Arab Debates over the Establishment of Palestinian Representative Institutions (the Revival of the Palestinian entity)

Discussion on this issue in the Arab League Council was integrally linked to the determination of the Arab position, or the position of every Arab state, on the Palestinian problem and its solution. In the debates in the Arab League Council on the issue of the Palestinian entity, or the establishment of representative institutions for the Palestinians, the antagonism and polarization of the stands of Egypt (and Iraq) and Jordan were prominent. The UAR/Egypt pressured for the passing of operative decisions on these issues. It applied all the weight of its leadership, diplomatic and propaganda channels, in order to impose its stand on this forum and mainly in order to make Jordan "submit" to it. Despite this, Jordan succeeded in withstanding the Egyptian and inter-Arab pressure and so prevented the passing of a *unanimous* decision which would have committed all the Arab states; if the decision was passed by a *majority* it would have obligated only those who voted for it, as stipulated in the Arab League Charter (article 7). Its main objective in the discussion was to postpone the passing of decisions concerning principles on the issue of the Palestinian entity in the ALC. In this way Jordan tried to gain time in the hope that circumstances in the Arab arena would change in its favor. Indeed, the decisions which passed unanimously on the issue of the Palestinian entity were generally related to "technical" subjects.

As stated, the question of reviving the Palestinian entity was raised on Egypt's initiative in the 31st session of the ALC on March 29, 1959. The council approved the political committee's recommendation:

1 In the very near future a high level meeting will convene to review the stages in the development of the Filastin problem in light of the present developments and conditions, and will consider the possible developments in the international arena that it will have to deal with. [The meeting] will draw up a united Arab policy that each member state in the League will be obliged to conform to, including practical solutions for the restoration of Filastin.
2 These are the articles that the [political] committee proposes for discussion:
   A The reorganization of the Palestinian people, highlighting its entity as a unified people rather than mere refugees, whose voice will be heard in the pan-Arab national arena [al-majal al-qawmi] and international arena through representatives elected by the Palestinian people.
   B The governments of states that are members of the League, in general, and of the states hosting the Arabs of Filastin, in particular, will establish [each state] a strong mechanism that will free itself from all other occupation and specialize in all aspects of the Filastin problem – political, military, economic, et al.[1]

In September 1959, the ALC convened at the foreign ministers' level. The issue of the Palestinian entity was on the agenda. The proposals on this subject were advanced by Saudi Arabia and supported by Egypt. As a result of the severe opposition of Jordan's prime minister, Majali, Egypt in addition to its reluctance to create a serious crisis with Jordan in the League, agreed to postpone the debate on this subject to the following session of the ALC.[2] The 32nd session of the ALC on February 29, 1960, from which Iraq was absent, occurred against the background of escalation of the struggle of Egypt against Israel which since 1956 had reached unusual proportions. Egypt intended to achieve progress on the issue of the Palestinian entity in this session. The Jordanian foreign minister, Musa Nasir (Palestinian), was faced with the Arab and especially Egyptian obstinate demand for the "concretization" of the Palestinian entity. Majali claimed that, "even the Jordanian government was struck with amazement at this stubborn attitude."[3] Indeed, the UAR succeed in isolating Jordan on this issue. The Jordanian foreign minister opposed every formulation of a decision which could be interpreted as realizing the idea of the entity. Nevertheless operative decisions were not passed. Instead, the ALC decided on "general principles" which would guide the Arab states in their treatment of the Palestinian problem.

1 The Palestinian people have a legal right in Filastin and the right to restore its homeland and determine its own fate [*yuqarir masirihi*].
2 [The Palestinian people] have the right, like every people in the world, to live a free and dignified life in its homeland, and to realize all of its national rights.
3 The Palestinian people's demand to restore its rights is a national movement for liberation from Zionism that with imperialism's assistance has expelled [*ikhraj*] the Arabs from their homeland and stolen their land and sources of livelihood.
4 The Arab Palestinian people's right to its homeland is an indelible natural right.
5 Zionism – [and later] Israel – from its first stages, is an aggressive movement based on racial–religious prejudice, and refuses to accept the Jews' loyalty to a homeland whose citizenship they carries.
6 The Palestinian people's [free and dignified] return to its homeland is a natural and noble right. The UN decisions pertaining to the Arab refugees' return to their homes is merely recognition and support of this right.[4]

There is no mention in these principles of the Palestinian entity and its various aspects. The importance of the decision lies in the wording of the principles of the Arab position on Arab activity toward a solution of the Palestinian problem. In fact this was a summary of the Arab position as it was formulated in the Arab League until then. Its most important point was the Palestinians' right to self-determination.

Nevertheless, the secretary general of the Arab League was assigned the function of forming the Palestine Experts Committee (PEC), composed of five members, in order "to complete the compilation of the plans for action concerning the Palestinian problem." This was a Jordanian achievement but a temporary one.

The 33rd session of the ALC at Shtura in Lebanon (August 22–28, 1960) took place against a background of worsening relations between the UAR and Jordan. The UAR made a renewed effort for the adoption of an operative decision on the issue of the Palestinian entity. Jordan was wise enough to understand that extreme opposition to the discussion of this subject would mean that no Arab state would support it because they all preferred not to oppose the UAR position concerning the

Palestinian problem. Hence, the decisions taken at this session on the issue of the entity embraced the stand of Egypt and Jordan in such a way that both seemed to be confirmed. On the other hand, the Egyptian recommendations that had been accepted in March 1959 were re-endorsed, but for the first time these recommendations became operative decisions favoring "the reorganization of the Palestinian people and highlighting of its entity as a unified people" and the "establishment of a Palestinian army in the Arab host states."

The manner in which this decision was to be actualized was not determined. A new term was added to the articles of this declaration, "The preservation of the Palestinian personality" and the prevention of its loss. This meant the rejection of plans for the settlement of the Palestinians and/or granting them the citizenship of the Arab states, mainly Jordan. On the other hand, it was determined that "the Arab Palestinian people . . . would act to restore its homeland through the aid and participation of the Arab states and peoples." The decision urged the secretary general of the Arab League to establish the Committee of Experts whose aim would be to "formulate a comprehensive plan for the restoration of Filastin." These last two articles suited the basic Jordanian stand and indeed Jordan considered them an achievement.[5] However, this Jordanian assessment was erroneous. The decision left room for pressuring Jordan. It served at a later stage as a point of departure toward a more concrete decision, even though more time and additional events would be needed to make its acceptance possible.

The Arab foreign ministers conference that took place in Baghdad in January 1961 occurred in the context of reconciliation between the UAR and Iraq, and was initiated by the former. The UAR revealed its will to compromise in the discussions and decisions, including the issue of the Palestinian entity; the conference therefore did not further promote the establishment of the entity.

At the Palestine Experts Committee that met in July 1962 to discuss the manner of highlighting the Palestinian entity, two basic positions were manifest: on the one hand, Jordan tried to exploit the forum in order to set forth its plan for Jordan to become the "Palestinian–Jordanian–Hashemite Kingdom" and the recognized representative of the Palestinian people. Egypt, on the other hand, perceived the Jordanian ruse, and reiterated its doubts about Jordan's ability to solve the Palestinian problem since Jordan's source of support was the West "that backs Israel." As expected, the conference ended in a deadlock.[6]

The disintegration of the UAR caused an escalation of the struggle in the inter-Arab arena. The Palestinian problem was not bringing the Arab world together in harmony. The issue of the Palestinian entity was put on ice at the inter-Arab forums for a period of two years during which time Egypt boycotted the meetings of the ALC in August 1962. This was followed by the Yemen War which broke out in September that year.

The 40th session of the ALC in September 1963 was an important landmark in the development of the issue of the Palestinian entity, i.e. the establishment of Palestinian representative institutions. The need to appoint a successor for Ahmad Hilmi, the head of the All-Filastin Government and Filastin representative in the Arab League, who died on June 29, 1963, served as a pretext for the Egyptians to eliminate once and for all this institution and to advance from the level of words to that of deeds in the establishment of Palestinian representative institutions. It partially succeeded. On Egypt's initiative, with the support of Iraq, Ahmad al-Shuqayri was invited to participate in the discussions in order to explain his proposals on the subject.

On August 24, 1963 Iraq presented the ALC with its proposals for the establishment of the Palestinian entity. The Iraqi proposal spoke about the establishment of a Palestinian National Council whose members would be elected in Arab countries including Jordan. These Palestinians would be divided into constituencies which would then each elect a representative. The council would elect a Palestinian government which would represent Filastin in the ALC and in the international arena. It would be responsible for the establishment of a Palestinian liberation army.[7] Jordan reiterated its basic stand against an operative decision on the issue of the entity or representation. Shuqayri stressed that:

> The Palestinian organization that would be established, would possess executive sovereignty (*siyada tanfidhiya*) but not territorial sovereignty (*siyada iqlimiya*), that is to say that during this period this organization would not have sovereignty over the West Bank or the Gaza Strip. The organization would only have territorial sovereignty over all Filastin following its liberation. The Palestinian people would decide its destiny only following the realization of its independence whether through the establishment of an independent state or through unity with an Arab state.[8]

The ALC eventually passed two separate resolutions on September 19, 1963:

1   On the issue of Palestinian representation: The appointment of Shuqayri as the "representative of Filastin" in the ALC "until the Palestinian people would be able to elect its own representatives." Thus the right of the Palestinian people to choose its own representatives was indirectly recognized and this was in opposition to Jordan's stand. Shuqayri was assigned the function of "forming and heading a Palestinian delegation" which he would take to the General Assembly of the UN. A precedent was created as a representative of Filastin in the League also became its representative in the UN. It was only natural that Jordan would register its opposition to this decision and the representative of Saudi Arabia would express his "disagreement with the principle upon which the decision was based" (meaning Shuqayri himself).

2   On the issue of the Palestinian entity: It was determined that the "right belongs to the Palestinian people to restore its homeland and to decide on its destiny and to realize its national rights fully." It was said that "the time has come for the possessors of Filastin to handle their problems by themselves and it is the duty of the Arab states to allow them to do this in democratic ways." The ALC expressed its support of the Iraqi proposal and recommended that this proposal, together with the other proposals which were suggested by the Arab states, be discussed in the ALC which was supposed to convene in February 1964. Jordan, in rejecting this proposal, suggested its substitution by another version which fitted its policy in stating that "the liberation of Filastin would be achieved through the aid and participation of the Arab states. Only after the completion of the liberation of Palestinian land from Israel would the Palestinians (*ahl Filastin*) decide on their political future in accordance with their wishes."[9]

To conclude, Egypt's idea to revival the Palestinian entity presented Jordan with a new challenge which threatened its existence and territorial integrity, both in the immediate and distant future. In addition to this threat, there was a more concrete threat to the existence of the regime in the violent Egyptian endeavor to overthrow the regime of the King Husayn. Thus in that period, the regime struggled with two challenges which complemented and assisted one another. Hence we learn that the struggle for the existence of the Hashemite Kingdom intensified precisely during the period when the regime was attempting to *"Jordanize"* the Palestinian population under Husayn's rule. Against this background, one may understand Husayn's bitter and obstinate opposition to the plan of the Palestinian entity in all its components. This opposition was expressed in unrestrained repressive means against the opponents who strove to overthrow his regime.

The Arab League Council was not capable of passing binding operative decisions on such an important issue as the Palestinian entity and the Palestinian representation within its usual framework; for that a senior-level meeting of the Arab heads of state would be required. However, without the prolonged penetrating discussions during the years 1959–1963, during which the significance of new political concepts in the arena of the Palestinian problem were clarified, the first Arab summit that was convened in January 1964 would not have been capable of passing those decisions which paved the way for the establishment of representative Palestinian institutions by Shuqayri.

The Arab–Israeli Struggle over Water

The water struggle was a major factor in the deterioration of Arab–Israeli relations that led to the Six Day War in 1967. The Arab states' struggle over Israel's water plans, especially the National Water Carrier (NWC) plan that was designed to carry water from the Jordan River and Sea of Galilee to the Negev, was an integral part of both the overall Arab struggle against Israel and the inter-Arab dispute over the method of solving the Arab–Israeli conflict. The struggle generated discussion on all aspects of the Arab–Israeli conflict and stood at the center of the conflict.

Following the debates the Arabs prepared, for the first time, a military plan for liquidating Israel, and long-term and short-term strategic goals in their struggle against the Zionist state. Water became the main topic in the Arab media and in inter-Arab forums such as the Arab League Council (ALC), Arab Defense Council (ADC), Arab chiefs-of-staff conference, and the highest forum – the Arab summit conferences-attended by the monarchs and presidents of Arab countries. Discussion in these forums centered on the *modus operandi* for meeting the challenge of Israel's water plan.

Since the Arab world viewed the Jordan River's water as a key element in the overall Palestinian problem and Arab–Israeli conflict, then its solution became part of the Arab, Egyptian, or Syrian strategy. Egypt had determined the strategy in the Arab–Israeli conflict and the Arab response to Israel's plans to divert the Jordan River. Just as Syria's position was the exact opposite of Egypt's on the first issue, so too was its position on the water issue.

The Jordan River is formed by the convergence of three rivers at a point 6.3 kilometers south of the closest point to the Lebanese border: the Banias in Syria, the Hasbani in Lebanon, and the Dan in Israel. From here the Jordan flows south (west of Israel's international border with Syria), through an area that was a demilitarized zone until the Six Day War, and spills into the Sea of Galilee. It then exits from the sea's southern end and flows through the Jordan Valley in Israel to Naharayim; from there until the Beit Shan Valley the river forms the border between Israel and the Kingdom of Jordan. From the Beit Shan Valley to the Dead Sea, the Jordan flows through the Kingdom of Jordan where it receives two major tributaries: the Yarmuk, whose sources lie mainly in Syria (the Yarmuk is an important source of the lower Jordan's waters, and its southern flank forms the Israeli–Jordanian border), and the al-Zarqa River that originates in the Kingdom of Jordan.

A regional cooperation plan for exploiting Jordan's water was first broached in the 1930s but until 1956, only 14 per cent of the river was used for irrigating riparian areas in Israel, Jordan, and Syria. Naturally the lack of cooperation stemmed mainly from the political situation: the Arab–Israeli conflict and differences of opinion among the Arab states.

On September 2, 1953, Israel began diversion operations of the river. For engineering reasons, the authorities had to choose an area south of the Banot Ya'akov Bridge (in the demilitarized zone along the Syrian border north of the Sea of Galilee). The plan included the digging of a 2.5 kilometer-long channel south of the bridge for transporting the water south to Tabha (at the northern shore) and using elevation differences for producing electricity. The plan called for the project to be carried out in the demilitarized zone – but not on Arab soil. While Israel proceeded with its operations, Syria issued its first complaint to the secretary-general of the United Nations on October 12, 1953. It accused Israel of violating the armistice agreement on three counts: it infringed upon the rights of the inhabitants in the demilitarized zone; it blocked the use of the Jordan's water for local Syrian irrigational needs; and it was occupying the demilitarized zone with military forces.

Syria issued a similar complaint to the UNSC (UN Security Council) on October 16, 1953, demanding that the UNSC convene for a discussion and resolution on the matter. Discussion began on October 27. The Israeli representative announced that his government was prepared to cease work temporarily in the demilitarized zone so as not to impede the UNSC's discussion. Operations ceased at midnight on October 28. At the conclusion of the debate on December 12, France, Britain, and the United States proposed a joint resolution, but when the resolution came to a vote on January 22, 1954, the Soviet Union cast its veto. The aim of the proposal had been to find a compromise between the parties in order to allow the plan's continuation.[10]

Israel ceased diversion operations in the demilitarized zone following the UNSC vote, mainly because of US pressure (including the threat of withholding economic aid). The background to this pressure was Washington's effort to find a solution to the region's water problem with a comprehensive plan for distributing the water to Israel and the Arab states.[11]

Israel turned its full attention toward an alternative diversion plan based on pumping water from the Sea of Galilee and transporting it to the Negev via the NWC. The details of this change of plans were first published in 1959.

Between 1952 and 1953, the United Nations Relief and Works Agency (UNWRA) asked that a regional plan be prepared for exploiting the Jordan's water, one that did not take the political geography and other political factors into consideration.[12] On October 7, 1953, Eric Johnston was named president Eisenhower's special envoy to the Middle East to promote a regional plan for developing the Jordan Basin's water and distributing it among the sides: Jordan, Syria, Lebanon, and Israel. The plan was part of US efforts to resolve the Middle East conflict and the refugee problem.

During technical and political talks with Israel and the Arab states, Johnston introduced a number of changes in the plan in order to reach a mutual agreement.[13] During the next two years (from October 1953 through 1955), Johnston came to the region four times to discuss water allotment and presented his final recommendations in October 1955. Israel accepted the redesigned plan, but the members of the Arab League's Technical Committee, having accepted the plan on principle, asked for more time to study its political ramifications. In practical terms, however, the Arab states rejected the plan for political reasons because they felt that signing a water distribution agreement with Israel meant the recognition of Israel's existence.

The "Johnston Plan" (whose official name was the "United Plan") was redefined as a "memo of understanding" for the parties' sake. The US version that became known to Israel only in 1959 determined the following allocation:[14] Lebanon would receive up to 35m cubic meters of water from the Hasbani (including the Wazani Spring). Syria would receive up to 20m cubic meters a year from the Banias, up to 22m cubic meters a year from the Jordan for use at the Butayha Farms (the northern shore of the Sea of Galilee) and up to 90m cubic meters a year from the Yarmuk.

Arrangements were made for a Jordanian–Israeli water exchange. There were two versions to the arrangements based on Johnston's discussions with Israel (July 1955) and the Arabs (The Jordan Valley plan – October 1955). While Johnston was finalizing the water exchange agreement between Israel and Jordan he believed that he could convince the Israelis, based on statements made by their representatives, to agree to greater concessions. According to the Israeli version (based on the July 1955 agreement), 100m cubic meters of water (30m cubic meters of brackish water and 70m cubic meters of freshwater from the Sea of Galilee) would be channeled into the Jordan River at a point south of the Sea of Galilee). Jordan promised to channel 40m cubic meters a year to Israel from the Yarmuk. On the other hand, according to the US–Arab version (based on Johnston's October 11, 1955 memorandum to the Arabs) Israel would channel 100m cubic meters a year into the Jordan (consisting of 15m cubic meters of brackish water and 85m cubic meter of freshwater from the Sea of Galilee); while Israel received 25m cubic meters from the Yarmuk.[15] In either case the brackish water should not exceed 2500 parts per million to the Sea of Galilee's freshwater.

The failure of Johnston's mission terminated further attempts at regional water cooperation. After 1955, the Arabs no longer raised the issue. Israel and Jordan gave the United States "a written promise to abide by the Johnston Plan, although Israel made it clear that its promise depended on an Arab agreement for a mutually accepted plan in the foreseeable future."[16]

The Arab Response to Israel's Plan to Divert the Jordan, 1959–1963

The 1953 water crisis was an Israeli–Syrian problem, but Israel's Jordan Diversion Plan became a general Arab–Israeli problem for the first time when the ALC met in Casablanca in September 1959. After a short discussion the ALC decided to establish a technical committee consisting of representatives of the UAR (Egypt and Syria), Jordan, and Lebanon who would study the problem and present recommendations at the next meeting.[17]

In late November 1959 the subject also came up for discussion in a UAR government session headed by Nasir, during which it was decided to convene a special session of the ALC to discuss the Israeli plan. The Technical Committee met between December 19 and 25, 1959 and resolved to call on the Arab countries to take appropriate steps to prevent Israel from pursuing its "aggressive plans."[18] From this point, the Arab media put the issue on the front burner.[19] Israel's diversion of the Jordan River became the subject of an Egyptian media attack that grew in intensity beginning in December 1959. The press trumpeted Nasir's absorbing interest in the Israeli plan and the steps that Egypt had to take to thwart "Israel's intrigue."[20]

Nasir stood at the head of the UAR – the Egyptian–Syrian unification – and was responsible for developments on the Syrian border. There were several direct factors for the Arabs' awakening and their determined, intense handling of the means to prevent Israel from carrying out water diversion:

During October and November 1959, Johnston initiated a number of meetings with the Egyptian foreign minister, Mahmud Fawzi, who was in the US attending the UN General Assembly, and informed him that Israel was about to implement – no later than by the end of November – its Jordan River diversion plan. Johnston stressed the problem's urgency and pressed Fawzi to discuss the issue and come to a general resolution on it by the end of November.[21] The Egyptians realized that Johnston was referring to Israeli engineering operations in the demilitarized zone along the Syrian border. Egypt attributed special meaning to Johnston's words because of his previous mission and his connections with the Eisenhower Administration. Washington knew about these meetings with Fawzi and may have even initiated them. The Americans wanted to renew negotiations with the Arab states in order to obtain a US-brokered regional water agreement. A new regional water plan could be based on the old one. Israel, however, responded negatively to these feelers. In December 1959 the US proposed to the Arab states, including Jordan and the UAR, the possible return to the Johnston Plan. Jordan rejected the proposal because debate on the issue was going on in the Arab arena. During the same period, early October, the Israeli finance minister, Levi Eshkol, and the chairman of Israel's Water-planning Authority, Aharon Weiner, were in the US discussing US aid for an Israeli water project. Johnston used this visit as a pretext to get the Arabs to agree to a regional water plan.[22]

Statements by Israeli officials added to the Arabs' fear that the water plan would be realized in the near future. On October 4, 1959 Moshe Dayan announced in an election campaign speech that the next government would divert the Jordan's water to the Negev – with or without the Arabs' agreement.[23] On December 17, 1959 he declared that "If the Arabs refuse to cooperate in solving the Jordan water problem [then] we'll proceed like we did in the Gulf of Aqaba and take the water by force."[24] Eshkol's statement of November 18, 1959 probably added to the consternation in the Arab world and stimulated it to frenzied activity. Eshkol stated that "the diversion of the Jordan has become a top priority plan and its first stage, at a cost of 150m Israeli Lira, would be completed in five years."[25]

The Arab states realized that Israel's water plan was a vehicle for strategic growth. It would enable the country to absorb masses of new immigrants, populate the Negev, and advance toward economic independence. An article appearing in the Egyptian press on December 5, 1959, noted that "the plan is also dangerous for political reasons since Israel intends to farm the Negev's land in order to guarantee employment for five million new immigrants."[26] The UAR sent a message to the Arab League on January 4, 1960 demanding that the ALC convene to discuss an Arab diversion plan of the Jordan. "The UAR had discovered an Israeli plot to divert the Jordan and exploit its water for irrigating large tracts of land in the Negev in order to absorb a huge number of new immigrants, and that this would be a serious danger to the security of the neighboring states and their territorial integrity, and is liable to undermine [a solution to] the Palestinian problem in the future."[27]

The Arab states feared that if Israel established facts on the ground and exploited the Jordan's waters, its acts would be recognized by international law. They saw the Israeli plan as the *de facto* realization of the Johnston Plan, and were disturbed about the removal of an important bargaining card for solving the Palestinian problem.

The water question became an inter-Arab problem, especially between 1959 and 1963 when inter-Arab rivalry was at its most intense since the Arab League's founding in 1945. The Arab world was polarized between two trends: the "national-revolutionary" trend under the leadership of Nasir, and the "moderate" trend under the leadership of Abd al-Karim Qasim who was a proponent of an Arab federative unification that would safeguard the "independence and sovereignty" of all the Arab states. The water problem exacerbated this rivalry, and each state tried to convince Arab public opinion that its position in the struggle against Israel was the more radical one.

The emergency atmosphere that pervaded the UAR leadership and infected the rest of the Arab leaders in October and November regarding Israel's allegedly immediate diversion intentions was also reflected in the Arab press – especially in Egypt. A December 5 *al-Aharam* article entitled "The President Demands an Immediate Report on Countermeasures. Israel is about to Conclude the Jordan Diversion Plan and Suddenly Announce its Implementation"[28] was based on information that Johnston had relayed to Egypt. Rooted in false information the Arabs believed that Israel was on the verge of initiating diversion operations. During October and November 1959, the Egyptians, and especially the Syrians, were convinced that Israel's diversion operations were at a much more advanced stage that they actually were. Furthermore, there was a great deal of opacity surrounding Israel's intentions, for example, the engineering operations in the demilitarized zone sparked the Syrians' fear that Israel intended to return to the original plan and pump the Jordan's water in the Banot Ya'akov Bridge region. Opacity can also be seen in a December 12 article by Salah Salim, a member of the Egyptian Revolutionary Council, on Israel's plan to divert the Jordan's water and link it to the Lake Hulah Drainage Project.[29]

Only later, after efforts at explanation and persuasion by Western states closely tracking Israel's progress, did the Arab countries begin to see that there would not be any water diversion and exploitation prior to 1963. The US convinced the Arab states that the actual use of the water would begin only in 1963 or 1964, that the Israelis intended to pump water from the Sea of Galilee, and that this project did not entail diversion operations in the demilitarized zone.

Given the centrality of the water issue and its influence on developments in the Arab–Israeli conflict, and the fact that the Egyptian leadership was largely responsible for developments on Syria's border with Israel in this period, Nasir took personal control of the matter. He apparently assessed that the problem had deteriorated after the dissolution of the UAR (September 28) because of the fear that a Syrian move on the border would not be in accord with Egyptian strategy in the conflict. This apprehension was behind Nasir's call for an Arab summit conference on December 23, 1963.[30]

The Syrian Position: The Use of Force

Israel's plans to divert the Jordan River worried Syria (the northern region of the UAR) and the Syrian Ba'th party more than it did any other Arab state prior to the Six Day War. In January 1961, the Ba'th claimed that Israel's water plan was "the most serious pan-Arab problem (qawmiya) on the Arab League's agenda today" in the struggle against Israel. The Ba'th kept to a militant, hard-line, uncompromising position: "[We must] forcibly halt Israel's diversion of the Jordan's water in order to prevent the eradication of the Palestinian problem." When the Nasir-led UAR government discussed Israel's diversion plan in December 1959, Akram al-Hourani, a founder of the Ba'th party, and leader and minister in the UAR government, called for "para-military activity,"[31] that is, limited military operations in the area where Israel was carrying out engineering work (considered then to be the central demilitarized zone).

The Ba'th's position stemmed from a number of basic factors: Israel's diversion of the Jordan was basically a Syrian problem since the project was planned to begin in the demilitarized zone and the Sea of Galilee's water would be pumped at a spot close to the Syrian border. The Banias, one of the Jordan's main tributaries, originated in Syria and flowed through Syrian territory. Syria reckoned that Israel was planning to use the water project to seize the demilitarized zone. In October 1960 the Ba'th had noted that "The demilitarized zone was the only place where the Jordan could be diverted."[32]

The Ba'th's position was rooted in Syria's view of the means for solving the Arab–Israeli conflict. The Ba'th perceived the blocking of Israel's water diversion project as the "main issue" on the pan-Arab agenda and the spearhead in the struggle to liquidate Israel. According to the party, "the diversion of the river's flow is the greatest danger threatening the Palestinian Arabs' rights since the nakba [the catastrophe of the Arabs] in 1948[33] and is also "a military threat of the first order that has to be dealt with by force . . . The Arabs' right to destroy the State of Israel is a legitimate right. The Arabs' efforts must be diverted to strangling Israel and preparing for its destruction. The correct position . . . is to prevent the diversion of the Jordan by every means available and under all circumstances . . ."[34] Syria favored the use of force in order to counter the diversion. It avowed in October 1960 that "Arab artillery could easily halt the [Israeli] diversionary works and destroy the equipment by force . . ."[35] In February 1962, the Ba'th requested the mobilization of all the forces necessary to destroy the plan's facilities . . ."[36] Only later did Syria realize that Israel had decided to pump water from the Sea of Galilee.[37]

The Ba'th position also stemmed from its rivalry with Egypt for public opinion in the Arab world. The Ba'th represented the opposing pole to Egypt's in the Arab–Israeli conflict. When the water crisis broke out in late 1959, the Ba'th, then a senior partner in the UAR, was quick to adopt a firm position on the issue. It expressed its stand not only in public statements by the Ba'th ministers and party spokesmen, but also in internal debates in the UAR government, in contacts with the Egyptians during the period of unity, and in (secret) internal circulars sent to party members in Syria and

Lebanon.[38] The dispute between the Ba'th and Nasir over the way of responding to Israel's diversion operations contributed to the Ba'th ministers' resignation from the UAR government on December 24, 1959.

The Debates in Inter-Arab Forums

The water issue was raised at the Arab League Council meeting held in Cairo at Egypt's initiative in February 1960. At the end of the meeting, on February 29, the council passed three decisions: (1) Israel's attempts to divert the Jordan's water are aggressive acts against the Arabs that justify legitimate self-defense by every Arab state. (2) The Jordan's water should be used for the benefit of the Arab states and the Palestinian Arabs. The council recommends setting up a special technical committee under the auspices of the Arab League. The committee will coordinate its steps on this issue and oversee their implementation. (3) The council appoints the Permanent Military Committee [subordinate to the Arab League Council and including staff officers of the Arab armies] to prepare a comprehensive plan for all contingencies.[39]

The issue was repeatedly discussed during the Arab foreign ministers conference held in Shtura, Lebanon, in August 1960, where it was decided to ask the special technical committee to continue its work and present a report to the Arab League's secretary general. In addition, the Permanent Military Committee was to prepare an inclusive report that would take into account all contingencies stemming from Israel's plans to divert the Jordan.[40]

The Permanent Military Committee's report to the ALC contained the following points: (1) A general evaluation of the situation shows that [Arab] preventive action against Israel's diversion of the Jordan's water could transform a limited series of border incidents into a battle involving all of the Arab military forces. (2) The Arab armies will have to be sufficiently strong to deal with this. Therefore, a unified, detailed, comprehensive plan will have to be drawn up for joint military activity, and at least a two-year period of preparatory activity will be necessary until any [Arab military] operations can be carried out. (3) The committee recommends convening the Arab Armies' Chiefs-of-Staff Committee (the Military Advisory Council) to discuss establishing a common mechanism capable of realizing this task, [a mechanism] that will include one hundred officers, instead of the [present] Military Committee made up of a number of officers most of whom are military attachés at Arab embassies in Cairo.[41]

During 1961, the debate intensified in Arab forums over the military aspects of an Arab response to Israel diversion plans. Talks also continued on an alternative option – an Arab "technical" response, that is, an Arab preventive diversion plan. The discussion proceeded under the shadow of Israeli warnings that any attempt to divert the Jordan's water "would be considered a threat to peace" – thus the Arab states assessed that military action would be inevitable.

The Arab League Council meeting in Baghdad between January 30 and February 4, 1961 reviewed the entire water issue, including the Permanent Military Committee's report. Sharp differences of opinion were voiced on whether to block Israel's diversion of the Jordan by force or by the Arabs' own diversion project. Whichever option was taken would evoke an Israeli response. Since the participants failed to reach an agreement on the recommendations of the Water Experts Technical Committee that had met in Cairo, it was decided that both the water issue and Israel's nuclear development would come under the handling of the Arab Chiefs-of-Staff Committee. The council reaffirmed its 1960 decisions, especially the recommendation to convene an Arab chiefs-of-staff meeting "at the earliest possible date" to discuss a military counter-plan as the basis for the general planning to prevent Israel's diversion of the Jordan River.[42]

The Arab chiefs-of-staff met in Cairo between April 22 and 26, 1961 and examined the chances of thwarting Israel's plans by military means. This discussion reflected the change in the inter-Arab agenda regarding water diversion *vis-à-vis* the 1960 talks when the military aspects of an Arab response had been emphasized. The Arab world correctly estimated the termination date of and details on Israel's diversion plan (the opening of the NWC).

The chiefs made the following secret decisions: (1) The Israeli project was expected to be completed during 1963 and would create a situation requiring the Arab states to take joint military action. Palestinians' cooperation in the overall [Arab] plan would also have to be taken into consideration. (2) Since Israel could be expected to employ all of its military might, including foreign assistance and atomic weapons that it may have obtained (or developed independently), the Arab states must be prepared to destroy Israel's military power. (3) The Arab states' military action calls for immediate, top secret preparations so that the [Arab armies] will be ready to take the initiative and begin moving before 1963. These plans require an efficient joint mechanism.[43]

The Joint Arab Defense Council (JADC, hereafter ADC) met between June 10 and 18, 1961, comprised of foreign ministers, defense ministers, and chiefs-of-staff; this was the first time that the council had convened since 1955.[44] The UAR (Egypt) favored the technical plan for diverting the Jordan as the preferred line of action. Nevertheless it also agreed to open military discussions and reconvene the Joint Arab Command (JAC) – in accordance with the articles of the 1950 Collective Security Pact.[45]

The ADC resolved that: "In light of the military situation estimate and the information brought before it, the third session of the council has decided in June 1961: "(1) To establish a joint general command of the Arab states' forces. (2) To approve the command's structure. (3) To approve the recommendations of the chiefs-of-staff conference for establishing the command staff or its core within two months from the date of the recommendations' approval. To determine the plan's general outline and provide an estimate of the forces and roles the Arab states will play in the budgeting within four months from the staff's establishment. (4) To have the states where the Jordan's sources are located prepare the technical and financial means as soon as possible and be ready within six months to implement the essential technical plans. (5) To have the Joint Arab Defense Council determine a realistic date for commencing the implementation of these plans."[46]

With the dissolution of the Egyptian–Syrian unification on September 28, 1961, relations between the two states changed over the water issue. Inter-Arab relations entered a new phase of disquiet when Nasir announced that "unity of the aim" takes precedent over "unity of the ranks." The dissolution strengthened Nasir's uncompromising national pan-Arab policy toward the Arab world.

In 1962, Israel's diversion of the Jordan went from being a common pan-Arab cause to a controversial issue between Arab camps. Egypt, for example, exploited the water issue for unleashing an attack on the new government in Syria, declaring that the "break-up of the UAR encouraged Israel to pursue its plan and lay the Jordan

Valley pipeline" (a project unconnected with the NWC Plan, and parts of which were completed before the dissolution of the UAR).[47] In early 1962 the Syrians, supported by Jordan and Lebanon, warned of the approaching danger involved in Israel's water diversion. All three states reported Israel Defense Forces (IDF) concentrations in the north of Israel – supposedly connected with the immediate implementation of the Jordan River Project.

Ba'th revolutions took place in Iraq and Syria respectively in February and March 1963, but a counterrevolution in Iraq in November brought an end to the Ba'th regime. Against the setting of the unstable situation in inter-Arab relations, at its meetings held in March 1962 and September 1963, the ALC had to adopt the defense council's earlier decisions. There were repeated incidents along the Israeli–Syrian border between July and September 1963, especially in the southern sector of the demilitarized zone. Following these incidents, and apparently due to a Syrian intelligence assessment, Syria feared that a large-scale Israeli offensive would occur in August 1963. Along with its grievances over the border incidents, Syria also complained of the approaching date of the opening of Israel's NWC in order to pressure the Arab states for their active support in case hostilities erupted.

In the autumn of 1963, with the approaching opening of the NWC, Syria's Ba'th regime found itself in one the most critical stages in its history. This stage was characterized, *inter alia*, by the struggle between factions and trends after the fall of the Ba'th regime in Iraq and especially by the need to respond to the approaching completion of Israel's water project and the pressure of Nassarite Egyptians plotting to topple the Ba'th regime. The president of Syria, Amin al-Hafiz, realized that if he threatened to obstruct Israel's diversion of the Jordan he could turn the tables on Egypt and force it to act by presenting it with the challenge that Syria really intended to go to war.[48]

The Arab League called for the convening of the Arab Defense Council and the Arab chiefs-of-staff conference in December 1963. In September, the ALC decided to summon the Arab Defense Council "at as early a date as possible to deal with the present critical stage." Prior to the conference, the Arab chiefs-of-staff (Advisory Committee) met between December 7 and 9. The following topics headed the agenda:

1 Defining the size of the force under the Joint Arab Command for carrying out the Arab military plan.
2 The amount of troops and material resources each Arab state would furnish the Joint Arab Command with an order guaranteeing the success of the Arab plan. In the course of the meeting, Egypt announced that it would not launch an attack from its border but was prepared to send troops to assist Syria. The Syrians rejected the Egyptian proposal, and the debate over an Arab offensive against Israel's NWC, if it became operational, ended without a decision. After discussing counter-measures, the Arab chiefs-of-staff committee recommended, *inter alia*, to the Arab Defense Council:
  A Setting up a headquarters or special staff or skeleton headquarters based on the previous decisions.
  B Calling on the Arab states to transfer selected officers to the League in order to establish a headquarters or skeleton staff (of about sixty officers).
  C Establishing a special mechanism for carrying out immediate and long-range technical counter-operations. The mechanism would begin

functioning before Israel began its diversion operations or shortly after-wards.[49]

None of these recommendations were discussed because the Arab Defense Council did not convene in January 1964 as planned. Instead, an Arab summit conference met in January following Nasir's initiative on December 23, 1963. Nevertheless, the decisions at this and the previous meetings served as the basis for the first summit's resolutions on the establishment of a United Arab Command, and the technical decision for the Arabs' own diversion of the Jordan's tributaries.

Part II   *The Crystallization of Arab Strategy: Decisions of the First and Second Arab Summit Conferences, 1964*

At the time when the Arab Chiefs-of-Staff Committee was convened (7–9 December 1963), the Syrians launched a virulent propaganda campaign against Egypt's reaction to Israel's impending opening of the NWC. Despite Egypt's claim to decided military superiority, the Syrians accused Nasir of lacking the will to stand up to Israel and cowardice in his treatment of the conflict. The Syrians further asserted that the Israeli water carrier was an issue involving all the Arab countries, not only Syria. Syria argued that "The dangers inherent in it threaten all of us; a unified Arab military strategy must be designed to thwart the [Israeli] diversion plan which is in reality a military ruse. By refraining from an armed confrontation to prevent the diversion of the Jordan's waters, Egypt has betrayed the Arab cause. The technical proposals for an [Arab] diversion scheme of the Jordan's sources are not a practical solution, but only a trick to confuse the Arab world. Nasir's subversive policy towards Syria is devastating pan-Arab relations while encouraging Israel to execute her own water scheme."[1] Shortly before the Arab chiefs-of-staff meeting began, *Radio Damascus* called on the Generals "to arrive at practical and conclusive decisions that will deter Israel and [western] imperialism from their plans to divert the Jordan River."[2]

Following the conference, Syria outlined (on December 15, 1963) six strategic threats to the Arab states which would result from the opening of Israel's NWC.

1   Israel would be able to absorb four million additional Jews into Filastin, an influx that would allow a heavier concentration of manpower in order to prepare itself for the decisive campaign in the future.
2   The project would forever separate the Arab East (al-Mashriq al-'Arabi) from the Arab West (*al-Maghrib al-'Arabi*) by means of a tightly crowded human wall in the Negev, and would thus destroy Arab plans for unity and the encirclement of Israel.
3   The project would increase Israel's manpower and economic strength, would place it at an advantage *vis-à-vis* the Arab forces.
4   The project was likely to bolster Israel's military potential, thereby encouraging it to launch new hostilities against Arab lands.

41

5   The Jordan River diversion was only one link in a series of Zionist-imperialist acts of expansionism against the Arab homeland.

6   The Jordan River project was another step in the aggressive policy of Israeli irredentism which defined its borders from the Nile to the Euphrates, and whose goal was to expel the Arabs from the entire region and settle in their place twenty million Jews.[3]

The Egyptians responded strongly to the Syrian charges and sought to repudiate this anti-Egyptian propaganda. They stated that the Arab states were feeble *vis-à-vis* Israel, and that while they masqueraded as "the protectors of Filastin," in reality they had not lifted a finger to oppose the Jordan River's diversion. Their basic motive was only to plot against Egypt. Two leading activists in defending Egypt's stature in the Arab world were Nasir al-Din al-Nashashibi, a senior commentator of the official organ *al-Jumhuriya* and Ahmad Sa'id, head commentator of *Sawt al-Arab*. Nashashibi bitterly criticized Arab leaders for denouncing Egypt as indifferent. He described "the empty-headed tumult they make in attacking Israel's diversion operations" as cheap and mindless propaganda, a transparent ploy to shirk away from taking responsible action.[4] "Syrian leaders are perfectly aware of their own ineptitude and will not dare to forcibly prevent [Israel's] diversion operations next spring," he charged. "What prevents you from diverting the Banias' waters which flow through your own territory," he piqued the Syrians. "Why do you not initiate a military campaign against Israel and announce the date, instead of bestowing upon the enemy the luxury of determining his own time-schedule?"[5]

Despite this, the Egyptian media was not remiss in pointing out the implications inherent in Israel's NWC. "The project would invest Israel with new economic powers through the irrigation of the Negev, and the absorption of millions of new immigrants would add decisively to Israel's military strength. Israel's enhanced strength would induce it to expansionism over Arab lands." Egyptian newspapers also emphasized the importance of the Negev as "a springboard into Sinai." "Israel's diversion of the Jordan would deny water to Syria, and turn the Kingdom of Jordan's agricultural soils into wastelands."[6]

Syrian propaganda diatribes against Egypt multiplied following an article written by Ihsan 'Abd al-Qudus in the Egyptian weekly *Ruz al-Yusef* on December 15, 1963:

The most lethal weapon that Israel holds in its arsenal for realizing its plans is that of schism in the Arab world. Israel is fully aware that the UAR [Egypt] wields the power and energy to disrupt its plans and annihilate it; however, it also knows that the Egyptian army cannot mobilize its full weight until the regime is absolutely convinced that the countries along Israel's borders are prepared [to fight]. Yet the regimes on these fronts are looking to ambush Egypt more than Israel! They would prefer Egypt to disappear instead of Israel. The propaganda machinery of these regimes is screaming for Egypt to extirpate Israel . . . [but] what they really desire is for Egypt to get bogged down in a war [with Israel] . . . and when that occurs they will withdraw seeing that the moment of truth has arrived to stab her [Egypt] in the back . . . but Egypt will not fall into that trap, it knows when and how to destroy Israel . . . The Arab fronts will not unite in a coalition for war against Israel unless they are politically united. There is no sense in a joint-military command unless it is backed by comprehensive and firm political unity . . . The UAR takes full responsibility as Arab leader. It has always taken the lead without getting itself bogged down or falling prey to another country's intrigues . . . Today [Egypt] knows when and how to destroy Israel.

In reaction to this article, published undoubtedly with the Egyptian government's backing, the Syrian authorities gave the following detailed reply:

1   *Ruz al-Yusef* deals with two major points: (a) Egypt will not initiate any military action against Israel's diversion of the Jordan River until a general political unification of Arab countries is achieved; (b) Egypt knows when and how to destroy Israel, and is capable of doing so by itself. This article, in effect, encourages Israel to pursue its river diversion plans and, at the same time, discourages joint Arab efforts from meeting the Israeli challenge. The conflict with Israel today is the struggle against its water scheme because execution of these plans will greatly diminish the chances of winning back Filistin.[7]

2   The Arab nation regards the *Ruz al-Yusef* article as a boost to imperialist circles to continue their stratagems for erasing the problem of Filistin. The battle against diversion of the Jordan is the task of all Arab countries. A call to divide the struggle should be seen as a flagrant national betrayal.[8]

3   It is beyond our comprehension how Cairo considers a national undertaking as a question of getting bogged down. On the other hand, we well understand why Egypt does not view the opening of the Straits of Aqaba to Israeli navigation and the stationing of UN forces along the borders as falling into a trap. But, we have yet to figure out why Egypt endeavors to befuddle the main struggle, for it is Israel, not Cairo, that day and night threatens to re-channel the flow of the Jordan, whereas the Arabs are stubbornly determined to prevent this. Should we announce to Israel: Go ahead, divert the Jordan, we will fight you only after we have become a united country?[9]

4   Will we face up to Israel's stratagems and guile with cowardice and fear of getting tied down in a war? If we are afraid of opposing Israel over water diversion today, how will we annihilate it tomorrow?[10]

5   Cairo's scheming and plotting are not strange to us. Egypt trades in all that is sanctified to the Arab nation, but we are steadfast in our conviction that the diversion of the Jordan is an Arab problem. Furthermore, it is a question of life and death, as well as a test of the Arab leaders, and the Arab nation's *raison d'être*.[11]

On December 23, 1963, in a speech at Port Saʻid on "Victory Day" (commemorating the evacuation of British and French soldiers from the city in 1956), Nasir called an Arab summit meeting "in order to deal with the Jordan River problem which is part of the question of Filistin." He also took note of the Syrians' extremist line regarding the Arab reaction to the opening of Israel's NWC in the summer of 1964. *Inter alia*, Nasir stated:

Filastin of 1948 will never return. It is impossible to deal with the Palestinian issue in the same way as in 1948. In 1960, during the period of unification, I asked the government, which included members from Syria, what could be done technologically and politically, but in the meantime not militarily, between 1960 and 1964 regarding Israel and the Jordan River project. At that time we came to the conclusion that Israel must be prevented from [diverting] Arab waters from the Hasbani, Banias, and Yarmuk Rivers. Afterwards we discussed military matters. The Ba'th press has stated that the UAR will not participate in a war over the Jordan River. I also know everything that was discussed at the Arab chiefs-of-staff conference [December 1963]. In my opinion, the Arab chiefs of staff should not have a say in this issue because, first and foremost, it is a political problem, and only secondly is it a military one. We in UAR (Egypt) believe that neither the chiefs-of-staff conference nor the Arab Defense Council meeting have been beneficial because in order to face the challenge of Israel's threat, there is no alternative but to convene Arab kings and heads of state at as early a date as possible. Conflicting views and opinions must be held in abeyance. We are ready to sit down with those who differ with us, and for the sake of Filastin we would even be willing to talk with them [the Syrians]. The UAR (Egypt) is ready to fulfill all her obligations. If necessary, we will recall our troops from Yemen and form new combat units. We will dispatch a call to the [Arab] League for convening a [summit] conference at the earliest date. We will enter into serious negotiations; it is not a dishonor to admit we are unable to exercise force if this is the case. The battle for Filastin may extend for a long time, and the question of the Jordan River is part of this problem. [Turning to the Syrians, he said] Either we declare that we can forcibly prevent them [the Israelis] from diverting the Jordan River, and our armies are prepared for this, or [we should not be hypocrites] by saying one thing behind closed doors while in the public the opposite. From my side I will publish all the discussions. If I cannot fight, then I will say without shame 'I cannot fight'.[12]

The Arab summit conference that Nasir summoned was a way out of the quandary he was stuck in since the end of 1959. He had come to realize that the opening of Israel's NWC was about to take place, and that he could not keep his 1959 promise that "1963 or 1964 would be the year of decision. This would be the time when Israel had completed its plans for re-channeling the Jordan, and Arab armies would be ready for combat."[13] Nasir needed the Arab leaders' consent for justifying his postponing the military option. He found this legitimacy in statements made by Yusef Shukur, the Syrian chief-of-staff. Shukur claimed at the Arab chiefs-of-staff meeting (December 7–9, 1963) that "Syria cannot divert the Jordan's waters in her territory otherwise Israel will attack, wrest away the river's sources, and we will be helpless to do anything about it." Therefore, Nasir admitted that Egypt and Syria found themselves "unable to act freely in their own countries."[14] Nasir aspired for "collective Arab action in facing the Israeli threat." He thus called for an Arab summit, confident that he would be able to dictate his strategy to the Arab countries. He believed that he could enlist the Arabs' financial and military potential for a long-term strategy that would guarantee sufficient military preparedness for the decisive victory in a total war against Israel. At the same time, this would be the Arabs' immediate response to the challenge of Israel's diversion of the Jordan's waters.

Two possible paths of action lay before the Arab heads-of-state at the first summit conference (January 1964):

1 To forcefully prevent Israel from expropriating the Jordan's waters by means of an Arab initiated military strike.
2 To carry out the Arab Plan [for re-channeling the Jordan's tributaries] within Arab territory, leaving them [the Arab countries] in possession of most of the river's water, while at the same time making military preparations to safeguard Arab lands from Israel aggression.[15]

During preparations for the summit conference and throughout its discussions, Egypt ascertained that the second alternative would eventually be approved. At the conference's opening, Nasir spoke of the dangers emanating from the Israeli plan and emphasized the importance of creating an Arab deterrent force for deployment during the execution of the Arab Plan. Nasir supported the Arab Defense Council's recommendation of June 1961 which had called for the formation of a Joint Arab Command (JAC) to obstruct Israel from engineering its plans to channel the Jordan's waters to the Negev. He reiterated the Defense Council recommendations that the "plan must be drawn up in its general format, assessing all available forces, and defining the role each Arab state would take – all this within four months of the creation of the JAC's nucleus. Arab forces would have to supply the JAC with all the required assistance and information."[16] Nasir complained that, "despite the 1961 decision, work had not been carried out due to political disagreements which allowed the enemy to exploit the Arabs' bickering by speeding up work on the water project." He added that Arab Defense Council's recommendations were reaffirmed by the Arab chiefs-of-staff in their December 1963 meeting.[17] On the other hand, Amin al-Hafiz, demanded total war against Israel and "putting an end to the subjugation of Filastin." In his view, "that was preferable to haggling over the diversion of the Jordan's waters." Nasir countered that "if we are unable to defend ourselves, then how can we cross over to an attack?" Nasir reiterated Shukur's own words at the conference of the chiefs-of-staff, for the need to "complete defense arrangements before an attack could be considered."[18]

The first summit conference "did not distinguish between: (1) Israel's plan for diverting the Jordan's waters; (2) the danger [to the Arab countries] by Israel's existence; (3) the final destruction of Israel." It dealt with all these issues *en bloc* "as a unified strategic concept." In the preface to first summit's resolutions, it was stated:

> The establishment of Israel is a basic threat, and the struggle against it is entirely agreed upon by the Arab nation. Since Israel's existence is considered a menace to the Arab nation, diversion of the Jordan's waters by Israel increases the dangers to the Arab people's existence. Therefore, the Arab states should draw up the necessary plans for dealing with the political, economic, and social aspects [of this menace] so that if the necessary results are not achieved there will be a last practical recourse, collective Arab military preparations to annihilate Israel.[19]

The first summit conference decided on three major issues:

1 *Diverting the Jordan River's tributaries* – creating "the Authority for Utilizing the Jordan River and Tributaries." Its role was to "plan, coordinate, and supervise the Arab diversion project." The project would receive an immediate £6.25 million (the total cost was £56 million). A detailed plan for diverting the water would be prepared by the "Authority." At the opening discussions on this issue, Ahmad Salim, chairman of the "Authority," surveyed the blueprints of the Arab Plan and pointed out that re-channeling the Jordan River would take up to eight years (the assessment was that the project would require 8 to 12 years). Initial costs would come to £70 million.[20]

2 *Setting up the united Arab command* (al-Qiyada al-ʻArabiya al-Muwahada) – It was decided "to immediately set up a United Arab Command (UAC) for the Arab armies. The UAC's main task would be to defend the Arabs' diversion of the Jordan River and its tributaries . . . The structure and authority of the UAC was to be based on the Arab Defense Council's decisions of 1961." Fariq Awal (General) Ali Ali Amer was appointed commanding officer of the UAC. "Organizing the UAC nucleus will take only one month, and the entire unit will be fully manned within two months . . . All of the Arab countries are required to set up units according to UAC demands. The major objectives will be determined by the Joint Arab Defense Council. All the Arab member states are obliged to facilitate the UAC, follow its orders, and carry out its recommendations." A total of £154 million were allotted for Syrian, Jordanian, and Lebanese arms procurements.[21] In accord with the first summit conference, the Joint Arab Defense Council decided (on January 30, 1965) to define the UAC's areas of authority: planning and directing operations, preparing forces for war, and coordinating military cooperation among member states. The Joint Arab Defense Council also ratified the UAC's plan for defending the Arab project for exploiting the Jordan River's waters and tributaries.[22]

3 *The establishment of the Palestinian entity* – The summit conference decided that "Ahmad al-Shuqayri, the representative of Filastin in the Arab League, will continue his contacts with the member states [of the Arab League] and with the Palestinian people in order to establish the proper foundations for the organization the Palestinian people, to enable it fulfill its role in the liberation of its homeland, and its self-determination."[23]

This was the first operational decision, ratified both unanimously and at the highest level, for reviving the Palestinian entity. It paved the way for Shuqayri to set up the Palestinian liberation Organization (PLO) in June 1964.

Nasir dictated a new strategy for the Arab world that was based on the concept of "stages". The principles of this strategy were endorsed at the second summit conference and its military phases were ratified at the third summit. This strategy "defined for the first time a comprehensive battle-plan for the struggle against Israel, [and it also defined] the final goal of collective Arab action and the means and stages, for achieving it."[24] The uniqueness of the strategy was its abandonment of the concept of a one-shot, all or nothing solution to the Arab–Israeli conflict by "liberating Filastin and returning the Palestinian people's rights." Instead, the second summit determined that "The Arab goal in the military sphere contains two stages":

The first stage: "The first immediate goal" (*hadaf awwali 'ajil*): "strengthening the Arab defenses in order to guarantee the Arab countries, through which the Jordan flows, freedom of conduct on their own soil." This meant creating an effective defense force by beefing up the Arab armies, especially building up the confrontation countries – Jordan, Syria, and Lebanon. Construction of this Arab force would take at least three years, according to the UAC commander, that is, until the end of 1967 or the beginning of 1968. A total of £150 million was earmarked for the task. It was also decided to concentrate the special units from Saudi Arabia, Iraq, and Syria along the Jordanian and Lebanese borders to aid Jordan and Lebanon and to be ready for rapid deployment in the event of an Israeli attack or even a threat of one. The other Arab states pledged to place their armies on immediate alert for repelling aggression of this sort. The summit granted the UAC commander "full authority to transfer military units" from one country to another.[25]

In the transitional period of organizing the united command, Arab states had to avoid border skirmishes that could escalate into all-out war. It was Nasir's intent that the Arab countries would regain their freedom of conduct in their own territory at the end of this stage if they established a powerful military presence to deter Israel from aggressive moves and thus pushed the enemy into a defensive position.

The second stage: "The final pan-Arab national goal" (*hadaf qawmi niha'i*) – it was decided that the "final goal [in the military sphere] was the liberation of Filastin from Zionist imperialism," or as Nasir put it, "the eradication of Israeli imperialism and the return of Filastin lands." The UAC commanding officer was given the task of drawing up a detailed plan for the annihilation of Israel. This was presented at the third summit conference, where it was ratified. At the same summit, £200 million were raised for bolstering the Syrian, Jordanian, and Lebanese armies in order "to cross over from the defensive stage to the offensive one."[26] In order to realize "the final pan-Arab national (*qawmi*) goal for the liberation of Filastin," the second summit made the following resolutions:

1 To complete the building up of an Arab force that was designed to realize this goal; and to mobilize all the Arabs' military, economic, and political resources for this [force].
2 The UAC will draw up a detailed plan to include order of the battle, equipment, financial resources, and estimated time needed to realize the goal.
3 To require each state to define the amount of aid it could expend on manpower and capital for reinforcing the military units of the Arab countries bordering Israel in need of such aid. Each state would also spell out the means by which it could share the burden for reaching this pan-Arab national goal (*qawmi*).
4 Within one year the UAC commander will draw up a detailed plan for the liberation of Filastin from Zionist imperialism according to the amount of troop under his command. He will present the plan at the next Arab summit.
5 The UAC commander has the authority to transfer troops from one country to the next on condition that he takes into account, prior to the outbreak of war, the existing laws in each state. [This special clause was appended at Lebanon's request.][27]

In Nasir's opinion, war with Israel was inevitable.[28] Nevertheless, at the center of his "stages" concept stood the desire of not getting caught in a war with Israel until victory was assured. Nasir promulgated this policy both publicly, in camera, and during talks with Arab diplomats. His strategy gained increased support in light of Syria's demands on the UAC (i.e. Egypt) in March 1965 to escalate the Arab reaction along the borders after Israel's attacks on Syria's diversion works.

After the first Arab summit, the issue of water diversion was discussed in inter-Arab forum – at the meeting of the heads of the Arab delegations to the Mixed Armistice Commissions with Israel that was held from February 27 to March 1 1964 in East Jerusalem and Amman. The Jordanian representative raised the question of "the degree to which Israel's diversion of the Jordan River violated the armistice agreements." At the end of the discussion, it was decided that:

"The diversion of the Jordan River by Israel to the Negev south of Beer Sheva is a violation of Article II of the Israeli–Jordanian Armistice Agreement, according to which neither side is permitted to commit an act that gains for it a military or political advantage." [According to the official English version of Article II.1 of the Israeli–Jordanian Armistice Agreement (April 3, 1949): "The principle that no military or political advantage should be gained under the truce ordered by the Security Council is recognized by the parties]." This was in violation of Article IV which stated that the armistice lines were determined without damaging existing arrangements in the border lines and their demand of the two sides in the future. [According to the official version of Article VI.9 "The Armistice Demarcation Lines defined in Article V and VI of this Agreement are agreed upon by the parties without prejudice to future territorial settlements or boundary lines or to claims of either party relating thereto."] This was also [in violation of] Article V of the Israeli–Syrian Armistice according to which the steps that pertained to the armistice line and the demilitarized zone should not be interpreted as though they are connected to the final regional (*iqlimi*) arrangements between the two parties. [According to the official English version of Article V.1 Israeli–Syrian Armistice Agreement (July 20, 1949): "It is emphasized that the following arrangements for the Armistice Demilitarized Zone are not to be interpreted as having any relation to the ultimate territorial arrangements affecting the two parties to this agreement."] This was also in violation of the rest of the armistice agreements that had similar articles since the diversion of the Jordan River: 1. Grants Israel a distinct military advantage since it removes military obstacles that existed at the time of the agreement, and their removal is a basic military change. 2. It gains [for Israel] a political advantage because of the population enlargement and an economic advantage by increasing income, and for this reason Israel will profit militarily and politically. 3. [The diversion] harms the Arabs economically because it prevents Arab lands from being farmed, and harms the industry in the Dead Sea area because it lowers the sea level, and in effect becomes Israel's military and political gain."[29]

In conclusion: at the first summit the Arab countries tried coping with the challenge of the Israelis' diversion of the Jordan River while at the same time not getting involved in a war. At the second summit (September 1964) the Arab states ratified the plans for water diversion and its military defense, and the green light was given for initiating operations. At the third summit (September 1965) it became apparent that Arab leaders were caught between their desire to continue diverting the Jordan's tributaries and their inability to prevent Israel from blocking the project due to its military superiority, especially in the air. In this light, it is clear why the UAC commander recommended at the third summit conference, that each Arab state, unable to withstand Israeli attacks, would have the right to determine whether to continue diversion operations.

Failure of the Arab Plan for Diverting the River Jordan's Tributaries

The Arab Plan for diverting the River Jordan's tributaries was based on the technical committee's recommendations that were ratified at the second Arab summit conference. The following is an outline of the plan's rationale:

1 Diversion of Tributaries in Lebanon
   A *The Upper Hasbani* – the excavation of a canal from the Hasbani Springs in the Hasbaya region and a canal from Wadi Shab'a for carrying water to the Kawkaba Tunnels and from there to the Litani River. (This project would transport 40–60 million cubic meters of water annually).
   B *The Middle Hasbani* – two diversion points – the first, in the Hasbani riverbed; the second, in Wadi Sarid. The Hasbani and Sarid would flow in a canal to the Banias and from there to the Yarmuk. According to the plan, 20–30 million cubic meters of water would flow annually to Syria (if Lebanon did not divert the Hasbani's floodwaters to the Litani, the Sarid Canal could transport up to 60 million cubic meters of water a year).
   C *The Wazani Spring in the Lower Hasbani Riverbed* – this would include an irrigation canal (carrying 16 million cubic meters of water a year) for local use in Lebanon; an irrigation canal in Syria (8 million cubic meters a year); and three pumping units to transport the Wazani's overflow to Syria via the Sarid–Banias canal at a rate of 26 million cubic meters a year.

The total plan was designed to divert 100–140 million cubic meters of water from the Hasbani for Lebanese use, as opposed to 35 million cubic meters allotted to Lebanon in the 1955 Johnston Plan. The cost of this part of the project was estimated at two million Pounds Sterling, and the estimated time for completion was eighteen months. To recall: the Johnston Plan assigned Lebanon 35 million cubic meters of the Hasbani's water, but nothing for Syria. The Arab Plan intended to divert 85–115 million cubic meters of Lebanese water to Syria.

2 Diversions in Syrian Territory
   A *Diversion of the Banias* – The diversion plan for the Banias called for a 73-

kilometer long canal to be dug 350 meters above sea level that would link the Banias with the Yarmuk. The canal would carry the Banias's fixed flow plus the overflow from the Hasbani (including water from the Sarid and Wazani). The Banias diversion would provide 90 million cubic meters of water for the irrigation of riverine areas. The designers calculated that eighteen months would be sufficient for executing the plan. The cost was estimated at five million Pounds Sterling (including two tunnels), that is, approximately two million pounds more than the Arab Plan.

B   *The Butayha Project* – The Syrians feared that if the Arabs implemented their diversion plan, Israel would block the Butayha Valley inhabitants' annual pumping of 22 million cubic meters from the Jordan as proposed in the Johnston Plan. In order to guarantee the villagers their vital water supply, the Arab Plan contained a proviso designed to incorporate primary and secondary canals from the Sea of Galilee.

3   The Water Plans in Jordan

The construction of a dam in the Kingdom of Jordan (the Mukheiba Dam on the Yarmuk River) was designed to hold 200 million cubic meters of water. Work on the dam would take 30 months at a cost of ten and one quarter million Pounds Sterling. The Mukheiba Dam (and the Makarin Dam) would hurt Israel if it was incorporated into the diversion plans for the Jordan River's northern sources, and without the Mukheiba Dam all of the diverted water would flow back to the Yarmuk and return to the Jordan's riverbed south of the Sea of Galilee. Excluding this plan, the rest of Jordan's water projects corresponded with the main parts of the Johnston Plan.[1]

When the Arab Plan was completed, Israel would have lost three-quarters of its water from the Banias and Hasbani (including the entire flow of the Wazani), as well as one-third of the water planned for its NWC – according to the Johnston Plan's original allocation for the Arab states and Israel. Naturally the loss of such a quantity of freshwater would increase the saline level in the Sea of Galilee.

The Arab Plan also enabled the local exploitation of the Jordan's sources in Syria and Lebanon, and the all-inclusive use of the Yarmuk and the diverted waters for vast areas inside the Kingdom of Jordan. The Plan was based on two principles: *one*, local projects for the maximum exploitation of the water in adjacent areas, in other words, projects that paralleled the Johnston Plan's distribution; *two*, projects aimed at diverting the water to greater distances in order to hurt Israel. These projects included the construction of a tunnel from the Hasbani to the Litani, the diversion of spillovers from the Lower Hasbani and Wazani to the Banias; and the diversion of the Banias to the Yarmuk.

The second Arab summit (September 1964) resolved "to begin at once the technical operations for exploiting the Jordan and its tributaries" and to "complete the concentration of the forces from Saudi Arabia, Iraq, and Syria assigned to assist Jordan and Lebanon by being rapidly sent to their target areas in the event of an Israeli attack. The rest of the Arab countries are committed to placing their forces on alert to repel such aggression."

In the UAC commander's report to the second summit, he estimated that "Israel would respond with military action during one of the Arab Plan's implementation stages," either at or close to the completion of the project. If Israel proceeded in this direction, the commander figured, it would find itself engaged in a war that the Arab countries were ready for.[2]

Partial Implementation of the Diversion Plan in Lebanon

Lebanon hoped that the second Arab summit's decisions would not force it to take immediate steps to implement the diversion plan in its territory. Lebanon tried to evade the execution of the plan's technical sections by all sorts of maneuvers: it pleaded for changes; it intentionally delayed carrying out area surveys; it handled the administrative sides of the diversion (such as land expropriation and financial allotment) with painstaking slowness; it raised objections on the military aspects of the diversion projects (the absence of an explicit order from the UAC to commence engineering operations and delays in the deployment of Arab forces for the defense of the operations); it demanded a fixed pumping station on the Wazani in Syrian territory; it foot-dragged over the issue of the final water distribution between Lebanon and Syria, and insisted that diversion operations in its territory be postponed until the diversion work on the Banias and Yarmuk was completed.

In December 1964 Egypt began pressuring Lebanon by various means to begin diversion operations. The first sign of this pressure appeared in the propaganda campaign that Egypt initiated in Lebanon's pro-Egyptian newspapers[3] and the Egyptian press.[4] The campaign was aimed indirectly against the new Lebanese president, Charles Helou, who entered office on September 23, 1964. In early 1965 Egypt increased its pressure on Lebanon, through the UAC and in inter-Arab forums, to commence engineering operations.

The Conference of Arab Prime Ministers (mini-summit) (CAPM) that was held in Cairo between January 9 and 10, 1965 demanded that Lebanon begin construction on the Wazani pumps inside its territory. The conference also discussed and ratified the decisions of the ADC, that had met before the CAPM, dealing with water diversion in Lebanon and the location of the Wazani's pumping station. The ADC confirmed the UAC commander's report and proposed two alternatives: *one*, to set up the pump in Syrian territory (at Maghar Shab'a, about half a kilometer from the Israeli border), which would entail the permanent deployment of a regiment-sized Syrian military unit on Lebanese soil in the Marj Ayoun area and the guarantee that the force received regular supplies; *two*, to set up the pump in Lebanese territory (in the vicinity of Kafr Rajar, two kilometers from the Israeli border), without the deployment of Syrian forces in Lebanon.

The Lebanese prime minister participated in the CAPM and agreed to the first option for military and technical reasons, but he opposed the deployment of a Syrian regiment on Lebanese soil for "parliamentary considerations" (that is, the Lebanese parliament had to approve such a step, as required by the second summit). Lebanon feared the introduction of Syrian forces and their influence on the internal affairs of state.[5] Since no decision could be made, the ADC handed Ali Amer, the UAC commander, the right to determine the location of the pumping station. He decided it would be built in Lebanon, and the council approved his decision. The ADC's decisions were ratified by the CAPM's plenum on January 10, 1965, and Lebanon was forced to submit to the UAC's (Egypt's) dictates and end its delaying policy.[6] But from Lebanon's point of view this was the lesser of evils, although according to the newspaper *al-Hayat*, and not without a leak from official sources, Lebanon "consented" to Amer's position for the following reasons:

A "If a pumping station is set up on Syrian territory, Lebanon will have to open its border to Arab forces so that it can fulfill its historical role."

B "If Lebanon's denies Arab forces entry into its territory it will have to set up the station on its own soil. Lebanon prefers this possibility for a number of reasons: the distance of the pumping site in Lebanon from Israel's border as compared to the site intended for construction in Syria; from a technical point of view it is preferable to channel the water flow from Lebanon from a low height rather than pump the water from a high area in Syrian territory; thus Lebanon will not have to bear the presence of Arab forces on its soil and suffer an Israeli response since all of the Wazani flows inside Lebanon and international law permits Lebanon to do what it wants with its water."[7]

These claims were undoubtedly in response to the Lebanese Christians' criticism of the government for giving in to Egyptian pressure. On the other hand, if Lebanon persisted in its refusal, the Lebanese Muslims would intensify their anti-government propaganda and incitement. The Lebanese government also feared that if Lebanon rejected the council's demand, nationalist responses would be awoken outside the country that would have an influence on Lebanon's domestic situation.

On the night of January 22, after debating the CAPM's resolutions, the Lebanese parliament voted in favor of the prime minister's line. Ali Amer's (or Egypt's) reason for pressuring Lebanon stemmed mainly from the desire to finally begin implementing the diversion plan – "the *raison d'être* of the UAC" (that had been obligated in the second summit conference to protect the diversion project). Syria's demand to deploy a brigade in Lebanon's Marj Ayoun area if the pumping of the Wazani's water was carried out on Syrian soil served as a stratagem to force Lebanon to actually participate in the diversion plan. Syria perceived the Marj Ayoun area as the "back door" to Damascus (on the Marj Ayoun–Meisalun–Damascus axis).

It should be noted, however, that Lebanon continued to dawdle over implementing its part of the diversion plan. It was criticized for this – albeit mildly – by Hasanayn Haykal in the Egyptian daily *al-Ahram:* "Up till now Lebanon has only been talking and not fulfilling its obligations."[8] The article generated anxiety at the highest level of the Lebanese leadership that Egypt was about to launch an anti-Lebanese propaganda campaign because of the delays in carrying out the diversion plan, a campaign that would have the effect of triggering a government crisis. Therefore, the Lebanese asked the Egyptians to tone down their criticism of the government and President Helou. The Lebanese leaders in particular feared that the "Filastin issue" would become the bone of internal-ethnic contention between Muslims and Christians.[9] It was against this setting that on March 20, 1965 the Lebanese minister of information announced that "Lebanon is ready to begin diversion of the Jordan's tributaries but the [official] order has not been received yet from the UAC."[10]

Under such intense pressure the Lebanese was forced to begin implementing the diversion plan. In March 1965 operations began on the Middle Hasbani (at Wadi Sarid) and preparations were made for the diversion route at the Hatzabani–Sarid confluence opposite the Syrian border. The amount of water planned at these diversion sites (10–30 million cubic meters) remained within the limits of the Johnston Plan, thus the Lebanese believed they were in no danger of an Israeli response. But they continued to disregard the Authority's demand to begin work on all the diversion plans in Lebanese territory.

As the opening of the second CAPM (mini-summit) approached in May 1965, the Lebanese tried to have Nasir agree to a halt in the diversion operations in Lebanon – mainly at the Wazani Canal and pumping facility – because of their fear of Israel's response. Israel's strikes against diversion operations in Syria (in March and May 1965), and the UAC and Egyptian response, encouraged the Lebanese president to raise the issue with Nasir in Cairo in May 1965. Helou requested that Nasir agree to stop the diversion operations in Lebanon until the UAC finished its preparations for defending the Arab states' borders. Helou explained his country's dilemma to Nasir: if diversion operations continued in Lebanon, Israel would probably attack; if Lebanon ceased operations on its own initiative it would be severely criticized by the Arab states – a rhetorical assault that could destabilize the Lebanese government. "We cannot ask Lebanon to do what we cannot do," Nasir replied. "If the Arab states cannot face Israeli attacks then we have no [choice] but to postpone the diversion of the Jordan's tributaries until our military preparations are completed. We will have to consult with the Arab states about this proposal."[11] Thus Nasir gave Helou the right to put off the implementation of the diversion plan. Ahmad al-Shuqayri, who also took part in the meeting between Helou and Nasir, sheds more light in his memoirs on Nasir's reply:

> What can we do, the Ba'th in Syria is the source of the problem, the Ba'th created the crisis . . . the Syrians have brought the problem on us. The Jordan [River] problem is part of the Filastin issue . . . The Filastin problem will take a long time and immense preparation [to solve]. The Ba'th wants me to liberate Filastin, I cannot liberate Filastin; the Ba'th raised the slogan 'Liberate Filastin Now – Not Tomorrow.' [But] until we produce planes and tanks we cannot liberate Filastin . . . What can we do? . . . The Ba'th wants to dominate Syria . . . and dominate the Arab states . . . We recently held summit conferences and agreed on everything . . . Israel has recently damaged the engineering areas in Syria . . . Syria cried 'We have to fight, we have to attack,' and I say we cannot attack. Under the present circumstances we cannot defend [ourselves], we have to complete our preparations . . . I have an idea. Let's put the subject of diverting the tributaries on hold until we complete our military preparations. We will consult the Arab states about this proposal. The Arab prime ministers [the CAPM mini-summit] are about to meet in Cairo on May 6 and I'll brief Zakariya Muhi al-Din, the head of our delegation, on our position; we will agree to whatever the states agree to.[12]

Lebanon, however, speeded up the pace of its work on the Sarid canal during June and July 1965. The Lebanese felt it safe to continue operations in areas that were further removed from the border, and they wanted to avoid criticism by domestic and external Arab elements. When the Lebanese delegation returned from the CAPM in June 1965, the foreign minister, Philip Taqla, told the government that work in hazardous areas would cease. After the Lebanese prepared the entire route, 5300 meters from Wadi Sarid to the Syrian border (excluding the last 200 meters), they started excavating the canal. By mid-July they completed a 4500 meter canal, 4.5–5 meters wide at the top, 2–2.5 meters wide at the bottom, and 1.5 meters deep. In mid-July they began casting the sides of the canal and building conduits along its length. While the digging was in progress, the Lebanese began excavating the diversion dam on the Hasbani approximately one kilometer southwest of Kafr al-Mari, and poured concrete onto the dam's floor in mid-July. They also started preparing the route of the canal linking the diversion facility with the canal being dug in the direction of the Syrian border.

Lebanon continued diversion operations even while the Western Powers (the United States and France) were pressuring it to halt the work and Israel was threatening to take forceful measures against the operations. Israel put teeth into its threats when it struck at diversion facilities in Syria and sent low-flying planes over the engineering operations in Lebanon.

The Egyptians knew that Israel had warned Lebanon. They believed that Israel's threats were intended to achieve a number of goals: to deter Syria indirectly from continuing diversion operations inside its territory and to emphasize the seriousness of Israel's intentions if Syria persisted in them. They also believed that Israel was aware that the diversion operations in Lebanon were only symbolic, and that its warnings were aimed at Cairo in order to squeeze it into an uncomfortable position in the Arab arena and underscore its (the UAR's) feebleness. The Egyptians were convinced that Israel's threats were meant to furnish Lebanon –and Jordan – with justifications for circumventing their obligations to the Arab summit's decisions. Based on this assessment, it appears that Egypt's willingness to allow Lebanon to halt the diversion works in its territory stemmed from the fear of a large-scale confrontation with Israel, especially in light of Israel's action against Syria's diversion facilities on May 17, 1965.

The cumulative effect of Western pressure and Nasir's approval to halt the diversion work finally convinced Lebanon to cease all engineering operations on the Sarid project and the al-Mari dam (July 4, 1965). The Lebanese press blamed the work stoppage on budgetary constrictions and the need to address the third summit conference for additional funding. Indeed, the Lebanese newspaper *al-Hayat* noted that, "the Lebanese Foreign Ministry decided [that Lebanon] would continue the mechanical diversion operations and renew the mechanical technical operations [such as road paving] and the diversion work itself when the expected budgeting is granted."[13] The third Arab summit conference officially backed Lebanon's work standstill.

In the third mini-summit, held in Cairo on March 14, 1966, the secretary general of the Arab League read the UAC's reports on the diversion of the Jordan's tributaries and the PLO. Afterwards – according to Shuqayri – George Hakim, the Lebanese minister and Lebanese representative lectured "in an academic style as though speaking in front of students": "The works on the Arab plan for diverting the Jordan's channel on Lebanese soil stopped when the technical operations in Syria were destroyed by Israeli forces . . . When Syria renews work on its soil, Lebanon will [also] be prepared to renew work in its territory . . . This depends on the guarantee of military protection."[14]

Syria's Dilemma in Implementing the Diversion Plan

Syria's strategy for dealing with Israel's diversion of the Jordan, and the factors that influenced the crystallization of Syria's response, were the same as in the previous period, except for one important difference – this time Israel's National Water Carrier was definitely about to begin functioning. The Arab world had to face a *fait accompli*. The form of Arab response to Israel's exploitation of the Jordan's water became a bitter controversy among the Arab states. At the center of the dispute were the opposing positions of Egypt and Syria, while Lebanon and Jordan stood in the middle. Syria's position, rooted in ideology, may be summed up:

1 "The Arab summit's decisions on the Jordan diversion issue should be seen neither as an adequate nor serious challenge to the approaching Zionist danger . . . The ideal solution [should be] to prevent Israel from starting its diversion of the Jordan's water. The summit's decisions are only a necessary step that needs to be supplemented with additional steps."[15]
2 "Diversion has to be integrated into a comprehensive military plan for liberating Filastin. The [Arab] diversion [plan] cannot serve as an alternative to the liberation of Filastin but is part of a practical plan to liberate Filastin . . . The diversion is accepted as a minimum alternative because the Arab states refuse to declare a war of liberation at present, but it is not a sufficient response."[16]
3 "The [Arab] diversion of the tributaries, although four or five years too late, is absolutely necessary in order to return our water and use it for developing our resources."[17]

Against the backdrop of this basic, ideological, hard-line position, it should be noted that in November 1964 (after the second Arab summit conference ratified it), Syria was the first Arab country to begin work on the Banias Canal route, adjacent to the Lebanese border, designed to convey the Banias's water south to the Yarmuk. Syria initiated the work without Arab pressure in the area most exposed to Israel. Syria was also the only Arab state that continued to work on the water route despite Israel's air strikes on the diversion sites (although the frequency of the strikes was inconsistent until the Six Day War). Nevertheless, it was careful not to get embroiled in an all-out war with Israel over the diversion operations.

On November 13, 1964, an incident occurred in the Tel Dan area when the Syrians fired on Israeli bulldozers on the patrol road encompassing the Tel. Tel Dan is the Jordan's only source located in Israel. Israel had paved a patrol road around Tel Dan in 1962 to protect the Dan's springs, but the Syrians claimed that the road cut through their territory. A week earlier, on November 3, 1964, the Syrians had opened fire on an IDF patrol at Tel Dan from their Nukheila position. The IDF responded with fire, including tank shelling, but the tanks missed their mark at the range of 700–800 meters.[18]

Following this incident the Israeli Armor Corps, under General Israel Tal (who assumed command on November 1, 1964), began to improve the tanks' range of fire. In the November 13 incident the Syrians again opened fire with tanks and machine-guns from their Nukheila position and then brought in recoilless artillery fire. The IDF

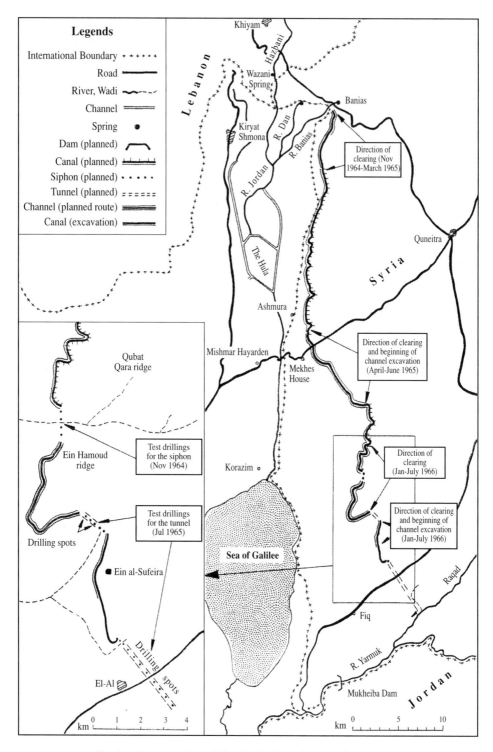

The Implementation of the Arab Diversionary Plan in Syria

56

responded and the incident began to escalate. From their other gun emplacements the Syrians quickly laid down an artillery barrage on Tel Dan and the Israeli civilian settlements of Kibbutz Dan and Shar Yishuv.

Chief-of-Staff Yitzhak Rabin asked Eshkol, who was also defense minister, for approval to call in the air force. When the approval came, Israeli warplanes went into action and silenced the Syrian artillery. This was the first time the air force had been called into action against targets deep inside Syrian territory for daily security needs. Two Israeli airforce planes (Mustangs) had attacked al-Hama in the 1950s, but in general the country's leaders exercised restraint before bringing in the air force lest Israel's political standing be harmed, the Syrians retaliate by shelling Israeli civilian targets, and the situation escalate into a major conflict. Immediately after the November 13 air strike an effort was made to halt the deterioration in the political and military theaters.

The Syrians linked the incident to the diversion operations going on in their territory and claimed that "Israel's aim was to test the seriousness of the Arabs' diversion [plan] and the [UAC] position on this decision . . . Syria has always opposed Israel's seizure of even one centimeter of Arab land . . . Syria is determined to carry out the summit's decision without being influenced by foolish aggression. The Syrian army is able to defend its plans and guarantee their implementation."[19] Despite the November 13 incident, the Syrians continued their diversion operations to the north and south of the Banias where they worked at four sites simultaneously with ten bulldozers.

The response to this incident in the Egyptian media paralleled Egyptian strategy:

> Israel wants to divert opinion from the general question of Filastin and direct it toward the secondary conflict over borders. Today the Filastin problem is not about refugees or borders – as Israel wishes to remind world opinion by this act of aggression." "The question is whether this aggression has been carried out in preparation for further acts according to its [Israel's] plans to thwart Arab projects for diverting the Jordan's waters.[20]

The March 17, 1965 Incident and its Aftermath

The incident on November 13, 1964 and the lesson derived from it served as the background for the next IDF operation on March 17, 1965, when agricultural work was renewed in the central sector of the demilitarized zone in the vicinity of Korazim (the Khirbet Qara tracts that had not been plowed since May 1951). The exchange of fire peaked on March 16, 1965 when an Israeli tractor driver was killed by recoilless artillery from Khirbet al-Dika, northeast of the Israeli settlement of Almagor. The IDF's battle-plan for March 17 had been prepared ahead of time. It was designed to take advantage of the Syrian diversion sites' proximity to the Israeli border by destroying the engineering equipment with tank fire and without having to cross the border. According to the plan, IDF tanks at Tel Dan would use an ordinary border incident as a pretext to knock out the water diversion equipment. The plan was drawn up by the general headquarters and received approval from the ministerial committee for security affairs. The air force was also placed on alert in case the Syrians began shelling Israeli settlements. The plan was based on the assumption that the Syrians would fire at a patrol traveling on the patrol road (built on November 3, 1964) as it had been doing routinely since February 1965. Until now the IDF refrained from returning fire. At three in the afternoon on March 17, while an IDF halftrack was checking the patrol road around Tel Dan, the Syrians fired on the vehicle from Nukheila. Two tank platoons deployed earlier shelled Nukheila and Syrian diversion equipment (at a range of 2000+ meters).[21] The Syrians were apparently surprised by the speed of the IDF response and failed to react – it seems they needed permission from a senior military authority. Up until this point the Syrians had cleared away a fifteen-kilometer route to the west and south of the Banias Village. Following the incident they completely halted their work in the section of the diversion project adjacent to the ceasefire line north and south of the Banias River.

Based on the official Syrian announcement of the incident, *Radio Damascus*'s broadcasts and commentaries between March 17 and 19, and the Syrians' report to the UAC – we may summarize the Syrian estimate of the incident: (1) Israel planned to shell the diversion project. The Tel Dan patrol was merely a provocation designed to disrupt diversion operations. (2) Israeli activity in this and previous incidents was designed to prepare the way for a large-scale operation whose goal was the seizure of the demilitarized zone and expulsion of its inhabitants. (3) Israel concentrated its forces on the Syrian border because it planned to launch a larger operation against Syria. (4) Syrian losses amounted to one killed and two wounded.

Conference of the Heads of the Arab Delegations to the Mixed Armistice Commissions

The Third Conference of the Delegations' Heads (from Egypt, Syria, Jordan, and Lebanon) to the Mixed Armistice Commissions took place between March 24 and 27, 1965. In his opening speech during the first of the conference's closed sessions, the assistant of the Arab League General Secretary discussed the implications of the Israeli response to the Arabs' diversion operations. He emphasized "the conference's special importance under the present circumstances when Israeli attacks persist and their scope is expanding, [and] after cooperative Arab work has begun in the united command and the implementation of the Arab Plan for using the Jordan's water, and after Israel and the imperialist exploitative powers that support it opposed the Arab Plan. Therefore we have to deal with the issue on a new basis, and submit a unified Arab plan based *only on the facts and backed by appropriate practical discussion*" [my emphasis – M.S.]. The hint to the Syrians was clear: the position would not be determined by sentiment, emotion, or ideological orientation, but only by "factual" considerations, that is, after an examination was made of the Arabs' ability to react forcefully and militarily to an Israeli response, and the dangers of a premature war were evaluated. The secretariat of the Arab League's protocol of the debates contains similar ideas to those brought by the assistant to the secretary general of the Arab League:

"The participants discussed the memorandum of the General Secretariat [of the Arab League] relating to [water diversion] and its developments, and they referred to the Arab League Council's March 13, 1965 decision that recommended renewed discussion on Israel's attacks at the Syrian border in light of the conference results. The participants agreed with the assistant to the secretary general of the Arab League to focus discussion on the following fundamental points: first, the nature and aims of Israel's attacks in the last fifteen months, and whether they were *sui generis* or a link in a chain of aggressive incidents since the establishment of Israel. What was the nature of the connection between Israel's attacks and the Arab plan, ratified in the two Arab summit conferences, for utilizing the water of the Jordan and its tributaries, and Israeli military concentrations along the armistice line? Second, how should the Arabs respond to Israeli aggression and how effective would their response be?" The participants in the conference asserted that there were Israeli military concentrations in the Hulah region, close to the Wazani River.

During the debate on the "the Lebanese border situation" it was agreed that "new Israeli concentrations had been discovered, extremely close to the Syrian border . . . [and] the estimate is that the enemy will probably attack the water plan in the al-Rajar-Banias region. The eastern [Syrian] side has taken the necessary steps for defense of the Banias."

The conference concluded *inter alia*:

1 In light of the facts and features of the actual border situation, the participants are aware that Israel continues to carry out its plan in order to complete the takeover of demilitarized areas that were originally Arab lands; [Israel intends] to create in this way a *de facto* border with the Arab states, in order to determine the international borders of Filastin as its border, finalize its previous gains, [establish] jump-off points for future attacks, and thwart the Arab Plan for using the Jordan's water.
2 By continuing its expansionist plan [Israel] has overcome Lake Hulah's problems by draining most of the lake and including the [entire] Tiberias Sea [Sea of Galilee] perimeter in its area of control; Israel has also seized most of the no-man's land and demilitarized zones, and is striving to take control of the rest [of the area]. The conference participants regard it as their obligation to safeguard Arab interests in the demilitarized areas and prevent new Israeli gains.

The conference's section on recommendations also noted – apparently under the influence of the Syrian delegate:

1   Israel has devoted a large part of its plan to seizing control of the no-man's areas and demilitarized zones. The aim of its present plan is to reach the international borders of Filastin.
2 Therefore, the situation has to be coped with by preparing a decisive plan. [It is imperative] to prepare a decisive Arab response to any Israeli aggression and take the steps to guarantee our resistance if this aggression develops into a general, full-scale armed confrontation.[22]

The Arab assessment comes into focus from the debates and recommendations at the conference as expressed by the Syrian representative and approved by the delegations' heads: "a repetition of incidents and an Israeli attack against the diversion operations can be expected." The Syrians also voiced their demand that the UAC respond "decisively" if the border situation deteriorates because of "wide-scale confrontations." These conclusions led the Syrians to ask the UAC for material aid for their army and a commitment to open additional fronts if Israel repeats its "aggression" against Syria.

The May 13, 1965 Incident and its Impact

After the March 17, 1965 incident, the Syrians ceased diversion operations for two weeks (until March 31), after which they brought several pieces of equipment to the southern end of the diversion route and hastily cleared out a 500-meter long section. Then they removed all their engineering equipment from the area. On April 15, a month after the incident, the Syrians returned to work on a new section, this time in the Banot Ya'akov Bridge area opposite the Israeli settlement of Mishmar Hayarden. Thus, the operations were transferred to the central sector, along the part of the route that runs north and south of the Banot Ya'akov Bridge–Quneitra road, 4–4.5 kilometers from the Israeli border and beyond the range of IDF light weapons.

In early May, the Israeli political leadership reviewed Syria's diversion operations and decided that the IDF would prepare its tanks for destroying the engineering equipment. Israeli armor moved into concealed positions, and again the plan was to exploit the Syrian fire in order to cripple Syria's diversion operations. On May 13, at 15:00 an Israeli patrol set out from Mishmar Hayarden and headed south. When the Syrians refrained from opening fire, the Israeli patrol began shooting and a firefight ensued during which the tanks started shelling the Syrian diversion equipment. Despite the long range (5000–5800 meters) the Israeli tanks crews managed to hit the equipment and knock out three tractors. The Syrians did not respond because of the fear that the IDF would call in their planes on patrol nearby. The Syrians had managed to clear a route of approximately five kilometers in this sector. Syrian work in the area ceased on May 22, following top-level discussions on May 19, 1965.

Following this incident, a number of elements could be discerned in *Radio Damascus* broadcasts:

1 Anger directed at the UAC for not coming to Syria's aid and leaving it to fend for itself against Israel.
2 A demand that the Arab leaders comply with the definitive plan for war and not limit themselves to tributary diversion (even though this was important in its own right).
3 A demand that the UAC prove its value by building a joint Arab deterrent force and deploying an Arab army "on all the fronts," otherwise each Arab state would return to conducting its own affairs separately.[23]

The timing of the Israeli reaction was important. On May 26 the Second CAPM convened, and the Israeli reaction seemed intended to serve as a warning sign to the participants. The main issue on the conference agenda was how to respond to Israel's attack on the Arabs' diversion operations. The IDF action undoubtedly had an impact on the discussion and resolutions of the CAPM: it was a challenge to the Arab's water diversion strategy and had caught the UAC commander and Arab leaders by surprise. Contrary to the UAC commander's estimate that was presented at the second summit (September 1964), Israel responded at the start of the Arab engineering operations and not at their completion, and the response was systematic and tough. The UAC commander realized that Israel was determined to prevent diversion operations by force.

The May 13 border flare-up confronted Syria with a serious dilemma: on the one hand, it had to continue the diversion operations otherwise the propaganda fallout would cause it harm in the domestic and inter-Arab arenas and tarnish its ideological credibility; on the other hand, Syria was isolated in the Arab arena because of its radical, militant orientation, and as long as Arab aid was uncertain it could not get involved in escalation that might lead to war – especially when Egypt opposed such a move. The IDF response reinforced the Syrian estimate (and that of the UAC commander, Ali Amer) that Israel was intent on blocking the diversion operations by force. The Israeli attack also corresponded with the Syrians' (and Amer's) basic assessment that in addition to bringing the Arab diversion plan to a halt, Israel intended to seize control of the demilitarized zones in a "large-scale operation". The Syrians perceived that the diversion works' proximity to the border made it easy for Israel to interrupt operations almost whenever it wanted to. This was the reason behind the Syrians' request that the UAC deploy a sufficiently strong air force in Syria to intervene immediately and neutralize Israel's air superiority in the area. The Syrians claimed that they could not return fire on May 13 because of Israeli air superiority. They proposed responding to every Israeli action with an immediate stronger response, even in areas "that serve as bases for IDF barrages" – that is, they would shell Israeli settlements where tanks or artillery were located. The Syrians also demanded that the UAC reinforce the "northern theater" with an Arab deterrent force and make the necessary preparations for immediate intervention "if Syria is threatened." Syria also demanded that the necessary preparations include a general Arab mobilization, the deployment of Egyptian military units in Sinai and the Gaza Strip, and the evacuation of the UN Emergency Force (a move that was undertaken on the eve of the Six Day War).[24] The Syrians wanted the Arab states to agree upon "a definite war plan against Israel and not be satisfied with the diversion plan." On this issue the Ba'th secretary general, Dr. Munif al-Razaz, declared in early June 1965: "We did not ask for any assistance for Syria itself, but demanded that the UAC reinforce the northern sector of the battle zone with a deterrent force. The water diversion is a joint Arab project. It would be wrong to say that Syria demanded opening all the fronts only [in response] to a strike against a tractor working on the diversion, but it demanded the build-up of an Arab deterrent force, a powerful build-up commensurate with the level of the struggle if went from local aggression to all-out aggression."[25]

At the CAPM that was held in Cairo on May 26, 1965, Nur al-Din al-Atasi, the Syrian deputy prime minister, charged that the Arab states had failed to come to Syria's assistance when Israel launched an air strike against diversion operations in Syria. He felt that "Egypt should have sent planes to retaliate against Israel." He demanded that "in a state of threat from Israel, Egypt should send troops into Sinai and the Gaza Strip and order the evacuation of the UN Emergency Forces," that is, open a front in Sinai and the Gaza Strip (as it eventually did in May 1967).[26] Zakariya Muhi al-Din, the Egyptian prime minister, reemphasized Nasir's position: " It is important to differentiate between a limited attack and an all-out attack. In the first case the responsibility for the defense lies on the country under attack, but in the second case Egypt and the other Arab states are obliged to go to war according to the articles of the Arab collective security pact." The Syrian chief-of-staff, Fahd al-Sha'ir, retorted that "there is no article in the Arab Collective Security Pact titled a limited attack and all-out attack," and again he criticized Ali Amer for not committing the UAC to Syria's assistance.[27] Mahmud Riyad defended the Egyptian position, writing: "Fahd al-Sha'ir is familiar with the military situation in Egypt and knows that dispatching Egyptian troops to Sinai and attacking Israel in the present circumstances would lead to defeat, nevertheless he has asked Egypt to do this, and this is the reason for the present distrust between Cairo and Damascus."[28]

During the debates in the Arab Defense Council on May 29, at the same time as the CAPM, the UAC commander who was committed to implementing the Egyptian strategy proposed that the diversion operations take place further from the border with Israel "until we have completed preparing the forces needed for blocking Israeli aggression."[29] Shuqayri wrote in his characteristically cynical style that in light of the Israeli aggression at the diversion operations "Arab political and military circles had no choice but to look to a *fatwa* to get them out of Jordan River crisis. The *fatwa* was that Syria would continue its diversion operations but in areas further removed from the armistice lines with Israel."[30] The UAC commander repeated, in effect, Nasir's position in his speech before the second Palestinian National Congress on May 29, 1965 in which he stated: "We cannot divert the Jordan's tributaries unless we have ground and air defenses . . . If we cannot divert them today then we should postpone diversion until we can defend it. We want to defend the diversion operations, but we must speak honestly, we have to be honest and state that first of all [their] protection must be guaranteed, and at the same time [we must] begin preparations for attaining our main goal."[31]

The Syrian response to Nasir's speech was immediate. The commentator on *Radio Damascus* imputed that Nasir was saying that "Syria will get itself involved in a war with Israel and Egypt will not participate in the war on the diversion of the water sources."[32] And the Syrian newspaper *al-Thawra* wrote: "Nasir initiated the summit conference despite Syria's opposition to the council's solution – [Arab] diversion for [Israeli] diversion . . . Syria alone responded and began operations . . . Aggression came but no [Arab] assistance [followed] . . . What remains of Nasir on the Filastin question?"[33] The Syrians also found themselves in hot water because of the technical problems involved in the diversion sites. The diversion route in the critical section closest to the Israeli border was at least twenty-five kilometers long, and the plan for diverting the Banias and channeling the Hasbani into Syrian territory depended on the completion of this section. But Israel's "concurrence" was needed in order to complete the work in this section, and Israel was determined to obstruct diversion operations. Syria's determination to complete the engineering task implied its readiness to escalate the border situation to a comprehensive war – when the Egyptians and UAC considered the timing inappropriate – and it was obvious that Syria was incapable of fighting such a war alone.[34]

On May 22, 1965, a week after the May 13 incident, the Syrians ceased work on this section and began operations at another site, further to the south, in the Wadi Fakhura area south of Sanbar. By the time they halted work there on July 15 they managed to excavate another six kilometers. Then they moved operations to the Qubat Qara sector deep in their own territory, roughly ten kilometers from the border, across from the Korazim area in Israel. The Syrians estimated that at this range Israel would have to escalate the situation by calling in its air force, and that such a step would not be easy. In light of the Syrians' progress in the Qubat Qara sector the IDF General Headquarters decided to farm the land at Khirbet Qara, near the Jordan River north of where the Jordan flows into the Sea of Galilee, an area that was still under dispute with the Syrians. If the Syrians opened fire, the IDF would hit their diversion equipment at Qubat Qara. The plowing began on August 12. When Israeli observers claimed that the Syrians were "aiming their weapons" (tanks and recoilless canons] on an Israeli tractor, IDF tanks and artillery opened fire. Two Syrian tractors and three tanks were hit. Israeli planes did not intervene as long as the Syrians avoided shelling Jewish settlements.[35]

At the third Arab summit that met on September 13, 1965, the secretary general of the Arab League reported that "diversion operations had, in effect, been discontinued in Syria, Lebanon, and Jordan because of Israeli aggression."[36] On the other hand, at a meeting of the Arab Defense Council on the eve of the summit, Fahd al-Sha'ir, the Syrian chief-of-staff, criticized the Arab press for condemning Syria for halting diversion operations. Al-Sha'ir described in detail the incidents that had taken place over the diversion operations since November 1964, and told his listeners that the August 12 incident had almost escalated into a much larger battle after Israel transferred a number of air squadrons to its northern area. He stressed that Syria had not ceased diversion operations and that he expected additional acts of "aggression" – perhaps against Jordan and Lebanon – for the fourth, fifth, and sixth time. Ali Amer's report to the participants in the third summit stated:

> We are facing an enemy who has openly declared his intention to attack if the Arab states continue carrying out their decisions on the technical operations; and indeed Israel has already attacked on more than one occasion. We must take the appropriate military steps in response to this aggression. On the other hand, the continuation of the technical work while we are aware the size of the gap in our military preparations and [our] disagreement over the rectification of [the situation], is a path that runs against logical thinking. [The second summit conference] estimated that the implementation of diversion operations would not lead to an Israeli attack. But the opposite happened. There is no longer any need to hide Israel's readiness to commit aggression. It has declared it openly. This situation forces us to reconsider our steps and our assessment of the situation.[37]

The UAC commander estimated, then, that the IDF action against the diversion project in Syria had caught the Arabs off guard. The Arabs' air inferiority called for a reexamination of the diversion plan since the Arabs had been unable to respond to Israeli aggression – either with a general response or a local one. In Amer's opinion Israel would probably continue its policy, carry out limited air strikes attacks against the diversion operations in border areas, and it was also conceivable that it would launch a massive air strike against the Arab states' air forces and vital services.

In the final analysis, the Egyptians (and the rest of the Arab states) believed that "Israel succeeded in disrupting the Arabs' plans to divert the Jordan's water, [therefore] engineering operations should cease until they could be defended militarily."[38] The summit conference resolved "to continue implementing the joint Arab plans for exploiting the water of the Jordan and its tributaries, according to the plan that had been decided on and the decisions for taking the necessary steps for military defense."[39] This meant that from now on diversion operations would depend on the evaluation of the states involved in them and would be their responsibility. In this way the summit conference gave an all-Arab approval to the halting of diversion operations to those states (Syria and Lebanon) unable to block Israeli military responses.

The issue of "work on the Arab plan for exploiting the Jordan River and its tributaries" came up for discussion at an emergency meeting of the Heads of the Arab Delegations to the Mixed Armistice Commissions with Israel, which was held in Cairo on January 9–11, 1966. The debates dealing with the situation along the Israeli–Syrian ceasefire lines concluded with the following statement:

> "The year 1965 has been characterized by two important events, one, the shelling of work operations centers in the plan to utilize the Jordan's tributaries in the Na'ran region, across from the central region, and in the Qubat Qara region, also in the central sector. The other event on the armistice line with Syria also occurred in the central region [and affected] Arab farmers working their land west of the armistice line, on occupied soil, in an area of 500 dunam [125 acres] called al-Hamamsa. The Jews had reconciled themselves to the '*status quo*', but this year tried to prevent Arab farmers from entering the area by plowing it with a number of tractors protected by artillery cover. Syrian artillery forced them to withdraw from the area."

> "Exchange of fire has continued in the area everyday from the beginning of last year until today, and the Jews have shot at any person or animal crossing the international Syrian–Palestinian border in the central region. This is why the demilitarized zone north of the Sea of Tiberias has been almost completely abandoned, and neither side can enter it."

> [Regarding the situation on the ceasefire lines with Lebanon:] "Israeli activity on the border in 1965 was marked by high altitude jet reconnaissance flights to monitor the operations for exploiting the water of the Jordan's tributaries and keep watch on Lebanese troop concentrations and their movements."[40]

The closing announcement of the third CAPM (March 14, 1966), in which Lebanon gave notice of the cessation of diversion operations in its country, gave only brief mention to the Arab Diversion Plan: "The conference expresses its gratitude to the Authority for its efforts in exploiting the water of the Jordan and its tributaries."[41] These words may be seen as a eulogy to the Arab Diversion Plan.

The July 14, 1966 Incident

After the IDF attack of August 12, 1965, the Syrians ceased work for three days and then renewed it at the Qubat Qara area until mid-October 1965, after which most of the equipment was moved south to the Ein Hamoud area, further from the Israeli border.

The work in the Qubat Qara area proceeded slowly until January 1966 with only a few pieces of equipment in operation. In all, five kilometers were prepared along this sector's route. From mid-October 1965 through mid-January 1966 a section was prepared in the Ein Hamoud area, east of the Butayha Valley, a route of seven kilometers. In mid-January 1966 the work was transferred to the Ein al-Sufeira area only twelve kilometers from the border. Work here progressed very slowly, and by July 1966 the Syrians managed to clear a route of only 3.5 kilometers and dig a one and a half kilometer long canal. As long as diversion operations in Syria continued, it was only a matter of time until Israel would launch another strike. Israel had another reason for attacking Syria: its support of the Fatah organization and its sabotage operations against Israel. Finally, on May 16, 1966 Israel had an opportunity to hit Syrian targets (until then Israeli responses had been concentrated only in Jordan) when an Israeli jeep drove over a landmine in the Almagor area and two passengers were killed. The perpetrators' tracks led to Syria. The IDF had two options: attack Syrian gun positions or diversion operations; an air attack was preferable and safer, but politically "more jarring" so the retaliation was postponed.

Another serious act of sabotage occurred two months later. On July 13 an IDF vehicle detonated a mine southeast of Almagor and two soldiers and a civilian were killed. This time the prime minister, who was also defense minister, gave his approval for an immediate strike against Syrian engineering operations at Ein Sufeira, including the use of the air force. Nine heavy earth-moving vehicles lay along the route, protected by three 14.5 mm. double-barreled anti-aircraft machine-guns, and a platoon of light infantry. The Israeli planes attacked the equipment on July 14 at four in the afternoon. This was the first air retaliation approved at the political level since the al-Hamma action in April 1951. Moreover, in contrast to the November 13, 1964 air sortie against Syrian gun positions that had been a quick response to silence the heavy shelling of Israeli settlements, the action of July 14, 1966 was designed to demonstrate with greater conviction Israel's determination to prevent Arab diversion operations by all means at its disposal, including the air force. The Israeli warplanes struck at the diversion equipment and destroyed the vehicles in the diversion area at Ein Sufeira east of the Sea of Galilee.[42] By six in the evening the Syrians announced that seven civilians, two soldiers and one woman had been wounded.[43] One of the Israeli planes on patrol bagged a Syrian MiG-21 in a dogfight – the first time in aerial warfare that a MiG-21 was downed by a Mirage.

In this incident too the Syrians' lack of response was clear proof of their air inferiority. The Syrian radio and press repeated their accusations against the pan-Arab position:

> Revolutionary Syria has a definite opinion on the water issue and insists on diverting the [water's] sources and forcibly preventing Israel from using the water. Syria sees this as the minimum line that it will not back down from, even though the Arab summit's position opposes this, just as it rejects the Syrian line on the liberation of Filastin. Syria will continue to maintain its revolutionary stand and position on the liberation of Filastin.[44]

The Syrian foreign minister's memo,[45] dated July 14, 1966, to the chairman of the Security Council and members of the UN, to the Arab League, and foreign diplomatic legations in Damascus, described Syria's diversion project as a constructive domestic project built on an economic basis with inter-Arab support, since Jordan and Lebanon were involved and the project was grounded in the rights of the Palestinian refugees. This was the first time that the diversion plan was presented as an economic project vital to Syria. It seems that this was connected to the bodies that the memo was addressed to. The memo referred, *inter alia*, to the following points:

1 Israel's disingenuous claims regarding infiltration from Syrian territory is merely a pretext, since it is obvious that this is a preplanned attempt to halt the constructive use of the Jordan's water.

2   The area where the incident occurred is a civilian area where civil engineers work on constructive economic project connected with the channeling of the Jordan's waters. Israel is trying to appropriate this water from Syria and prevent the Syrian plan to raise the people's standard of living from being realized.

3   Israel has disseminated false information about infiltration in order to steal the water from Syria, Jordan, and Lebanon and from the refugees who dwell on the borders of the usurped homeland.

4   This is not the first time (a similar attempt was carried out by the Israelis on November 13, 1964) that the chairman of the Security Council and participants in the discussion condemned Israel for its activity.

5   Syria has announced – and reiterates – that it is not responsible for the action of Palestinian organizations that strive to return to their homeland. It [Syria] is not the only state that has armistice borders with Israel. If Israel's intentions were pure it would refer [the issue] to the Syrian–Israeli Armistice Commission, which is authorized to discuss this issue, but this body is paralyzed because Israel boycotts it.

The July 14, 1966 attack was the last IDF combat activity until the Six Day War. After the incident the Syrians performed no work of substance on the diversion operations in this sector but continued it in the southern sector where they prepared approach roads and linked up various sections of the route. The Syrians cleared another 900 meters along the route in the central sector, but the work pace was so slow that the entire operation had only symbolical significance.

In sum, from November 1964 until September–October 1966 the Syrians blazed a thirty-eight kilometer route and dug a canal almost three kilometers long. Until the July 14, 1966 incident Syria's diversion operations proceeded almost continuously despite the shooting exchanges. After each flare-up the Syrians moved to other sectors along the route, at a greater distance from the border. After the July 14, 1966 air strike, work halted for a month and renewed in mid-August, but the pace was negligible. Five bulldozers were used in earth-leveling operations in 1965, seven bulldozers beginning in February 1966, and nine from June 1966.

Water Diversion in Jordan: the Yarmuk Project

It is difficult to speak of an Arab Diversion Plan in Jordan since it was actually the original "Yarmuk Project" that the Jordanians had drawn up to irrigate half a million dunam (2 million acres) in the Jordan Rift Valley. The Yarmuk Project was based on the diversion the river's water, its tributaries in the Rift Valley, and ground water. The principles of the Yarmuk Project included: (1) Reservoirs and retaining dams on the Yarmuk (the Mukheiba and Makarin dams) and on the Jordan's tributaries on both sides of the river. (2) Major canals on both sides of the Jordan and a network of lateral canals for water distribution. (3) Pumping stations to bring up ground water.

The Yarmuk is the Jordan River's largest tributary, lying between the Sea of Galilee and the Dead Sea, with a drainage basin of 7250 square kilometers, mostly in Syria, with a small section (1410 square kilometers) in Jordan. Most of the Yarmuk's water in the summer comes from the Muzeirib Springs (over 3.7 cubic meters a second) that flow from the Syrian heights north of the Tel Shihab Falls. From here the water flows west to Makarin (at a height of 80 meters) where it joins with its main sources. It flows from Makarin to the mouth of the Jordan (at a height of 202 meters) in a narrow channel, 300 meters beneath the heights from which it drains. The annual rainfall on the Yarmuk's northern drainage basin is between 600–1000 millimeters. The following data determines the river's regimen: in the winter its channel is filled with flood waters; in the summer water is sparse; in the rainy season (from October to April) its flow increases and reaches its climax in February; the river gradually subsides each month in the spring and summer (May to September).

Jordan presented the Yarmuk Project at the first Arab summit conference as the first stage in the implementation of the general Arab Plan for diverting the Jordan's tributaries, and as a basis for diverting the Banias and Hasbani Rivers to the south at a later stage. Within this framework the Yarmuk dams were designed to collect the diverted water from the Banias and Hasbani. Without these dams all of the Yarmuk's water would flow into the Jordan south of the Sea of Galilee. The first stage envisioned the construction of the Mukheiba Dam and a retaining dam at Makarin, and the elevation of the sides of the Ghor Canal.

Jordan's irrigation projects were announced at the first Arab summit conference to the proponents of the plan for diverting the Jordan's sources, and entire project came under the supervision of the "Arab Authority for Diverting the Jordan's Tributaries." However, in practice, Jordan did not have to diverge from the Johnston Plan. The Jordanian water plan fit the plans to divert the Jordan's tributaries, and depended mainly on Jordan's willingness to receive the spillovers diverted to the Mukheiba Dam and to invest Arab finances in its irrigation plans. Unlike the diversion plan in Syria, Jordan only implemented its part of the plan that Israel had also agreed to, in other words, only in the event that the Jordanian plan became part of Syria's diversion project could Israel perceive it as directed against Israel. But in the end Jordan did not have to face such a test. The second Arab summit conference approved a budget of 10.25 million Pounds Sterling for the construction of the Mukheiba Dam. The dam, described as a "top priority project," was to be built in the "immediate operations" stage.

Finally, in the absence of any progress in the Arab diversion plan Jordan was its chief beneficiary. Jordan fulfilled its share of the Arabs' financing without becoming militarily and politically entangled with Israel or the Arab states. Jordan carried out its water plan in a silent agreement with Israel, while avoiding any deviation from the Johnston Plan. This Israeli–Jordanian agreement remained intact from the 1960s until 1994 when the two countries signed a peace treaty, which included a new allocation of the Jordan's and Yarmuk's waters.

Failure of the Arab Strategy

The first Arab summit conference ratified the Arab strategy to thwart Israel's NWC Plan. The strategy was designed to divert the Jordan's tributaries and prepare the Arab armies for the defense of the engineering operations. The second Arab summit (September 1964) gave the green light to start the implementation of diverting the Jordan's sources. But only a few months after the conference, the strategy became bankrupt. The failure stemmed mainly from the timing of the Israeli military response, which was devised to damage and halt the diversion operations. The UAC commander (and the Arab leaders) at the second summit estimated that an Israel attack would come close to or at the end of the diversion operations, instead it came at their beginning. The Israeli response in March and May 1965 confronted the Arab world – especially Egypt, Syria, and Lebanon – with a serious dilemma. The Arab states realized that Israel was determined to prevent the implementation of the diversion operations even if it meant calling in its air force and escalating the situation into a full-blown military clash.

Egypt, the main force behind the Arabs' water strategy, did not consider the Israeli attack against diversion operations in Syria sufficient enough reason to enter into a full-scale war at a time when the Arab armies were still unprepared. This assessment was reinforced by the superiority that Israeli warplanes had shown in border incidents. Egypt viewed these incidents as local clashes involving Syria alone rather than matters requiring a comprehensive Arab response – especially an Egyptian one – as Syria demanded.

Lebanon was caught in the vice between Egypt and Syria on the one hand, and Israel on the other; the Western states also pressured Lebanon to avoid participation in the Arab Diversion Plan. The Lebanese president and the leaders of the country's Christian communities feared a military clash with Israel and a political confrontation with the Arab world in general, and Nasir in particular, and their impact on the "fragile balance" of Lebanon's political regime if the "Palestinian issue" became the bone of contention in a domestic ethnic dispute. Israel's offensive against the diversion operations in Syria helped President Helou convince Nasir and the Arab world, albeit unofficially, of the need to freeze the Wazani diversion operations even though Israel was aware of Lebanon's dilemma and the cessation of work in June 1965.

Syria stuck to the consensus reached at the summit conference, although after the third summit it was "solely responsible" for diversion operations which it continued to carry out at a distance from the border with Israel and at an extremely slow pace. Syria's military inferiority, especially in the air, and the lack of Egyptian support, forced it to be heedful not to deteriorate the situation to the point of an all-out confrontation and to maintain a minimum response to IDF strikes, sometimes even avoiding any response at all. It was careful to remove the diversion operations from the border. The Syrian military headquarters made sure that every response to an IDF attack on Syria's diversion sites would be issued only by senior commanders at the front so as to minimize an uncontrolled deterioration of events – even though at the same time some senior officers were calling for stronger retaliation against the IDF strikes. Under these circumstances the Syrian leadership was in a perpetual state of frustration from 1964 until the Six Day War regarding all aspects of the conflict in general and the water issue in particular. Egypt and the rest of the Arab world also shared this frustration because of their failure to act when faced with the most serious challenge in the struggle against Israel between 1959 and 1967. Syria found some consolation in its support of the Fatah organization that incorporated the strategy of a "popular liberation war" against Israel.

The inevitable conclusion is that the Arabs' water struggle against Israel, in all its aspects – political, technical, and military – was the main contributing factor to the exacerbation in the Arab–Israeli conflict that led to the Six Day War. The water struggle forced the Arab world to crystallize a comprehensive strategy in the Arab–Israeli conflict, and the Palestinian problem became the central issue in the inner Arab discourse. The struggle over water also catalyzed the Arabs' military rearmament in preparation for a military struggle that both the Nasir-led Arab world and Israel regarded as inevitable. The frustration of the Arab world, and especially Syria, because of the failure in the water struggle only strengthened Arab resolve to free itself from the sense of defeat by the strength of a comprehensive solution to the conflict. The main question was the timing of the confrontation.

The Rise of the Palestinians as a Factor in the Arab–Israeli Conflict

Part I *Establishment of the PLO –*
The Jerusalem Congress, May 1964

The first Palestinian National Congress (PNC) held in East Jerusalem (May 28–June 2, 1964) approved Shuqayri's proposal to set up the Palestinian Liberation Organization (PLO). The second Arab summit, which was held in Cairo, September 5–11, 1964, "welcomed the establishment of the PLO as the basis of the Palestinian entity and as a pioneer in the collective Arab struggle for the liberation of Filastin." Moreover, "the PLO's decision to establish the Palestinian Liberation Army (PLA) was endorsed." There was agreement over the general formulation that "the PLO represents the will of the Palestinian people in its struggle for the liberation of its homeland, Filastin."[1]

The quality of the PLO as representative of the Palestinians and of the composition of its institutions was central to Shuqayri's political concept and to his activities as chairman of the PLO. After the first summit Shuqayri had to come to grips with the composition of the first Palestinian National Congress (PNC) that convened in East Jerusalem.[2] The crystallization of his ideas on the question of the Palestinian entity and the composition of its institutions was influenced mainly by the following factors:

1 Shuqayri was not elected by any Palestinian bodies as "representative of Filastin" in the Arab League or as the founder of the PLO. He was imposed on the Palestinians by Arab states. In fact he was appointed by Egypt so that Jordan, which regarded him as the least of all evils, would agree to the establishment of the Palestinian entity.[3]

2 Shuqayri was obsessed by the fact that the PLO "was born in the bed of the summit conference" and was constrained by the conditions of the Arab arena. In the composition of the PNC he put "most of his energy into gaining the support of the maximum number of Palestinians and Arab states" alike.

3 Shuqayri was connected umbilically to Nasir. Before embarking on anything significant he always attempted to gain Nasir's approval, such as for the

Palestinian entity program and the policy towards Jordan.[4] Nasir's support and Shuqayri's harnessing himself to Nasir's policies gave Shuqayri and the PLO a position of strength in the Arab arena and among the Palestinians.

4 Shuqayri worked in an almost total vacuum in the Palestinian arena. There were no popular Palestinian organizations or institutions in which the PLO could be built; he did not have the "Palestinian territory" or "Palestinian population" which were necessary for the establishment of an independent Palestinian political entity.

5 Shuqayri had a strong motivation for succeeding in his task and thereby improving his image. He was dogged by the negative image of his personality which continued even after the founding of the PLO. He did not shrink from any means in order to establish successfully the PLO, even exercising deceit, which became for him a "national obligation."[5] Within the circumstances of 1964 he was the most suitable person for the post, but in the end his qualities militated against him.

The decision of the first Arab summit deliberately avoided stating how the Palestinian people would be organized. The only way to reach a unanimous decision was to agree on the lowest common denominator. In this, Nasir adopted the right tactic in attempting to obtain Husayn's approval, at any price, including a "watered-down" decision, even if it meant acceding to King Husayn's demand that the phrase "Palestinian entity" should not be mentioned. To the Arab heads of states, including Husayn, it was clear that what was meant was the establishment of Palestinian representative institutions. They left decisions about the way in which these institutions would be set up and composed to deliberations between Shuqayri and Husayn.[6]

Shuqayri had no alternative but to choose the system of appointment as the procedure for composing the PNC. No Arab state – excluding Egypt – would allow elections to the PLO institutions on its own territory. This system was particularly convenient to Jordan. In every Arab country where there was a large concentration of Palestinians, Shuqayri appointed a Preparatory Committee which elected a list of candidates for the PNC. With Jordan's agreement Shuqayri appointed a Supreme Preparatory Committee which decided on the final list of members. The PNC did not represent the Palestinian population democratically, but the vast majority of PNC members were appointed in close cooperation with Jordan and only with its agreement. The PNC represented interests and pressure groups whose representation Shuqayri thought was necessary to secure the establishment of the Palestinian institutions without disruption. To this end Shuqayri was obliged to give way to Jordan's demand for complete control of the PNC. The identity of interest between Shuqayri and Jordan in their desire to see the Jerusalem Congress succeed, together with Nasir's support for Shuqayri, ensured in advance that the Congress would succeed and the aims of the three leaders would be achieved. As detailed below, close examination shows that Jordan was promised almost 65 percent of the total number of PNC representatives.

Shuqayri tried to prove that the members of the PNC represented the groups of Palestinians "from the sea to the Gulf." In his report to the second Arab summit he devoted a special section to classification of the PNC members according to their geographical representation and intentionally made out that he was including representatives from the East Bank of Jordan. Accordingly Jordan allocated 216 places out of 396 (391 actually in attendance) that is 54%, while the West Bank received 118 and the East Bank 98; Lebanon – 22; Qatar and Doha – 7; Libya – 8; Algeria – 9; Gaza Strip – 47; Kuwait – 20; and Iraq – 3. Shuqayri also tried to show that the PLO represented all the strata of Palestinian society. He did this by emphasizing in his report to the second summit the representation of women, workers, and journalists, and further, by pointing out that the members of the PNC also represented "members of the House of Deputies, ministers, mayors and local council leaders, chambers of commerce, unions of doctors, lawyers, engineers, students . . . who were elected by the people." To the representatives from Jordan must be added members of the Preparatory Committee, press representatives, most of the women representatives, trade union representatives, and municipalities – in all, Jordan accounted for nearly 255 representatives.

Among the "Jordanian" representatives were: 25 members of municipalities in the West Bank; 39 members of the House of Deputies and senators; 16 who were past members of the Jordanian House of Deputies; six clergymen, including two Christians – in all, over 100 members of the PNC from Jordan (in other words, 20 percent of the PNC members) served or had served the Jordanian government in an official capacity.[7] In this way the PLO and the Jordanian establishment overlapped considerably, with the "Jordanians" representing Jordanian rather than Palestinian interests.

The 47 representatives from the Gaza Strip included at least 26 who served in some official capacity in the Strip, among them 11 members of the Supreme Executive Council (25 members) of the Palestinian National Union (PNU) appointed by the governor of the Gaza Strip in May 1962; six (out of ten) members of the Legislative Council of the Gaza Strip; and nine members of the regional committee of the PNU in the Gaza Strip.[8] In this way Shuqayri and Egypt ensured the loyalty of the Gaza Strip representatives. Lebanon was supposed to have 22 representatives; four were absent (one was forbidden entry into Jordan).[9]

In addition, there were a number of Independents and supporters of the Mufti. Most of the Syrian delegation was made up of members of the Preparatory Committee in Syria, appointed by Shuqayri. Naturally, these representatives inclined towards the policies of the Syrian Ba'th party. The Fatah representatives participated as individuals and were put on the list of Kuwait and Qatar representatives; similarly, representatives of the Arab Nationalists Movement (ANM) were included in the Jordanian and Lebanese delegations.

In response to criticism voiced by Palestinians against the pro-Jordanian composition of the PNC and his obvious pro-Jordanian bias, Shuqayri set up an Executive Committee (EC) (August 1964) with a "balanced" composition showing an "independent line," even though the majority in fact supported him. His attempts to co-opt Fatah representatives to the EC failed. Academics and financiers similarly resisted attempts to co-opt them to the EC. Shuqayri did succeed, however, in co-opting representatives of the ANM. On August 9, 1964 he made public the names of the 14 members of the EC. The c-in-c of the Palestinian Liberation Army became the fifteenth member, but this only after the second summit when the establishment of the PLA was approved. Apart from himself (Shuqayri) as chairman, the EC consisted of seven members known to support him (thus ensuring a majority for himself), four or five known for their independent line (including two from the ANM), and one from Syria.

Shuqayri appointed seven members with higher academic degrees. Jordan was dissatisfied with the appointment of members to the EC who belonged to the Jordanian opposition, such as Bahjat Abu-Gharbiya and Walid al-Qamhawi. The composition of the EC found general approval among the Palestinians.[10]

Shuqayri saw the PLA as a vital representative element in the Palestinian entity. He wanted to set up the PLA as an organization that would represent "the independence" of the Palestinians. For him the PLA was an expression of the fact that "the Palestinian entity is not words alone." With his usual hyperbole Shuqayri proclaimed to the summit that "the PLO without the PLA is like a body without a soul." He believed that by placing the PLA under the control of the PLO, the PLO would be more readily accepted as a representative body of the Palestinians and that it would give the PLO a military image.[11]

The Egyptian Attitude

The setting up of the PLO was the realization of Egypt's initiative in establishing the Palestinian entity. Egypt gave Shuqayri full support, while simultaneously conducting a flexible policy and tactics in order to break, at any cost, the deadlock over this issue. To this end Egypt, together with Shuqayri, reassured Husayn about the purpose of the entity with regard to his kingdom, and presented it as "support for the Jordanian entity." The Egyptian media embarked on an unprecedented campaign in support of Shuqayri and the Palestinian entity. They praised the results of the PNC, and the Jerusalem Congress was likened to the First Zionist Congress held in Basle in 1897. It was emphasized that the "PLO saw itself as the sole representative of the Palestinians."[12] Egypt advised senior West Bank politicians to support Shuqayri, on the assessment that this support was essential to his success in convening the PNC and in establishing the PLO. These politicians gave Egypt's stand serious consideration. In September 1963, Hikmat al-Masri and Walid al-Shak'a, two leaders of Nablus, went to Beirut to meet the Egyptian ambassador there. It is reasonable to assume that the purpose of the meeting was to discuss Shuqayri's plan. In March 1964, Hikmat al-Masri and Qadri Tuqan went to Cairo for the same purpose. Egyptian newspapers, which were now allowed once more into Jordan, helped put over the Egyptian position to the Palestinian inhabitants of the West Bank who had harnessed themselves to Shuqayri's efforts.

The Jordanian Stand

Husayn made his first major error in the history of the struggle over the existence of the Palestinian entity and the Jordanian entity when he signed the summit decision on the question of the entity. Husayn looked for short-term advantages. He did not consider the political developments that would emerge from setting up the Palestinian entity within the Palestinian population in his country. When he agreed to the summit decision, he was obliged to take the next step, namely the convening of the PNC and setting up of the PLO. In this way Husayn speeded up the process which threatened the existence of his kingdom.

The considerations for his agreeing to set up the Palestinian entity at the first summit included:

1 The support of all the Arab heads of states for the establishment of the Palestinian entity. Husayn was impressed with the compliments Nasir paid him during the summit, and happy at finally being accepted into Nasir's "nationalist club" after "seven lean years" of isolation in the Arab world and constant attempts to overthrow his regime.[13]

2 Husayn believed he had the ability and the means to turn the PLO into an organization of the regime. He relied on his intelligence and security network and on his control over the Palestinian population of the West Bank.

3 Husayn was satisfied with Nasir's and Shuqayri's promises that the Palestinian entity would not harm "the unity of the kingdom" and his sovereignty over both banks. The summit declaration avoided mentioning the Palestinian entity and accepted Husayn's request to discuss the notion of Palestinians' self-determination only after the stage of "liberation." Husayn believed he could handle someone like Shuqayri.[14]

Husayn left nothing to chance. In his talks with Shuqayri he made sure that the composition of the PNC would be a guarantee that the PLO would be totally subject to Jordanian control and that the decisions of the PNC would reflect Jordan's conception. In this he succeeded; Shuqayri accepted all his demands. The steps Jordan took were:

1 Apart from ensuring a "Jordanian" majority in the PNC, Jordan intervened in the appointment of delegates from Jordan. Husayn made sure that only a few days before the congress convened (May 28, 1964) the West Bank members of the Senate and House of Deputies would join the PNC. In order to sustain his control over the PNC, Husayn ensured that the Jerusalem Congress was turned into a permanent National Congress and that Shuqayri was elected chairman of the Executive Committee, with the authority to appoint members to it.

2 Husayn was the dominant person in the congress. He personally made sure that the decisions of the congress were "flawless." Husayn's headquarters, including the staff of security services, were located near the congress.[15]

3 The final decisions of the congress, including items of the Palestinian Covenant and the Constitution of the PLO, were at one with Jordan's position and relieved its fear concerning the setting up of the PLO. These two documents emphasized the following:

A "The PLO will not assert any territorial sovereignty over the West Bank, nor over the Gaza Strip, nor over the al-Hamma area."

B "The Palestinian people will achieve self-determination after completing the liberation of its homeland." The basic Jordanian standpoint was accepted as it was defined in the White Book of 1962. This stated that "the liberation of Filastin is a pan-Arab national obligation; the responsibility for this lies entirely with the Arab nation, government, and peoples, and at their head the Arab Palestinian people." It was emphasized that the PLO would not interfere with the internal affairs of the Arab states.

C   The question of the PLO's representativeness of the Palestinians was not mentioned at all in the covenant or the constitution. It was circumvented with the statement that one of the functions of the EC was "representation of the Palestinian people." The decisions of the PNC emphasize that "the PLO will represent *Filastin* [but not the Palestinians] in the Arab League, in the United Nations and its institutions . . ."

4   Non-acceptance of the decision to set up the Palestinian Liberation Army. In the early talks between Husayn and Shuqayri, Husayn and senior officers of the Jordanian Arab Army strongly objected to the establishment of separate and independent Palestinian units in Jordan. Shuqayri displayed tactical flexibility in this sensitive area, and in his talks with Husayn before the PNC, a formula was agreed whereby "the Palestinian battalions will be set up with the agreement of the states concerned."[16]

5   The regime took strenuous security measures before and during the congress in Jerusalem in order to prevent even the smallest disturbance to the gathering and its deliberations. It succeeded beyond expectations. The basic situation assessment by the Jordanian intelligence and security services was that "the existing divisions of opinion among the Palestinians in everything connected with the congress and the subjects it will debate are likely to cause agitation and disturbances." The assessment was that "demonstrations and violent clashes between demonstrating groups are expected, including the use of arms, [and these are] likely to develop into activity against the kingdom." It was no wonder then that the following steps were taken:

A   The West Bank was turned into a military camp during the congress and even Jerusalem was turned into a "detention camp." The responsibility for internal security, as from 05:00 hours on May 27, 1964 was turned over to the army. The commander of the Western Front became a kind of military governor of the West Bank. Military forces were concentrated in central places in the large towns. The Jerusalem police force was reinforced by 100 policemen and four officers. A unit of the army engineering corps regularly examined the area where the congress was taking place for fear of sabotage.

B   The security forces were given strict orders to prevent demonstrations and gatherings, and even to open fire if necessary.

C   The movements of the opposition parties' members who were under surveillance, were limited; entry into Jerusalem during the congress was allowed only to those bearing special permits.

D   During the congress, entry into Jordan was forbidden for *personae non grata*, among them ten people from Lebanon, including two leaders of the ANM, Ghassan Kanafani and Ahmad al-Yamani (the latter a PNC member).[17]

Syria's Antithesis

If it depended on the Syrian Ba'th party, the PLO would not have been established in 1964. The Ba'th proposals regarding the setting up of the Palestinian entity were rejected by Husayn. The problem faced by Nasir and Shuqayri was to put forward not a maximalist program like that of the Ba'th which encompassed the bases for the establishment of a "Palestinian state" on the West Bank and the Gaza Strip, but rather a practical program taking into account the inter-Arab conditions of 1964. The Ba'th was strongly critical of Shuqayri, his "non-rational" program and the way in which the PNC was constituted and the PLO established. The Ba'th argued that "the PLO is the outcome of the compromise between the Arab heads of state," and its establishment was meant "to support the Palestinian people's demands for the establishment of a revolutionary entity." The Ba'th also claimed that the Jerusalem Congress had not been democratically elected. At the congress "Jordanian tactics dominated." "The entity was born at the Jerusalem Congress without land and lacking autonomy in its activity." Despite this criticism, the Ba'th was not without hope that the PLO activity "could be reformed in a revolutionary direction."[18] The National Command of the Ba'th concluded on the eve of the Jerusalem Congress that it was not enough to criticize Shuqayri and his plan but that it had to present an alternative plan for debate at the congress. On May 20, 1964 the National Command published its own plan for the Palestinian entity as an antithesis to the Shuqayri – Husayn – Nasir plan. The elements of this plan were:

1 The Palestinian entity must include the basic components of all entities – land, people, and government (*sulta*).
2 The Palestinian people have a legal right to its homeland within its borders which are not subject to partition and which include the conquered land of Filastin, the Gaza Strip, the West Bank of the Jordan River, and the al-Hamma area of southern Syria.
3 The entity will have two ruling institutions: a national assembly (*majlis watani*) and a Supreme Executive Committee. The national assembly will be established through direct elections by the Palestinians of Filastin and in the other Arab countries. Jerusalem will be the capital of the entity. The national assembly will have the right to establish a government and to decide on the setting up of a Palestinian national army. The supreme executive committee will be elected by the national assembly in a secret ballot. It will have no fewer than 15 members. It will represent the Palestinian entity and will speak in its name in the Arab and international arenas.[19]

In effect these components of the Palestinian entity would, of course, in practice be "the state of Filastin." The National Command deliberately avoided using the word "state," apparently in order to hide the clear similarity between this plan and Qasim's plan for the establishment of a Palestinian republic. The Syrian antithesis was a synthesis of Qasim's plan and of Shuqayri's and Egypt's earlier plan.

The aim of the plan was clear – to upset Jordan's territorial integrity and to establish a "Palestinian state," as a first stage, on the West Bank, the Gaza Strip, and al-Hamma, and as a second stage, in all of Mandatory Palestine. But for tactical reasons Shuqayri rejected it out of hand. Internal struggles and changes within the leadership of the Syrian Ba'th led to this plan being pushed aside. The eighth National Congress of the Ba'th (April 1965) did not consider this plan, and the Ba'th began to emphasize a new phenomenon in the Palestinian arena – Fatah and fida'iyyun activities.

Fatah's Reaction

From the start Fatah had reservations about the way the PLO was set up, "directed by the Arab regimes." The Fatah leaders feared that Shuqayri's activity would undermine their attempt to recruit Palestinians to their organization and its aim of leading "the Palestinian National Movement." They decided to meet him in Cairo in early 1964, and Abu Iyyad told him that "an organization set up from above will be inoperable if it does not rest on an active [popular] base." He proposed a package deal according to which there would be secret coordination between the PLO's public activities and Fatah's secret activities. Accordingly, "the PLO would become a kind of Jewish Agency, that is, the legal public body of the armed struggle which [Fatah] was waging." The link between the two organizations "would be made through the Fatah representatives who would be appointed by Shuqayri as members of the PLO EC."[20] Their purpose was clear: behind the scenes Fatah would be the dominant factor in the PLO. Shuqayri understood their intentions and rejected the proposal.

The Jerusalem Congress put Fatah on the horns of a dilemma. On the one hand, the composition of the congress, Shuqayri's objectives and the "patronage" he had from the Arab states, including Jordan, compelled Fatah to boycott it. On the other hand, there was "the need not to be absent from a Palestinian political life," and "the more essential need to penetrate a rich and strong organization in order to exploit the means that stand at its disposal." Fatah decided in favor of participation in the congress but not in the institutions of the PLO. It had seven representatives at the congress. Two of the Fatah's leaders, Khalid al-Hasan and Hani al-Qadumi, rejected Shuqayri's offer to join the PLO EC.[21] Fatah's organ, *Filastinuna* (April 1964), called for the establishment of a "revolutionary Palestinian entity based on a military organization." Fatah was in favor of "making the entity more prominent through the conduct of pure elections, if it is possible." But it warned that, "it is impossible to conduct free elections, because these would arouse [a new] hatred and blind factionalism."[22] In 1964, Fatah had not yet made its mark in the Palestinian arena.

Palestinian Organizations' Alignment

Shuqayri's activities in establishing the PLO brought about attempts at cooperation and alignment among Palestinian organizations with the intention of setting up a roof organization as a counterbalance, an alternative to the PLO. At the end of January 1964 contacts were made to unite a number of clandestine Palestinian organizations in one framework and under one leadership. In these discussions disputes arose regarding the organizational framework of cooperation among them, the form of unity between them, and their stand regarding Shuqayri and the PLO. Two developments should be noted. On March 14, 1964 a joint declaration was made on behalf of four Palestinian organizations calling for the establishment of the institutions of the Palestinian entity on "revolutionary principles," free elections, the formation of regular army units, and the election of a national congress to elect an executive committee which would be a collective leadership. A more meaningful organization was established at the end of May 1964 – that of The Political Bureau of the Palestinian Revolutionary Forces for

United Action. The Bureau was composed of six representatives of six organizations to coordinate their activities on the basis of a single political platform, while preserving the organizational and ideological independence of each. The joint platform called for the establishment of "an active, revolutionary Palestinian entity" and for "unity of action" between all the organizations.[23]

In the Palestinian arena itself, the year 1959 witnessed three important phenomena. In October, at a meeting of the Fatah founders, the Fatah organizational structure was finally established; in November the General Union of the Palestinian Students was set up; and also in that year *Filastinuna,* the Fatah organ, made its appearance. It is symbolic that the process of the elimination of the Arab Higher Committee headed by the Mufti Haj Amin al-Husayni had also begun in that year.

Still, it was only towards the end of 1962 and especially in 1963 that additional, secret Palestinian organizations began to form in Lebanon, Kuwait and to a lesser extent in the Gaza Strip. There were (1964–1965) "some 40 organizations with memberships from 2 to 400."[24] They called for the establishment of such institutions as a Palestinian government and national assembly, for recognition of the West Bank as "a part of Filastin" and for the establishment of a Palestinian army. Among these Palestinian organizations were: Jabhat al-Tahrir al-Filastiniya, Jabhat Thuwar Filastin, Jabhat al-Tahrir al-'Arabiya al-Filastiniya, al-Jabha al-Thawriya li-Tahrir Filastin, Kata'ib al-Fida'iyyin, Jabaht al-Tahrir al-Watani al-Filastini, and Talai' al-Fida' li-Tahrir Filastin. A number of these organizations had secret contacts with West Bank inhabitants with the aim of organizing branches there – activity that did not go unnoticed by the Jordanian security authorities.[25] At their meetings in the Arab states during this period, these Palestinian organizations demanded that the Palestinian entity be elevated to the level of a top-priority issue.

Nevertheless, any Egyptian initiative, Iraqi reaction or inter-Arab discussion stemmed merely from Egyptian and Iraqi considerations and not from pressures by a massive Palestinian popular movement. The reaction of the Palestinian population to such activities in the period 1959–1962 was generally one of passive sympathy or of activity inspired by the authorities rather than arising out of any institution initiative. In the years of the Egyptian–Syrian union there were no visible signs that the issue of the Palestinian entity had led to any independent Palestinian political movement. Instead, the Palestinian intelligentsia showed a strong tendency to act within the pan-Arab framework (except for the founders of Fatah) and to support Nasir's dictum that "unity is the road to the liberation of Filastin." Even *Filastinuna* began to relate to the Palestinian entity only at the end of 1960, when it called for the establishment of "a Palestinian revolutionary national rule on the Arab parts of Filastin,"[26] that is, the West Bank and Gaza Strip. It seems, therefore, that Fatah was also influenced by Egypt and Iraq's stand on that issue.

Part II *Jordan's Confrontation with the PLO – National Awakening in the West Bank*

In his book, *Jordan and Palestine: An Arab Perspective* (1984) [Arabic], the former Jordanian Minister of Education, Sa'id al-Tal, writing with the hindsight of two decades, pointed to the creation of the PLO in 1964 as the watershed in Jordanian–Palestinian relations:

> Unity between the Jordanian and Palestinian people developed quickly in all areas of activity without much difficulty until 1964, when the First Arab Summit voted to establish the Palestinian Liberation Organization (PLO) as the institutional representative of the Palestinian people . . . [The PLO] was transformed into the instrument for severing the unity between the two people, Jordanian and Palestinian. The conflict that erupted due to the PLO's aim of taking over the government in the West Bank led to the deepening of local division between the Jordanians and Palestinians . . . This conflict, which impaired Jordan's internal stability, lasted until early June 1967.[1]

In my opinion, the creation of the PLO should be seen as a turning-point in Jordanian–Palestinian relations. The historical testimony from a member of the Jordanian political elite was the first overt sign of the country's official re-assessment of "Jordanization" that had been imposed on the Palestinian population since the 1950 annexation. Moreover, the first inkling of this change can be traced to Egypt's initiative to "revive the Palestinian entity" in March 1959 and in later inter-Arab colloquies.[2] Internal Jordanian developments, relations between Jordanians and Palestinian citizens (or "Jordanians of Palestinian origin" as they were officially termed), and the creation of the PLO, all served as expressions of the strengthening of "Palestinianization," that is, the increased awareness of Palestinian identity. The process culminated in a life-threatening crisis to the regime following the IDF raid on the village of Samu' in November 1966. The roots of Jordan's internal crisis can be traced to the Palestinian national awakening in the West Bank where anger against Jordanian discrimination and prejudice had been growing since the 1950 annexation. During times of crisis or national convulsion pent-up feelings erupt in a storm of protest. This is what happened in April 1963 and November–December 1966 after the Samu' raid.

To establish himself as a representative of the Palestinians, Husayn had to rule both the territory and the population of the West Bank. The PLO, on the other hand, needed only the political allegiance of the population. From this stemmed the inevitable bitter struggle between Jordan and the PLO for the soul of West Bank Palestinians. As for the Palestinians in Jordan, they now faced a dilemma: was their allegiance to the Hashemite regime, or to a Palestinian organization which had been set up to represent them? Both Husayn and Shuqayri used the phrase "Jordan is Filastin and Filastin is Jordan," but they meant diametrically opposite things.

Shuqayri's Goals

His short-range aim was "personal autonomy" for the population on the West Bank. The Palestinians would be permitted "to express freely their national activities, like the other Arab peoples, in the stages of their struggle." Thus independent political and military institutions were needed for the West Bank Palestinians, to be integrated with the political institutions of the PLO – for example, participation in elections to the PNC, in the Popular Organization and in the PLA. Shuqayri believed that, since the Palestinians were the majority in Jordan and superior to the Jordanians in, for instance, education, this would lead in the long term to Jordan being taken over by the Palestinian entity. This meant achieving "territorial sovereignty" after having achieved "personal autonomy." West Bank politicians understood Shuqayri's intentions and supported them. After the PLO's confrontation with Jordan erupted in 1966, Shuqayri stated that the West Bank was "the launching area for the liberation of Filastin" and that the "the way to Tel Aviv passes through Amman," that is, "the liberation of Filastin must begin with the liberation of Jordan from Husayn's regime through the establishment of a nationalist regime." There is no doubt that in his view the next step, after the overthrow of the monarchy, had to be "Palestinian self-determination" and the setting up of a Palestinian state in Jordan. He stated that, "the East Bank is an integral part of Filastin," "Jordan has no right to exist as a state" and that "Jerusalem must be the capital of all Filastin."[3]

Shuqayri adopted Nasir's approach that these objectives could only be attained in stages while pacifying Jordanian leaders regarding the PLO's intentions. Only if these methods failed would it be necessary to resort to a popular uprising by the Palestinian population, but political circumstances in the Arab arena and his dependency on Nasir led Shuqayri to steer a zigzag course. Early in 1965, after setting up the PLO and getting the second summit's approval for forming the PLA, Shuqayri turned to the central problem: PLO activity in Jordan. He formulated several demands from Jordan.

In the military sphere, Shuqayri demanded conscription for the Palestinians in Jordan, and permission for the Palestinians to form, arm and train PLA battalions in Jordan subordinate to PLA command and in accordance with the UAC plan. The PLO also presented Jordan with a plan for strengthening the villages on the front line with Israel militarily, economically, and socially. He also demanded permission to set up "popular training camps" for civil defense exercises for the West Bank population and to provide them with weapons for emergencies. Furthermore, the PLO asked to set up and run ideological military summer camps for youth and students, in cooperation with Jordanian officers.

Shuqayri also demanded free and general elections for the PNC among the Palestinians in Jordan in accordance with procedures approved by the Executive Committee of the PLO. The PLO would apply the Law on the Palestinian Popular Organization in Jordan. The PLO demanded that Jordan grant diplomatic immunity to the PLO center in Jerusalem, members of the EC and PLO officials.

The PLO demanded permanent allocation of time on Jordanian radio for broadcasting of "nationalist" programs and permission to conduct propaganda campaigns in both print and speech.

Finally, Shuqayri demanded the imposition of a 3 percent tax on the salaries of Palestinians in Jordan for the PLO, and permission to conduct popular fund-raising campaigns. He also demanded that the Jordanian government put into effect the protocol prepared by the Arab League regarding freedom of movement, place of residence, and work for the Palestinians.[4]

These demands implied duality in the government, and the creation of a kind of a state within the state. The PLO would become an additional executive authority in Jordan, responsible for the "Palestinian section." Since this section comprised two-thirds of the population, it seemed clear that Jordan would have to turn into a "Palestinian state" with the Jordanians in a minority or at least only a part of a confederal state.

The Jordanian Conception

The starting point of the Jordanian conception continued to be the White Paper of 1962. Wasfi al-Tal's view was that in this program "the subject of the Palestinian entity was included, and the principles and implications of the Palestinian personality [were] thereby defined as essentially one with the Jordanian entity. These principles were accepted by the participants in the summit conferences, as a result of which the Palestinian entity was set up with the support of King Husayn and the government."[5] Tal now attempted to put this plan, devised under his inspiration, into practice. The principles of the Jordanian concept regarding the PLO, as Tal conceived and executed them, can be summarized as follows.

First of all, the PLO had to be "the prop of the Jordanian entity, all of whose activity is directed at becoming a center of power of the campaign for Filastin." In other words, "the concentration of Palestinian potential by the PLO complements the role embodied in the Jordanian entity in all its constituent elements and complements the activity of the state and the people since Jordan was established." In this capacity the PLO is "the Arab arm of Jordan and Filastin."

Second, "the state is responsible . . . for directing [its] citizens, organizing and training them in accordance with the laws. All activities, in whatever framework, connected with the citizens, must be directed by the state apparatus or with its permission. Thus every action connected with PLO activity must be based on the following principles: wholeness of the entity of the Kingdom of Jordan, its interests and internal unity, the laws of the kingdom, its sovereignty and security consideration, the foreign and internal policy of the state."

Third, since the majority of its citizens are Palestinians, Jordan is the sole representative of the Palestinians. Therefore, there is no need to establish separate "Palestinian bodies" in Jordan. "Jordan, both its banks, is Filastin, and represents the launching point for its liberation"; the Palestinians in Jordan are "Jordanians of Palestinian origin."

Finally, the Palestinian entity is a diplomatic necessity whose aim, first and foremost, is to further Arab efforts in the international arena. "The setting up of the PLO is meant to keep the Palestinian problem in existence and to help organize and mobilize the Palestinian potential outside of Jordan."[6]

These policy principles left no doubt about Jordan's position regarding Shuqayri's demands. The Jordanian regime, however, tried to show that it was actually satisfying these demands by its own methods. In fact, Jordan's attempt to identify the Hashemite state with Filastin stood in contrast to its actual policy of "Jordanization" of the Hashemite Kingdom with special emphasis on the East bank.

Jordan's reactions to the demands put forward by Shuqayri and the PLO were as follow. In the military sphere, Jordan refused to cooperate, repeatedly asserting that 60 percent of its soldiers in the Jordanian army were Palestinians and that all Palestinians in Jordan receive Jordanian citizenship. Conscription would hurt many workers in Jordan and beyond, as well as their families in Jordan. Instead Jordan preferred a volunteer army: "Jordan is forming new battalions whose number is four times what the PLO demands and these are deployed on the front lines."[7] The government passed the Law on Defense of Front-Line Towns and Villages, and army headquarters issued a special order for its implementation. Training and distribution of arms to the villages began on June 16, 1965. Jordan claimed that it was implementing a plan for "popular training" of all its inhabitants, and as a proof pointed to exercises by the Civil Defense and summer camps for military training of students and youth (20,000 were trained in 1965).[8]

As for PLO institutions, Jordan agreed in principle to hold elections to the PLO institutions so long as this was done through the Jordanian Interior Ministry. It argued that all Jordanian citizens already participated in "popular organizations," such as the House of Deputies, the Senate, the government, the army, town councils, trade bureaus, professional and labour unions, schools and educational institutions. It agreed to grant diplomatic immunity to the PLO offices and officials.

Jordan did agree to cooperate with the PLO in the sphere of media and information, in accordance with Jordan's own national guidance plan. Also, Jordan agreed in principle to the demand for a "liberation tax," but this was conditional on its being imposed on all Jordanian citizens and not only "on those of Palestinian origin."[9]

The Confrontation

Disputes between the PLO and Jordan were inevitable once the summit deliberately avoided defining the role of the PLO in Jordan. As a result each party acted according to its own conception and interest. The second summit made the location of units of the PLA conditional on "the agreement of the Arab state concerned." Shuqayri failed to obtain from the third summit a pan-Arab seal of approval for his demands on Jordan, in view of Husayn's resistance to these demands. Furthermore, Husayn opposed Shuqayri's referring to the West Bank during the summit debates as "Palestinian territory." Husayn demanded that the PLO's role in Jordan be defined, but the summit refrained from this, and contented itself with a decision regarding the Popular Organization and "general direct elections to the PNC," and a statement that "the PLO will maintain contact with the member states concerned in order to achieve understanding regarding the steps necessary" for such elections.[10] No decision was taken on the question of conscription.

Thus no agreement between Husayn and Shuqayri was possible. In the period 1964–1967 the relationship between the PLO and Jordan went through a number of stages.

In the period up to September 30, 1965: The relationship developed against the background of Nasir's desire to sustain the summit's atmosphere and purpose – namely Arab solidarity. Husayn, aware of this policy, rejected Shuqayri's demands, but was also aware of the mood on the West Bank and so avoided an open split with Shuqayri. On June 19, 1965 the PLO and Jordan approved in principle a draft agreement prepared and presented by Amer Khamash, the Jordanian chief-of-staff, involving fortification of the front lines and the formation of guard units of 15,000 to 20,000. This force, which would be armed only with light weapons, would be subordinate to the Jordanian army exclusively; its formation would be financed by the PLO. The agreement did not deal with the question of forming the PLA in Jordan.

Other demands of Shuqayri were settled according to the Jordanian basic positions, since Shuqayri was under pressure from Nasir, who wanted an agreement which would alleviate Jordanian's misgivings about the PLO's intentions in Jordan so that the PLO could gain a foothold there. The June 1965 agreement was never put into effect because of strident opposition within the PLA HQ, which insisted that the Palestinian commando and fida'i units in Jordan be under PLA command, and even threatened to censure the plan openly "as treacherous." Faced with this pressure Shuqayri withdrew from the agreement, and returned to the third summit with his earlier demands.[11]

October 1965 to June 1966: Nasir, hoping to pressure Husayn into carrying out the summit's decisions, hinted to Shuqayri about embarking on a limited propaganda campaign against the king. Shuqayri did this in his speech on *PLO Radio* on October 1, 1965. Jordan counter-attacked: Husayn appealed to Nasir to restrain Shuqayri. Nasir advised Husayn and Shuqayri to reach an agreement between themselves.[12] On December 24, 1965 an agreement was reached between Shuqayri and the Jordanian ambassador to Cairo, Anwar al-Khatib, who was pro-Egyptian.

According to this agreement the PLO would conduct a popular fund-raising campaign in Jordan; summer camps would be set up for training youth and students by Jordanian teachers and officers chosen by agreement between Jordan and the PLO; elections to the PNC would be conducted by the PLO under Jordanian supervision; Jordan would allocate a "corner" for the PLO on *Radio Amman* under control of the Jordanian Information Ministry; Jordan would put into effect the Arab League Protocol concerning the Palestinians; both sides agreed that the UAC would consider the question of the formation of PLA battalions in Jordan; the issue of the "popular organization" and "the popular training" would be reconsidered as soon as possible between the two sides.

However, within the Jordanian government there was serious dispute regarding stipulations that entailed Jordanian concessions, and Husayn refused to approve the agreement. Khatib seems to have erred in assessing flexibility on his government's part.[13] The mutual propaganda attacks now became even bitterer. Through the mediation of the secretary-general of the Arab League, representatives of the PLO and Jordan reached a temporary agreement (January 10, 1966) on cessation of the propaganda attacks and postponement of the PNC convention; they also agreed that the two delegations would meet on February 21, 1966 to continue the negotiations – on the basis of both the Khatib – Shuqayri accord and the Jordanian Foreign Ministry announcement (December 6, 1965) on Jordanian policy.[14]

Jordan, not wanting to be attacked during a forthcoming mini – summit meeting of Arab heads of government (expected in mid-March 1966), and especially in view of Nasir's support for Shuqayri's demands, concluded the discussions with the PLO by signing an agreement of March 1, 1966. Its terms can be divided into three categories:

1 On some matters Jordan did not compromise and its stand was accepted: conscription, arming of the front-line villages, and the form of a "popular fund-raising campaign" for the PLO and a "liberation tax" imposed on the entire Jordanian population. (The "liberation tax" caused much resentment among officials and army officers, which Jordanian authorities directed toward the PLO.) A decision on the formation of PLA units was transferred to the UAC.

2 On some matters Jordan had already made concessions – PLO information, summer camps for the training of youth and students, freedom of movement for the Palestinians.

3 There were also important matters on which Jordan made new concessions – "full freedom for the PLO to implement the law on elections to the PNC as approved by the PLO EC." The PLO was permitted to set up centers of the Popular Organization in Jordanian districts. Significantly, the agreement said nothing that could be interpreted as showing any special attitude towards the inhabitants of the West Bank; the words "Palestinian" and "West Bank" were not mentioned, not even in the section on "freedom of movement and work."[15]

Jordan signed the agreement without any intention of implementing it, desiring simply to obtain peace within and without. In a secret memorandum (March 5, 1966) to his ministers and the directors of the General Security and General Intelligence, Tal gave clear directives about exactly what PLO activities would actually be allowed in Jordan. All avenues for penetration into the PLO by "opportunists, destroyers, saboteurs who serve party and opportunist interests" must be closed. "All contacts between the PLO and citizens, for whatever purpose, without permission of the state or its special offices and not in accordance with its laws, must be prevented." "The PLO must be warned against employing party members or saboteurs. The War Laws regarding communism and parties must be carried out immediately and literally." "Any printed or photographed material (of the PLO) must be prohibited." Tal also warned that "The moment it is proved that the doors of this cooperation [between the PLO and Jordan] lead to confusion and sabotage, the states will reconsider" this cooperation.[16] The document speaks for itself. All that was left to Shuqayri if he wanted to be active in Jordan was to turn the PLO into a Jordanian organization.

A few weeks after the agreement was signed, first steps were taken to carry out the spirit and letter of the prime minister's directives. In early April 1966 a wave of arrests began which involved about 300 activists of the Ba'th, the Communist Party and the ANM. This was a crackdown on the PLO or pro-PLO activists also included leaders of the Popular Organization, which the PLO had begun to set up in Jordan and which the Jordanian authorities feared would turn into an insurgent national movement on the West Bank. The authorities also wished to prevent demonstrations being organized for Filastin Day in May 15, 1966.[17] All in all, an open split was imminent between the PLO and Jordan. Shuqayri prepared for it by attempting to transform the PLO in Jordan into an underground organization.

From June 1966 to May 1967: the Jordanian leadership assessed the situation confronting them. Their conclusions were to break off contact with the PLO; to eliminate completely the PLO activities in Jordan while undermining its representativeness of the Palestinians; and to cast aspersions on Shuqayri's leadership. Husayn first openly expressed this decision in a speech in Ajlun on June 14, 1966. In a message to Nasir on July 14, 1966, Husayn stated that, "in view of the PLO's deviation from the purpose for which it was established, it was not possible for us to cooperate with it."[18]

Husayn had correctly assessed that Nasir intended finally to terminate the "solidarity" of the summit, which would mean a worsening of relations between Egypt (and Syria) and Jordan, and a renewal of Egypt's campaign to undermine the Jordanian regime, signs of which were already apparent. The Jordanian leadership considered Nasir's speech of June 22, 1966 a turning point in his attitude towards Jordan.[19] The regime received decisive information regarding subversive activity by the PLO and Syria in Jordan, in addition to PLO attempts to penetrate the army. In March 1966 Jordanian intelligence warned of an increase in PLO activity on the West Bank; the Popular Organization, whose activity increase after the March 1966 agreement, began to take on a secret character and became inimical to the regime. Election committees set up by the PLO throughout the West Bank drew up the electoral rolls independently and made direct contact with the inhabitants. It was clear to the regime that, in the PNC about to be elected, Jordan would lose its absolute majority and thus the basis on which Jordan had agreed to the setting up of the PLO would collapse. The deliberations and decisions of the 3rd PNC (May 20–24, 1966), concentrated on attacking Jordan, left no doubt in the regime's mind about the PLO's future goals in Jordan.

In the light of all the above Jordan concluded that the PLO intended to set up a "Palestinian state" stage by stage in the West Bank and the Gaza Strip. It judged that in the first stage the PNC (to be elected) would elect a government which would demand authority over internal matters of the West Bank and the Strip; in the second stage this government would attempt to have Jordan's annexation of the West Bank revoked and would then declare an independent "Palestinian state."[20] Husayn once again had to choose the lesser of two evils: he could reorient Jordan's policies and join the "revolutionary camp," which meant submitting to Nasir's and Shuqayri's dictates regarding the Palestinian entity with all the danger that entailed for his regime; or he could wipe out the PLO entirely from Jordan in the full knowledge that this would lead to increasing attempts to undermine and eventually overthrow him. He chose the latter, believing that he could rely on the loyalty of his army, security forces and intelligence. Shuqayri, with Nasir's support, embarked on a vitriolic propaganda campaign which questioned the kingdom's unity and its very right to exist. Jordan replied with a massive personal counter-attack on Shuqayri. After Nasir's decision not to participate in the Arab summit, Shuqayri stepped up his campaign against the Jordanian regime; Fatah activities from the Syrian and Jordanian borders, which received considerable support form the West Bank population, gave the campaign impetus.

The Palestinians' National Awakening in the West Bank: In the Aftermath of the Samu' Raid

An important aspect to understanding the rise of the Palestinians as a factor in the Arab–Israeli conflict is the national awakening of the West Bank inhabitants in the wake of the establishment of the PLO and emergence of Fatah and other Palestinian fida'i organizations during the sixties. This national awakening became especially pronounced during the events in the West Bank following the IDF raid on Samu' (November 13, 1966) in which a national leadership emerged.[21]

On the night of 11–12 November, mines had been laid inside Israeli territory south of Hebron. That night an IDF halftrack went over a mine that left three soldiers killed and six wounded. The tracks of the perpetrators led across the border into Jordan. Because of this the units of the Jordanian Arab Army (JAA) in the Hebron area had been put on a high state of alert out of fear of Israeli retaliation.

On 13 November 1966 the IDF launched a large-scale attack on the village of Samu', south of Hebron, in response to acts of fida'iyyun sabotage. According to the Jordanian defense minister's report to the prime minister, fifteen military personnel (including two officers) and five civilians were killed; thirty-four soldiers (including the brigade commander) and six civilians wounded; ninety-three houses destroyed (including the police station and a girls school). The defense minister pointed out that "the enemy's goal was to blow up homes thought to be Fatah bases near the cease-fire lines . . . A very large force of the enemy's infantry, armor, artillery, and engineers had been committed." During an air strike one Jordanian plane was shot down and the pilot killed.[22]

In the afternoon a Jordanian military spokesman emphasized the Jordanian "victory", the IDF retreat, and the fact that "the attack was much wider in scope than any previous raid." He stressed the "size of IDF losses" compared to the JAA's, and "the superb conduct of Jordanian troops."[23]

The blow to Jordan by the IDF raid gave vent to an angry outburst of Palestinian national sentiment due mainly to the pent-up rage at the discrimination suffered in Jordan. The PLO, Egypt, and Syria seized the opportunity to institute a virulent propaganda campaign against the Hashemite regime with the goal of shaking it up. The intensity of response also reflected the huge gap between the Palestinian population and the regime. The raid sparked unprecedented anti-Hashemite ferment along with demonstrations and riots that occasionally involved gun-fire. These disturbances were more violent than those of April 1963. The agitation in the West Bank – especially in Nablus – became so severe that the army had to intervene for the first time (November 21). The demonstrations were fueled by Damascus, PLO and Cairo broadcasting incitement aimed at encouraging a civil uprising involving the army. The agitation on the West Bank continued until early December 1966.

At a press conference on November 21, Prime Minister Wasfi al-Tal assessed the IDF raid:

> As a limited local campaign, the battle of Samu' was a sweeping victory for our armed forces. Israel concentrated an armored force and artillery brigade at half the level it had deployed in the [1956] Sinai Campaign. In the Jerusalem area it deployed even greater forces, and directed a larger army group in the north at Jenin . . . The military assessment was that . . . Samu' was intended as a diversionary attack in order to launch a massive strike elsewhere. This estimate too was correct . . .[24]

While he emphasized that the Samu' raid was a major move in Israel's preparations for capturing the West Bank, his message was also intended for domestic ears by presenting the battle as a Jordanian victory and an outstanding display of JAA valor.

The simultaneous eruption of the demonstrations in urban centers and refugee camps on the West Bank, as well as the reliable information gathered by Jordanian Intelligence, all pointed to a guiding hand behind the unrest. The smoking-gun led to activists in the West Bank's "National Leadership" which included veteran opposition leaders, communists, and members of the Arab Nationalists Movement (ANM) and the Ba'th party. Added to the list were agents that Shuqayri had recruited in Jordan. There is truth then in Jordan's claim that the ringleaders were PLO and communist activists equipped with money from foreign sources. Similar to the April 1963 riots, high-school pupils, refugees, and people on the street stood out prominently among the demonstrators. But unlike the April 1963 riots, a well-coordinated West Bank "National Leadership" emerged in November 1966 that organized protests against the Hashemite regime and its policy towards Shuqayri, the PLO, and Fatah.

The most active members of the "National Leadership" belonged to the local national leaderships in Nablus and Jerusalem. Two "National Leadership" meetings (Nablus, November 21) and (Jerusalem, November 23) called for the convocation of a "people's convention to discuss core issues regarding the Homeland." The convention would be organized by committees from various districts in Jordan, and the signatories included MPs, senators, and members of the Jerusalem and Nablus municipalities. The announcements made by the two national leadership meetings demanded:

1 The arming of border villagers and reinforcement of the front lines in accordance with UAC military experts.
2 The organization of popular resistance according to UAC recommendations.
3 Compulsory conscription.
4 The deployment of Arab military units in Jordan to strengthen the JAA, and Jordan's membership in the Egyptian–Syrian defense pact.
5 Full cooperation with the PLO, permitting it to operate independently inside Jordan.
6 Free rein to Palestinian fida'iyyun.
7 Allowing the people freedom of discussion regarding their future.[25]

The nationalist characteristic of the leadership's demands stands out prominently, especially support for Fatah activity, the call to permit the opposition to engage in political activity, and the right to free assembly. This was the first time that a nationalist organization established on both banks of the Jordan River was comprised of representatives from all of the public institutions and political parties on the West Bank. The newly-formed leadership succeeded in consolidating its position regarding the Jordanian government, a policy not always supportive of the regime and occasionally extremely radical. Almost the entire national leadership identified with Shuqayri's demands of Jordan and his political-propaganda activity inside other Palestinian groups, especially his collaboration with the Fatah organization. This type of radical activity sent shockwaves through the regime and compelled the king to devise an appropriate response to the turn in Palestinian – Hashemite relations.

Following the national leadership's decision to convene a popular convention, a preparatory committee was held in Jerusalem (December 1966) to formulate a "national manifesto." Over 150 representatives from cities and villages of both banks were invited. The manifesto's text was to be ratified at the 5 December convention.

Jordanian security services were aware of the plans for a popular convention and were resolved to obstruct it at all costs. Several of the leading organizers were arrested and their papers confiscated. The convention was declared illegal, and on 5 December, the day it was to have convened, the head of Jordanian security circulated a message to all police commanders in the district stating that the government had decided to prohibit the meeting from taking place . And, indeed, the convention did not take place.

The text of the manifesto, however, was circulated in poster-form throughout the West Bank and publicized the same day in the Arab media:

1 This convention has been called in response to the people's rage . . . The [people's] will is being expressed and it is the source of authority claiming the right to determine the policy of its Homeland.
2 [The convention] demands that the constitution be honored . . . that basic freedoms be recognized, honor of the citizens respected, and the restrictive emergency laws terminated.
3 [The convention] believes that armed Arab struggle is the only path to destroy the Zionist-Imperialist base and return the stolen Homeland.
4 The convention] demands the presence of Arab armies on Jordanian soil.
5 [The convention] supports the PLO as *the only representative of the Palestinian people's will* [my emphasis – M.S.] . . . The convention demands that the Jordanian government allow the [PLO] to carry out its sacred nationalist obligations [*qawmiya*] by granting it the necessary freedom to execute its military, economic, and organizational plans, and mobilize the Palestinian people . . .
6 The convention recognizes the importance of fida'iyyun activity as part of the Filestin liberation struggle, and therefore demands all Arab states bordering the occupied areas not to hinder fida'iyyun activity.[26]

The convention "manifesto" was the climax of the Palestinization and radicalization of the West Bank population since the establishment of the PLO and the beginning of Shuqayri's activity. It reiterated the demands of the Nablus and Jerusalem posters, but went even further by strongly inclining to Egyptian – PLO and Fatah positions. The manifesto's tenets also posed a flagrant challenge to the Amman regime. Equally significant were the demands that the "National Leadership" be seen as party to the Jordanian opposition on all aspects of democratization, such as equal representation, freedom of political activity, and viewing "the people as the source of government." This was a subtle call for proportional representation in elected institutions and government based on demographic size (the Palestinians made up two-thirds of Jordan's population). If the government adopted the manifesto's key sections it would mean converting Jordan into a "Palestinian state," accepting the Egyptian – Syrian nationalist line, and turning Jordan into an Egyptian satellite.

Summing up the situation on the West Bank following the raid, a Saudi diplomat in Jerusalem reported (December 25, 1966):

No conditions exist under which the West Bank residents will accept the present situation; they will remain steadfast in their clearly defined, publicized demands . . . Namely, limited royal constitution, freely held elections according to a population census and the establishment of parliamentary government based on the majority of parliamentary members (two-thirds Palestinian). Without the realization of these demands, the West Bank will remain in a state of discord and unrest . . . The government will be in a precarious position and find itself constantly on the lookout, especially under the present circumstances where the Egyptian, Syrian, and PLO media are stepping up their virulent anti-Hashemite attacks, and reaching always attentive ears . . .[27]

The "moderates" (here the Saudi diplomat was probably referring to Palestinians in government offices or affiliated with the regime) felt that certain demands of the radicals would have to be accepted before calm was restored. The diplomat added that this could be achieved if the regime avoided provocative statements against the Palestinian public and discontinued its use of harsh measures.

Conclusion: The Struggle for Control of the West Bank and the Fate of the Hashemite Regime

The distrust between the regime and the West Bank Palestinians deepened in the wake of the November crisis. Also, a lack of trust developed in the relations between the regime and moderate West Bank leaders who served in key government posts. The confrontation with the West Bank Palestinian population could have quickly spread to the Palestinians on the East Bank too.

The "National Leadership" that had incited and led the demonstrations included veteran opposition leaders from the 1950s whom the regime believed it had won over through government jobs and lucrative financial offices. During the November crisis many of these notables fled the Hashemite camp and joined the opposition leaders, probably with the intent of guaranteeing their futures if the regime toppled. The young leadership, made up of Ba'th activists, communists and Arab nationalists, had been silenced in April 1966 and later in the wave of arrests of PLO and opposition activists, thus it was not prominent among the organizers of the riots.[28]

The fate of the Hashemite regime hung on the outcome of the struggle for the West Bank. The organized demonstrations proved that underneath the apparent calm, in effect since the confrontation between the government and Shuqayri in mid-1966, the PLO had managed to build up a network of activists and agents inside Jordan who could bring the population out to the streets at a moment's notice. The Samu' raid afforded such an opportunity. Despite the regime's reservation at calling in the army to quell the rioting, and despite the military's demand for a retaliatory strike against Israel, the army acted decisively and aggressively in putting down the demonstrations. There was no manifestation of disloyalty among the officer cadre. The crisis proved that even violent protest, foreign agitation, and sabotage lacked the power to bring down the regime as long as the army remained loyal. The East Bank remained quiet throughout the entire crisis, even in the north of Jordan, an area known for its anti-Hashemite inclination.

Mutawi quotes "a well-informed Jordanian source":

> So intense was Palestinian feeling that leading figures on the West Bank pushed for declaring the creation of an independent Palestinian state on the West Bank. They believed that Egypt and Syria would not hesitate to grant it recognition and in such circumstances the Jordanian government would find it difficult to resist.

Mutawi added that according to Hazem Nussaibah (foreign minister four times between 1962 and 1966),

> Leaders of the West Bank were called to the Royal Palace and given a stiff reprimand by the King and Tal for their alleged support of Shuqayri and their threat to break away from Jordan.[29]

The real impact of Samu' came in the form of the tremors it sent through the Jordanian elite because of events on the West Bank and the burst of Palestinian national awakening. Jordanian leaders, especially the king, had to re-think a change in the government structure. This could be accomplished by providing the West Bank with some degree of "autonomy" in response to nationalist demands being made following the Israeli raid and in order to prevent radical elements from taking unilateral steps. This recalls the spirit of the later March 1972 plan for a "United Arab Kingdom" that proposed dividing Jordan into two autonomous regions under the Hashemite crown. Sa'id al-Tal (Wasfi al-Tal's brother) wrote:

> For the sake of historical truth, the foundations of [the 1972] plan were laid in 1966 [probably after the Samu' raid] when King Husayn accepted its principles. But reservations over the plan by certain officials postponed its implementation. It remained on the back burner until the June War . . . [In the aftermath,] many of the organizational reforms that Jordan was prepared to carry out, including the plan for the United Arab Kingdom, were suspended.[30]

After the Six Day War, the idea of granting "autonomy" to the West Bank was considered in November 1968 by King Husayn,[31] but its official announcement came only in March 1972 in the form of the United Arab Kingdom Plan.[32]

The Fida'iyyun Organizations' Contribution to the Descent to the Six Day War

In the interim between the Sinai War in 1956 and the Six Day War in 1967, the Arab–Israeli conflict continued to simmer and intensify until it culminated in the outbreak of war. The Palestinian problem stood at the center of the Arab world's political discourse. During these years the borders were not as quiet as Israel's leaders maintained. Tension became especially pronounced on the Jordanian and Syrian borders in January 1965 when fida'iyyun organizations (*fida'i*, Arabic for one who sacrifices himself for a noble cause) commenced sabotage operations inside Israel. Fatah launched its first operation on January 1, 1965. The fida'i activities that followed triggered Israeli retaliations whose high-points were the Samu' raid in Jordan (November 13, 1966) and the large-scale operation in Syria (April 7, 1967). Thus the guerilla – fida'iyyun organizations played an important role in destabilizing the border situation and contributing to the descent to war. In this light, the Six Day War was the fulfillment of Fatah's basic goal: to ensnare (*tawarit*) the Arab states in a war with Israel.

The fida'iyyun organizations' contribution to the descent to war can be observed in the following areas:

1 Sabotage operations continued despite Israel's warnings. Israel demanded responsibility for these actions from the Arab states that harbored the fida'iyyun and allowed them use of their countries as staging bases for operation. The continuation of guerilla operations led to increasingly violent Israeli retaliations whose high-point was the raid on the Jordanian village of Samu'. The IDF's responses were part of its overall effort to counter the Arab plan for diverting the Jordan River and its tributaries.

2 Syria provided the fida'iyyun organizations, and especially Fatah, with generous backing and served as Fatah's logistical hinterland for training and weapons and ammunition supply. Syria increased its support despite Israel's admonitions. Israel had no doubts that Syria was aiding and abetting Fatah activity, including Fatah operations emanating from Jordan (which Fatah operatives entered from Syria). After Jordan and Lebanon took determined

measures in countering Fatah activity on their soil, Syria, since the autumn 1966, remained Fatah's only secure operations base. Nevertheless the Syrian regime imposed limits on Fatah's activities in Syria and on using Syria as a base for attacking Israel. In June 1966 a number of Fatah leaders, among them Arafat and Abu Jihad, were detained in Damascus, interrogated, and then released.

3   The IDF's retaliations led the Jordanians, Syrians, and later the Egyptians, to believe that Israel intended to seize the Jordanian-controlled West Bank or topple the Syrian regime. On the one hand, Syria's frustration at the failure of the Arabs' water diversion plan and, on the other hand, the turnabout in Jordan's position toward Israel after the Samu' raid, contributed to the process that led to the Six Day War and to Jordan's participation in it.

4   The change in Egypt's position (and the PLO's) toward support of fida'iyyun operations began in mid-1966. By the end of the year the PLO, the Arab Nationalists Movement, and other organizations – such as Ahmad Jibril's group, the Palestinian National Front – also started taking an active part in sabotage operations.

Border tension also increased because of sabotage acts inside Israel. It continued despite orders from the United Arab Command (UAC), or more correctly from Egypt, to the Jordanian, Syrian, and Lebanese chiefs of staff to suppress fida'iyyun activity because it went against the Arab strategy that had been approved at the Arab summit meeting; such activity was liable to entangle the Arab states in a war they were still unprepared for. Jordan obeyed the order with some reservations; Lebanon was even more reluctant to comply with it; and Syria continued to support Fatah and other Palestinian organizations, declaring that it had no intention of safeguarding Israel's security.

The Emergence of Fatah (Harakat al-Tahrir al-Watani al-Filastini)

The Fatah organization appeared in the Arab domain following Israel's January 12, 1965 announcement of a sabotage operation against Israel's National Water Carrier in the Galilee that took place on the night of January 1. A Fatah squad set off a small explosive device that caused no damage whatsoever, but Israel's near-hysterical publicity of the incident reflected its surprise. Israeli intelligence learned of Fatah and its operational plans two or three weeks prior to the incident, even though the organization's name first appeared in Fatah's Beirut-based mouthpiece *Filastinuna* in 1959.

Fatah's internal publications reveal that during Israel's occupation of the Gaza Strip (from October 1956 to March 1957) the idea of a "Palestinian armed movement" emerged. After the occupation, "several young educated Palestinians – most of them members of the Palestinian Student Association in Cairo – met. Their common interest was [to forge] a new path in the struggle [against Israel] . . . that would pave the way for a popular armed revolution and the organization of the people and its leadership toward [the goal of] liberation." Fatah's internal publications relate that, "crystallization of the organization's core took two and a half years . . ." In 1958 the founders formed a unified group calling itself *Harakat Tahrir Filastin* (The Filastin Liberation

Movement). They chose the acronym H.T.F. and reversed the letters to spell FaTaH. Between 1958 and 1965 Fatah's founders spread their ideas among the dispersed Palestinian masses, recruited followers, trained them militarily, armed them, and prepared them for the revolution.[1]

In 1958 the main ideas of the movement were consolidated and appeared in the monthly *Filastinuna* that was published in Beirut. According to Abu Iyyad, one of the founding members: "Fatah's founders met in Kuwait in October 1959 and set up [the movement's] organizational structure."[2] Only in late 1962, and especially throughout 1963, were secret Palestinian organizations established in Lebanon, Kuwait, and to a lesser degree in the Gaza Strip. In 1963 Fatah opened its first bureau in Algeria, and its members underwent military training there. A new period in the history of the Palestinian National Movement began on January 1, 1965 when the military arm of Fatah, al-'Asifa launched sabotage operations against Israel thus inaugurating the "New Palestinian National Movement." Other fida'iyyun organizations emerged in Fatah's wake, some of which had been active underground. In 1964 and 1965 there were "close to forty organizations with membership ranging from 2 to 400."[3] Fatah's organ, *Filastinuna*, began to circulate in October 1959. Its slogan proclaimed that, "long-range, popular armed revolution is the path to the liberation of Filastin."[4]

At first Fatah saboteurs crossed into Israel from the Jordanian and Lebanese borders, later they infiltrated from the Syrian border. In its early years the organization was isolated in the Palestinian arena. It recruited Palestinians as well as mercenaries from among veteran fida'iyyun who had served in the Egyptian or Syrian intelligence services in the 1950s.[5] At first the Palestinian public "offered only quiet and passive support, and was unwilling to take part in fida'iyyun activity or provide the necessary backing, but it did not conceal its admiration of the fida'iyyun operations executed by Fatah."[6] The widespread publicity that the Arab and Israeli media accorded Fatah operations created a much greater impression of the organization's size than the number and practical results of its sabotage acts would indicate. Unlike the PLO (the Palestinian Liberation Organization), founded by Ahmad al-Shuqayri in 1964, that loyally supported Egyptian strategy, Fatah adopted a militant, independent path that broke ranks with Arab strategy over Shuqayri's leadership and the nature of the struggle. The outpouring of sympathy that the Palestinian masses showered upon Fatah upset the PLO's representation of them, jolted the organization, and undermined Shuqayri's leadership. The emergence of additional fida'iyyun organizations exacerbated these phenomena.

A number of features characterized fida'iyyun activity from early 1966, one year after the organization's debut, until the Six Day War in June 1967:

1 The low volume of guerilla operations – five a month – though this was a fifty percent rise since 1965 – the first year of Fatah activity.[7] The increase in operations was noteworthy in view of the Jordanian and Lebanese governments' decision to obstruct fida'iyyun activity on their territory. Several operations had been foiled in both countries. The Jordanian regime tried to block infiltration from Syria into Jordanian territory and from there into Israel. Syria played a major role in directing fida'iyyun activity in Fatah's early stage, but later it supported other Palestinian organizations too – whether they operated out of Lebanon and Jordan or crossed directly into Israel from the Syrian border.

2 The gap between Fatah's reportage of the damage it wreaked on the IDF, and what really happened can be seen in the imaginative description of Fatah's "encounters" with the IDF and the damages it inflicted (wounded, killed, and loss of equipment and vehicles). For example, Fatah published its "tally of military operations" carried out between January 1, 1965 and June 5, 1967: number of operations – 183; enemy troops killed and wounded – 546 soldiers, 5 officers; mines detonated – 44; water stations destroyed – 25; military vehicles destroyed – 50; guard posts destroyed – 23; ammunitions dumps destroyed – 7; settlements attacked – 53; military trains blown up – 1; factories destroyed – 2; Fatah wounded – 13; Fatah killed – 5.[8] The Palestinian public found it comforting to believe these reports since they boosted morale and magnified the glory of the Palestinian fida'iyyun or the "new Palestinian." No open criticism of the exaggerated reports was heard publicly during this period. After the Six Day War, when the volume of Fatah activity increased, criticism would be heard.

3 The ineptitude in handling sabotage equipment (that was in decrepit condition but later improved). The level of performance improved when the fida'iyyun began employing mechanical and chemical delay fuses and even electric timers. On the other hand, sabotage squads – including members of the Syrian – Palestinian commando battalion that Syrian intelligence had taken under its wings – were better equipped, better trained, and achieved better results. At this stage, however, the level of damage perpetrated by the fida'iyyun was not taken as a yardstick for the success of an operation for Fatah and other organizations. The operations' significance lay in their demonstration that an active "armed struggle" was being waged by the Palestinians.

The Egyptian Position

Egypt favored the step-by-step strategy that the first Arab summit had approved, which was based on an avoidance of an all-out military confrontation with Israel until the Arab states were fully prepared. Nasir claimed that Israel should not be allowed to decide on the date for confrontation, but that the Arabs, that is he, Nasir, should.[9]

With the first publication of Fatah's sabotage operations in Israel in early January 1965, the Egyptians vigorously opposed them. They estimated that this activity could drag them into a war with Israel before they were sufficiently prepared for it. They reckoned that Israel would probably respond with a heavy hand to these provocations, and a situation might develop whereby Egypt would be enmeshed willy-nilly in an armed conflict. This view was reinforced by the assessment (made as early as 1965) that Fatah activity was part of an "imperialist plot."

A few months after Fatah's first sabotage operations against Israel, Egypt's security and intelligence services obtained considerable information about the organization and its activities. According to Egyptian intelligence accounts:

1 Fatah is one of many Palestinian underground organizations. It has branches in a number of Arab states: Kuwait, Lebanon, Syria, Jordan, Lybia, Algeria, and the Gaza Strip. Those in charge of the organization are in contact with

several Arab or foreign states in order to receive financial and military assistance. Some of the organization's leaders have tried to make contact with [Arab leaders] such as Nasir and Ben Bella.

2 Fatah was established five years ago. The center of the organization's activity is in Kuwait where conditions are favorable to its activity: Kuwait's material resources, the large number of Palestinians working in various government apparatuses, and Kuwait's distance from the political struggles in the Arab world. Most [Fatah] members come from the Muslim Brotherhood. There are also a number of Christians among its members [but this is for] deception. The organization calls its branches by various names such as, "The Islamic Revolutionary Movement," "The Sons of Filastin Group," and "The Palestinian Liberation Front," even though those responsible for supervising the organization circulate the organ *Filastinuna* and coordinate the training and enlistment of political support of Arab states. The reason for the organization's pseudonyms in the Arab states is for camouflage purposes so that the organization can pursue its activity in case any branch is paralyzed.

3 The organization's membership comes to 2,000. Fatah has a training base in northern Tripoli in Lebanon, at the farm of Tawfiq Khuri, where its members undergo instruction before being transferred to areas adjacent to Israel. The organization's aim is to carry out harassment operations in Israel. Syria has promised [Fatah] military and material assistance, and has provided the organization with a supply of weapons that were [smuggled] into Jordan in August 1964. The organization has established contacts in the Gaza Strip, and has training areas in Syria, Lebanon, and Algeria.

4 Fatah sent a delegation to the People's Republic of China to obtain approval for . . . training in China and the use of a training base in Albania.

5 The organization has informed its branches in the Arab states to be prepared to carry out sabotage operations after the second summit (September 1964) regardless of the operations' results. The organization has assigned tasks to its branches in Arab states, and has selected the Gaza Strip as the area for its activity. Fatah began to distribute weapons and money to activists in Jordan, especially in the Hebron region, for operations against Israel. The fact that the organization penetrated Israel from Syrian territory confused the Palestinian public's perception of the organization.

6 There is room to believe that the organization serves reactionary and imperialist plans in the region. Most of the members running [the organization] come from the Muslim Brotherhood or are agents known for their links to Britain, therefore it is impossible to find out the truth of [the organization].

7 Fatah opposes the PLO – the official representative of the Palestinian entity [according to the resolutions of] two Arab summit conferences. Fatah opposes the PLO's policy and accuses the Arab states, especially Egypt, for the loss of Filastin. There is room to believe that the organization serves reactionary and imperialist plans in the region. Its military communiqués are exaggerated and bloated. These communiqués will probably result in . . . Israel's exploitation of them in order to enlist sympathetic public opinion; a blow to the PLO's stature among the Palestinians; intensified regional tension; the Arab states [will be] in an awkward position . . . when water diversion operations of the Jordan River's

tributaries commence; Israel [might] gain an excuse to launch military operations, even if they are of [only] a limited nature.

4　Egyptian security authorities have concluded that Fatah activity has to be kept under watch, and that the PLO, whose establishment was approved by all the Arab states, is the only organization representing the Palestinians. In [the Egyptians'] opinion, any operation carried out by an organization other than the PLO weakens its [the PLO's] influence and activity. [In their opinion] Fatah's leaders must act responsibly and carry out their activity within the framework of the PLO.[10]

Based on this report, the Egyptians adopted sweeping measures to counter Fatah activity, undermine its recently gained popularity in the Arab and Palestinian arenas, and whittle down its status as the sole representative of the Palestinian people. Fatah's challenge to the Arab states and the PLO forced Egypt to act as the main backer of the PLO and its leader – Ahmad al-Shuqayri.

From early 1965 to mid-1966, the Egyptians waged an anti-Fatah campaign both overtly and covertly. They vigorously inhibited the organization's sabotage activity by taking tangible steps to intercept the saboteurs operating out of the Gaza Strip. During this period the Egyptian media avoided publicizing Fatah's announcements. It also pressured other Arab states to clamp down on the fida'iyyun. Egypt took the following measures:

1　It waged a smear campaign against Fatah in Lebanon's pro-Egyptian Press that stressed "Fatah's link with agents from Central Treaty Organization (CENTO) and Israel."[11] In line with Egyptian policy and under its influence, PLO spokesmen declared on January 2, 1965 that their organization had no connection with Fatah; it opposed Fatah's sabotage acts, regarding them as deviations from the general Arab policy. PLO circles claimed that "they knew nothing about [Fatah] and that in their view unclean hands were behind these acts especially since they took place at a time when the Arabs intended to begin diversion operations. [In their opinion] The majority of Fatah's members belong to the Muslim Brotherhood and want to entrap Nasir in an open war with Israel."[12] The PLO undoubtedly viewed Fatah activity as an attempt to undercut its status in the Arab world as the flagship of the Palestinian struggle. Later, an attempt was made to explain the Egyptian line: " fida'iyyun operations are liable to drive Israel to retaliatory acts at a time unsuited for the Arabs; only when the Arab armies have become strengthened will the enemy be deterred from retaliating."[13] Shafiq al-Hut, the PLO representative in Beirut, wrote in *Filastin*: "As for the limited fida'iyyun activity that certain Palestinian revolutionary organizations are engaged in . . . we fear that this activity will lead to retaliatory acts by the enemy as in Qalqiliya and Jenin, so that our loss will be greater than our gain."[14]

2　In inter-Arab forums, Egypt dictated its antagonism toward Fatah, trying to force the Arab states to move against Fatah members and prevent them from carrying out operations in Israel. Jordan and Lebanon accepted Egyptian policy because of Israel's response to Fatah sabotage and Israel's placing responsibility for Fatah infiltration on the Arab states from which it emanated. In January–February 1965, following Israel's January 12 disclosure of Fatah's sabotage operation, the UAC, which had been established at the first Arab Summit in January 1964 and whose commander was Ali Amer, the former Egyptian chief-of-staff, ordered the chiefs of staff of Syria, Jordan, and Lebanon to suppress fida'iyyun operations against Israel. The UAC condemned these acts and demanded that "irresponsible people be forbidden from executing such acts at so inappropriate a time." It stressed that "these operations are incompatible with UAC-approved plans . . . Every operation that is superfluous from the point of view of [our] joint military plan is liable to precipitate hostilities with the enemy before the Arab states have completed their preparations for these battles so that the enemy alone will benefit from them." These orders remained in force until the Six Day War.[15]

When the heads of the Arab delegations to the Mixed Armistice Commissions met (March 24–27, 1965) they shunned concrete reference to Fatah operations. The assistant to the Arab League's secretary general proposed "discussing the published material on the al-'Asifa and Fatah forces and their operations on the four Arab fronts, and exchanging information on this issue." The secretariat of the Arab League classified the official protocol of this debate as "top secret." According to the protocol:

> The participants discussed [material] that had been published on the al-'Asifa and Fatah forces. The heads of the delegations made it clear that they had no information on these two organizations. The head of the Jordanian delegation stated that Israel claimed on several occasions that members of the two organizations had infiltrated from Jordan, but investigations always discovered discrepancies in the claims. The head of the Lebanese delegation noted that his government had undertaken a painstaking investigation that failed to yield any information on either organization, and that it had taken decisive steps to prevent infiltration into occupied Filastin by members of these organizations, if indeed they were operating in Lebanon. The pictures and investigations by the Armistice Commission proved that the Israeli patrols had encountered three [sabotage] squads and succeeded in capturing four or five Palestinians and one Lebanese. Two [saboteurs] managed to escape and two others were killed. Members of the [al-'Asifa] forces had entered the occupied area armed, which made their discovery easy. The heads of the Syrian and Egyptian delegations stated that they had no information on this matter, even if a great deal of information was available on their activities.[16]

In sum, the conference's recommendations did not refer to this subject. The claims of the delegations' heads notwithstanding, the intelligence agencies of the four countries possessed, in fact, information on Fatah activity against Israel emanating from their respective territories.The reference to al-'Asifa and Fatah as two separate organizations was obviously an error and apparently stemmed from confusion over Fatah's publications.In effect, al-'Asifa was Fatah's military arm.

Fatah sabotage inside Israel was again brought up in an emergency meeting of the heads of the Arab delegations to the Mixed Armistice Commissions held between January 9 and 11, 1966 in Cairo and chaired by the assistant to the Arab League's secretary general, Sayyid Nofel. Nofel proposed discussing "the situation on the armistice lines, and [Israel's] attacks [carried out] on Jordanian, Syrian, and Lebanese soil and that were linked to Fatah raids or Arab operations for exploiting the water of the Jordan and its tributaries." The only participant who related to Fatah activity in his general survey was the head of the Lebanese delegation. Referring to the situation on the Israeli–Lebanese border, he noted:

> The outstanding feature in the events of 1965 was the threats that Israel made in the course of the meetings of the Mixed Armistice Commission after numerous acts of sabotage had been carried out close to the armistice line and that Israel claimed had been perpetrated by saboteurs who infiltrated from Lebanese territory. Although sabotage was committed, it was insignificant and harmless, but Israel promised to exact revenge. Indeed, on the night of October 28/29, 1965 it blew up a house in the village of Hulah and three water tanks in Mis al-Jabil. Israel acknowledged these acts. Lebanon lodged a complaint in the Security Council. Israel began nighttime vehicle-patrols along the border, it used searchlights especially in areas convenient for infiltrating across the armistice line so as to prevent infiltrators who might be coming from Lebanon . . .

The issue was discussed in a separate section of the agenda that the delegations' heads referred to as the "So-Called Fatah Organization activity" (*parentheses in original* – M.S.). According to the conference protocol:

> The participants exchanged views on Fatah and the effects of the infiltrators' attempts to enter Israel from Arab countries. There was no accurate information forthcoming on this organization, its establishment, its base, and the source of its funding. Furthermore, its operations appeared amateurish, and caused little damage. [Although its sabotage] included nothing more than knocking down a wooden hut, [banging] a hole in a wall, or uprooting wooden railway ties, Israel has exploited these acts in order to exaggerate and inflate [the importance] of this organization, with radio stations and propaganda machinery supportive of Israel joining in the uproar. [Therefore] we should be suspicious of the substance of this organization and wary of information on it.[17]

The following announcement was made at the conclusion of the conference: "The participants discussed *inter alia* Fatah's regular activity in the occupied land. [They] agreed that it has been ineffective. These operations are [a source of] suspicion, and the Arab states should be wary of [them] and skeptical of information about them."[18]

The positions of the delegations' heads and the conclusions of the two meetings are interesting for a number of reasons:

1   The participants' pretension regarding information on Fatah, even though the conference was held behind closed-doors. The "pretension" in the March 1965 conference was obvious, but in the January 1966 conference it was not obvious coming after a whole year of Fatah activity, including publication of their announcements, contacts between its founders and the heads of Arab states, and even a Fatah communiqué to the Third Arab Summit (September 1965). The pretension of the Syrian delegation was especially blatant considering the Syrian authorities' close ties with Fatah leaders, and their assistance in training the organization. (See below: Syria.) This was also true for the heads of the Jordanian and Egyptian delegations. In the Syrians' talks with Western diplomats, including Americans and British, and in other inter-Arab conferences, they insisted they knew nothing about the organization.

2   On the other hand the Lebanese delegation detailed the steps its government was taking in order to counter Fatah infiltration; the Egyptian representative

exhibited indifference to the guerilla acts; and the Syrian representative completely ignored the matter.

3 The impression is that the delegations' position and the conclusion of the January 1966 discussions were designed to correspond with the official position of Egypt or the UAC to limit Fatah activity. This explains the attempt, even in a closed-door conference, to shed all responsibility for Fatah activity. Only Lebanon displayed special sensitivity to the issue, but this stemmed from the influence of its position on the country's fragile ethnic balance and in the Arab arena. In the spirit of the UAC's recommendations, in September 1965 the Lebanese government prohibited the publication of information on Fatah (including its communiqués) in the Lebanese press.[19]

In late December 1964 Egypt's intelligence agencies and "general investigation" bureaus became aware of Fatah's organizational activity in the Gaza Strip and its preparations to infiltrate Israel. They kept up surveillance of its activities. Preventative arrests of Fatah members foiled sabotage operations. Nevertheless, Fatah managed to carry out three operations across the Gaza Strip in February 1965. On February 8, 18, and 20, fida'iyyun infiltrators laid mines on the Israeli patrol road along the border. Egyptian security forces conducted another wave of arrests in Gaza in July 1965. They tightened surveillance, detained the leaders of the organizations, and seized ammunition dumps, thus ending sabotage operations from the Gaza Strip until the Six Day War. The detainees were released only after they signed an affidavit to cease their activity "unless it was approved by the special authorities." For example, a Fatah activist in Gaza, Musa Arafat al-Qudwa, signed an affidavit on January 26, 1966 "not to collect contributions for the family of the fida'i, Muhammad Bakir Hijazi, and the 'shahid' Jalal Ka'ush family unless the special authorities in Gaza approved of it." At the head of Fatah activity in the Gaza Strip stood a number of wealthy families. Fatah leaders and activists in the Gaza Strip included Musa Ali Arafat al-Qudwa, Awni al-Qishawi (Abu Mu'in), Muhammad al-Ifranj, Dr. Umar Sekik, Hasan Khalil Husayn, and Muhammad al-Khawaja. From Beirut and Damascus Fatah sent communiqués to dignitaries and government officials in the Gaza Strip, while Gaza's Fatah branch also circulated an internal bulletin among its members. The attempts by Fatah leaders to meet with Egyptian government officials, including Nasir, ended in failure in 1965.[20]

The Change in Egypt's Policy toward Fida'iyyun Activity

By mid-1966 Egypt's official position on Fatah's fida'iyyun activity tended to support the organization. At first Egypt had reservations in implementing this change in policy, but later it implemented it more vigorously. Nevertheless, it still was not pleased with the timing of Fatah's operations outside the framework of inter-Arab policy based on UAC resolutions. Despite this, the PLO remained "the supreme realization of the Palestinian entity."[21] The change in the Egyptian position stemmed from two main reasons:

1 Nasir's termination of the summit spirit in July 1966, after which the Palestinian

issue became the rallying point for Egypt, Syria, and the PLO in subverting the Jordanian regime.

2 The positive reaction that Fatah operations aroused in the Arab world in general, and the Palestinian arena in particular, vis-à-vis the PLO's "blunders" and "crises." Syria's categorical support for Fatah activity also contributed to this changed attitude. Thus, the Egyptian media and the Lebanese pro-Egyptian press expressed support and sympathy for Fatah's sabotage operations.[22]

Despite its policy volte-face, Egypt still opposed Fatah operations into Israel from the Gaza Strip, and continued tracking and overseeing Fatah supporters and activists who tried to renew their activity. Nevertheless, a let-up can be observed in the severity of Egypt's measures. Fatah leaders (Yasir Arafat and Faruq al-Qadumi) tried to contact Egyptian officials to gain their support because of Egypt's "paramount influence" in the Arab world. Finally, in mid-July 1966, Egypt agreed to meet with the heads of Fatah. The meeting took place in Cairo and was attended by the head of Egyptian General Intelligence, Salah Nasr, but it ended inconclusively. A second meeting was also held in July 1966. This time several leaders from the government party, "Socialist Union" showed up. The Egyptians explained to the Fatah leaders that " fida'iyyun acts should only be carried out within the framework and according to the Arabs' comprehensive planning for the liberation of Filastin." Kamal Rif'at, one of the leaders of the revolution and a senior figure in Egypt's intelligence community, who also served as the secretary to Arab affairs of the Socialist Union, stated on August 3, 1966:

> At a recent meeting between the al-'Asifa Command and Socialist Union, we made it clear that fida'iyyun operations had to be based on preplanning and continuity. [These operations] could not pose a threat to Israel's survival. We also tried to convince the al-'Asifa Command that fida'iyyun operations had to be connected and coordinated with the overall Arab plans for the liberation of Filastin . . . I must point out that al-'Asifa people are excellent revolutionaries and elite fida'iyyun fighters.[23]

By the end of 1966 Fatah tried to develop working relations with Egypt on a "defined and limited basis." According to Abu Iyyad's account, when Shams Badran, Egypt's minister of war, and Fatah leaders met, the latter proposed "setting up of fida'iyyun squads in the Negev [Israel's southern desert] to harass the Israeli army in peacetime or during a war. Fatah would supply the manpower, and Egypt the logistical assistance." But Badran "scoffed at" the proposition and demanded details on Fatah and its leaders. This meeting, too, ended without any results.[24]

The third stage in Egypt's position on Fatah began in February 1967 and continued until the Six Day War. The Egyptian attitude shifted from public support to a basic agreement on limited sabotage activity (by Fatah and the PLO-affiliated organization "Abtal al-'Awda") though not from Egypt's borders (the Gaza Strip and Sinai).

This policy change should be seen against background of a two-year experience that taught the Egyptians that Israel went no further than small-scale retaliatory raids and did not consider the size and nature of the sabotage acts as a casus belli. In the Egyptians' eyes, "all the signs indicate that fida'iyyun activity, in its present form, can go on for a long time if the Arabs are prepared to pay the price of limited Israeli retaliatory strikes . . . and as long as Egypt protects the Arab countries from Israeli occupation . . ."[25]

Egypt did not want to trail behind the Syrians in supporting Fatah and basking in the glory of fida'iyyun operations. There was also a tendency to retain the Palestinian card for use in subverting Husayn's regime. In practice, the Egyptians began aiding a fida'iyyun group affiliated with the Arab Nationalists Movement that identified with Nasir and his policy and cooperated with the PLO.

The Egyptian media and the Lebanese pro-Egyptian press noted that Egypt's new policy identified with the rights and struggle of the fida'iyyun,[26] reported Fatah communiqués,[27] and recognized the PLO's right to carry out acts of sabotage inside Israel.[28]

Despite these changes, the Egyptian authorities continued to detain Fatah members in the Gaza Strip and hamper guerilla infiltration from the Strip. In February 1967, Egypt estimated that "under the present conditions, Israel would view fida'iyyun activity emanating from the Gaza Strip as officially sanctioned activity, and on the basis of this assessment would determine the manner of its response . . . Thus, fida'iyyun activity was liable to exacerbate the problem and create a climate of tension and high-alert . . . [However] this is not a case of provocations aimed at creating a pretext for initiating a full-scale conflict. Every act that could precipitate a full-blown confrontation before [we are prepared for it] must be seen as [involuntary] entanglement . . ."[29] In the first quarter of 1967 the Egyptians were extremely apprehensive about preserving quiet on the border and did everything possible to avoid giving Israel a pretext for escalating border tension. This included reducing the Egyptian army's field exercises along the border.

In May 1966, "Gaza intelligence" received information on the return of al-'Asifa (Fatah's military arm) to activity in the Gaza Strip. The General Investigations Department in the Gaza Strip failed to turn up any evidence for this, though it seized Fatah leaflets and communiqués that had been distributed or mailed to various people in Gaza. Surveillance of known Fatah activists was tightened. In November 1966, Fatah tried to renew its activity in the Gaza Strip (after a hiatus in its operations following the roundup of activists in 1965). It circulated leaflets, and acquired landmines and explosives for use in Israel. Awni al-Qishawi, a Fatah officer in the Gaza Strip, also resumed operations following his release from jail in 1965. The Egyptian security authorities caught wind of this activity and again arrested Fatah activists in December 1966. Thus, in accordance with their policy, the Egyptians curbed sabotage activity into Israel emanating from the Gaza Strip.[30]

The PLO naturally adopted Egypt's policy *volte-face* on the fida'iyyun. This freed the PLO from the dilemma of representing the Palestinians, on the one hand, and denouncing sabotage operations because of Egypt's previous policy, on the other hand. The PLO extended its support of the fida'iyyun on two levels: in public declarations, and by supplying them with material aid and actively participating in their operations.

In May 1966 the PLO's propaganda organs, and Shuqayri himself, announced their backing of the fida'iyyun and lauded their activity inside Israel. The PLO now gained the status of a "revolutionary" or "fida'iyyun" organization.[31]

In the next stage, the PLO assisted the fida'iyyun in practical ways. On August 1, 1966 it seems that Shuqayri received approval from the PLO's Executive Committee to set up fida'iyyun squads among Palestinians living in Lebanon. The PLO (Shuqayri), through the commander of the PLA, that was subordinate to the PLO,

Wajih al-Madani, cooperated with Shafiq al-Hut, the PLO representative in Beirut, in organizing a group of fida'iyyun called Abtal al-'Awda. Al-Hut, the founder of the Palestinian Liberation Front and one of the ANM leaders in Lebanon, joined this organization. Thus, Abtal al-'Awda was in fact a "front" that was used as a cover in an agreement between the PLA commander Madani and the ANM. Al-Hut was part of this set-up and was responsible for the enlistment, training, and activation of approximately fifty guerillas. He was in close contact with Egyptian intelligence officers in all aspects of his men's training, weapons supplies, and operations. The PLO intentionally avoided taking sole responsibility for acts of sabotage.[32] Fatah praised the PLO for the positive change in its attitude toward the fida'iyyun, its active partic-ipation in fida'iyyun operations, and its involvement in founding Abtal al-'Awda.[33]

In conclusion, because of Abtal al-'Awda's limited operations, it remained on the sidelines of Palestinian activity in comparison with Fatah. It gained the protection of the Arab Nationalists Movement rather than that of the PLO. Together, the Palestinian Section of the Arab nationalists (*Shabab al-Thar*) and Ahmad Jibril's organization (The Palestinian Liberation Front) and Abtal al-'Awda established the "Popular Front for the Liberation of Filastin" in December 1967 under the leadership of George Habash.

Syria's Position

The Period prior to the February 1966 Revolution

Before discussing the Ba'th (Syria's ruling political party) and its position on Fatah and fida'iyyun activity, a number of passages will be presented from the report that the Ba'th's "Filastin Branch in Lebanon" submitted to the 8th National Ba'th Congress in April 1965. The report served as a basis for recommendations to the congress. The heads of the Ba'th's Lebanese branch were on good terms with Fatah leaders in Lebanon, and probably in Kuwait too, from whom they obtained details on the organization. The report stated *inter alia*:

1   "[We learned] from our party's connections in Kuwait that Fatah was the more serious of the liberation movements . . . Our colleagues [from the Ba'th branch in Kuwait] learned that Fatah branches in Jordan had acquired weapons and were ready to carry out operations in the occupied land."

2   "Fatah seemed to be on the verge of completing preparations [for Sabotage incursions into Israel] when the PLO was established, which caused [Fatah] embarrassment and annoyance. The Lebanese press, excluding *al-Ahrar* [a pro-Ba'th paper], refrained from publishing Fatah's military communiqués, later the rest of the papers followed suit. At first it was impossible to publish Fatah's bulletins in the Syrian, Jordanian, or Egyptian press since this would have implied official recognition [of the organization] and endangered [these countries] for their responsibility in operations against Israel. This would have also hurt al-'Asifa by revealing its connections [to these countries]."

3   "The fida'iyyun's expanded activity calls for large-scale recruitment (and) a great deal of material aid that they hope to receive from Syria. But, in addition

to the time [needed] for expanding the leadership cadre and [developing] leadership skills at the organization's local level, [Fatah] also has to [develop] political skills together with fida'iyyun military training."

4   "Fatah has demonstrated its willingness to cooperate with us; it held contacts at the leadership level because of the above mentioned possibilities [of obtaining aid from] our party."[34]

Unlike the Egyptian intelligence's unfavorable assessment of Fatah, the report of the activists in the "Filastin section" of Lebanon's Ba'th party revealed a sympathetic approach that they tried to instill in the party's leadership. Although they overstated Fatah's operational capabilities and the impact of its sabotage activity on Israel, they tried to convince the Ba'th leadership that Fatah was an organization worthy of Syrian material, propaganda, and military assistance.

The report recommended that "the congress, in conjunction with military experts, discuss the possibility of waging a war of liberation, [in other words, a guerilla war,] in the mountainous and rocky regions of Filastin just as Fatah [is doing]; and discuss the possibilities of fida'iyyun training [for] Palestinians who were party members; [it also recommended] preparing Palestinian and Arab public opinion for moral and material participation in this undertaking."[35]

"After [the 8th National Ba'th Congress] reviewed the report and discussed the condition of the Palestinian people and the present stage of the Filastin problem," it proposed the following recommendations to the new national leadership:

1   "The [Ba'th] party must support every action in the armed struggle carried out by Palestinian groups."
2   "[The party must] furnish the Palestinian people with arms, train them adequately for the conditions of the struggle, and prepare them for the war of liberation."
3   "A secret committee must be established for discussing the Palestinian Liberation Movement – Fatah and the party's position on it."[36]

The Syrian position on Fatah was characterized by "dualism" – the gap between declared party policy, on the one hand, and its practical accomplishments, on the other hand. Some senior officers held a view opposite to that of the official one. Syria was the only Arab state that overtly sponsored Fatah activity. The Syrian media served as a mouthpiece for Fatah's announcements. On January 21, 1965 *Radio Damascus* was the first station to broadcast a lengthy bulletin by al-'Asifa, Fatah's armed branch. The Fatah organ, *al-'Asifa*, was distributed in Syria and from there to other Arab states and the Gaza Strip.[37]

Also, *Radio Damascus'* "the Filastin Corner" gave almost continuous encouragement to fida'iyyun activity while portraying it as the Palestinians' only practical venue. Lebanon's *al-Ahrar* and the Damascus press and radio were the only media publicizing Fatah's military communiqués in 1965.[38]

Despite this, the Syrian regime, or party, lacked a clearly-defined Fatah policy in 1965. As a centralized regime, the Ba'th looked upon Fatah with suspicion and distrust. It feared an independent militant element in Syria that might become an instrument in the hands of a rival group and undermine the regime one day. The Syrians tried "to take the organization under its wing and bring it under its control" by developing relations with the "moderates" in the Fatah leadership and infiltrating supporters of Syria into key positions. Fatah wanted to be an ally of the Ba'th regime in order to obtain material goods as well as military and political assistance. This explains why Fatah made contact with the Ba'th leaders in Syria, Lebanon, and Kuwait. At the same time, the organization was sensitive to its autonomy, and rejected Syria's conditions for cooperation that would have transformed Fatah into a Ba'th protectorate. The first time that a Fatah squad crossed the Syrian border, without government permission, on an operation into Israel (August 1965), Syrian intelligence arrested several Fatah leaders who were in Syria for official negotiations, although it soon released them. Later that year the Syrians again hauled in a number of Fatah leaders, including Yasir Arafat, on suspicion of sabotaging the Tapline (Trans-Arabian oil line) but freed them when the charges could not be proven. [39]

The Second Stage: February 1966 – June 1967

The revolution that brought a group of young left-wing officers into government in February 1966 was also accompanied by a change in Syria's strategy in the Arab arena and the Arab–Israeli conflict in general, and toward the Palestinian problem in particular. The new strategy was based on the concept of a "comprehensive popular war of liberation" as the only path for the liberation of Filastin and the only justification for the regime's existence. Algeria and Vietnam were presented as examples of this doctrine, and thus worthy of emulation. The main points of this strategy were:

1 "The Palestinian problem is the key issue in the party's struggle in the domestic, Arab, and international domains, and [as such] demands the mobilization of all means and resources for the liberation of Filastin.
2 "The popular war of liberation is the sole guarantee for victory in Filastin.
3 "The Arab Palestinian public must become the vanguard in the popular war of liberation . . . The progressive Arab forces must organize the [Palestinian] public and prepare it for participating in the campaign."[40]

When the Ba'th leadership approved this doctrine in March 1966, it also accepted fida'iyyun activity as an integral part of it. The Arab world had been polarized after the demise of the summit atmosphere (and rise of progressive and conservative camps). Syria cooperated closely with Egypt, the PLO, and Fatah in trying to undermine Jordan's regime under the slogan: "Today We Liberate Jordan – Tomorrow Filastin; The Liberation of Jordan Means the Liberation of Filastin." Classified Syrian documents from this period refer to the West Bank as "the Palestinian part of Jordan."[41] The Ba'th leaders and its propaganda organs openly defended fida'iyyun operations, though they denied responsibility for them. Indeed, Israel's policy of placing the burden of responsibility for sabotage acts on Syria, forced Damascus to clear itself of the charge by claiming, as Hafiz al-Asad, the minister of defense and air commander, did in May 1966, that "we have no desire to enter an argument over al-'Asifa since we know nothing about it."[42] On the other hand, when the Israeli foreign ministry stated in August 1966 that Israel would view Syria as responsible for Fatah activity even if launched from other countries, the Syrian foreign ministry spokesman avowed that "all of Syria's moves stem from the [goal] of revolution, and not from the fact that [Syria] is a state . . ."[43] Syria also asserted that "it did not watch over Israel's security, and that it would never impede the revolution of the persecuted Palestinian people."[44]

For all practical purposes, Syria became the principal supporter or coordinator of fida'iyyun operations emanating from the Syrian, Lebanese, and Jordanian borders.[45] The overthrow of the government in March 1966 led to changes in Syria's intelligence branch. Until now it had been responsible for liaison with Fatah and supervision of its activity within Syria and its infiltration into Israel from the Syrian border. The head of the Syrian intelligence's "foreign branch," Major Lewis Awad, who had been in charge of Fatah activity, was arrested. The ascendancy of new officers to government paved the way for smoother cooperation between the army and Fatah. On the one hand, Fatah's guerilla operations became the highest realization of the "popular war of liberation" and the "new strategy;" while on the other hand, for security reasons similar to those of the previous Ba'th regime, the new government could not allow an armed organization like Fatah to operate freely and uncontrolled inside Syria. The regime also feared that Fatah's incursions into Israel from Syria might heat up the border – a development that ran counter to Syrian policy. Nevertheless, the Syrian army provided Fatah with training facilities and military equipment. Syrian officers instructed Fatah recruits in Syrian army camps. At the same time, the regime tightened its surveillance of Fatah's activity and tried to gain a domineering influence over the organization and its *modus operandi*. The Syrian army ran operational fida'iyyun units of its own (mainly for reconnaissance and intelligence objectives) – one such unit was the 68th commando battalion.

Fatah's need for a "secure staging base" forced it to cooperate with Syria's intelligence agencies, but at the same time it sought to retain maximum independence. It came to an agreement with the "Filastin section" of the Syrian Ba'th party (established in 1966) that the Filastin Ba'th section would assume responsibility for reconnaissance and intelligence operations inside Israeli territory, as well as the transfer of weapons, explosives, and money to the Palestinian Ba'th in Jordan.[46] This probably explains why Fatah ceased its infiltration into Israel from the Syrian border. Although a wave of operations was carried out from Syria in July 1966 by groups linked to Syrian intelligence, the Syrians temporarily halted the infiltration because of Egyptian pressure following the signing of the Egyptian–Syrian military agreement on November 4, 1966. The Syrians saw armed incursion as the only form of response to the April 7, 1967 incident in which six Syrian planes were shot down. Sabotage operations carried out by combined Fatah squads and Syrian commando teams increased over a wide area along Israel's northern border. After a lengthy suspension, sabotage activity also resumed from the Golan Heights. The targets chosen lay relatively deep inside Israel, and the planners' aim was to hit major population centers. There was a marked improvement in operational effectiveness and the devices employed, which included mortars.

Despite the apparent harmony and cooperation between Fatah and the Ba'th regime, each side was apprehensive of the other and unsure of the other's ulterior motives:

The Syrian perspective. Syria's dilemma lay in its conflict of interests. On the one hand, the regime had to safeguard its own national security by taking control of Fatah's activity in Syria and cross-border incursions, and by trying to influence the organization's leadership to adhere to Syrian policy; on the other hand, Damascus was devoted to its Ba'th ideology that advocated a popular war of liberation and that viewed fida'iyyun (and Fatah) activity as the cornerstone of its struggle.

Fatah's perspective. Fatah's leaders realized the importance of Syria and its geographic location as a base for fida'iyyun operations and as a purveyor of military assistance, especially military instruction. This was crucial at a time when Fatah activity was curtailed in Jordan, Lebanon, and the Gaza Strip. Nevertheless, Fatah endeavored to preserve its organizational and decision-making "autonomy," though it was aware that it had to coordinate its moves with Syrian authorities.

Fatah's dilemmas prevailed until after the Six Day War. On December 31, 1969 an internal Fatah resumé dealing with Syria's policy toward the organization stated that, "Syria has been the staging area, secure zone, and [source of] oxygen for our [lungs]."[47]

In conclusion: if the fida'iyyun organizations had not emerged, Syria probably would have created them (just as it established "al-Sa'iqa" after the war). Syria was unquestionably the main backer of Fatah and other fida'iyyun organizations that had sprung up before the war. Syrian support was an integral part of Ba'th strategy in the Arab–Israeli conflict. But Syria's military aid and encouragement brought on Israeli retaliation, heightened border tension, and hastened the processes that eventually led to a full-blown armed clash.

Jordan's Dilemma: Between an Israeli Invasion of the West Bank and the Campaign against Fatah

Between 1949 and 1967 two issues dominated Israel's relations with its Arab neighbor to the east, Jordan: security along the border and the fate of the West Bank in case of a radical change in the Jordanian government. Throughout these years a complex relationship developed between the two states based on their common interest in safeguarding the integrity of the Royal Hashemite Kingdom of Jordan. Israel regarded Jordan as an ally handling daily security issues and as a potential partner in a lasting peace agreement. Israel further believed that Jordan's independence and territorial integrity under King Husayn were strategic assets, and it let it be known that any change in the Hashemite regime by military take-over, foreign subversion (Egyptian–Syrian), or the introduction of Iraqi army units, would be seen as a major security threat and, therefore, justification for Israeli occupation of all or parts of the West Bank. At the same time, Israel held the Jordanian government responsible for maintaining a peaceful border and preventing any form of infiltration or sabotage. Although the Israelis were keenly aware of Husayn's serious efforts at stanching guerilla attacks, Jerusalem persisted in punitive–retaliatory acts that sometimes had a jarring effect on the Jordanian regime.

Husayn inherited from his grandfather, King Abdullah, a special relationship with Israel characterized by dialogue for dealing with routine security matters, the exchange of intelligence data, either directly or through third parties, and the mutual pursuit of a political solution. In contrast to other Arab leaders, Husayn harbored no offensive designs against Israel and, like his grandfather, preferred to settle the Palestinian problem and the Arab–Israeli conflict by peaceful means through the recognition of Israel's right to exist. At the same time, he informed Israeli leaders that he would adamantly adhere to the Arab consensus on the means of resolving the conflict. Despite this, he had no qualms at viewing Israel as a "supporter" of his regime during periods of crisis when the Hashemite government was threatened by internal or foreign subversion.

Concern Over an Israeli Invasion: the April 1963 Crisis

Remaining high on Israel's agenda up until the Six Day War was the possibility of a military operation for seizing all or part of the West Bank (such as Mt. Scopus in Jerusalem), in the event of a political upheaval in Jordan or the presence of Iraqi troops on Jordanian soil. Israel harbored a deep concern over the prospect of a change in Jordan's status quo, and gave ample warning of its implications. In a Knesset speech on October 15, 1956, Ben-Gurion clearly stated Israel's position regarding the eastern border:

> We have long known that the Egyptian dictator [Nasir] has ambitions to dominate Arab countries . . . The first victim in his ambitious scheme is Jordan . . . It seems that plans are underway to unite Jordan with Iraq . . . The military deployment inside Jordan, even if only on the East Bank, by an Arab country that is not a signatory to an armistice agreement with Israel would undermine the region's *status quo* and violate article one of the armistice agreement . . . The Israeli government honors the *status quo* based on this agreement with the Hashemite Kingdom . . . [and] will feel free to take action if the *status quo* is violated and a foreign military force is deployed inside Jordan.[48]

Twice in the past this issue had been intensely debated: the first, during the crisis in the wake of the revolution in Iraq (July 1958); and the second time, in April 1963 following the declaration of the Tripartite Federation between Syria, Egypt and Iraq. Following the coup in Iraq, Israel foresaw a change in the Jordanian regime and sought diplomatic contact with Great Britain and the United States to learn their position on an Israeli initiated military action against the West Bank. In discussions Ben-Gurion held, the possibility of seizing Mt. Scopus or all of the West Bank was raised, but he expressed misgivings that "an additional one million Arabs would be the end of the country."[49]

Jordan did not hide its fear over Israel's threats to occupy the West Bank. Husayn seized Israel's bellicose warnings for justifying his objection to the introduction of foreign troops onto Jordanian soil in a no-war situation, even though this position ran counter to UAC policy. Between 1965 and 1967, the king took advantage of the Israeli threat to legitimize the steps he took against the Fatah organization and its use of Jordan as a base for sabotage against Israel. Husayn also used Israel's intimidation in order to clamp down on hostile elements, especially those emanating from Egypt and Syria, engaged in plotting against his government. In this way a common Israeli–Jordanian interest developed. Husayn accurately defined his dilemma:

> Always in our mind, and in my mind in particular, was the fact that the West Bank was the most important target as far as Israel was concerned. We were in the hills and close to the sea in some places. If the Israelis were to implement their plan, attack at their convenience, and extend beyond the area of Filastin, their first objective would obvi-

ously be Filastin itself. Therefore the most important area, apart from Jerusalem, was the West Bank.[50]

During the April 1963 crisis, Jordan grew acutely aware of the likelihood of Israeli capture of the West Bank in the event of a pro-Egyptian putsch or the rise of an Egyptian puppet-state in Jordan. All of the parties involved in the crisis endeavored to convince Egypt to cease its propaganda broadcasts and subversive activity for no one had any doubts that Egyptian intrigue was behind the events.

The crisis arose on March 17 following an announcement of the tripartite federation uniting Egypt, Syria and Iraq. This declaration caused great agitation among the Jordanian Palestinians concentrated in the West Bank who were pro – Nasir to the core. In nationalist and opposition circles hope grew for the long-awaited revolution or, at the very least, the establishment of a nationalist government, especially following the Ba'th revolutions (Iraq, February 1963; Syria, March 1963). Jordan, however, admonished the new Syrian government that if the Hashemite regime collapsed, Israel would move to seize the West Bank. Throughout the 1963 crisis the fate of the Hashemite Kingdom hung in the balance.

The crisis began on April 20 and lasted until April 26 when normalcy slowly returned to the kingdom. For an entire week angry demonstrations flared up throughout the West Bank, the likes of which had not been seen since December 1955. The protestors chanted pro-Nasir slogans and demanded Jordan's participation in the new Arab federation. Pictures of Nasir and UAR flags were put on massive display. The demonstrations peaked on April 20–21 when the number of protestors in some cities approached 4,000. After the Jordanian parliament gave a no-confidence vote to the government (April 20), the army was sent into action to suppress the demonstrators and return law and order. A curfew went into effect in the West Bank cities, and the army exchanged shots with demonstrators in Jerusalem, Nablus, Jenin, and Tulkarm. During the clashes, thirteen protestors were killed and ninety-seven wounded. Most of the wounded were between the ages of seventeen and twenty. The curfew was gradually lifted on April 26; schools re-opened on May 9, and the soldiers returned to their bases on May 11.[51]

King Husayn exploited the fear of Israeli military intervention in order to block the Egyptians and domestic elements from attempting to shake up his government. In a press conference on April 23, at the height of the crisis, Husayn reiterated: "I have often referred to the danger that Israel might seek to benefit from the [present situation] and pursue a policy that would result not only in a loss to Jordan but to the entire Arab nation . . ."[52]

At the height of the crisis, Jordan endeavored to convince the Egyptians, with the assistance of American diplomacy, that it would be against Egypt's interests to have the Jordanian government replaced with a pro-Egyptian proxy because it would lead to Israel's seizure of the West Bank, the United States would condone the Zionists' motives, and American aid to Egypt would suffer in the end. The UAR would also be hurt. Husayn was letting Nasir know that any ill to Jordan would rebound on Egypt. The Egyptian response was meant to pacify the Jordanians by informing them that Egypt had no subversive intentions and would not allow itself to get involved in a militarily adventure while its forces were still bogged down in Yemen. During the crisis Husayn asked the British and Americans to warn Egypt publicly against fomenting trouble, but the Americans rejected this because they feared a breakdown in relations with Nasir. The United States ambassador to Amman also advised against this step because of the bitter reaction it would awaken in Jordanian public opinion, especially on the West Bank.[53]

Although the actual ground conditions did not indicate a threat to the regime's stability, there was often exaggerated concern in the American and British foreign offices over the danger of Egyptian and Syrian subversion. This was apparent during the climax of the crisis when the United States and Great Britain frantically combined their intelligence estimates and coordinated their moves in the eventuality of the ouster of the Hashemite regime and an Israeli invasion of the West Bank. The British Embassy in Tel Aviv reported on April 11 that: "The Israelis have told us *ad nauseum* that they would have to move into Jordanian territory on the West Bank if a collapse of Jordan seemed to threaten Israel's security – as it well seemed to do."[54]

Both Britain and the United States strove to persuade Egypt, in the first phase, to silence its propaganda campaign against Jordan, especially the venomous broadcasts over *Sawt al-Arab*. The US ambassador to Cairo submitted an official protest to the Egyptian authorities, arguing that this agitation was threatening the stability of the Jordanian regime.[55]

In talks between the US ambassador and Nasir's minister of information, Sami Sharaf, on April 27, 1963, the ambassador notified the minister that "if there were an armed coup in Jordan, the present profitable relations between the US and the UAR would be irreparably ruptured. He referred to the possibility that Israel might possess herself of most of the West Bank, from which it would be difficult to dislodge them. He drew attention to the tone of Cairo broadcasts." Washington also instructed the ambassador "to confirm his presentation [via Sharaf] to President Nasir. He should emphasize that Nasir could not count on the US being able to restrain Israel. The US had much to lose from armed conflict in Jordan, but they thought the UAR had even more to lose." The ambassador sent a personal letter to Nasir "making all these points on April 28."[56]

Egyptian forces were put on alert as the situation grew explosive, but with three infantry divisions tied down in Yemen, an Egyptian confrontation with Israel was an unlikely option. Furthermore, Nasir was aware of the weakness and dissension inside the Jordanian opposition and the army's loyalty to the king; he also understood that the disturbances had been spontaneous outbursts rather than the product of Egyptian intrigue. Under these circumstances, it seemed to him that the chances of pulling down the Hashemite regime seemed remote, and that the king would overcome the crisis. Thus, when Nasir relayed to the Americans in late April that he was not involved in actually trying to dispose of Husayn, he was saying the truth.[57]

Nasir disavowed Egyptian military action for hastening the downfall of the Jordanian regime if it meant that the Israelis would see it as justification for occupying the West Bank. Egypt endeavored to show that political developments in Jordan were an internal matter that did not warrant an Israeli incursion. Nevertheless, because of its obligations to pan-Arabism (*qawmiya*), Egypt could not allow itself to refrain from intervening in case of an Israeli invasion.[58]

Throughout the crisis, a constant flow of information had crisscrossed between Washington, London and Jerusalem. It was crucial for the United States and Britain to have as accurate a picture as possible of Israel's expected moves. The Americans and British were intent on preventing an Israeli military thrust that, in their estimate, would leave them in an awkward situation, enflame the whole region in an all-out war, and pave the way for Soviet intervention. But the two powers knew perfectly well that they could not obstruct an Israeli grab for the West Bank if the Hashemite government collapsed.[59]

In conclusion, Arab fears of an Israeli incursion, and the April 1963 crisis brought a number of points into sharp focus for Jordan, Egypt, and Syria that would reach acute expression three years later in the November 1966 crisis. These included: the likelihood that Israel would intervene militarily in the case of a change in Jordan's *status quo*; the Hashemite regime's ability to overcome domestic crises as long as the army remained loyal; the limited ability of the West to intervene; and the deep mistrust between the Jordanian regime and the Palestinian population in Jordan.

The Campaign Against Fatah[60]

Fatah's sabotage from Jordan (beginning in January 1965) and Israel's responses exacerbated the border situation. This development together with Jordanian – PLO friction led the regime to adopt a tough approach toward Israel on the armistice commission and in Jordan's propaganda organs. Jordanian leaders perceived Fatah as a dangerous factor not only because of its involvement in border incidents that triggered Israeli retaliations, but also because of its potential threat to the regime's stability (as proved true after the Six Day War). Like other Arab countries, at first Jordan had only a vague concept of the body that stood behind the organization; the Jordanians thought the mufti, Haj Amin al-Husayni, might be the culprit since his goal was to force the Arab states to go to war with Israel.

In February 1965, King Husayn warned the Arab states of the danger of permitting or encouraging fida'iyyun groups to operate against Israel. When the first fida'i was killed by Jordanian soldiers as he was returning from an operation in Israel on January 4, 1965, the fida'iyyun organizations saw the incident as a symbol of the violent struggle between the Palestinian entity and the Hashemite regime. Tension increased when Jordanian security forces arrested a colleague of Mahmud Hijazi, a Fatah member, who had been captured by Israel during an operation on January 7, 1965.

Jordanian authorities treated Fatah with kid-gloves throughout 1965, making no special effort to suppress it, lest a second front develop in addition to the PLO front. Fatah operations in 1965 were limited to cross-border raids and the recruitment of fida'iyyun – activity that was less menacing to Jordan's internal security than that of the PLO. In 1965, the Jordanian authorities launched a campaign aimed at tracking and supervising Fatah and fida'iyyun activity in the West Bank, mainly in the villages bordering Israel that had become staging bases for fida'iyyun operations.

Some of the Fatah activists who carried out missions in Israel in the first months of 1965 were recruited from refugee camps in the Nablus region and were veterans of sabotage squads that had been run by Syrian intelligence agents in the 1950s. The Jordanians tightened surveillance and investigation of Fatah squads especially in the Qalqilya, Tulkarm, and Nablus regions. Military and police units in the Nablus area were ordered to stiffen their patrols and checkpoints. In this way, the Jordanians

110

managed to capture the fida'iyyun who attacked the Israeli village of Kfar Hess (February 28, 1965) on their return to Jordan (the Tulkarm region in the West Bank), and keep them in detention in Tulkarm for two months. Later, the governor of the Nablus district deferred their trial indefinitely.

The Jordanian regime justified its moves against Fatah (earning inter-Arab – especially Egyptian – approval for them) by claiming that the Arab countries and PLO distanced themselves from an organization whose activity only intensified border tension. Amman also pointed out that Fatah operations were contrary to UAC policy and the UAC's explicit orders that it had repeatedly issued in January and February 1965. The Jordanian Army general staff took full advantage of these orders, circulating them among officers in 1965 and 1966 and emphasizing that "Fatah and al-'Asifa posed a threat to the Jordanian border."[61]

In the wake of continuous Fatah operations across the Jordanian border, their widespread reportage, their support by the second Palestinian National Congress – May 1965, Israel's complaints to the Israeli–Jordanian armistice commission, and Jordan's fear of Israeli retaliation, the Jordanian chief of staff, Amer Khamash, sent a memo to the commanders of the "western" and "eastern" fronts on May 24, 1965 relating to "the Fatah organization." (The memo eventually filtered down to battalion commanders.) It detailed Fatah operations and hinted that Israel might be behind the organization's activity. The main points of the memo:

1 A number of guerilla operations have taken place recently in the occupied area. The other side [Israel] has complained to the mixed armistice commission that an organization by the name of Fatah is responsible for these acts.
2 This organization is probably trained and activated by authorities in the occupied area [Israel] to create an atmosphere of tension along the armistice line and get the attention of the superpowers in order to gain support in international circles for military aid to maintain the region's power balance. Destructive elements that care nothing for the public's interest may be running this organization.
3 The UAC condemns operations such as these that do not fit in with its approved plans. [The UAC] demands that these irresponsible elements be forbidden from arrying out operations at this inappropriate time. Therefore, you must order your units to curb the infiltrators' movement and forbid them entry into the occupied area [Israel] for sabotage purposes that heighten border tension and undermine the general interest.

Two points stand out in the chief of staff's memo: *first* – its "supposed unawareness" of Fatah's true nature despite Jordanian intelligence's information on the organization, its leadership, and objectives. This approach parallels the position of the Arab states, including Jordan, in the closed Arab conferences held in March 1965 and January 1966 by the heads of the Arab delegations to the armistice commissions, when they resolved that Arab states would assume no responsibility for Fatah activity in and from their territory. *Second* is the broad insinuation that Israel was deeply involved in Fatah activity in order to justify Jordan's moves against Fatah.

The contents and accusations in the chief-of-staff's memo reflect the regime's dilemma in dealing with Fatah:

1 On the one hand, Fatah operations were bound to increase border tension and lead to Israeli retaliations. This concern appears in many instructions from brigade and battalion commanders on the West Bank related to the prevention of Fatah operations and the arrest of infiltrators. For example, on June 18, 1966. a communiqué from the commander of the "Western Front" (West Bank), Liwa (Maj. Gen.) Mahmud Ahmad Salim, to his brigade commanders stated:

A Information from a reliable source has warned that a group of guerillas (*mukharibin*) has entered Jordan in order to carry out acts of sabotage in the occupied area on [the nights of June 18/19 and 19/20, 1966]. The group is located in Irbid and northern Shuna [along the Jordan River in the West Bank]. The source has observed unusual military movement in the Beit Shean – Afula and Ramlah regions that indicate a general or partial [Israeli military] mobilization in these regions.

B The enemy [will probably] exact revenge on Jordanian territory by dynamiting the Eastern Ghor Canal and Khalid Ben al-Walid Dam [Mukheiba]. [The enemy] is keenly interested in this dam because it is the [first] of the Arab summit decisions to have been carried out for diverting [the Jordan's] tributaries.

C The Qadisiya Brigade has been ordered to increase surveillance of the Ghor Canal and halt all movement to and from the canal. It will also report on all enemy movement and prevent anyone suspected of affiliation with a Fatah organization from approaching the armistice line or attempting to infiltrate into occupied territory.

2 On the other hand, at this stage, Jordan could not openly criticize operations supported by the Palestinians in this country, otherwise it would appear to be obstructing the struggle against Israel. The Jordanians raised two claims in justification of their arrest of Fatah activists and suspension of their activity: *one*, they cast doubt on the organization's intentions, presenting it as serving Israel's interests, and intimating that Israel was manipulating it; and *two*, they took advantage of the UAC's orders in January and February 1965 to the Jordanian, Syrian, and Lebanese chiefs of staff to curb Fatah activity in order to prove that this was an issue of inter-Arab (especially Egyptian) policy that had been approved at the Arab summit.

3 Jordan's relations with Shuqayri, the head of the PLO, also began to deteriorate in 1965, and reached their low-point in 1966. Jordan sought to avoid opening a second front in the struggle with the Palestinians. During these two years, Fatah's status among the Palestinians had strengthened, and the Hashemite regime feared that an all-out struggle against the organization would spark internal problems since two-thirds of Jordan's population was Palestinian. Therefore, the regime proceeded with great caution in dealing with Fatah.[62]

Jordan's response to the IDF raid on the night of May 27/28, 1965 testifies to the seriousness with which the regime viewed sabotage attacks emanating from Jordan. At a general staff meeting the king ordered the army to root out Fatah training areas and arrest Fatah members. The staff officers' mentioned that the fida'iyyun were probably entering Jordan from Syria. The king called for restraint before opening fire on the border so as not to provoke an escalatory incident. In this spirit and probably on orders from the chief of staff and commander of the "western front," the brigade commanders issued a communiqué to their battalion commanders on June 8 stating, *inter alia*, that "al-'Asifa forces under Fatah control are imperiling the Jordanian border because of their operations in the occupied area; [these acts] run counter to Arab and UAC policy and are having a [deleterious] impact on our current military situation. Therefore, [you] will order [your] frontline units to remain alert, keep the border under close surveillance, and halt these organizations."

In 1965 the regime took limited steps – such as preventive arrests and warnings – against Fatah. Some detainees were released after they agreed to work for the authorities at a higher price than what Fatah was paying them. The regime cast a veil of silence over its measures, and refrained from holding trials in order to avert public dissension. Furthermore, the regime encountered a lack of cooperation at certain operational levels and among security forces in the field when it came to suppressing Fatah activity.

The first time the king made a public reference to Fatah activity was on October 4, 1965 in a speech critical of the organization: "We do not believe in the impassioned, hastily executed activity of [certain] organized bodies nor do we recognize its usefulness [since it] deviates from the UAC framework and joint Arab plans . . . at a time when we are building up our forces and increasing our strength, [fida'iyyun activity] interferes with Arab planning, weakens Arab unity, provides the enemy with an opportunity to commit aggression and take the initiative out of Arab hands, and leads to a confrontation before our preparations are completed . . . This is the first time these organizations have tried to take such preposterous action, and it is a cause for concern . . ."[63]

Two interrelated processes began in 1966: Fatah intensified its activity in Jordan and infiltration into Israel from Jordan; and the Hashemite regime stepped up its operations against Fatah, especially in border areas. The United States was concerned about Israeli–Jordanian tension and pressured Amman to clamp down on infiltration. The UN and the United States conveyed Israel's messages and warnings to Husayn to make a stronger effort at controlling sabotage activity.[64] Against this background, the king launched a sweeping campaign against Fatah members who had been under surveillance, and other Palestinians suspected of affiliation with the organization. Large quantities of weapons and explosives were uncovered. The army was issued strict orders, some by Husayn himself, to stop the fida'iyyun from crossing Jordan's borders. The UAC's orders were frequently reissued to Jordanian officers in order to emphasize that this was a matter of inter-Arab policy. The regime also publicized the UAC's orders in order to preclude criticism of its anti-Fatah campaign.

As in the previous year, orders to reinforce border surveillance and to hamper penetration into Israel filtered down the ranks from brigade commanders to battalion commanders to company commanders, but when the orders reached the local commanders, the latter were often lax in obeying them. This was especially true of National Guard troops on night watch. The Hitin Brigade commander met with his battalion commanders on December 28, 1966 and reviewed the lessons of the Samu' raid, the conditions on the armistice line, and the fida'iyyun acts and their ramifications. The brigade commander ordered them "to take control of the armistice lines and prevent anyone from crossing them whether to or from the occupied territory because every act of sabotage operation is injurious for us right now."

In a speech on May 25, 1966 the king repeated his earlier position on Fatah activity, basing it on UAC orders: "The return of the stolen homeland cannot be [accomplished by] irresponsible behavior, since there is no quick or sentimental way for restoring [this] stolen right . . . The UAC must be allowed to carry out its assignment within the collective framework. Every operation outside this framework is a spontaneous deed that detracts from [our] strength and gives the enemy an opportunity to commit aggression and entangle us in a confrontation before we are prepared [for it]."[65]

Israel's Samu' raid on November 13, 1966, and other Arab attacks against Jordan because of its steps against Fatah and PLO activists, and the attempts by the PLO, Syria, and Fatah to undermine the regime, forced Husayn, Wasfi al-Tal, and the Jordanian media to relate decisively, directly, and much more determinedly toward Fatah activity than in the past. The following examples illustrate this point:

1   On November 20, 1966, *Radio Amman* commented on a Jordanian Arab's answer to the question of whether "Jordan's position on the fida'iyyun issue differs from that of Egypt, the UAC, or the Arab summit's decisions" as follows: "The UAC and the Arab states backing it have repeatedly warned of reckless activity [by the fida'iyyun] that provided the enemy with an opportunity to choose the time and place for his response. In the event of an all-out war of liberation, Jordan will not oppose fida'iyyun activity . . . Why do Cairo, Damascus, and Beirut inhibit fida'iyyun activity [and at the same time] reproach Jordan?"

2   At a press conference on November 21, Wasfi al-Tal stated: "The summit conference decided to curb fida'iyyun infiltration. The UAC sent us and the other Arab states on Israel's border dozens of directives on this issue . . ."[66] At another press conference on November 28, King Husayn spoke in the same vein as Tal: "If fida'iyyun cross-the-border action is Arab policy, then why don't they operate out of Sinai, the Gaza Strip, and Syria? The essence of fida'iyyun [activity lies in] . . . their training and experience in sabotage operations inside enemy territory before the final battle begins."[67]

3   In the first half of 1967, up until the Six Day War, Jordan's leaders continued to expound the above-mentioned claims, sometimes even more vigorously. For example, during Husayn's visit to Abu Dhabi in February 1967, he announced that "Jordan is blocking the fida'iyyun from operating in the occupied territory. Indeed, we are [doing this] but [we are following] a resolution [made at] the Casablanca conference [Arab summit meeting in September 1965]. Kings and presidents decided this based on the UAC's recommendations that came in the wake of an irresponsible, uncoordinated operation by the fida'iyyun that interfered with UAC planning. Have you heard of a fida'iyyun operation in Israel originating in Sinai or the Gaza Strip?"[68]

During 1967, until the war broke out, Jordan's security authorities maintained surveillance over Fatah activity, especially its recruitment of new members, the smuggling of money into Jordan, and distribution of leaflets. The arrest of Fatah members continued, although it generally fell short of legal prosecution. The Jordanians increasingly realized, and with much justification, that the Syrians were deeply involved in Fatah activity in Jordan and from Jordan into Israel, and in undermining Husayn's regime. On February 20, the deputy commander of the Jordanian army estimated that

"Syria is currently training Fatah members in top secret places in Darʿa and Quneitra. The training includes infiltration paths and the use of explosives and automatic weapons . . . A number of squads have been sent from their training bases to the [border] regions of Suwayda and Salhad and police stations close to the Jordanian border . . ." The facts on the ground – the arrest of armed fida'iyyun, the sabotage operations themselves, the distribution of Fatah leaflets in Amman and other places by Fatah activists who snuck into Jordan from Syria – substantiate these estimates.

On November 17, 1966 a few days after the Samuʿ raid, Husayn and Tal met with Arab representatives in Amman. The king fumed over the failure of Egypt and the UAC to come to Jordan's aid, and pointed to the similarities between the present conditions and those of 1956. He believed that Israel was about to launch a major attack against Jordan or Syria. The king and the prime minister were also furious with Lebanon because one of the fida'iyyun who admitted to taking part in the sabotage that preceded the Israeli attack belonged to Shafiq al-Hut's group (Abtal al-ʿAwda) and had infiltrated from Lebanon. The Lebanese ambassador replied that Lebanon forbade any element to conduct actions that hurt Jordan, and he asked the Jordanians for evidence to show his government. The king avowed that Jordan's information was incontestable.[69]

The commander of the Jordanian army sent a communiqué to the acting commander of the UAC, Fariq (Lieutenant General) Abd al-Munʿim Riyad, stressing that "the Samuʿ attack was neither the first nor the last of its kind in response to what are termed 'Arab fida'iyyun operations' in Israel. As you may recall, Fariq Awal (General) Ali Amer, the UAC commander, wrote a letter in your honor, which you circulated to all of the Arab states involved in this matter, and in which he ordered the suppression of these acts because they interfered with the UAC's coordinated military plan. Any operation, whatever its nature, that is not part of the coordinated military plan, can serve as grounds for getting dragged into a war with Israel before the Arab states have finished their preparations . . . and only the enemy will benefit."[70]

On November 29, King Husayn held a large press conference and spoke candidly about the Samuʿ raid and the lessons he learned from the event. He felt that this was similar to what happened in 1956 and that Israel intended to make a major military move against Jordan or Syria in the near future. The following two points are especially worth noting:

1   "The Israeli raid did not surprise us. We were expecting this type of an aggressive action for several weeks and had taken precautionary steps to meet the danger, but the raid exceeded the usual proportions, consisting of an armored brigade, a heavy artillery brigade, and a large concentration of fighter aircraft and bombers.

2   "When the raid began we thought it was the start of an all-out war; we expected major complications along the armistice line; we hung onto all necessary steps. Despite the large [enemy] military concentration, our forces performed gallantly in repulsing the aggression. The Jordanian air force helped relieve the pressure on our ground forces, enabling them to repel the enemy that had crossed the armistice line [and inflicting] heavy losses."

Husayn listed Jordanian losses in battle: army – fifteen killed and thirty-five wounded; civilian – six killed and two wounded. Eleven houses destroyed; stores, a police station, and a mosque damaged. "We admit these details because we want to tell the truth and learn from [our] mistakes."[71]

The JAA commander-in-chief estimated that "the attack on Samu' was not the first or last of its kind in response to Arab fida'iyyun raids inside Israel."[72]

The Impact of the Samu' Raid on Jordan's Participation in the War: A Turning-Point

Jordan's basic assessment, as expressed by the country's leadership from the start of sabotage activity in January 1965, was that guerilla acts carried out by Fatah and other organizations would be used as a pretext by Israel for launching a general war. According to this estimate, Israel would carry out a number of retaliatory raids to prepare the ground for an all-out war or the capture of the West Bank. The raid on Samu', therefore, was seen by Husayn not as a typical act of retaliation but as part of a comprehensive design to occupy the West Bank by attacking from the sparsely defended south. Husayn's goal in suppressing PLO and fida'iyyun activity inside Jordan should also be seen as an attempt to thwart Israel from carrying out its plans.

The Samu' raid and its domestic backlash were a jolting experience for Husayn and the regime's leadership. They were forced to reconsider Jordan's short-and long-term relations with Israel. The military and political leadership had been expecting an Israeli response but were caught off balance by its size and intensity. The king was furious and astounded at Israeli logic in hurting him this way. His anger was proportional to the raid's ruinous influence on internal affairs in his county for the following reasons:

1 The Samu' raid was a reaction to cross-border fida'iyyun activity but it was clear that Syria was providing assistance to Fatah whereas the Jordanian government was taking steps to disrupt Fatah activity. The regime's assessment was that Israel preferred taking revenge on Jordan instead of on Syria, even though Israel was aware of Jordan's efforts at blocking fida'iyyun activity. Several days prior to the raid, Husayn informed the Israelis, both directly and via the Americans, that he was punishing those responsible for guerilla activity against Israel. Also, shortly before the raid, Ya'akov Herzog, political advisor to prime minister Levi Eshkol, met with King Husayn in London where the king repeated his promise to do everything in his power to prevent border incidents. He asked [his Israeli listener] that his difficulties in moving against the Palestinian organization be taken into consideration.[73]

2 The IDF's raid wreaked havoc on Jordanian Arab Army (JAA) morale because of the heavy losses and because, in fact, the Jordanian troops had already been ordered to halt infiltration and sabotage. Therefore the widespread outcry and JAA pressure for revenge should come as little surprise. The army evinced signs of bitterness over the regime's floundering and there was talk of turning to the Soviet Union for weapons. Nevertheless, the military remained loyal to the regime and proved to be the linchpin in preserving political stability.

3 The raid took place at a most unpropitious time for Husayn. He was in the midst of a painful struggle against the PLO and deteriorating relations with Egypt

following Nasir's tirades against him because of Jordanian support of a Saudi Arabian initiative to establish an Islamic Pact [74]

For all of these reasons the Samu' raid should be seen as a turning-point in Jordan's attitude towards Israel, from a state of guarded coexistence to one of disappointment and pessimism, although clandestine meetings between the two neighbors continued. At the heart of Jordan's military and civilian estimate stood the unequivocal conclusion that Israel's main design was conquest of the West Bank, and that Israel was striving to drag all of the Arab countries into a general war, in the course of which it would make a grab for the West Bank. According to this appraisal, in light of Jordan's military weakness and the Arab world's dithering, Israel believed it would have little trouble in seizing the West Bank. After Samu', these apprehensions so obsessed the Jordanians that they should be regarded as the deciding factor in King Husayn's decision to participate in the Six Day War. He was convinced that Israel would attempt to occupy the West Bank whether Jordan joined the fray or not.

Additional conclusions reached by the Jordanians:

1 Since Israel viewed the Jordanian border in the same manner as the Egyptian and Syrian borders, Jordan would not be spared the consequences in a general war; therefore it would have to join an Arab alliance during a time of war. Both King Husayn and Fariq (Lieutenant General) Amer Khamash (JAA chief-of-staff) pointed out that "the [Israeli] attack was a reprisal for sabotage undertaken not by Jordan, but by Syria. One of the goals of the attack, they reasoned, was to demonstrate to the Arab world that Israel regarded all Arabs as its enemies whether Syrians, Egyptians, or Jordanians . . . Jordan's weak defense line made the West Bank a prime target."[75]

2 Israel's basic aim was to escalate the border situation into a full-scale war when it was convenient for Jerusalem and then capture the West Bank. The huge concentration of forces in the Jerusalem area and along the border with Jordan north of Jerusalem indicated that the Samu' raid was a diversionary maneuver in a larger battle plan to force Jordan to retaliate. Israel could then claim that it was only responding to Jordanian and fida'iyyun attacks that in effect would provide Israel with the *casus belli* for seizing the West Bank. Therefore, according to Wasfi al-Tal, "Jordan refrained from taking any reprisal action and tried to prevent commando activity along the armistice lines."[76]

3 The Samu' raid was planned to test the efficiency and ability of the UAC, especially regarding air cover and ground deployment simultaneously on several fronts. It became clear that the UAC failed the test. Hazem Nussaiba (foreign minister four times between 1962 and 1966), Adnan Abu Odeh and Ahmad Salim (commander of the Western Front – the West Bank) believed that Samu' was designed to: "provoke West Bank citizens to rebel against the government, which Arab propaganda had already accused of being too soft on Israel. This increased the possibility that unrest in the West Bank would be so severe that it could be used as an excuse by the Israelis to invade. They could claim that the danger of the Palestinians gaining the upper hand in Jordan presented a threat they could not tolerate."[77]

To conclude: The Jordanian leadership's appraisal of the repercussions of the Samu' raid was a major factor in King Husayn's decision to join Nasir's war chariot by signing a joint defense pact with Egypt on May 30, 1967. This was the determining factor for Jordan's participation in the war that would soon break out. Against the backdrop of the Palestinian national awakening, which received explosive expression after Samu', it was only natural that the Palestinians, who were pro-Nasir and revered him as their savior, immediately allied themselves to the nationalist wave sweeping the Arab world after Nasir blockaded the Straits of Tiran (22 May 1967). Convinced that the day of reckoning with Israel was approaching and the liberation of Filastin was just over the horizon, the Palestinians demanded Jordan's integration into Nasir's war strategy. With domestic upheaval endangering his regime, Husayn "pleaded" with Nasir to accept Jordan as an ally in arms and was willing to accept all of Nasir's terms. This earned Husayn accolades of enthusiasm from the West Bank Palestinians and instilled in them a sense of national pride.

Convinced after the Samu' raid that Israel's strategic goal was the West Bank, Husayn allied himself to Nasir out of genuine fear that, in a comprehensive war, Israel would invade the West Bank whether or not Jordan was an active participant. Concern over Israel's response to the deployment of Arab forces for defense on Jordanian soil, therefore, was no longer relevant. The moment that Husayn understood that war was inevitable, he hastened to sign a defense pact with Nasir and to request additional troops from Saudi Arabia and Iraq for the defense his country in accordance with the UAC plan. Husayn felt that he had to participate in the Six Day War even if his chances of victory were slim. He faced a choice between the lesser of two evils, and because of this, he was elevated to the status of national hero in Arab eyes.

The Arab Military Build-Up

The first Arab summit decided to immediately establish the United Arab Command (UAC) based on the structure and authority that had been approved by the Arab Joint Defense Council (ADC) at its third session in June 1961. The summit also confirmed the appointment of Fariq Awal (General) Ali Ali Amer – chief-of-staff of the Egyptian army and military assistant to the secretary-general of the Arab League – to supreme commander of the UAC, and the promotion of Fariq (Lieutenant General) Abd al-Mun'im Riyad to chief-of-staff of the UAC. In addition, the summit determined that Ali Amer "would begin organizing the nucleus of a headquarters within one month, and that the entire process . . . would be completed gradually within two months." The summit also decided that "all the Arab states would commit themselves to establishing and allocating the forces that the UAC proposed and the ADC approved. The Arab states pledged to assist the general commander in his work and to implement his recommendations and orders."[1] The first summit resolved to appropriate a total sum of £150 million to be distributed over a ten-year period. This sum was intended to augment the budget for strengthening the states (excluding Egypt) that bordered Israel. In other words, £15 million would be apportioned annually for arming and equipping Jordan, Syria, and Lebanon. This financial burden fell upon: Kuwait (£5 million), Egypt (£3 million), Saudi Arabia (£2 million), Iraq (£1.5 million) and the remaining Arab states (£3.5 million). Half a million pounds were also designated for the ongoing management of the UAC. (In the first year already Jordan received approximately £4 million).[2]

On January 30, 1965, the ADC approved the decision that defined "the roles of the UAC of the Arab armies," starting with the UAC's tasks in planning, operations, war preparation, the coordination of military cooperation among member states of the Arab League, and the unification of military regulations in the member states' armies.[3]

The UAC's work between 1964 and 1967 was characterized by two lines of action:

1 Accomplishments in staff work. This included the preparation of Arab defense plans against an Israeli attack; and the preparation of plans for defending Syria, Lebanon, and Jordan where diversion operations of the Jordan's tributaries were underway. According to the UAC's operational plan (prepared in 1964) for defending the diversion plans:

A Local armies were to be reinforced with Arab forces – the Jordanian Army with Iraqi and Saudi troops, and the Lebanese army with Syrian troops – and would thereby provide defense for the areas where water diversion operations are taking place.

B Forces not under attack would carry out limited acts of aggression to relieve the pressure on the other fronts. The UAC designated each Arab state a role in the event of an Israeli attack on diversion operations. It also defined the requirements for implementing the military plans, especially in the preparation of the theater of operations, air bases, order of battle, and weaponry. In 1964–1965 the Arab states' progress in organizing and armament was deemed to be success. The UAC also drew up plans for strengthening the Arab states, including the confrontation states with Israel, and kept track of their progress. Close coordination between the UAC and the GHQs (general headquarters) of these states was expressed in daily intelligence reports and a communications network was set up between the UAC and the confrontation states.

2 However, the UAC fell short of the mark in the area of operations and logistics. It failed to become a headquarters with command authority – the transfer of forces or control over local headquarters – in either wartime or peacetime. The UAC's operations and status were adversely affected by the summit atmosphere and inter-Arab wrangling that resurfaced in 1966. Thus, on the eve of the Six Day War, for all practical purposes the UAC was without operational ability and influence. The following factors contributed to this shortcoming:

A Basic distrust existed among the Arab states, especially the confrontation states (Egypt, Jordan, Syria, and Lebanon). Relations between Nasir and the Syrian Ba'th regime festered in an atmosphere of mutual suspicion. Given Egypt's and Syria's centrality in the conflict, the UAC's success depended to a large degree on political cooperation between the two, and less so on political cooperation between Egypt and Jordan.

B The UAC's "chain of command" had been compromised by two weak links: Jordan and Lebanon. Both countries were particularly sensitive to any form of foreign involvement in their armies (especially by the two nationalist regimes – Egypt and Syria) since such involvement was liable to arouse security problems that might threaten the stability of their regimes. Therefore, Jordan and Lebanon opposed the deployment of Arab forces on their soil. (Syria, too, balked at having Egyptian air force units stationed on its soil under Egyptian command.)

C Some of the Arab chiefs-of-staff who felt that the UAC had in effect curtailed some of their authority and intruded on matters concerning their headquarters were reluctant to cooperate with it and hampered its efforts.

D The political considerations had a crucial influence on the UAC's basic decisions which were, in effect, subordinate to the summit's policy that Egypt had dictated. Since the UAC was a pan-Arab organization that depended on the willingness of its member states for military cooperation, and since it was obvious that Egypt had a powerful influence on this machinery, the UAC's performance depended on the ongoing atmosphere of the Arab summit and on inter-Arab political cooperation. Thus, in the first half of

1966, when Nasir abandoned the summit institute and inter-Arab rivalry intensified, the UAC ceased to function. When Nasir's speech of July 23, 1966 blocked the fourth Arab summit, it symbolized the UAC's bankruptcy. Indications of this situation were already apparent at the third summit. Against this background the UAC failed on two counts:

(1) *The Syrian view*: In 1965 the UAC rejected Syria's demand for the "pan-Arabization" of Syria's water struggle with Israel. This came at a time when Israel was disrupting diversion operations in Syria. The UAC regarded the IDF operations as a local affair that did not warrant UAC involvement; that is, intervention by the rest of the Arab states – first and foremost Egypt.

(2) *The Jordanian view*: The UAC did not come to Jordan's aid during the Samu' raid (November 13, 1966) nor afterwards; and it was especially unwilling to supply Jordan with an (Egyptian) air umbrella even though this militant step had been planned if war broke out.

The Authority and Status of the UAC and its Commander

The first major problem that the UAC commander encountered was the extent of his and his staff's authority. Did he have control of the land forces in wartime which were subordinate to the ADC, or did he have command of the Arab armies that had been assigned missions according to the summit's decisions so that he was subordinate to the heads of the Arab states. The UAC commander, Ali Amer, strove to realize the second option. There was another major issue linked to this distinction. Did the UAC commander have the authority to transfer forces from one combat theater to another in non-combat periods as well as in wartime?

The question of the UAC commander's authority was discussed for the first time during the second Arab summit (September 1964). Amer's report to the second summit introduced a comprehensive plan for arming and training the Arab forces. If the weapons arrived in the time frame that he determined, and the operational theaters remained unified, and the UAC had unqualified freedom to transfer Arab forces from one theater to another in periods of quiet, then within *three years* [my emphasis – M.S.] the UAC would be able withstand an Israeli attack. "After Israeli aggression, it would be too late," he claimed.[4] He also demanded granting the UAC the authority to carry out the necessary military operations. He assumed that unity of command would guarantee success in realizing his strategy. Within this framework, he demanded full authority to send Arab troops to Lebanon, Syria, or Jordan, as he saw fit. Ali Amer complained that Lebanon refused to permit Arab forces entry into its territory according to the UAC's orders but only after Lebanon specifically requested as such and the Lebanese parliament sanctioned their entry.[5] The plenary debate at the second summit failed to reach an agreement on this issue, and the discussion passed into the ADC which convened for this reason on September 7, 1964. During the meeting Lebanon, Syria, and Jordan expressed their reservations about having Arab forces under UAC command stationed on their soil.

Lebanon's Position

In his memoirs, the Egyptian foreign minister, Mahmud Riyad, recalled the discussion at the second summit: "Ali Amer was rational in his survey [of the situation] and realistic in his planning. But Amer's way of realizing his demands underscored the problem that the Lebanese president had raised regarding the UAC commander's right to transfer troops from one Arab theater to another. President Hilou had pointed out that the Arab forces deployed in Lebanon 'would stir up domestic problems because of fear of the role of these forces'." Lebanon was obviously apprehensive over Syrian forces entering its country and their influence on Lebanon's fragile internal situation. Riyad claimed that he had discussed this issue with President Hilou and had asked for another formula that would enable him to overcome this obstacle and that would be acceptable to him. In Hilou's opinion, "an agreement by the Lebanese parliament would be sufficient for the entry of Arab forces into Lebanon in order to deal with the problem." Riyad reported this to Nasir who supported the formula that President Hilou proposed. Ali Amer also agreed with Hilou's formula, and the second summit approved the decision "to grant the commander of the UAC the full right to transfer troops, on condition that the movements from one state to another prior to the outbreak of war were considered the constitutional rules and regulations in each state."[6]

After the UAC commander ordered work on the water diversion to commence, he also ordered "Arab forces to amass close to Israel's borders. The countries involved informed him that the concentrations had been carried out." The UAC also ordered a plan to be drawn up for the deployment of forces if Israel attacked one of the states engaged in diversion operations. But the Lebanese GHQ refused to carry out the UAC's orders regarding troop concentrations on the Lebanese border or the entry of Arab forces into its territory unless its government sanctioned the order and decided where the main pump on the Wazani's sources would be set up. In November 1964 the Lebanese army commander asked the UAC commander to bring Lebanon's demands before the ADC. Thus, on December 1, 1964 the UAC chief-of-staff, by order of the UAC commander, met with the Lebanese chief-of-staff, Yusef Shmayit, to discuss Lebanon's demand. However, no progress was made. Lebanon's chief-of-staff stated that "the constitutional situation in Lebanon requires Lebanon to convene the ADC."[7] It was obvious that Lebanon had adopted a tactic of foot-dragging. Lebanon claimed that the UAC commander's demand was a political matter that would have to be decided by Lebanon's foreign and defense ministers.

The issue was readdressed at the Arab prime ministers' mini-summit in Cairo on January 9–10, 1965, following the UAC commander's detailed report to the conference on Lebanon's position. The conference listened to the UAC commander and moved the matter to the ADC that convened on January 10 at Lebanon's request. The Lebanese foreign minister, Philip Taqla, outlined Lebanon's position, and concluded by saying that Lebanon was determined to oppose the entry of Arab forces into its territory, despite the UAC request, until Lebanon's legal institutions (the president of Lebanon, the parliament, and the Lebanese government) approved of the move. He demanded that a decision be made that would be in force "in all circumstances" (in peacetime and in wartime) that Arab troops would not be sent to Lebanon until the Lebanon's legal institutions had agreed to such a move. Thus, Taqla set forth a stand more hard-line than the position of the second Arab summit which had differentiated between "peacetime" (when the entry of Arab troops into Lebanon was conditional on the agreement of the authorities) and "wartime" (when the UAC commander had the authority to transfer forces into Lebanon after consulting with Lebanese army commander). Ali Amer's response to Taqla was a repetition of his criticism of Lebanon's position, emphasizing that Lebanon's approval for the entry of Arab forces was urgent. Amer asked Taqla, "If the Lebanese Parliament refuses the entry of Arab forces into Lebanon, then what? " Taqla replied determinedly, claiming that the democratic way was standard procedure in Lebanon for all crucial decisions. Furthermore, he considered the whole discussion on decision-making in the Lebanese Parliament as intervention in Lebanon's internal affairs. He stressed that the Lebanese House of Representatives was the country's highest authority as decreed in the constitution, and the prime minister and foreign minister had to receive parliament's approval for all decisions of this kind. Taqla requested that the decision for the entry of Arab troops into Lebanese territory be made in the spirit of Lebanon's demand. At the end of the meeting a formula was decided on that won general approval. It was added to the decisions relating to the UAC's authority to transfer forces. The mini-summit plenary ratified the decision, which meant that Lebanon's reservations had been accepted:

1 The conference has taken note that the entry of Arab forces into Lebanese territory in time of need requires *prior approval* [my emphasis – M.S.] by the Lebanese government.
2 The Lebanese government must receive the immediate approval of its legislative authority as circumstances dictate.

According to the mini-summit's decisions, the Lebanese government undertook to obtain prior approval from the House of Representatives to allow the entry of Arab forces when necessary and under the following conditions:

1 The commander of the Lebanese army agrees to the need.
2 The House of Representatives will be informed of the matter (theoretically, after being informed, parliament could meet urgently and reject the government's decision).[8]

Thus, on the morning of January 22, 1965 the parliament concluded a seven-hour closed-door debate on the mini-summit's aforementioned decision and approved the government's line. The decision contained the following contents:

It [the Lebanese parliament] authorizes the government, after consultation with the Lebanese army's GHQ, to permit Arab troops to enter Lebanese territory when aggression is taking place that threatens the country, or when emergency military events require urgent steps and preclude the convening of the parliament on short notice. On each occasion, parliament must be informed of the Lebanese government's steps. When acts of aggression against Lebanon occur, the government must implement Section 2 of the collective security pact that was passed by the Arab League Council in 1950.[9]

With reference to Section 2, the Lebanese parliament asked the government to ascertain that the Arab states were obligated to rush to Lebanon's aid if it was attacked.

The UAC commander's report to the mini-summit (May 26–30, 1965) recalled Lebanon's and Jordan's opposition to the entry of Arab forces "for strengthening their defenses until the establishment of local formations were completed a year from now."[10] Until the Six Day War no decisions were made in Arab forums on the Lebanese issue. The debates in the Arab forums concentrated mainly on the question of Arab forces in Jordan and the deployment of Arab air units in Syria.

Jordan's Position

The UAC commander attributed special importance to the reinforcement of the Jordanian front with Arab forces from Iraq and Saudi Arabia. This was because of Jordan's geopolitical status, and especially because of the length of its border with Israel and the commander's estimate of Jordan's difficulty to withstand a full-scale Israeli attack. Jordan had supported the creation of the UAC and had high hopes for receiving special financial assistance for implementing a military build-up. Liwa (Major General) Amer Khamash, the Jordanian chief-of-staff, explained that Jordan's operational plans for defending the West Bank had been revised in 1965 according to the UAC's general operational plan, because "a joint Arab operation that would not enable Israel to take up arms against one Arab state, and would enable it [Jordan] to deal with the danger it was facing from Israel. Therefore, if we fight together, we expect the assistance of an air umbrella and the entry of Arab troops into Jordanian territory in order to strengthen its defense."[11]

Despite Husayn's support of the UAC's establishment and role, he vigorously opposed the UAC commander's demand for the entry of Arab forces into Jordan, except in wartime. Husayn's stand led to an increase in tension between Jordan and the UAC; and between Jordan and Egypt and Syria in 1966. The Jordanian regime viewed this refusal as a matter of survival. These were the main reasons for Jordan's hard-line position:

1 *Intervention in Jordan's internal affairs* – If Arab forces were stationed in Jordan, King Husayn feared they would become a subversive element, and instead of protecting the kingdom they would compromise his regime's stability. The king was concerned about ties that might develop between the officers in the Arab force and Jordanian officers, and the ideological and nationalist influence that Iraqi officers, in particular, might have on their Jordanian counterparts.

2 *Israeli intervention* – The Jordanians estimated that Israel might use the entry of Arab forces into Jordan as a pretext to attack and realize its dream of capturing the West Bank. Husayn claimed that "Israel might exploit the entry of non-Jordanian Arab troops in the kingdom to justify a large-scale military operation . . . What worries us is our enemies' plan to force us into a battle that we [the Arabs] are not ready for. On more than one occasion they [the Israelis] have declared that they would view these forces as a reason to launch a large-scale operation ... They [the Arab forces] are liable to create a situation in which the Arab world goes to war before being one hundred percent certain of the results"[12] (this was a hint at Egyptian and particularly Nasir's policy). Husayn's fear appears to have been genuine. Nevertheless, Jordan agreed to the entry of Arab forces only when war with Israel was imminent. Jordan claimed that its

army was strong enough to deal with a small-scale Israeli attack and had no need of token forces for defense purposes. It also asserted that as long as the Arab world's military strength was unequal to Israel's then everything had to be done to prevent Israel from finding an excuse to launch an attack.[13]

3 Jordan contended that *Arab reinforcements would not be deployed in time* to respond to an Israeli strike. It also noted that since it was the first line of defense against Israel, it had an abiding interest in acquiring the capability to repulse an Israeli attack with its own forces until the arrival of aid from other Arab states.[14] The defense plan that Jordanian GHQ formulated was based on this assumption.

In his report to the second summit conference, the UAC commander discussed the issue of reinforcing the Jordanian front. He pointed to two conditions that were needed to rectify the Arab military situation:

1 Reinforcements to the Arab states bordering Israel that would enter and take control of militarily appropriate areas of concentration according to the UAC's plans.
2 The number of aircraft under the UACs command would be augmented by at least four squadrons and deployed in areas bordering Israel. Without these [air] units, the situation in the northern countries – Lebanon, Syria, and Jordan – would remain uncertain and the ground forces would be incapable of defending their borders.[15]

In January 1965, the UAC commander repeated his demand at the meeting of the Arab prime ministers mini-summit, to grant him the authority to transfer forces from one Arab country to another. His orders "to amass Arab forces on Israel's borders," meant, of course, the entry of Saudi and Iraqi forces into Jordan, and that the UAC would determine the troops' missions according to operational plans for the defense of water diversion operations in Jordan. In his report to the mini-summit, Ali Amer discussed Jordan's response to these orders:

> In contacts with Jordanian authorities about the reinforcements they needed from the Iraqi and Saudi forces, it was agreed that only administrative service units would enter Jordan, and that military advisors would be dressed in civilian attire. [Since Jordan] refused entry of [foreign] forces into its territory, the UAC had to deploy the Iraqi units at H3 [a large military base and airfield inside Iraq on the Jordanian border] and the Saudi forces in Tabuk. The UAC still believes that by stationing the force a good distance from the theater of operations the military situation in the Jordanian kingdom is thereby jeopardized since the movement of these forces [into Jordan] during [wartime] might be carried out under unfavorable conditions for the Arab air force. [This in fact did happen to the Iraqi force in the Six Day War.] [Amer felt that] such a situation would imperil the entire Jordanian front. [The UAC] was still convinced that the deployment of Saudi and Iraqi support units in [Jordanian] territory was the correct military move to make in the Jordanian front.[16]

The UAC commander's report was referred to the Arab Joint Defense Council which had also convened at this time. At the end of the meeting, the council reached the following decision: "The UAC report has informed the council of the possibilities of concentrating Iraqi and Saudi reinforcements in Iraqi and Saudi territory [on the Jordanian border] before being employed in the theater of operations in Jordanian territory. While the council respects and accepts the UAC's opinion on this matter, it has decided to convey its [the council's] recommendation to the prime ministers so that they can make the necessary decisions." The Jordanian representative proposed that the matter be transferred to the summit conference. The mini-summit plenary that met on January 10, 1965 ratified the Jordanian representative's proposal and the vague wording of the defense council's decision, and stated that the conference "has decided to transfer the matter to the Casablanca summit conference which will be held in September 1965."[17] Jordanian prime minister Talhuni asked to register his country's reservations about the entry of Arab forces into Jordan other than in wartime. He also stated that Jordan would refuse the UAC's commander's request to allow Iraqi and Saudi forces to enter Jordan.[18] The prime ministers preferred to avoid taking a position on this matter, thus freezing the situation – that is, Arab forces would not enter the Hashemite Kingdom without Jordan's permission.

The Arab prime ministers conference (mini summit) in May 1965 focused on Israel's strikes against the diversion sites in Syria. The UAC commander's report discussed Jordan's refusal to allow Arab forces to enter its territory "[which were intended] to strengthen Jordan's defense, for one year until the process of setting up the units as the UAC demanded was completed." The UAC commander repeated his demand to permit "Arab forces entry [into Lebanon] and Jordan in order to strengthen their defenses and provide the UAC with the freedom to respond to enemy aggression." Wasfi al-Tal, head of the Jordanian delegation, voiced his opposition to the entry of Iraqi and Saudi forces "until the UAC forces completed their military preparations," that is, until "they were sufficiently trained and equipped." When the ADC met to discuss the UAC commander's report, the Jordanian foreign minister claimed that Israel might use the entry of Arab forces into Jordan as a pretext to retaliate. He added that the first Arab summit's decision – which stated that the UAC would not "take command" of any Arab state's border during peacetime – had to be implemented. The UAC chief-of-staff, Abd al-Mun'im Riyad, responded to al-Tal, saying that "the entry of Iraqi and Saudi forces to specific areas of concentration in Jordan was part of the military preparations, and Jordan's opposition was obstructing all our military plans and exposing us to danger."[19] In the Prime Ministers Conference, too, no new decisions were made on the issue.

Despite the Jordan's rigid position, the only progress that the UAC made – albeit minor progress – on the issue of troop movement was ironically in Jordan. Ali Amer reported that stockpiles had been prepared in Jordan for the Iraqi and Saudi expeditionary forces, and that steps had been taken for planning the integration of the Iraqi expeditionary force into the Jordanian defense layout. Jordan agreed to permit the entry of only the administrative mechanism of the Iraqi and Saudi forces, and a number of military advisors in civilian dress. In September 1965, the possible integration of Arab expeditionary troops during wartime was mentioned in the operational orders for the defense of the West Bank. Nevertheless, the Iraqi expeditionary force that was designated for Jordan, and that gradually approached the border in late 1964, was so reduced in size that it consisted of one armored brigade, rather than a division as the UAC had demanded, and did not enter Jordanian territory. During the third summit (September 1965) no more than one brigade headquarters and two tank platoons were deployed in H3 on the Iraqi side of the Jordanian–Iraqi border. The Iraqi expeditionary force entered Jordan only at the outbreak of the Six Day War – at King Husayn's summons. The Saudi brigade remained in Tabuk.

Syria's Position

Given the distrust between Egypt and Syria's Ba'th regime, the Syrians were extremely wary over a situation that might call for Egyptian forces, especially Egyptian air units, to be stationed in Syria. Already at the January 1965 mini-summit, the Syrians had reservations about Egyptian and/or Iraqi forces entering its territory without its permission. Following Israeli air strikes against the diversion operations, the UAC offered to send an Egyptian air squadron to Syria to provide air support. While the mini-summit was in session in May 1965, the UAC commander answered the Syrian chief-of-staff, Fahd al-Sha'ir, who charged that the UAC had failed to dispatch an Arab air force to Syria's assistance. According to Amer, the reason was that Egypt had agreed to send a squadron to Syria on condition that the Syrian base, where the squadron would be operating, came under Egyptian command, but Syria had refused, insisting that the squadron should be under direct Syrian command.[20]

Immediately after the May 1965 incident, the Syrians demanded that the UAC determine that Arab borders are one single border, and that the northern air theater (Jordan, Syria, and Lebanon with Iraqi air support), whose strength was sufficient for dealing with the Israeli threat, would become operational. On May 29 the Syrians proposed in the ADC the establishment of a deterrent force of five air squadrons containing fighters and bombers that would provide strong air support in the event of an Israeli attack. It was clear to the Syrians that only the Egyptian air force was capable of performing this mission. But the presence of Egyptian air squadrons in Syria would precipitate a collision with Israel, a development that Nasir had no interest in at this time. Egypt rebuffed Syria's demand and insisted on extraterritorial rights over Syrian airfields that would come under Egyptian command so as to deploy Egyptian security forces to protect them "from Syrian intervention." While the defense council was engaged in discussions, Syria agreed to allow Arab forces (including Iraqi troops) to enter its territory on condition that they included air contingents and radar units. Syria also agreed that Arab forces would be stationed on its soil before their entry into Jordan and Lebanon in the event that they were urgently needed there.[21]

The Syrians' direct request to Iraq – not to the UAC – in mid-October 1966 for military aid if Israel attacked, testifies to the UAC's situation and Syrian policy toward the organization. The Iraqis replied that they were willing to extend military assistance to Syria in conjunction with their obligations to the UAC on the northern front, after they received the UAC's permission to do so. As part of their commitment to the UAC, they were prepared to send units that had been assigned to the UAC to assist Syria. This force would include: one reinforced infantry brigade, one tank battalion, one squadron of fighter aircraft, and one squadron of bombers. In making a direct request to the Iraqis, the Syrians went behind the UAC's back because they were averse to having Egyptian forces deployed on Syrian soil (excluding an air squadron) according to Egypt's conditions. The Iraqi response left their ambiguous position intact. On the one hand, they agreed, in principle, to the Syrian demand; on the other hand, they

127

maintained their loyalty to the UAC. On November 4, 1966, against the background of the collapsed summit atmosphere, the Syrians' attitude toward the UAC, and Iraqi waffling over a direct agreement with Damascus for sending support troops to Syria, Egypt and Syria finally signed a defense pact. Discussion in the Arab arena now focused on the Jordanian issue.

Continuing Discussions on the Dispatch of Arab Forces to Jordan

The UAC commander's report to the third summit meeting (including the defense council and summit plenary) still focused on Jordan's and Lebanon's opposition to the entry of Arab (Saudi, Iraqi, and Syrian) forces into their territory. Amer summed up the issue, noting the substandard military situation in these two counties and that improvement could not be expected "in the near future" since the effects to strengthen the two countries would only be felt in two years at the earliest. He reaffirmed the estimate that he presented to the second summit that improvement in the Arab military situation depended on two conditions: the entry of reinforcements into the border states (Jordan, Syria, and Lebanon) and the forces' deployment in tactical positions; and an increase in the number of fighter aircraft under UAC command to at least four squadrons and their deployment in the border states.

Ali Amer pointed out that the UAC had already demanded both conditions in 1964 in the realization that they would improve the situation in the northern theater of operations. But no real progress had been made in either case. King Husayn repeated his position, stressing that "the entry of these forces into Jordan would induce Israel to attack Jordan." In light of Husayn's position, President Arif of Iraq immediately declared that in this case he intended to return his troops to Iraq since their deployment on the border with Jordan was a burden on Iraq. Naturally, Husayn was not opposed to this,[22] and the Iraqi forces were called back to their bases.

While discussions were being held at the third mini-summit (March 12–14, 1966) the ADC also met and reviewed, *inter alia*, the UAC commander's report; but no progress was made on the issue. Ali Amer especially pointed to the fact that the Arab states were not keeping to the financial commitments they had pledged to the UAC. It was decided that a fourth mini-summit would be held in Algeria in early September 1966.

The question of Arab forces entering Jordan was raised acridly in the ADC emergency session (December 7–10, 1966) following the IDF raid on the village of Samu' in the southern Hebron hills (November 13). Jordan accused the UAC of impotence and failure to abide by its commitment (that Egypt would supply Jordan with air support, for example). Egypt retorted that Jordan's failure to comply with the UAC's demand had contributed to the Israeli victory. A week before the ADC meeting, the UAC set the atmosphere by ordering the Arab forces to go on alert, that is, by concentrating forces for the defense of Jordan. In this way the UAC could show it was making decisions and moves in the crisis. The question of Arab forces entering Jordan was expected to head the meeting's agenda, but due to the crisis that had enveloped Jordan and the Arab world because of the IDF raid, Egypt and the UAC preferred to avoid having the session erupt in an upheaval. Therefore, they adopted a flexible tactical position.

Jordan tried to avert disagreement by presenting the ADC with a memo laying out the terms for its agreement to allow Arab forces to enter its territory:

1   The authorized Arab institutions will be prepared to take responsibility for the results of this decision [or response] – that is, the danger of being hurled into a war with Israel. (Jordan made the Arab states aware that it believed the entry of Arab troops into Jordan would precipitate war with Israel.)
2   The amassment of the Arab states' full military power on the border with Israel would include Egyptian forces in Sinai (which meant Egypt's evacuation from Yemen). Jordan estimated that the Iraqi and Saudi expeditionary forces would be inadequate to guarantee the kingdom's security.
3   An appropriate level of alert was guaranteed for the reinforcement forces before their entry into Jordan, and the forces' freedom of action on the various fronts was also guaranteed. Jordan demanded the evacuation of the UNEF from borders of Sinai and the Gaza Strip, or an unqualified Egyptian guarantee that the UN force would not prevent the Egyptian army from engaging Israel in combat if Israel attacked Jordan. Jordan claimed that "the presence of UN forces on Arab soil obstructed the implementation of the UAC's plans," that is, it impeded the Egyptian military move designed to aid Jordan.
4   The UAC had to carry out its financial commitments to Jordan. The reason that Jordan demanded this was that Egypt and Saudi Arabia had failed to honor their commitments to Jordan because of the exacerbation of relations.[23]

This session of the ADC revolved around the UAC commander's report which raised the following points:

1   The IDF's build up and Israel's nuclear development. The report discussed the balance of power between Israel and the Arab states, and affirmed that the plans for strengthening (arming and establishing new units) the Arabs' ground forces were acceptable. Nevertheless, the report warned that the balance of air forces was unequal, and especially noted the tardiness in Jordan's system of equipping its aircraft and procuring planes from the United States.
2   The report estimated that Israel would continue its policy of limited land and air operations against diversion sites or border regions. For the first time, the possibility was broached of a large-scale Israeli air strike (retaliation) against the air force and strategic facilities of one of the Arab states.
3   The UAC commander pointed to Jordan's opposition to the entry of Arab forces into its territory other than in wartime, and Jordan's conditions for agreeing to their entry. He believed that unless the UAC's basic decision on the reinforcement of the Jordanian front with Arab forces was implemented, Israel was liable to have complete freedom to take the initiative against the Arab nation. In Amer's opinion, the situation could be amended if Jordan consented to the entry of Arab reinforcements into its territory as agreed upon. This force would be made up of one Iraqi armored brigade, two Iraqi infantry brigades, and one Saudi infantry brigade – and if an air defense was promised, it would consist of two or three squadrons of fighter aircraft (MiG 23s or British Lightnings) since Jordan did not have planes of comparable quality.

4 The UAC commander emphasized that the forces had to be concentrated on all of the fronts and kept on an operational state of alert in the likelihood that Israel would mount a full-scale attack against Jordan. Thus, Ali Amer agreed with the Jordanian assessment that the entry of Arab forces into Jordan might trigger an Israeli military response. In this way his decision was an answer to Jordan's demands.

5 Amer complained that the Arab states were not fully honoring their financial commitments to the UAC. In 1966 the payments by the Arab states for strengthening and maintaining the UAC were less than 30 percent of the total promised, and funds were not transferred to the regular budget.[24]

In view of the "gravity of the hour" and the smoldering passions in the Arab world after the Samu' raid, at the conclusion of the ADC meeting all of the participants agreed to reach an Arab consensus regarding Jordan's basic position. Amer also pressed for a unanimous decision on the entry of Iraqi and Saudi forces into Jordan within two months at the latest. Jordan could not – and did not – want to oppose this proposal too since it would have delayed the implementation of the decision. The final decision included the following sections:

1 Jordan agrees to allow Iraqi and Saudi forces to enter its territory in accordance with the UAC plan, within two months at the most. The ADC will reconvene on January 15, 1967 to examine the preparations and steps [to be taken] for the Arab forces' entry into Jordan.

2 The required funds must be channeled for the establishment of the military units that the ADC has determined [that is, the Arab states have to honor their financial pledges to the UAC).

3 Syria had to be paid 50 percent of the UAC's budgetary reserves.

4 The council had complete confidence in Ali Amer, the UAC commander.[25]

At the end of the ADC meeting a consensus was reached due to the willingness of Egypt and Syria to "come around" to Jordan's position. They did this in order to prevent the collapse of the meeting, thereby "saving" the UAC's status, which was close to bankruptcy because of its failure to respond to the IDF's Samu' attack. Therefore, the UAC and Egypt avoided applying excessive pressure on Jordan. Also, Jordan's agreement was only tactical since it went from a negative position to a conditional agreement. In reality, Jordan relinquished nothing, since the conditions for the agreement made the decision impractical. The agreement to implement it within two months bought Jordan time and enabled it to leave the council meeting intact and without the council having decided on the agreement's immediate implementation. The removal of Jordan's extreme demands from the agenda (the evacuation of UN forces and troop concentrations) also helped to temper the debate and soften the decisions on Jordan's obligations.

Following the ADC meeting, and after Jordan realized that its conditions for the entry of Arab forces into its territory would not be accommodated, it refused to honor the ADC's decisions, declaring that its basic position on this issue had not changed. On December 28, 1966 Jordan informed the Arab League secretariat that it viewed the ADC's decisions as a single bloc and would not implement the provision concerning the entry of Arab forces into its territory unless the sections relating to the flow of funds to the UAC were fulfilled. The Egyptian propaganda organs were in an uproar over Jordan again, accusing it of failing to provide adequate defenses for the West Bank. On January 25, 1967 King Husayn repeated in detail the reasons for Jordan's opposition to the entry of forces into its territory.[26]

In late November, early December 1966, before the ADC emergency meeting (December 9–10) and against the background of the heated inter-Arab dispute over the Samu' raid, Iraq took an unprecedented initiative, apparently without instructions from the UAC, and sent a token expeditionary force to the Iraqi–Jordanian border. Iraq wanted to prove its readiness to come to Jordan's aid in an emergency, an act that would also shower it with prestige in the Arab arena. The Iraqi force that deployed in the area known as H3 on the border with Jordan, included a reinforced battalion and a squadron of fighter planes. The Iraqi force seems to have been one of the factors that propelled the UAC to order the concentration of reinforcements on the Jordanian border in late November. Soon afterwards, in January 1967, the Iraqi forces returned to their bases, since the ADC made no arrangement for the entry of Arab forces into Jordan.[27]

Egypt and the UNEF on the Israeli Border (1965–1966)

The UNEF's deployment on the Egyptian–Israeli border (Sinai and the Gaza Strip) was one of the consequences of the Sinai War. From Egypt's point of view it was a negative result. Not only was it a thorn in Egypt's eye, but it was also traumatic reminder to the Egyptian political and military leadership. Thus, the removal of the UN forces became a goal in itself. The UN's presence on the border with Israel detracted from the regime's prestige in general, and Nasir's in particular. For Nasir the Filastin problem was the key element in his concept of Arab nationalism. Nasir's opponents in the Arab world – especially Jordan, Saudi Arabia, and even Syria – exploited the UNEF's presence to launch an anti-Egypt propaganda campaign that claimed the UN's presence afforded Egypt a convenient excuse to avoid taking action against Israel. Nasir and his deputy, Mushir Amer, had been obsessed with the goal of removing the UN force ever since it was deployed in the region in 1957. Muhammad Fawzi, who was appointed Egyptian chief-of-staff in March 1965, relates in his memoirs: "When the first Egyptian brigade returned from Yemen in 1965, as part of the unit exchange between Egypt and Yemen, Nasir and Amer attended the welcoming reception at Port Tawfiq. An argument broke out between the two leaders at the [official] event over the possible transfer of the brigade from Suez to Sharm al-Sheikh which would also have the effect of coming as a big surprise for the world. The conversation ended only on a note of hope. The brigade returned to its base in Cairo as planned."[28] Mushir Amer apparently suggested moving the brigade to Sharm al-Sheikh, intending it to replace the UN unit stationed there across from the naval passage through the Straits of Tiran.

After the Samu' raid and the deterioration in Egyptian–Jordanian relations, Jordan's propaganda machine mainly targeted Egypt on the issue of the UNEF's presence in Sinai, Gaza, and the Straits of Tiran coast (Saudi Arabia also joined the anti-Egypt propaganda campaign, though its invective was less voluble and persistent than Jordan's). Jordan alleged that Egypt's Yemen policy had removed Egyptian forces from Israel's borders. On November 21, 1966 Wasfi al-Tal stated that the UNEF in Sinai "was now an obstacle [preventing Egyptian] military action. The Egyptian army had to leave Yemen and redeploy in the Sinai."[29] On January 7, 1967 he gave a press conference and declared that "the agreement that misters Nasir and Ben-Gurion signed through the mediation of the Hammarskjöld [after the Sinai War] put an end to Egypt's military presence in Sinai and on Filastin's borders. The UN forces would remain deployed in these territories until permanent peace was established between the two sides. Nasir laid down the real weapon and turned to the cudgel of rhetoric. It is childish to claim the UN force was not an obstacle [as the Egyptian foreign minister declared in the ADC]."[30] On January 25, 1967 King Husayn stated:

> What justification is there for the UN's presence on our [Arab] territory today? We boycott countries and companies, and try to pressure Israel, our enemy . . . but the Gulf of Aqaba has been open since 1956. From Israel's point of view, is not the withdrawal of our brethren from the Straits of Tiran and their replacement by] the UNEF more important than the boycott we are trying to impose on companies? We hope that the Egyptian forces will not stay in Yemen but [will take up positions] in the region where both they and we can proceed to regain our rights. If the UNEF remains, then there is only one explanation for its presence, which is, the [1956] agreement according to which it [the UN] will remain [in the region] until the Filastin problem is solved or a settlement reached. [31]

In this period, the Jordanian press obviously adopted the official line of the regime's leaders.

During Mushir Amer's visit to Pakistan (December 10–11, 1966) he repeated his proposal. This came in light of Jordan's propaganda campaign and its effect – the issue was discussed in pan-Arab forums and heard throughout the Arab world. Amer sent Nasir "an open cable" in which he recommended "dispatching [Egyptian military] units to Sharm al-Sheikh to threaten the closure of the Straits of Tiran to Israeli vessels." Amer also proposed that "Egypt [simultaneously] announce in the ADC its decision to oust the UNEF from the straits." This announcement, he believed, would require an Egyptian force, that had been sufficiently prepared for the task, to take control of Sharm al-Sheikh. According to Amer, this move was aimed at "taking the wind out of Husayn's sails" and from Jordanian propaganda, and at the same time it would serve Egypt's interests in the Arab arena "after completing a positive move to meet the challenge of Israel's aggression against Jordan."[32] Amer apparently thought that such a move entailed no military risk for Egypt and no new military challenge since Israel was not expected to respond.

Nasir objected to Amer's claims. He seems to have believed that if Egypt took control of the straits, it would have to block them to Israeli shipping, and this would trigger an Israeli response at a most inconvenient time for Egypt (on May 22, 1967, Nasir's prediction proved right). Nevertheless, he decided to pursue a line that officially guaranteed that the emergency force would not be a stumbling-block to an Egyptian military move against Israel.

According to this line, after Jordan raised the issue in a letter addressed to the ADC meeting (December 7–10, 1966), and immediately after Ali Amer presented his report, Riyad, the Egyptian foreign minister, hastened to reply to Jordan's accusation that the

UNEF was an obstacle to Egypt, and to Jordan's demand to remove the UN force. Riyad reviewed the history of the UNEF, its missions, and the circumstances under which it had been established and stationed on the border: "They were originally deployed to monitor the Israeli withdrawal." He noted that the Jordanian authorities had recently begun to allude to the UNEF in their criticism of Egypt. "The UNEF is not an impediment to Egypt or its freedom to do what it sees fit. We can demand the evacuation of these [UN] forces whenever we want . . ." In order to prove his point, Riyad reminded his listeners that "when Israel amassed its forces on the Syrian front after the Tawfiq battle in February 1960, Egypt amassed its forces in Sinai in preparation for intervention, if Syria was attacked. Egypt never took into account that it might have to confront the international emergency forces on the armistice line . . . [Furthermore,] . . . the emergency forces cannot restrict the Palestinian people's freedom to establish its army and train it on Filastin soil or in Sinai . . . When Egypt approved the UAC's plans, it obligated itself to implementing them. It regarded this as the fulfillment of the Arab national commitment, and could not accept any condition by any party that would limit [Egypt's] right to work for the Arab homeland and Arab honor."[33] Little wonder then that the Egyptian authorities took pains to leak Riyad's statements to the Egyptian media. The Jordanian foreign minister responded positively to Foreign Minister Mahmud Riyad's lecture: "We did not raise the issue in Jordan in order to reproach [anyone] but to be sure [of Egypt's position] and [to be sure] that security has definitely been achieved . . ."[34] (See Chapter 7 for the UNEF evacuation)

The Convening of the ADC in March 1967: Jordan Is Again the Center of Discussion

Hostility toward Jordan was expressed in the ADC meeting (March 11–14, 1967). Jordan and Saudi Arabia were absent because their conditions had not been met, that is: the ADC meeting should be preceded by an Arab summit conference. Jordan was certain that Egypt and Syria would criticize it and that Jordan would gain nothing of practical value by attending the meeting. The main issue on the agenda was the UAC commander's progress report that he had been asked to provide, according to the decision of the ADC emergency meeting in December 1966. Amer's report is noteworthy for its objective description of the UAC's situation. He read his report "nervously and laconically for five minutes." Here are the main points:

1 The UAC has made impressive progress in organization, arms build-up, and operational planning; and has, in effect, almost attained the goals it set for itself in the Arab summit's three-year plan.
2 Remaining obstacles:
   A The unstable inter-Arab relations prevent the UAC from exerting its authority.
   B The Arab states' lateness in payments to the UAC.
   C In these circumstances the UAC is unable to bear the responsibility it was granted at the second summit.
3 The UAC commander's recommendations:

A The UAC is willing to consider the present situation as an intermediate period, in the hope that political circumstances will change for the better. The UAC will continue to operate only if the states honor their financial commitments.

B If the situation does not improve and money is not received on a regular basis, the UAC will remain a "future hope."[35]

During the debate on Amer's report, all of the speakers expressed their confidence in the UAC and its staff, and reaffirmed their pledge to uphold their financial commitments. Discussion focused mainly on the position to be adopted toward Jordan. The Syrian foreign minister demanded that Jordan and Saudi Arabia be censured and a new debate held on the UAC's plans without taking Jordan, Saudi Arabia, and Tunisia into consideration. The Egyptian foreign minister, Mahmud Riyad, called for a new UAC plan that would exclude Jordan "because it had broken ranks with joint Arab activity." He added that Egypt respects its commitment to protect other Arab states – including Jordan and Saudi Arabia – if Israel attacks them – regardless of whether or not the UAC continues to function. He proposed canceling the financial aid promised to Jordan and the other Arab states that had failed to honor the ADC's decisions. Amer insisted that if Jordan refused to take part in the UAC plan, the Iraqi forces would carry out their mission on Syrian soil exclusively.[36]

Indeed, the ADC voted to deny Jordan the budgets that the summit had allotted it and transfer the funds to Syria, Lebanon, and the Palestinian Liberation Army (PLA).

The council's decision included the following points:

1 Arab member states will honor their financial obligations on time – no later than July 1967.
2 Any state that fails to fulfill the military commitments that the council has decided will have its financial allotments frozen. After Jordan is excluded, the sums collected for the UAC will be divided among recipient states, that is, Syria, Lebanon, and the PLA.
3 The council asks the UAC's c-in-c to draw up a military estimate of the current situation among the Arab states, on the assumption that it is transitory [referring to the exclusion of Jordan, Saudi Arabia and Tunisia].
4 The ADC has decided that it will convene on July 4, 1967 to discuss the new estimate of the situation, and whether the financial commitments have been honored.[37]

On March 20, 1967, the Syrian newspaper *al-Ba'th* responded to the decision, demanding that Jordan and Saudi Arabia be expelled from the ADC.

Jordan claimed that there was a basic error in the defense council's decisions. An "official Jordanian source" acknowledged that "the arms consignments recently arrived in Jordan from the United States are gift consignments that were obtained according to bilateral agreements and outside the framework of the consignments that Jordan purchased with UAC funds." In response to UAC reports that Jordan had received £21 million to procure new weapons and at the same time had received weapons from the United States free of charge, the Jordanian source stated that "Jordan had actually received only £14 million and that £12 million was needed to complete its purchases." The source also confirmed that Jordan had received an additional £5.5 million from the UAC "to continue setting up military formations" and claimed that Jordan had, in effect, paid £8.5 to cover the necessary costs for maintaining these forces.[38]

The UAC's Contribution to the Build-up of the Arab Armies

The first summit conference determined that the Jordanian, Syrian, and Lebanese armies were too weak to repulse an Israeli attack in the near future, but the Egyptian army could effectively defend the Egyptian front. Another problem was that these states opposed, on principle, the entry of Arab forces into their territory. This meant that their armies and weapons had to be strengthened in order to ward off an Israeli attack, even if they were only minimally successful, until the main Arab force in the rear arrived. Therefore, the summit decided to augment the quantitative and qualitative strength of the Jordanian, Syrian, and Lebanese armies, that is, to supplement them with additional units and equipment. Thus, after the UAC was established, it made an inventory of the border-states' armies, and the Iraqi army, in order to determine how they should be strengthened and the forces to be placed under UAC's disposal. As stated, the first summit decided on a sum of £150 million over a ten-year period as financial assistance for strengthening the states bordering Israel, excluding Egypt, that is, £15 million a year. The UAC divided the annual sum in the following manner: Jordan and Syria – £6 and £7 million respectively, and Lebanon – £2 million.

The UAC also assumed the task of financing and maintaining the new units that had been established on its initiative at £5 million annually over a five-year period.[39] At the time the UAC was established, it approved plans for procuring equipment and arms for the Syrian, Jordanian, and Lebanese armies, and financing them by means of the military build-up budget it had been granted.

Excluding the sums allotted for the military build-up, the sections of the UAC's budget that were presented to the mini-summit for its approval in January 1965[40] included:

1　A budget for establishing the UAC: a one-time payment of half a million pounds.
2　Maintenance of the UAC: an annual budget of one-quarter of a million pounds.
3　Maintenance of the new forces (their armament according to the military build-up plan): £25 million to be paid in five yearly installments of £5 million.
4　The Arab states' participation in the establishment of the PLA (Palestinian Liberation Army) – £5.5 million.
5　Maintenance of the PLA: £2 million annually.

During 1964, and also in the UAC commander's report to the second summit in September, Ali Amer demanded that the weapons in the Arab armies be of the same type by increasing Jordan's and Lebanon's military strength with Soviet arms, including combat planes. During the second summit's discussion on Ali Amer's report, the UAC commander replied to Nasir's question, saying that eastern bloc weapons were preferred because they were less expensive than western arms and the conditions of payment were more flexible. During the ADC meeting at the second summit, Jordan and Lebanon remained adamantly opposed to this proposal. Husayn justifiably estimated that the eastern bloc's willingness to sell weapons to the Middle East at such "reasonable" prices stemmed from its interest in securing a foothold and influence in the Arab world. Besides creating difficult coordination problems with the Jordanian army's current western equipment, Husayn felt that the Soviet planes it was being offered were inferior to the American aircraft that Jordan would be acquiring.[41] The Egyptians also tried to exert pressure "from below" by influencing the Jordanian officer cadre. They did this through information campaigns and organized visits to Egypt in which Soviet arms were ostentatiously displayed. All this had no effect on Husayn's basic position. He correctly understood that a positive reply to Egypt regarding Soviet weaponry would "cut the rug from under" the main backer of his regime (Britain and the United States) and boost Nasir's and the Russians' influence on his army. Thus Egypt's attempt – via the UAC – to unify the weapons of the confrontation states ended in failure in the second Arab summit, which agreed that Lebanon and Jordan would continue to be stocked with western arms.

The UAC's influence on the Jordanian army was enormous in 1964 – the euphoric period of inter-Arab relations – because of the UAC commander's marked success in convincing Husayn to replace his senior military staff. During his visit to Jordan in June 1964, Amer inspected several of the army's units and met their commanders. He received an unfavorable impression of the veteran commanders who had been appointed to their positions in the period of the domestic turmoil in 1957 and 1958, when the only standard for officer promotion was loyalty to the regime and the ability to secure the loyalty of the troops. Amer bluntly voiced his criticism to the King and the director of the army's planning and organization. Amer's stinging disproval led to the removal of one hundred officers on July 12, 1964 – including four brigade commanders and sixteen battalion commanders. The ousted officers were replaced by new commanders who had received advanced military training, but they too were Bedouin, loyal to the regime. Thus, the UAC commander's attempt to drive a wedge between the Jordanian officer cadre and the king failed.

Amer's report to the second summit on the balance of power between Israel and the Arabs stated that the IDF was stronger than the Arab forces. In his opinion, the UAC had to make an effort to attain Arab military superiority. He also pointed to both the strong and weak points in the Arabs' defensive and offensive lines. According to his estimate, the UAC currently needed seven to ten days to repulse an Israeli attack on one of the Arab states engaged in water diversion operations. In such a case – Israeli victory was certain.[42]

The UAC prepared a plan for strengthening the Jordanian, Syrian, and Lebanese armies in coordination with the commanders of these forces. The second summit (September 1964) ratified the plan. The plan dealt especially with the strengthening of the land forces more than the air forces.

Strengthening (Reorganizing) the Jordanian Army[43]

The UAC's plans for strengthening the Jordanian army enabled Husayn to realize his long-held dream of doubling his army's power. Jordan would be allocated five to seven million pounds a year from the UAC treasury over a ten-year period. This sum was intended to establish and maintain five infantry brigades and two tank battalions (with all their necessary support and service units) within five years. At the same time Jordan's National Guard would be disbanded. It should be noted that the decision to disband the National Guard and establish four infantry battalions in its place was made in October 1963. Another part of the plan called for the purchase and formation of a squadron of jet fighters.

On September 28, 1964 the Jordanian GHQ, headed by King Husayn in the role of supreme commander of the armed forces, approved the plan for "reorganizing the armed forces." This reorganization was based on the establishment of five infantry brigades, with each brigade comprised of its own staff and three infantry battalions. Two field artillery battalions and six 4.2 inch mortar batteries would also be established. Thus the Jordanian army would have six field artillery battalions. A new engineer battalion would also be formed and added to the current battalion. The GHQ meeting decided to implement the army's reorganization in two stages:

1 Reorganization would begin at once in accordance with present possibilities.
2 Reorganization would begin with the set up of new units financed by UAC funds once the budgets were transferred to Jordanian banks. According to this plan, four infantry brigades would be established in 1965:
    • In the first stage: six months would be required for the first two brigades to be set up.
    • In the second stage: six more months would be needed for the establishment of an additional two brigades.

The National Guard units would withdraw to the rear of each military area as decided. At each stage the National Guard would be replaced by regular brigades responsible for the defense of the border. In early 1966 a fifth brigade would start to be formed. Artillery and engineering units and other support and administrative elements would begin to be constructed in early 1965.

The January 1965 the mini-summit approved the allocation of Jordan's build-up budget for 1965:

1 Two and a half million pounds for the facilities and equipment needed to absorb the division (the establishment of the new brigades).
2 One and half million pounds (of the above-mentioned two and a half million) for the establishment of an airfield in H5 (on Jordan's territory).

The UAC commander, in his report to the third summit (September 1965), reviewed the progress made so far in strengthening the Jordanian army in 1964–1965:

1 As of March 31, 1965, five (new) infantry brigades had been established consisting of: one brigade at one hundred percent strength; the rest at eighty percent strength. General staff units also began to be set up and pilots and technicians were being properly trained.
2 The UAC transferred funds for the units' facilities, the new formations, and an airbase (£4 million). A number of facilities have already been completed and the rest are still in under construction.

3 Seventeen thousand pounds were transferred to the building of administrative warehouses for the Saudi and Iraqi forces (that would enter Jordan in wartime or after Jordan consented to their entry).
4 Jordan signed arms deals worth twenty-two and a half million pounds for land forces; four and a half million pounds of this sum was provided by the UAC. A small amount of the weapons already arrived; the rest would come between the 1965 and 1967.
5 No deals had been signed yet for air supplies, and construction on the airbase had not commenced either.

From Amer's point of view, the strengthening of the ground forces was satisfactory, but the fortification of the Jordanian air force had not progressed noticeably. The strengthening or reorganization of the Jordanian army continued in 1966 until the Six Day War. Husayn's January 25, 1967 speech revealed in unprecedented detail the build-up of the Jordanian army:[44]

1 Infantry – nine infantry brigades (four veteran units and five that had been organized in March 1965 with the disbanded National Guard. Added to this was the Royal Guard brigade).
2 Armor – two brigades (approximately 300 tanks, consisting of 250 Patton 48 tanks).
3 Air force – Husayn reported that the five new fighter squadrons would soon reach full strength (this number also included the Hunter squadron whose strength was equivalent to two squadrons [twelve planes in each squadron], and the thirty-six F-104s that Jordan had ordered from the United States and were to arrive in the coming years).

The details that Husayn supplied regarding the Jordanian army's order of battle and strength were undoubtedly designed to discredit the UAC accusation and the Egyptian and Syrian propaganda organs, that had been active after the Samu' raid, regarding Jordan's feebleness in demonstrating its army's strength at home and abroad. Husayn wanted to prove the Jordanian army's capability to withstand an Israeli attack until Arab reinforcements arrived at the front. In this way he intended to counter Egyptian and Syrian censure of Jordan's refusal to allow Arab forces to enter its territory and their claim that this had impaired Jordan's defense (to prove their point the Egyptians and Syrians mentioned the Samu' raid).

The Strengthening of the Syrian Army

In January 1965 the mini-summit approved the UAC commander's budget for the Syrian build-up in the coming year:

1 Approximately £1.4 million of the initial budget was designated for the construction of an airbase.
2 Approximately £65.000 for the establishment of two infantry brigades in the first year.
3 Approximately £325.000 – for general staff units in the first year.

4 Approximately half a million pounds for maintenance costs.

The UAC recommended giving priority to the air force rather than the ground force even though this recommendation clashed with the Syrian build-up plan. The Syrians accepted the UAC's list of priorities. The UAC reported to the third summit on the progress being made in the strengthenin of Syria's armed forces.

A New units
Land forces – Three new infantry brigades were in the planning stages. One of these brigades already had 60% of its manpower, with 70% of the troops' weapons and equipment in storage.
The air force – Syria announced that a fighter squadron was being formed, and that a bomber squadron, whose planes had already arrived, would be operational by October 1, 1965. An air brigade was being formed: 60% of the soldiers were in training, 80% of their weapons and equipment were in storage, and the planes would be arriving a few at a time between 1966 and 1968.
Navy – a squadron of missile boats was being set up: 70% of the manpower was in training, 80% of their weapons and equipment were in warehouses; and the vessels could be expected to arrive in 1966–1967.
General staff units began to be formed in 1966. Work on this matter was still in progress.
B Facilities
The UAC transferred £2.7 million to establish military camps for the new (infantry) forces and airbases. The locations of the two infantry brigades' camps had been selected. Work had begun on the construction of two airfields. The money for them came from the budget for the construction of the airbase.
C Acquisitions
Syria signed acquisitions deals valued at £40 million land and air equipment (excluding communications, engineering and air defense). The UAC allotted the Syrians £3 million.
The UAC commander expressed his satisfaction that the build-up was "progressing in orderly fashion."[45]

The Strengthening of the Lebanese Army[46]

The following budget proposal was approved in the January 1965 mini-summit for strengthening the Lebanese army in 1965:

1 Approximately £130,000 for the establishment of the ground forces in the first year.
2 £124.000 for the local needs of two infantry battalions and one artillery battalion in the first year.
3 £900.000 for the construction of an airbase in the first year.
4 Approximately £24,000 to complete facilities for general staff units.
5 Approximately £198,000 for maintenance.

The UAC recommended postponing the decision on the naval forces until the air force issue was decided since the latter had priority. Amer informed the third summit that the Lebanese build-up had been limited to its ground forces. The following details describe the build-up of the Lebanese army:

A New units
1 On September 1, 1964 the Lebanese army began forming two infantry battalions at 80% manpower and 90% of the equipment and weapons.
2 In August 1965 a third infantry battalion began to be formed.
3 An artillery battalion was being set up at 75% of its manpower and 90% of its equipment and weapons.
4 No progress had been made in strengthening the Lebanese air force, so in this area the Lebanese are noticeably weak.
B Acquisitions
Lebanon signed an agreement for acquiring equipment for its land forces at a cost of £400,000. The UAC approved the purchase and provided the sum. Acquisition deals were also signed for planes and air defense radar.
C Facilities
The UAC transferred to Lebanon approximately £1.2 million for the construction of an airbase and absorption facilities for the new units. Lebanon announced that its airbase could begin absorbing aircraft from March 1, 1966. Construction also began on three camps for receiving the forces being formed.

The Palestinian Liberation Army (PLA)

The UAC commander conveyed to the third summit that he and Shuqayri had coordinated their positions and decided that Arab states hosting the Palestinians would be provided with assistance to establish the following PLA units in their territory:

A Egypt – On August 1, 1965 instructions were given to set up two infantry brigades and one commando battalion in the Gaza Strip.
B Syria – The formation of a commando battalion was completed. On July 1, 1965 two additional battalions began to be formed. According to UAC commander, the number of volunteers in the permanent ranks had reached 60% and was raising costs. The UAC demanded that the number of permanently serving volunteers be kept at a maximum of 20%.
C Iraq – The establishment of a commando battalion would begin on September 1, 1965. An acquisitions deal for equipping the battalion had been signed. The battalion's men would be volunteers from different Arab countries because of the small number of Palestinians in Iraq.

The following **progress report** was presented by the UAC commander, Ali Amer, at the third Arab summit (September 1965) on the military strengthening of states receiving UAC assistance:

A The Jordanian, Syrian, Lebanese armed forces began their build-up in 1965 according to the UAC plan that was approved at the second summit. The result was a vast improvement in the size of the ground forces. Nevertheless, their influence on the military situation should not be expected before the middle of 1966, that is, until the weapons of the above-mentioned ground forces arrived and their level of training improved.

B If Israel attacks before the Jordanian and Lebanese ground forces complete their training in mid-1966, the ground forces of these two counties will not be adequately prepared, especially since they oppose the entry of Saudi, Iraqi, and Syrian forces into their territory. Therefore the military situation in these two countries is unpromising and is not expected to improve in the near future. Even if arms deals are signed today, their effect on the military will be felt only in another two years at earliest.

C Although Jordan and Lebanon have not signed deals yet for their air forces, an improvement has taken place in Syria's air force. This improvement can be expected to continue when Syria receives the weapons it purchased and when the new air formations are completed in two years. These will provide Syria with the ability to partially assist in the defense of Lebanon and parts of Jordan.

D The intermediate-range aircraft (in Syria and Lebanon) cannot protect Jordan and Lebanon from a great distance even though most of Lebanon's territory can be defended from Syrian airbases.

E Israel has exploited this air weakness and employed its air force against the Arab states. This occurred, for example, in November 1964 in the northern sector of the diversion operations in Syria, and on May 13, 1965 in Syria's central sector. When Israel put up an air umbrella, Syria was unable to provide an answer.

F Iraq has asked to pull its forces out of H3 because of the area's harsh desert terrain. The UAC rejected the Iraqi argument even though Iraq's claims were justified.

Given the developments in the diversion operations, that is, the Arabs' failure to meet Israel's challenge of their military inadequacy – especially in the air –the third summit decided to shorten the timeframe of the build-up plan from four years to three, beginning in late 1965.[47]

In ADC discussions on March 14, 1966, at the same time as the mini-summit meeting convened (March 12–14, 1966), Ali Amer pleaded with the Arab states to honor their financial commitments to the UAC so that it could carry out its missions against Israel. Amer stated that the commitments (to the UAC, the diversion plan, and the PLO) amounted to £40 million.

Amer reported to the ADC emergency session on December 7, 1966, that the pace of the build-up of Arab land forces was sufficient (he was referring to the Egyptian, Syrian, and Iraqi acquisitions deals with the eastern bloc and the changes that the Jordanian army had undergone in the preceding year). On the other hand, the report pointed to the abysmal situation in the balance of air forces, and especially Jordan's weakness in planes, although the report noted Jordan's aircraft deal with the United States. The UAC apparently continued to insist on introducing advanced fighter aircraft (MiG 21 or Lightnings) and was unwilling to accept American F4s.

The UAC at the Operational Level

Like any military command, the justification for the UAC's existence and its status was measured by its ability to serve as an operational headquarters whose orders were carried out by the units under its command. Here too, like the entry of Arab forces into Jordan, Lebanon, and Syria, the UAC failed. Nevertheless, we should take note that as long the spirit of the Arab summit (i.e. Arab solidarity) was maintained and the skeleton of Arab solidarity preserved, especially in 1964–1965, and as long as Jordan, Syria, and Lebanon found it convenient to adhere to the UAC's instructions, then UAC could chalk up a certain degree of success at the operational level.

As the second Arab summit was about to convene (September 5–7, 1964) and order diversion operations to begin, the UAC prepared an operational plan for their defense. The plan stated:

A Local armies will be responsible for defending the diversion sites. Iraqi and Saudi forces will enter Jordan in order to strengthen the Jordanian army; and Syrian forces will enter Lebanon in order to strengthen the Lebanese army.

B In order to relieve the pressure on other fronts, Arab forces not under attack will carry out limited acts of aggression so that [enemy] forces will be tied down in these sectors.

The UAC plan listed all the possible moves – in accordance with the forces under its command – for defending the Arab states once technical operations commenced. The plan defined the forces' roles and coordination in the event of a major Israeli attack against an Arab state. The January 1965 mini-summit approved and confirmed the plan which included the commands responsible for employing the forces and the use of Syrian air and naval forces for reinforcing Lebanon. The UAC plan also determined that *"every state was responsible for responding to the enemy's attack, as long as it was not a case of [the enemy] capturing part of its territory"* [my emphasis – M.S.].

After the second summit approved the decision to commence the diversion operations, it decided on the following goals:

A The most pressing issue is the strengthening of the defense layout in the states involved in diversion operations.

B The immediate start of diversion operations.

C The speedy completion of the concentration of Iraqi, Saudi, and Syrian forces to assist Jordan and Lebanon.

In the last week of September, as part of the preparations designed to guarantee the defense of the diversion works, the UAC ordered the forces under its command to amass close to the area of their operations. This was carried out according to the following plan:

A Egyptian forces in Sinai; Jordanian forces on the West Bank; Syrian forces south of Damascus; and Lebanese troops south of the Tyre–Marj Ayoun line.

B The concentration of Saudi forces in the Tabuk sector; and part of the Iraqi

142

forces in H3. The amassment of these forces was intended to help Jordan in the event it was attacked (given Jordan's refusal to have foreign forces stationed on its territory).

In addition, the UAC ordered:

A   One Syrian brigade to deploy on the Syrian–Lebanese border, to maintain in a state of alert, and to be ready to come to Lebanon's assistance.

B   The level of alert to be raised for moving the above-mentioned reinforcements.

C   The level of alert to be raised for air and naval forces.

The forces under the UAC's command were assigned the following tasks:

A   Defense.

B   States that were not in such danger of an Israeli attack would carry out limited initiated actions against Israel in order to relieve the pressure on those states that were under threat of an Israeli attack.

In October 1964, the UAC's instructions were implemented, but not in their entirety, and especially not regarding the Iraqi expeditionary force assigned to Jordan. Changes were also made in the deployment and movement of forces in Iraq, Jordan, Egypt, and Saudi Arabia (on the Jordanian border). The UAC's original plans called for an Iraqi expeditionary force of divisional strength (one armored brigade and two infantry brigades) to be deployed in the Rutba region – H3 on the Jordanian border.[48]

It must be stressed that following the first summit and second summit conferences (1964) the confrontational states were definitely interested in cooperating with the UAC (excluding of course Jordan and Lebanon that opposed the entry of Arab force into their countries). Thus, preparations began for transferring the Iraqi expeditionary force to the Jordanian border according to the UAC's orders. In reality though, the Iraqi force that eventually deployed in H3 consisted of only a single armored brigade. Appropriate steps were also taken in Jordan's defense layout to concentrate forces on the Jordanian front, especially in the area of diversion operations (the Mukheiba dam) and in places where the canals of the Eastern Ghor were being elevated. Saudi forces in the Tabuk – Gulf of Eilat region were also part of the defense plan, and some of these troops were designated to enter Jordan if a flare-up occurred. A Saudi infantry brigade was intended to reinforce the Jordanian army. The Egyptian forces in Sinai would also be reinforced by an armored brigade. In the friendly spirit of the summit atmosphere in October 1964, Jordanian, Iraqi, and Saudi GHQ representatives coordinated activity and held staff meetings with UAC representatives headed by the officer-in-charge of the UAC staff and attended by the heads of the UAC's air and administrative branches.[49]

Jordan's and Lebanon's refusal to allow Arab forces to enter their territory naturally impeded the UAC's planning and operational ability. Therefore, Arab reinforcements remained on the borders of Jordan (and Lebanon), and the Iraqis eventually decided to cut back on their troop strength and return their forces to Iraq. The ADC convened at the same time as the mini-summit was in session (January 1965) and received a report from the UAC commander about the possibility of concentrating Iraqi and Saudi reinforcements inside their respective countries before being ordered to move them into operational areas in Jordan. Although the ADC agreed with the UAC on this matter, it decided to pass the UAC recommendation on to the prime ministers' forum for the final decision. The Jordanian delegate proposed that the issue be addressed at the summit conference. The prime ministers' forum approved the UAC report, and accepted the Jordanian and Lebanese reservations on the question of the transfer of forces (see preceding section).

As for the implementation of the UAC's orders for the concentration of forces, it will be noted that although the Saudi brigade was deployed in Tabuk, the UAC's order for an Iraqi division to be sent to the Jordanian border was an important step. Until late 1964 only one armored brigade had been amassed in area H3. But since it had nothing to do, and in light of the deterioration in inter-Arab relations, the brigade was gradually scaled down; the third summit (September 1965) was informed that only brigade headquarters and two tank companies remained in area H3. The Saudi brigade, however, maintained its position Tabuk, but the Iraqi force was pulled out after the summit because of King Husayn's refusal to allow Arab forces into his country. It should be emphasized that the UAC regarded the dispatch of the Iraqi force to the Jordanian border as evidence of its own importance and contribution to the Arab military effort.

The only progress made at the operational level occurred in Jordan. Administrative stockpiles or warehouses were prepared for the Iraqi and Saudi expeditionary forces, and steps were taken for the integration of the Iraqi expeditionary force into Jordan's defense layout. In November 1964 it was decided that an Iraqi radar unit would be stationed in Jordan and that an Iraqi team would operate it and serve as the vanguard for the transfer of Iraqi air units to Jordan during wartime.

There was considerable cooperation in operational planning between the Jordanian GHQ and the UAC. The Jordanian command was fully aware of its army's capability to withstand an all-out Israeli attack on the West Bank, a scenario that the Jordanian GHQ assessed as quite likely in the event of a Jordanian–Israeli clash or a military engagement between Israel and the confrontational states. Despite the king's reservations over the entry of Arab forces into his country in peacetime, he attributed importance to the Arab assistance intended to protect Jordan in time of war. Thus, the UAC and Jordanian general staff worked out a joint plan in 1965 for Jordan's defense within the UAC's all-Arab defense plan known as *Tariq*. The Jordanian plan for the defense of the West Bank received the UAC's approval in September 1965. Operational command number 1/65 *Operation Husayn* (Jordan's part in the *Operation Tariq*) of September 26, 1965 that was issued by the "Western Front (West Bank) Command" and signed by Muhammad Ahmad Salim, the commander of the Western Front, stated the following in the "General Situation" section:

1 Israel may carry out an aggressive act on one of the Arab fronts across from its border aimed at preventing the diversion of the Jordan's tributaries that the conference of Arab kings and presidents decided on in September 1964.

2 Israel aspires to expand its territory by capturing the crests commanding the West Bank in order to secure the defense of the vulnerable coastal regions where the majority of Israeli settlements are located.

The section "The Enemy's Possible Methods of Activity" listed four methods. Each one described the possible order of battle that Israel would employ on the Jordanian front:

1   A limited-scale attack against the diversion areas of the Jordan's tributaries in Syria and Lebanon; their capture and retention until international conditions were met that guaranteed the cessation of diversion operations in the future. The enemy would employ the following forces in this attack: four infantry brigades and one armored brigade. The enemy would hold in reserve one infantry brigade, one armored brigade, and one paratroop brigade, and an additional paratrooper battalion. The rest of the force would be sent to the Syrian and Egyptian fronts.

2   The capture of the entire West Bank, cutting it off from the Hashemite Kingdom. The enemy would probably employ the following forces on the Jordanian front: ten infantry and two armored brigades, and one paratroop brigade.

3   An attack against the Egyptian front. The enemy would probably employ the following forces on the Jordanian front: four infantry brigades, and reserve forces consisting of: one infantry brigade, one armored brigade, one paratroop brigade, and one paratroop battalion.

4   Raids against diversion facilities in Lebanon, Syria, and Jordan aimed at destroying them and then withdrawing. The estimated size of the raiding force is one brigade supported by engineer units and the air force.

According to the *Operation Husayn* estimate, if the second scenario (the capture of the West Bank) was carried out, "then the enemy would probably make its main attack in two directions: one in the direction of Jerusalem and eastwards toward the Dead Sea; and the other in the direction of the Jordan Valley and southwards toward the Dead Sea."

The section "Friendly Forces" in sub-section (1) stated: "The Hashemite Kingdom of Jordan relies on its defensive units on its borders to repel any surprise attack by Israel until the [Arab] forces, that the UAC has allocated, come under the command of the Jordanian armed forces."

According to the *Operation Husayn*, the order of battle on the western front, that was designed to protect the West Bank, would include: the front's headquarters, seven infantry brigades (each containing three infantry battalions) and one National Guard battalion; the western front artillery would include: two field artillery battalions and one battery of 4.2 inch mortars; one engineer battalion, and administrative and service units.

The order also determined that two independent armored brigades (the 40th and 60th) would serve as GHQ support reserves on the western front with its headquarters in Ramallah.

In the first year (1965), the UAC succeeded in establishing good working relations with the various Arab headquarters and gaining limited command authority for itself which was mainly expressed in receiving regular intelligence reports (from the various Arab headquarters) on IDF activity and in declaring a state of alert in all of the Arab armies bordering Israel whenever there was fear of an Israeli operation.

The Failure to Establish a Northern Air Theater

In November 1964, after the Israeli aerial attack against Syrian positions in the Dan region, and after the Syrian request for Arab air assistance, the UAC proposed (apparently at Syria's initiative) to set up a "northern air theater" that would fully coordinate air defense among Syria, Jordan, Lebanon, and the Iraqi air units assigned to this theater of operations. All the parties accepted the proposal, and some progress in coordination began to be made, especially in air communications which was operated from a control center in Ajlun, Jordan. However the Egyptians demanded that an Egyptian officer be in charge of the "theater" and be under the command of the UAC commander, and acceptable to him. The Egyptians believed that the officer would make certain that the Syrians were restrained. But the Syrians rejected the proposal. On January 9, 1965 the ADC (that met within the framework of the mini-summit) approved the UAC's recommendation to establish an "air operations group" (or air operational theater) that would be staffed by officers from the aforementioned countries and that would deal with coordination of the air effort and command of the air units of these countries. The idea was to establish a unified command for air defense consisting of Syria, Lebanon, and Jordan. Practical discussions were held in Lebanon and Jordan, and progress was made in coordinating the air communications that would be run from an air control center in Ajlun, Jordan.

On May 25, 1965, during the ADC discussions (that were held within the framework of the Arab prime ministers conference), and against the backdrop of Israel's attack on water diversion operations in Syria, the Syrians demanded air reinforcements with " enough clout" to intervene immediately if Israel attacked again. Ali Amer replied to the Syrian demand by suggesting that a command center for the "air operations group" (*majmu'at 'amaliyat jawiya*) be set up and directed by a senior officer. He proposed appointing "a capable Egyptian officer" for the role; but Syrian prime minister Atasi wanted a Syrian commander to be in charge since Syria would be the largest air power in the group. Amer opposed this, claiming that "it was his direct responsibility to choose senior commanders lest the responsibility of command be divided into separate secondary commands that would not be subordinate to the supreme command." Amer demanded that the air units include ten to twelve squadrons (for reinforcing all the fronts) subordinate to the UAC command. In discussions that took place at the mini-summit, the Syrian chief-of-staff charged that the UAC had taken no action, the Arab states had stayed out of the battle, and the Egyptian air force should have carried out a retaliatory operation in response to the IDF's attack against the diversion works. The UAC commander rejoined that Egypt had been prepared to send a squadron to Syria under Egyptian command, but Syria had rejected this and insisted that the squadron come under Syrian command.[50] As noted, Amer repeated his demand at the third summit for an increase in the number of the air combat units under UAC command to at least four squadrons and their deployment in countries neighboring Israel since the planes were unable to operate at greater distances.

During the ADC discussion on the UAC commander's report (within the framework of the third Arab summit in September 1965), the Syrians repeated their demand to have Iraqi, Saudi, Syrian and Egyptian forces concentrated in Jordan and Lebanon and on the Sinai border, and to transfer fighter squadrons and air defense equipment from countries neighboring Israel, and from more distant countries that could supply them, in order to strengthen the air defense layouts in Syria, Lebanon, and Jordan. Syria demanded that the UAC receive more than the four squadrons (the amount the UAC commander had asked for), but six or ten squadrons in addition to air defense weapons such as anti-aircraft cannon. The Syrian chief-of-staff, Fahd al-Sha'ir, reaffirmed Syria's right to appoint a Syrian commander to the "air operations group." He stated that Syria was contributing the largest number of aircraft and airbases that would be coming under the group's command, and that the Syrian commander was more familiar with conditions in the theater. He claimed that Syria had no wish to become an obstacle to the UAC, and would accept the UAC's choice of an Egyptian officer-in-charge on condition that the UAC reexamine the commander's and the group's authorities in joint talks between Syria and the UAC. When the ADC met on September 11, 1965, it sanctioned the decision for the establishment of "an air operations group whose task would be to coordinate its members' air operations." The UAC commander was authorized "to alter the military plan that has been approved in the present council meeting if the need arises, without having to return to the council."[51] Until the Six Day War no substantial progress was made on this matter.

Jordan felt that the UAC had proved inadequate in the Samu' raid of November 13, 1966. Jordan accused it of ineptitude. The UAC regarded the ADC's emergency meeting of December 7, 1966 as an attempt to reaffirm the ADC's faith in the UAC, its operational plans, and its plans for a build-up. On the eve of the ADC meeting, the UAC put the Arab armies on a state of alert and ordered the amassment of forces for the defense of Jordan.

The Arab (UAC) Position on Israel's Nuclear Project

The issue of nuclear research or, as the Arabs claimed, Israel's development of a non-conventional weapon, was raised in inter-Arab forums during the period under discussion, as the Arab–Israeli conflict and the water struggle deteriorated. Nasir's declaration of December 23, 1960 received wide publicity: "If we are convinced that Israel is producing an atom bomb, this spells the beginning of war between us and Israel, since we cannot allow Israel to produce an atom bomb. Our attack against the source of aggression will be unavoidable."[52]

This statement was made during the period of Egyptian–Syrian unity and at the height of Nasir's campaign to promote the Palestinian problem. A different position on Israel's nuclear development had been expressed, as stated, in the Arab chiefs-of-staff meeting in April 1961. The subject was brought up for discussion especially in light of publication in the West about Israel's nuclear plans. During these talks the Syrians exhibited an aggressive position in line with their position on the conflict in general. The Syrians raised the issue in the second Arab summit. They demanded the strengthening of the Arab armies' atomic, bacteriological, and chemical (ABC) capability. At the end of the discussion, the second summit decided to establish the "Joint Arab Council for Atomic Research for Peaceful Purposes (JACARPP) within the Arab League."[53]

On January 9, 1965, the secretary-general of the Arab League circulated the mini-summit's agenda which included section 6, entitled "the Joint Arab Science Council for the Use of the Atom for Peaceful Purposes [JACUAPP]." The secretary-general's detailed report and section 6 stated that only a number of Arab states – Jordan, Saudi Arabia, Egypt, and Lebanon – had appointed representatives to the council. Yemen had not sent a delegate. He called on the rest of the Arab states to comply with the second summit's decision and dispatch representatives to the council.[54] The issue of appointing representatives to the council resurfaced in the mini-summit in May 1965. The summit's decisions included the request that member states in the league that "had not joined the JASCUAPP yet" do so. The current members of the council were Jordan, Sudan, Syria, Iraq, Egypt, Lebanon, and Morocco.[55]

The third summit engaged in a more detailed discussion following the increase in the number of publications dealing with Israel's nuclear development. The UAC commander's report to the third summit acknowledged the growing number of reports about Israel's widespread activity in ABC weapons. Amer claimed that although Israel was trying to camouflage this activity in civilian guise, it fully intended to develop its ABC capability. He estimated that Israel's motives were based on the objective logic that it had to pursue development this area because it was the only way it could freeze the present situation and guarantee its survival in a hostile environment. He concluded by saying that if Israel succeeded in producing a nuclear weapon, the Arab states would find themselves in an inferior position that Israel was likely to exploit in order to dictate conditions. The UAC commander asked that the implementation of the second summit's decision to establish the JASCUAPP be advanced. He emphasized that it had to be advanced even if this entailed enormous material output since the borderline between the goals of war and peace was thin.[56]

When the ADC met (during the third summit in September 1965), the Syrian chief-of-staff, Fahd al-Sha'ir, reiterated Syria's demand (that had been raised in the second summit) to strengthen the Arab armies' ABC capability, after claiming that Israel had already gained possession of bacteriological and chemical weapons. He even alleged that Israel had armed various sized bombs with these weapons, and that Israel's nuclear reactors were capable of producing radioactive material for use in bomb production. He also professed that Israel was likely to complete its production of a nuclear bomb in a few years. The Syrian chief-of-staff expressed his concern that the Arab states' conventional arsenal would prove incapable of repelling Israel's ABC weaponry. For this reason he demanded that the Arabs draw up plans as soon as possible for the production of similar weapons. He was referring in particular to countries like Egypt, Iraq, and Syria that were capable of developing research in this field and at any rate were already engaged in it (Egypt was known to have used chemical weapons in the war in Yemen, and Iraq had employed them in its struggle against the Kurds in northern Iraq).

Nasir contributed to the Arab debate on the nuclear issue by declaring on February 20, 1966: "If Israel produces an atomic bomb, then I believe the only answer will be a preventive war. The Arab states will have to move immediately to destroy everything that can allow the production of the bomb."[57] Prior to this, on October 15, 1965, Hasanayn Haykal had written in the same vein: "If Israel becomes a nuclear superpower, Egypt would definitely not sit on its hands and refrain from preventive action.[58] Against this background, the question of "preventive war against Israel" was raised in ADC discussions that were held on March 14, 1966 (at the same time as the mini-summit was in session). The UAC commander's report to the summit was apparently based on Egypt's intelligence estimate that Israel would be capable of producing an atom bomb in 1967. The conference discussed Nasir's announcement of a preventive war aimed at destroying Israel's nuclear power. During the talks a number of basic questions were raised: who would launch the war; how would the superpowers – especially the United States – react; was this intended as an all-out war or a limited operation since Nasir himself had admitted that the Arabs were not ready yet for a full-scale war with Israel. Some of the delegates were of the opinion that even if Israel developed a nuclear weapon it would be incapable of using it since the superpowers would not allow it. Egypt claimed the Soviet Union seemed to be unconditionally disinclined to help the Arabs obtain nuclear arms. In any case, it was agreed that the superpowers had to be convinced – especially the United States and the Soviet Union – to act jointly to halt Israel's nuclear activity and make it clear to Israel that the Arab states would not permit it to be the only state in the Middle East with nuclear weapons.

The matter was again brought up for discussion at the mini-summit on March 14, 1966 (which was preceded by the Arab foreign ministers meetings held between March 12 and 14, and the ADC conference on the morning of March 14). Citing "reliable sources," *Radio Beirut* announced that Wasfi al-Tal, the Jordanian prime minister, had spoken in the ADC meeting (for two hours) on the growing danger of Israel's intention to produce a nuclear bomb, and had avowed that it was currently producing bacteriological weapons. He warned that the Arab states had to "take appropriate steps to meet this danger. The sources noted that the council decided to establish a committee subordinate to the UAC to discuss defensive measures."[59]

According to the ADC's decision of March 1966, Egypt approached the superpowers – the Soviet Union, France, and the United States – and warned them that Israel might be developing nuclear weapons. Egypt hoped to obtain an international arrangement that would prevent Israel from engaging in any form of concrete activity in this field. In this way Nasir's declarations of "an Arab preventive war" should be seen as a means of countering Israel's nuclear weapons development and forcing the superpowers to pressure Israel to cease its nuclear research. Egypt relayed its fears to the Soviet Union in 1966. But it mainly turned to France and the United States because of their strong ties with Israel. In October 1965, Mushir (Field Marshal) Amer went to Paris and told De Gaulle that Israel was using its nuclear reactor in Dimona for military purposes and was trying to obtain enriched uranium from various countries. In Amer's opinion, Egypt could not sit with its arms folded in the face of such a security threat. The French tried to calm the Egyptians by pointing out that according to a French–Israeli agreement, everything that Israel produced in Dimona would be brought to France's knowledge. The Americans, too, tried to soothe the Egyptians. President Johnson himself, conveyed the message to Nasir that the United States would not allow Israel or any other state in the region to build a nuclear bomb. Still on this issue, Husayn Khalaf, the head of Egypt's delegation to the Geneva Disarmament Convention (March 1967) that discussed an agreement to prevent nuclear proliferation demanded that the agreement must have a section that stated, *inter alia*, "monitoring would be carried out by the International Atomic Energy Commission and this monitoring would be obligatory, not voluntary, and on a global, not regional basis."[60]

Toward the end of 1966 and early 1967 Egypt's apprehension seems to have been allayed thanks to the superpowers' response, especially that of the United States. In an interview in the British newspaper *Observer* in February 1967, Nasir replied to the question if Egypt was worried about a possible atomic threat from Israel: "We stated that we would sign an agreement prohibiting the proliferation of nuclear weapons, but Israel refused. Actually, we are not concerned because if Israel continues working on the production an atomic bomb, then the final solution will be a preventive war to thwart this danger and destroy it."[61]

Ali Amer's report to the ADC's emergency meeting on December 7, 1966 contained his view of Israel's nuclear development. He discussed Israel's nuclear research and the Arab potential, and evaluated Israel's military nuclear strength, its capability for building an atom bomb, and the UAC's desire to have the Arab states make progress so that their military potential would overtake Israel's. He spoke about published reports of Israel's intentions to operate a thermal laboratory for producing fissionable material, and thought that Israel's preparations in the production of a nuclear bomb testified to its success in the field. He insisted on inter-Arab coordination, especially on the establishment of the "Joint Arab Council for the Use of Nuclear Energy for Peaceful Purposes."[62] During the ADC meeting, no military solution to the problem was raised. At the end of its discussion on the issue, the council reached the following decision regarding "joint Arab cooperation on the use of atomic energy for peaceful purposes":

1 The Arab governments that had still not endorsed the agreement for cooperation on the use of atomic energy for peaceful purposes had to do so. This was necessary so that it could go into effect as soon as possible for the sake of national interests.
2 The Arab Science Council (ASC) would convene in the first half of January 1967 in order to complete arrangements for the establishment of special mechanisms.[63]

Thus, in early January 1967 the ASC convened attended by representatives from Egypt, Syria, Jordan, and Iraq, but it adjourned without issuing a final statement. Until the Six Day War, the Arabs made no practical progress on this issue.

In conclusion: the following points characterize the Arab assessment and position on this issue during the period under discussion:

A Israel was making progress in nuclear development, especially in light of the published reports on its intention to operate a thermal laboratory capable of producing fissionable material, and its advances in the production of nuclear weapons.
B Israel was striving to develop nuclear weapons in order to freeze the Arab–Israeli conflict in its present state. These weapons would be the first step toward giving it the opportunity to cement its existence, unite its supporters in the international arena, and prepare for the final settlement of the Arab–Israeli conflict. Israel was exploiting the region's concern over its nuclear activity in order to perpetuate its presence in the region.

C However, Israel's nuclear development did not play a major role in the developments on the Arab side that led to the Six Day War. No evidence exists that the issue was brought up in discussion on immediate military matters. On the contrary, the military implication, that is, the production of nuclear weapons, was estimated as a problem still several years off. Arab forums did not discuss the military aspect of Israel's nuclear program or nuclear weapons that it might employ for achieving a solution to the conflict. The Arabs emphasized that Israel's development of nuclear weapons would gain for Israel political leverage to force the superpowers (especially the Soviet Union) to agree to the status quo and guarantee Israel's security. It was for this reason that the Arab confrontation states worked intensively with the superpowers, threatening a preventive war so that the superpowers would pressure Israel to avoid the development of these weapons.

Changes in Jordan's Position on the Eve of War [64]

The Jordanian position on the entry of Arab forces into its territory began to change after Egypt closed the Straits of Tiran to Israeli shipping on May 22, 1967. As it became clear that a major Arab–Israeli war was on the horizon, Husayn asked Iraq to dispatch an expeditionary force to help in defending Jordan against an Israeli invasion of the West Bank. Iraq answered Husayn in the negative, since the king had heretofore refused such a move.

King Husayn and Prime Minister Sa'ad Jum'a participated in the general staff meeting that convened to reassess the developments and deterioration in the region's security situation. The main issue on the agenda was the defense of the West Bank. The meeting came to the conclusion that Israel was primed to attack the West Bank. Husayn decided to take the initiative and travel to Cairo to coordinate positions with Nasir. On May 30, he flew to Cairo. The meeting resulted in the signing of an Egyptian–Jordanian military pact that stated: "Each side regards an armed attack on one [side] or its forces as [an attack] on both [sides]." During military operations "the Jordanian armed forces would come under Egyptian command." Fariq (Lieutenant General) Abd al-Mun'im Riyad, the UAC chief-of-staff, was appointed commander of the UAC's forward headquarters on the Jordanian and Syrian fronts with Israel. He was supposed to run his command from Jordanian headquarters in Amman in coordination with the Egyptian GHQ.

Husayn agreed to the entry of Arab forces from Egypt, Iraq, Syria, and Saudi Arabia to strengthen Jordan's defense layout at the front. Following the signing of the Egyptian–Jordanian defense pact, President Arif reversed his previous refusal to send forces to Jordan. Now he ordered Iraqi units to be sent immediately to Jordan. Husayn, too, arranged with Nasir that Egypt and Iraq supply Jordan with air support. Nasir assured Husayn that the Egyptian air force would protect the Jordanian army. It was agreed that two Iraqi "Hawker Hunter" squadrons would be operated from the H3 base near the Iraqi–Jordanian border. The Jordanians awaited the arrival of an Iraqi armored division (two infantry brigades, one mechanized brigade, and an armored brigade, all told – 150 tanks); a Saudi infantry brigade; a Syrian mechanized brigade; two Egyptian commando battalions; and two Iraqi bomber squadrons.

151

The following is the list of units that arrived in Jordan and their contribution during the war:

Iraqi forces – The Eighth Mechanized Brigade moved from northern Iraq to H3 on the Iraqi–Jordanian border on June 2, 1967; it arrived in Mafraq on June 5 where it was ordered to proceed to the Jordan Valley, deploy in the Jericho region, and advance in the direction of Ramallah. Close to midnight on June 5, the bulk of the brigade arrived in the area of the Damia Bridge, but while it was moving, the Israeli air force attacked. Most of brigade's equipment and supplies were destroyed so that when it finally arrived in the Jericho area its fighting capacity was severely reduced. Abd al-Mun'im Riyad, the "Eastern Front" commander, ordered the Iraqis to send more forces. Thus, on June 6 another Iraqi brigade arrived in Jordan (the First Brigade) but it came too late to participate in the war. Following this, the Twenty-seventh Infantry Brigade and Sixth Armored Brigade arrived.

Saudi forces – On June 1 the Saudis informed the Jordanian chief-of-staff that their units would arrive that day from Tabuk. Actually, the Saudi units arrived only on June 6 (one brigade less one battalion) at al-al-Mudawara – a crossing point on Saudi–Jordanian border. Riyad ordered the brigade to move to Quweira (north of Aqaba) on June 7, but the Saudi commander refused until he received orders from his headquarters in Tabuk. Finally, on June 8, the first battalion's vanguard arrived in Ma'an (southern Jordan). It was joined on June 9 by the rest of the brigade (the remainder of the first battalion, the second battalion, and the brigade's staff). The Saudi expeditionary force – one brigade – was completed on June 12 when the third battalion arrived. In other words, the Saudi force arrived too late to participate in the fighting.

The Egyptian units – Egyptian assistance to Jordan numbered two commando battalions (the Thirty-third and Fifty-third) that landed in Jordan after Fariq (Lieutenant General) Abd al-Mun'im Riyad arrived there, who, as mentioned, had been appointed commander of the UAC's forward headquarters, and was in effect the commander of the Jordanian army. The two commando battalions arrived in Amman on June 3. The Thirty-third was sent to the "Khalid ben al-Walid" Brigade's area in the Jenin region, and the Fifty-third joined the "Hashemite" Brigade in the Ramallah area. On June 5 the two battalions were ordered to cross into Israel and destroy six military bases (airfields and radar stations). The Thirty-third battalion was assigned the Lod, Ramle, and Ekron airfields; and the Fifty-third was assigned the airfields at Kfar Sirkin, Herzlia, and Ein Shemer. They had to cross the border at nightfall. The Thirty-third entered Israeli territory but failed to accomplish its mission. Only one unit of the Fifty-third battalion managed to penetrate Israeli territory, but it too failed in its mission. On June 6 the Egyptian forces were ordered to retreat, but during the withdrawal some troops got separated and others were captured or killed in an exchange of fire with the IDF.

Syrian aid – On June 6 the Syrians told the Jordanians that the Seventeenth Mechanized Brigade would arrive on the Syrian–Jordanian border within one hour, but after midnight (June 7) there was still no sign of it. Riyad contacted the Syrian war room in Damascus and requested the immediate dispatch of an additional armored brigade. He informed the Syrians that the Seventeenth had not arrived yet. The vanguard of the Seventeenth Brigade reached Ramtha on the Jordanian–Syrian border only on the morning of June 7. The Syrian commander was ordered to immediately take up defensive positions on the Wadi Shu'eib axis (leading from the Allenby Bridge to Salat, and from there to Amman) after all his forces arrived in order to allow the Jordanian forces to reorganize. At 22:00 on June 8, the Syrian commander asked for a time extension of one day in order to dig into his assigned positions. On June 9, Riyad informed him that he could return to Syria that evening, which the Syria commander did forthwith. In other words, Syrian forces, too, played no part in the war in Jordan.[65]

Conclusion: The Failure to Establish an Arab "Power Center"

Nasir failed to realize the main element in his strategy: to establish an Arab "power center" for war with Israel. Without operational command there was no justification for the UAC. The UAC's weakness – the UAC was one of the three basic elements in Arab strategy in the conflict as formulated in the first and second summits – was conspicuous already in early1966 and, to a certain degree, at the third summit when it was clear that the UAC could provide neither protection for diversion operations nor an answer to Israel's challenge to them. The UAC (and its missions) was the military guarantee and the main instrument for attaining the Arabs' strategic objectives. Its military capability bankruptcy was clearly demonstrated to the Arab states – especially to the confrontational states. The breakdown of Arab solidarity in the summit atmosphere in Nasir's speech of July 23, 1966 put an end to the likelihood of reviving the institution. Against the setting of this failure, and under the pressure of the deterioration in the security situation on the border with Israel, the confrontational states found an alternative to the UAC in bi- or trilateral agreements, such as the Egyptian–Syrian defense pact (November 4, 1966), the Iraqi–Syrian defense pact (May 13, 1967), and the Egyptian–Jordanian military agreement (that went into effect on May 30, 1967, and which Iraq joined on June 4).

Fariq Awal (General) Muhammad Fawzi, the Egyptian chief-of-staff in the Six Day War, described the UAC's situation and military coordination between the Arab states in his memoirs:

> The UAC drew up a military plan whose goal was the merger of all of the Arab states' military potential against Israel. According to the plan, two independent fronts were established: the eastern front (Syria, Jordan, and Iraqi and Saudi reinforcements), and the southern front (Egypt, and nominal forces from Algeria and Sudan). But this command achieved nothing of practical importance. The name 'United Command' was merely symbolic; it was of no influence either in peacetime or wartime. Fariq (Lt. Gen.) Ali Amer and his headquarters played no sort of an active role because they lacked *bona fide* authority that would have furnished them with command and control of the Arab forces as was planned prior to the 1967 war. Thus, it was a united command without united armies [under its command]. Furthermore, despite the bilateral agreement between Egypt and Syria for joint defense against Israel's expansionist activity, coordinated operations [between Egypt and Syria] was nothing more than theoretical planning; many alternative plans were decided on, most of which were defensive that I personally drew up with the Syrian chief-of-staff, Liwa (Major General) Ahmad Suwaydani; among these plans was an air attack in one wave by one of the two countries. But when the time came for carrying them out, none of the plans materialized.[66]

The UAC's chief-of-staff, Fariq (Lt. General) Abd al-Mun'im Riyad, who was appointed "commander of the forward UAC's headquarters" in Amman on the eve of the war, also discussed the UAC's role in his report of June 19, 1967. His report was entitled: "The Operational Move on the Jordanian Front – Lessons and Conclusions":

> The entry into the campaign against the enemy required early planning. But what happened was that the UAC, which as assigned this task, was already paralyzed in the year before the start of the campaign, so that coordination, in the usual sense of the word, was non-existent. Furthermore, the combat theater had not been adequately prepared, and the forward headquarters, which had been organized [only] a few days before the outbreak of hostilities, was incapable of doing anything more than it did. This was a glaring mistake of Arab policy that ruined the Arab military force even before Israel did.[67]

The UAC, established in 1964, lost its right to exist and became a headquarters without troops, a mere symbol, and an empty shell. The fate of the bilateral military pacts, too, was no better, since bilateral coordination was characterized by improvisation and slapdash coordination. The mismanagement and incompetence was expressed in the way the Iraqi, Syrian, and Saudi reinforcements entered Jordan after the outbreak of war. From Jordan's point of view, they had no influence on the war's stages and results. The Jordanian leadership claimed that "Jordan had entered the war believing that the Arab states would provide it with reinforcements and an air umbrella. But in practice neither of these two crucial demands materialized and the Jordanian army was left to fight practically alone."[68]

The UAC had been established to protect the diversion works, but it failed in its task because of its objective incapability and the timing of the Israeli response. Its failure to prepare the Arab armies for war stemmed from the Arab states, basic distrust of each other, especially between Egypt and Syria, and from the fear of intervention in their internal affairs. The UAC did not become a military operational command with the authority to move forces from one theater to another. The UAC commander's report to the second summit conference (September 1964) offered a comprehensive plan for arming and training the Arab armies. Ali Amer stated that it would require three years to prepare the Arab armies for defense against an Israeli initiated attack, and only if the Arab armies kept to the timetable of the build-up plan that he had worked out.[69] "Instead of commanding the armies, the [UAC] became a body that channeled money and dealt with logistical matters," that exchanged information and intelligence reports on the Arab armies and Israel, financed arms deals, and prepared training and instructional programs. In the end, Amer proposed to the ADC (in January 1967) the dismantling of the UAC or freezing its activity. An Arab diplomat serving in Cairo in this period summed up the situation: "The outcome of the creation of the UAC, that the Arabs had pinned great hopes on, was only a rise in salaries and the granting of special benefits and cars to officers from the various different Arab countries attached to the UAC."[70]

Syria, too, contributed to the UAC's failure. For example, it refused to allow an Egyptian air unit on its soil, and demanded that the force come under Syrian command because it feared the force would intervene in Syria's domestic politics. Against this backdrop, the Syrian Ba'th party faced a dilemma: between the commitment to its stated radical position (the forcible prevention of Israel's operation of the NWC) and its inability to realize this strategy because of military weakness and the lack of military backing from the Arab states.

At the opening of the third summit in Casablanca (September 13–17, 1965), Nasir summed up the results of the two previous summits regarding UAC activity, the authority for diverting the Jordan's tributaries and the establishment of the PLO. He stressed that "the actions that had been carried out are insufficient since the Arab states' potential is great and allows them to realize their primary goal which is the liberation of Filastin." He spoke unambiguously at the summit's closed meeting "about the Arab states' military weakness, including Egypt's. He pointed to [the Egyptian] one hundred million dollar arms deal that had recently been signed with the Soviet Union that was intended to strengthen Egypt's defense capability." The participants at the summit heard Ali Amer's "most important report dealing with the way to achieve Arab national security." Mahmud Riyad noted that the report "was based on in-depth research and included a comprehensive plan for [a military] engagement with Israel."[71]

However, in the wake of these developments, and especially in light of the freeze in the summit's mechanisms, Nasir's strategy of stages came to a dead-end. Nasir had to face the following dilemma:

A On the one hand, "Filastin's liberation from Zionism and imperialism [became] the Arab national goal [al-hadaf al-'Arabi al-qaumi]," as determined in the second summit. This summit decided that "in order to realize this goal, the Arab force had to be properly prepared and had to muster all of the Arabs' military, economic, and political potential." Indeed, under pressure from the Syrian president, the second summit decided "to order the UAC commander to draw up an offensive plan against Israel." Nasir infused the Arab world with the awareness that Egypt had "assumed the main responsibility for meeting the challenge of Israel and preparing for the liberation of Filastin." He convinced the Arabs that the "strategy in stages" had a chance of succeeding. Within one year from the convening of the first summit, he managed to raise the curve of expectation in the Arab world and instill in it the belief that he was finally on the track to the liberation of Filastin. For the first time since the dissolution of the UAR, the Arab world recognized that a real well-defined plan had been decided on for destroying Israel. This was "the era of strategy and goal."

B On the other hand, following the failure of Nasir's wahdat al-'amal (unity of deed) (Arab solidarity in the summit spirit) and the return of divisiveness in the Arab world (July 1966), "a wave of desperation began to flood Arab public opinion, especially among the Palestinians." For a while Nasir avoided openly admitting his policy's failure in the Arab arena "lest the Arab nation become despondent of itself after abandoning hope in its rulers." Haykal's articles in al-Aharam (between July and August 1966) on the "crisis in the Arab revolution" were actually expressions of Nasir's own "revolutionary crisis" and his attempt to explain his strategy's failure.

Nasir arrived at a dead-end because of his inability to realize his strategy for the liberation of Filastin, a goal he had been declaring to the Arab world he was committed to since 1957. This dead-end also contributed to his decision in the intermediary period between May 15 and June 5, 1967 to risk moves designed to prove that the time was ripe to fulfill what he had promised.

Against the background of the failure of the Arabs' water plan and the failure of the UAC, the third element in Arab strategy – the establishment of the PLO and revival of the Palestinian entity – was the only positive outcome of the first two summit meetings. Shuqayri played a salient part to bring about this outcome (see Chapter 4).

7

Nasir's Steps toward the Six Day War

May 13 to June 5, 1967

Assessing Israel's Intentions

The events that culminated in the Six Day War began with the Syrian leadership's assessment on May 12, 1967 that Israel was planning a large-scale operation sometime between May 15 and 22 – one week after Israel's Independence Day. Syria relayed its warnings to Egypt on May 12. The Syrian foreign minister informed the Egyptians of the "Israeli–Imperialist plot" against Syria and expressed his country's hope that Egypt would not remain on the sidelines. Of special importance was the May 13 report by the Syrian chief of staff, Liwa (Major General) Ahmad Suwaydani, to the Egyptian chief of staff, Fariq Awal (General) Muhammad Fawzi that detailed the Syrians' assessment of Israel's intentions:

1 [According to] information obtained from a reliable source Israel has mobilized the majority of its reserves and concentrated its main armed force, approximately fifteen brigades, on the Syrian front, and is planning a large-scale attack against Syria that can be expected to take place between May 15 and 22, with the use of a large paratroop force.[1]
2 The declarations by Israeli leaders (a reference to statements made beginning on May 15 relating to Syria's responsibility for acts of sabotage against Israel).
3 The fear that Israel would perceive UN General Secretary U Thant's May 11 condemnation of Fatah's sabotage operations as though it granted international legitimacy for a strike against Syria.
4 Israel's diversion works in the Almagor region [that Syria apparently regarded as preparations for a military strike].

When Syria informed Egypt details of its estimate – including information from the Soviets regarding a possible Israeli attack during the week after Israel's Independence Day – they emphasized the gravity of the threat and the reliability of the information. The manner of Syria's presentation seems to indicate that they tried – and succeeded – to instill fear into the Egyptians of a large-scale Israeli strike.

On May 14, Mushir (Field Marshal) Abd al-Hakim Amer, the Deputy Supreme Commander of the Egyptian Armed Forces, sent Fariq Awal (General) Muhammad Fawzi, the Egyptian chief of staff, to Syria: "to ascertain the truth of the reports received from the Soviet Union and other countries regarding the concentration of Israeli forces on the Syrian border." Fawzi made the twenty-four hour visit to Syria in order to study the situation on the Syrian front and question staff officers and other military commanders at the front. His conclusion: "I found no incontestable evidence to corroborate the accuracy of the reports. On the contrary, I saw air photos the Syrians had taken of the Israeli front on May 12 and 13, but could not discern any change in the regular military situation." [On May 13, a Syrian MiG-21 carried out photo reconnaissance over the Tiberias–Safed sector to uncover "Israeli troop concentrations."]

On May 15, Fawzi returned to Cairo and handed Mushir Amer the results of his visit that "disproved the presence of any [Israeli] concentrations on the Syrian front."[2] Amin Huwaydi, the Egyptian minister of state in charge of general intelligence, recalled that Fawzi came back from Syria with an entirely different picture from that of the Soviet reports. According to Huwaydi: "I also remember in that period – when I was minister of state – traveling to Damascus with the delegation headed by Zakariya Muhi al-Din. At the airport Abd al-Karim al-Jundi, the head of the Syrian Military Intelligence who was one of the hosts, told me there were no troop concentrations. He even asked in surprise why we were making such a fuss over this in Cairo."[3]

Thus, the questions that must be asked: why – after the Egyptians and Syrians learned the truth of the reports about Israeli troop concentrations – did this warning continue to worry them more than earlier ones; and why did the Egyptians and Syrians continue taking belligerent steps toward war? Did events simply get out of control? Did Nasir want to avoid war but find himself gradually caught up in one? Or perhaps the opposite is true? If events proceeded methodically under Nasir's control, then when did the critical turning point occur? In mid-April, following the April 7 incident, the Egyptians asked the Syrians to weigh their steps very carefully lest they get embroiled in a situation that would result in a catastrophe for both countries. Was mid-May the right time for Nasir to change his estimate and decide that he was ready for war?[4]

How can we explain why Egypt heeded Syria's warning this time and took the steps that the Syrians had demanded in the past? After the May 13, 1965 incident, the Syrians demanded that the UAC prepare for immediate involvement "in [case of] a threatening situation against Syria." Measures included a general Arab mobilization, the transfer of the Egyptian army into Sinai and the Gaza Strip, and the evacuation of the UNEF from these areas. On May 26, 1965, during a meeting of the heads of Arab governments, Nur al-Din al-Atasi repeated Syria's insistence that "if Israel threatened [Syria], Egypt should send troops to Sinai and the Gaza Strip and demand the withdrawal of the UN Emergency Forces"; in other words, open a front in Sinai. Egypt, naturally, rejected these demands, claiming that this was a local incident and Syria's responsibility.[5]

Furthermore, how can we explain that shortly after the outbreak of the crisis, the entire Arab world – "from the sea to the gulf" – mobilized for the struggle against Israel? How can we comprehend the hysterical fervor that united the Arab masses behind Nasir? How can the incredible phenomenon of mass belief in Israel's approaching destruction be explained? Was it only because Ahmad Sa'id's radio broadcasts on *Sawt al-Arab* inspired the certainty that the march to Tel Aviv was at hand and within reach of the Arab armies? How can we account for the conduct of the most moderate Arab leader, King Husayn, who ran frantically to Nasir and practically begged him to allow Jordan to join the war wagon as soon as possible, and who agreed to all of Nasir's conditions including placing the Jordanian front and Jordanian army under an Egyptian commander?

I believe that the background to Nasir's moves to war are not to be found in immediate factors, such as the Syrian–Soviet warning, but in deeper, long-range processes that took place in the Arab world in general, and Egypt in particular, after the Sinai War, and that it required only a sudden factor, or catalyst, to ignite the flames that had been amassing in the Arab world since 1957, or even 1948, in order to erupt into an all-out Arab–Israeli war. Against this setting we can discern the stages of the crisis: the first stage – tension in Syrian–Israeli relations; the second stage – development into a crisis in Egyptian–Israeli relations; and the third stage – confrontation between the entire Arab world and Israel. The widespread feeling in the Arab public was that the Arab world, led by Nasir, was marching toward a war that would resolve the 1948 problem.

Nasir's steps toward war can be explained in light of the historical developments and processes of the two major players as revealed in this research – Syria, which initiated the move that led to a war which resulted in an Arab national disaster, and Egypt, which responded to Syria's move and brought the war to its fatal conclusion.

Part I   *Basic Factors in Syria's Estimation*

Unlike their previous warning, this time the Soviets awakened the Syrians' latent fears about Israel's intentions to deliver a military strike aimed at undermining the Ba'th regime, or even toppling it, because of its radical, militant anti-Israeli position. The outcome of the April 7, 1967 incident created a situation in which only one move was needed to transform Syria's fears into the sense of a tangible threat, especially since the Ba'th leadership was engaged in an internal struggle for control of the government. This time the Syrians responded with near-hysteria that an attack was about to take place, even after it soon became clear that there was no solid basis to the reports of IDF concentrations on the border. The Ba'th leadership exploited the Israeli "threat" as another means for strengthening its domestic position. The basic factors behind the Syrians' May 12 assessment are as follows:

Deep Fears of an Israeli Attack

Since early 1965 the Syrian assessment reflected the fear of a large-scale Israeli attack that would include the exploitation of a local incident as a pretext for a major military operation. During the third Arab summit conference (September 1965), the Syrian chief of staff spoke about the IDF's damage to diversion operations in Syria: "Syria expects that aggressive acts will be made against it for the fourth, fifth, and sixth time . . ."[1] Because of their near-obsessive fear, the Syrians presented a number of excuses and pretexts that it believed Israel would employ for carrying out its planned offensive. Syria's anxiety heightened in 1966, especially after the Samu' raid, and peaked after the April 7, 1967 incident whose lessons served as a starting point for its May 12–13 estimate of the situation. The following factors magnified Syria's apprehensions:

Israeli Declarations and Warnings

The Syrians took seriously declarations by Israel's leaders that Israel would respond harshly to acts of sabotage perpetrated with Syrian support or from Syrian territory. Israel's tone grew more menacing as it became clear that the Syrians were playing an increased role in sabotage operations – especially in actions committed by the Fatah. A climax was reached in the period prior to the Six Day War when Syria openly supported Fatah sabotage inside Israel – this was Syria's realization of the doctrine of a "popular liberation war." Furthermore, according to Israel, the IDF attacks on Syria's diversion works were also in retaliation to Fatah sabotage being carried out with Syrian support. For example, chief of staff Rabin described the background of the IDF's July 14, 1966 operation against Syrian diversion works in the following manner:

> Since the beginning of the year we have witnessed a noticeable deterioration [in the situation] along the Syrian border. The last four acts [of sabotage] in the Syrian sector could not have been carried out without the Syrian army's compliance . . . Therefore the Syrians have been told that we will not allow these provocations, perhaps the worst in the last two years, to continue. The [July 14 operation] was a protest in the language the Syrians understand best – that until there is quiet on [our] side of the border, there will be no quiet on [their] side . . . I advise the other side to remember that Israel alone will decide the rules of the game . . . The IDF has a long arm, an abundance of stratagems, and a large array of means . . .[2]

This was an unequivocal message that placed the responsibility for the Fatah's acts and Israel's future counter-responses on the Syrians. Rabin's August 13, 1966 announcement was even more explicit: "For a number of months now the Syrians have been organizing, training, and running sabotage units for a popular war against Israel . . . Syria is aching for war. As in the past, we will continue to hold states abetting (guerrillas) responsible [for their acts], but now it seems that Syria is responsible for organizing and training these units even though they pass through other countries."[3]

Rabin's forceful interview in the September 11, 1966 edition of the IDF weekly, *Bamahaneh*, offered a precise, comprehensive formulation of his strategic concept toward Syria and had a strong impact in Syria and the Arab world:

> Israel currently faces two main problems with its daily security: the Syrian problem in all its aspects, and the Fatah and sabotage problem . . . The question that confronted Israel [was] how to cause those countries that oppose [sabotage] activities to take effective measures so that [they] would not be perpetrated from their borders. These countries are Egypt, Jordan, and Lebanon. A strike against their regimes might contribute to a quelling of sabotage activity but I doubt it is the most effective remedy. Therefore methods of action have been selected for the IDF that will avoid loss of life, on the assumption that [our operation] across the border will in itself be a limited strike against the regimes and rouse them to take action against the saboteurs . . . This type of activity is unsuited

for Syria . . . The response to Syria's activities – whether sabotage, [water] diversion, or border aggression – must be directed against those who carry out the sabotage and against the rulers who support these acts . . . Here the objective needs to be *changing the government's decision and eliminating the motives for the actions. The problem with Syria is basically one of a clash with the government* [my emphasis –M.S.][4]

This announcement evoked sharp responses in the Arab world in general, and in Syria in particular, which regarded it as Israel's declaration of intent to topple its regime. From this point and until the outbreak of war, this basic Syrian–Arab assessment provided the background for the Syrian estimate of the situation. The Syrians – together with other Arab leaders, including Nasir – repeated this interpretation of Rabin's statements in order to justify their fear of a massive Israeli operation.

On September 18, 1966, prime minister Eshkol responded to the Arabs' interpretation of Rabin's declaration and the demands of Western countries and the United States for an explanation of Rabin's meaning: "The State of Israel does not intervene in the internal affairs of other countries . . . We have information that the Syrian government has taken sabotage units under its wing and is training them to commit murder inside Israeli territory. Israel holds the Syrian government responsible for every hostile incident or act of sabotage in which the perpetrators operate out of its territory."[5]

The Samu' raid served as a warning to Syria. Eshkol declared: "We hope that the [Samu'] lesson will be studied by the Damascus regime and that influential figures will advise the Damascus government to keep the borders quiet."[6] Eshkol reiterated the warning: "Syria is heating up the borders again – the border with Jordan and the border with Israel. I am warning it that this will not be allowed."[7] In a press conference on January 16, 1967, Foreign Minister Abba Eban said that the Syrian attacks must end and that Syria should have no illusions about "[our] strength and resolution to halt [them]."[8] On January 17, Eshkol stated in the Knesset that the situation on the Syrian border was "grave and perilous."[9] The week before Independence Day, beginning on May 15, 1967, offered Israel the opportunity to issue stronger caveats to Syria (see below). The Syrians regarded the blunt signals with extreme seriousness in view of the reports coming in from intelligence and diplomatic sources of Israel's "aggressive" intentions.

Tension on the Syrian Border

The tension on the Israeli–Syrian border also heightened Syria's fears of a massive Israeli attack. *Three main problems* amplified the border tensions that the Syrians generally feared Israel would exploit to attack them:

1 The conflict over the status of the demilitarized zones. The legal status of these areas had been defined in the Armistice Agreement signed by Israel and Syria. The Syrians were opposed to any form of Israeli use of these areas[10] within a two-mile radius of the Israeli part even if only for agricultural purposes. On occasion the dispute over the zones had developed into an exchange of fire and serious clash, such as the April 7, 1967 incident. In closed Arab forums the Syrians expressed their anxiety that "Israel would continue to implement its plan to gain control of demilitarized zones that had originally been Arab lands. [Israel's] goal is to attain the international borders of Filastin, and to achieve this goal it wants to dominate all of the lands necessary. Hence, we must take steps that will enable us to deal with this aggression if it develops into a large-scale armed clash." The Syrians figured that Israel intended "to create a viable border between itself and the Arab states – with Filastin's international borders as the border – so that it could be used as a springboard for further offensives and counter the Arab plan for making use of the Jordan's water."[11]

In light of Syria's assumptions, we can understand the extremely hard-line position it exhibited toward Israeli activity in the demilitarized zones – especially, the shooting at Israeli "agricultural" workers. Syria expressed its basic position during a series of unofficial talks proposed by General Odd Bull, head of the UN Observers, which was aimed at resolving the question of work operations in the demilitarized zones. In January 1967 the talks were held within the framework of the Armistice Commission under UN mediation after Syria and Israel agreed to the secretary general's proposal.

On January 6, 1967 the Syrian spokesman announced that Syria had agreed to take part in the talks: "The situation on the Israeli–Syrian border confirms Israel's aggressive plans that include the concentration of forces, to pressure Syria. Syria holds Israel responsible for any aggression and links Israel's suspicious movements with plots now being made against the interests of the Arab people."[12] The same day, Foreign Minister Abba Eban explained Israel's position, noting that the dispute along the northern border with Syria was much larger than the question of the demilitarized zones: "The sovereignty of the demilitarized zones has been on the Israeli–Syrian Armistice Commission's agenda for many years as the leading issue for discussion. This issue runs counter to the Armistice Agreement. Israel cannot allow the Syrians any form of intervention in the demilitarized zones. This is why Israel no longer participates in the commission's meetings." And he added, "The question of farming operations is only one part of a long list of Syrian provocations, including sabotage penetration by gangs of murderers."[13]

The first meeting of the Israeli–Syrian Armistice Commission took place on January 25, 1967, with both sides agreeing to the UN's outline of the agenda: "To determine practical arrangements for the problem of cultivation in the demilitarized zones with the goal of guaranteeing the farmers and settlers in the region a peaceful atmosphere." At the end of the first meeting and in the wake of Israeli maneuvers, the UN published the following announcement: "Both sides re-affirmed their commitment to refrain from any type of hostile or aggressive activity during the period of the talks."[14] Syria was not pleased with the UN announcement since it made Syria appear to have capitulated to Israel's demands. Therefore the regime embarked upon an information campaign emphasizing that Syria had made no commitments and that no agreement had been reached. On January 24 the Syrian spokesman declared: "Israel's claim to sovereignty in the demilitarized zone is totally unfounded, and according to the Armistice Agreement and Security Council resolution no armed Israeli or military personnel is allowed to enter the demilitarized zone." The Syrians also stressed that they would not serve as Israel's policeman in the future. "Quiet in the demilitarized zone does not mean there will be quiet in the occupied territory."[15] The Syrian minister of information announced: "Israel must evacuate the areas, and Odd Bull must demand this of the state of gangs."[16] Thus, on January 29, 1967 during the commission's second meeting, the Syrians countered Israel's proposal with the demand that the commission accept the five conditions that Syria would agree to for the continuation of the debates:

A The implementation of the Armistice Agreement and Security Council resolutions for the demilitarized zone. The Syrians expressed their willingness to implement them immediately.

B Evacuation of military and para-military forces from the demilitarized zone. Demolition of military fortifications and removal of arms from the demilitarized zone and a return to the ceasefire line of July 20, 1949.

C The return of Arab citizens to their homes and the guarantee for all to work and live under the supervision of the Mixed Armistice Commission.

D Concerning the line of cultivation in the demilitarized zone, the Syrian side would make their point of view known in due time.

E Concerning the use of lands on both sides of the cultivation line in the demilitarized zone, the Syrians insisted that each side should be free to use the land as it saw fit.

In addition to these proposals the Syrian delegate demanded that the commission chairman affirm the commission's authority to discuss problems of the demilitarized zones and Israel's claims to sovereignty in the area in light of the Armistice Agreement (Israel opposed this demand). The Syrian delegate pointed out that "These proposals do not detract from Syria's basic position on a comprehensive solution to the Palestinian problem."[17]

The talks quickly came to a dead-end because the UN and Israel refused to add the Syrians' first three demands to the agenda, claiming that they deviated from what had already been decided. But on February 2, at the third meeting, the Syrians stuck to their demands and insisted on discussing all five points. The UN continued in vain to pressure Syria to change its position and abide by the agenda that had been agreed upon. The talks were on the verge of collapse, with the blame leveled at the Syrians. Odd Bull, the head of the UN Observers and chairman of the talks, suggested that the meeting be postponed until February 9. Both sides agreed,[18] but on the day before the meeting was to take place, the Syrians asked for a further delay, till February 16, claiming they had to study the subject. Odd Bull and Israel consented. The meeting was postponed without fixing a new date. Odd Bull realized that the Syrians intended to repeat the same demands that Israel had rejected at the second and third meetings.

With the talks in a logjam the Israeli government decided to renew cultivation (in areas near Kibbutz Ha'on) that had been halted in mid-January at the start of the talks. Cultivation began on April 2. The Syrians fired on the tractor. The following day the Syrians again shot at the tractor.[19]

The April 7 incident in the demilitarized zone offered the Syrians a way out of an awkward position. They made it clear to the UN that Israel's wide-scale operation in the demilitarized zone had been carried out while the talks were in progress, and "proves Israel's fundamentally aggressive position and removes all legal and moral basis for a continuation of the talks. Therefore Syria regards the operation as an act that terminates the series of talks that began on January 25, 1967, according to the UN Secretary General's call." On April 8 the Syrian minister of information, referring to the previous day's incident, praised Syria's hard-line position in the Armistice

Commission's talks over the demilitarized zone, and added: "we knew that Israel was planning an aggressive act, and we made all the necessary preparations for it."[20]

Thus the status of the demilitarized zones, sovereignty over them, and Israel's right to cultivate them remained central issues of disagreement between Syria and Israel up until the Six Day War. The Syrians were fearful that this issue would serve as a pretext for the start of a large-scale aggressive initiative by Israel. This estimate was confirmed and reinforced by the April 7 incident. On April 9, Hafiz al-Asad, the Syrian defense minister, issued "operational order No. 67/1" to the commander of the southwest region (Syrian front) and to the air force and air defense commander to take necessary measures in view of "the enemy's reinforced movement opposite the southwest sector and the various indications that the enemy is likely to try . . . to seize the entire demilitarized zones adjacent to the border."[21] The reinforcements that Asad mentioned were probably Israeli armor units that the Syrians had observed and estimated at 200 tanks.

2 The fear of an Israeli response to Syrian diversion operation. Israel's unwavering determination to prevent the implementation of the water diversion plan in Syria sowed fear in the hearts of the Syrians that Israel intended to exploit the diversion operations in order to escalate a local incident into a large-scale action. These fears grew as long as IDF attacks continued against the diversion sites. Two examples will illustrate this point. In early May 1965, on the basis of reports that the Syrians received, or collected by themselves, indicating that Israel had mobilized its forces and deployed at least one armor brigade and one infantry brigade in the Galilee, they braced themselves for a large-scale Israeli attack in the diversion operations' area. Both this assessment and the May 13, 1965 incident correlated with the UAC's basic estimate of Israel's "aggressive" intentions and added to Syrian fears. Accordingly the Syrians requested that the UAC guarantee sufficient air strength for immediate intervention.[22]

In late September 1966, the Syrians again fretted over an Israeli attack following reports from Arab sources that Israel would use a local incident as a pretext for launching a massive operation deep into Syria that would include the bombing of airfields. This information was relayed to the UAC that passed it on to the Jordanians along with the order to heighten military alert. In light of reports of IDF troops concentrations on the Syrian border, the UAC ordered the Jordanians to prepare to implement "*Tariq*" (the UAC's Arab Defense Plan). Together with this the Syrians feared that Israel would renew cultivation in the demilitarized zone in order to exacerbate the border situation and carry out an aggressive move against the diversion operations' sites.[23]

3 The fear of Israeli retaliation against acts of sabotage. The Syrians' fear of a massive Israeli retaliation against sabotage activity stemmed from Israel's accusation that the Syrians were unconditionally accountable for it because of the patronage they extended the Fatah organization, for example, in the form of training. The Ba'th regime mulled over this issue. On the one hand, it supported Fatah in accordance with the concept of a "popular liberation war" against Israel, but, on the other hand, an announcement of this support was essentially a *mea culpa* of incursions into Israel emanating from Syrian territory and thus a justification for Israel to retaliate against the regime. Nonetheless, the Ba'th regime in Syria acknowledged its support of sabotage acts against Israel and claimed that it was not obligated to safeguard Israel's security.

In early May 1966 the Syrian foreign minister, Ibrahim Makhus, voiced his country's fears and warned of the danger of an Israeli attack.[24] He also discussed this with the ambassadors of the Great Powers in Damascus. On June 5, 1966 the Jordanians received reports (that they relayed to the UAC and Syrians) about Israeli military concentrations extending from the region south of Tzemah to the northern part of the Hulah, opposite the Syrian front. According to the reports, a partial mobilization of reserves had taken place in Israel's northern area. The Jordanian intelligence estimate that was brought before the Syrians and UAC noted that one of the probable aims of the troop concentration and partial mobilization was "an attack on the Syrian front [in] revenge for the Fatah operations. [It was also necessary] to take into account the Israeli leaders' declarations about Syria's support of Fatah and continuous operations in the Syrian front area even after Israel had issued its warnings." Jordanian intelligence estimated that if its assessment was correct then Israeli troop concentrations in the central and southern regions were designed to prevent the intervention of Jordanian or Egyptian forces in case of an Israeli attack on Syria.[25] In late August 1966, after a number of Fatah sabotage actions in the Syrian sector, the Syrians were seized with a palpable fear that Israel was about to launch an "aggressive act" in the Syrian [Golan] Heights. The Syrian army went on alert. As already mentioned, fearing an Israeli air and ground attack against Syria, the UAC ordered Jordan to prepare to initiate the "*Tariq Plan*." The heads of the Arab delegations in Damascus were invited to the Syrian foreign ministry and "learned about Israel's aggressive plan against Syria while it [Israel] prepared world opinion."[26]

In addition to fears based on these reports, the Syrians also believed that "Imperialists, Zionists, and [Arab] reactionaries were conspiring" against the regime. The Soviets – whom the Syrians turned to for intelligence information and political aid – tended to strengthen this belief and publicized the existence of the alleged scheme in the Soviet media. Moreover, the Syrians perceived Israel's anti-Syrian diplomatic activity in the international arena and especially in the UN as a way of preparing the political groundwork for a military operation. They compared this endeavor to the one made just before the Sinai War when Israel had warned the international community about Egyptian-supported fida'iyyun operations. Armed with these claims, Syria launched an information blitz in the international arena, especially in the West and United States, but the Americans tried to calm them about Israel's plans.[27]

The signs of an Israeli attack boosted the Syrians' anxiety especially between October 1966 and April 1967. Following Rabin's statements in the IDF weekly, *Bamahaneh* (September 11, 1966) they concluded that Israel's was preparing to topple the regime in Damascus by initiating an overwhelming military act. In mid-October the UAC also became infected with this fear and asked the Syrians (and Jordanians) to find out whether Israeli troop concentrations had been seen on the Syrian front. At the same time the Jordanians learned that the Syrians had received information that "Israel has decided to implement the imperialist plot with the use force within one week."[28] In October, the Syrians increased their warnings of an Israeli attack. On October 19 the Syrian minister of the interior, Muhammad Ashawi, admonished: "The Zionist announcements and behavior prove beyond any doubt that the battle is approaching, and the situation now resembles that which prevailed on the eve of Suez.

Syria awaits the battle that Israel is threatening to wage so that it can rid itself of [Israel]."[29] The Syrian foreign minister, Ibrahim Makhus, delivered a speech at Damascus University on October 23 stating that "Wide-scale Israeli aggression against Syria is very likely, after Imperialist and [Arab] reactionary forces failed to subvert the revolutionary regime in Syria."[30]

November 1966 marked the IDF raid on Samu' that came in response to acts of sabotage carried out by Fatah. Several days before the raid, the UAC reported that Israel might launch an operation against Syria (as the Syrians feared). The Samu' operation itself was reason for the Syrians to worry since they feared that it was a preview of events about to befall them. The Syrian newspaper *al-Thawra* expressed this fear on November 15: "The Syrian people will wage a popular war of liberation against Israel if it attacks Syria." The article also referred to the tense border situation. Only toward the end of November, in order to fulfill its obligation toward Jordan, and claiming that an Israeli operation against Syria was likely, did the UAC order the Arab forces to be deployed in their positions according to the Arab Defense Plan and the Iraqi forces to be concentrated in Rutbah and H3. The order was cancelled in the middle of December.[31]

January 1967 was also fraught with tension on the Syrian border. In mid-January the Syrians informed the UAC of the deteriorating situation and repeated their assessment that a large-scale Israeli operation was probable. Eshkol's Knesset speech that "the situation [in the north] was grave and serious" served as justification for the Syrians' assessment. Their mid-January evaluation noted:

A The situation on the Israeli–Syrian armistice line has grown tenser because of the dispute over the demilitarized zones and the continuation of acts of sabotage in the conquered area [Israel].

B The enemy has begun to concentrate large forces in the northern area. Armor and artillery reinforcements have been seen heading toward the Syrian border, in addition to the two armor brigades [already] deployed there.

C The enemy has two possible modes of action on the Syrian border: (1) A ground attack and paratroop drop with large air assistance to capture the Syrian [Golan] Heights. At this point the UN might intervene and a new situation would be created that would include the dispatch of a UN Emergency Force [as in Egypt]. (2) Satisfaction with a powerful air strike against Syrian military bases and headquarters on the Syrian Heights.

In response, the UAC ordered the Jordanian, Syrian, and Lebanese armies to be on alert and ordered an intelligence effort to discover Israel's military intentions.[32] *Radio Damascus* described Israel's information campaign regarding Syria's responsibility for the border tension as though "it was designed to pave the way for an Israeli military operation."[33]

In April 1967 the border tension reached its peak and was accompanied by a genuine fear in Syria of Israel's plans. The April 7 incident left no doubt in the Syrians' minds of Israel's intentions. This time Syria succeeded in infusing the Egyptians with their trepidation.

In conclusion: From the beginning of 1965 the Syrians were increasingly fearful of new factors affecting the relations between the two sides. Along with warnings and "calls" for help to the UAC, the Syrians tried to involve the Arab military establishment in general and the Egyptian military establishment in particular, in their problems with Israel. Under Egyptian instruction, the UAC steered clear of such involvement. Nevertheless, the Syrian fears that peaked in the first half of 1967 were genuine since their assessment was based on "reliable" information from various sources.

The Soviet Factor

Given the Russians' warnings to Syria and Egypt prior to May 12, 1967 about the supposed concentration of Israeli forces on the Syrian border, it is of special interest to review the Soviet Union's positions on the Israeli "threat" to Syria in the two years before the war. The Syrians found it necessary to turn to the Soviet Union as long as border tensions continued or as long as they estimated that Israel was planning a military operation against them, an assessment that was based, *inter alia*, on reports of IDF border concentrations. From the Syrian point of view the Soviet Union's importance was two-fold: on the one hand, it was the only superpower that was Syria's ally and patron, and supported the regime *vis-à-vis* the Western superpowers. The Soviet Union was the only country that could force the West to put pressure on Israel. On the other hand, the Soviet Union had diplomatic relations with Israel and the means to exert direct or indirect pressure on Israel to deter it from attacking Syria (at least the Syrians thought as such). The Syrians also believed that Soviet intelligence was able to obtain reliable information on Israel.

The Soviet media served as a mouthpiece for Syrian information and propaganda and constantly supported Syria's positions. It was only natural that Russian diplomats and the Soviet media bolstered the Syrians' belief in an "Imperialist, Zionist, reactionary conspiracy" in order to preserve and strengthen their position in Syria and especially to demonsrate that the Soviet Union was the defender of the Arab cause. The Russians exploited the Syrians' fear factor to the hilt.

The Soviet Union's typical conduct on this issue was their response and stand – that they had no knowledge of Israeli plans to attack Syria – to Syria's May 1966 "cry" that was based on information it had obtained regarding Israel's border concentrations and partial mobilization of its reserves. At the same time the Russians noted that an offensive against Syria was possible in light of American activity in the region and Israeli retaliations. On May 25, 1966 Semeyonov, the Soviet deputy foreign minister, informed the Israeli ambassador in Moscow that "the Soviet government has information that Israel is currently concentrating its forces on the borders of Arab countries. This troop concentration is dangerous since it is taking place along with a hostile anti-Syrian campaign in Israel." He added that "it is impossible not to see the martial statements that Israeli military figures are making to the Arab states, for example the announcement by the Israeli chief of staff, General Rabin, threatening to take military steps against Syria . . . The Soviet government *hopes* [my emphasis – M.S.] that the Israeli government will adopt a realistic approach to the possible implications of implementing such a dangerous plan against the non-aligned Arab states, including Syria." In the spirit of Semeyonov's statements, the *Tass News Agency* published the following announcement on May 26: "The United States, Britain, Israel, and the reactionary circles in Jordan and Saudi Arabia are scheming to topple the left-wing Syrian government." The announcement emphasized that "the Soviet Union *cannot remain indifferent* [my emphasis – M.S.] to the attempt to upset the peace in a region so close to the Soviet border . . . Israeli provocations against neighboring states have grown more frequent. The IDF stands in a ready position. All leaves have been cancelled and Israel's armed forces are deployed along the Syrian border. The Israeli chief of staff, Lieutenant General Rabin, made speeches antagonizing the Arab states, under the illusion that Israel is capable of determining its neighbors' political ties."[34]

This was the first time that Semeyonov's warning and the *Tass* announcement sounded like a Soviet "*threat*" to respond to events in the Middle East. There was special significance to this since the *Tass* announcement appeared as an official Soviet statement, and the threat itself ("cannot remain indifferent") was worded in non-committal terms if the situation began to decline. The Russians' emphasis – both in the oral message and *Tass* announcement, even if minimal – on their opposition to Israeli action against Syria stemmed from genuine concern, even if unsubstantiated, over their interests in Syria and the Middle East and their intention to defend them if necessary. The publication of the message and commentary on *Radio Moscow in Arabic* (May 30, 1966) that was based on the *Tass* announcement were meant as additional proof of the Soviet Union's support of Arab interests. The Arab media naturally responded positively to the Russian move.

The Soviet media – the press, commentary, and especially *Radio Moscow in Arabic* – continued to hash over the report (that was totally fictitious) about *Israeli troop concentrations on the Syrian border* [my emphasis – M.S.]. In early June 1966 the Russians exploited Syrian fears by continuing to raise the "Israeli threat to Syria" message in both the media and diplomatic channels. This tactic undoubtedly benefited Soviet interests in Syria and the Arab world.

October 1966 was a turbulent month for the Syrians and increased their fears of an Israeli move. The Soviet media also tried to prove, as it customarily did, that the Soviet Union wished to protect Arab interests, especially because Syria's apprehensions were an all-Arab matter. The following items were published on October 3, 1966: "Israel is making aggressive plans because of the increasing pressure exerted on Syria by the imperialist superpowers and Arab reactionaries. The Soviet Union is closely watching developments in the Middle East and Near East that are taking place near its borders."[35] "Syria is not alone. The UAR stands next to it and so do all the Arabs. The United States and Britain have united with Arab reactionary states in an imperialist collusion against Syria."[36] On October 13 *Pravda* announced that, "*as of today several Israeli military brigades are deployed on the Syrian border*" [my emphasis – M.S.] On October 26 *Radio Moscow in Arabic* spewed out a venomous anti-Israeli diatribe: "Israel, with the support of the imperialists, is waging a political battle against Syria and openly threatening war on the pretext that squads of Palestinian refugees have crossed into its territory from Syria to carry out acts of sabotage."

On the other hand, the Soviet diplomatic channels played an important role in calming the Syrians and trying to deter Israel from striking Syria. Also in October, in the shadow of the growing fear of an Israeli attack, three "revolutionary" Arab states – Egypt, Iraq, and Syria – sent an official message to the Soviet government asking Moscow to defuse the tension on the Israeli–Syrian border. These countries were told that the Russian ambassador in Tel Aviv met with Eshkol and warned him not to attack Syria, and Eshkol's answer was that Israel had no intention of attacking Syria.[37] The Russians tried to calm Syrian nerves, pointing out that by their reckoning there was no danger of an Israeli attack and that the main problem was the Imperialists' exploitation of Israel, therefore it was best to reduce tension and avoid giving the Israelis and Imperialists a pretext to launch a strike. The Russians also advised the Syrians to safeguard their regime, and promised them full political support in the Security Council.[38]

The Soviet Union's position on the border tension (after the Samu' raid and January 1967 incidents) was essentially the same as the political support and propaganda it had given the Syrians in the past. It is worthwhile to look at the Soviet Union's reaction to the April 7, 1967 incident because of the severity of the response and because it was the last Israeli retaliation before the war. The immediate reaction was heard on *Radio Moscow in Arabic* just after the incident and merely repeated the announcement of the Syrian spokesman. On April 8 the *Radio Moscow in Arabic* commentator quoted parts of an article from the Syrian newspaper *al-Thawra* from the same day: "At this overt stage in the battle we should remind the leaders in the White House that we recognize the nature of the battle and know its dimensions." Interestingly, the Soviet commentator did not read the rest of the *al-Thawra* statement: "Whether they believe this or not, when imperialism threatens world peace, then the explosion will not be limited [to the scene of the events]." Soviet diplomatic response came later.

On April 21, 1967 as in May 1966, the Soviet deputy foreign minister, Ya'akov Malik, relayed an oral message to the Israeli ambassador in Moscow: "The government of the Soviet Union sees the need to warn again the government of Israel that the hazardous policy it has been waging for several years is fraught with danger, and [Israel] will be held solely responsible. The government of the Soviet Union expects that the government of Israel will carefully reconsider the present situation and avoid being dragged behind circles that wish to transform its country into a weapon in the hands of hostile foreign forces that will jeopardize the vital interests of its people and the fate of its country." On April 26, as in May 1966, the Soviets published, via the *Tass News Agency* and *Izvestia*, the contents of a message that Malik had given to the Israeli ambassador (though he told the ambassador at the time that it was decided not to publish the message because "it is a matter between the two countries"). The message stated that, "Following the armed attack against Syria on April 7 the government of the Soviet Union has repeatedly warned the government of Israel about its brazen policy toward its neighbors. The warning was included in the announcement of the Soviet government that had been relayed a few days earlier to the Israeli ambassador in Moscow."[39] The contents of the warning, as they appeared in the two publications, were essentially identical to the oral message given the Israeli ambassador on April 21, the only difference being one major point. While the original wording was mainly a request for Israel to cease its adventurous policy that was serving foreign interests, the published version employed a more threatening tone to Israel as well as concern for the peace and security of the Arab states.

Ironically, the "message" was presented to the Israeli ambassador two weeks after the incident, at a time when the border situation was considerably quieter. The Syrians and perhaps the Egyptians and Iraqis too may have asked their Soviet allies to exert pressure on Israel not to move against Syria. The timing of the publication was apparently influenced by the Iraqi foreign minister's visit to Moscow and the talks during his visit when the Syrian border situation and the Soviet Union's role in the region were discussed. The joint statement on the talks contained a paragraph condemning the "Israeli aggression."[40] At all events, the publication of the message with the special emphasis not appearing in the message to the Israeli ambassador was obviously designed to show the Syrians and the entire Arab world the extent of the Soviet Union's friendship toward them, its concern for their peace and safety, and its ability to pressure Israel and take diplomatic action capable of deterring Israel.

Almost two weeks after the publication of the message the Soviets warned the Syrians and Egyptians of a large number of Israeli troops allegedly deployed on the Syrian border. Considering the Soviet Union's policy until this time, it seems that the Soviets were surprised by the Syrians' frenetic response and even more so by the chain reaction in Egypt that the warnings elicited. A year earlier, the Soviets had informed the Syrians about Israeli border concentrations but the Syrian response had been relatively low-keyed. Later, when the Russians realized the consequences of their warning, they tried together with the Americans to reduce the tension lest it escalate toward war; and this, despite their continued support of the Arab position in general and Egyptian position in particular. The Syrians' (and Egyptians') confidence in the information that the Soviets had been relaying to them for the past two years and their recognition of Soviet support undoubtedly contributed to their acceptance of the Soviet warning about an Israeli build-up. Although the Syrians depended on the Soviet Union's backing, they considered Egypt's guarantee of political support and especially military assistance to be of much greater importance.

The Syrians Attempt to Drag Egypt into a Military Operation – The Cairo Agreement, November 4, 1966

The increasing gap between Syria's radical strategy toward Israel and its military weakness that rendered it incapable of implementing its strategy alone put the Syrian Ba'th regime in a state of perpetual frustration. This frustration intensified in proportion to the deterioration in the border situation. Syria remained uncompromisingly bent on a military solution to most of the issues in the conflict with Israel. The Syrian Ba'th regime's main declared ideological goal was the elimination of Israel, since "the Arabs' right to annihilate Israel is a legitimate right." This objective even justified the regime's existence. It also explains the Ba'th regime's ambivalence toward Nasir's struggle with Israel and the dispute with him over the manner of solving it. On the one hand, the regime supported Nasir's pan-Arab nationalist view and his basic positions on the Arab–Israeli conflict but, on the other hand, Syria was in conflict with the Egyptian way of implementing this strategy. Basically, Syria's air weakness precluded its involvement in a war with Israel on its own; therefore it tirelessly sought to drag Egypt into opening a second front or at least taking part in a para-military operation against Israel. In other words, it tried to get Egypt to commit itself to come to Syria's aid, and especially to provide air assistance, in a serious incident with Israel. But the Syrian efforts were in vain. The results of the April 7, 1967 incident, the severest from Syria's point of view, gave heightened expression to its frustration. The attempt to involve

Egypt in a war with Israel became Syria's obsession. But the most the Syrians could obtain from the Egyptians in this period was the November 4, 1966 defense agreement.

By the same token, Nasir struggled vigorously with Syria's militant, extremist positions, venturing to make unpopular declarations and incur sharp counter-propaganda. He avoided any move that could be interpreted as a capitulation to Syrian demands beyond Egypt's commitment to the Arab strategy that had been ratified at the Arab Summit Conference according to his initiative and dictates. He weathered Syria's criticism after the May 13, 1965 incident when Syria demanded that Egypt send its planes on a retaliatory mission against Israel. He rejected Atasi's statements at the Conference of the Heads of Arab Governments (mini summit) (May 26, 1965) calling on Egypt to launch its planes against Israel after IDF aircraft attacked diversion operations in Syria. Atasi demanded that Egypt dispatch forces to Sinai and the Gaza Strip when Israel made threatening moves, and he also demanded the evacuation of UN Emergency Forces. Nasir perceived the Syrian border incidents as local matters that Syria had to cope with, and not as Arab–Egyptian events that required an Egyptian or Arab response that could develop, he feared, into an all-out war that he still wanted to avoid in this period. His position naturally invoked the Syrians' bitter criticism.

On November 4, 1966, in the wake of the changed summit atmosphere (the disintegration of Arab solidarity, the return to two camps in the Arab world, the breakdown of the UAC, the deadlock in inter-Arab military cooperation, the deterioration of the border situation, and the fear of a massive Israeli military operation) the Egyptians agreed, under Syrian pressure, to sign a defense agreement with Damascus whose main clause dealt with bilateral political–military cooperation and coordination. The agreement was presented as "a meeting of progressive forces." According to the Syrian chief of staff, "the new agreement is primarily a political step even in its military context." Syrian Prime Minister Zu'ayein claimed that the agreement would be implemented "in any instance of aggression by any side, even if the threats turned out to be coming from Arab reactionary forces."[41]

Both sides seem to have perceived the importance of the agreement in the political meaning they attributed to it, that is, in the act of mutually signing it and in Egypt's renewed commitment to Syria. Indeed, the agreement made no mention of actual military matters. The two sides were satisfied with the general political formulas, such as a mutual commitment to lend assistance if either side is attacked. This assessment received further backing from the fact that only after the agreement was signed did talks begin for the coordination of bilateral military assistance. Most issues, however, remained unresolved, especially those dealing with air assistance. This may be attributed to Syria's demands regarding the nature and conditions for Egyptian military aid.

The Syrians' growing concern over a major Israeli operation seems to have led them to try wringing from the Egyptians a binding commitment to provide military assistance, mainly air support, in the event of a major Israeli move or even a precarious local incident. They probably reiterated the demands they made at the Arab Summit, in debates in the Arab prime ministers' conference, and in meetings of the Arab Defense Council (ADC). But all of these efforts came to naught. The Egyptians stuck to the strategic position they adopted in 1965 regarding the extent of assistance they were willing to give to Syria. The Syrians' only achievement was Egypt's consent to strengthen its commitment to aid Syria if Israel threatened or embarked upon a large-scale military action that included the seizure of territory. During the talks on military coordination after the signing of the agreement, both sides agreed that if Israel attacked one of the two countries, the other would bomb Israel's airfields.[42] The need to strengthen this commitment following the April 7, 1967 incident was an important factor in Egypt's moves that began on May 14.

The April 7, 1967 Incident and its Repercussions

This incident was of great significance to the Syrians and added another milestone on the final path to war.

Background details: The flare-up took place in the Ha'on sector of the southern demilitarized zone where the Syrians held topographical superiority. Their positions were located on heights that afforded a commanding view of the entire area of Israeli farming operations, which explains why the Syrians preferred to initiate an incident in this particular sector. The entire area was under dispute. The border meandering between the tracts was complex, and difficult to demarcate. A status quo had eventually been worked out for land cultivation. In practice three areas were designated: areas that Israel farmed up to the border which had been marked by the UN; areas in the Syrian part where Israel agreed to Syrian grazing; and disputed areas west of the UN demarcated line, that the Syrians rejected Israel's right to cultivate but did not object to or interfere with the cultivation of areas further west. In January 1967 the Syrians fired on the farther western tracts a number of times, but the incidents usually ended with a short exchange of fire, and Israel continued to cultivate the lands without obstruction.

In early April 1967 Israel decided to farm the more distant western tracts of the Ha'on sector and sent out a tractor to begin work. On April 2 and 3 the Syrians shot at the vehicle with machine-guns and anti-tank weapons. After the IDF returned fire, the tractor drove out of harm's way. On April 7, following three consecutive days of rain during which the work stopped, the Israelis renewed the farming operations. When a tractor entered the western area at 09:30, the Syrians opened fire on the vehicle. An exchange of shots ensued and the Syrians brought down artillery and tanks fire on the tractor, and then began shelling civilian settlements in the Ein Gev and Gadot sectors. Thus the Syrians employed the new strategy they had declared, according to which, Israeli settlements would be shelled in response to IDF fire on Syrian positions. The Israeli air force attacked the Syrian positions that had bombarded the kibbutzim. In the ensuing dogfight, six Syrian aircraft were shot down. In the course of the entire incident the Israeli Air Force (IAF) performed 171 sorties (84 attacks, 52 interceptions and patrols, and 35 scrambles that remained outside the combat zone).

The Israelis suffered one killed and one wounded. One hundred and fifty Syrian shells fell on Kibbutz Gadot. Most of the artillery aimed at Kibbutz Ein Gev landed in the Sea of Galilee and a few shells hit Kibbutz Tel Katzir.[43]

The incident did not surprise the Syrians. They expected that the Israelis would try to cultivate the land. On April 7 they were prepared for a "routine" flare-up in which both sides would use various weapons, including tanks. Their expectation stemmed from earlier Israeli declarations and from Israel's cultivation of the farther westerns tracts at the beginning of April. At the start of the incident the Syrians were careful not to overstep the standard "rules of the game" by shelling Israeli settlements lest they give Israel a pretext for calling in its air power. The second stage of the incident began when the IDF ordered its planes to bomb Syrian artillery positions and fire-bases. After the IAF entered the battle at 13:35 and penetrated Syrian airspace between Quneitra and Damascus, two Syrian planes were bagged at 13:58. Between 14:57 and 15:30 the Syrians started shelling the civilian settlements of Kibbutz Ein Gev and Kibbutz Gadot. Two other reasons for Syria's heavy-handed response: April 7 was the anniversary of the founding of the Ba'th regime, and the decision had been made for the immediate implementation of the "new strategy" of targeting civilian settlements. In the ensuing dogfights four more Syrian MiGs were downed. Syrian losses amounted to six planes, five soldiers killed, and several wounded.

The Syrians undoubtedly felt that the severity of the incident, and in particular the heavy losses, were a major departure from their predictions. A top-secret report dated April 27, 1967 from the commander of the southwest region (Syrian front), Aqid (Colonel) Ahmad al-Amir Mahmud, to the Syrian defense minister, contained a summary of the main lessons derived from the incident. The report's analysis rather candidly discussed the positive and negative sides in the Syrian army's fighting methods. The following points are worthy of mention:

1 The combat actions of April 7, 1967 are considered to be the largest operations to have taken place in the region. The enemy had preplanned these operationst all levels. Their direct reason was the forcible cultivation of a tract that we were determined to prevent. According to observations of the enemy's response and their concentration of forces in the air and on the ground, *it seems obvious that he planned and decided ahead of time to engage in combat* [my emphasis – M.S.].

2 The main features of the operations: The enemy's total reliance on its air force, and its concentration of direct-laying ground fire on the important frontline positions that it wanted to destroy and paralyze.

3 The enemy succeeded in determining the timing of the battle and achieving the surprise factor that he had been lacking for considerable time. On the other hand, the enemy failed to conceal his preparations, so that the battle was expected.

4 The enemy made intensive use of his air force in order to silence our artillery emplacements and destroy our positions. He relied on his air superiority, as he perceives it, in order to overcome our topographical advantage.

5 The enemy acted according to the principle of concentrated power in order to achieve superiority. He deployed a tank company and a base for launching anti-tank guided missiles as well as mortars, static weapons, and Spanu-type heavy machine-guns in the Ha'on–Tel Katzir sector.

6 The enemy's planes dropped bombs weighing 250–500 kilograms that accurately hit their targets because of the enemy's domination in the air.

7 The enemy tried to limit the cause of the incident to the cultivation of land. When the first and second tractors were hit, the enemy exchanged them for a third one and then a fourth that also received hits.[44]

The Armistice Commission was handed an official complaint from the Syrians, and at the same time the Syrian military spokesman made a statement that was broadcast on *Radio Damascus* on April 7 at 21:20:

> For the third time in one week an Israeli tractor entered the disputed area in the demilitarized zone. Since the Israelis persisted in their aggression, and despite a warning, the only thing left to do was answer the Israelis in the only language they understand, and we opened fire and destroyed the Israeli tractor. Our forces destroyed two additional tractors and two tanks, and then the Zionist state went berserk and at 13:40 called in its planes to join the battle. At the same time our artillery shelled the enemy's positions in the occupied areas, completely destroyed its military positions, and caused severe damage to the kibbutzim of Ein Gev, Tel Katzir, and Gadot. Our losses: five killed, several wounded, and five planes [shot down].

The Syrians' propaganda-information campaign that was designed for both domestic consumption and the Arab world focused on two main points: *first*, the April 7, 1967 incident proved that Syria had successfully implemented the "new strategy" which caused the Israelis heavier losses than the Syrians suffered. *Second*, the Syrians were not satisfied with the defense strategy but with integrating it into an offensive within the framework of a "popular liberation war." The Syrian minister of information responded to the incident by stating: "This aggression did not come at all as a surprise to us . . . We knew that Israel was preparing an aggressive move, and we prepared for it accordingly. We believe that yesterday's battle was neither the first nor the last of its kind. Our goal has been declared – the liberation of Filastin and annihilation of the Zionist entity." On the other hand, in the international arena and UN, the Syrian information machine claimed that the latest incidents had been contrived and preplanned by Israel. Syria requested that its general demands regarding the demilitarized zones be observed, that is, the removal of all Israeli military installation and the return of Arab citizens to their homes.[45]

On April 8 *Radio Damascus* reiterated that Syria was not responsible for Israel's security and that the Syrian army would not stand in the way of the fida'iyyun. Indeed, in the period between April 7 and May 15 the focus of Israeli–Syrian tension transferred from the cultivation of disputed areas in the demilitarized zone to the escalation of sabotage activity carried out with Syrian support from both the Syrian and Lebanese borders, and perpetrated by Syrian Palestinian commandos. According to the Syrians this activity was in retaliation for the April 7 incident.[46]

In conclusion: According to the Syrian assessment of the incident, as relayed to the Egyptian delegation headed by the Egyptian prime minister during his visit to Syria on April 22, the Israeli action had been preplanned. The Syrians found evidence for this in statements made by Eshkol and Rabin. The Syrians were strongly convinced that Israel was planning a "large-scale aggressive move" aimed at capturing parts of the Golan Heights, including the city of Quneitra. Their apprehension mounted a few days after the incident when they observed IDF armor reinforcements on the frontlines which they believed signaled an Israeli attempt to seize all the demilitarized zones.

The Syrian assessment that was delivered to the Egyptians claimed that the IDF had concentrated almost two hundred tanks on the Syrian border. The Syrians noted that the hands of American intelligence were involved in every event in the Middle

East. They were firmly convinced of an "Imperialist, Zionist, and Arab reactionary" collusion to topple the regime in Syria. The Syrians relayed this assessment to other Arab countries via diplomatic channels, and Syrian politicians stated it officially. Syria tried to convince its Egyptian allies that the incident put the Egyptian–Syrian agreement that was signed in Cairo on November 4, 1966, to its ultimate test.[47]

The Formulation of Syria's May 12, 1967 Assessment

The Syrian estimate of the situation formulated during the week of the April 7, 1967 incident remained valid until May 12 and paved the way for the facile, unquestioning acceptance of the Russian warning. Actually, the verification of the estimate received an additional boost following the Soviet warning and other reports that the Syrians claimed to have obtained from their own sources. In light of their experience they attributed the highest credibility to the Soviet information, if not to Israeli military concentrations then at least to Israel's aggressive intentions. Syria's fears since early 1965 of a large-scale Israeli attack came to expression in its May 12, 1967 estimate of the situation subsequent to the Russian warning. From the Syrian point of view the hour had come for the Israeli attack they had been anticipating for over two years. Little wonder that after a day or two without any clear signs of Israeli troop concentrations, the fear of the approaching attack still lingered. The Syrians believed, or wished to believe, that an Israeli attack was imminent. They probably viewed Israel's armor reinforcements on the border, after the early April incident, as proof of the credibility of the Soviet warning and the reports they received from other sources.

The declarations of Israeli leaders in the week before Israel's Independence Day (that began on May 15, 1967) confirmed the Syrians' assessments. Israeli leaders accused Syria for the escalation in sabotage activity after the April 7 incident. Eshkol and other Israeli politicians warned Syria that if it did not put an end to the increased sabotage activity, Israel would be compelled to retaliate. These warnings were transmitted not only through the media but also via diplomatic channels. Some of Eshkol's statements should be recounted. On May 11 he told Mapai representatives that Israel regarded the latest sabotage activities with utmost gravity, and if left with no alternative Israel would strike the saboteurs' nests in retaliation. He notified Syria that Israel would take measures "no less drastic than those of April 7, 1967."[48] He declared in a May 13 radio broadcast: "We have proved that we will not allow our borders to be open to attack. We have shown that we are capable of responding where, when, and how we choose. We do not recognize the limitations that they attempt to put on our operations and responses. Arab states and Arab nations should be aware that a quiet border on their side means a quiet border on our side. If they sow unrest on our borders, theirs too will suffer from unrest."[49] Rabin repeated the warning, directing it to Syria. In a press interview published on May 14 he stated: "The manner of the [IDF] response against Jordan and Lebanon was adapted to states averse to sabotage activity emanating from their territory against their will. The situation in Syria is different because the regime abets the saboteurs. Therefore the objective of an operation in Syria is different from one in Jordan and Lebanon . . . Since the Syrians realize that we are aware of their encouragement of acts of sabotage they would be wise to cease them –

and the sooner the better."[50] The Syrians got the message but it only strengthened the assessment they had formed after Rabin's September 1966 interview in *Bamahaneh* that Israel's goal was to overthrow the Ba'th regime in Syria.[51]

A United Press report from Jerusalem on May 12 received special attention in Egypt and Syria. It stated that "a senior Israeli source [Major General Aharon Yariv, the head of Israeli military intelligence] discussed in his briefing today an Israeli answer that would convince the [Ba'th] regime that the advantage it seeks to gain from what it refers to as a popular war of liberation will be its detriment." The source pointed out the connection between the border incidents and acts of sabotage with the politics of the regime in Damascus whose popular base was "very narrow." Regarding the scope of a military operation against Syria, the source expressed its personal opinion: "The most certain and effective response to the problem is a powerful large-scale military operation." But, the source added, "not everything that is certain – is possible, I think that the chances of finding a solution other than by military means, this type of operation included, are good." The Israeli source noted that an operation was required that would convince the Syrians of the dangers of a "certain, possible, or approaching all-out military confrontation" with Israel; "but in order to achieve this goal, there are alternatives between the extremes of counterinsurgency and an invasion of Syria and takeover of Damascus."[52] The original wording of the briefing was without any direct threat by Israel to undermine the Syrian regime – in contrast to what Arab commentators and other elements tried to attribute to it. For example, *Radio Damascus* commented on the report in the following manner: "On May 12, 1967 the *UP* [*United Press*] *News Agency* reported an announcement by Israeli leaders in Jerusalem that if Syria continued its sabotage campaign, it would suffer from a military operation intended to overthrow the regime."[53] This report would have only strengthened Syria's assessment of Israel's intentions.

Thus, when Syria received information of Israeli troop concentrations and aggressive intentions it launched a propaganda-information campaign aimed at mobilizing the international arena against the expected Israeli move. On May 11 the Ba'th Party's Foreign Affairs Department sent a message to "friendly revolutionary and progressive Arab parties," explaining the background and causes for "the aggression of April 7, 1967," and making it clear that "the dimensions of the aggression are likely to be renewed at any moment." The message emphasized that "the chances of aggression are increasing, and its main features and threats are extremely clear. They are being expressed in the public declarations of Israeli leaders . . . and in the Imperialist-Zionist offensive campaign against the revolutionary regime in Syria."[54]

The Syrian representative to the UN, George Tu'ma, met with the UN Secretary General U Thant on May 13. The meeting was designed to discuss the secretary general's May 11 declaration that Tu'ma charged had encouraged Israel to continue with its threats against Syria. Tu'ma repeated to UN reporters his position on U Thant's announcement: "I regret to say that Fatah operations are on the rise. These operations are taking place near the Syrian and Lebanese borders and should be condemned. This type of activity is harmful and is opposed to the spirit and word of the armistice agreements and jeopardizes the peace in the region. All of the states involved must take every step to put an end to these acts." After the Tu'ma–U Thant meeting, the UN spokesman published an announcement stating it was superfluous to say that U Thant's denunciation against Fatah operations "granted approval of the use of force by any of the sides [and]," the spokesman added, "the secretary general repeats his call for all parties to respect the armistice agreements."[55]

On May 13 the Syrian foreign minister called on the delegates of the member states of the UN Security Council and claimed that "the threats that Eshkol, Abba Eban, and Israeli military figures have been making are only new warnings for international consumption and their goal is to cover the next Zionist aggressive act." In his opinion, "Imperialist and Zionist circles are planning an aggressive move against the revolutionary regime in Syria; this goal has been recognized in the declarations of Yitzhak Rabin and was renewed today in a statement by Israeli sources that have decided . . . to terminate the revolutionary regime in Syria."[56] On May 15 Syria delivered a message to the Security Council calling its attention "to the threats against Syria that Eshkol and Abba Eban have been making." On the same day the Syrian representative in Washington met with Lucius Battle, the American assistant secretary of state. The Syrian claimed that his country "could not prevent the Palestinians from pursuing their struggle to retrieve their homeland."[57]

To conclude the Syrian assessment: The Syrian request of May 13 for Egyptian help that ignited the conflagration was fueled not only by the Soviet warning but also by Syria's growing fear of a massive Israeli attack over the last two years. It was also fed by the Syria's increasing frustration over its inability to meet the Israeli challenge that climaxed after the April 7 incident. The Syrian regime came to the conclusion that Israel had decided to topple the regime because of its radical position on the conflict's issues, even if this meant the use of military force. The failure to draw Egypt into military involvement on the Syrian front added to the frustration of the rulers in Damascus. Nevertheless, they succeeded in strengthening Egypt's commitment to come to Syria's aid if Israel threatened or attempted to seize Syrian territory. Once the Egyptians believed that such an attack was about to occur, they came to the Syrians' assistance as promised, and they did this for all they were worth.

Part II *Nasir and the Arab World March toward War*

Strengthening of the Egyptian Commitment to Syria after the April 7, 1967 Incident

After the April incident Egyptian and Syrian leaders met for two meetings in Damascus. On April 10 Fariq Awal (General) Muhammad Sidqi Mahmud, the commander of the Egyptian air force, arrived in Damascus for talks with Syrian military leaders about Egyptian air assistance. Between the 18th and 22nd of the month Egyptian Prime Minister Muhammad Sidqi Sulayman visited Syria accompanied by the Egyptian minister of state, Amin Huwaydi, and Nasir's personal representative, Sabri al-Khuli. The aim of the visit was to discuss all aspects of bilateral relations and coordinate positions on the Arab arena and Israel. The visits were also intended to placate Syria after criticism of Egypt by hostile elements, especially the Jordanians, but also Syrian military and Ba'th circles that accused Egypt of failing to help Syria during the April flare-up and reneging on its part of the bilateral defense agreement. In response to the allegations, and in order to pacify domestic criticism, the Syrian leaders had to emphasize that "the two states had been in contact during the April 7, 1967 incident and that the events had not required Egyptian intervention." After the incident, the Egyptians, too, leaked to the pro-Egyptian Lebanese newspaper, *al-Anwar*, a report that was also broadcast on *Radio Cairo* (April 10) stating that "Egypt offered Syria assistance during the Israeli aggression, but the Syrian command, which was in continuous contact with Cairo, said that it was capable of repulsing the Israeli attack."[1]

These visits were of great importance because they contributed to the strengthening of Egypt's commitment to Syria. The Egyptians repeated their promise to step in if Israel seized Syrian territory. Nevertheless, they were interested in restraining the Syrians from heightening border tensions so as not to give Israel an excuse to attack Syria. The Syrians repeated their belief in Israel's "aggressive" intentions and its "collusion" with the United States, and, it seems, they succeeded in convincing the Egyptians.

The Egyptian air commander and his Syrian colleagues discussed the question of Egyptian air assistance. The Syrians rejected the Egyptian proposal to set up their own base on Syrian soil or deploy Egyptian planes under Egyptian command on a Syrian base. The rejection stemmed from the Syrians' worry over the political fallout from such a move. A joint statement published on May 12, 1967 at the end of the visit stated that steps had been discussed to bolster the defense systems of both countries against the common enemy.[2] The Syrians regarded the visit of the senior-level military delegation "as an irrefutable answer to reactionary propaganda criticizing Cairo's lack of military support for Damascus and absence of an Egyptian response on April 7, 1967." The Egyptians were told that because of this propaganda the Syrian leadership had to convince party leaders that Cairo was totally committed to Syria's defense and their joint plans. Three major issues – Egyptian air assistance, Jordanian propaganda against Egypt, and the Syrian high command's criticism of Egypt – forced Nasir to discuss his views on them in his May 1 speech:

"When the Israelis began their aggression against Syria, Husayn's radio station claimed that the Joint Defense Agreement with Syria was not being implemented and that Husayn was furious over this . . . This radio station accused Egypt of not protecting the Syrian people . . . Everyone knows that the range of combat aircraft is limited, and that if our combat aircraft take off from Egypt and intend to return then they cannot reach Syria's borders. How can our planes lift off from here? I want to tell the Arab nation and Arab people that we have signed a defense agreement with Syria and we are prepared to honor it and to stand on the right-hand side of Syria and the Syrian people. The Egyptians are just like any other Arab people, but under no circumstances will we overstep this [commonality]. If an air battle erupts between Syria and Israel, [our planes] cannot take off from Egypt and come to Syria's aid. The only way to help the Syrians is to deploy our planes on Syrian soil. When we signed the agreement we said to our Syrian brothers that we are prepared to offer you every kind of assistance. If you need planes, we'll give them to you. If you need pilots, we'll give them to you too, without any limit on the numbers. Our Syrian brothers said that they had enough pilots, and we felt rest assured [about this]. Even Fariq Awal Sidqi restated this in Syria after the last air battle, and our offer is still binding. We also claimed that if

Syria were attacked, then Syrian pilots and Egyptian pilots would take off together in order to counter any aerial aggression against Syria."[3]

The visit to Damascus by the Egyptian delegation, headed by Prime Minister Sidqi Sulayman, was of even greater importance than the military delegation's visit. The talks centered on relations with Israel and Syrian–Iraqi relations – the latter because of the distrust still rife between the two Ba'th regimes. As for the Israeli issue, the Syrians probably reviewed the details of the April incident, stressing that it had been preplanned as Eshkol's statements indicated. When the Syrians had reviewed the incident with the Egyptians, they tried to lessen the magnitude of the blow and exaggerated the number of Israeli losses (seven aircraft and heavy damage to the Ein Gev, Gadot, and Ha'on settlements) while minimizing their own losses (four planes, and ten soldiers and civilians). The Syrians claimed that Israel had amassed 200 tanks on the border during the flare-up. The Syrians also were convinced that American intelligence was involved in every incident, and that Imperialist and reactionary forces had tried to underrate the significance of the Egyptian–Syrian Joint Defense Agreement. The Syrians asked the Egyptians to coordinate positions and plans with them, and even made suggestions for role allocation. They also requested establishing joint surveillance of the border (the Syrians were particularly worried that Egypt would take unilateral steps. Their suspicions of their ally would remain throughout the crisis and during the war). The Syrians expressed fear of a massive Israeli attack that would include the capture of Quneitra. The Egyptian delegation assured them that if Israel seized Syrian territory, Egypt would enter the battle "in full force," in other words it would intervene militarily if Israel captured Syrian territory – whether Quneitra or other parts of the Golan Heights. Nevertheless, the Egyptians made it clear that Syria would have to weigh every move it made on the border so as to preclude situations that could endanger the two countries. They also explained to the Syrians that according to the current Egyptian strategy on all phases of a war with Israel, it was of the greatest importance to make sure that the timing was right. The Egyptians' intention was that Israel must not be given an excuse to carry out its plans against Syria. The Syrians tried to glean more commitments from the Egyptians, such as the opening of an Egyptian front or taking of operative steps even in cases that Egypt regarded as exclusively Syrian matters, such as the April incident. The Syrians also demanded that Egypt provide direct air intervention, but this Egypt refused. The Syrians repeated their suspicions of Israel's aggressive plans and the American "conspiracy."[4]

On April 22, 1967, a joint statement was published at the close of the delegation's visit. It stated *inter alia*:

> . . . Both sides wish to inform the Arab masses that contact was maintained between [Egypt and Syria] during and after the April 7, 1967 incident. They also maintain their constant and resolute intention to implement the joint plan that was agreed upon in the joint defense pact between the two countries . . . [5] [This paragraph was obviously designed to counter criticism of Egypt for not fulfilling its commitment to the agreement.]

If the April incident furnished the Syrians with incontestable proof of their assessment regarding Israel's "aggressive" aims, then the discussions and conclusions by the two Egyptian delegations to Syria in the three-week period before the outbreak of the crisis should be seen as the starting point for understanding Egypt's moves that began on May 14. The visits strengthened Egypt's commitment to help Syria in the case of a large-scale Israeli military operation or seizure of Syrian territory. When the moment of truth came, the Egyptians kept their promise that under these conditions they would enter the battle in full force.

In the Wake of Soviet and Syrian Warnings

The Syrians' warning did not surprise the Egyptians. The Soviet Union had informed both the Egyptians and Syrians about "Israeli military concentrations." The Soviet Union told the Egyptians of the possibility of an aggressive Israeli action against Syria on as early a date as the May 1 celebrations. The Syrians received the information in the form of a detailed report on IDF concentrations in the north of Israel. At any rate, we should accept Nasir's version (that Mushir Amer was partner to) of the elements of Egypt's May 14 estimate, following which the order was issued to transfer troops to Sinai the next day. The following data stood at the basis of the situation estimate:

1   "Solid information" was received on about May 13 that "Israel was concentrating a large military force (11–13 brigades) on the Syrian border. This force was divided into two fronts – the first, south of the Sea of Galilee; and the second to the north of it."[6] The Egyptians confirmed that there was an Israeli military concentration but they ascertained "with certainty" that there were thirteen brigades and not eighteen as the Syrians had relayed.[7]

2   The reports that the Egyptians collected from various sources referred to an imminent Israeli invasion of Syria. The reports coming from Syria and the Soviet Union were "confirmed by reliable Egyptian sources."[8] The Soviets informed Sadat – who led the parliamentary delegation to the Soviet Union between April 27 and May 14, 1967 – that approximately "ten Israeli brigades were deployed on the Syrian border" and "the invasion of Syria was forthcoming." The Egyptian ambassador to Moscow, Murad Ghalib, reported that the soviet deputy foreign minister, Semiyonov, confirmed the Israeli troop concentrations on the Syrian border. When Ghalib tried to corroborate this with Soviet Defense Minister Grachko, the latter expressed surprise at the attempt to question [the truth of] Israeli concentrations and pointed out that he even had a list of the brigade and battalion commanders in this force (the list was given to Egypt by the Soviet military attaché in Cairo). It should be noted that when Kosygin spoke with the Egyptian minister of war on May 26, he felt it necessary to confirm this information by stating, "When Israel concentrated its forces against Syria we informed [the Syrians] . . . The reports were clear. We reported them to you and you acted on them."[9] Nasir chose May 17 as the date of the Israeli attack.[10]

2   The Egyptians estimated that the declarations by Israeli political and military figures were overt threats to invade Syria in response to the acts of sabotage emanating from Syria. According to Nasir, these declarations "left no doubt in anyone's mind of the reliability of the information [therefore there was no time] to wait or deliberate."[11] Nasir went so far as to charge that Eshkol was threatening to conquer Damascus and that Israel had been threatening Syria for

several years: "On May 12, 1967 this threat reached a climax that no one could accept . . . . I did not choose the timing. Israeli Prime Minister Eshkol himself chose the timing when he threatened to march on Damascus, conquer Syria, and overthrow the national regime in Syria."[12]

Huwaydi notes that "on May 14, 1967 Amer convened the senior staff at the air command headquarters and informed them about the large Israeli force concentrated on the Syrian border, and the contents of hostile declarations currently being uttered by the Israelis about sabotage attempts against their country, the obstruction of the Jordan River Plan, and their determination to defend the freedom of navigation in the Red Sea. Moreover, the political and military visits of British and American officers in Israel, Jordan, and Saudi Arabia testified to the fact that this concentration was directed against the Syrian regime. Thus, if Israel attacked Syria, captured part of its territory, or destroyed the Syrian air force, then Egyptian troops would be forced to intervene according to the Joint Defense Agreement signed by Cairo and Damascus." Afterwards "Amer ordered the deployment [of Egyptian] forces in Sinai in order to protect [Egypt] and even carry out limited offensives if necessary."[13]

As in Syria, in Egypt too the reports of Israeli troop concentrations and Israel's intention to attack Syria fell on attentive ears. A few months before the crisis the Egyptian leadership inclined to accept the Syrians' assessment of a massive Israeli offensive that would include the takeover of Syrian territory. On May 14, 1967 Egypt's political and military leadership appear to have accepted this estimate. This belief was further reinforced when Egyptian military intelligence added its view of Israeli concentrations on the Syrian border and submitted a report on the 15th of the month that stated: "Israeli military concentrations are still located in Israel's northern region – [numbering] 5 to 7 brigades."[14] Interestingly, the report avoided mentioning that the concentrations were on the Syrian border, and sufficed to note that they were generally deployed in the northern region. This wording was probably influenced by Fawzi's report after his visit to Syria on May 14. The Egyptians replied to the Syrians' May 13 warning, saying that they were following the situation's developments. The decision to deploy forces in Sinai was probably made on May 14 around noontime. Simultaneously the Egyptians admonished Syria to halt sabotage operations so as not to provide Israel with a reason for attacking. In the same vein, the Egyptian Headquarters issued a strict order to the government in Gaza to prevent infiltration into Israeli territory.

The elements that went into formulating the Egyptian assessment appeared in Battle Order No. 1 that Mushir (Field Marshal) Abd al-Hakim Amer, Deputy Supreme Commander of the Egyptian Armed Forces, issued in the afternoon of May 14 at the end of discussions in the Egyptian High Command. The order outlined the political background of the operational steps:

Reliable reports have been obtained lately attesting to massive Israeli [troop] concentrations on Syria's borders with the aim of carrying out an aggressive action against Syria in order to: (1) Overthrow the Arab liberation government in Syria and replace it with a reactionary proxy government. (2) Terminate the liberation movement for Filastin.The Israeli prime minister and chief of staff have confirmed these aims in their militant and brazen declarations which should be seen as flagrant provocations to the

Arab liberation forces led by Egypt . . . We must stand firm in the face of any aggressive action against any Arab liberation state, since these states are, in effect, Egypt's first line of defense . . . It appears that Israel has found the time practicable for delivering a crushing military blow to Syria, the Arab national movement, and the Palestinian problem . . . In our estimate the enemy probably thinks that we are likely to get embroiled in a battle at a time unsuited for us, [therefore] after examining all the possible [scenarios] we have decided to take a decisive step in the face of Israel's military threats and intervene immediately in the event of Israeli aggression against Syria.[15]

At the same time, 12:00 on May 14, the first operational orders and decisions were issued by the Deputy Supreme Commander "confirming the possibility of an Israeli attack on Syria, and the resolve of the Egyptian military and political leadership to send its armed forces against Israel if Syria is attacked."
The decisions:

1 To put the armed forces on the highest level of alert (commencing at 14:30, May 14).
2 To deploy forces in Sinai immediately and implement the "Qahir" Defense Plan.
3 To cancel instruction in military academies and instructional institutions.
4 To deploy the Ein Jalut forces in the Gaza Strip according to the "Qahir" Plan and reinforce them with heavy units waiting for them at el-Arish.
5 To prepare the feda'iyyun for carrying out the "Fahd 2 Plan" [murderous attacks] inside Israel.
6 To coordinate military operations with Syria.[16]

On May 16 Amer appointed Fariq Awal (General) Abd al-Muhsin Kamil Murtaja, the commander of the ground forces, to "general commander of the Egyptian front" with Israel. The situation estimate remained in effect on the next day even though it became clear from the report of Muhammad Fawzi, who returned from Damascus on May 15, that no proof existed of Israeli military concentrations. It seems that Egypt, like Syria, concluded that a massive Israeli attack was expected against Syria and that the lack of Israeli troop concentrations did not mean that Israel's basic intentions had changed. Egypt's was so staunchly determined to intervene if Israel attacked that it was willing to enter a confrontation with Israel even outside the Syrian context. Fawzi's report notwithstanding, Egyptian military intelligence maintained that Israeli forces were concentrated in the north. Only at a later stage, after Israel had amassed its forces in its southern front, did the Egyptians turn their attention to their own border.

It should be noted that the Jordanians reinforced the Egyptian and Syrian assessment by the reports they (the Jordanians) apparently obtained from armistice commission sources about Israel's preparations for an offensive against Syria aimed at capturing Syrian positions overlooking Israeli territory and holding them until an international emergency force was brought in. The Jordanians also expected that Israel would attack the Hebron Mountains.[17]

The crisis with Egypt developed in a number of stages.

The First Stage, May 15–17, 1967: Deterrence and the Evacuation of UN Forces

The Egyptians' goal in this stage was to do the maximum to deter Israel from its (alleged) intention to attack Syria, and clarify to Israel, the Arab world, and the international community the seriousness of Egypt's intention even if it carried the risk of a military confrontation with Israel. Thus, Egypt took a number of steps.

Deployment of a Deterrent Force in Sinai

Egypt's immediate reaction, following the May 14 situation estimate, was to dispatch forces to Sinai and seize defense positions according to the "Qahir" Defense Plan (that included stationing combat aircraft in Sinai). The Egyptians expected that this threat would reduce the pressure on the Syrian border by forcing the IDF to transfer units from the north to the south. The Egyptians estimated that Israel would be incapable of fighting on two fronts simultaneously. The concentration of Egyptian forces in Sinai was intended to convince Israel of Egypt's determination to launch an offensive on its front if Syria was attacked. On May 15 Egyptian military intelligence assessed that "Israeli military concentrations – five to seven brigades – were still deployed in Israel's northern region." The Egyptians estimated that Israel would initiate a ground attack against Syria whose inferior forces would collapse before "seven IDF brigades." If this happened, the Egyptians realized they would have to intervene, which they intended to do mainly by providing air assistance. They also estimated that their defense alignment in Sinai would have to be ready to cope with an Israeli response. They expected Israel to begin with a heavy air strike, probably followed by a ground attack. Egypt's military steps were designed, then, to serve two purposes simultaneously: deter Israel and prepare the Egyptian forces for intervention if required. On May 16 Egyptian military intelligence reported that "Israel will think twice before escalating the situation" – an assessment that indicated Israeli equivocation. The May 17 intelligence report came to the far-reaching conclusion that "Israel's morale is low and a general atmosphere of fear and doubt prevails."[18]

The Egyptians planned to take a radical step that they judged would prevent an Israeli attack against Syria. In addition, the military preparations were accompanied by an unprecedentedly large-scale information campaign designed to deter Israel and "its supporters" and make it clear that the "scheme" would fail and that any aggression on their part would precipitate an explosion throughout the region that would be far greater than anything they had planned. By May 18 the Egyptians had emplaced over three infantry divisions and two tank brigades, as well as two Palestinian infantry brigades and a Palestinian commando battalion, in Sinai.

On May 15 the Egyptian published only preliminary reports – not headline articles – of the events, but the next day the military aspect of the events began to appear in the leading stories of the media. The Egyptian media continued to report on the movement of military units from Cairo through Sinai via Ismailia, and on Egypt's "military preparations for the termination of all Israeli aggression against Syria."[19] On May 16, Ahmad Sa'id, station manager of the Radio Cairo's *Sawt al-Arab*, began his broadcasts that incited the Arab world against Israel. In a special commentary at noon that day he announced: "Cairo stands on Damascus's right-hand side with all its might and potential both in weapons and equipment. Egypt's missiles have been set up on the border and are aimed at Israel." The next day Sa'id boasted: "All of Egypt with its entire human, economic, and scientific potential is now prepared to embark upon a total war that will wipe out Israel's threats."[20]

On May 17 two Egyptian MiG-21s carried out a photo reconnaissance mission, *inter alia*, over Israel's nuclear reactor at Dimona, penetrating Israeli airspace from Jordan and crossing into Sinai via Nitzana. Their mission was probably to search for IDF concentrations and positions based on intelligence reports or the assessment that Israel had started transferring units to the Egyptian front. The MiGs' aim does not seem to have been to gather information on the Dimona reactor in order to bomb it, as the IDF assessed. Whatever the mission's goal, there are no clear indications (not even in Egyptian documents captured in Sinai by the IDF) to confirm operational plans for such a move. During the crisis the Egyptians carried out additional air reconnaissance flights over the Negev whose aim was obviously the same: to uncover IDF deployment along the Egyptian front. The discussion in the IDF and at highest echelon of the defense ministry (with Eshkol, who was serving as defense minister) over the possibility of an Egyptian air strike against the reactor derived more from the Israeli intelligence assessment than from concrete evidence. The issue was also discussed in the Ministers Committee for Security Affairs on May 21. Based on intelligence assessments, Eshkol stated that the Egyptians might take offensive steps such as bombing the Dimona reactor or closing the Straits of Tiran.

The Evacuation of the UN Forces

The important step taken after the Egyptians' dramatic announcement of its military concentration in Sinai was its decision to remove the UN Emergency Force from the Israel's border and Sharm el-Sheikh. (For the background to this move see pages 131–133). Discussion over the evacuation of the UN Emergency Force took place on May 15 and was followed by the decision to oust them because the deployment of Egyptian forces in Sinai was not sufficient in itself to deter Israel. The Arab world assumed that as long as the UN force stood between the Egyptian army and IDF, the Egyptian concentration of military power in Sinai was not proof enough of Egypt's resolve to fight. In February 1960 an Egyptian force had been deployed in Sinai to deter Israel from attacking Syria, and a warning had been given to the UN Emergency Force about the possibility of its evacuation (without its actually being asked to decamp). Therefore, when Nasir and Amer now decided on the large-scale deployment of troops in Sinai they believed that this move also required the removal of the UNEF from the border. The brief discussion given to the ouster of the UNEF proves the extent to which the subject had occupied Nasir and Amer since 1957. They were just waiting for the opportunity to get rid of the UN troops.[21]

When the decision was made, Amer ordered Chief-of-Staff Fawzi to prepare a special letter to the commander of the UN Force demanding the withdrawal of his troops. On May 16 Amer issued the following instructions to the army: "It was decided to remove the UN Forces that have been operating on *our land* and that were stationed here according to our request, but who were used by the Arab states opposed to our regime in their political propaganda campaign, claiming that the [UN] Forces protect Egypt . . . The ouster of the UN Forces may serve as a pretext for an Israeli military operation and there are already signs of Israeli troop movement toward our border." The Mushir ended his instructions on the note: "There is nothing to fear about Sharm al-Sheikh." Afterwards he issued detailed instructions to the Egyptian forces in the event of an Israeli attack.[22]

On May 16, in accordance with Amer's order, Fawzi, the Egyptian chief of staff sent a message to General Indir Jit Rikhye, commander of the UNEF: "I hereby inform you that I have instructed all Egyptian armed forces to be ready for action against Israel the moment it commences aggressive action against any Arab country. By these orders our forces have been concentrated in Sinai on our eastern border. In order to guarantee the safety of the international emergency forces located at observation points on our eastern border, I request that you order them to withdraw and redeploy in Gaza. I have issued orders on this matter to the eastern region's military commander and requested that he inform me that the orders have been carried out."[23] (The wording of the Egyptian request was blunter this time than it was in 1960, when the Egyptians asked the emergency force to draw up plans for its withdrawal.) According to Rikhye, the Egyptian officer, Aqid (Colonel) Mukhtar, handed him Fawzi's message at 22:00 (Egyptian time) and added a curt oral demand: "General, you are requested to order the immediate withdrawal of UN Forces from as-Sabha and Sharm al-Sheikh this evening. Our high command expects an immediate Israeli response when it discovers our demand. Our army must be in control of as-Sabha and Sharm al-Sheikh this evening." In reply to Rikhye's comment that Fawzi's letter mentioned nothing about a withdrawal from these two vital points Mukhtar made it clear that "the Egyptian chief of staff wants a withdrawal from Sinai including as-Sabha and Sharm al-Sheikh."[24]

It seems likely that Rikhye informed U Thant about Egypt's formal demand, including Fawzi's letter, and also Mukhtar's verbal message, calling for the withdrawal of the UN forces from the north to Sharm al-Sheikh. U Thant understood the implications of the Egyptian demand. Thus, on May 17 the UN secretary general, informed the Egyptian ambassador: "The withdrawal of UN forces from their front positions will be carried out only under orders of the secretary general. If Egypt insists on its demands then the withdrawal will be total – not partial, and final – not temporary." Also on the same day (14:00 Egyptian time) Fawzi delivered to Rikhye a second message demanding that the Yugoslavian units evacuate Sinai within twenty-four hours. (The Yugoslavian force was deployed along the international border with Israel and at Sharm al-Sheikh.) Fawzi added that he was giving Rikhye forty-eight hours to withdraw, but already on the same day Egyptian troops took over the UN positions. On the morning of May 18 (06:00) *Radio Cairo* announced: "As of sunrise on May 17 Egyptian forces have been deployed along the lengthy Egyptian border running from Rafah to the Gulf of Aqaba." On the evening of May 17 the Egyptian foreign minister sent a message to the UN secretary general in the following language: "The Government of the United Arab Republic [Egypt] has the honor to inform your Excellency that it has decided to terminate the presence of the UNEF from the territory of the United Arab Republic and Gaza Strip. Therefore, I request that the necessary steps be taken for the withdrawal of the Force as soon as possible." The next morning Egyptian troops forced the UN forces to evacuate al-Sabha and Kuntilla.

Egyptian soldiers appeared in the Yugoslavian camp at Sharm al-Sheikh and told the commander that they had come to take control the position at Ras Nasrani.[25]

The question that needs to be asked is whether the first demand the Egyptians made to Rikhye – to evacuate the UN Forces – was intended only from Sinai's eastern border with Israel or from the entire peninsula, including Sharm al-Sheikh. Most scholars and Egyptian officials who discussed the matter in their memoirs, including Hasanayn Haykal, Mahmud Riyad, and Abd al-Ghani al-Jamasi,[26] believe that the Egyptian intention was to remove the UN Emergency Force from Sinai's border with Israel but not from Sharm al-Sheikh. This view maintains that Nasir did not consider closing the straits at this point – a move that would have been unavoidable if the UN Force had abandoned Sharm al-Sheikh. In my opinion, Nasir's and Amer's intention to evict the emergency force from Sharm al-Sheikh was linked to their demand to oust the force from Sinai's eastern border:

1. Amer's orders of May 16 included "the removal of the forces acting on our land." He did not refer to evacuating part of the forces when he linked this demand to the Arab propaganda against Egypt over this issue. Therefore the addition, "there is nothing to fear about Sharm al-Sheikh" was meaningful.

2. When the Egyptians issued their demand on May 16, their forces were already deployed in the northern half of Sinai facing the eastern border with Israel. Therefore, Fawzi wanted to mention precisely the location of the Egyptian forces whose deployment was the reason for the Egyptian demand. If Egypt had demanded explicitly in writing the withdrawal of the Emergency Force from Sharm al-Sheikh, then even at the outset of the crisis this would have been considered an offensive act toward Israel and proof of Egypt's intentions to close the straits.

3. The Egyptians' response to the UN secretary general's reply was positive and immediate. From this point of view the secretary general performed their (the Egyptians') task magnificently. It was he who asked the Emergency Force to evacuate all their positions, including Sharm al-Sheikh. On May 17, the day after Fawzi's letter, the Egyptians already requested the withdrawal of the entire UN Force from all of its positions, including Sharm al-Sheikh. The demand arrived in a letter to Rikhye, in the Egyptian foreign minister's letter to the UN secretary general, and in a private meeting with Rikhye in which the Egyptians requested the deployment of the Emergency Force at three points that would serve as possible alternatives to the Gaza Strip: Kuntilla, Ras al-Naqab, and Sharm al-Sheikh area. At the same time *Radio Cairo* began to advocate Egypt's right to oust the entire UN Force. On May 17, according to the minister of war, Shams Badran, even before the Egyptians presented the demand to the UN secretary general for the pullout, they had been in contact with the Yugoslavian forces and coordinated the withdrawal of the Yugoslavian units from Sharm al-Sheikh. In other words, the Yugoslavian commander agreed to abandon Sharm al-Sheikh even before receiving the order from General Rikhye.

4. The close proximity between the decision to evacuate the UNEF and to close the straits shows that the second move depended on the first. It will soon be shown that the question of closing the straits came up in the same discussion over the evacuation of the UNEF. Actually, the basically political decision to

close the straits was made late in the evening of May 17, that is, at the same time as the Egyptian demand for the general evacuation of the UNEF. The two issues were linked to propaganda in Jordan and Saudi Arab and to Nasir's statements about "eradicating the results of the 1956 aggression."[27]

Thus the withdrawal of the UNEF created, *ipso facto*, another major problem: The closure of the Straits of Tiran–Gulf of Aqaba to Israeli shipping.

Implementation of the Defense Agreement With Syria: The Commitment to Defend the Arab Homeland

When Egypt responded to Syria's challenge, it decided to honor to the letter its commitment to the bilateral defense agreement. It perceived the threat facing Syria as though it was also a genuine threat to Egypt since Syria was the "front line of defense for Egypt's national security." Nasir felt it was important that the entire Arab world, not only Syria, realize that Egypt would honor the conditions of the agreement that obligated it to defend Syria. Indeed, Egypt took all the necessary steps for the implementation of the defense agreement

During his visit to Damascus on May 14, Fawzi, the Egyptian chief of staff, promised the Syrians that Egypt would carry out the clauses of the defense agreement dealing with assistance to Syria in case of an Israeli attack. Fawzi recalls that during the visit he "informed the Syrian chief of staff, Liwa (Major General) Ahmad Suwaydani, of the military steps Egypt was taking. I emphasized for the last time the need to coordinate the military plans as agreed upon."[28]

The Egyptian media made sure to give wide publicity to this policy. Ahmad Sa'id, the popular commentator and station manager of *Sawt al-Arab*, set the propaganda tone at every stage in the crisis and the entire Egyptian media followed suit. In the broadcast on May 16, Sa'id's style of extremism is readily observable: "Cairo stands with all its power next to Damascus . . . This will be an all-out war; this time we are prepared for it and have decided that all the Arabs will take part in it. Let Eshkol apply his threat and he will find himself surrounded by Arab armies from Syria and Sinai . . . . [Yes Misters] Eshkol and Rabin, [you] agents of imperialism – we are waiting for you at the border."[29]

On the same day the newspaper *al-Ahram* reiterated this taunt: "Egypt will declare war on Israel if the Syrian homeland faces Israeli aggression [against] its land and security . . . This position comes not only from the defense agreement but also from Egypt's unwavering position on any instance that Israel wages war against an Arab state."[30] On May 17 *Radio Cairo* added: "Egypt has succeeded in mobilizing its full military potential to meet the challenge of the schemers of intrigues against Syria and the entire Arab homeland, and defeat them."[31]

Egypt exploited to the hilt its demand to evacuate the UNEF. It goaded the Arab states that had criticized it on this issue, proving once and for all when the moment of truth arrived Egyptian power would overcome every obstacle in the way of defending an Arab state. "The UN Emergency Force has never been an obstacle on our path when we were asked to protect an Arab country or Arab right . . . These military steps attest to our sense of responsibility toward every revolution, Arab state, and nation that struggles for its freedom."[32]

It was equally important for Egypt to prove its commitment to other Arab states on matters of national security. This commitment was encapsulated in the role that Egypt assumed as the expounder and engineer of Nasir's brand of Arab nationalism. Egypt openly proclaimed that it would fulfill its obligation to this commitment, thus it not only enhanced its obligation but also awakened expectations in the Arab world for its realization.[33] The Arab public believed that Egypt "intended to carry out its policy and meet the Israeli challenge if attacked." The Egyptians claimed that "this position stemmed from Egypt's basic principle that any Arab country under attack must be helped. A few years earlier Egypt had put this principle into practice in Iraq, as well as in Syria and Yemen when there loomed a threat to the revolution."[34]

Israel's Fears

From May 17 Egypt's estimate indicates that the concentration of its armed forces in Sinai and the open announcement of this had caused Israel great concern. The Egyptians also believed that their vigorous activity "had provided a conclusive answer to Israel's threats." A victory atmosphere prevailed in Egypt. Israeli headlines proved this. *Radio Cairo* cited examples from the Israeli press: "Israel Frets over Egypt's Announcement to Support Syria"[35] or "Deep Concern in Israel over the Massing of Egyptian Forces near Israel."[36] *Radio Cairo* blared: "The Israeli leaders are now convinced beyond doubt that Egypt is absolutely resolved to intervene if Israel attacks Syria." [37] On May 18 *al-Akhbar* described "the fear that has seized Israel" since Egypt concentrated its forces on the borders.[38]

The Second Stage, May 18–22, 1967: The Center of Gravity Shifts to the Egyptian Front and the Closing of the Straits

The second stage was the decisive stage. It determined the direction the crisis would take, and was the stage in which the decision to block the straits – the *casus belli* – was made. Also in this stage, the Egyptian political–military leadership deliberated the question of implementation and timing of the blockade. When the final decision was made, Nasir harnessed all the power of his leadership in order to deal with its consequences. The Egyptian leadership was fully aware of what the closure of the straits implied for Israel.

On May 18 an Egyptian Borders Guard unit took over the UN camp and facilities at Sharm al-Sheikh. Two days later (May 20) a battalion of paratroopers was dropped into the area and took complete control of Sharm al-Sheikh and Ras Nasrani. News agencies reported that "Egyptian forces have seized the fortified base at Sharm al-Sheikh and have gained control of Israel's shipping lane in the Straits of Tiran. This step puts Israeli shipping in jeopardy."[39] At 17:00 on May 19, when the UN flag was lowered in the Emergency Forces camps in the Gaza Strip, the force essentially ceased to exist. On May 21 Egyptian shore batteries were installed in Sharm al-Sheikh (Ras Nasrani), completing the preparations for the blockade of the straits. The following day Nasir announced their closure.

The withdrawal of the UN Force thrilled the Arab world. It symbolized Egypt's release from the shackles of the 1956 war, appeared as a challenge to Israeli military power, and was especially seen as a step that restored Arab honor. For the Arab world the UN's departure was tangible proof of Nasir's firm intent to meet Israel on the battlefield. It was also an expression of Egypt's autonomous decision to liberate itself from the chains placed on it after the Sinai War. From Egypt's point of view "this meant that Egypt does not want UN forces protecting militant Israel from a punitive act of deterrence against it."[40] Accordingly, Egyptian propaganda highlighted the significance of Nasir's demand by emphasizing the American and British opposition to the UN's withdrawal and their "self-righteous claim of preserving the peace."[41] After the evacuation of the UN Force the Arab world expected that Egypt's next move would be to halt Israeli shipping. "Now that Egyptian forces have returned to Sharm al-Sheikh, Nasir is free to block Israeli shipping through the passage, as before 1956."[42]

A major turning point in the crisis occurred at this stage. The greater the Egyptian force in Sinai grew and the more that Israel aligned its forces in the south opposite it, the more the center of gravity moved from the Syrian–Israeli border to the Egyptian–Israeli border. If on May 16 Israel began a partial call-up of the reserves as a security measure, then on May 19 a large-scale mobilization went into effect because of the continuous build-up of Egyptian forces in Sinai. The Israeli call-up did not elude Egyptian eyes.[43] On May 18 Egyptian military intelligence reported "the continuous flow of Israeli reserves to the front line." The report estimated the strength of the Israeli force as six infantry brigades, one armor brigade, and one tank battalion. An Egyptian intelligence report of May 19 summed up: "Events in the region have reduced Israel's chances to pursue its initiative and forced it to adopt a cautious position."[44]

The Egyptian army continued its build-up by pouring men and matériel into Sinai. On May 18, the 118th infantry brigade was ordered to pull out of Yemen and return to Egypt. A May 21 Israeli military intelligence estimate put the total Egyptian force in Sinai at four divisions (three infantry and one armor) numbering 600 tanks, 600 artillery pieces, and eighty thousand troops. By this time Israel too had mobilized eighty thousand troops.[45]

The carefully-briefed Egyptian headlines announced "the conspicuous change in Israel's position and its retreat from its threats." On May 17 "informed sources" in Cairo noted that as a result of Egypt's moves, "Some of the Israeli forces concentrated on the Syrian border in the north have begun heading south on the roads. A reinforced Israeli armor brigade and three infantry brigades have been traveling at full speed to the Egyptian borderlines."[46] "Based on informed sources" in Cairo, *al-Ahram*'s political correspondent summed up the events of May 18: "The major activity has been the movement south of Israeli forces. The [Israeli military] concentrations on the Syrian border three days ago that numbered eleven brigades have been divided into three attack groups and are moving south today. The force heading south is estimated at six brigades. Nitzana appears to be the concentration zone. Air units that were deployed in the north have also been transferred to airfields in the southern region. The Israeli force now deployed in the south or in transit to the Egyptian border is estimated at nine brigades." Nevertheless, on May 20 *Radio Cairo* continued to report Israeli fear of the flow of Egyptian forces to Sinai.[47]

A trace of irony can be detected in this assessment. The Egyptian leadership believed that its concentration of forces in Sinai had achieved the goal of removing the so-called Israeli threat from Syria. Little wonder, then, that the Egyptian media bally-hooed the Egyptian "victory." This belief reinforced the Egyptian leadership's self-confidence and led it to make provocative boastful declarations toward Israel that carried with them the potential of a new problem – a confrontation with Israel.

On May 19, Mushir Amer made an unprecedented announcement in *al-Ahram* that contained elements of the Egyptian assessment:

> Egypt's armed forces have recently seized positions that now enable them to respond and deter. I wish to leave no room for doubt in the mind of anyone in the Arab east (Mashriq) or outside it that Egypt will use all its strength to smash any attempt at aggression. The time has come to put an end to the Israeli enemy's policy of boasting and arrogance. This policy has recently reached its peak.
>
> The Israeli enemy sometimes seems to act as though he is capable of attacking and establishing facts [on the ground] from the result of the attack. [Egypt's] transfer of [its] armed forces – with great power, skill, and vigilance – to the front lines has overturned the Israeli enemy's position. The main force of the Egyptian army is capable of smiting the enemy a decisive blow. At the same time, the Egyptian army operating in Yemen is fulfilling its heroic role and is being helped by revolutionary forces in the Arab south. I will only say that the armed forces facing the enemy will quash any hostile move on any battlefield from any direction.

Such a declaration made by the head of the military pyramid provides a key for understanding the *volte-face* that transpired in the Egyptian perception and estimate. Amer's braggadocio undoubtedly reflects the atmosphere prevalent among the military leadership and the switch that occurred in the Egyptian command's situation estimate of its own handling of the crisis till now. Of special note is the Egyptian army's confidence that it had successfully implemented the deterrent factor. The sense of self-assurance reinforced Amer's appreciation of this strategy, and the evaluation that the balance of forces inclined in Egypt's favor led Nasir to determine Egypt's next strategic move in the crisis. According to this estimate the military command was ready for an armed duel with Israel, and an Egyptian military initiative was not to be ruled out. The change in Egypt's assessment had special significance: namely the May 17 decision in principle to close the straits and accept the consequences (an inevitable military clash with Israel). Interestingly, even at this late date Nasir refrained from making any open reference to the crisis, and Amer restricted his above-mentioned declaration to a discussion on the military implications alone.

On May 19 Fariq Awal (General) Murtaja also expressed himself in the spirit of Amer's statements: "The Egyptian forces have moved into the UNEF positions and are prepared to transfer the campaign beyond Egypt's territory." And on May 20 he declared: "We are ready for any contingency. Our forces are on a state of alert and prepared to bring the battle, if [war] breaks out, to [the enemy's side] . . . Any Israeli attack, no matter what its proportions, against Syria or any other Arab state means for us the start of a holy war."[48]

The changed atmosphere and revised estimate of the situation also called for a re-assessment of the attitude toward fida'iyyun activity whose importance had been overshadowed by the approaching war. Furthermore, open support of this activity would provide an additional boost to the regime's already soaring popularity. Therefore, Egypt had nothing to fear by overtly supporting fida'iyyun operations against Israel. On May 19 *Radio Cairo*'s commentator expressed an outspoken stand on an issue that Egyptian propaganda had been silent on till now: "fida'iyyun penetration into Israel is a legal act that Israel must now understand. Egypt supports fida'iyyun activity from a military and political point of view."[49] This emphasis was also designed to demonstrate the success of Egyptian deterrence in causing Israel to cower before the Egyptian threat.

At the same time, anti-Israel and anti-American invective reached unprecedented levels of boasting and crudity. On May 18 and 19 *Radio Cairo* blared: "Israel again feels itself locked between two jaws – Egypt and Syria. Rabin's bluster is shrinking. Israel's forces that were concentrated on the Syrian border in cahoots with the United States and the stooge Husayn have begun withdrawing and fleeing in disarray. Where are the threats and swaggering of the colonialist dogs? They run to the UN and Washington hoping that they will save them from their mess now they realize Egypt's forces can crush them with a powerful blow. We know who you are – you murderers of Bernadotte and Hammarskjöld. The initiative is ours and we know what we are doing and what we will do. We know that we will pulverize Israel and emerge victorious." Ahmad Sa'id boasted: "Our only method against Israel is war, an all-out war that will finally annihilate the Zionist entity."[50]

The Arab Arena: Solidarity with Egypt

As the crisis darkened Nasir redoubled his efforts to win the Arab world's support of Egypt by emphasizing that the crisis was an all-Arab struggle as much as it was an Egyptian–Syrian one. This task was not difficult considering his impressive achievements to date: the removal of the "threat" on Syria and withdrawal of the UNEF, while the war trumpets of the approaching confrontation with Israel sounded. The Arab world also experienced a metamorphosis in its attitude to Egypt's moves. Given Nasir's past declarations, it was far from clear in the first stage of the crisis whether his intentions were genuine. But as the crisis deepened, when large forces were moved into Sinai, the UN Force evicted from Sharm al-Sheikh, and especially after Egypt's strident propaganda campaign, the Arab public became convinced that Nasir meant business this time and was marching to a war with Israel. The belief in Nasir, his leadership, and willingness to fight was the prime motivating force of the Arab masses that began in this stage and peaked on the eve of the war.

The regime's propaganda-information campaign directed at the Arab world stressed that the recent success of Egypt's policy toward Israel stemmed from the strength with which it implemented its policy, and that "Egypt's power created a new situation in the Arab world, one in which Arab rights are protected by force."[51] This stage witnessed the Arab world's mobilization in support of Egypt's moves and the concomitant rise in expectations of Egypt. Since Nasir was well aware of these expectations it should not come as a surprise that the Egyptians were optimistic about Arab reactions to Egypt's moves in this stage.

Syria

The Egyptians estimated that they had proven to the Syrian public that Egypt was the center of power in the Arab world. They also reckoned that official circles in Syria and inside the Ba'th leadership had much more faith now in Egypt's ability to fulfill its promise to come to Syria's aid. The regime in Damascus used the crisis to bolster its own stature in the public. At this stage the political leadership put a freeze on any suggestions of independent, Syrian-initiated military action against Israel. The Syrian order, issued before the outbreak of the crisis, that prohibited fishing in the Sea of Galilee, remained in effect;[52] in other words, the Syrians, like the Egyptians, avoided instigating a border incident that would give Israel grounds for escalating a local incident into a major confrontation.

The Syrian media easily adopted the Egyptian propaganda line and even exceeded it in virulence toward Israel and the United States. On May 21 *Radio Damascus* proclaimed: "The decisive battle that the Arabs have been waiting for since 1948 is at the gate . . . Israel is like a mouse trapped between [armed] concentrations in the north and south."[53]

In the military sphere: On May 16, while the crisis was still in its early stage, the Syrians informed Egypt, apparently on the advice of Nasir who was interested in displaying inter-Arab military cooperation among the Arab states, that they were ready to absorb Iraqi air units and wanted to know the size of the force and when it would be arriving in Syria. Syria's consent to allow Iraqi planes based on Syrian soil was a major turnabout in its position and testifies to the gravity the danger that it believed Israel posed. Previously the Syrians had agreed only to bomber assistance taking off from Iraqi airfields. In the end, Syria's willingness on this issue was not translated into reality.

On May 16 and 17 an emergency defense line was extended along the Syrian border – mostly tank and infantry battalions were advanced to the existing defense positions. Artillery positions at the front were reinforced with reserves from bases at Quneitra. On May 18 the Syrian front entered a state of full emergency layout and two more brigades were brought in. The air force was put on the highest level of alert. By May 17 the Syrians had mobilized their entire reserve force. Three days later, on May 20, 40,000 Syrian troops stood on the front lines.

Iraq

The main goal of Iraq's activity was to secure its status in the "revolutionary" camp. Military coordination between Iraq, Syria, and Egypt increased in this stage, especially in the realm of Iraqi air assistance to Syria. The Egyptians pressured the Syrians to accept Iraqi air assistance. On May 20 an Iraqi military delegation – led by the deputy chief of staff accompanied by the deputy commander of the Iraqi air force and a number of officers from the air force headquarters – visited Damascus. The visit's aim was to discuss cooperation between the two air forces and the possibility of introducing Iraqi planes into the Syrian arena. It was agreed, *inter alia*, that Iraqi ground and air liaison officers would come to Damascus to study long-range operations flying from Iraqi airfields.

On the same day the Iraqi government convened an extraordinary meeting to discuss the regional situation. At the conclusion of the meeting the Iraqi war minister declared that the Iraqi army was prepared to assist any Arab state attacked by Israel.[54] Also on May 20 a high-level Iraqi delegation, headed by Deputy Prime Minister Tahir Yahya, arrived in Cairo to participate in the meetings of the joint Iraqi–Egyptian political leadership. The delegation discussed the crisis, Egypt's aims, and the scope of Iraqi assistance required.

Lebanon

The upswing in Nasir's stature was strongly felt in Lebanon by both his traditional supporters, and his opponents (the Christians) who feared the consequences. The fervor in nationalistic, pro-Nasir circles amplified, and their high morale recalled the prevalent mood in 1956. Nationalist circles that wanted to increase Lebanese support of Egypt underscored the danger of an Israeli operation against Lebanon that would pave the way for an Israeli invasion of Syria.

On May 18, demonstrations broke out in south Lebanon and the city of Sidon during the funeral procession of a Palestinian Fatah member from the Ein al-Hilwa camp who was killed on the border while trying to infiltrate into Israel. The demonstrations – expressions of a nationalistic awakening in the Lebanese public – had to be suppressed with force.[55]

Lebanon's contribution to the military preparations was the deployment of an armed force in the south of the country. In this way, Lebanon displayed its solidarity with Egypt. On May 18 the Lebanese army mobilized its emergency defense line in South Lebanon. Most of the force was concentrated in the eastern sector (Marj Ayoun). At the same time a Lebanese military delegation arrived in Damascus to discuss military coordination.

Saudi Arabia

The Egyptians judged that Nasir's prestige in the general Arab public had risen to an unprecedented level since 1956. But the Saudi broadcasts continually disparaged Egypt's moves and prodded Egypt into an armed clash with Israel. The Saudis hoped that such a clash would turn the Egyptians' attention away from Yemen and force them to withdraw. The Egyptians felt that the Saudi rulers would sooner or later join the Arab bandwagon in a show of solidarity with Egypt and Syria. On May 20 Saudi Arabia declared that "it would support the Syrian people against the aggression now threatening its security and peace." On May 23 King Faysal, who was in London, called a press conference to announce Saudi support of the Arab countries aligned against Israel and that his country's armed forces had gone alert.[56]

An interesting editorial appeared in the May 22 edition of the Saudi newspaper *al-Bilad*: "If the Egyptian forces intend to prevent Israel from attacking Syria, force it to remove its troops from the Syrian border, and in this way return peace and quiet to the Egyptian border . . . then this is not our wish, [we prefer] a positive, united action to destroy Israel." The Royal House of Saud, on the other hand, expressed "its unconditional support of Egypt's closure of the Gulf of Aqaba to the passage of Israeli and foreign ships carrying strategic materiel, including oil, to Israel." The Saudi government gratefully acknowledged the rapprochement between Husayn and Nasir following Husayn's visit to Egypt on May 30.[57] In response to Egypt's request that Saudi Arabia try to persuade Iran to cease supplying Israel with oil, the Saudi government declared that it knew nothing about an oil supply from Persia to Israel.[58]

Jordan

Nasir's elevated status was also observed in Jordan. Nasir's moves had sparked enthusiasm and exultation in the Palestinian public of the West Bank, winning him tremendous support. On the other hand, the official Jordanian position toward Nasir's moves had not changed at this stage. Jordanian propaganda continued as before the crisis in its aggressive line against Egypt and Syria. Jordan led those states calling on Nasir to oust the UNEF and blockade the Straits of Tiran. The Jordanians expressed satisfaction over the UN pullout from Sinai, a step that "returned faith and hope to the Arabs" but they also demanded that the Egyptians "bring back the cannons to the Straits of Tiran and prevent Israeli shipping in the Red Sea. If [Egypt] fails to do so, the goal of its military steps will be cast in doubt."[59] They also criticized the publicity the Egyptians gave to the troop concentrations and harbored a suspicion that the Egyptians were collaborating with the Americans.

Furthermore, Jordan did not remain silent over Syria's propaganda attacks and subversive activity against it. In response to Syrian intrigue the Jordanian newspaper *al-Dustur* asked on May 18: "Does Syria intend to attack Jordan?" and answered: "Syria's propaganda machine continues to threaten and insult Jordan more than Israel does, an attitude that raises suspicions that Syria's target in all this dramatization is Jordan, not Israel."

The PLO

Ahmad al-Shuqayri launched an awareness campaign among the Palestinians. *Radio PLO* adopted Egypt's information-propaganda line and went even further, boasting that fida'iyun activity was the reason for the current "grave circumstances . . . fida'iyyun will operate tenaciously until war becomes certain and unavoidable, and then we will join the battle."[60]

Other Arab States

Kuwait, Sudan, Yemen, Algeria, and Lybia voiced their support of Nasir and Syria and their willingness to offer assistance.

The Closure of the Straits: The Decision and its Repercussions

Nasir and Amer realized that the eviction of the UN Emergency Force obligated Egypt, *ipso facto*, to take over Sharm al-Sheikh and the then close of the straits. It was impossible to separate the three moves. The timetable for the closure might be flexible, but the act itself had to be done. Nasir was fully aware that the seizure of Sharm al-Sheikh and blockade of the straits would lead to a clash with Israel. In 1968, at his trial, Shams Badran, the ex-minister of war, described the link between these moves:

> The Mushir said to us [during his visit to Pakistan in December 1966] 'We should send President Nasir a telegram explaining the idea of evacuating the UN forces and taking control of Sharm al-Sheikh. The battalions are ready for this.' I sent a telegram with this message to the president but did not receive an answer since he was not convinced of this idea. I told Mushir Amer that I had reconsidered the issue and came to the general conclusion that if we evacuate the UN Forces from Sharm al-Sheikh, the gulf will be closed and war might erupt. He answered, 'No, I don't intend to forbid shipping, only to take over Sharm al-Sheikh so that there won't be cause to criticize [us].' I said that in

that case they would talk about the closure of the straits, and it might intensify the propaganda campaign against us. When [the president] did not reply, I told Mushir Amer that this step would probably raise problems that we were incapable of dealing with. The Mushir answered, 'We only intend to take control of Sharm al-Sheikh, without blockading the straits.' I told him that this was only half a solution.[61]

On May 17 the "political decision" was made to block the straits to Israeli shipping. The day this decision was approved by a unanimous vote in the Supreme Executive Committee of the Arab Socialist Union, Egypt demanded the unconditional withdrawal of the entire Emergency Force. Only the prime minister, the engineer Sulayman Sidqi, was opposed. Before the vote was taken, discussion focused on the political and military situation that could result from the evacuation of the Emergency Force. Amer noted the prospect of gaining control of Sharm al-Sheikh. Sulayman and another participant tried to distinguish between the seizure of Sharm al-Sheikh and the closure of the straits to Israeli shipping. Sidqi raised the possibility of the takeover of Sharm al-Sheikh while allowing shipping to continue. Amer interrupted, "How could my forces be stationed there and just watch the Israeli flag pass by in front of them?" The discussion ended on that note. Nasir decided to bring the issue to a vote because of "its importance [and to preserve] unity of opinion."[62] It also seems that political conditions in this period precluded a separation of the two moves. A decision to separate them would not only incur a propaganda attack but would also be interpreted as capitulation to Israel due to fear of its reaction. Nasir wanted to prove to the Arab world that the exact opposite was true.

Once the political decision was made (May 17) the headquarters began taking steps to implement it. The following day Amer convened the high command to discuss operational plans for reoccupying Sharm al-Sheikh. In the course of the meeting Amer appointed Amid (Brig. Gen.) Abd al-Mun'im Khalil as commander of the Sharm al-Sheikh region. Thus, the region came under the direct command of the armed forces' headquarters. Khalil was given a battery of coastal artillery (130 mm.) that decamped from Suez at midnight of May 21 and arrived in Sharm al-Sheikh on May 23. Amer ordered the rapid dispatch of paratroopers to Sharm al-Sheikh even though they had received a different assignment. The paratroop battalion was dropped on Sharm al-Sheikh on May 20, thus securing the takeover of Sharm al-Sheikh. Amer fretted that the Israelis would take advantage of the departure of the UN Force in order to seize Sharm al-Sheikh.[63]

Nasir realized the significance of the decision – war with Israel – therefore he had to make sure that the decision was unanimous. He needed time to absorb the ramifications of the decision and carefully weigh this step. To further this aim he probably devoted the time between May 17 and May 21/22 preparing for the military takeover of Sharm al-Sheikh (U Thant was scheduled to visit Egypt on May 23 to discuss a compromise on the straits). A sign of Nasir's deliberation was his eschewal of any public statements during this five-day period until he decided on the path to take. Thus, only in the evening of May 22, after military preparations for seizing the area had been completed did detailed instructions to blockade the straits to Israeli shipping finally reach the commander of the Sharm al-Sheikh region in charge of operations.

When Nasir finally evaluated the consequences of this move he realized that the chances of war had shot up from 80 percent to 100 percent, and he took full responsibility for his strategic move. He relied completely on the estimate of Amer and his staff regarding the Egyptian army's ability to cope with the military implications of the decision. Now, after Nasir was completely convinced of the need to declare the straits blockaded and was assured that all of the military preparations had been made, he led Egypt and the entire Arab world with unparalleled élan to war. His campaign began on May 22 in his Sinai speech. This was his first speech since the beginning of the crisis, and was broadcast over *Radio Cairo* early the next morning. From this moment Nasir became the most exalted figure in the Arab world, even more so than after he nationalized the Suez Canal Company (July 26, 1956) and gained a political "victory" in the Suez Campaign–Sinai War.

On May 23, at 05:30 *Radio Cairo* broadcast his speech that he had delivered to pilots at an Egyptian airbase in Sinai the previous day. Amer had accompanied him on his tour there. Nasir declared the straits blocked to Israeli shipping and expressed his readiness to go to war with Israel:

> [Unlike in 1956] today Egypt faces Israel without Britain and France by its side. The United States supports Israel politically now and supplies it with weapons. Israel has recently threatened Syria with aggression, and today Egypt and Israel stand opposite one another. Israel made its [threat] on May 12, 1967 and everyone who heard it asked what the limit of its arrogance is. This is why Egypt can no longer remain silent. Israel threatened to carry out a military operation against Syria in order to conquer Damascus, and Israeli pundits estimated that Egypt would do nothing since it was occupied in Yemen. The whole world is talking about Sharm al-Sheikh and the navigation in the Gulf of Aqaba and Port of Eilat. This morning *Radio London* stated that in 1956 Nasir promised to open the Gulf of Aqaba. This is an out and out lie. Nasir cannot surrender any of Egypt's rights. Today the armed forces are in charge after taking control of Sharm al-Sheikh and returning our sovereignty to the Gulf of Aqaba, which is located in our territorial water and where our rights [have jurisdiction]. We will never permit the Israeli flag to pass through the Gulf of Aqaba. *These Jews threaten war, and we say to them ahlan wa sahlan [welcome, come right in!] we are ready [for war].* [my emphasis – M.S.]. War may provide Israel and the Jews with an opportunity to test their strength with ours, then they will find out that what they wrote about the 1956 campaign and conquest of Sinai was only fantasy and lies. Egypt is prepared to enter the battle if Syria or any other Arab state is attacked.[64]

Before the broadcast of the speech, the announcer said: "Nasir officially declared yesterday that the Gulf of Aqaba is blocked to Israeli shipping with a ban on strategic matériel to Israel through it, even on non-Israeli ships. This means that Egypt is conducting operations in the Gulf of Aqaba as it did up until the Suez War in 1956."

In the evening of May 22, after the military preparations for the seizure of the positions overlooking the straits (Ras Nasrani) were completed, Mushir Amer gave special instructions to the Egyptian commander at Sharm al-Sheikh on how to close the straits:

1 Beginning at 12:00 noon on May 23 ships bearing an Israeli flag will be prevented from entering the Gulf of Aqaba on their way to Eilat.
2 On May 24, at the first light of day, oil tankers from any country will be prevented from entering the Gulf of Aqaba on their way to Eilat.
3 Ships of all countries will be allowed to leave the gulf.

4 If a ship does not respond to a warning shot, firing will commence to force it to cease its movement and afterwards to sink it.
5 Ships accompanied by warships will be allowed to pass. It will not be necessary to oppose [prevent] or engage in a confrontation with a ship or warships, even if the ship accompanying it carries an Israeli flag.[65]

On May 26 Nasir explained the significance of the blockade of the straits, as he saw it when he made the decision:

[Seizing] Sharm al-Sheikh means confrontation with Israel. Taking such a step requires the readiness to enter into a full-scale war with Israel. This act cannot be distinguished from others, therefore we had to weigh [the consequences] and decide when we can come to Sharm al-Sheikh and retrieve our rights. This has been the principle behind these moves. The truth is that I was authorized by the Supreme Executive Committee [of the Socialist Union, that is: the political leadership] to implement the step in the proper time. And the right time was the [Israeli] threat of aggression against Syria.[66]

With the announcement of the straits closure, a new chapter was opened in the crisis. Both sides, the Arabs and Israelis, realized that a military confrontation was inevitable. Now the Egyptians and Israelis asked themselves who would strike first.

The Third Stage, May 23–28, 1967: The Crystallization of the Second-Strike Strategy

The third stage in the crisis was marked by a new strategy: Nasir's initiative in dealing with both the closure of the straits and the inevitability of war with Israel. Under the prevailing political–military conditions he had to devise the best path of action for guaranteeing Egypt's victory in the approaching confrontation.

The Military Alignment and Offensive Plans

Only after the First Arab Summit (January 1964) approved an Arab strategy for solving the Palestinian problem, and only after the UAC made plans for defending Arab diversion operations, did Egypt draw up its military–security strategy. The Egyptian Armed Forces GHQ ordered the Eastern Military Region Command (Sinai) to prepare the "Qahir" Defense Plan. The fundamentals of the plan were decided on in early 1966, and approved by Amer on December 21, 1966. A derivative of the plan was the "Fahd" Air Plan for providing direct assistance to ground forces and reconnaissance units. The "Qahir" Defense Plan was designed "to prevent the enemy from breaking through to the Suez Canal, to destroy [enemy] forces that penetrated [Sinai], and to prepare a major counterattack, in cooperation with strategic reserves, . . . for destroying the enemy." The Egyptian answer to the IDF's *modus operandi* called for the creation of a security belt (*nitaq amni*) that ran the length of the border with Israel, and the construction of a "tactical defense depth" (*'umq difa'i taktiki*) comprised of two defended forward areas (*nitaq difa'i*).[67]

However, the plan did not materialize for a number of reasons: the extreme fluidity of the political and military crisis that began of May 14, 1967; Egyptian intelligence estimates that generally failed to correspond (to put it mildly) to developments on the Israeli side; and the personality of Mushir Abd al-Hakim Amer, who stood at the head of the military pyramid and directed most of the troop movements and deployment in Sinai during the crisis. These reasons led to improvisations and substantial deviations from the original plan to defend Sinai. The first change – the order to withdraw the UNEF from the Gaza Strip and Sharm al-Sheikh – had not been taken into consideration when the "Qahir" Defense Plan was drawn up. Military units were frequently transferred to different deployment areas. For example, the "Qahir" Plan called for the 4th Brigade to seize the Sharm al-Sheikh area; instead, Amer ordered a paratroop unit to quickly carry out the assignment. On May 16 the Deputy Supreme Commander, Amer, ordered his forward command post to be established on the eastern front, and the Gaza–Kuntilla sector secured. Immediately afterwards Amer ordered plans drawn up for a limited attack in the northern and southern Negev in case "the enemy tries to perform a counter-operation against the Gaza Strip and gulf region." According to chief of staff Fawzi, the army's assignments were seriously altered from the original "Qahir" Plan. On May 18 the air branch issued orders to complete the preparations for air strikes and an air umbrella to protect the ground forces attacking the Eilat area (codenamed "Asad 1"). The ground forces also prepared an offensive plan for taking Eilat – codenamed "Fajr" – that required the reshuffling of missions of various units. On May 20 the Straits of Tiran–Gulf of Aqaba crisis intensified with the arrival of Egyptian paratroopers. The Egyptian Command estimated that Israel would respond by attacking the Gaza Strip and Kuntilla area.[68] Amer introduced a major change in combat plans after the announcement of the straits' closure. The Mushir feared that Israel and its backers would initiate hostilities in the gulf region. This prospect led to Amer's offensive concept and the order to prepare plans for a limited attack against Israel.[69]

Thus, following the new assessment of Israel's possible moves after the closing of the straits, Egyptian deployment in the Sinai underwent a major deviation from the "Qahir" Plan. The Egyptian headquarters believed that the IDF would concentrate its effort on capturing the Gaza Strip in order to use it as a bargaining chip in negotiations. They reckoned that Israel would agree to withdraw from the Gaza Strip in exchange for the opening of the straits to Israeli shipping (as it did in 1956). Egypt prepared for an Israeli offensive on Gaza by dispatching an armored task force to the Rafah area for a counterattack and for a secondary effort to capture the Israeli settlements of Kerem Shalom and Nir Yitzhak. On May 24 the Egyptian 4th Armored Division entered Sinai (according to the "Qahir" Plan it was supposed to wait in the canal zone) and concentrated in the Meliz region in order to provide strategic depth to the forward defense zones. At the end of the month the Egyptian estimate of the situation changed again: the high command assessed that Israel would not be satisfied with a limited response in the Gaza Strip or al-Hasaneh region but might launch a large-scale offensive against the Canal Zone. In other words, the IDF's main thrust would come at the Quseima and Lutz Passes, and Wadi Faran. To meet this contingency, Egyptian Command introduced basic changes in the deployment of its forces.[70]

On May 23 Mushir Amer issued operational order (No. 1967/16) to prepare an offensive plan for cutting off the southern Negev from the rest of Israel. The "Fajr" Plan was a combined land, sea, and air operation with air units from the "Asad" Plan and naval units participating (two ships would embark for Eilat). Simultaneously,

Amer issued order (No. 1967/17) to prepare the "Saham" Plan for a surprise air strike against Kerem Shalom (Rafah) forty-eight hours after the "Fajr" operation commenced. On May 26 orders (No. 1967/18) were issued for securing the Rafah region and preparing the 7th Infantry and 14th Armored Brigades for offensive operations in the northern Negev.[71]

The following are the offensive plans that Fawzi claims were prepared "[too] quickly and without reconnaissance [data] or exact information on the enemy."

1 The "Fajr" Offensive (Mushir Order No. 1967/16, May 23). The goal: to cut off the southern Negev and Eilat. Air forces: to take part and provide air coverage according to the "Asad" Plan, and so forth. Maritime forces: to shell the Eilat coast and destroy the enemy's coastal artillery, and so forth. Completion of preparations (isti'dad): 20:00, May 26, 1967. The commander of the ground forces, Fariq (Lt. Gen.) Salah Muhsin, presented the plan to Fariq Awal (General.) Murtaja at 20:00 on May 25 and received Murtaja's approval. The commander of the eastern front ordered its implementation. Mushir Amer then issued orders to the commander of the air force, Fariq Awal (General) Mahmud Sidqi, to carry out the "Asad" air plan at dawn on May 27. The air force headquarters staff quickly dispatched detailed orders to air units, including those at the el-Arish airfield. Fawzi recalls that, "it was later proven these orders and their time of implementation were leaked to the enemy. The base commander and his adjutant had to face a military trial after the war." This was the only plan that came close to being carried out but was cancelled at the last moment.
2 The "Sahm" Attack Plan was intended as an attack on the Rafah axis "to repulse any enemy force threatening the Gaza Strip." The plan was cancelled when a light-armored force (Force Shazli) was moved south.
3 The "Ghasq" Attack Plan was designed to attack on two axes: (1) Against Birin. (2) Against the Rachel Hill (the plan was shown to Fariq Salah Muhsin on May 28 at 10:00). Also, on June 3 the Second Army commander asked for strafing by a squadron of fighters and bombers to assist the ground forces during Operation "Ghasq." He also asked for an air umbrella.
4 The "Sulayman" Attack Plan: This plan was drawn up to repulse the Israeli force threatening the Gaza Strip and to make a powerful assault on Kerem Shalom and Nir Yitzhak. The plan was rejected because of differences of opinion between the ground commander and division commander (between May 29 and June 1) over the axes for the offensives.[72]

None of the offensive plans were implemented.

On May 26 four Egyptian MiG 21s approached Israel's Nitzana area at a great elevation (45–50 thousand feet) apparently on a reconnaissance mission in preparation for the Fajr Plan. The quartet split up into two formations. One pair flew to Dimona, banked to the left, and headed back to Sinai. The second pair veered south and flew along the border to a point north of Eilat before returning to Sinai. In my opinion, this patrol, like the one on May 17, was not looking for the reactor, but was collecting intelligence data on IDF troop concentrations in the south in preparation of the above-mentioned plans.[73]

Formulation of the Second-Strike Strategy

Amer planned to implement the "Fajr" Plan at dawn of May 27 after he redeployed his forces. The Israeli deception had succeeded beyond all expectation, thus Mushir Amer and the Egyptian command believed that the attack would come on the southern axis. But, between May 23 and 25, Nasir altered his strategic thinking that had clashed directly with Amer's recently developed offensive concept. This change of strategy was based on Nasir's sound assessment that the closure of the straits would lead to an inevitable military confrontation with Israel. Now he had to figure out how to assure the maximum gains in the approaching war. On the one hand, Nasir wanted Egypt to win international support, including that of the United States; on the other hand, he wanted to prevent Israel from acquiring the same support. His new strategy was based on the principle that Egypt would not initiate a military move, sustain the first strike, and then retaliate with a decisive second strike. According to Haykal's statements on May 26: "We can expect the enemy to make the first strike in the war, but at the same time we must reduce its impact to a minimum. Afterwards, the Egyptian's second strike will come when we counterattack and repulse [the enemy] to the maximum."[74]

From Egypt's point of view, although the initiative would be in Israel's hands, this did not imply that Egypt was unwilling or unprepared for an all-out war. Actually, Egypt overestimated its military power. It had developed an exaggerated self-confidence in its ability to withstand the first blow, respond with a mighty second one, and carry the fighting over to Israeli territory. The adoption of the second-strike strategy stemmed from a sense of power and the assessment that the Egyptian army could not only surrender the initiative but also absorb a first strike, get its nose bloodied, and despite this win by means of a counterattack. The Egyptian High Command supported this assessment because it had received highly optimistic evaluations from military intelligence regarding the balance of forces. Mushir Amer also accepted this estimate. Moreover, if Israel did not launch a war, then Egypt would be satisfied with the *status quo* that it viewed as a great political achievement. Therefore, given the current political and military alignment, the Egyptians felt that they were prepared for, and even eager for, an all-out confrontation with Israel, but because of strategic (international and military) considerations they preferred to let Israel initiate the first strike.

Nasir decided on the second-strike strategy no later than May 25, after consultations in which Haykal participated. The strategic turnabout was revealed in an article written by Haykal on May 26 and in the debates during a High Command meeting on the previous evening. Haykal analyzed the new strategy even better than Nasir did, and he became the national mouthpiece of Nasir's view. Fawzi describes the High Command meeting in which Nasir first outlined his strategy:

> Nasir was present at the High Command meeting on May 25, 1967 in which an estimate of the situation was made and operational plans discussed. Talk revolved around the possibility of an IDF attack on the Gaza Strip region along the southern axis and at Kuntilla. Military plans were reviewed that were designed to protect these two targets. Offensive plans were presented, that Amer had ordered the ground forces commander to draw up in order to counter IDF forces in the southern Negev and on the northern axis. Amer approved them and demanded close coordination [between units] in order to guarantee their success. Toward the end of the meeting Nasir stressed the military and morale-boosting importance of the Gaza Strip, especially for the Palestinian people.

Later he met privately with the Mushir for a half hour, after which Amer returned to the meeting and canceled the air operation – the 'Asad Plan' that he approved earlier that day for implementation at dawn on May 27.[75]

If Fawzi's testimony is correct, the Mushir listened to Nasir's political analysis during their closed-door parley, and then came out in favor of Nasir's second-strike strategy.

Even before the new strategy was approved, there were many indications of Egypt's interest in preserving the quiet on the border so that Israel would not have an excuse for a initiating a military operation backed by the international community, especially the Americans. Therefore, Egypt sought to prevent acts of sabotage emanating from the Gaza Strip and to avoid hostile incidents on the Egyptian or Syrian borders with Israel. On May 18 the minister of war, Shams al-Din Badran, ordered Fawzi and Gaza's governor, Liwa (Major General) Abd al-Mun'im Husni, to take steps to ensure that the Fatah organization would not move around freely in the Gaza Strip and infiltrate into Israel, so that "our operational planning will not go awry." Four days later (May 22) Badran sent a sharp letter to the governor of Gaza complaining that *Voice of Israel* announced that fidai'yyun had burnt fields inside Israeli territory across from the Gaza border. He reiterated that steps had to be taken to curtail these acts. Furthermore, following an Egyptian army investigation of mine-laying at Kerem Shalom, instructions were issued to Egyptian forces not to open fire on IDF forces in the area that "could lead to war."[76] Shortly after the closure of the straits the Egyptians asked the Syrians (or to be precise, ordered them) not to initiate any activity on the border with Israel. Nasir and his foreign ministry staff were careful to stress to Western diplomats Egypt's interest in preserving the peace and refraining from starting a war. Nasir purposely emphasized to the West that Egypt had no intention of launching a war, and he was telling the truth. On May 24 U Thant asked Nasir that, "considering the Israelis' fear that you intend to begin hostilities, would you promise me not to attack Israel?" Nasir's reply: "We have never declared that we would attack Israel, it is Israel who threatens to invade Syria. Our moves have been defensive measures designed to prevent the implementation of this threat. We will not begin the attack."[77]

The Fundamentals of Nasir's Second-Strike Strategy

1 Egypt's "Ten Days of Glory"

From the onset of the crisis Egypt gained a number of major political windfalls. Nasir boasted that "for the first time in Egypt's relations with Israel, Egypt succeeded in forcibly changing a *fait accompli* that had been thrust upon it." He was referring to the international demand of Egypt after the Suez – Sinai War to allow Israeli vessels passage through the Straits of Tiran. Now Egypt had restored the border situation to its previous condition, that is, Egypt "has erased the results of the 1956 aggression." Haykal explained this in the following way:

> As for the Gulf of Aqaba, Imperialism appeared in 1956 in the form of the armed might of Britain and France and created a fait accompli from the autumn of 1956 to the spring of 1967. I mean the weapons of Imperialism did this, not Israeli arms. Now for the first time the Arabs have dared change a fait accompli that was forced upon them by creating a new fait accompli that guarantees Arab rights and interests. The

forced blockage of the Gulf of Aqaba is a fait accompli that Arab weapons have enabled and protected . . . from Israel's point of view this is the most compelling factor in the present situation. But in effect the most compelling factor is the fait accompli that [we] have created and are capable of defending. This is not just about the Gulf of Aqaba; this is a larger issue: it's about Israel's entire security philosophy since the establishment of the state. This means that Israel has no choice but to resort to arms, that is, an armed clash between Egypt and the Israeli enemy is inevitable.[78]

The prestige of Egypt and Nasir skyrocketed. More important, almost all the chips were in Nasir's hands. Egypt had flung a security–strategic challenge in Israel's face, perhaps the most serious challenge in Israel's history. Haykal summed up Egypt's "ten days of glory" in the following words:

The Egyptian military operation has achieved three goals that have changed the balance of power in the region and surprised even Egypt: the failure of Israel's planned initiative against Syria – the invasion of Syria is now impossible because the enemy has had to move all its forces to the south to meet the Egyptian military concentration; the return of Egypt's armed forces to a direct face-off with Israel; and the blockage of the Gulf of Aqaba to Israeli navigation.[79]

Nasir was undoubtedly satisfied with the political gains he had achieved so far, including the closure of the straits, as long as the *status quo* was upheld without the danger of war. The question was whether Israel would accept the present situation, and Nasir believed that it would not.

2 Sustaining Israel's First Strike; the Force of Egypt's Second-strike

The Egyptian air commander estimated that an Israeli first strike would cause his forces no more than 10–15 percent losses. This estimate satisfied Nasir. Defending Nasir's decision, Huwaydi pointed out that "In addition to the political situation which precludes our opening the war, the air force commander's assessment contributed to the decision against launching a first strike."[80] Egyptian intelligence, too, estimated that the balance of forces was in Egypt's favor, and that Egypt could withstand a first strike and respond with a second, more powerful one. The Egyptian high command assessed that after the first strike the army would be capable of repelling an Israeli attack and launching a counteroffensive. Even if the Egyptian attack did not end in Israel's military defeat, it would definitely weaken the enemy. This estimate was totally wrong and out-of-touch with reality; nevertheless Amer adopted it, and no commander – not even chief of staff Fawzi – dared speak against it.

During a field forces command meeting on May 24, in the presence of all the divisional commanders, military intelligence presented the following balance of forces on the Egyptian front: armor – three to one in Egypt's favor; infantry – three to one in Egypt's favor; artillery – one thousand Egyptian guns compared to an unknown Israeli quantity. But Fawzi noted that the true ratios were: armor – 0.6 to 1 in Israel's favor; infantry – 1 to 1.7 in Israel's favor; artillery – 1 to 0.5 in Egypt's favor; aircraft – 1 to 2.5 in Israel's favor; pilots – 1 Egyptian pilot to every 2.7 Israeli pilots. In his opinion, "military intelligence's error gave the impression of belittling the enemy's strength."[81]

Given Egyptian military intelligence's statistics, little wonder that an atmosphere of optimism pervaded the High Command regarding the outcome of a clash with Israel. On May 29 Amer told Mahmud Riyad, the Egyptian foreign minister: "If Israel attacks, only one-third of our force will be needed to reach Beer Sheva." Such optimism was rife in Nasir's May 26 speech: "We have waited for the right moment to be fully prepared so that if war with Israel breaks out we will be guaranteed of victory and we will take firm steps [to ensure it]. I say this for a reason . . . We have felt lately that our strength is sufficient to meet Israel in battle, and with God's help, we will make the right moves and emerge triumphant."[82]

Like Haykal's article that day, Nasir's speech resounds of arrogance. Nasir came to the conclusion that Egypt had been preparing for a test of strength with Israel since the 1956 War; now the time had arrived. He realized that since the crisis began, he had revised his estimate of Egypt's strength. On June 4 he declared: "The situation in the Gulf of Aqaba in 1956 was similar to today's, but after the Anglo-French aggression, we brought our forces back from Sinai and the UNEF appeared. This is the reason that we had to prepare for the final battle with the enemy, and when we felt we were ready we regained our rights, forced the emergency troops to withdraw, we returned to the Gulf of Aqaba, and blocked it [to Israeli shipping]."[83]

The regime tried to infuse the Egyptian and general Arab public with the military's sense of confidence. In a May 25 article, probably written after a round of background talks, Mamduh Rida, the senior correspondent of the Egyptian daily *al-Jumhuriya*, expressed the Egyptian military–political elite's assessment:

In 1956 the Egyptian people courageously withstood three countries and managed to defeat them . . . [Today it] is capable of doing this infinitely better. The situation in 1967 is different from that of 1956. Today the nation is not going into battle with Israel out of an emotional urge, but out of a deep awareness, a determined resolution, and belief that it is a matter of necessity. The nation is not going to fight Israel merely to contain it, but to destroy it. The nation knows that it is stronger than Israel not only in numbers but also in equipment. It is not proceeding into battle against Israel without knowing the outcome . . .[84]

3 The Egyptian Plan Was Basically Defensive

Years later Huwaydi added a point that justified Nasir's strategy, a reason that neither the media nor Nasir or Haykal mentioned either during or after the crisis – probably because it might have called into question the military estimate that they were trying to convey:

An air strike is a prerequisite in an offensive plan, that is, if our plan had been offensive then there would have been an initial air strike as in October 1973. [In 1973 we carried out] an air strike deep in Sinai before we crossed the canal. But in 1967 the situation was different because the plan was strategically defensive. Indeed, some changes were introduced because of the limited offensive activity in one or more places that some of our forces were supposed to carry out, but this did not mean that the plan was offensive. It meant that if an air strike was implemented the ground forces would not be able to take advantage of its results. [The first strike would have been only] an air strike, while the rest of our force was waiting for the response. The documents confirm this. The question is – assuming that the air forces delivered the first strike, how would the military command have seen the development of the operations? The official documents do not reveal such thinking. Also, nothing in the official documents suggests that there were plans for exploiting the success of the first strike had it been carried out.[85]

Huwaydi added this claim in the defense of Nasir at a later stage, apparently without either Nasir or Amer having referred to it during the crisis or afterwards, because at the time they had tried to show that the Egyptian army was capable of delivering a second strike on land and in the air, and transferring the war to Israeli territory. Nevertheless, Huwaydi correctly claims that the basic plan in Sinai – the "Qahir Plan" – was essentially defensive. Actually, there was no plan for a strategic attack. Until May 26 all of the military plans were based on the Mushir's concept of "preventive defense" (*al-difa' al wiqa'i*) alongside the preparation of land, air, and sea plans for a limited attack. A change occurred on May 26 when the limited offensive plans were canceled. From this point the Egyptian army went over to the second-strike plan and the "traditional defense" approach.[86]

4 International Pressure for Restraint

Nasir attributed special importance to the international arena, the superpowers, and to the United States and the Soviet Union in particular. The Soviet Union guaranteed its support; and France's position (de Gaulle's) suited his plans. His main objective was to neutralize, or at least reduce, the US level of commitment to Israel in the event of war. After the closing of the straits, the Egyptians presumed that they would reap a political victory whether or not war broke out. If Israel made a successful move in the first stages of the campaign, then the Egyptian forces would be able to counter on the ground and in the air before Israel could claim any irreversible gains. In other words fighting would cease at an early stage because of superpower intervention, and Egypt would be the winner. According to this scenario, even if the United States intervened militarily in Israel's favor, it would do so only after a few days of combat in which Israel would suffer heavy losses in men and matériel since the fighting would be on its soil. As for the Soviet Union's position, the Egyptians believed that it would not intervene militarily but would prefer to extend military aid to the Arabs while it supported them politically. United States intervention would result in the strengthening of anti-Americanism in the Arab world and perhaps even induce pro-Nasir reorientations in the "reactionary" states. The Egyptians did not rule out the possibility of a revolution in "one" of the Arab "reactionary" states. (This naturally refers to the Egyptian assessment before Husayn's May 30 *volte-face*.) After the freeze in international activity in trying to resolve the crisis, and after the closure of the straits, the Egyptians estimated that Israel was losing the struggle to secure military backing from its Western friends. Israel's isolation heightened Egypt's self-confidence. Egyptian radio stations stressed that the balance of forces was in Egypt's favor, emphasized Israel's isolation, and pointed out that most of the Arab states, the neutral states, the eastern bloc, and especially the Soviet Union, all supported Egypt's position, while only the United States stood on Israel's side.

The Soviet Union and the United States influenced Egypt's crystallization of the second-strike strategy:

The Soviet Union

When the crisis broke out, the Syrians tried to gain hefty Russian support by claiming that the threat to Syria was part of an overall Imperialist scheme to besiege the Soviet Union. Therefore they asked the Soviets to discard the passive approach and display forcefulness. The Soviets reaffirmed their promise to stand by Syria and continued to warn Israel. On the eve of the announcement of the closure of the straits the Egyptians asked the Soviets to publicly deny Western reports that the Soviet Union was prepared to discuss the crisis within a four-way superpower framework and join the 1950 tripartite declaration with the United States, Britain, and France. This request attested to the Egyptians' anxiety that the Soviet Union might adopt a position unfavorable to Egypt. The reasons for Syria's diplomatic activity and Egypt's apprehensions were the Soviets' avoidance up to this point of making any official public clarification of their position in the crisis other than vague calls for peace and stability in the Middle East; their reluctance to commit themselves on American reconciliation feelers; and their evasion of Arab pressure, especially pressure coming from Syria, Iraq, and Egypt. At this stage the Soviets were still formulating their estimate of American willingness to get involved and of the danger of a military clash. Thus, the Russian information organs in Arabic, unlike those in the rest of the eastern bloc countries, made no mention of Egyptian troop concentrations in Sinai and the evacuation of the emergency forces – excluding references to official Egyptian reports. For example, on May 21 *Radio Moscow in Arabic* discussed the question of southern Arabia, which changed its position after the Egyptians announced the closing of the straits and the Arabs began pressuring it to take measures to deter Western intentions of a military intervention.

After the Syrians' talks with the Soviet leadership at the beginning of the crisis, they understood that the Kremlin was prepared to aid the Arabs – even with military intervention if necessary. But on May 19 the Syrians realized that Soviet support would not go that far. The Egyptians also realized this. Furthermore, after Nasir's May 22 announcement of the closure of the straits, the Soviets advised the Syrians and Egyptians to proceed with patience and self-restraint lest "Imperialism intervenes, and Israel and the Imperialists have a so-called pretext to launch an attack." They especially tried to prevent the Egyptians from initiating a military move that would lead to full-scale war, stressing before the Syrians and Egyptians that according to Soviet sources Israel was panicky and interested in reducing tension in the region because of the Syrian and Egyptian positions and the Arab's coordinated effort against Imperialism.[87]

The more obvious it became that the Western superpowers were disinclined to take a tough stand and would limit themselves to oral gestures that implied their acceptance of the new situation, the more the Soviets perceived that Israel was isolated and that the danger of superpower intervention was abating. The Soviet estimate was probably influenced by Egyptian reports, following talks between Cairo and Washington, that the United States had accepted the *status quo*.

Given Russia's consistent support of Egypt, Nasir's radio announcement of the closure of the straits, and the fear of a possible Israeli or American response, the Soviet government published the following official statement on May 23:

> Whoever ventures to initiate an offensive in the Middle East should realize that he will be confronted by the combined power of the Arab states and the unflinching opposition of the Soviet Union and all peace-seeking nations . . . Israel made a hostile move against Syria on April 7 – [after] it concentrated its forces on the Syrian border and [Israeli] leaders threatened this country . . . The Soviet Union is doing and will continue to do

everything in its power to maintain peace and security in the Middle East and defend the just rights of the nations.[88]

The wording of the statement was non-committal, cautious, and void of any mention of direct intervention. Another Soviet announcement stressed that Arab solidarity "is the bulwark against aggression." The Soviet Union's basic position was expressed in diplomatic contacts, most of which were initiated by Arab states and the Western superpowers. In their contacts with the French and Americans the Soviets took a hard-line on Israel's responsibility for starting the crisis, but at the same time they expressed their hope for achieving quiet in the region. On May 22 Soviets sent a non-committal message to Nasir, the Egyptian people, and the Arab nation – "supporting Egypt and the Arab nations in the defense of their homelands and their anti-Imperialist ideologies, and expressing solidarity with them."[89]

Following Eban's May 25 warning to the Americans that an Egyptian attack was imminent, the United States administration sent a note to Kosygin asking him to restrain the Egyptians. Kosygin obliged. The Soviet ambassador in Cairo woke Nasir up at 03:00 on May 27 and told him not to commence military operations, saying that "Egypt must not be the party that initiates a military offensive otherwise world public opinion would turn against it." Simultaneously the Soviet ambassador in Tel Aviv delivered an identical message to Eshkol at 03:30, demanding that the Israeli leader take all the necessary steps to avoid a military clash with Syria and Egypt, that is, to abstain from a preemptive strike. The note expressed the Soviet Union's belief that Israel did not want war, and it called on Israel not to let itself be pushed into armed aggression because of pressure from interested parties. Although the ambassador tried to find out if Israel intended to initiate hostilities, he failed to receive a direct answer. Eshkol invited him to visit the northern border and see with his own eyes if there were any Israeli troop concentrations there, but the Soviet ambassador declined. Kosygin also sent a message to Johnson warning that the Soviet Union would come to the aid of the Arabs if Israel attacked. The Russian leader asked the United States to exert its restraining influence on Israel in order to avoid a military conflagration, while he, Kosygin, promised to work toward the same goal on the Arab side.[90]

On May 25 the Egyptian minister of war, Shams Badran, and the director-general of the Egyptian foreign ministry, set out for Moscow on an "urgent mission." In an urgent meeting with the Soviet leadership they discussed military aid to Egypt and political and moral support for the Arabs' position, first and foremost Egypt's position. Each side interpreted differently the results of the visit. Fawzi recorded Badran's version: "When Badran took leave of Grechko, the Soviet defense minister, at the airport, he felt that the Soviet minister's behavior [or statements] implied that the Soviet Union would intervene politically and militarily on the Arabs' side. Badran added that he believed that this would be [in the form of] direct intervention." When Badran returned to Cairo on May 28 he informed Nasir that, "the Soviet Union would support the Arab position against Israel and provide direct assistance in the Arabs' armed struggle." On the basis of this report Nasir declared on May 29 that, "When I met with Shams Badran yesterday he delivered an [oral] message from Kosygin stating that the Soviet Union is standing on our right hand side in the present struggle and will prevent any country from reverting the situation to its previous, pre-1956 condition." According to Fawzi: "Badran voiced this misunderstanding in a government meeting

206

on the day after his return [from Moscow]. [He] tried to convince his listeners that if the American fleet in the Mediterranean intervenes in the military struggle between Israel and us, then our bombers – TU-16s – along with our fleet's fast-moving ships could easily destroy the largest aircraft carrier in the American fleet." Fawzi notes that, "On the other hand, according to the Foreign Ministry director-general's report that reached Nasir only on June 13, the Kremlin leaders had asked Shams Badran 'not to let the situation deteriorate,' and that Grashko had only said to Badran at the time of their departure, 'We'll always be on your side.' "[91]

Huwaydi strengthens the foreign ministry director-general's version regarding the influence of the superpowers on the crystallization of Nasir's second-strike strategy: "International pressure and efforts were underway to prevent the two sides from starting a war. De Gaulle, too, pointed out that France would oppose any state that initiated an attack. The Soviet Union, too, exerted constant pressure in this direction. Official protocols reveal that during the meeting with the minister of war, Shams Badran, the Soviet leadership in Moscow made it clear that it was in Egypt's interest to avoid starting a war [especially] since Cairo had garnered enough political and military victories, and that political efforts should be given a chance to restore quiet in the region." Kosygin clarified his position to Badran during their May 26 meeting:

"In my opinion, you have already won both politically and militarily. What do you want now? I think you should be satisfied with what you have attained: the withdrawal of the UN forces; your takeover of the straits; your forces deployed in Gaza; what more do you want? . . . Generally speaking I prefer roundtable talks instead of military conflict and [I believe] this is in your interest . . . You should stabilize what you have achieved without resorting to war. If you accept this line of thinking, then our thoughts coincide, but if you think otherwise, let us know."[92]

After Badran's visit to Moscow the Soviets decided to engage in much closer cooperation with Egypt and Syria and coordinate their political moves with the Arabs. But, on the diplomatic level they still sought to pacify the situation. They also proposed a "constructive" solution based mainly on international recognition of Egyptian sovereignty in the straits and the guarantee of protection of shipping by means of navigators under UN auspices. The Soviet Union definitely intended to adhere to the Egyptian position on preserving the *status quo*. Taking all these developments into consideration, Egypt asked the UN to convene an emergency session of the UNSC on May 28 in order to gain international backing for the new *status quo*. The Soviet media continued to assert the Kremlin's unqualified support of Egypt's moves even after the crisis deteriorated and war broke out.[93]

Nasir and the Egyptian media lauded the Soviet Union's political and military support. On May 29 Nasir stated:

> I met with the minister of war, Shams Badran, and learned the details of his talks in Moscow, and I want to state that the Soviet Union is our friend and as such it stands by us. Since 1955 [it] has demanded nothing of us, nor has it interfered in our internal affairs or beliefs [*madhab*] . . . When I visited [Moscow] last year I asked for an assortment of weapons, and they responded positively. Yesterday Shams Badran brought me an [oral] message from Kosygin, stating that the Soviet Union stood beside us and would not allow any state to intervene in order to return the situation to what it was before 1956. In the name of the Egyptian people, I thank the Soviet people for the generous, friendly, and honest attitude that we can expect from them.[94]

During the crisis and throughout the struggle for Arab public opinion, the Soviet Union saw no better exchange for its aid and support of Egypt than this section of Nasir's speech that reverberated throughout the Arab world via the Arab media.

At the time of the Syrian leadership's visit to the Soviet Union on May 29, the Russians repeated their promise to extend political and military assistance to Egypt and Syria. After the signing of the Husayn – Nasir defense agreement, the Soviet media ceased almost all of its criticism of the Arab "reactionary" regimes, denouncing only Israel. On June 2 in a message to the Israeli government that was given to the Israeli ambassador in Moscow, the Russians repeated their warning to Israel. "The Soviet government wishes to reiterate that it will do everything in its power to prevent a military confrontation. It is presently focusing its efforts in this direction. But if the Israeli government decides to assume responsibility for the outbreak of war, it will pay for the consequences." In a conversation between Kosygin and Badran on May 26, Kosygin said that "reports from Israel point to the likelihood that [Israel] will initiate military operations in the end of May 1967."[95]

The reason behind the Soviet Union's intensive diplomatic activity, besides the desire to cool tempers and stave off a military confrontation, was its assessment that an Israeli attack would jeopardize Nasir's position and its achievements in the region. The assessment was based on the assumption that an Israeli operation was likely whether Eban's talks in Washington succeeded (as part of an American–Israeli plot) or whether they failed and Israel would be forced to act alone. This explains the Soviets' decision to fulfill their promise and ship an unlimited supply of military equipment into the region after Badran's visit to Moscow. *In conclusion*: Soviet efforts were aimed at taking diplomatic steps and preventing an Egyptian military initiative while Nasir was at the pinnacle of his political success.

The United States

Nasir's attitude toward the United States during the crisis was complex and multifaceted. He frequently joined in the anti-American propaganda campaign that reached strident tones at times. The following factors contributed to Egypt's hot – cold relationship with the United States:

1 Both countries put great value on their longstanding ties and understood its complexity. Nasir regarded Egypt's relations with Washington as a counterweight to the close relationship with the Soviet Union. His interest in financial aid was a major motive for the special importance he attributed to American–Egyptian relations. He set great store by the United States as a superpower and its influence in the Western world and international arena. Since the United States was the key to the Western world's moves in the present crisis, he endeavored to maintain direct channels of communication with Washington. It appears that the two countries even exchanged intelligence information (after the war intelligence links between them became official). During Badran's trial in February 1968, the ex-minister admitted that the Americans had been the source of Nasir's information on June 2 that Israel would attack within two or three days.

2 Nasir viewed America's support of Israel as the major "fly in the ointment" in

American–Egyptian relations. He attributed great importance to the United States role during and after the Sinai War and hoped that it would play the same role in the present crisis. He regarded its relations with Israel as a yardstick for measuring its support of the Arab cause as well as determining the Arab position toward it. He feared that if Egypt initiated hostilities, the United States' would rush military aid to Israel, that is, it would embark upon a military operation against Egypt. Indeed, Badran informed Kosygin on May 26 that he "received a telegram from the Field Marshal today with reliable information that the United States would supply Israel with planes with Israeli markings flown by American pilots and operating from Israeli airbases." He added that "In all events, we are prepared to face Israel and whoever is behind Israel as along as we do not initiate the aggression."[96]

Nasir's estimate of US policy fluctuated between two poles during the crisis:

1 On the one hand, he believed that the United States completely identified with Israel and its right to use force to guarantee the principle of freedom of navigation through the straits. Furthermore, he did not rule out the possibility of direct military aid to Israel if Egypt launched an attack. Nasir's fear was one of the important factors in his justification of the second-strike strategy.
2 On the other hand, Nasir felt that his contacts with the American administration after the closure of the straits revealed a change in Washington's position. The United States had become a "positive mediator." In the wake of the superpowers' failure to reconcile the issue of the straits, the United States appeared willing to accept the *status quo*.

When Eban arrived in Washington on May 25, a message awaited for him from Eshkol stating that Egypt had brought more troops into Sinai and was recalling its forces from Yemen; the Egyptian fleet had returned from the Red Sea to the Mediterranean; and last but not least "the Arabs were planning to launch a full-scale attack against Israel." Eshkol added that, "the main problem is not the straits. It is a question of Israel's survival. A deterioration in the Western position encourages the Arabs, and their appetite grows by the hour." Eshkol concluded his message on a decisive note: "You have to find out what practical steps Johnson intends to take." On the same day, the head of Israeli military intelligence presented his assessment: "All signs show that [Egypt] will probably make a confrontational move against us." Israeli intelligence obtained information about Operation Fajr and estimated that Egyptian bombers were likely to attack airfields and vital objectives on the night of May 26/27.

The head of military intelligence reported to the ministers on May 26 that, "numerous reports indicate [Egypt's] intention to launch an offensive." This assessment crystallized just as the Egyptian 4th Armored Division moved into Sinai on May 25, an additional Egyptian armored brigade was formed, an armored brigade returned from Yemen, the part of the Egyptian fleet sailed from the Red Sea to the Mediterranean, and other military movements were carried out all of which pointed to the likelihood that Egypt would initiate an attack. Israeli intelligence estimated that Egyptian forces in Sinai stood at four infantry divisions, two armored divisions – 800 tanks and 80,000 troops. With the Egyptian fleet back in the Mediterranean arena, the ground forces in Sinai would be supported with naval fire power.[97]

Eban conveyed these warnings to the American administration and demanded a staunch declaration of backing for Israel. This resulted in Washington's message to Kosygin on May 25 asking him to curb the Egyptians. (The Soviets complied with the request, it will be remembered, at the meeting between the Soviet ambassador and Nasir on the night of May 26/27.) The following day the American ambassador in Cairo met with Nasir and handed him an urgent message from Johnson stating that an Egyptian-initiated attack would damage Egypt's international standing. According to Fawzi "a high-priority telegram arrived from the Egyptian ambassador in the United States [probably after his meeting with Secretary of State Rusk on May 26] mentioning the United States anger [*inzi'aj*] after it had received reliable information from Israel about Egypt's plan to attack and the date of the attack. This refers to the 'Asad Plan' that was supposed to have taken place on May 27." Fawzi notes that, "It was clear to President Nasir that Israel's information was correct."[98]

On the morning of May 28, the American ambassador to Israel, Walworth Barbour, handed Eshkol messages from Johnson and Rusk. The messages repeated the promises given to Eban and advised the Israeli government not to take hasty steps. Johnson's message stated that Kosygin had already informed him that "the Soviets had information that Israel was planning to attack the Arab states and that the Soviet Union would assist the Arabs if Israel attacked." The Israeli government convened that day and decided, in light of the American warnings, to wait for the results of the diplomatic activity in the international arena.[99]

On May 26 Nasir harshly criticized American policy. "Today we see America's hypocrisy toward the Arabs. It supports Israel one hundred percent . . . The United States is unquestionably an enemy of the Arabs because it acts with flagrant partiality toward Israel."[100] But the American position continued to vex Nasir, especially against the background of American efforts to obtain Western support of a forced solution to freedom of navigation in the straits. He was particularly worried over the possibility of American–Israeli collaboration similar to the tripartite British–French–Israeli collusion in 1956. Nasir's statements at the May 28 press conference revealed Egypt's growing fear of American moves while Egypt pursued international efforts to secure its recent political gains. He emphasized that "We have no direct quarrel [with Washington]. The basic problem between the United States and Egypt – is Israel. The Americans favor Israel and alienate one hundred million Arabs . . . We admired the Americans during the tripartite aggression against Egypt in 1956. Today the situation is completely different . . . They claim that the [Gulf of Aqaba] is an international [waterway]."[101] In his May 29 speech, Nasir intensified his attack on the United States:

> We are not afraid of the United States and its threats, nor of Britain and its threats, we are not even afraid of the entire Western world and its support of Israel . . . One hundred million Arabs are not worth a scrap of garlic peel to them . . . If the United States and Britain back Israel, this means that not only Israel is our enemy but that the United States and Britain also are.[102]

Johnson's message reached Eshkol prior to the Israeli government meeting. It asked Eshkol not to use language more explicit regarding America's obligation than what had been said to Abba Eban. The president again admonished Israel not to make a preemptive strike. Under the influence of the message the Israeli government decided on May 28 to avoid a military initiative for three weeks. The next day the American administration announced its official policy lines:

1 Following the Israeli promise not to precipitate hostile activity, the United States reaffirms its guarantee to safeguard Israel's economic and political independence.
2 The Israeli government's decision allows the United States to engage in diplomacy, especially through the UN, to ward off a conflagration.
3 If this path fails, the United States will continue to work at gaining international support, especially among the maritime nations, until a formula is found that will pacify the situation and remove the danger to Israel.

Washington stressed in this announcement that the continuation of American aid depended on Israel's avoidance of military activity. Thus, the United States hoped to allay Nasir's suspicions that it was conniving with Israel against Egypt or goading Israel to attack. The policy statement was also intended to serve as a balanced approach that would be acceptable to the Egyptians.

Once Nasir announced the closing of the straits, the United States tended increasingly to shift its political effort from trying to influence the Soviet Union and the Arabs to diplomatic activity. The Americans based their argument on the assessment that it was impossible to get the Egyptians and Russians to take steps that made them appear as retreating, since they would not allow the tension to subside unless they emerged from the crisis with a tangible gain in their hands. Given the United States' involvement in Vietnam, American policy in the Eastern Mediterranean was geared to avert a confrontation that could lead to a direct clash with the Soviet Union – especially since the administration was uncertain how far the Soviets would go in such a face-off.

Toward the end of May, when Washington realized that the crisis had bogged down in a dead-end – that is, that America's allies would not cooperate in political action or force a solution that guaranteed maritime freedom in the straits – then the United States began to prepare for the possibilities that still remained open to it in the Middle East, including the ensuring of Nasir's achievements. It grew increasingly aware that the present crisis had an impact not only on Arab–Israeli affairs but also on America's status in the Arab world and perhaps in other regions too. Furthermore, Washington began to perceive that the Soviet backing of Egypt's moves and the new situation that was created contained grave dangers to America's Middle Eastern and global position. For this reason an American State Department official, Charles Yost, arrived in Cairo on May 30 for talks with the Egyptian foreign minister Mahmud Riyad, and on June 1 the American envoy, Robert Anderson, met with Nasir in Cairo. At the same time Nasir and Johnson exchanged messages (on May 30 and June 3 respectively) related to their ongoing bilateral dialogue. In the wake of Washington's new estimate of the situation, the administration displayed a keen interest in the normalization of relations with Egypt and a willingness to mediate (to serve as a "positive intermediary" as the Egyptians put it), on the basis of the *status quo*, in order to assuage Cairo's apprehensions. Whatever the case, based on past experience, the Americans refrained from pressuring Egypt to make concessions. They were careful not to give the Egyptians any cause for suspecting an American–Israeli "conspiracy," and they strove to demonstrate to the Egyptians that the United States was not involved in any Israeli offensive plans. This orientation became increasingly important to the United States the more it realized that an Israeli military initiative was inevitable. Therefore it endeavored to prepare the ground for fending off accusations when hostilities broke out of being in collusion with Israel. (Indeed, such incriminations were not long in coming after Israel's air strike on June 5.)

Yost proposed a compromise to the Egyptians: they would immediately grant unconditional free passage to all Israeli ships without cargo checks, and in the next stage, they would negotiate with the maritime states; the United States would guarantee that the Gulf of Aqaba was considered Egyptian territory (that is, under Egyptian sovereignty) but a strict restriction would be placed on Egyptian surveillance of shipping passage. In times of peace any ship, including Israeli vessels, would be permitted to pass through the straits without interference. In wartime the Egyptians would have the right to halt Israeli vessels. The Egyptians rejected this proposal outright. They stated their willingness to negotiate the passage of Israeli ships through the straits only within the framework of renewed discussions over the Palestinian problem on the basis of UN resolutions since 1947.[103]

Both the United States and Egypt wanted to keep their dialogue intact – the United States, in order to prove its good intentions to reach a compromise with Egypt and prevent the crisis from deteriorating; and Egypt, in order to neutralize American–Israeli cooperation or at least preclude American involvement if war broke out. The two sides decided that Vice President Humphrey would visit Egypt, and the Egyptian vice president, Zakariya Muhi al-Din, would come to the United States. Muhi al-Din's visit was scheduled for June 6 and, naturally, never took place.

Egypt's propaganda campaign against the United States was an important element in the bilateral relations. Egypt wanted to signal to the United States what could happen if it supported Israel in a military confrontation. The Egyptians hoped to deter the United States from giving massive aid to Israel. Nasir, along with the Syrian and Iraqi leaders, portrayed the Soviet Union as a friend and the United States as "standing behind everything going on [in the Middle East], just like Israel. America was Israel, and Israel was America." Nasir set the tone for the anti-American propaganda offensive, and the media in Egypt and other Arab states followed suit. As the crisis escalated the Egyptian media (as well as the Syrian and Iraqi media) attacked the United States daily, even hourly. The authorities seem to have issued sweeping instructions to the media to brazenly denounce the United States.[104]

On July 23 Nasir summed up the international factors behind his decision for "a second-strike strategy":

> After our troop movement [into Sinai] and taking the initiative in removing the threat from Syria, we realized . . . that if we struck the first blow in an armed struggle, we would suffer drastically from the consequences. *First*, we would have to deal with American military operations against us [because they] would claim we fired the first volley . . . [President Johnson] asked for restraint and said that he had asked the same from Israel . . . *Second*, the following day the Russian ambassador handed me a message from the Soviet prime minister asking us to hold our fire and informing me about his [similar] message to the Israeli prime minister. The Soviet prime minister also pointed out that any action we initiated would seriously endanger world peace. *Third*, the entire international community was opposed to war. President De Gaulle stated explicitly that France

212

would determine its position on the basis of [who fired] the first shot. Then the American presidential envoy arrived. He suggested that an [Egyptian] vice president leave for the United States. I agreed with the idea. Next the Americans welcomed Muhi al-Din's trip to Washington to meet with Johnson, and asked if the date Tuesday, June 6 would be suitable. We all know that [Israeli] aggression began on June 5. In other words, in the middle of all this political, diplomatic activity, we were correct in thinking that the explosion was still far off.[105]

The Fourth Stage, May 29–June 5, 1967:
Waiting for the First Strike

The crisis now peaked. The Egyptians, Israelis, and entire Arab world realized that a massive confrontation was only a matter of time. The Egyptian–Israeli clash had become full-blown between the Arab world and Israel (the culmination of the Zionist movement). This explains why the Arabs determined that their goal was to solve the Palestinian problem in its widest sense. In the Arabs' eyes Israel's very existence was in doubt, that is, even if war were avoided, Israel would collapse because of the blockade imposed upon it.

This stage also witnessed Nasir's attainment of his primary goal, or vision: the unity of an Arab front and the mobilization of the entire Arab world's resources for a military confrontation with Israel. The notion of "unity of the ranks" [or "unity of aim"] had been successfully accomplished. It is no wonder, then, that Arab passions were whipped to a frenzy as "the final battle" against Israel approached.

Egypt's Assessment of the Military Situation

Both the Egyptians and Israelis were in a state of high tension – but for different reasons. Egypt waited for Israel to strike the first blow, and Israel waited for the right moment to strike.[106] Both sides were on full alert. The Egyptians continued to receive reports of IDF activity and troop deployment. This information, however, reflects unflatteringly on Egypt's military intelligence that had swallowed the IDF's deceptions regarding the main axis of attack. Since the Egyptian high command was glued to the concept that the main attack would come on the southern axis, it deployed most of its forces there.

On May 29 Egyptian military intelligence reported that enemy activity in the Negev's southern sector was preparing an offensive on the southern axis. The report emphasized that "Israeli ground forces headquarters had ordered the southern axis to be strengthened." On June 1 intelligence reports from el-Arish also highlighted the "enemy's intention to attack along the southern axis and perhaps parachute forces south of Kuntilla." A June 3 intelligence report differed from the others, noting "the size of Israeli troop concentrations on the Egyptian confrontation line . . . [on] the southern axis . . . stood at no more than one infantry battalion and one minority's battalion of lookouts, backed by a mechanized brigade and a few tanks." Fawzi points to "the accuracy of the reports on enemy troop strength on the southern axis and that they were based on *the Egyptian air force's first successful air reconnaissance at noon of June 2 over the southern Negev, at a depth of fifteen kilometers into enemy territory*" [my emphasis – M.S.]. Fawzi also adds that "these reports on enemy strength on the southern axis were accurate, but they arrived too late . . . and Mushir Amer did not attempt to change the battle order in Sinai. Furthermore, during the High Command meeting in Sinai that day nobody questioned the reason for the concentration of the bulk of our forces on the southern axis opposite the enemy's weaker forces, as noted in that day's intelligence report." Fawzi comes to the conclusion that "this was due to the mental obfuscation of the commanders and combat forces because of the excess of orders, vagaries in the deployment of forces, and military intelligence's imprecise reports [or assessments] since May 15, 1967."[107]

On Friday June 2, three days before the war, Nasir, Amer, Badran, headquarters officers, field commanders, and Amer's and Fawzi's bureau chiefs convened for a High Command meeting during which Nasir predicted almost the exact date of the Israeli attack. According to Fawzi:

> Nasir opened the meeting with a political analysis of the international situation, after which he discussed world public opinion, especially that of the United States, and the possibility that [Washington] would extend direct aid to Israel if its military security was threatened . . . The president concluded his analysis emphasizing that Israel would launch a preemptive first strike after it had finished organizing its affairs . . . [as it did] in 1956. He expected that war would break out within two or three days – on June 4 or 5 . . . He [repeated] his warning that Israel would begin its offensive on June 5. Afterwards he discussed the details of [Israel's] preventive war that called for its implementation of the first strike, [and he] recalled the events in 1956 [Israel's surprise attack, a short-term war, the fighting on Egyptian soil]. He aimed his words especially at Fariq Awal (General) Muhammad Sidqi Mahmud, the commander of the air force and air defense, concentrating his argument on the estimated damage to our air force and [our] vital counter-response. Sidqi Mahmud estimated a 15–20% damage to the air force in an Israeli first strike, and that the forfeiture of our initiative would lead to the weakening of our air force. The debate in which Nasir, Amer, and Sidqi Mahmud participated came to the conclusion that it would be preferable to suffer an Israeli first air strike and retain international support – especially of the United States – since the president believed [the United States] would intervene on Israel's side if we initiated the first strike. Moreover, the United States would document and publicize our attack on Israel, which would be detrimental to Egypt in the international arena.
>
> At the end of the meeting we agreed to take the necessary preventive steps [wiqa'i] to limit Israel's first strike damage to our air force and allow us to counterattack in the air. Amer agreed and instructed Sidqi Mahmud to do what was necessary to protect the air force against a first strike, especially since our forces' task has become generally defensive, 20% of the forces would be damaged in the first strike in a war with Israel, and since this possibility was preferable to a first strike on our part and a war with Israel and America. The president ended the meeting by stating that he knew exactly which steps Israel would take since circumstances and events were similar to those of 1956, that is, [Israel would attempt] a surprise attack, short-term war, and transfer of the campaign onto our territory.[108]

Fawzi's report of the meeting appears reliable up to this point. He goes on to describe his impression of the participants and Amer:

> The president's political and military assessments did not convince Mushir Amer. He made no comment on the president's warning of the exact date of the campaign, as proof

of this he kept to his schedule and visited Sinai on the day war was supposed to break out [according to Nasir's evaluation]. The rest of the command officers, too, were antagonistic since Amer had not warned them about a possible Israeli attack on June 5. In fact, some of the commanders were heard muttering, 'What's he saying? What about his [Nasir's] estimates in 1956?' I believe the Mushir was the source of this grumbling. In any event, the commanders were skeptical over the president's position and admonitions, and they identified with their commander – Amer . . . On the other hand, Amer, whom the president's views had failed to convince, circulated the June 2 intelligence report among most of his forces. The report (that apparently reflected the Mushir's estimate on purpose) stated that 'Israel will not embark upon an offensive [because] the current Arab determination will undoubtedly force the enemy to realize the consequences of war erupting in the region,' even though one day before this report [June 1] the el-Arish intelligence bureau noted the enemy's intention to launch an offensive on the southern axis and possibly drop airborne troops south of Kuntilla.[109]

Following Egypt's revised strategy regarding the stages in the confrontation according to the second-strike concept, Amer issued order No. 1967/18 on May 29 that redefined the operative war aim: "To repulse the enemy's surprise attack, defeat and destroy his forces, and prepare to transfer offensive operations in the direction of Sinai–Filastin as quickly as possible according to the Qahir Plan." Fawzi comments: "We see, then, that the Mushir backed away from his [original] intentions; he canceled all of the offensive plans, and no longer opted for interdictory defense, but for traditional defense."[110]

On June 2, the day of High Command meeting (and probably as a result of it) Amer, who was serving as Deputy Supreme Commander of the Armed Forces, issued the following order to "the officers, NCOs, and soldiers of the armed forces:

Israel has tried and continues to try to obtain direct American support for its military activity against Egypt. It is obvious that the United States will not dare to get directly involved for Israel's sake because [it knows] the Soviet Union's firm position and decision to intervene in case of aggression by a superpower against the United Arab Republic. Israel cannot sustain the burden of lengthy mobilization . . . which has totally paralyzed its economy.

Two major events have occurred in recent days:
1 Jordan has entered the joint defense.
2 Iraqi forces have joined the large force [gathered] on the Jordanian border.

My analysis of the situation – especially after Israel formed an emergency government that included extremists clamoring for war – is that it apparently believes that the Iraqi forces stationed on the Jordanian front will require at least two weeks to become effective. Israel might attack the UAR [Egypt] in the very near future before this concentration is completed. Therefore I have drawn up a plan and issued instructions to prepare operations. Our goal is to destroy Israel's main force. Our army can accomplish this with its vast resources.[111]

Amer's certainty about the United States position naturally stemmed from the strategic implications of the second strike that had been analyzed in the June 2 High Command meeting and that were accepted by Amer. The certainty also originated in Egyptian diplomatic contacts with the Americans prior to the meeting, and Badran's report of his visit to the Soviet Union must have influenced Egypt's perception of the Russians' position. Thus, Fawzi's impression seems correct regarding the response by

Amer and his officers to Nasir's predicted date of the Israeli attack. Amer linked his assessment to the deployment of Iraqi forces in Jordan. He spoke of "a quick attack" but, unlike Nasir, he made no mention of the timing. And on the morning of June 5 he left for Sinai to inspect the troops.[112]

In conclusion, the Egyptian army remained on full alert waiting for an Israeli air strike, after which it planned to deliver the decisive second blow. The Israeli first strike did take place, but the Egyptian second strike never had a chance. Nasir's strategy never got off the ground.

Widening the Circle: A Solution to the Palestinian Problem

After Nasir blocked the straits, he realized that an all-out confrontation between Israel and the Arab states was inevitable, and that if he failed to take the initiative, then Israel would. It was only natural of him, and perhaps even expected, to present the aim of the approaching war as the solution to the Palestinian problem (or 1948 problem); that is, the "restitution of Palestinian rights and the establishment of a Palestinian government on liberated Filastin land" as enshrined in the UN resolutions. Thus Nasir turned the straits issue, mainly an Egyptian–Israeli bone of contention, into the solution of the 1948 problem. In this way he skillfully excited the Arab world (or Arab nation) and at the same time recruited it into his campaign; in both endeavors his success was unprecedented. Another reason that the Palestinian issue was raised at this rather late stage in the crisis seems to have been in preparation for the eventuality that the military leadership's assessment proved correct and the war was carried over onto Israeli territory. Nasir wanted to prove that he was fulfilling his long-range commitment to resolve the Palestinian problem.

Even before the May 29 speech in which he defined the strategic goal as "a solution to the 1948 problem," the Palestinian political issue had cropped up in the Egyptian leadership's political–military discussions – mainly on Nasir's initiative. The degree of Nasir's involvement in the Palestinian issue and its importance in his plans can be seen in his intention to set up a Palestinian government in the Gaza Strip or Palestinian government institutions in Filastin territories at the end of the campaign. In other words, Nasir intended to fulfill Egypt's promise ever since the idea of reviving the Palestinian entity was broached in 1959, and from the time it shifted its position on the PLO and fidai'yyun activity. This issue probably surfaced when Nasir was discussing the steps to be taken in the Palestinian political field if the *status quo* was maintained, or if war erupted that he was sure would end in an Egyptian victory, even if only a partial one after the fighting was transferred to Israeli territory. On May 21 the Lebanese newspaper *al-Nahar* published an article by its senior writer, Michel Abu-Jawda, stating *inter alia*: "According to information from Lebanese sources, Egypt has planned or is planning to announce the following step – to establish a 'Palestinian Arab Republic' on Filastin soil, the Gaza Strip, and the West Bank, and to call on Arab and friendly states to recognize [it] and help its army regain its occupied land: whether in one campaign or gradually."

On May 25 Nasir raised the Palestinian issue in a High Command meeting that was discussing and approving operational plans. He stressed the importance of hanging on to the Gaza Strip because of its political and moral significance, especially for the Palestinian people.

He turned the participants' attention to the importance of the Gaza Strip. Its capture [by the Israelis] would have a deleterious impact on Egypt's prestige. He believed that the forces assigned [to defend the strip] were insufficient to withstand an Israeli attack. Therefore, he saw the need to reinforce the Gaza Strip with more combat-ready troops in order to force Israel to reconsider its attack.[113]

If Nasir's May 26 speech was worded in general terms, ("We hope to see Israel surrounded by a single front, and we will not surrender the Palestinians' rights"), then the rhetorical escalation in his May 29 speech reflected the intensification of the crisis. In a speech before members of the Egyptian People's Council (Parliament) who had come to express their support of "his steps in the face of the Israeli threat," Nasir declared:

After (the events of 1956) we have succeeded in production and building . . . since then eleven years have elapsed . . . Materially we have returned to pre-1956 conditions but in my opinion this has been a minor accomplishment. The importance lies in the moral realm: bolstering the Arab people, reviving the Palestinian problem, and restoring self-confidence to every Arab and Palestinian, on the assumption *that if we succeed in returning the situation to what it was before 1956, then God will undoubtedly help us return [it] to what it was before 1948 . . . and not to the absurd condition of 1948. With God's help we shall triumph* [my emphasis – M.S.]. The preparations have been completed and we are now ready to meet Israel's challenge . . . *Today the problem is not the Gulf of Aqaba or the UN Emergency Forces, but the rights of the Palestinian people; the aggression in Filastin in 1948, with the abetment of Britain and the United States; the expulsion of the Arabs from Filastin; the abrogation of their rights and expropriation of their property; the rejection of every UN decision that benefited the Palestinian people* [my emphasis – M.S.]. Today's problem is much greater than what they're talking about. They want to reduce it to a question of the Straits of Tiran, international emergency forces, and navigational rights, but we demand full rights for the Palestinian people . . . Arab rights will never be surrendered.[114]

The significance of Nasir's *volte-face* and the deep thought that must have gone into it, appeared in a leading article in *al-Ahram*, published in conjunction with Nasir's presidential office, and perhaps under its instructions. The article was entitled "Filastin is the Problem":

Nasir has presented the ultimate challenge in the Palestinian problem. The Arab position was not determined by Israeli border provocations and its relentless political provocations. The problem is not about the Straits of Tiran or the withdrawal of the international emergency forces. Egypt's military and political moves on these two issues have been a kind of rectification of the after-effects of the 1956 aggression and the restoration of our rights. Our main problem is the disappearance of a country [Filastin] from the political map of the Arab East. In 1948 the Zionist gangs that came from the four corners of the world committed acts of aggression against the Filastin homeland that are still being felt. Indeed, this is the problem.[115]

All of Nasir's statements on the Palestinian issue prove how high it stood on his agenda and that his commitment to the problem was a major factor in determining his political and even military steps.

Closing the "Arab Ring"

In the inter-Arab domain: When Egypt closed the straits, it was sufficiently confident to exploit its achievements and assemble a front of progressive states, while denouncing the Arab "reactionary" states. The popular enthusiasm in Jordan, Saudi Arabia, Lybia, Kuwait, Yemen, Algeria, and Lebanon of Nasir encouraged him to pursue this policy. Even the king of Morocco tried to "cozy up" to Egypt, advising Nasir to take advantage of his position above the general contention in the inter-Arab sphere. On May 29 Tunisia declared its return to Arab League activity. King Husayn's attachment to Nasir's camp on May 30 was the highpoint in the pro-Egypt trend. In other words, during the week prior to the war the entire Arab world cast its lot in with Nasir's military campaign – an outstanding achievement in inter-Arab relations that had not been witnessed since 1949.

Jordan

Husayn had the political acumen to sense the prevailing mood in his country and the Arab world after the blocking of the straits. He realized that Nasir's unilateral act implied war, and on May 25 he asked Iraq and Saudi Arabia to dispatch troops to Jordan in order to strengthen its defense system and "deter the inevitable Zionist attack, or at least lessen its damage."[116] He estimated that the Israeli invasion of the West Bank was now a palpable danger. Jordan's fear that Israel would use the entry of Arab forces into Jordan as a pretext for seizing the West Bank now became irrelevant. Saudi Arabia agreed to send troops. On May 26 Jordanian and Saudi officers met in Tabuk (northern Saudi Arabia) to coordinate their moves. Iraq, however, turned down the Jordanian request because Husayn had spurned Baghdad's offer to station forces on Jordanian soil a few months earlier. Iraq now claimed that it needed UAC (Egyptian) approval.[117] When Iraq consulted Nasir, he vetoed the matter and supported Iraq's refusal to dispatch military forces to Jordan as long as Husayn still shunned the Arab (Egyptian–Syrian) campaign. Nasir had no desire to extend an all-Arab backing to Husayn until the king reversed his inter-Arab policy. Nasir also perceived that Jordan's consent to have Iraqi forces in its country was a ploy designed to weaken the "progressive front" while gaining a pan-Arab image for Jordan.

King Husayn came to the conclusion that Jordan had to integrate into the general Arab atmosphere and could no longer allow itself to trail behind the rest of the Arab countries; he also had to pacify the Palestinians on the West Bank. Therefore on May 24, the Jordanian prime minister, Sa'ad Jum'a, published the following official statement: "The Jordanian government fully supports the Egyptian position on its restored sovereignty over the territorial waters of the Gulf of Aqaba and the prevention of passage to Israeli vessels in this gulf . . . The Jordanian government has mobilized all its resources and forces in order to handle the situation and supports Arab rights and sovereignty."[118]

In the meantime tension was building in Jordan's domestic sphere and was liable explode with repercussions more injurious than those of the November 1966 riots. Government circles and security agencies fretted over the public mood in general and among the West Bank Palestinians in particular. Nationalistic fervor was soaring, especially among opposition elements, and the Jordanian public was ebullient over the prospect of Israel's certain downfall. The army and its junior officers were infected with a martial spirit and hunger for battle, and the Jordanian high command feared that if fighting erupted some units might go into action before ordered to. On May 25, in a token gesture, the Jordanian government ceased its propaganda campaign against "certain Arab states" (excluding the issue of the May 21 Ramtha explosion that was carried out by Syrian intelligence). Jordan cancelled its intention to recall its ambassador from Damascus and sever relations with Syria following acts of sabotage perpetrated by fida'iyyun working for Syrian intelligence. Instead, it limited its response to expelling the Syrian ambassador from Jordan. On May 24 the King met with several Arab ambassadors, and including the high-profile presence of the Egyptian ambassador. Jordanian propaganda began to amplify its anti-American volume in official statements and the media. On May 26 Jordan agreed to prepare airfields for maintenance of UAC aircraft "if the need arises," that is, for Iraqi planes to operate from Jordanian territory. Beginning on May 28 *Radio Amman* joined the Arab world in broadcasting nationalist slogans calling for the march to war.

Developments in the Arab arena, growing domestic unrest, and the rising wave of nationalism on the West Bank shook Husayn's self-confidence and increased his fear that Jordan's continued political isolation would undermine the regime. Furthermore, when he learned of Egypt's plans to renew its propaganda campaign against him, beginning on June 4, in order to jolt his regime and perhaps even overthrow it, he hastened to ask Nasir personally for reconciliation. On May 28 he sent Nasir a message, via the Egyptian ambassador in Amman, asking to meet with him in Cairo, outlining Jordan's precarious situation, promising to establish a nationalistic government in Jordan compatible with Egypt, and expressing his willingness to discuss any conditions that Cairo saw fit to broach. Nasir's reply the following day contained a number of stipulations: (1) the immediate removal of Jordanian forces from the Syrian border; (2) the cessation of Jordanian schemes against Syria; (3) the expulsion of Syrian political fugitives seeking asylum in Jordan; (4) the refusal to permit the deployment of Saudi troops on Jordanian soil, and (5) the deployment of Jordanian units on Israel's border in order to draw Israeli forces to the Jordanian front. If King Husayn accepted these conditions, Egypt promised not to resume its propaganda campaign against Jordan.

Husayn arrived in Cairo on May 30, the same day he signed a joint defense pact with Nasir. The agreement's wording was identical to the Egyptian–Syrian defense agreement signed on November 4, 1966. Nasir's prior conditions were overshadowed by Husayn's complete willingness to sign the agreement, and especially to have the Jordanian army placed under the direct command of Abd al-Mun'im Riyad, the UAC chief of staff, in time of war. After the two leaders affixed their signatures to the agreement, *Radio Cairo* immediately broadcast article 7: "If military activities commence, the chief of staff of the Egyptian armed forces will take operational command of both countries." (Iraq joined the pact on June 4.) Nasir had not anticipated such a windfall. Now Riyad was personally in charge of the war on the Jordanian front.[119] Two days later Husayn gave a press conference in which he dwelt upon the importance of the pact:

> The joint defense pact that I signed in Cairo is not merely an historical event that is quickly relegated to memoirs; it is a major operational document [that expresses our]

determined decision. The wording and aims of the pact are identical to those in the pact signed by Egypt and Syria last autumn . . . I also regard the pact as though it was a Jordanian–Syrian document . . .[120]

The pact had meaning not only for Egyptian–Jordanian relations. Husayn's joining the Egyptian-led camp symbolized a turning point in the Arab world's political and military alignment toward the war. The pact reinforced Nasir's confidence in the inevitable clash with Israel. Now that a united front of confrontation states had been formed, Nasir's optimal conditions had been attained for war with Israel. He perceived that the lengthy Jordanian front would tie down Israel's troops, thus alleviating pressure on the Egyptian front. The two leaders noted these implications during the signing ceremony that took place in the presence of Shuqayri, who was there as a symbol of Husayn's "reconciliation" with him.[121] The agreement also opened Jordan's border to expeditionary forces from Iraq and Syria. During their meeting, Nasir and Husayn telephoned Arif asking him to retract his previous refusal to send an expeditionary force to Jordan. Arif now readily agreed. In the wake of Husayn's step, the moderate or "reactionary" Arab bloc – Saudi Arabia, Tunisia, and Lybia – also hopped on board Egypt's war wagon. In effect, Husayn contributed to the closing of the "Arab ring" now that the entire Arab world was united behind Nasir. The Egyptian–Jordanian pact was also an expression of the success of Nasir's policy. It gave a push to Egypt's propaganda campaign in the Arab world now that the leading "reactionary" state, Jordan, had joined the Nasirite camp. Furthermore Nasir's stature in the international arena, and especially in Egypt's relations with the United States, strengthened. This was apparent in American policy toward Nasir.

The signing of the pact generated enormous enthusiasm in Jordan and raised the King's prestige. Crowds of cheering people greeted Husayn and Shuqayri on their return from Cairo; in Nablus a large demonstration chanted, "Long live the king" and "Long live Nasir." The Arab media, excluding the Syrian press and radio, went overboard in praising the pact, its military and political implications, and Jordan itself. They considered the pact a "dazzling historical victory for the Arabs now that the Arab armies have completely encircled Israel."[122] Thus, Husayn's participation in the war was irreversible once hostilities broke out. Eshkol's message to the king on the morning of June 5 to avoid hostilities was meaningless for Husayn – therefore he brushed it off.

Jordan's "descent" to the all-Arab consensus, which began with the blockage of the straits, compelled the regime to change its information-propaganda line. This reorientation was also necessary because of the increasing nationalistic fervor, especially on the West Bank, demanding Jordan's integration into Nasir's militaristic plans. In other words, along with Husayn's "historical step," Jordan's information line changed, especially after Nasir "responded" to Jordan's propaganda campaign demanding the evacuation of the emergency force and closure of the straits. On May 27 *Radio Amman* joined the Arab chorus, and succumbed to the deepest feelings in the Jordanian public in general, and Palestinian West Bank public in particular: "The Jordanian people will fight for Filastin. No obstacle will deflect it from the main goal. The Palestinian people lives for Filastin and is ready to sacrifice itself for Filastin."

Following the Husayn–Nasir pact Jordan became a full-fledged partner in the Nasirite camp and in the crusade against Israel. The Egyptian president was much pleased by this. But for Husayn this move was a calculated risk. If he lost the West Bank, he could at least salvage the Hashemite regime on the East Bank.

In conclusion, Husayn's participation in the war on June 5 was unavoidable. The Jordanian leadership's estimate of the implications of the Samu' raid had been decisive in the king's May 30 decision to jump on board Nasir's war machine by signing the mutual defense pact. After Samu' Husayn estimated that if war erupted Israel would invade the West Bank whether or not Jordan was a belligerent. A few days before the Six Day War Husayn still believed that Israel would attack light-weight Jordan rather than mighty Egypt. On the other hand, Jordan's internal situation, especially on the West Bank, was on the threshold of an explosion that threatened the king's regime. Jordan's Palestinian population was pro-Nasir. It perceived Nasir as the savior of the Palestinian people and called for Jordan's integration into Nasir's war policy. Against the backdrop of the Palestinian national awakening it was only natural that this population was quickly caught up in the nationalistic wave sweeping across the Arab world after Nasir's announcement of the closure of the straits to Israeli vessels.

Husayn's considerations were correct: On the one hand, he knew that Jordan's participation in the war meant that Israel would occupy the West Bank. On the other hand, Jordan's non-participation in the war would expose him as a traitor to the Arab cause and jeopardize his regime's stability. Therefore the choice was between the lesser of two evils. This time, as in the past, the king chose wisely and became a national hero in the eyes of his people and the Arab world. In retrospect, and taking into consideration the development of the Palestinian National Movement in the wake of the war and the morale of the Palestinian people after the Samu' operation, Israel's occupation of the West Bank undoubtedly freed the Hashemite Kingdom of a heavy burden. This burden would have been difficult for the regime to cope with if the West Bank had remained within the framework of the Hashemite Kingdom.

Syria

When the political and military balance shifted from the Syrian arena to the Egyptian arena, and after Egypt's relations with Israel and the superpowers became the main focus of political activity after the closure of the straits, Syria found itself relegated to the sidelines. This new situation had an impact on Syrian–Egyptian relations and on political camps inside Syria. Syria had been at the center of political and military activity since the outbreak of the crisis and now returned to its "traditional status" of near-total dependency on Egypt's moves. The military and political initiative naturally gravitated to Egypt, and Cairo now assumed the leadership role in place of Syria and the Ba'th Party. The Syrians saw that the nucleus of activity was shifting from the military realm, the area they preferred, to the political realm where Egypt pursued it without coordination with Syria. The Syrians realized that Egypt would continue to handle the political activity according to its own considerations and special interests.[123]

This resulted in mutual distrust. At one point the Egyptians feared that Syria might initiate a move on its front that would undermine Egyptian strategy. Since May 26 Egypt had adopted the second-strike concept that called for the avoidance of any action by either Syria or Egypt that might be a pretext for an Israeli attack. The Egyptians discussed this matter with Syria, and Damascus assured its ally that it had no intention of taking an independent initiative and would coordinate its steps with Egypt. On the other hand, the Syrians were dismayed that the Egyptians had not consulted with them on major issues, such as closing the straits or U Thant's visit to Cairo, and had not told them of their intentions, such as appealing to the Security Council. The Syrians suspected that Egypt's approach to the UNSC on May 27 implied Egypt's interest in securing a compromise, especially since this move had been taken without prior consultation with Damascus. After the *fait accompli*, the Egyptians explained to the Syrians that their appeal to the UNSC had been a means of preparing the ground for a Soviet veto, if the need arose. Nevertheless, the Syrian leaders insisted that Syrian military activity had been the main "reason for Israel's panic." The Ba'th leaders found that they had to convince the party's rank and file that their moves toward Egypt were justified, especially their continued reliance on and coordination with Egypt. Evidence of inner-party dissension over this point appeared in a Syrian newspaper article on May 20 written by Hafiz al-Asad, the minister of war and commander of the air force:

> Our forces are prepared not only to respond to aggression but also to initiate the liberation operation itself and smash the belligerent Zionist entity [that lies] in the midst of the Arab homeland. All our forces . . . are now eager for battle and waiting for the sign from the political leadership. As a military man I believe the time has come to launch a liberation campaign, and that we should take the minimum steps necessary for punishing Israel, forcing it to open its eyes, bend in subjugation, live in an atmosphere of fear and terror, and never think about aggression again. I am certain that our Egyptian brothers feel the same.[124]

Asad must have been referring to the Ba'th political leadership. He had qualms about Syria's policy of coordinating its moves with Egypt because it prevented Syria from undertaking an independent initiative. The regime responded quickly. On May 22, in a speech before the Association of Arab Workers, President Atasi refuted Asad's call for a Syrian military initiative: "We agreed to commence the liberation campaign with the Egyptians immediately after Israel's first step." Atasi promised that fidai'yyun operations would continue, and he praised Egypt's deeds.[125]

The Nasir–Husayn defense pact created additional problems in Egyptian–Syrian relations because of Syria's bitterness over another Egyptian *volte-face*, one that had additional repercussions in Syria. Egypt had initiated another strategic move without consulting Damascus, and this time ideology also played a part in Syria's indignation. The Syrians found it difficult to accept Egypt's inclination toward reconciliation with "Arab reactionary" states in general, and Jordan in particular. They raised the notion of an "encounter of progressive forces on the battlefield." The Syrians held high-level talks with the Egyptians, including Vice-President Zakariya Muhi al-Din in Damascus on May 31 during which they stated emphatically that they opposed any agreement with Arab reactionaries. The Egyptians had the impression that the Ba'th regime was loath to appreciate even the military value of the pact with Husayn. The talks with the Egyptians revealed inconsistencies among the Syrian leadership. Salah Jedid and Suwaydani vehemently opposed the Egyptian–Jordanian defense pact. The Algerians failed to influence the Syrians on this point. The Ba'th regime even forbade the circulation of *al-Aharm* beginning on May 31, the day after the signing of the pact, when the details of Husayn's visit to Cairo were published.

Despite the advantages of the Egyptian–Jordanian pact in the struggle against Israel, the Syrian media continued to assail the Hashemite regime and foment against it until the eve of the war. On May 31 *Radio Damascus* announced: "The liberation of Filastin will come about through the liberation of Jordan." On June 3 the radio commentator announced that "The [Western] agent's regime in Jordan continues its activity against the Arab fidai'yyun and progressive fighters and fills its prisons with them"[126] On June 4 the *Radio Filastin* commentator on *Radio Damascus* declared: "O Arab people on the two banks! . . . [Stand] outside the Mandelbaum Gate in Jerusalem next Wednesday and block the Jewish convoy. Be prepared to turn the Mandelbaum Gate into the second Island of Tiran and the road to Sheikh Jarrah [Jerusalem neighborhood where the convoy was supposed to pass] into the second Gulf of Aqaba, and the Hebrew University on top of the mountain into the second Eilat."

Because of these attitudes behind the scenes, it was essential for Syria to be a partner of equal status in the talks, situation assessments, and decision-making taking place in Cairo – if not in practice then at least in appearance. The Syrians found it unthinkable that they had learned about major events – such as the closing of the straits – only after the fact. The Syrian leadership had to take a number of steps in order to demonstrate their country's ongoing active involvement in the political developments. In addition, the Ba'th regime made an effort to demonstrate it was an independent, influential player in the Middle East, and not merely Egypt's lackey. It embarked upon a series of high-level diplomatic moves that included President Atasi's journey to Moscow and Foreign Minister Makhus's trips, first to Paris where he relayed an oral message from Atasi to President de Gaulle, and then to Algeria. The leadership also hoped that this activity would benefit it for internal party reasons. Atasi's brief visit to Moscow on May 29 and the Syrian announcement after his return highlighted the visit's publicity aim. While the Soviet Union noted that it had been a "goodwill visit," Syria sought to exploit the trip for elevating its own international and inter-Arab stature, equating it with Egypt's. Naturally the Egyptians were unhappy that Atasi's made his visit at the height of the crisis, and they let the Syrians know that they viewed the trip as unnecessary. In fact the visit had been forced upon the Soviet leadership at a time when it had planned to be outside of Moscow. Makhus met De Gaulle on June 1 "and outlined the Imperialist-Zionist plot."[127] On June 2 he held talks with President Boumedienne of Algeria.[128]

In their effort to coordinate their moves with Egypt, Prime Minister Zu'ayein and chief of staff Suwaydani traveled to Cairo on May 23 to discuss with Nasir the latest developments in the crisis, especially following the closure of the straits. They also held talks with the Prime Minister Sidqi. The next day they returned to Damascus. The visit was held on the same day as the leadership of the National (Qawmi) Ba'th Congress of the Ba'th Party's convened in order to give the appearance that Syrian activity and decision-making were taking place in conjunction and coordination with the Egyptian political and military leadership.

On May 23 the Ba'th leadership met in Damascus and decided to convene the national and regional leaderships in order to rally the party's nucleus around its position, and discuss "the latest developments in the Arab people's momentous campaign against Imperialism, Zionism, and the Arab reactionaries." The Ba'th leadership felt that it needed unanimous party support for its policy because of the criticism in the ranks that Syria was being led by Egypt, especially after Egypt closed the straits without informing Damascus. Indeed, support and justification of Egypt's moves was the main theme in the Ba'th leadership's announcement published on the eve of the congress's adjournment:

> Israel's threats and barefaced provocations have forced Egypt and Syria to take the initiative and carry out their historical mission for the Arab nation: facing up to Zionist and Imperialist military concentrations and mobilizing all of their military and popular resources for the liberation of Arab soil from all forms of Zionist and Imperialist occupation . . .
>
> Egypt has made the historical decision to terminate the role of the emergency forces, restore [Egypt's] legal right to control the Gulf of Aqaba, and close [the gulf] to Israeli navigation . . .
>
> In the name of the party and its [branches], we express our full approval of this brave revolutionary decision and Egypt's right to complete control over the Gulf of Aqaba which is Arab territorial water, and we extend all of fighting Syria's revolutionary resources to the support and defense of this right.[129]

On May 25/26, as part of Syria's vigorous diplomatic activity, the Foreign Ministry summoned the heads of the foreign diplomatic missions in Damascus and explained in detail the current military situation "justifying the Arab–Syrian position." Three days later, on May 29, Foreign Minister Dr. Ibrahim Makhus's reply to the Americans' moderate, non-committal oral message was published in Damascus. The Syrian answer was mainly an attempt to refute the American position by presenting "historical" and "special" claims. Regarding fidai'yyun activity against Israel, Makhus reiterated the government line that Syria took no responsibility for fidai'yyun operations, although it recognized "the justice of their struggle."

The friction in Egyptian–Syrian relations also came to expression in the military sphere. A large gap appeared between the joint planning of operations and their implementation, especially after fighting broke out on the Egyptian front. The Syrian military, unlike the political leadership, seems to have been most reluctant to take orders or dictates from the Egyptians, in particular when they stemmed from Egypt's battlefield exigencies and the Egyptian staff's desire, under Amer's instructions, to alleviate the pressure on the Egyptian front by making use of the Syrian front – at any rate this was the Syrian High Command's perception of events. It also seems that Syrian generals still held a grudge over the Egyptian General Staff's high-handed arrogance toward them during the Egyptian–Syrian unification.

Thus, in the last stages of the crisis, just after the war erupted, the Syrian High Command greeted the Egyptian staff's overtures with a large dose of reservation and agreed to them only after Syrian interests were first thoroughly examined. Furthermore, the Syrian high command seems to have opposed Egypt's second-strike concept, preferring an Arab military initiative, that is, an "Egyptian–Syrian" one, as Asad referred to it, and was against allowing Israel to make the first strike. Indeed, the Egyptian operational demands were generally linked to the Egyptian military situation. On May 30, for example, when Egypt assessed that Israeli reinforcements were moving down from the Syrian sector and an Israeli attack was imminent, the Egyptian chief of staff asked his Syrian counterpart to order the Syrian air force to carry out aerial reconnaissance over Israeli airfields in the north in order to determine the size and type of enemy aircraft, and to concentrate the bulk of Syrian armor on the frontlines in order to tie down Israeli forces, thus easing the pressure on the southern front. The Egyptian chief of staff even warned that it might be necessary to activate their joint plan: a Syrian attack on Israel's northern airfields and an Egyptian strike against Israeli airbases in the center and south of the country. The Syrians, however, did not follow these orders, claiming that they lacked MiG 21s and aircraft tires.

On May 31 the Syrian headquarters issued an attack order codenamed "Nasr." The "Nasr Plan" called for crossing the Jordan River at dawn, capturing the city Safed, and severing the Galilee with two army groups (the 12th and 35th). On June 3 the brigades on the first line began preparing advanced staging areas. On June 4, the assemblage was completed and the forces ready to attack. The 12th Army Group was given the task of breaking through the central axis and capturing Safed; the 35th would have to cross the Jordan estuary and cut the Tiberias–Rosh Pina road near the settlement of Elifeled. On the night of June 4/5 the Syrians informed the Egyptians that they were waiting for an order to commence operations, that is, to carry out the joint war plans – including offensives.

Even in the first stage of the fighting, when the situation on the Egyptian front was unclear and reports of an Israeli air offensive were coming in, the Syrian High Command still refrained from implementing the Egyptian orders. Late in the morning on June 5, the Syrians also came under air attack. Abd al-Mun'im Riyad's request that an armored brigade be sent to Jordan was not immediately answered. The brigade arrived too late to be of help. The Egyptian chief of staff's request from his opposite number on the Syrian side on the first day of the war to attack Israeli airfields in the north was only partially answered – three hours after the Egyptian signal was received – despite Syria's declared intention of the previous night to attack Israel. According to Fawzi:

> At 11:00 the Mushir had me order the Syrian High Command to implement the air offensive against Israel's northern airfields as we had decided with the Syrian chief of staff, Ahmad Suwaydani. I made radio contact with [Suwaydani] and asked him to carry out the attack plan codenamed 'Rashid', but I received no positive reply. He uttered only one sentence: 'We'll try, sir.' Later I learned that the Syrians issued no orders whatsoever for a counteroffensive or engagement in any form of operations against Israel.[130]

Fawzi's report is not accurate. Syrian planes did attack a few places in the north of Israel in the late hours of the morning of June 5. Among the targets hit were Kibbutz Ein Hamifratz and Kurdana in the Haifa Bay region, the Megiddo airfield, Tiberias, Tzalmon, and the Arab village of Ilabun. Ten Syrian planes were shot down. The Syrian military spokesman mentioned the offensive at 11:35. At 12:45 *Radio Damascus* reported that according to the Syrian military spokesman, "The planes inflicted heavy damage on the enemy's airfields in the northern region." The spokesman added that Haifa's oil refineries had been bombed.

On the night of June 5/6 the Syrian forces were ready to carry out "Nasr Plan." Some of the preparations, especially on the forward lines, were disrupted because of Israeli aircraft and artillery activity. The Egyptian order notwithstanding, the Syrians balked at implementing the plan, claiming there were difficulties in fording the Jordan

River. On the night of June 6/7 the Syrians reorganized their troops in defensive positions. The IDF offensive on the Golan Heights began June 9.

Iraq

Despite Iraq's eagerness to join Egypt's war effort and its willingness to come to the aid of Syria and Jordan with air and land forces, when the moment of truth came it dallied over the execution of these commitments. Even on May 30, after Arif approved the preparations for sending expeditionary forces to Jordan, the Iraqis still dawdled. Nasir wanted Iraq to rush military assistance to Jordan and Syria in order to boost morale and make a display of a united front of "progressive Arab states."

The Iraq leadership disagreed over the dispatching of Iraqi forces abroad. Some officers believed, even after the signing of the Nasir–Husayn pact and just one week before the war, that Nasir was bluffing and that his moves were only saber-rattling. One week before the war the Iraqi chief of staff informed the Egyptians that the Kurds in northern Iraq might renew their fighting at the end of the harvest month (May), and that he was reluctant to reduce his forces in northern Iraq [that included troops designated for Jordan]. The air lift to Egypt of an Iraqi infantry battalion was also put on hold despite Egyptian pressure. The Iraqis were adamantly opposed to sending their forces to Syria, claiming that they had to review Syrian plans for these forces first. A few days before the hostilities, when the Iraqi military leadership was absolutely certain that war was imminent, actual steps were afoot to send an expeditionary force to Jordan but the troops arrived too late to be of help to the Jordanian army.[131]

Part III   *The Arab Propaganda Campaign*

The political crisis and the war were the biggest media events in the Arab–Israeli conflict since 1948. The Arab media, especially the Egyptian, not only played a major role in awakening and shaping public opinion but also had an unprecedented influence on the Arab leaders' decision-making. Egypt's press and radio set the tone (and volume), and the Syrian and Iraqi media naturally followed suit. The Egyptian radio commentator, Ahmad Sa'id, of *Sawt al-Arab* was conspicuous in his personal admiration for Nasir, his extremism toward Israel, and his ability to incite Arab public opinion.

In the press, the daily *al-Ahram* and its editor and confidant of Nasir, Hasanayn Haykal, stood out. Egypt's cause was also served by pro-Nasir newspapers in Lebanon (most of which received financial backing from Egypt). At the same time there also appeared "moderate" or "independent" Lebanese newspapers such as *al-Hayat*, *al-Nahar*, and *al-Jarida* that tended to support independent positions close to the "conservative" camp – Jordan and Saudi Arabia. The Egyptian media also made use of television (although this medium was not as widespread and sophisticated as it is today). Thus, the shaping of Arab public opinion was systematic, consistent, and deliberate. It took place on a daily and even hourly basis. Little wonder then that in the week before the war the Arab world was in a frenzy against Israel, filled with pride and revived hopes; it felt as though it was living in the "Golden Age" of a new Arab renaissance. The following survey illustrates the tone and content of the Arab information-propaganda campaign.

The Enhancement of Nasir's Personality Cult

At sunrise (05:30) on May 23, *Radio Cairo* broadcast Nasir's first speech since the crisis. The president had delivered the speech the previous evening before a group of pilots at an airbase in Sinai. From this point Nasir became the preeminent orator and most hard-line spokesman in the Arab arena. His speeches went over extremely well because of his political accomplishments during the "ten days of glory" – as Haykal termed the period between May 14 and 23. Nasir's prestige in the Arab world had not attained such heights since in the days of glory after the nationalization of the Suez Canal Company and Suez–Sinai War, and during the Egyptian–Syrian unification. In four speeches – on May 22, 26, 28, and 29, 1967 – he set the political agenda of the Middle East until war finally erupted.

The pinnacle of his fame was reached on May 31 when two Lebanese newspapers likened him to the twelfth-century Arab warrior Saladin (Salah al-Din al-Ayubi). An article in the Lebanese weekly *al-Huriya* entitled "Nasir – The Guardian of the Arabs," compared Nasir to Saladin "whose command a million and a half Palestinian refugees await." Another Lebanese weekly, *al-Hawadith*, described Nasir "as a unique leader, not only in the region but in the entire world, because the decision to go to war is an earth-shaking decision that demands rare courage not always found even among leaders of great nations. The Arabs have not had a leader like Abd al-Nasir since the time of Salah al-Din al-Ayubi." On the previous day, May 30, *Sawt al-Arab* extolled the magnificent leadership of Nasir who "has been victorious in every battle he has fought. The Arab nation has complete faith that Nasir's leadership will demonstrate the power of the Arab nation. We say to our enemies in a loud and clear voice that the nation that produced Saladin, has now given birth to Nasir." It should come as little surprise, then, following this vaunted image of the Egyptian president's invincibility "that all Arabs, from the Atlantic Ocean to the Persian Gulf, support Nasir; and the Arab nation expect his signal to launch the war." On May 31 Ahmad Sa'id boasted:

> Nasir has accustomed us to new victories daily in the forward lines of attack aimed at smashing the Imperialist base. Nasir has presented us with new victories: the threat to Syria has evaporated like a cloud, the emergency forces have pulled out, the Gulf of Aqaba is closed to the Zionists, and Arab military concentrations – Egyptian, Kuwaiti, Iraqi, Syrian, Jordanian, and tomorrow Algerian, Sudanese, and Moroccan – are deployed along 950 kilometers of border. Nasir has not forgotten the rebellion in the south [Yemen], he reaffirms his support of it and declares its connection to the campaign against Israel – a victory in [Yemen] means the defeat of the Zionists and a blow to Imperialism.[1]

The Egyptian and Arab media magnified Nasir's image as a leader "who succeeds in projecting the main goals of the Arab revolution. Nasir, the leader of the revolution, is an integral part of the Arab nation and leads it from victory to victory. He will lead the [Arabs] to triumph over Israel and to a solution of the 1948 problem." Nasir became identified with the Arab nation "by his dedication to Arab rights, he expresses the aspirations of the nation's masses."[2]

The Call for Israel's Destruction

On May 15 when the Arab–Israeli crisis erupted, and especially with war looming on the horizon after the closure of the straits, the Arab world intensified its call for Israel's annihilation. Cairo broadcasts, such as *Sawt al-Arab*, greatly contributed to the war fever – and *Radio Damascus* and *Radio Baghdad* joined in the campaign.

Ahmad Sa'id's extremism and his demand for Israel's eradication reached an unprecedented level of stridency in Arab broadcasts. As the clouds of war approached, Arab propaganda blared louder and more impulsively. Moreover, since extremism had become the propaganda machine's main tool for mustering the masses' support of their leaders and regimes, radio stations competed with each another in adopting a more fanatical tone against Israel.

On May 30 *al-Hayat*, a Lebanese newspaper known for its moderation and its ties to the Saudis (who supported it financially), summoned the Arabs and Arab armies "not to miss the great opportunity that has fallen into their hands for the first time in twenty years, enabling them to deliver a decisive knockout that will incapacitate Israel . . . Israel seems to have reconciled itself to the *faits accomplis* in the region and prefers to shun a confrontation with the Arabs in order to survive and wait for a better hour [to resume its struggle]."

The Baghdadi daily *al-Arab* wrote in the same spirit on May 20: "Now that the Arab states have planned a second round that will lead to Israel's devastation, instead of wasting time they must deliver the knockout punch to their historical enemies, the robbers of their land." On May 21 *Radio Damascus* trumpeted: "The battle that the Arabs have been waiting for since 1948 is upon us. The masses are determined to fight and seek revenge for their stolen land. Our nation has always been eagerly awaiting this moment." The Jordanian daily *al-Dustur* published an article by Issa Na'uri on June 1 claiming that "The Arabs now have the opportunity that they lacked in 1948. They lost the first opportunity; they must not miss the second one. The blockade of Israel is complete and the Arabs' anger toward [Israel] is greater than in the past. The time has come to exterminate Israel."

Thus, agitation against Israel intensified. Israel's extermination – the dream of the Arab masses and the entire Arab nation – was guaranteed: "Israel lacks the strength to prevail against the Arabs for even a single hour. The Arab people are adamant in their decision to wipe Israel off the face of the map and restore Arab honor to Filastin."[3] The Arab media instilled certainty into the masses that Israel was on the verge of disintegration. "Thanks to the blocking of the straits Israel faces two possibilities, both of which will be soaked with its blood: it can either die by strangulation from the Arab military and economic siege or be consumed by fire from the Arab forces encircling it on the south, north, and east."[4]

The outcry for Israel's extirpation reached its climax on the eve of the war when the commentator of *Sawt al-Arab* announced: "There is no backing away from expunging Zionist aggression. This is the decision of all the Arab forces. Our troops will soon exterminate the aggressor and restore Arabs' rights, as the commander of the eastern front told his soldiers and officers: we can return Israel's corpse to its creators, that is, to Britain and the United States."[5]

Swagger and Confidence in Arab Power

Starting on May 23/24, and especially after May 30, the level of Arab contempt, braggadocio, self-confidence in Arab military prowess, especially Egypt's, and ability to cripple, if not annihilate Israel, that appeared in Arab newspaper articles and radio broadcasts, is astounding. The Arab masses swallowed the propaganda with relish since the message suited their aspirations and expectations. The Arab world had been waiting twenty years to hear their leaders' speeches guaranteeing the "fulfillment" of their promises: an all-Arab mobilization for "the battle to end all battles" against Israel, the realization of Arab solidarity and "Arab unity of aim," visions of "dazzling" Arab victories, excellent conditions created for attaining this goal, and above all the emergence of a leader capable of bringing all these aspirations to their fruition.

A good example of the propaganda is the article published in the Egyptian weekly *al-Musawar* on May 30 after the writer's visit to a bomber airbase. The article, accompanied with pictures, boastfully describes the preparations in this and other bases, the new aircraft, their missions, and the Israeli targets. The writer noted that "Egypt's long-range bomber crews received precise lists of enemy targets to attack inside Israeli territory. The flying fortresses are lined up . . . waiting for H-hour to take off over Israeli territory and turn their targets into an inferno . . . When the clash with the enemy finally commences and the first radio signal is given, the flying fortresses will take off, carrying death and destruction in their bellies . . . [with air superiority] we can expect a total victory immediately after the opening shots."

Even Hasanayn Haykal, Nasir's backroom advisor, who was generally level-headed and balanced in his writing, became infected with the martial spirit and added his own view of events to convince the Arab public of the incontestable Arab victory around the corner. On June 2, three days before the fighting began, he wrote of Israel's plight in the wake of Egypt's moves:

> The [Israeli] government has no room to maneuver: surrender or revolution. Israel has to either strike in order to break the Arab siege that surrounds it or not strike and be broken from within. Israel is headed toward collapse, this is all but certain, whether internally or externally. Israel never was and never will be a natural entity capable of adjusting and adapting quickly and easily to the winds of change. This state was and remains a creation of cheap and unstable material, it is like a plaster figurine incapable of change unless it is broken.[6]

On June 3 the pro-Egyptian Lebanese weekly, *al-Ahad*, following Haykal's line, wrote: "If war breaks out one can expect Israel's total destrucion, but if the Cold War continues then the Arab military seige will force [Israel] to mobilize, and this will lead to its demoralization and economic collapse, and hasten its demise."[7]

Two days before the war, *Sawt al-Arab* boasted: "The Arab nation is stronger today, more organized, better equipped and prepared for battle. Today we have the initiative. It can be felt in [our] growing strength, the nation's military and technological advances, the people's heightened awareness, and the organization of the entire nation."[8]

These moods reflect the depth of the "*nakbat Filastin*" (Filastin catastrophe) in the mind of the Arab masses. The Arab propaganda broadcasts that called for war against Israel or a solution to the Palestinian problem and the extirpation of Israel were not only the hidden wishes of the masses; they also awakened a mass frenzy that encompassed all levels of society in the Arab world. Such powerful public expression of Israel's coming destruction had not been heard since 1948. The Arab broadcasts instilled confidence in the heart of the Arab people that Israel's annihilation was a forgone conclusion. The public was confident that Israel was not only about to be destroyed, but that the restoration of the Filastin homeland and establishment of the Palestinian state were also within reach – after all, president Nasir himself had made this promise, and Nasir always kept his word.

Arab Solidarity

It is interesting to note that the term "Arab nationalism" that Nasir used so frequently after 1956 was omitted from his speeches and from Egyptian and Arab propaganda. The commonly used terms were: the Arab nation, Arab consolidation, the Arab homeland, and Arab solidarity. Since the dissolution of the Egyptian–Syrian Union (September 1961) the concept of Arab solidarity had not received such popularity in so short a time as it did after the signing of the Nasir–Husayn defense pact. But it is important to emphasize that Arab solidarity was reinvested only after the Arab world realized that Nasir was dead serious about going to war, that war was close at hand, and that Israel's eradication was within reach. No Arab leader wanted to miss the opportunity to contribute his part to the "great moment" – the victory over Israel.

On May 31 *al-Hayat*'s political commentator praised "Arab consolidation and solidarity that has come to fateful expression at this moment in the form of the Nasir–Husayn rapprochement and the signing of the Egyptian–Jordanian joint defense pact." The commentator pointed out that "by this historical step Husayn has bridged the abyss that divided several Arab states, and he has brought about the Arabs' full consolidation *vis-à-vis* Israel." On June 3 the Lebanese newspaper *Sawt al-'Uruba* wrote: "The Arab solidarity that we are witnessing today was absent during the Filastin catastrophe (*nakba*), that is now twenty years old. This solidarity will result in the destruction of the criminal state, now twenty years old." At a press conference on May 29 the Lebanese minister of science, Michel Ede, a Christian, gave his view on the unfolding events: "It seems that Israel's perception of Arab divisions was wrong; it forgot that the Palestinian problem [unites] the Arab states. Israel now faces a solid array of Arab states that have declared without any hesitation or misgiving that they will stand united against the Israeli foe."[9]

Arab solidarity can also be seen in the announcements that nearly all of the Arab states hastened to ballyhoo their armies' state of alert and their willingness to assist in the fighting. Arab chiefs of staff and political leaders began making a pilgrimage to Cairo in order to express their support of Nasir and his strategy. In the last week before the war the rabid masses became the motivating factor that spurred their leaders to take part in the certain victory over Israel.

Husayn's dash to Cairo was a good example of this. Furthermore, demonstrations of support and sympathy for Nasir and the Syrians and their position on the Palestinian problem were held throughout the Arab world. On June 2 a Jordanian newspaper described one such outburst of support:

On June 1, 1967 traffic on Baghdad's main thoroughfare, al-Rashid Street, came to a halt for more than three hours as thousands of members of the trade unions marched in support of Egypt's position on the Palestinian problem. The demonstrators carried pictures of Iraq's President Abd al-Rahman Arif and President Gamal Abd al-Nasir.[10]

Regarding propaganda, crowd agitation, and the media's role in whipping up the masses to wild excitement, mention should be made of the system of radio broadcasts during the first two days of the war before the Arab public learned the dimensions of the defeat. The broadcasts from Cairo, Damascus, Baghdad, and other Arab capitals echoed the public's mood and expectations. Thus, the radio stations announced imaginary air and land victories; extravagant reports of attacks against the Israeli air and ground forces (for example, 156 Israeli planes were shot down on June 5); and cries of encouragement and enthusiasm emboldening soldiers and the masses to sally forth to battle for the "liquidation of the Zionist entity," a battle "whose objective is Tel Aviv." More examples follow:

"We will stand up to Israeli aggression and annihilate it so that the stain of the Zionist-Imperialist entity is erased." (*Radio Cairo*, June 5, 09:15).

"Forward to the capture of Tel Aviv!" (*Radio Cairo*, June 5, 09:24).

"We'll all meet in Tel Aviv." (*Radio Cairo*, June 5, 09:28).

"Destroy, avenge, crush, and liberate occupied Filastin from the Zionist thugs." (*Radio Cairo*, June 5, 09:27).

"Every Arab must avenge the honor of 1948." (*Radio Cairo*, June 5, 09:25).

"Seize your weapons, O Arabs, [and proceed] to the heart of occupied Filastin. We shall meet in Tel Aviv." (*Radio Damascus*, June 6, 04:15).

"Onward, Soldiers of Jerusalem! You have a rendezvous with Rabin in Tel Aviv." (*Radio Amman*, June 6, 11:55).

"We've entered Israel, our goal is Tel Aviv." (Baghdadi headlines, *Radio Baghdad*, June 6, 07:30).

The broadcasts, especially those of Ahmad Sa'id from *Sawt al-Arab*, were not satisfied with these cries of encouragement and incitement. Later that day (June 5) they began to state "facts" about Arab "accomplishments." For example:

"In a few hours Tel Aviv will fall into our hands. O Arabs, the return to Filastin has begun." (*Radio Cairo*, June 5, 14:30).

"We're on our way now to the heart of Israel, we're on the road to Tel Aviv." (Egyptian Television, Cairo, June 5, 17:30).

Part IV *Conclusion and Evaluation*

Once Nasir decided to concentrate his forces in Sinai, a move designed to deter Israel from attacking Syria, he realized that the presence of the UNEF in Sinai completely belied his aim and proved Egypt's unwillingness to fight. Therefore the UN forces had to be removed. Nasir's goal was to convince Israel and the Arab world that he was ready for a confrontation. But this was not enough. The withdrawal of the UNEF was linked to Egypt's seizure of the border with Israel in the direction of Sharm al-Sheikh.

Nasir was fully aware of the trap he was setting for himself by demanding the pullout of the UNEF; still, he planned his steps according to a clear-eyed assessment of the political and military repercussions. Four or five days elapsed between the May 17 political decision to close the straits and the official declaration of implementing the decision. During this interim Nasir remained silent. He gave the green light to implement the closure only after he was absolutely convinced that his historic move was correct, and only after he had carefully weighed its political and military ramifications and saw that Egyptian troops were in complete control of Sharm al-Sheikh. His famous slogan taunting Israel, *"ahlan wasahlan,"* testified to his certainty of the justification and correctness of his decision, even though it presaged war.

The implications and historical significance of the closure of the straits were not lost on Nasir who sought a unanimous decision at the highest level of political leadership. He was fully aware of the risks at every step; therefore he constantly assessed the dangers of a military confrontation. Vice-President Shafi'i recalled that Nasir calculated that the evacuation of the UNEF would boost the prospects of war from 50 percent to 80 percent, and that the blocking of the straits would raise the likelihood of war from 80 percent to 100 percent.[1] Nasir's evaluation was correct, as was his June 2 assessment that Israel would launch an air strike on June 5.

Nasir progressed consciously and methodically toward the Six Day War. He was impulsive and unpredictable toward his external opponents, including his Western foes, but he was a tough and sober statesman in his basic positions. He was also a brilliant tactician and master at political maneuvering. He had no qualms about expressing clear, undisguised, scathing positions against his adversaries in the Arab world. He surprised a Palestinian delegation in June 1962 when he revealed that he had no plans for the liberation of Filastin. Thus, his decision to lead Egypt and the Arab world to war seems to have been reached only after deep consideration and level-headed awareness of the consequences, and after consultation with the High Command and his innermost circle (Amer, and probably Haykal). He calculated the impact of his moves on Israel and the prospect of war. Whether or not his calculations were correct, he accurately assessed the implications of the straits' closure to Israeli shipping and even foresaw almost the exact date of the Israeli air strike.

Naturally when political leaders and generals go to war – whether they initiate it or are forced into it – their aim is to win. Nasir was no exception. After Amer and the high command handed him data on the army's strength and capability and its comparability to the IDF, he was confident that Egypt would emerge victorious. Little wonder then that he chose to deliver his first fiery speech since the onset of the crisis before pilots at an airbase in Sinai. There he coined the expression – *"ahlan wasahlan."*

In addition to the long-term processes surveyed in this study, the following factors also influenced on Nasir's decision-making from the start of the crisis.

Nasir's Commitment to Solving the Palestinian Problem and Liberating Filastin

From the moment the crisis erupted and proceeded toward an armed clash with Israel, Nasir was deeply conscious of his commitment to solve the Palestinian problem. Since the Palestinian problem, or liberation of Filastin, was at the core of his concept of Arab nationalism (or Nasirism) he strengthened his commitment and thus raised the expectations of the Palestinians and the Arabs that under his leadership Filastin would be liberated. His commitment to a solution received greater weight between 1964 and 1967. Nasir knew exactly what was expected of him and waited for the opportunity to "come through with the goods" even if much time and preparation were needed. The golden opportunity came during the May 1967 crisis.

Nasir tried to convince the Arab world that everything he had accomplished in the field of domestic and foreign policy had been for Filastin. He placed the Palestinian issue at the center of the dispute in the Arab world, claiming that, "a successful confrontation with Israel demanded a united and developed Arab nation." The Palestinian problem served as a legal, emotional, political, and strategic justification for Nasirism and its dissemination in the Arab world. The Palestinian problem was the reason for Nasir's opposition to the Baghdad Pact. Arab unity was the "path to liberating Filastin." In this light, the Egyptian–Syrian unification had been for the benefit of Filastin, and its dissolution was a blow to the Palestinian problem. The war in Yemen had been for Filastin's sake, as were the wars against Arab reactionaries and Western Imperialism. If the Palestinian problem was the focal point of Egypt's foreign policy, it also justified the strengthening of Egypt's domestic front and the steps taken by the government, such as the economic revolution in industry and agriculture, adoption of Socialism, nationalization of Egypt's resources, and quashing of the opposition to the regime. The liberation of Filastin was also the reason for breaking up the monopoly of arms supplies to the Middle East. This explains the praise that a senior Lebanese journalist heaped on Nasir before the war, referring to him as "the most outstanding Palestinian leader in the region . . . [who] is responsible for the future of the [Palestinian] problem."[2]

Nasir imposed his way of liberating Filastin on other Arab states and claimed that an Arab state's national, pan-Arab orientation (qawmi) would be judged by its attitude or contribution to the liberation of Filastin. Therefore most inter-Arab disputes revolved around the Palestinian issue, especially since the majority of the Arab states had been freed of the yoke of Imperialism or reactionary governments (as the revolutions in Iraq and Yemen attested to). Thus, after the Six Day War when Nasir cemented Egypt to the Palestinian problem, which had become the main pivot of Arab nationalism, he solved Egypt's historical dilemma of having to decide between Egyptian nationalism (wataniya) and Pan-Arab nationalism (qawmiya). Nasir regarded the New Palestinian National Movement as an outgrowth of Nasirism.

He convinced the Arab world that only Egypt, with its human and material resources, could lead it to victory over Israel. Despite his commitments and Arab expectations, Nasir had the experience of the 1948 War and Sinai War behind him; therefore he had no illusions that meticulous preparations would have to be undertaken to achieve a decisive victory on the battlefield. He would go to war when he determined the time was appropriate. He admitted that "If I decide to initiate a war, then there can be only one outcome – a cut-and-dry [Arab] victory. We cannot open a war without first defining its time and place, without being fully prepared." This was Nasir's strategy in a nutshell. He touted it openly and in discreet diplomatic conversations. Several times he postponed the solution claiming that Egypt was not ready yet. This was the reason that he convened an Arab summit meeting in January 1964. He had to prove that although he had put off the showdown with Israel, he was still preparing for it, and would challenge anyone in the Arab world who accused him of selling the Palestinian issue short. Nasir's main critics were Jordan, Saudi Arabia, the Ba'th regime in Syria, and Qasim's regime in Iraq. He defended his steps, declaring, "Everything I am doing is to help solve the Palestinian problem." During the prewar crisis he came to the overall conclusion that this commitment obligated him to the Arab world and Palestinians, and that he was ready now to pay off the debt. At the height of the crisis he summed up this point in the following words:

> If Israel initiates hostilities against Syria or Egypt, an all-out war will be fought aimed at annihilating Israel. I could not say this five or even three years ago . . . Now, eleven years after 1956, I can make such a statement because I am convinced of Egypt's and Syria's capabilities. Today I also know the position of other Arab states.[3]

Nasir wanted to demonstrate his commitment to solving the Palestinian problem, therefore he declared in unmistakable language that the goal of Egypt and the entire Arab world in the coming war was to restore the Palestinian people's rights. Unlike his position before the crisis, he now felt that "we are prepared to meet every possible contingency and solve the entire Palestinian problem since today's issue is not the Gulf of Aqaba, the Straits of Tiran, or the UNEF, but the rights of the Palestinian people, the issue is the aggression that took place in Filastin in 1948 with British and American collusion, [the issue is] the Arabs' expulsion from Filastin. Today's issue is larger than what is being discussed, we want the Palestinian people's full rights [returned]."[4]

His words speak for themselves.

Nasir's Commitment to Defend Every Arab Country

Nasir preached Arab nationalism, unity, and solidarity because he believed in Egypt's Pan-Arab national mission. He assumed the role of protector of Arab countries from direct or indirect foreign military intervention; defender of pro-Nasir, revolutionary regimes; and champion of Arab countries bordering Israel if the latter invaded or even threatened to invade them. The most conspicuous example of Nasir's commitment to this course was his massive military involvement in Yemen (1962–1967). He explained Egypt's unification with Syria in 1958 as the need to safeguard Syria from internal disintegration. I believe his concern was genuine and stemmed from his belief in Egypt's Pan-Arab national mission in the "Arab ring," as defined in *The Philosophy of the Revolution* that he wrote in 1954. When riots erupted in Jordan's West Bank in April 1963, in the wake of the announcement of the tripartite (Egypt–Syria–Iraq) union on April 16, Nasir weighed the possibility of Egyptian intervention in the event that Israel invaded the West Bank. On April 2, 1963 he stated, "Israeli aggression against any Arab country would be considered aggression against Egypt."[5] When Jordan was rocked by internal crisis, he placed the Egyptian army on alert.

Egypt's transfer of forces into Sinai on May 14, 1967 in order to deter Israel recalls a similar move made by Nasir on February 1, 1960, during the Egyptian–Syrian union. On the night of January 31/February 1, 1960 IDF soldiers raided the village of Tawafiq Tahta, in the Syrian part of the demilitarized zone. The Syrians claimed that the raid failed and that the IDF "suffered a humiliating defeat." The Egyptian High Command acknowledged the Syrian version and estimated that Israel would not suffer such a "defeat," and that a second large-scale IDF operation could be expected. On February

1, the Egyptian forces were put on a high state of alert and two days later a reinforced infantry brigade advanced into Sinai from the Suez Canal. By mid-February the Egyptian High Command concluded that the IDF would attack Syria around February 17. Beginning on the night of February 17/18 and throughout the following two days the majority of Egypt's combat troops flowed into Sinai. This was the largest concentration of Egyptian forces in Sinai prior to the Six Day War. The army was deployed in both defensive and offensive positions. In 1960, unlike in May 1967, the Egyptians did not publicize their concentration of forces. When the IDF did not attack Syria, the Egyptians saw this as proof of their "deterrence's effectiveness." The troops returned to their home bases in the second half of March 1960.[6] During the crisis Nasir, Amer, and the Egyptian media highlighted the Egyptian commitment to aiding Syria, in accordance with the defense pact, and helping any Arab state that came under attack. Nasir genuinely believed that Israel was about to invade Syria. Therefore, he had to deter Israel like he did in February 1960 because of his commitment to Syria and Egypt's pan-Arab national mission. This time, however, things developed differently. He must have seen the damage his emage and prestige would suffer if Israel did indeed attack Syria, and Egypt sat on the sidelines. He would be considered a "paper tiger" who had violated his Pan-Arab commitment. Nasirism, based on Arab nationalism, would be forfeited. He also feared that Egypt would lose its respect and leadership status that was rooted in its ability and commitment to come to the aid of Arab countries in trouble, especially in the case of a tangible Israeli threat. For Nasir this commitment was "something more durable and binding than agreements and pacts."[7]

Egyptian Sovereignty in the Gulf of Aqaba Restored and Erasing the Results of the 1956 Aggression

The term "expunging the results of the aggression" that Nasir coined and frequently used in the postwar period came from the Sinai – Suez War. On December 23, 1958 Nasir summed up the accomplishments of 1957: "The major feature of 1957 was the elimination of the remnants of the [1956] aggression. Throughout 1957 we were engaged in expunging the vestiges of [this] aggression . . . the struggle against the economic embargo . . . and political isolation. This was a decisive year for Arab nationalism."[8] Of course when he used the term "elimination of the traces of aggression" he was not referring to Israel's freedom of navigation in the Gulf of Aqaba or the presence of UN Emergency Forces.

Nasir could not tolerate the opening of the Straits of Tiran to Israeli shipping. Israeli navigation in the gulf (and the stationing of UN Forces on Egyptian soil) had been forced on Nasir by an arrangement whereby Israel evacuated Sinai after the Sinai War. Since that time Israel's maritime freedom in the straits had been a major headache for him. He waited for the right moment to annul it. Jordan and Saudi Arabia exploited the navigation issue and UN presence on the Egyptian–Israeli border in order to taunt him during times of inter-Arab discord. Israel's Maritime freedom in the gulf contradicted the exacerbation of the Arab–Israeli conflict in the years following the Sinai War, and also ran counter to the principles of the Palestinian problem that Nasir himself had elevated to the forefront of the Arab agenda. During the Arab summit conferences and the debates on Arab strategy to solve the Palestinian problem, the

Israeli navigation issue became almost irreconcilable. It harried him even more from mid-1966 when the summit atmosphere faded, inter-Arab relations deteriorated, and the Arab world split into two camps: the "progressive states" (Egypt, Syria, Iraq, and Algeria) and the "reactionaries" (Jordan and Saudi Arabia at its core). Saudi Arabia wished to formulate an Islamic pact to serve as a counterweight to the Nasirite camp. In their tirades against Egypt, Jordan and Saudi Arabia made explicit mention of the UN Forces in Egypt and Israeli vessels' freedom through the Straits of Tiran. There was little Nasir could do in the face of such effective propaganda. He dared not tackle it head on since they had exposed his Achilles' heel. Nasir's only counterclaim was that Egypt could remove the UN Forces any time it wished to.[9] In December 1966 Amer suggested a way out of the quandary: remove the UN Emergency Force without closing the straits. But Nasir rejected this plan. He justified Egypt's position on May 26, 1967: "Should we utter empty rhetoric or should we build up and train our army as long the international emergency force is stationed here and until we have completed our preparations? Then, as I have said, within one half hour we'll tell the international Emergency Forces to get out. The same holds true for Sharm al-Sheikh. Some Arabs have chided us. This is totally unacceptable. Sharm al-Sheikh means a clash with Israel."[10]

Egypt did not acknowledge the political background for stationing the emergency force or opening the straits to Israeli navigation. It pretended not to recognize that this had been the result of Israel's victory in the Sinai War. It preferred to avow that Britain and France had forced these terms. Naturally Egypt assumed this attitude in order to diminish Israel's achievement and offset the impression that it had yielded to Israel. Egypt's attitude also illustrates the extent to which Israel's maritime freedom piqued Nasir. As the conflict intensified, this situation became increasingly unbearable for Egypt. Little surprise then that on May 26 Hasanayn Haykal boasted that the straits had been blockaded again: "Egypt has forcefully succeeded in changing an act that had been forced on it. The opening of the Gulf of Aqaba to Israel was a *fait accompli* that had been railroaded through by the might of Imperialist arms. The *status quo* in the gulf was imposed by the 1956 Anglo-French invasion and not because of the Israeli army, even though Israel benefited from it."[11] Thus, Egypt's removal of the emergency force, its takeover of Sharm al-Sheikh, and closure of the straits were considered as the means of "expunging the results of the 1956 aggression," "returning the situation to what it was before the aggression," and reestablishing Egyptian sovereignty over the straits. As Nasir announced on May 29, 1967: "They're making a big uproar because we returned the situation to what it was before 1956."[12] Nasir took pride in this. The commentator on *Sawt al-Arab* got carried away in his passionate depiction of this achievement: "No party has the power to change the fact that the Gulf of Aqaba is now an Arab gulf banned to Israeli shipping and will remain banned to it in the future. For this goal the Arabs have prepared a mighty force beyond the enemy's imagination. If Israel has no right to exist, how can it have any rights in the Gulf of Aqaba?"[13]

Arab Honor and Pride Restored

For the first time since 1948 an Arab state, and not incidentally Egypt, took the initiative in challenging Israel to a confrontation on the battlefield. The Arabs perceived this step as retrieving their honor that the Western states, including Israel, had badly tarnished by portraying the Arab world as weak, fractured, and inadequate in comparison to Israel. Nasir had been devastatingly insulted by Western descriptions of Israel's strength in contrast to the Arabs' alleged impotence. The outstanding expression of the Arabs' restored honor, following Egypt's initiative, can be seen in Haykal's characterization of Egypt's accomplishments in the period of May 14–23 as "the ten days of glory." "This is the first time that Egypt has forced its moves on Israel" or threatened it with the use of force. This explains why Nasir was identified with Saladin. Never had Nasir referred to Arab honor with such intensity and in such a short time, and he described his feeling in his May 29 speech:

> The Arab revolution and the Arab masses' enthusiasm that we witness in every Arab country and everywhere is not just because we have returned to the Gulf of Aqaba or expelled the UN Forces, but because we have recaptured Arab honor and Arab hope. Israel has always bragged [about its strength], and the Western countries, first and foremost the United States and Britain, continued to ignore, humiliate, and underestimate us. But the time has come – and as I've already said: we have determined the time and place [for the confrontation with Israel], and will never return to the absurd situation of 1948, and with the help of Allah we will emerge triumphant – the preparations are completed and we are ready to deal with Israel. If Western states brush us aside and disdain us, we will teach them to respect and value us, otherwise all of our talk on Filastin and the rights of the Palestinian people will have been mere bombast.[14]

After the signing of the Egyptian–Jordanian joint defense pact on May 30, Nasir announced that "while the Arabs deal with the American and British challenge, they must be united in order to [regain] their rights, enshrine these rights, and defend Arab honor."[15]

It is difficult to describe Nasir's mood, pride and sense of Arab honor that he imparted to Egypt and the Arab world after he closed the straits and expressed his challenge to Israel with the words "*ahlan wasahlan*." This was the hour of greatness that Nasir had been waiting years for – instead of making excuses to the Arab world that he had neither the ability nor a plan to fight Israel, now he could say these two words "*ahlan wasahlan*" which meant "I am ready and I invite you to battle." Little wonder, then, that the Arab masses were swept off their feet by euphoria. Nasir spoke of "a very different Arab world than that of ten days ago. The despair that had overtaken the Arabs would never return." He went so far as to speak of an Arab renaissance. He described the mobilization of the Arab world behind him as "a genuine Arab regeneration." Filled with pride and esteem Nasir recalled Egypt's glorious past: "We are capable of doing things, we are not petty states. Our countries are major players."[16] He also looked back on the Arabs' glorious past and their victories over the Crusaders: "We are an ancient people, our culture is seven thousand years old. The Crusaders conquered our land, and we waited seventy years. Where are the Crusaders today? They abandoned [the land] and left behind only fortresses. No Arab will depreciate the rights of the Palestinian people."[17] Now that the region was on the threshold of war, and Nasir could prove that he was fulfilling his commitment to fight Israel only when his armed forces were ready and the time was auspicious, he could clarify his past statements on the Crusaders:

I was once asked if I meant that we'll have to wait seventy years, like the Arabs who waited seventy years until the Crusaders were expelled. I said these things and people claimed that Nasir is postponing the solution to the Palestinian problem for seventy years. Look, I didn't mean seventy [years] as a [specific] time frame. I said that given our staunch decision and the Arab nation's ancient culture, it is impossible to terminate our [the Palestinian] problem. We have to wait for the right opportunity to realize our goals and [in the meantime] prepare ourselves relentlessly.[18]

Mushir Abd al-Hakim Amer, the Military Commander

In the Sinai War of 1956 Nasir dominated the political and military handling of the war, while Amer was still "new" to his role and lacked actual combat experience. In 1967 Mushir Amer dominated the military side of the crisis and the war itself. Amer had responsibility for the army, while Nasir, the political leader, had responsibility for the overall strategy and the handling of political events. After the Sinai War, Amer vigorously introduced a division of labor between the political and military spheres when he took sole responsibility for the military and administrative running of the army, including the appointment of officers, placing the army on a war footing, and equipping and training the troops. Moreover, because of Egypt's involvement in political developments after the 1956 War, Nasir also transferred civilian functions to Amer.

Huwaydi is convinced that the Mushir surrounded himself with people loyal to him until Nasir was no longer able to replace him even if he wanted to and "was unable to intervene in any matter, large or small, related to the armed forces."[19] Amer blocked Nasir's attempts to promote certain officers or dismiss others – such as the navy commander and some of Amer's staff officers – who were derelict in duty. Amer had reservations about Nasir's proposal to appoint Muhammad Fawzi as chief of staff, and when he was forced to accept this appointment Amer made sure to limit Fawzi's authority.

The struggle between the two men was generally kept concealed because Nasir feared its influence on the army and Amer's concentration of authority. The conflict between them began after Amer's failure in Syria – where he served from 1959 to 1961 as the sole vice-president in Syria with presidential authority in the northern region (until the dissolution of the Egyptian–Syrian union) – and continued until the Six Day War. Nasir tried unsuccessfully to oust Amer on two occasions, after the Sinai War and after the break-up of the UAR.[20] Nasir's attempt to limit his authority also failed. Amer was successful in keeping Nasir away from military matters. Thus, the Mushir became an "autocrat" in full control of the army, even though Nasir officially bore the title of "Supreme Commander of the Armed Forces." The tense relations between the two men came to expression in the following areas during the crisis and the war itself:

1 Amer was the supreme military authority. He issued orders on both large and small matters. Senior officers turned to him for every concern. Military commanders, including the top brass, were personally loyal to him and dared not express opinions opposed to his. But his military skill proved his undoing

when he failed to meet the exigencies of a high-pressured crisis and a major war that was much greater than the Sinai War that he had mishandled eleven years earlier. During the 1967 War he circumvented the military hierarchy, and gave orders directly to divisional commanders and even brigade commanders. His conduct and state of nerves on the first and second day of the fighting reflected his military capability – he had a breakdown and lost complete control of himself and the army.

2 Nasir avoided involvement in purely military matters, preferring to leave them in Amer's hands. Amer, for his part, does not appear to have been an obstacle to his strategic and political moves. In fact, he fully cooperated with Nasir in these areas. For example, in high-level talks headed by Nasir, Amer supported Nasir's second-strike strategy even though a few hours earlier he had ordered a limited attack against Israel. The same held true in talks over the removal of the UN Force and closure of the straits.

3 Above all, Amer's greatest influence lay in his fervor for a showdown with Israel. He appears eager for battle, anxious to prove his military "skills." His optimistic assessment of the Egyptian army's capability in a large-scale military confrontation with Israel was a decisive factor in the Egyptian leadership's decision-making during the crisis. Since Amer was, in fact, the supreme commander, everyone, including Nasir (who really had no choice), unquestioningly accepted his estimates. Egyptian military intelligence also was on his side.

4 In practice, a split developed in the state's leadership (or even in Nasir's one-man rule). "A split was created in decisive decision-making, and a conceptual gap in the implementation of decisions. While President Nasir ruled the state and the nation, Mushir Amer and his entourage controlled the armed forces outside the state's natural framework." Therefore, the High Command that was unequivocally loyal to Amer and undoubtedly aware of his feud with Nasir did not take the president's status into consideration and may even have scoffed at his warnings and assessments. "The main result of the [Nasir – Amer] struggle was that neither of them could ascertain the true fighting capability of the armed forces until they were pinned down in combat."[21]

In conclusion, Amer, who stood at the head of the military pyramid and directed the military side of the crisis, bore the main responsibility for the military defeat. The second-strike strategy was based on the army's ability to withstand the first strike, but when Amer and the air force commander failed to take the necessary steps to prepare for it, such as putting the air force on high alert, and ignored Nasir's warnings, the entire strategy fell apart in the first hours of hostilities.

During the Free Officers' Revolution in 1952 Amer had been a major, a battalion commander. Fifteen years later he still lacked the necessary tactical and battlefield skills to manage a military operation of such vast proportions. He had made a mess of the Suez – Sinai War; bungled his administrative tasks in Syria during the period of the union; and it turned out that he also failed in rebuilding the Egyptian army and preparing it for war as Nasir expected. The chiefs of staff of the air force and navy and senior staff officers shared the responsibility for the 1956 debâcle. But loyalty to the Mushir allowed some of them to remain in their roles, and others to be promoted. Military intelligence also had its share of shortcomings. During the crisis it mistakenly held to a rosy picture of the balance of forces that matched that of the Field Marshal. The military intelligence even "fell for" the IDF's deceptive maneuvers, especially regarding the main axis of attack. This was a classic case of a "political" thinking over-taking sound intelligence analysis.

Nasir's second-strike strategy came to nothing; in effect, the IDF's first strike decided the war. Therefore it is difficult to evaluate Nasir's strategy, even in historical retrospect. But in light of the disintegration of the entire Egyptian military complex, including the field command, and the army's deficient fighting ability, we may assume that even if the results of the first strike had been according to Amer's and the air force commander's expectations, the second strike would still have missed the mark. The Egyptian army was abysmally unprepared for such a war. From an historical point of view it was Nasir's gravest political mistake not to have drawn long-range conclusions from the Sinai War about Amer's competency and the senior command's qualifica-tions. Nasir learned his lesson after the Six Day War and took personal responsibility for the management of military affairs and reorganization of the army for another round designed "to expunge the results of the aggression." It fell to Sadat to reap the harvest.

8

In the Wake of the
Six Day War

The Khartoum Summit, August 29 – September 1, 1967:
A New Arab Strategy

The Six Day War and its results symbolized the end of a process in which the Arab–Israeli conflict had been the central – almost exclusive – axis of Arab nationalism, and the beginning of a process in which the Palestinian problem became the heart of the conflict.

Two major consequences of the Six Day War had an impact on the conflict: *First*, the change in Arab strategy that Nasir, beyond all his expectations, managed to dictate to the fourth Arab summit in Khartoum. Inter-Arab relations entered a period of reconciliation, and a new agenda was established in the Arab world. *Second*, the fida'iyyun organizations became the dominant factor in the Arab–Israeli conflict, winning the recognition of the Arab states as the leaders of the New Palestinian National Movement. Eventually they became a major party in the Arab–Israeli conflict. The Arab summit that convened in Khartoum between August 29 and September 1, 1967 ratified a new Arab strategy based on a solution in stages to the Arab–Israeli conflict. Nasir asked the Arab states to agree to what was "possible." The following decisions were arrived at:

1 The conference agrees on the need to unite all efforts to eradicate the traces [results] of the aggression, on the basis of [the fact] that the occupied lands are Arab lands whose return all the Arab states are responsible for.
2 The kings and presidents agree on consolidating their political efforts in the international and diplomatic arenas to eradicate the traces of aggression and to guarantee the withdrawal of Israel's warmongering forces from occupied Arab lands following the June 5 aggression. [This will be done] within the framework of the Arab states' basic commitments, which are: no peace (*sulh*) with or recognition of Israel; no negotiations with Israel; and adherence to the Palestinian people's right to their homeland.[1]

Thus, the summit decided that the solution to the Arab–Israeli conflict would be in two stages:

The first stage would be "the elimination of the traces of the [Israeli] aggression" in other words, the solution of the "1967 problem," through "liberation of the Arab territories occupied by Israel" in the June war. Nasir believed that at this stage this was the primary goal. He fostered the belief in the Arab world that this goal was realizable.

The second stage would see the achievement of the long-term strategic goal. According to the joint announcement made by the heads of the Arab states at the conclusion of the summit: "The preservation of the Palestinian people's hallowed right to their land."[2] that is, dedication to a solution to the "1948 problem," or the "liberation of Filastin" in the prewar sense.

Explaining the Khartoum decisions, Hasanayn Haykal wrote in December 1967: "The Arab struggle . . . placed as its goal the elimination of the June 1967 aggression, without deviating from its efforts to eliminate the results of May 1948 aggression."[3]

The consequences of the [1967] war have given rise to doubts in the Arab world, especially among the Egyptian leadership, regarding the likelihood of realizing this goal. A cautious Egyptian assessment admitted that since "the eradication of the aggression of 1948 is an abstract goal," then the elimination of 1967's results would mark a turning-point toward a solution to the "1948 problem."[4]

With the hindsight of forty years and the publication of almost the entire protocol of the Khartoum summit, it is possible to reassess the summit's results and its impact on the path to a solution to the conflict. Whereas the Arab strategy that was approved in the second and third summits focused on a comprehensive military solution, the Khartoum summit was a watershed not only in declaring a solution in stages, but also in perceiving a new dimension – the political one. This path comprised:

1 The Arab agreement for overt political activity designed to attain the first stage of the solution to the conflict, namely, "the eradication of the results of the aggression." This agreement also included political activity aimed at attaining the objectives of the second stage, according to the conditions determined in the summit. Nasir's and Husayn's starting point on the issue, and that was accepted by the summit, was that a long period would elapse until the first stage could be accomplished by military means.

It must be stressed that the three "no's" of Khartoum were not the result of a demand or proposal by Nasir or any other Arab leader, but were the absolutist demand of Ahmad al-Shuqayri, head of the PLO, who wanted to curtail Husayn's steps toward a political solution for the West Bank. Arab leaders – including Nasir – were forced to submit to Shuqayri's demands lest it appear that they had succumbed to Israel's demands following the Arabs' military defeat. Nasir's willingness to commence political activity did not stand in contradiction to his view that "what was taken by force – will be returned by force." On the contrary, from his perspective the military option complemented the political path.

2 Based on Nasir's initiative and support, the summit authorized Husayn to take all steps necessary to return the West Bank and (East) Jerusalem to his kingdom, as long as these steps were within the limitations of Khartoum. Nasir and Husayn both realized that time was working against the Arabs on the West

Bank where Israeli rule was becoming more entrenched everyday. During the discussion Nasir stated:

> Time is working against us, the [people's] condition there is difficult . . . Political activity is the only way to quickly regain the West Bank. Everyday that passes strengthens the occupation on the West Bank . . . I think that Husayn will arrive at some kind of agreement with the Americans . . . We must do our utmost to return Jerusalem and the West Bank with the means currently at our disposal, that is, if we delay, neither Jerusalem nor the West Bank will be retrieved. This is why I told King Husayn that he is permitted to take all measures necessary, excluding negotiations with Israel, to regain the West Bank and Jerusalem.[5]

3   A byproduct of Nasir's agreement to the political path was his agreement to UNSC Resolution 242 of November 22, 1967. In his opinion, this decision laid the foundation for Israel's withdrawal from the territories it had captured in the war, in other words, it could help implement the first stage of the Arab/Egyptian strategy – "the eradication of the results of [Israeli] aggression." But Nasir still felt that there was not enough bite in this to solve the Palestinian problem, that is, the "1948 problem." Nasir's agreement enabled the Jarring mission, which was designed to implement the resolution, and American mediation whose climax was Secretary of State William Roger's 1970 initiative for a political solution to the conflict. Nasir's and the Arab summit's decision to turn to the political process undoubtedly paved the way for Sadat's political initiative in February 1971, and even more so his peace initiative in 1977. Sadat was keenly aware of the factors making up the Arab–Israeli conflict and, as he stated, he sometimes disagreed with Nasir on the issue. (After the Six Day War Sadat worked closely to Nasir and was able to learn and master Nasir's strategy as well as his tactics for carrying it out).

4   The new status on the West Bank and the Gaza Strip created a linkage between the solution to the West Bank territorial issue and the solution to the Palestinian-national issue. In other words, the solution to the Palestinian problem was also divided into two stages: the liberation of occupied Palestinian lands and the liberation of Filastin. Thus Egypt, Jordan, and the Palestinians had to determine their position on the future of the occupied Palestinian territories. Nasir decided in favor of the Palestinians, even if he did so obliquely because of his improved relations with Husayn. On February 1, 1969 he announced that the Palestinian problem is the "problem of a people that possesses a homeland." This meant that when Israel withdrew from the West Bank and Gaza Strip, a Palestinian government would be established there. Sadat was more explicit on this issue.

5   Amin Huwaydi, the Egyptian war minister and head of the general intelligence after the Six Day War, presented his view on another aspect of the war's conclusion and the turn to the political path – the American–Egyptian dialogue. In his opinion "one of the signs of the post-Khartoum period was the numerous channels that opened between Egypt and the United States, including official, personal, and secret channels between the two countries' intelligence services."[6] Nasir reckoned that in the political process the United States would be his key for influencing Israel.

In view of Jordan's participation in the war and the rise in Husayn's prestige in Jordan and the Arab world, the summit regarded the king as a hero and national leader. He won more sympathy and admiration in the Khartoum summit than he ever received since his ascension to the throne. He remained Nasir's closest ally until the Egyptian president's dying day. He and Nasir dominated the summit's debates. Husayn was elevated to this status even though he lost two important elements that had justified his claim that Jordan was the representative of the Palestinians. He lost the West Bank and the largest concentration of the Palestinian population. After the war Husayn realized that his government's paramount objective was to return the West Bank to his kingdom. Nasir supported this approach. Husayn understood that by assuming responsibility for the recovery of the West Bank he still represented the Palestinians and the West Bank still belonged to his kingdom. Indeed, with Nasir's help, the summit authorized Husayn "to do everything possible [within the limits of the Khartoum no's] to retrieve the West Bank and Jerusalem."[7]

Like Nasir, Husayn assumed that if the West Bank remained under Israeli influence for the next year or two, then the lengthy separation would work against its return to Jordanian rule. He emphasized this in the following statement at the summit:

> The situation on the West Bank is very bad and difficult. If we leave the West Bank in Jewish hands for a long period, it will be difficult to retrieve it afterwards. The West Bank is not the sole problem. The future of Jerusalem is important not only for Palestinians and Arabs, but for Muslims and Christians too. We cannot cast responsibility on the people (in the West Bank) alone without trying to save them. I ask that my responsibility and commitment are defined. Is this an Arab or Palestinian problem? We cannot leave here without reaching an understanding on this issue. I personally cannot tolerate [how things stand at present]. We must come to a united position.[8]

Unlike Husayn, after the defeat Shuqayri was pushed so far onto the sidelines that "they forgot" to invite him to the Khartoum summit. From this position he waged a rearguard struggle. Sensing that his ouster from the Palestinian–Arab political arena was a matter of time, he decided to shed the image affixed to him up until the war by proving that he was not being dragged behind the wheels of the Arab leaders. During the summit he revealed, to the surprise of the heads of Arab states, a radical uncompromising position, even to the point of walking out of the last session in protest against the summit's rejection of his position. But the main concern of the Arab world after its defeat was to obtain Israel's pullout from the territories. The Palestinian problem had still not assumed its new role in the Arab arena. Shuqayri was considered one of the symbols of defeat. Shafiq al-Hut, along with Shuqayri a member of the PLO delegation to the summit, testifies in his memoirs:

> Shuqayri ['s statements at the summit] toward the [Arab] kings and presidents were as acrimonious as theirs had been toward him, and even more so . . . Actually, there was no difference between [the attitude] toward Shuqayri the man and toward Shuqayri the PLO leader. . . . I admit that I was often surprised that his replies failed to distinguish between the wheat and the chaff, and I felt that he tended to 'exaggerate.' When I followed the Arab leaders and listened to what the PLO leader was saying, I believed that a 'new approach' had to be taken in the Arab homeland and Palestinian arena . . . Shuqayri thought that he would lead this 'new approach' single-handedly! Shuqayri was

a symbol that had played out its part in solving the problem and the entity. His role had been great, and this credit should not be taken from him.[9]

Shuqayri's summit speech (which was circulated as a memo) contained his views and his demands of the summit. He proposed six principles for dealing with the heart of the Palestinian problem. The following are excerpts from his speech:

1. "No peace (sulh) or coexistence with Israel."
2. "No negotiations with Israel."
3. "No settlement that would harm the Palestinian problem and lead to its elimination."
4. "Neither the Gaza Strip, West Bank, nor the al-Hama area will be surrendered; Jerusalem's Arab-ness must remain intact.
5. "No Arab state will accept a separate solution to the Palestinian problem."
6. "The Palestinian people have the basic right to a homeland and the right to self-determination."[10]

The Arab leaders' attitude toward the memo reflected their attitude toward Shuqayri the man; in other words, they ignored him. His speech intruded a great deal of tension into the summit, and the chairman hastened to close the session. Nasir made no comment.[11]

Shuqayri's position (especially his six-point plan) incited a bitter argument with Husayn. Shuqayri's obvious goal was to stymie Husayn's political effort (that had Nasir's full backing) to return the West Bank to his kingdom. The argument became so caustic that Nasir had to intervene. At the beginning of the discussion on the political solution, Shuqayri brought up the following points: "A withdrawal is needed from two types of land: Arab land, such as Sinai, that belongs to the UAR, and the Golan Heights, that belongs to Syria; and Palestinian land – al-Hama, the Gaza Strip, and the West Bank. This is Palestinian land and its fate is in the hands of the Palestinian people."[12] When Husayn heard Shuqayri assert that the West Bank is Palestinian land, he lashed back: "We have to do more than register positions; we have to quickly regain our position prior to the aggression. The problem now is to discuss every decision that will lead to the withdrawal of Israeli forces. We do not wish to [differentiate] between Arab land and Palestinian land. [People] in Jordan do not feel that there is a difference between the leadership and the people. I repeat that I will not hurt anyone who disagrees with me, but I ask you to define my responsibility. Is this an Arab or Palestinian problem? We cannot leave here without [reaching] an understanding on this issue, at this stage I personally find this intolerable."[13]

Nasir, who understood the rift between Shuqayri and Husayn, especially Shuqayri's insinuations that Husayn should not be the one allowed to get a settlement for the future of the West Bank, decided unequivocally in favor of Husayn's position and ignored Shuqayri's speech:

We must act as quickly as possible to return Jerusalem and the West Bank with the means currently at our disposal. The only way to do this is through political activity. When I met King Husayn, I told him that he could take all the steps necessary – excluding peace (sulh) or negotiations with Israel – to return the West Bank and Jerusalem, including an improvement in relations with Britain and America. I think that every day the West Bank remains in Israeli hands it becomes more strongly linked to Israel . . . Since we are unable to carry out a military operation, we are left with political action.[14]

Abd al-Majid Farid, who served as the secretary-general of the Egyptian president's office and who took part in the Egyptian delegation to the Khartoum summit, describes the atmosphere during the discussion:

> After Nasir's statements the atmosphere in the conference heated up. The direct cause of this was King Husayn's statements. Shuqayri interrupted and threatened to walk out of the conference. Nasir tried to put out the fire in the conference hall, but to no avail. He tried a second time to cool the passions. When he failed again, he ceased his efforts, and the fracas continued though the fire was contained within a narrow circle so it would not influence the positive results that had been attained in the conference up to this point. The meeting hall became a verbal battlefield between the Jordanian delegation headed by King Husayn and the Palestinian delegation headed by Shuqayri. Things were said that everyone – especially Nasir – considered unnecessary, and need not be repeated.[15]

The following are the key sections of the debate:

Ahmad al-Shuqayri: "The West Bank issue is crucial. The six principles mentioned in the memo . . . must serve as the basis of any phased or final solution. We agree with you that the enemy has to withdraw from the Gaza Strip and West Bank; but the question is what price will we have to pay to regain the West Bank? If the price is too high [exorbitant], then it would be a great mistake. The aim of United States policy is to totally eradicate the Palestinian problem. The Johnson Plan's five points are a heavy price for the West Bank. As an Arab citizen and chairman [of the PLO] I refuse to pay such a price, and I state here and now that I oppose it. The Yugoslavian Plan seeks a final solution and lasting peace in the region. We reject every plan that will result in the total eradication of the Palestinian problem."

Nasir: "I take issue with Shuqayri regarding the final solution to the problem. The final eradication means sitting with Israel at the negotiating table, and this is what the United States basically wants. In the past we had one catastrophe (*masiba*) and now [there are] two: the catastrophe of 1948 and the disaster of 1967; therefore I said that we are willing to pay the price to recover the West Bank, and I meant a price that is reasonable. We must not forget that half of Filastin was lost in 1948, and the second half was lost in 1967. The price is not the eradication of the problem. The price may call for closer ties between Husayn and the Americans. If the truth is always bitter, we must accept it. I disagree with Shuqayri who sees President Tito's plan as the eradication of the Palestinian problem. There's a difference between political activity and the eradication of the problem. Unless we embark upon positive activity aimed at recovering the West Bank, then the land the Jews have seized will gradually become Israeli land. We must fight with political means until the appropriate time comes and we regain our right through military action." In the ensuing exchange, Shuqayri stated: "We support giving full backing to King Husayn's efforts [and] intentions, but the man does not have the [authority] to reach a [separate] political solution."

King Husayn replied testily: "Of course our position will be strong if we reach a general agreement. We must not forget that this is a problem of all the Arabs and of Arab existence; it is impossible to reach an agreed-upon solution to the problem by individual contacts, whether through me or anyone else. Within this framework I am prepared to take on any role and assume responsibility, but others [referring to Shuqayri] must understand that this is not a public auction or a registering of positions. We heard Shuqayri speak about the six principles. Gentlemen, let's take a look at the first Arab summit's decisions that determined Shuqayri's precise mission. And another question: I would like to know who wrote these six principles? This evening I heard many things [again referring to Shuqayri] that may be interpreted as though I am concerned about my self-respect. The issue at hand is far more important than this. It is not a case of preferring one person over another. Jordan was the frontline bulwark against the danger; and it is from this starting point that I am speaking. I agree with every idea that you agree with or with whatever responsibility you define, but I am not willing to take advice from any man about what should and should not be done [referring to Shuqayri again].

Shuqayri responded acidly: "The truth is that the Palestinian problem is our problem. But no one among us has the authority to agree to any type of a solution to the problem – neither King Husayn nor the PLO. If you want the PLO merely to be an audience, then our presence is not needed here, and we are prepared to walk out of the conference right now. But before I leave the hall, I want to say something bluntly in the PLO's name. No king or president has the authority to solve the Palestinian problem. If such a person exists, it will be a dangerous turning-point for the [pan-Arab] national problem, which is an issue and responsibility not only for the present generation but also for the following ones." In the course of the debate, Shuqayri added: "If the conference limits itself [to approving] the political effort without a commitment to the principles that I mentioned, I will leave the conference."[16]

On the morning of September 1, 1967, the last session of the summit was held during which the proposals for the decision were approved. Shuqayri intended to boycott the session but the heads of the Sudanese and Iraqi delegations persuaded him to return by telling him that the following two principles were adopted:

1 No Arab state will accept on its own a political solution to the Palestinian problem.
2 No solution to the Palestinian problem will be accepted unless it is first discussed and approved in a general Arab meeting that includes the PLO.

Despite the above principles, in a separate meeting, the foreign ministers continued their efforts to draft a commitment that did not reject "peace" and a "separate solution" while omitting the need for a general Arab meeting that included the PLO. During the foreign ministers' meeting Shafiq al-Hut insisted on listing the PLO's reservations, including the two principles mentioned above. When these sections were brought to the summit plenum for approval, it turned out that they had not been put on the agenda. Shuqayri demanded that the two principles be added, but when he realized that this was not going to happen, he left the meeting in protest. Although the summit accepted the proposal that opposed peace with Israel, it rejected the second one regarding a separate agreement. This was because of Husayn's unrelenting opposition to it.[17]

After the announcement of the summit's close (September 1, 1967), Shuqayri explained "to the Palestinian people and the Arab nation" the reason that he walked out of the conference:

The main reason is that the PLO presented the summit conference with a memo containing six principles that any solution to the Palestinian problem would have to be based on. The memo stated that no Arab state is allowed to accept on its own any solution to the Palestinian problem. It also stressed that the Palestinian problem is a major Arab problem, and a political solution to it is forbidden unless all the Arab states agree on the agreement in a general meeting that includes the PLO. But the summit conference did not agree to the PLO's proposal. [Thus] the PLO delegation had no alternative but to walk out of the conference as an expression of its protest of the summit conference's decisions on the Palestinian problem.[18]

Shuqayri's participation and aggressive demeanor at the Khartoum summit were, in effect, his "swan song." It was clear that he had reached the end of his political tether. He admitted as such in his memoirs: "I am certain that the Khartoum summit and its decisions will force me to resign sooner or later." He considered the Khartoum conference "the greatest political defeat that the Arabs bought upon themselves in modern history." He explained his aggressive position in the summit by claiming that "King Husayn wants the summit conference to invest him with the authority to discuss the Palestinian problem outside its jurisdiction, and he wants to know the limits of this authority. I had to speak from the standpoint of my historical responsibility to the Palestinian people, a responsibility that will follow me to the grave."[19]

Conclusion

The Arab–Israeli Conflict between the *Nakba* and the *Naksa* – The Emergence of the New Palestinian National Movement

The Six Day War was the culmination of the deterioration in the Arab–Israeli conflict, which began in 1957 when Nasir started espousing Arab nationalism, whose main feature was the Palestinian problem or the liberation of Filastin. The decade was characterized by the preparations that both sides made for an all-out confrontation, which both saw as inevitable. Also during this period, the Arab countries formulated their positions for a solution to all aspects of the conflict and chose their objectives and the means of realizing them. The main objective that served as a beacon stayed the same until the Six Day War, although differences of opinion broke out between Egypt and Syria. The main stages, on the road to the Six Day War were: the water struggle; the convocation and decisions of the first Arab summit; the second summit's resolutions that determined the Arabs' goal in the conflict for the first time; the rise of the New Palestinian National Movement whose representatives, the fida'iyyun organizations, advocated an armed struggle against Israel; Israel's battle against them, and against Jordan and Syria to get them to halt the fida'iyyun's activity; the deterioration of the security situation on the borders due to the water struggle and Palestinian sabotage activity; the military strengthening of the Arab states – first and foremost Egypt; and the Palestinian problem, which was the decisive factor in Arab political and military activity. Each element added another layer to the long process in the conflict that intensified and culminated in war. Although Nasir wanted to decide the time and place for war when he was ready and certain of its results, that is, when he felt assured of an overwhelming victory, in the end neither side decided the outbreak of war, expected it, or foresaw it until the crisis erupted. When Nasir sent his forces into the Sinai, after careful consideration, in effect he let Israel choose the timing for the opening attack, which he foresaw with uncanny accuracy.

At the base of all the stages that preceded the war, the *nakba*, the festering residue of 1948 felt by Arabs of all classes – especially their leaders, intellectual circles, and politically aware citizens – lay at the heart of issue. The results of the 1948 war had become embedded in the Arab soul and sank even deeper following the Sinai war.[1] The written material exuding hate-filled messages against Israel, Arab newspaper articles, Arab broadcasts, and above all the inciting, vitriolic speeches of the Arab leaders, added oil to the flames of animosity against Israel's existence in the region. The Arab states began competing over radical expressions against Israel until it seemed that extremism became the main goal. The overt extremist position toward Israel served as a vehicle for butting political rivals, attaining political legitimacy, gaining public favor, covering up domestic shortcomings or neglect, achieving foreign policy objectives, and above all functioning as the reason and background for military armament. Arab propaganda presented Israel as the Arab world's most dangerous enemy – even more menacing than Western imperialism. A number of books published in the Arab world elucidated this danger. *The Protocols of the Elders of Zion* was published in new editions.[2] These books compared the coming confrontation to a war against the Crusaders, promising that Israel would be destroyed just as the Crusaders had been.[3] The war's goals were defined as "revenge for [Arab] honor, the return of their country, and the cleansing of Filastin soil." Arab hostility toward Israel was expressed in the crisis that preceded the Six Day War and could be seen in the behavior of the Arab public in general and the Arab leaders in particular. "*Nakbat Filastin*" was deeply ingrained in Nasir's political consciousness and was a central element in the crystallization of his strategy for conflict resolution.[4]

The allegiance that nearly all of the Arab states gave to Nasir's moves a few days after the crisis broke out testifies not only to the president's charismatic leadership, but also to the depth of the *nakba* trauma and the Arabs' powerful urge to rid themselves of it. This phenomenon clarifies the extent to which the *naksa* (the June 1967 defeat) deepened the *nakba* trauma and expanded it into the popular levels of the Arab public. Given the Arab public's rage on the eve of the war, the humiliation that the Arab world suffered was a personal blow to every Arab. Israel not only decisively defeated the Arab armies, it also captured large chunks of Arab territory, making it the *de facto* ruler of a large Arab population – this was the exact opposite of the former glories that every Arab was reared on. Little wonder then that after the war there was a great anticipation for a new Salah al-Din, and the expectation for an Arab victory was even stronger than on the eve of the war. This explains the great importance of Sadat's strategic victory in the Yom Kippur War.

During the period under discussion, the Arabs saw Israel as the source of the Palestinian problem – in its broadest sense – whose solution lay in Israel's destruction and the recovery of the Palestinian people's legal rights as defined in the Arab strategy as approved by the second summit and the military planning approved by the third summit. The Arab states embarked upon a process whose final goal was to make sure that the Palestinians were a separate party in the conflict, even if they had not gained formal recognition of this status due to inter-Arab reasons. The Arab states had not yet absorbed the changes that the Palestinian problem had undergone – the rise of a new generation of Palestinian leaders and the growth of the New Palestinian National Movement that was expressed in the establishment of the PLO and especially in the emergence of Fatah and other fida'iyyun organizations. The recognition of the status of these organizations increased following the results of the war and with the rise and strengthening of the fida'iyyun organizations' position. This is why every attempt by Israel to separate a solution to the Arab–Israeli conflict from a solution the Palestinian national problem – by presenting the conflict as a border issue and the Palestinian problem as a refugee issue – was doomed to failure.

This research presented in the preceding chapters concludes that only within the context of the political and military processes that developed in the Arab–Israeli conflict after the Sinai war is it possible to understand the crisis that led to the Six Day War, the development of Nasir's view of the factors with regard to the solution to the conflict, and his moves toward war. The domestic political system and circumstances in Egypt, Syria, and Jordan can also be understood within this context. Explaining Nasir's moves after May 13, 1967 by other factors in the conflict, or solely by political and military moves he made after the outbreak of the crisis, is only a partial explanation.

Furthermore, it has clearly been demonstrated in this study that the development of the Palestinian problem as a national movement for self-determination was linked to events in the Arab–Israeli conflict and the Arab states' position toward the conflict; in effect, these were two sides of the same coin. The inevitable conclusion is that an inseparable connection existed between developments in the Arab–Israeli conflict and developments in the Palestinian problem as it was perceived until the Six Day War. This connection grew stronger after the war, when it became a joint simultaneous Arab–Palestinian struggle for the liberation of Arab territories and a solution to the Palestinian national problem, i.e. the liberation of the Palestinian territories and "the return of the Palestinians' legal rights." The Palestinian problem that became an inseparable and indelible part of the conflict supplied the New Palestinian National Movement with a powerful impetus for its advancement and gains.

Only a leader of Nasir's stature could survive the results of the *naksa*, continue to lead the Arab world, and dictate a new strategy of conflict resolution. The Arab public completely identified with Nasir during the crisis that preceded the war and perceived Nasir's failure as its own failure. Indeed, their loyalty to him and their belief that he could deliver them from the deep postwar crisis increased the more that he persisted in the struggle against Israel – this time by waging a war of attrition. Moreover, there was no alternative to Nasir as leader of Egypt or the Arab world. This was shown by the hysterical responses in Egypt and the Arab world when Nasir announced his intention to resign on June 9, 1967. Nasir learned the lesson from the 1967 defeat and took personal responsibility for preparing the Egyptian army for the next war. His credo was: "What was taken by force will be retuned by force." He believed in this principle and implanted it in the Egyptian people and the Arab world.

After the *naksa*, Arab leaders, especially Nasir, were determined to extirpate the trauma and restore Arab honor that had been trampled so ignominiously. Thus, Sadat's strategic victory in the Yom Kippur War was perceived as the first Arab triumph since Salah al-Din defeated the Crusaders in the twelfth century, and it paved the way for his peace initiative in 1977, a continuation of his initiative of February 4, 1971. No wonder then that on the twenty-fifth anniversary celebration of the October War in 1998, Egyptian propaganda asserted that it was directly linked to the Arabs' military defeat in the Six Day War and their strategic victory in the Yom Kippur War (October War). Egyptian spokesmen claimed that the 1967 defeat was the motivating force behind the Egyptian victory in the October War.

251

Throughout the period under discussion, Nasir instilled in the Arab world the awareness that a solution to the conflict was attainable only if the Arabs knew how to prepare for it correctly. But, when the moment of truth came, this conception collapsed. A new generation arose, a generation of intellectuals that had not only been reared on the 1948 Arab–Palestinian *nakba*, but that had actually experienced the 1967 *naksa* which became another layer of the 1948 *nakba*; both defeats now shaped the young generation's position toward Israel. The *naksa* generation bequeathed to its successors the hostility toward Israel that fed on the Arab world's frustration in its failure to match Israel's progress and achievements in all fields, and its inability to vanquish it on the battlefield. Furthermore, the results of the Six Day War deepened the popular level's hatred toward Israel. The Palestinians dwelling on the West Bank, including the refugees, experienced a double trauma. In addition, the vast body of Arab literature published after the Six Day War, which analyzed and explained the causes and results of the defeat, widened the abyss between Israel and the Arab world.[5] Hostility toward Israel was nourished on the linkage that Arab propaganda made between Israel and Western imperialism or colonialism.

The hysterical war fervor in the Arab public during the crisis – the waiting period before the outbreak of hostilities – and the certainty that Israel's demise was imminent and that the *nakba* trauma would soon be relieved embedded the conflict into the consciousness of additional layers in the Arab populace, especially among the Palestinians. Thus, a gap was created between the Egyptian and Jordanian leaderships, on the one hand, that had signed peace agreements with Israel and that adhered to their commitment to the peace process, and on the other hand, the popular strata and intelligentsia in Arab society that were against any move toward opening a new leaf with Israel after the Oslo Accords. This was true especially after the Israeli–Palestinian conflict reignited with singular ferocity in the two *intifadas*. In this light it is possible to understand Sadat's difficulty, and after him, Mubarak and Husayn's problems in getting their nations accustomed to the idea of peace with Israel. Israel's attitude toward the Palestinian problem and its resolution was the gauge for Egypt and Jordan's relations with Israel and their degree of commitment toward the Palestinian problem. Sometimes the compromise was a "frozen peace." The perpetuation of the Israeli–Palestinian conflict influences Arab public opinion, especially in Egypt and even more so in Jordan where the Palestinians make up about half of the population.

The military defeat that Israel inflicted on Egypt and the Arab world in June 1967 caused the Arab leaders to reassess the practicality of the view that an all-out military solution alone would solve the Arab–Israeli conflict, i.e. the Palestinian problem, especially in light of Israel's military superiority. It should come as no surprise then that after such a large-scale military defeat the Arab world in general, and Nasir in particular, were not willing to accept any political solution offered by Israel. From the Arab point of view to do so would be tantamount to surrender. Nasir's new approach was accepted by Arab leaders. It called for an integration of the military struggle with a political struggle aimed at exerting pressure on Israel to make concessions toward the Arabs until the first stage – the eradication of the results of Israeli aggression – was achieved. Echoes of this view were heard in discussions at the Khartoum summit (August 29–September 1, 1967). The summit conference adopted the political path for solving the conflict until a military solution was attainable. These considerations and the readiness to discuss a political solution had a long-term effect on the willingness to find a political solution capable of satisfying Arab expectations or at least "eradicating the results of aggression." The War of Attrition that Nasir initiated in April 1969 expressed the integrated political–military struggle that he advocated.

Amin Huwaydi, who served as the minister of war and head of general intelligence after the Six Day War, wrote: "After the 1967 defeat there were two schools of thought in the Egyptian political leadership: the first school favored an immediate turn toward a political solution in order to arrive at a peace settlement; the second school claimed that the only hope of a political solution was the build-up of military power, not necessarily for its exertion, but for convincing the other side that a just solution would have to be based on a balance of interests and on the principle of 'what was taken by force will be returned only by force'." In his opinion, "the second school emerged victorious, but the first school came back in greater strength after Nasir's departure." It is not hard to discern the signs of the second school that dominated Nasir's presidency after the war, whereas the first school was dominant during Sadat's tenure.[6]

Eventually the War of Attrition wore Egypt out,[7] though Israel, too, was considerably exhausted, and the Jarring Mission failed to advance the political process. The Egyptian–Israeli agreement on the Roger's Initiative in June 1970 for a three-month ceasefire illustrated, on the one hand, the stalemate that Nasir's attrition policy had led to, and, on the other hand, the Jarring mission's failure to broker a political arrangement. Nasir died without his two-pronged strategy for a political–military struggle achieving any tangible results. Sadat reaped the fruit, but not before he embarked upon a new strategy in the conflict.

The June 1967 Arab military defeat (naksa) greatly reduced the likelihood, if there ever was one, of a political solution acceptable to both sides, even if the Arab side was willing, unlike in the past, to enter political negotiations. The war's results entrenched the Arabs more deeply in their positions. Since any concession was considered surrender, the Arab side refused to make any allowance – territorial or political – acceptable to Israel; and Israel spurned Arab demands that were territorial or Palestinian-related. Nasir's slogan "what was taken by force will be returned by force" described the Arab position accurately. Historically Nasir was right. An Arab military move was needed that would undo the results of the Six Day War, that is, a strategic victory that would bring both sides to the negotiating table and jumpstart the peace initiative. Sadat was wise enough to exploit the success of the Yom Kippur War in order to reap political gains by changing his strategic approach to the conflict.

The Palestinians benefited from the war's results and the impasse in the attempts at conflict resolution that lasted until the 1973 Yom Kippur War. Fifteen years after the 1959 Egyptian initiative to revive the Palestinian entity, and nine years after Fatah began operations (January 1965), the New Palestinian National Movement scored impressive gains in the seventh Arab summit that was held in Rabat in October 1974. These included, inter alia, recognition of the PLO as the sole legitimate representative of the Palestinian people, and approval of the PLO resolution (June 1974) for "the establishment of a Palestinian national government [or Palestinian state] over any Palestinian areas that will be liberated." This, in effect, was the Arab states' political recognition that the PLO (or the Palestinians) was a separate party in the conflict and represented the Palestinian people in all talks on a political resolution of the conflict and the future of the Palestinian territories. This was the realization of Nasir's vision. The Jordanian option raised in this period – Palestinian self-determination within the

Jordanian–Palestinian framework – was already anachronistic. The Jordanian option had become irrelevant even before the Rabat decisions and Yom Kippur War, since the Arab countries already recognized the PLO as the Palestinians' representative and rejected, although not officially, the return of the West Bank to Jordanian rule. Following "Black September" (September 1970) there was no likelihood that the West Bank populace would want to return to Jordanian rule. After Palestinian awareness and political ties to the PLO strengthened, the Palestinians viewed the organization as their legal representative. Thus, another stage in bolstering Palestinian consciousness and identity was completed after the Yom Kippur War.

The pan-Arab system and its institutions (the Arab League Council, the Arab chiefs-of-staff, the Arab Defense Council, the UAC, and above all the Arab summit conference) – despite their weaknesses and shortcomings in joint military cooperation and the implementation of the Arab plan for diverting the Jordan River's tributaries – contributed to the revival of the Palestinian entity, *inter alia*, because of the status of the Palestinian problem in Arab public opinion and the Arabs' commitment and guilt feelings toward the Palestinians following the 1948 *nakba*. In this area the pan-Arab system's contribution was of great importance. For the first time, inter-Arab forums devised a strategy that committed the Arab states (at least officially). Despite his criticism of this system and the way its official bodies functioned, Nasir, at any rate, benefited from them. For example, when he summoned the summit forum to help him out of the deadlock in late 1963 and prevent Syria's ill-devised actions. The third summit approved his proposal for suspending water diversion operations and his statement that Israeli actions against Syrian diversion operations were a local matter and Syria's responsibility, and one that did not require an all-Arab or Egyptian response. The Khartoum conference helped lighten his burden of defeat and return him to the center of leadership in the Arab world. In retrospect, the inter-Arab system had an aggregate influence on the Palestinian question even if proximate to and during the events themselves a different impression was received.

After the war, Nasirism (or Nasir's view of Arab nationalism) that had driven Arab politics between the two wars gave way to the Arab–Israeli conflict. Even after the defeat, Nasir determined the elements of the conflict, calling for the mobilization of the Arabs' political, economic, and military resources for war with Israel. The main objective of his policy and that of the rest of the Arab leaders was "the eradication of the results of [Israeli] aggression." The conflict also supplanted Arab nationalist ideologies (Ba'th and the Arab Nationalists Movement) that were now bankrupt. There was no argument in the Arab world over this foregone conclusion. When the dispute over the way to solving the conflict sprang up again, the Arab world retuned to the polarities in the Egyptian and Syrian positions that, as in the Six Day War, converged in preparation for the Yom Kippur War (October War). The components of the conflict continued with even greater intensity to be the center of political discourse in the Arab world. This was also the new-found strength of the conflict and its influence on the Arab states' foreign and domestic policy. The Arab–Israeli conflict became the decisive issue.

Egypt's status and contribution stood at the forefront of the advancement and development of the Palestinian national issue. Egypt's stand became an "historical position." No other Arab state contributed as much to the Palestinian issue as Egypt did under the leaderships of Nasir, Sadat, and Mubarak. It is hard to describe the growth of the New Palestinian National Movement – which was represented in the PLO under the leadership of Fatah – its achievements and stature, without Egypt's assistance, support, and tireless efforts beginning in 1959. Egypt initiated the resurgence of the Palestinian entity and determined its goal: a Palestinian state to be established on Palestinian territory in the West Bank and Gaza Strip. Egypt never recognized Jordan's annexation of the West Bank in 1950. Unlike Syria, Egypt sought to establish an independent Palestinian entity unaffiliated with any Arab country. The leaders of Fatah–PLO realized that only Egypt could help them attain their goal: the establishment of a Palestinian national government in the liberated Palestinian territories. The Fatah leaders saw Nasir as their undisputed ally in the region, as their patron, pathfinder, and commander as no other Arab leader was.

Husayn, whose kingdom had shrunk to its original size before the annexation of the West Bank, was regarded after the war as a national hero in his own country, and in the eyes of Nasir and the majority of the Arab world. He remained Nasir's close ally until the Egypt's president's dying day. The two leaders depended on one another for realizing their goal of returning the West Bank to the Arabs as soon as possible. Husayn needed Nasir's support to prove his nationalism and enable him to enter negotiations with the United States and Israel for a political solution. Since ascending to power in 1953 Husayn had not enjoyed such close relations with Egypt for so long a period. In order to preserve this alliance, he had to adopt a nationalist-oriented domestic and foreign policy that in practical terms put his regime at risk. He participated in the War of Attrition, supported the fida'iyyun organizations, allowing them to operate in Jordan, and went along with the Roger's initiative – all to win Nasir's cooperation. His pact with Nasir enabled him to weather "Black September" and the Syrian invasion without disrupting his regime. Moreover, his cordial relationship with Egypt gave him freedom of action in dealing with Israel, which included secret meetings with Israeli leaders to discuss their respective positions on a possible settlement. He sought a separate agreement with Israel, on condition that it did not deviate from the Arab consensus and was acceptable to Nasir, or at least complied with his conditions for an Israeli withdrawal from the West Bank and a solution to the Jerusalem problem. In secret meetings with Israeli statesmen, such as Yigal Allon and Abba Eban, Husayn rejected the principles of the Allon Plan. After his talks with the Israelis, he came to the conclusion that a separate agreement with Israel would require major concessions that he could not afford to make. Therefore he reckoned that the West Bank's return would be possible only in the framework of a final agreement under the auspices of Egypt. Like Nasir, Husayn too understood that an agreement on Sinai was more obtainable than an agreement on the West Bank. Sadat, who was not fettered with commitments to Husayn, supported the PLO and fida'iyyun organizations at Husayn's expense, broke off relations with the King, and announced that the Palestinian organizations were the representatives of the Palestinian people. He made all these steps after Husayn published his plan for the United Arab Kingdom in March 1972. Sadat then used his influence to get the Rabat summit to declare that the PLO was the sole legitimate representative of the Palestinian people. His goal was to integrate the PLO into the political process and discussions for a solution to the conflict by according it with the status of the party representing the Palestinians and Palestinian territories.

Husayn had no control over developments in the Arab–Israeli conflict in general and the Palestinian problem in particular. Time was working against him. He waged "holding battles" that by their nature could not advance his agenda. They only contributed to the withdrawal from one political "defense line" to another. Nevertheless, he partially managed to slow down processes and postpone Arab decisions, but he could not ultimately prevent them. His anachronistic initiatives worked to his detriment. Husayn had no choice but to swim against the current. As he saw it, there was no room for compromise. In the struggle for survival between the Palestinian entity and the Jordanian entity, Jordan did not decide on any Arab move regarding the Palestinian problem in general and the Palestinian entity in particular, although it took full advantage of its right of veto, that the Arab League's bylaws granted member states, to postpone Arab moves that could not be prevented. Jordan did this in Arab League forums that discussed the revival of the Palestinian entity until the first summit (January 1964) and the Algeria summit (November 1973) by vetoing an Arab decision to recognize the PLO as the sole legal representative of the Palestinian people. In the end Jordan yielded to the Arab consensus at the Rabat summit (October 1974), as it had done in the first Arab summit.

Husayn did not pursue a long-term policy since he was dependent on developments in the Arab arena. His main goal was to preserve his regime. Therefore his policy in the Arab arena was characterized by zigzags. He made tough decisions which he carried out with exemplary determination, as when he dealt with Shuqayri's subversive activity in Jordan, and when he realized in 1970 that the activity of the fida'iyyun organizations – as a state within a state – threatened the loss of his kingdom, or when he drew the conclusion that in the short run there was no chance of returning the West Bank to Jordan under the conditions that he had set. He won the struggle against Shuqayri in 1966 and the "Palestinian resistance" in 1970-1971, thereby safeguarding his regime's stability. He acted with decisiveness and truculence when he ousted the organizations from his country in 1971. His regime demonstrated remarkable survivability despite subversive activity designed to pull it down and despite the fact that the major Arab states questioned, at one time or another, his right to exist. He regarded his consistent position on issues concerned with the Palestinian entity and the PLO's status as a forward defense line for the East Bank. Considering the developments on the Palestinian question, it should be emphasized that Jordan's Palestinian population remains a key factor in the regime's stability.

The basic weakness of the Palestinian entity in this period was its lack of territory and population on which to establish its rule. Only in the Gaza Strip did the PLO enjoy extensive freedom of action, within the Egyptian authorities' limitations. All the parties involved understood this limitation. The Ba'th expressed it openly and explicitly in its May 1964 plan. When Shuqayri tried to implement one of the two elements – territory or population – in order to cement the connection between the Palestinian inhabitants and the PLO, Husayn justifiably regarded this as a threat to his throne and his kingdom's integrity, and he opposed it with all means at his disposal. In this round of the quarrel over who represented the Palestinians or in the long struggle of their existence, the Jordanian regime found that political means were sufficient in both the Jordanian and pan-Arab arenas. As long as the West Bank remained under Jordanian hegemony, the regime's chances of winning this round were good. But victory was only a temporary solution; it merely prepared the way for the more difficult struggle to come, between 1968 and 1971.

In retrospect, Israel's occupation of the West Bank in the Six Day War saved Husayn's regime. It liberated him from the turbulent Palestinian factor in his kingdom. Even before the war the Palestinians in Jordan had undergone a Palestinian national awakening, that is, an accelerated Palestinianization that was expressed in opposition to the Hashemite regime (e.g. the Palestinian intifada in the wake of the Samu' operation). The strengthening of the national awakening among the West Bank Palestinians would have eventually endangered the kingdom and hastened its Palestinianization with the potential of Jordan becoming a temporary "alternative homeland" (*al-watan al-badil*) for the Palestinians.

After the war, the Syrian Ba'th acted as though no new geopolitical conditions had been created in the region. The Ba'th retained its positions, political views, and ways of solving the conflict. It remained glued to the same positions it held before the war. From the Ba'th's point of view, any deviation or change in its position was an admission of strategic failure on the part of the ruling group that had been in power since February 1966, and could lead to its ouster. The Syrian Ba'th not only remained faithful to the strategy of a "popular liberation war," but enhanced it with the dimension of "armed struggle." Therefore the Ba'th opposed Nasir's strategy, boycotted the Khartoum conference, and dispatched low-level delegates to the 1969 Rabat summit conference. During the Ba'th regime, Syria wanted to lead the "rejectionist camp" rather than be towed behind Nasir's policy. The Ba'th's attempt to extricate itself from the stalemate and the internal struggles that were intensifying at the highest level of the regime, and its desire to strengthen its position in the Arab arena – pushed it into the ill-fated military invasion of Jordan in September 1970, after which Jedid's regime fell, and Asad came to power on November 16, 1970. Asad tried to tighten his grip on the regime by exploiting the conflicting and presumably deep-rooted characteristics in Syrian politics: pan-Arab nationalism (*qawmiya*) on the one hand, and the advancement of Syrian nationalism (*wataniya*) on the other. As for the Syrian Ba'th – Asad called for a separate Syrian strategy on the Arab–Israeli conflict that would prove Syria's independence and uniqueness. Regarding the Syrian leadership, the "revolutionary strategy" was supposed to transform Syria into a "powerful stronghold in the struggle for the liberation of Filastin." In this way Syrian domestic politics and Syria's position in the conflict remained mutually connected.

After the war Ba'th strategy in the conflict was interspersed with "lofty" nationalist slogans such as: "historical responsibility" and "the fateful holy struggle." The strategic principle was based on a "comprehensive and total solution" whose goal was the liquidation of Zionism – in the form of the State of Israel – in Filastin. The Ba'th emphasized the Arabness of Filastin (*'urubat Filastin*), according to which, the territories' fate would not have to be decided after the liquidation of the traces of aggression. The Ba'th believed that "a solution to the Palestinian problem depended on the triumph of the Arab revolution, the struggle against imperialism, including Israel, a national struggle [*watani*], a pan-Arab struggle [*qawmi*], and a social struggle in Arab society." The second principle was "the armed struggle" within an "all-out war of liberation [*shamila*]." Syria rejected Resolution 242, charging that it ignored Arab rights in Filastin and intended to establish permanent peace between the Arabs and the "artificial Zionist entity." The third principle was the establishment of a forum of "progressive forces" as an alternative to the Arab summit. Syria proposed that this forum should combine the military, economic, and political resources of Syria, Egypt,

Algeria, and Iraq for the "joint battle." Thus, Egypt and Syria parted ways after the war, but, as stated, the two sides made a rapprochement prior to the Yom Kippur War as they had done on the eve of the Six Day War.

If the fida'iyyun organizations did not exist, Syria would have had to invent them, if only to justify its view of a popular liberation war and the armed struggle. The Palestinian organizations served the Syrian Ba'th in the period after the war just as the Palestinians served Nasirism in the 1950s and 1960s in the struggle against Israel and the reactionary Arab regimes. Although Syria's support complemented Egypt's political support of the "Palestinian resistance," it could not serve as an alternative. Syria regarded itself as the responsible party or patron of the Palestinian issue no less than the Palestinians themselves. Therefore Asad revived the Syrian slogan that "Filastin is Southern Syria." Ba'th policy did not conform to the PLO–Fatah view of an independent Palestinian decision (*Istiqlaliyat al-qarar al-Filastini*). The confrontation between the two sides was the inevitable consequence of reality.

An interesting and perhaps natural phenomenon is that the more the conflict intensified after the PLO's establishment and Fatah's rise to power, the greater the awareness of the Palestinian issue grew among the Palestinians and the Arab world, and the more the need became for a Palestinian political or paramilitary organization to wage a struggle for self-determination. During the period 1962–1967, Palestinian organizations – both civilian and fida'iyyun – grew to several score by 1967. The source of this phenomenon was the new Palestinian national awakening whose foremost expression was the commencement of Fatah sabotage activity in January 1965. The establishment of the Palestinian entity in the form of the PLO fulfilled the aspirations and latent yearnings harbored by Palestinians since the *nakba*. An expression of this can be seen in the enthusiastic response to the establishment of the entity and the intense political activity among Palestinian activists in the West Bank, Gaza Strip, refugee camps in Lebanon, and other Palestinian concentrations.

Before the war, these aspirations and yearnings did not go beyond passive responses; at the most they roused activity in the clandestine organizations that were established at the time, including Fatah. This grassroots activity was unable to exert pressure on the Arab leaderships to resuscitate the Palestinian entity and introduce changes in their policies on the conflict. It was natural that the Palestinians greeted enthusiastically any activity they considered a step toward the "return" (*al-'awda*) and "liberation," and that they also expressed their willingness to take part in it. The only country where the Palestinians acted as a political pressure group was Jordan. Although in private talks local Palestinian political activists supported the PLO and discussed their dream to establish a Palestinian state, their pressure was not translated into a separatist popular movement but remained within the internal Jordanian political game that sought to alter the trend in Jordan's domestic and foreign policy. In 1965 neither Israel nor the Arab world viewed these organizations as indicators of a New Palestinian National Movement. The 1967 Six Day War contributed to the Arab world's recognition of the movement. Thirty years after it first appeared on the Middle East stage, the movement could chalk up impressive gains (the Oslo Agreement) on the path to realizing its goals of self-determination and the establishment of a Palestinian state.

From an historical perspective, the establishment of the PLO (with Egyptian support) was undeniably a major turning point in the growth of the Palestinian problem, a milestone in the history of the Palestinian National Movement in general, and in Jordan's future and fate in particular. The role that Shuqayri played was equally as important as the Egyptian initiative and support. They complemented one another. Despite personal drawbacks, Saudi reservations, and Jordan's vigorous opposition to the idea of reviving the Palestinian entity and establishing its institutions, Shuqayri succeeded in creating the PLO *ex nihilo* and winning for this move and the organization not only Palestinian legitimacy but also – via intrigue and guile – pan-Arab legitimacy and the status as the Palestinians' representative body. His chief contribution to the New Palestinian National Movement was the establishment of the PLO. In the political conditions in the Arab and Palestinian arenas in this period, he appears as the only figure among the Palestinian activists capable of filling this complex role. This is why Nasir's choice was proven correct. Shuqayri symbolized the lowest common denominator that the Arab states could agree on for the role of "organizing the Palestinian people." He performed this task skillfully, passionately (sometimes overdoing it), and successfully. He knew how to take advantage of the summit atmosphere and the polarity in the Arab world. Under his leadership the PLO survived longer than its leaders expected. The concern over the PLO's fate, following the termination of the summit atmosphere in 1966, and Shuqayri's fears of such a development, did not materialize, mainly because of Egypt's support and the Palestinian leadership's efforts to maintain the official framework. However, the fida'iyyun organizations, i.e. the alternative to Shuqayri, could have set up a representative Palestinian establishment, such as the PLO, but this would have been taken place years later, perhaps after the Six Day War. The Egyptians, with Shuqayri's help, shortened the process. From this viewpoint, the fida'iyyun organizations received a cake already baked which they owed to Shuqayri.

With the emergence of the fida'iyyun organizations – first and foremost Fatah – the Palestinian problem experienced an historical turning-point in addition to the establishment of the PLO. A new political generation of Palestinians arose, a generation comprised of the sons of the *nakba* (whose parents were the *nakba* generation itself) that became the leadership of the New Palestinian National Movement. This generation had matured on the lap of Arab nationalism *à la* Nasir, and on the Arab world's disappointment with the fabrication of Egyptian–Syrian unity. This younger Palestinian generation broke ranks with the veteran Palestinian leadership, headed by Shuqayri. In 1968, three years after Fatah started its activity, it succeeded in establishing itself as the Palestinians' leading organization. The Palestinianization that the Palestinians underwent, and the handling of the Palestinian problem,received a push in this period whereas the Jordanianization of the West Bank proved a failure. The Palestinian nationalist awakening that was strongly demonstrated after the Samu' raid accurately reflected these two parallel processes.

In the aftermath of the Six Day War, when the Arab–Israeli conflict became the central focus and *raison d'être* of Arab nationalism, Nasir defined the meaning of the Palestinian problem in unambiguous terms (February 1969) as "a nation that has a homeland," and by "homeland" he meant the Israeli–occupied Palestinian territories. The fact that the solution to the West Bank's future was based on two stages that had been defined at the Khartoum summit only strengthened the linkage between a solution to the Arab–Israeli conflict in general and the Palestinian national problem in particular, so that the solution to the Palestinian national problem became an incontrovertible condition to the solution of the entire conflict. This situation stemmed from a number of factors:

1 The official and popular Arab recognition of the New Palestinian National Movement now operated openly. Unlike the Palestinian leadership under Shuqayri, the movement's new leadership came up from the grass roots, which explains its popularity among the Palestinians who regarded it as the authentic leadership. Egypt was considered patron of the New Palestinian National Movement, and Nasir viewed the movement as the byproduct of Nasirism. For this reason he won the most esteemed title: "the Palestinian leader" and "the person responsible for the fate of the Palestinian problem."

2 The West Bank and the Gaza Strip, also known as the "inner arena" (*al-dakhil*), underwent two parallel processes that intensified under the Israeli occupation: (1) accelerated Palestinianization, i.e. the heightening of the Palestinian awareness for self-determination (the territories eventually became the main stronghold of the struggle against Israel); (2) the process of separating the West Bank from political affiliation with Jordan. The result of "Black September" was the near-total political separation from the Hashemite Kingdom. The resolutions at the Rabat summit that recognized the PLO as the sole legitimate representative of the Palestinian people closed the door to any official bonds between the two banks, thus ending the "Jordanian option" – that was an Israeli formula – as a solution to the Palestinian problem, and the possibility that Jordan would represent the Palestinians in the territories in talks on a settlement for the return of the West Bank. Husayn's only card for remaining in the political process was Israel's refusal to recognize the PLO as the representative of the Palestinian people or as a party in the political process. Since the king was constantly aware of this predicament, he was finally forced to declare the administrative and legal separation of Jordan from the West Bank in July 1988. In this way he recognized the *status quo* and in effect ceded the West Bank.

3 In contrast to the assessment that I broached in my book *The Palestinian Entity 1959–1974, Arab Politics and the PLO* (London 1988, 1996), while undertaking the current research I realized that the Palestinian national awakening on the West Bank, which developed in early 1968 after the occupation, was in fact a strident continuation of the national awakening highlighted during the riots on the West Bank after the Samu' operation. In this way the struggle against the Israeli occupation replaced the opposition to the Jordanian regime and precipitated the Palestinian national awakening on the West Bank. In fact, the Israeli occupation nourished that awakening with new national tenets. The local or "traditional" leadership joined and became an inseparable part of the general Arab struggle for the "eradication of the results of the aggression."

4 The adherence of the "traditional leadership" in the West Bank to the Arab position that was agreed upon in the Khartoum summit, on the one hand, and the strengthening of its affiliation to the PLO under the new leadership of the fida'iyyun organizations, on the other hand. This "traditional leadership" held administrative roles in the West Bank during the Jordanian period, and most of its politicians headed the national leadership on the West Bank during the

November 1966 riots. Owing to its dependency on the Arab position in the conflict, there was no chance whatsoever that the traditional leadership, which represented the inhabitants before the Israeli administration, would agree to any proposal that contained a separate agreement with Israel – a proposal that failed to subscribe to the Arab position of the Khartoum summit or the PLO. The Khartoum decisions unconditionally rejected a solution to the Palestinian problem based on autonomy, or even a Palestinian state, resulting from an agreement with Israel. They rejected the proposals that the local Palestinians in the West Bank had raised for establishing a Palestinian state on the basis of the partition resolution. Therefore all of the various proposals that the Israeli administration placed before this leadership had no chance of being accepted. For all practical purposes the leadership was unable to make independent decisions on its own. It turns out that the Israeli administration's assessments regarding the local leadership's freedom of action and the prospects that it would accept the Israeli proposals were too optimistic and often just plain wishful thinking. In my opinion, this stemmed from a misreading of the traditional leadership's weakened status and the national awakening that the West Bank had undergone, as stated, during Jordanian rule – circumstances that had been clearly apparent in late 1966.

5　The resistance by the West Bank and Gaza Strip inhabitants to the Israeli occupation fueled the Palestinian struggle for self-determination with nationalist content. The Arab desire to abolish "the traces of the aggression" strengthened the Palestinian demand that the West Bank and the Gaza Strip be recognized as Palestinian territory, and not part of the Jordanian kingdom as Husayn claimed. The occupation of Palestinian land gave legitimization to the establishment of a Palestinian national movement dedicated to fighting for liberation from Israeli occupation of the West Bank. The occupation not only reinforced the Palestinian national awakening, it also strengthened the demand to restore the West Bank to Palestinian – not to Jordanian – hands after its "liberation."

With the rise of the New Palestinian National Movement working for "the liberation of Filastin" and establishment of a Palestinian national government in the Palestinian territories, and in light of the Arabs' recognition of the legitimacy of this demand after the war, a close linkage was created between the liberation of West Bank (Palestinian) land and the first stage of the Arab strategy, "the eradication of the traces of the aggression." Therefore, already in the first stage of the discussion on the "liberation" of the West Bank, or the Israeli withdrawal from it, an Arab decision had to be made on the West Bank's future after its "liberation." The question over who represented the West Bank Palestinians in political discussion on the territories' future had to be resolved. A struggle then ensued between Jordan and the Fatah-led PLO over Palestinian representation in the political process.

The New Palestinian National Movement that emerged after the Six Day War was a militant–radical political movement with more of a pan-Arab (*qawmi*) coloring than any other political movement in the Arab world, excluding perhaps the Islamic movements. As such, it replaced bankrupt Arab radical movements. The New Palestinian National Movement swirled around a ring of contradictions that spurred its development and strengthening. It wavered between pan-Arab character (*qawmi*) and

"Palestinization" (*watani*); between Arab unity and Arab division; between, on the one hand, the desire for an independence in decision making and, on the other hand, depending on Arab support and guardianship; between freedom of action for the fida'iyyun organizations, and the need to take into consideration the Arab states' territorial sovereignty and national security requirements. The movement had to choose between the linkage to progressive, militant, yet poverty-stricken states, on one hand, and conservative, monarchic, wealthy states, on the other..

Ironically, because the "Palestinian resistance" (i.e. the fida'iyyun organizations) was the pan-Arab expression (*qawmi*) of the conflict, the New Palestinian National Movement's "revolutionary" doctrine clashed with the Arab confrontational states when they attempted to defend their sovereignty and national interests (*watani*). In other words, the Arab commitment to the Palestinian cause was valid as long as it did not collide with Egypt's principles of national security or Egypt's strategy in the conflict, and when in Nasir's opinion this strategy was not only the result of Egypt's commitment but also corresponded with the interests of the Palestinians as he perceived them. From Nasir's point of view an overlap existed between Egyptian strategy in the conflict and Palestinian interests. The Syrian Ba'th regime, too, and especially Hafez al-Asad's regime, claimed that it represented the Palestinians' interests better than the Palestinians themselves. In this situation a clash between the New Palestinian National Movement – that was represented by the PLO after the Six Day War – and Nasir (and Asad at a later date) was inevitable when Egyptian strategy opposed the PLO's position. This occurred after Nasir accepted the Roger's Initiative in July 1970. Hence the saying: "fida'iyyun freedom of action within the limits of the sovereignty of the state."[8] The continuous clashes from 1968 to 1971 between the Jordanian regime and "Palestinian resistance" symbolized more than anything else the dilemma that culminated in "Black September." In its "armed struggle" during the years prior to the Six Day War, the "Palestinian resistance" exacerbated the security situation on Israel's borders thereby contributing to the descent to war. Following the organizations' activity against Israel, civil war erupted in Jordan in 1970 (and to a large degree in Lebanon too in 1975). Arafat was expelled from Damascus in 1976 following hostilities between the PLO and Syria. It should come as little surprise then that as the Yom Kippur War approached "Palestinian resistance" was a greater problem for the Arabs than Israel was. The number of Palestinians killed in clashes with Arab states was higher than the number killed in engagements with Israel.

Although these confrontations with the Arab states and Israel physically hurt the Palestinians, paradoxically, due to the Palestinian problem's important place as the heart of the conflict and the Arab states' involvement in and commitment to it, the New Palestinian National Movement managed to survive and make impressive gains. Its endurance enabled the movement to overcome all the crises that befell it since it first appeared on the stage: the "Black September" (1970) crisis; the civil war in Lebanon (1975–1976); the Syrian invasion of Lebanon in 1976; Sadat's peace initiative in November 1977; the Israeli invasion of Lebanon in June 1982; Arafat's expulsion from Damascus in June 1983 and his expulsion from Lebanon in December 1983. It is interesting to note that after each crisis, Arab support for the PLO strengthened; Palestinian national consciousness increased among the Palestinians; and their determination to continue the armed struggle against Israel in order to attain their goals grew stronger. Ironically, against the background of these crises, the Arab commitment toward the Palestinians in general and the PLO in particular was more conspicuous for the realization of self-determination in the West Bank and Gaza Strip.

It is also ironic that the Egyptian–Israeli peace agreement that the PLO and other Arab states vigorously opposed, paved the way to the Oslo Agreement, even though Sadat deviated from the Arab consensus approved at the Rabat conference in October 1974, which forbade the signing of a separate treaty with Israel. Interestingly, because of this, Sadat did his best to include in the peace agreement a solution to the Palestinian national problem whose goal was Palestinian self-determination as part of the autonomy plan. Indeed, sections of this plan served as guidelines for the Oslo Agreement which led to the Jordanian–Israeli peace agreement. Husayn – because of his commitment to the Palestinian problem, his attachment to the Arab consensus, and the Palestinian majority in Jordan's population – could not allow himself to sign a peace agreement with Israel until the Palestinian national problem was resolved. Jordan still regards the Palestinian problem as a crucial factor in its national security.

From Hafiz Asad's point of view the Oslo Agreement and the Jordanian–Israeli Peace agreement slipped the rug from under Syria's claim to be the patron of the Palestinian problem, a position that the elder Asad often emphasized. The peace agreement with Jordan weakened and even abrogated the validity of his demand for an overall solution to the conflict. Asad, the leader of the Ba'th party, who engraved on its banner the most radical position toward Israel in the Arab world, would have had a hard time digesting the results of a Syrian–Israeli peace agreement that was liable to symbolize, from his point of view, the end of the Arab–Israeli conflict. For this reason he did everything in his power to make certain that if he signed a peace agreement, it would enter the conflict's history as the best treaty that the Arabs had ever achieved. It would have had to include Syrian gains that were greater than those in other peace agreements with Israel, including the Egyptian–Israeli peace treaty. All indications show that Bashar, Hafiz Asad's son, is taking the same path.

Looking back on the struggle between the Zionist movement and Palestinian National Movement (from the pre-state period, through the British Mandate, through the 1948 war and establishment of the State of Israel, through the subsequent Arab–Israeli conflict which gave rise to the New Palestinian National Movement that advocated armed struggle, and until the Palestinians became a separate party in the conflict alongside the Arab countries), the necessary conclusion is that the Oslo Agreement was an historical turning point. This watershed was a great achievement for the Palestinian National Movement and the Arab national movement, both of which had struggled together for decades for Palestinian self-determination and the establishment of a Palestinian state, as the agreement implied.

Since 1957, and perhaps even since 1948, the Arab world has been trapped in the greatest dilemma in its modern history: its commitment to solving the Palestinian national problem (or the Arab–Israeli conflict) through a solution that "will restore to the Palestinian people their rights." The dilemma intensified after changes occurred in the tenets of the conflict and the Palestinian problem following the Arab military defeat in the Six Day War. On the one hand, the Arabs demanded that Israel withdraw to the June 5, 1967 lines; on the other hand, the Palestinians gained the status of a separate party in the conflict and demanded recognition of their right to self-determination. The autonomy plan that Egypt and Israel signed as part of the peace agreement only highlighted this dilemma and Egypt's desire to reach a solution. The peace agreement that

Jordan signed – only after the Oslo Agreement was approved – did not absolve it of the need to continue working toward a permanent settlement between Israel and Palestinians. Therefore, as long as the conflict between Israel and the Palestinians persists, and Syria keeps the embers of the conflict smoldering, Egypt and Jordan will remain bound to their commitments to the Palestinians. Only a permanent solution to the Israeli–Palestinian conflict, a solution that includes the establishment of a Palestinian state in the West Bank and Gaza Strip, and a solution to the Jerusalem issue, will free Egypt and Jordan from their commitments.

Three key issues in the Israeli–Palestinian conflict demand solutions: the territorial problem (the degree of Israel's withdrawal); the Jerusalem question; and "the right of return" (al-'Awda). A solution to the Jerusalem question is even more difficult than the right of return since it is not only a Palestinian problem but also an Arab and Islamic one, and could pave the way for a solution on "the right of return." Without an agreed-upon solution to Jerusalem's status, it seems doubtful that the Palestinian leadership, whoever may comprise it, will be able to sign a permanent agreement with Israel. As the Palestinians see it, their hegemony over East Jerusalem, including Islam's holy sites, that will enable them to declare Jerusalem the capital of an independent Palestinian state, appears to be a *sine qua non* for a permanent settlement with Israel, and in particular for an end to the Israeli–Palestinian conflict.

But even if leaders should appear who had the necessary foresight to cut a deal to the benefit of both parties, the Arab dilemma will continue, although at a lower level of intensity, until the conflict with Syria is resolved. An Israeli–Syrian agreement (simultaneous to or after the signing of a permanent settlement with the Palestinians) would free the Arab states from the decades-long vicious circle and extricate them from their intractable dilemma, that is, it will bring the Arab–Israeli conflict to a "conclusion." In the meantime Israeli–Palestinian relations continue to cast their shadow on Israel's relations with Egypt and Jordan in particular, and with the Arab world in general. The continuation – or heating up – of the Israeli–Palestinian conflict is likely to have a pejorative effect on Israel's relations with these two Arab countries despite their commitment to peace, which they see as a strategic objective inextricably bound to their national interests.

Appendices

Fatah, Jordanian, Egyptian and Syrian Documents, Letters and Operational

1 Cover page of Fatah's monthly journal *Filastinuna*, No. 2 (November 1959).
2 A letter from the commander of the Nablus region, dated April 11, 1960, relating to information on efforts being made by West Bank notables to dissuade West Bank ministers from cooperating with the government.
3 An order from Jordan's minister of the interior to district governors, dated May 27, 1964, authorizing military commanders to open fire when necessary in the case of demonstrations during the coming PNC.
4 A warning issued by the commander of the Fourteenth Battalion (Jordanian army), dated March 21, 1965, regarding possible Israeli action against Jordan because of the Arabs' water diversion plan.
5 A letter, dated May 21, 1966, from the commander of the Gaza intelligence to the director of general internal security referring to the evidence of renewed activity by al-'Asifa branch in the Gaza Strip.
6 The headquarters of the Western Front, Operational Order 1/65, dated September 26, 1965 – "Operation al-Husayn" for defending Jordan.
7 An announcement by the Popular Convention [not] held in Jerusalem on Monday, December 5, 1966.
8 A letter from the minister of defense and commander of the Syrian air force, Hafiz al-Asad, dated April 1, 1967. Operational Directives No. 1/67 regarding increased enemy movements opposite the southwestern area and a possible [Israeli] attempt to seize the demilitarized zones.
9 Egypt: Operational Order No. 2/67, dated May 21, 1967, by the commander of the Eastern air region regarding targets in Israel for various regional air wings.
10 A letter, dated May 27, 1967, from the commander of the southwestern region (the Syrian front opposite Israel) to the commander of the 123rd Brigade forbidding unauthorized patrols or visits in the forward positions.
11 Jordan GHQ: Information regarding acts the Palestinian Liberation Front is likely to perpetrate in Israel, dated September 18, 1965.

12 Letter from the Jordanian chief of staff, dated May 24, 1965, to the commanders of the western and eastern fronts regarding the "Fatah Organization" and the possibility that Israel is behind it. The letter emphasizes that the United Arab Command condemns Fatah's operations and demands that steps be taken against the infiltrators and countermeasures be taken to prevent infiltration into the occupied area [Israel] aimed at carrying out sabotage activity.

13 Jordan: A letter from the commander of the Hittin Brigade, dated December 2, 1966, to battalion and brigade commanders regarding the arrest and interrogation of guerilla squads that infiltrated into Jordan from Syria and were caught in Irbid. Details are given of the targets of sabotage and quantity of weapons found in the squads' possession.

14 Syrian situation estimate, dated February 1, 1967, regarding a possible Israeli attack against Syria.

15 Egypt: Operational Order No. 3/67, dated May 19, 1967, from the commander of the eastern air region regarding the air force role in an attack for isolating the Negev and capturing Eilat.

16 Letter, dated June 8, 1965, from the commander of the Hashemite Brigade regarding activity by the Fatah Organization "that poses a danger to the Jordanian border and runs contrary to the policy of the Arab states and UAC."

17 Egypt: Operational Order No. 6/67 of the Second Air Brigade, eastern region air headquarters, regarding Wing 25's missions: the concentrated bombing of the Port of Eilat, state of alertness beginning at dawn, May 26, 1967.

18 Operational Order No. 5/67 from the commander of the eastern air region regarding missions of the air force and air defense units, and including the bombing of the Port of Eilat and its vicinity. The timing of the operation will be determined by the commander of the air force. The operation's codename: "Asad."

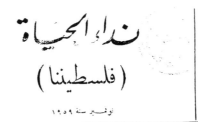

بشرف عليها
توفيق حوري
ص. ب ١٦٨٤
بيروت

ندا، الحياة
(فلسطيننا)

نوفمبر سنة ١٩٥٩

السنة الاولى
العدد
٢

كلمة التحرير

حمداً لله وشكراً للقراء الاعزاء على هذه الثقة الغالية التي اوليتموها لنا والتي ملئت نفوسنا أملاً وزادتها عزة. كيف لا وهذا هو العدذ الاول نفذ في كثير من مناطق التوزيع.

كيف لا وهذه الرسائل تنهال علينا، بعضها يهنيء وبعضها يوجه. فيها انتقادات وفيها مطالب. وهي في مجموعها الكبير ذخيرة ضخمة نعتز بها. ودليلا حيا رائعاً على ان هذه المجلة قد وجدت في قلوب اخواننا صدى طيباً. وملئت ذلك الفراغ الضخم في المحيط الصحفي لقضية وطننا السليب.

وإننا امام هذه الارادة القوية لشعبنا المناضل الابي لنعلن بعزم واصرار على اننسير في الدرب الى النهاية غير مبالين بالمصاعب والعراقيل التي وضعت أمامنا بتعمد لتعيق سيرنا. والتي وصل بعضها الى حد محاولة حجب هذه المجلة عن القراء.

ومع هذا يا اخي فانا نمد ايادينا لتكاتف معك، لنقاوم معاً، ولنسير معاً، ولنناضل معاً، مضحين في سبيل استرداد الوطن السليب بكل مرتخص وغال. واضعين نصب اعيننا هذا الهدف السامي لا نحيد عنه مهما ازدادت اهوال هذا السبيل.

ومرحباً بك ايها الزميل حيث تكون مشرداً بعيداً عن فلسطيننا المغتصبة، لنخلق من هذا التشرد وتلك المحنة قوة جبارة تعيد الحق الى نصابه وتقودنا لاسترداد الوطن الحبيب.

فحمداً لله .. ثم حمداً لله .. وشكراً للقراء .. واننا لنعاهدكم ان نكون دائماً في الصف الطويل المجاهد المناضل. نسير دائماً بهدى من ايماننا العميق وثقتكم الغالية. واضعين نصب اعيننا هدفنا السامي لا نحيد عنه ولازوم غيره والله الموفق والمعين.

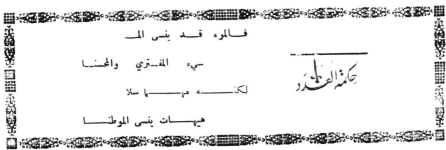

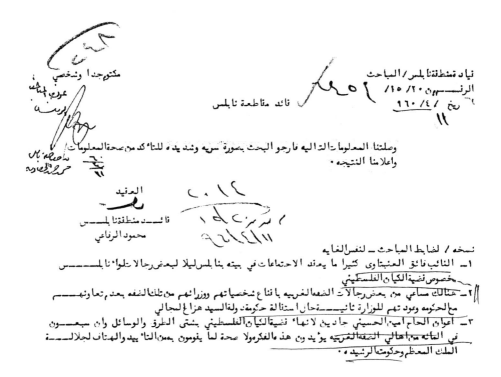

2 A letter from the commander of the Nablus region, dated April 11, 1960, relating to information on efforts being made by West Bank notables to dissuade West Bank ministers from cooperating with the government.

وزارة الداخلية

عمان

مكتوم جداً

الرقم م.د/٦٦/

التاريخ ٢٧/٥/١٩٦٤

معالي محافظ القدس
محافظ العاصمة
متصرف لـواء نابلس

لا حتمال وقوع مظاهرات اثناء انعقاد المؤتمر الفلسطيني
ولا حتمال اضطرار وحدات الجيش لاطلاق النار على المتظاهرين
في حالة عدم اذعانهم . ارجو تزويد القادة العسكريين في
المناطق التابعة لكم باوامر تخولهم اطلاق النار اذا ما تفاقم
الشغب والتظاهر الى حد يتعذر معه ان البلد وسلامته
للخطر لا سمح الله .

واقبلوا احتراماتي ،

(خال المجالي)
وزيـر الداخليـة

نسخة ـ الى سيادة رئيس الوزراء الافخم
نسخة ـ الى معالي وزيـر الدفاع
نسخة ـ الى عطوفة القائد العام للقوات المسلحة
نسخة ـ الى مدير الامـن العام

٢/ب/١

3 An order from Jordan's minister of the interior to district governors, dated May 27, 1964, authorizing military commanders to open fire when necessary in the case of demonstrations during the coming PNC.

مكـــــتوم

قيادة كتيبة الملك محمد الخامس/ ١٤

الرقم/ ١٢/٢٤/ ٢٤٤

التاريخ ٢١/آذار/ ١٦٥

قائد الكتيبه / ٣٠١

قائد الكتيبه / ٣٠٢

قائد الكتيبه / ٣٠٣

قائد الكتيبه / ٣٠٤

قائد الكتيبه / ٣٠٥

قائد الكتيبه / ٣١٢

قائد السرايـــا

الموضوع/ تحويل روافد نهر الاردن

٠١ علم مندوب الاردن الدائم في هيئة الامم المتحدة ان جريدة (لوموند) الفرنسيه
نشرت بعددها الصادر بتاريخ ٣/٣/ ٦٥ ان امريكا تشجع اسرائيل علـــى
تقديم شكوى الى مجلس الامن الدولي ضد تحويل الروافد العربيه بقصـــد
اصدار قرار لاحالة القضيه على محكمة العدل الدولي وتجميدها هناك .
واميركا فكرت بهذا بعد ان فشلت في اقناع اسرائيل بعدم اللجوء الى
مقاومة التحويل بالقوه .

٠٢ يستنتج من ذلك انه قد تكون نوايا عدوانيه لدى المسؤولون اليهود ضـــد
الاردن وغيرها من البلدان العربيه لذلك يرجى اخذ الحيطه والحذر
والاستعداد لمجابهة اية اعتداءات قد تقوم بها اسرائيل .

الرئيس الاول الركن
قائد كتيبة الملك محمد الخامس/ ١٤
محمـــد الحمـــد

نسخها الى/
قيادة لواء بلدس للعلم
حفظ

4 A warning issued by the commander of the Fourteenth Battalion
(Jordanian army), dated March 21, 1965, regarding possible Israeli action
against Jordan because of the Arabs' water diversion plan.

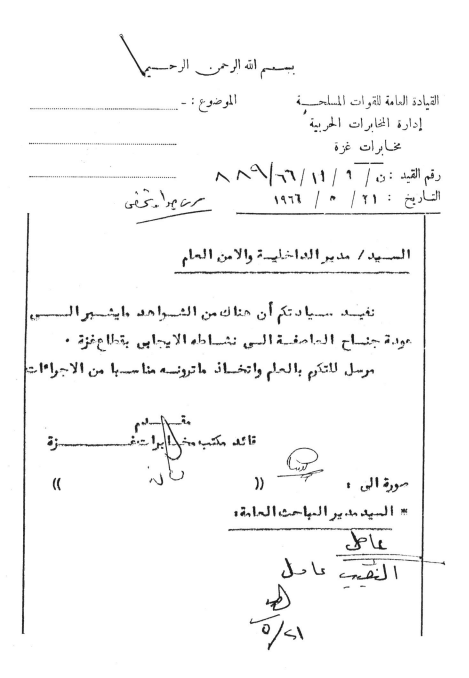

5 A letter, dated May 21, 1966, from the commander of the Gaza intelligence to the director of general internal security referring to the evidence of renewed activity by al-'Asifa branch in the Gaza Strip.

مكتوم جداً

رقم النسخة (\ )

قيادة الجبهة الغربية
العمليات

الرقم/١٤ / ١/ ح
التاريخ/ ٢٦ ايلول ١٩٦٥

تعليمات حربية رقم ١ / ٦٥

عملية الحسين

خرائط المراجعة / مجموعة خرائط المملكة
للضفة الشرقية والضفة
الغربية ١٠٠٠٠/١

٠١ الموقـــف

أ. عــــام

(١) من المحتمل أن تقوم اسرائيل بالتعرض على جبهة احدى الدول العربية
المتاخمة لحدودها هادفة في ذلك منع تحويل روافد نهر الاردن الذى
أقر تنفيذه مجلس الملوك والرؤساء العرب المنعقد في ايلول ١٩٦٤ .

(٢) تتطلع اسرائيل الى توسيع رقعتها وذلك بالاستيلاء على المرتفعات
المسيطرة الموجودة في ضفة الاردن الغربية لتأمين الدفاع عـــــن
المناطق المفتوحة على الساحل التي تعتمد عليه معظم المستعمـــــرات
الاسرائيلية .

ب. قوات العـدو

(١) القوات البرية

ما يعادل ٢٠ لواء مشاة (عامل / احتياطي خـــــط أول ،
احتياطي خط ثاني ، دفاع اقليمي وكتائـــــب
ناحال)

٢ لواء مظلات زائد كتيبة مظلات

٥ لواء مدرع (عامل واحتياطي)

١٥ كتيبة مدفعية ميدان
وحدات من الصواريخ المضادة للطائرات من طراز
هوك .
وحدات من المدفعية المضادة للطائرات

مكتوم جداً

6 The headquarters of the Western Front, Operational Order 1/65, dated September 26, 1965 – "Operation al-Husayn" for defending Jordan.

مكتوم جداً

(٢) القوات الجوية

٧٠	طائرة مقاتلة ميـراج
٢٥٠	طائرة مقاتلة قاذفة ، منها (١٣٢) أنواع حديثة والباقي أنواع قديمة
٢٦	طائـرة قاذفـة
	طائرات نقل تكفي لنقل لواء مظلات من كتيبتين

(٣) القـوات البحرية

٢	مدمــرة
١	فرقاطـة
٣	غواصـة
٢٤	زورق طوربيد
١	قنـاص
٦	زورق سريع
١٤	زورق انـزال

(٤) امكانية العدو في جمع الاحتياط

لدى العدو الامكانيات السريعة لاستدعاء احتياطه في سرعة تامة للقيام بعمل مفاجئ سريع ضد احدى الجبهات المتاخمة لحدوده .

(ه) الاعمال المحتملة للعدو

(أ) هجوم محدود العمق على مناطق تحويل روافد نهر الاردن في سوريا ولبنان واحتلالها وعدم الانسحاب منها الا بشروط د ولية تضمن عدم التحويل مستقبلا وفي حالة كهذه يخصص العدو والقوات التالية امام الجبهة الاردنية /-

٤	لواء مشـاة
١	لواء مـدرع

ويحتفظ بقوات احتياطية تقـدر /ب-

١	لواء مشـاة
١	لواء د روع
١	لواء مظلات زائد كتيبة مظلات

ويوزع باقي قواته امام الجبهة السورية وجبهة الجمهورية العربية المتحدة .

(ب) القيام بعمليات تستهدف احتلال الضفة الغربية بكاملها واقتطاعها من المملكة الاردنية الهاشمية ، وفي حالة كهذه قد يخصص العدو والقوات التالية امام الجبهة الاردنية /-

١٠	لواء مشـاة
٢	لواء دروع
١	لواء مظلات

مكتوم جداً

بيان من المؤتمر الشعبي المنعقد في القدس
يوم الاثنين ٥/١٢/١٩٦٦
=========================

• ينعقد هذا المؤتمر في ظرف بالغ الخطورة على وجود الشعب ووطنه وحرياته ومصالحه القومية

• ينعقد في الوقت الذي تبددت فيه آمال الشعب التي انعقدت على الاجماع العربي بحتمية تحرير فلسطين وذلك لنجاح الاستعمار في دفع القوى الرجعية للتآمر على العمل الجماعي العربي وتخريبه

• وكذلك في جو العدوان الصهيوني على السموع ، ذلك العدوان الذل لكرامة شعبنا واحدا ، والذي لم يكن ثمة رد طيبه ، وبالرغم من مضي ثمانية عشرة سنة من النكبة ، الا الشكوى على المعتدى الى الهيئة الدولية التي خلقته

• ينعقد هذا المؤتمر اثر خيبة الشعب العارمة التي رد فيها ردا صادقا على الصهيونية وحماتها المستعمرين سادة وجودها وعلى رأسهم الولايات المتحدة الاميركية — رد بإثبات عجزها من ارهابه ، وانه الان اقوى تصميما وعزما من اي وقت مضى على استرداد وطنهم السليب

• وفي الوقت نفسه ثورت هذه القضية من ارادة الشعب في اسماع السلطة الحاكمة في وطننا ، ان هذا الشعب هو مصدر السلطات وصاحب الحق في رسم سياسات وطنه ، وتمكينا له من ذلك لابد له من ممارسة حرياته واتخاذ سياسة التعاون وتقليح روابط التجمعة التي تربط وطننا بدول الاستعمار على اي شكل جاء هذا الارتباط ، وغير ذلك لا تنشأ ولا تنمو الثقة بين الشعب والحكم

• وتحقيق هذه المطالب تهيء الفرصة لقيام تعاون عربي فعال ومخلص ، تسوده الثقة بين الاردن والدول العربية في مقدمتها الجمهورية العربية المتحدة ، والخروج من الطوق الاستعماري المفروض على الاردن الى مجال التعاون مع دول العالم على اساس التكافؤ والاحترام المتبادل ضمن قواعد الحياد الايجابي وعدم الانحياز وطبعا اساس يستوجبه تحرير فلسطين وتقتضيه المصالح القومية العربية العليا

• لذلك فان هذا المؤتمر ادراكا منه لمسؤوليات تجاه الشعب والوطن والاخطار المحدقة بهم

وإعرابا عن ارادة الشعب يعلن انه :—

١— يؤمن ايمانا راسخا بوحدة الشعب العربي في الاردن نضالا ومصيرا ، وانه جزء لا يتجزأ من الامة العربية ، وان تحقيق الوحدة العربية هو هدفه العصري

٢— يطالب باحترام الدستور وسيادة القانون ، واطلاق الحريات العامة ، وصيانة كرامة المواطنين ، وتوقيف المسلسل بالقوانين الاستثنائية التي تحد من الحريات العامة

٣— ان الكفاح العربي المسلح المتحالف عن سياسة عربية عندرة هو السبيل الوحيد للقضاء على القاعدة الاستعمارية الصهيونية واسترداد الوطن السليب

٤— يؤمن ان الاردن هو الخط الامامي وساحة التدعم للقوات العربية لمعركة تحرير فلسطين ، ولذلك يطالب بانه بادخال وحدات من الجيوش العربية الى الاردن لتدعيم الجيش العربي الاردني الباسل تنفيذا لخطط القيادة العربية الموحدة

٥— يؤيد المؤتمر منظمة التحرير الفلسطينية بوصفها الممثل الوحيد لارادة شعب فلسطين والعصبة لطاقاته وتواء ليأخذ مكانه الطبيعي في معركة التحرير ، وانطلاقا من ذلك فان المؤتمر يطالب السلطة في الاردن بتمكين العدالة من ممارسة واجباتها القومية المقدسة واعطائها الحرية في تنفيذ خططها العسكرية والمالية والتنظيمية بما في ذلك الاتصال بالشعب الفلسطيني لتعبئته وتنظيمه واعداده عسكريا على اساس الميثاق الوطني الفلسطيني ، وقرارات القيادة العربية الموحدة

٦— يطالب المؤتمر بايقاف حملات التهاتم الشخصية التي تخرج عن نطاق النقد البناء

٧— يعتبر المؤتمر بأهمية العمل الفدائي كجزء من معركة تحرير فلسطين ولذلك يطالب جميع الحكومات العربية المحيطة بالعدو المحتلة بعدم التعرض للفدائيين

٨— يؤكد وجوب تسليم وتحميل الخلايا الامامية بشكل فعال وفق خطة توضع بالاتفاق مع قيادة الجيش العربي الاردني ومنظمة التحرير الفلسطينية والقيادة العربية الموحدة

٩— يحيي المؤتمر ارواح الشهداء عسكريين ومدنيين الذين سقطوا في معارك الشرف والفداء

١٠— يحيي المؤتمر الجيش العربي الاردني سياج الوطن ويطالب بان لا يوضع هذا الجيش الباسل في اوضاع تنحره للاصطدام بالشعب الذي هو منه والوجه

١١— يطالب المؤتمر باطلاق سراح المعتقلين

×××××××××××

7 An announcement by the Popular Convention [not] held in Jerusalem on Monday, December 5, 1966.

الجمهورية العربية السورية
وزارة الدفاع

رئاسة هيئة أركان الجيش والقوات المسلحة
شعبة لعمليات - فرع الخطط والعطيات
الرقم / ٥٣٥ / ٣٠٠ م
التاريخ / ١ / ٤ / ١٩٦٧

سري للغاية

- ((توجيهات عمليات رقم ((٦٧/١)) -

ــ الى , قائد المنطقة الجنوبية الغربية ـ عطيات
قائد القوى الجوية وقائد الجو والجو ـ عطيات

١ـ عدل حركات التعزيز التي يجري بها العدو مقابل المنطقة الجنوبية الغربية والاشتباكات المتكررة الواردة
من احتمال قيام العدو بـ :
ـ فلاحة الاراضي المجردة في : منطقة الدكة ـ منطقة الدردارة
ـ محاولة الاستيلاء على كافة المناطق المجردة المتاخمة للحدود

٢ـ تتخذ الاجراءات التالية لمنع العدو ومن تنفيذ الاحتمالين المذكورين :
أ ـ تقوم الجبهة بـ : تعزيز المرتفعات المطلة على الدكة بفصيلة دبابات و ٢ مدفع هاون
ـ تعزيز المرتفعات المطلة على اراضي الدردارة بفصيلة دبابات و ٢ مدفع هاون
ـ حماية هذه التعزيزات بأسلحة م/ط مناسبة
ـ تكون المدفعية جاهزة للتدخل في كافة الاتجاهات المحتملة
ـ تعديل أوامر الهجمات المعاكسة الخاصة بمسترجع المفتوحة واللحمة
ـ يعطى انتباه خاص لتعزيز الدفاع عن اللحمة
ـ زيادة الحذر واليقظة
ـ تنفذ هذه التدابير اعتبارا من آخر ضوء هذا اليوم

ب ـ يطلب من القوى الجوية :
ـ أن تكون جاهزة لدعم الاعمال الدفاعية من المناطق المجردة والدبابات المذكورة
ـ أن تكون جاهزة لحماية التشكيلات الارضية في الجبهة وحماية المطارات والاهداف الحيوية في البلاد
ـ نشر وحداتها الجوية في المطارات الميدانية بالشكل الذي تراه مناسبا
ـ أن تحضر تنفيذ القنابل لاستعمالها عند الضرورة لحرق الطريق المشجر في الاوسط
ـ تنفذ الاجراءات في نفس ثقل هذه التوجيهات

اللواء الجوي حافظ الاسد
وزير الدفاع م الخارة والتوقيع

الجمهورية العربية السورية
وزارة الدفاع
قيادة المنطقة الجنوبية الغربية
فرع العمليات ـ عطيات
رقم / ٣٨٠ / ٥٠٠ م
تاريخ / ١ / ٤ / ١٩٦٧ م

نسخة طبق الاصل السـ : نسخ
ـ صورة طبق الاصل السـ
ـ قيادة القطاع الشمالي رقم لعلت عدت

ـ يطلب اليكم تنفيذ ماجاء بالتوجيهات اعلاه واعداد الفترة الخاصة
بتعزيز المرتفعات المطلة على الدردارة بناء على دلي قرارئيس الاركان العامة للقوى
السيد الركن احمد الامير محمود
قائد المنطقة الجنوبية الغربية

8 A letter from the minister of defense and commander of the Syrian air force, Hafiz al-Asad, dated April 1, 1967. Operational Directives No. 1/67 regarding increased enemy movements opposite the southwestern area and a possible [Israeli] attempt to seize the demilitarized zones.

9 Egypt: Operational Order No. 2/67, dated May 21, 1967, by the commander of the Eastern air region regarding targets in Israel for various regional air wings.

برقية محمولة رقم / ٧٧٥ /   تاريخ ٢٧/٥/١٩٦٧   سرى للغاية   فورى
======

من : قيادة المنطقة الجنوبية الغربية ــ فرع العمليات ــ عمليات
الى : قيادة اللواء ١٢٣ قسم العمليات ــ عمليات

اعتبارا من تاريخه يمنع القيام بأى استطلاع غير مقرر أو القيام بزيارة للنقاط الامامية وفي حال القيام بالاستطلاع
المقرر يجب التقيد بالشروط التعبوية ضمن النقطـــــــة •

على فروع المنطقة الجنوبية الغربية ابلاغ الوحدات المرتبطة بهم بمضمون البرقية •

العقيد الركن احمد الامير محمود
قائد المنطقـــــــة الجنوبية الغربيـــــــة

الجمهورية العربية السورية
وزارة الدفاع
اللواء ١٢٣ ــ قسم العمليـــــات
الرقم ٢٥١/م ل ١٢٣
التاريخ ٢٨/٥/١٩٦٧•

صورة طبق الاصــــــل :
==================
تعمـــــــيم
الى كافة الوحدات للتقيد بمضمونها •

العقيد الركن محمد احمد عيد
قائد اللواء ١٢٣

ن/ع

10 A letter, dated May 27, 1967, from the commander of the southwestern region (the Syrian front opposite Israel) to the commander of the 123rd Brigade forbidding unauthorized patrols or visits in the forward positions.

القياده العامه للقوات المسلحه الاردنيه   تكتم جــدا
الاستخبارات العسكريه

الرقـم : م غ غ / ل / ٢٨ / ٣٥
التاريخ : ١٨ / ٩ / ١٩٦٥

شابط مركز استخبارات منطقة القدس
شابط مركز استخبارات منطقة نابلس
شابط مركز استخبارات منطقة الخليل
شابط مركز استخبارات اللواء الجنوبي
شابط مركز استخبارات اللواء الشمالي

الموضوع : ـ جبهة التحرير الفلسطينيه   ش ع / ٥ / ٢٨ / ٢
السريه .
                                     م ٥ / ٩ / ٢

١. وردت ا معلومات من جبهة التحرير الفلسطينيه السريه تفيد بان العمليات
     الاجراميه التاليه هي : ـ

     ا . تستهدف لتمويه الجيش الاسرائيلي جيشا ومؤلف من ستة
          شابات ومستودعات الأرهيـه للحم بحول بـه بعـد ذبح البقر
          ملب لاحمـه .

     ب . تستهدف الفعل الثوري لاسرائيل بمعاونة رجال فدائيين من خسزم
          رئيسه من العمليات يعلم الثاهـرو .

٢. بتاريخ ٣ / ٨ / ١٩٦٥ دخل الفدائيون من نفس المنافه المنافذه الحاليه
     وحتى ٣ / ٨ / ١٩٦٥ لم يعودوا للاردن وان الاتصالات كانت تصادو
     وان وجمـه الصعوبات من المنافه لهذا النشـاط .

٣. بتاريخ ٣ / ٨ / ١٩٦٥ اكد رجال المنافه ان الفدائيين عادوا ليلـة
     ٨ ـ ٩ / ١٩٦٥ مالمين ويصدر بيان من المنامـه .

٤. فدائيون مجموعة اخرى من فدائيين جبهة التحرير الفلسطينيه السريه سيماح
     يوم الخميس ٨ / ١٩٦٥ القيام باعمال النسف والتخريب .

يرجى الاطلاع واعلامنا ما تتوصلون اليه من نتائج حول حسنـه
النافذه .

د. المقدم الركن
مدير الاستخبارات العسكريه

11 Jordan GHQ: Information regarding acts the Palestinian Liberation
Front is likely to perpetrate in Israel, dated September 18, 1965.

12 Letter from the Jordanian chief of staff, dated May 24, 1965, to the commanders of the western and eastern fronts regarding the "Fatah Organization" and the possibility that Israel is behind it. The letter emphasizes that the United Arab Command condemns Fatah's operations and demands that steps be taken against the infiltrators and countermeasures be taken to prevent infiltration into the occupied area [Israel] aimed at carrying out sabotage activity.

قائد كتيبة عبد الله بن رواحة
قائد كتيبة جعفر بن أبي طالب
قائد كتيبة صلاح الدين الأيوبي
قائد كتيبة عبد الرحمن الغافقي

الموضوع : المخربين

١ . الساعة ٢٢٠٠ يوم ٦٦/١١/٢٩ ألقي القبض في مدينة أربد من قبل رجال الأمن على الجندي السوري عبد الله محمد حسن أبراهيم من عشيرة المجاربه ومن سكان أم البساتين الأردنيه سابقا ويقطن حاليا قرية مسعيه السوريه قضاء القنيطره وضبط معه ما ن :-

  أ . رشاش ستن تشيكي
  ب . ٢١١ طلقه للرشاش
  ج . ٣ قنابل يدويه
  د . ٧ قطع مفجرات جلفنايت

٢ . بالتحقيق معه اعترف انه دخل الأردن مع أربعة أشخاص آخرين وجهوم النسف والتخريب وان هناك عشرة أشخاص آخرين يريدون دخول الأردن لنفس الغايه وموجودين في قرية المنشيه السوريه استعدادا للدخول .

٣ . الساعة ٢٢٣٥ يوم ٦٦/١١/٣٠ اصطدمت احدى الدوريات العسكريه مع مجموعه من المخربين السوريين قرب قرية برشتا الأردنيه وتبادلت معهم اطلاق النار واستعمل المخربون الرشاشات الخفيفه والقوا على الدوريه ثلاثة قنابل يدويه وبالتالي تمكنت الدوريه من القاء القبض على احد المخربين ويدعى (عبد الهادي قاسم خليل) من سمنع اصلا ويسكن درعا وضبط معه ما يلي :

  أ . رشاش ستن تشيكي
  ب . ١٦٢ طلقه رشاش ستن
  ج . قنبله يدويه واحده
  د . اربعة مخازن للرشاش

٤ . بالتحقيق مع المذكور اعترف بما يلي :-

  أ . انه يعمل مع منظمة الفتح منذ مدة شهر تقريبا وقد تدرب في تدريبات على قوم أنواع المتفجرات والأسلحة الخفيفه مع ما يقارب من ٤٥ شخصا وكان يشرف على تدريبهم الملازم الأول المتقاعد محمود تمسم وهو ضابط في الجيش السوري سابقا اصلهم من حيفا .

13 Jordan: A letter from the commander of the Hittin Brigade, dated December 2, 1966, to battalion and brigade commanders regarding the arrest and interrogation of guerilla squads that infiltrated into Jordan from Syria and were caught in Irbid. Details are given of the targets of sabotage and quantity of weapons found in the squads' possession.

مكتوم جداً ومستعجل

ـ ٢ ـ

ب ٠ وبمنتصف ليلة ٢٨ ـ ٢٩ / ١١ / ١٦٦ تبلغ مع تسعة اشخاص آخرين مسربين منهم كل من المدعو عبد الحميد سيحخاني كردى الاصل ويوسف دايل بأذن بالاستعداد لدخول الاردن ٠ ثم جهزوا بالاسلحه والذخيره والمتفجــرات وحضر نقيب (رئيس) من شعبة مخابرات درعا مع سيارتين لاند روفر ونظمهـــم بنفس الليلة الى قرية المنفيه السوريه ٠

جـ ٠ أعطيت لهم التعليمات بالدخول الى الضفه الغربيه من الاردن لمساندة المتظاهرين ضد الجيش العربى والقيام باعمال التخريب وخصوصا الجسور والدوائر الحكوميه ٠

د ٠ دخلوا الاردن من طريق وادى المغير بين الطره والشجره ليلة ٢٩ ـ ٣٠ / ١١ / ١٦٦ وقاموا تلك الليله شرق بلدة بيت راس ٠ وصباح يوم الاربعاء الموافق ٣٠ / ١١ / ١٦٦ شاهدوا سلطات الامن والجيش الاردنى تفتيش تلك المنطقـــه فقرروا العوده الى سوريا خوفا من اكتشاف أمرهم ٠

هـ ٠ بدأوا بالعوده الساعه ١٩٠٠ يوم ٣٠ / ١١ / ١٦٦ وفى طريقهم وضعــوا متفجرات موقته تحت جسر وتحت عامود تلفون قرب قرية خرجا الاردنيه ٠

٥ ٠ أزيلت المتفجرات من تحت الجسر وعامود التلفون وتبين ان عددها ٣٨ اصبح وضعت لتتفجر الساعه ٠٧٠٠ يوم ١ / ١٢ / ١٦٦ ٠

٦ ٠ صباح يسوم ١ / ١٢ / ١٦٦ القى القبض على احد هؤلاء المخربين فـــى وادى الثلاثه ويدعى محمد الكردى حيث اضطرت الدوريه لاطلاق النار عليه عندما حاول الفرار الى سوريا واصيب بجراح خطيره نقل الى المستشفى للمعالجه ٠

٧ ٠ طيا الملحق (ا) والملحق (ب) يتضمنان المؤسسات والمنشآت الهامـــه والجسور والعبارات فى قاطعى الخليل وبيت لحم ٠

٨ ٠ يرجى اجراء التنسيق مع مسؤولى الامن فى محافظة الخليل وقضاء بيت لحم لحراسة هذه المؤسسات والمنشآت والجسور والعبارات كما يطلب تشديد الحراسه على القيادات والمستودعات والمعسكرات بشكل هام والقاء القبض على كل من يشتبه بأمره لهذه الغايه أوكل من يحاول تعكير صفو الامن واعلامنا ٠

د/العقيد الركن   نسخه الى :
قائد لواء حطين   قيادة الجبهه الغربيه اشاره لكتابكم
رائد ركن / نايف المعايطه   رقم ع ٢ / ٢٤ / أ /   تاريخ
                                    ١ كانون أول ١٦٦
                                  قائد كتيبة الدبابات العاشره ٠
                                    الركن العسكرى ٠

مكتوم جداً ومستعجل

دفتر رسمي جل

قيادة لواء الأمام علي بن أبي طالب
(التعليمات)

الرقم - ع /٢٤/٨ \\
التاريخ - شباط ١٩٦٧

قائد كتيبة اسامه بن زيد
قائد كتيبة زيد بن حارثه
قائد كتيبة عبد الرحمن الداخل

الموضوع / التحركات الاسرائيليه مقابل
الجبهة السوريه

لاحظا لبرقيتنا رقم ح /٢٤/٨ تاريخ ١٩٦٧/١/٢٥

١ • ان الموقف يزداد توترا على خط الحدود (السوري – الاسرائيلي) بسبب النزاع
على المنطقه المجرده بين الطرفين واستمرار اعمال التخريب داخل المنطقه المحتله •

٢ • قام العدو باجراء حشودات كبيره وتحركات عسكريه وفيما يلي اهم المعلومات بهذا
الصدد : –

أ • الجـو

(١) وضع سلاح الجو الاسرائيلي تحت الانذار الفوري وقد تام خلال
الفتره من ١٢ – ٢٦ كانون ثاني ١٩٦٧ بحطيط ترحيل لحوالي اربعة
اسراب مقاتله من توابت (قصاينا) ودائره والقالوجه بشر السبت ثاني الجنوب
الى قاعدة رامات ديفيد دحيفا وموجدون في الشمال • وقد كانت شبكة
الرادار تسجل اعداد واوقات هذه التحركات •

(٢) افاد السوريون ان شبكة الرادار لديهم قد سجلت ترحيل (٨٠)
طائره من القواعد الجنوبيه الى القواعد الشماليه •

(٣) التعليق • من المؤكد ان العدو واخذ في الارنه الاخيره يحسن
تواجده الجويه في الشمال باعداد كبيره من الطائرات المقاتله • مما يحزز
الاحتمال بان العدو سيعتمد الى درجه كبيره على سلاحه الجوي في اية
عمليه مقبله ضد سوريا •

ب • الدروع والمدنحيه

(١) وردت معلومات تفيد بانه خلال يومي ١٦ و ١٧ /١/١٩٦٧ شوهدت
تجمعات من الدروع والمدنحيه الاسرائيليه (المتوسطه والثقيله) في منطقتي
مبنيون وتفوريا شمال الناصره تسير باتجاه منطقة الحدود •

(٢) قام العدو باغلاق الطريق المؤديه الى المنطقه الشماليه بسحر
١٨ كانون ثاني بوجه المركبات المدنيه ولمدة ٢٤ ساعه •

(٣) التعليق • يحتمل بان لواء الدروع الثامن • كانون المقيم عسا
عند في منطقة صوفيت قد تحرك للشمال بالاضافه الى تعزيزات اخرى من
سلاح المدنحيه • وهذا يعني ان هنالك لواتي دروع الان مقابل الجبهه
السوريه •

ج • التوجيه الاسرائيلي

14 Syrian situation estimate, dated February 1, 1967, regarding a possible Israeli attack against Syria.

سِرّي ومستعجل

ـ ٢ ـ

تُرَى سوريا أن أي الحكومة تحاول أن تستنزف حصن أوسائل الدبلوماسيه بواسطة هيئة الأمم رفجنة الهدنة المشتركة قبل اللجوء الى اللجوء ·

(ب)   التحذير · تم تجريد الحكوماﺕ المراقبيه الى عدم اللجوﺀ للشروﺀ فنرو وأن لن يتجاوز أول حادﺙ تخريبي بنسب الى سوريا ·

٣ ·   التحليل العام · يستنتج من دراسة الموقف ومجريات الحوادﺙ ورﺩوﺩ الفعل المعبره لدينا أن العدو وأن بقو العدو وأحدﺙ الاحتطابين على الجبهة السوريه ·

أ ·   القيام بدبو مدبر ـ مشاﺀ ـ فروﻉ ـ متمديه ـ متنديه ـ متجدﺩه ـ محدﺩه ـ حول مناطق جرﺩ
كبير وأنزال مظلي وذلك من أجل احتلال المرتفعاﺕ السوريه وتدمير المواني الدفاعيــه
ليما أو أجزﺀ منها وعندئذ ستتدخل هيئة الأمم وتبدأ المفاوضاﺕ من جديد لأجـــرﺀ
تسويه تد يكون من بعدها أرسال قواﺕ طوارﺉ ﺩولية بين الطرفين كما هي الحال لذي
الحد ريه الحربيه المتحدة · وهذا ما تتطلبه أسرائيل وتوقه أسرائيل عن ذلك نسي
أكثر من مناسبه ·

ب ·   الأعتداﺀ يجحم حوﺩ حوﺩ كبير (تحاشيا لوقوع الخسائر في القواﺕ الأرضيه الأسرائيليه
وأنزال قواﺕ شديده على مراكز القواﺕ السوريه والقياﺩاﺕ في الجبهه السوريه ·

٤ ·   لكن لم يتوصل الطرفان الى أي اتفاق حول المناطق المجرﺩه وأستغلالينا من العدو
بأن أول أجتماع عقد يوﻡ ٦ كانون ثاني رأجل ليوﻡ ١١ كانون ثاني بسبب اثارة المطلوب الأسرائيلي
يتعلق بقضايا التخريب التي تخذيما سوريا ما دعه المندوب السوري للأحتجاﺝ بشده ويطلب هذا
التأجيل وعدم الخوﺽ في هذه النقطه لكونها خارجه عن جدول الأعمال ·

٥ ·   يرجى العلم بذلك ·

ﺩ/ العزيم
قائد لوﺀ الأمام علي بن أبي طالب
الرائد الركن / حسان القضاه

سرّي ومستعجل

الجمهورية العربية المتحدة
قيادة المنطقة الشرقية الجوية
مكتب رئيس الأركان

صورة رقم (٢)

الرمز : ٢٤/١٩٦٧/٢/٣٥
التاريخ : ١٩٦٧/٥/١١

أمر عمليات رقم ٣/٦٧

١ـ من المنتظر القيام بعمليات تعرضية لعزل منطقة النقب الجنوبي واحتلال ايـــــلات .

٢ـ يخصص المجهود الجوى التالى لاستخدامه بواسطة قائد القوات البرية لصالح العمليــة .

أـ ٢٧ طلعة سرب قاذف مقاتل من الالوية الجوية ٧ ، ١٢ المتمركزان حاليا فــــى القاعدتان ٢٥١ ، ٢٤٨ .

بـ ٣ طلعة سرب قاذف خفيف من اللواء الجوى ١١ المتمركز بالقاعدة ٢٢١ .

ـ كما تخصص طلعة سرب قاذف ثقيل من احتياطى قائد القوات الجوية والدفاع الجوى لصالح العملية . تطلب بمعرفة قائد القوات الجوية والدفاع الجوى .

٣ـ الحد الأقصى للمجهود اليومى :

ـ ١ طلعة سرب قاذف مقاتل ، طلعة سرب قاذف خفيف .

٤ـ سوف تطلب الطلعات مباشرة بواسطة جماعة المعاونة الجوية من المدارات وستكـــون الشبكة ٥٥ مستمعة على نفس التردد .

٥ـ سيقوم بالتوجيه/على الاهداف ضباط توجيه من نقط توجيه متقدمة . ستخبار التشكيـــلات الجوية بأسمائها الكودية والترددات اللاسلكية التى تعمل عليها فى حينـــه .

٦ـ الالوان الكودية للتشكيلات الجوية أثناء توجيه الطائرات على الاهداف :

أـ الطائرات التى ستقوم بالعمل فى معاونة الاتجاه الرئيسى ورمزها الكودى (أحمر)
بـ ٥٥ ٥٥ ٥٥ ٥٥ ٥٥ ٥٥ ٥٥ الثانوى ، (ايلات) ورمزها الكودى (أصفر)
جـ ٥٥ ٥٥ ٥٥ ٥٥ ٥٥ فى عزل ميدان المعركة ورمزها الكــــــودى (أخضر)

٧ـ ستقوم الطائرات الجوية بضرب مطار ايلات وضرب محطة الارسال ومستودعات البترول بهـــا بمجهود منفصل لذلك من قيادة الطائرات الجويـــــة .

لواء طيار/ عبد الحميد عبد السلام دغيدى
قائد المنطقة الشرقية الجويــــــــة

(التوقيع)

15 Egypt: Operational Order No. 3/67, dated May 19, 1967, from the commander of the eastern air region regarding the air force role in an attack for isolating the Negev and capturing Eilat.

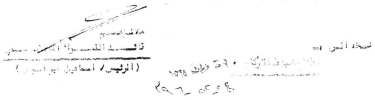

16 Letter, dated June 8, 1965, from the commander of the Hashemite Brigade regarding activity by the Fatah Organization "that poses a danger to the Jordanian border and runs contrary to the policy of the Arab states and UAC."

(سرى للغاية)

قيادة القوات الجوية والدفاع الجوى

قيادة منطقة شرق القوات الجوية

اللواء الجوى الثانى

القيد / ٦٧/١/١/٦٣

التاريخ / ١٩٦٧/٥/٢٦

أمر قتال رقم ٦/٦٧

١ ـ خرائط المراجعة

مجموعة خرائط مصر وفلسطين ١/ ٥٠٠٠٠٠

٢ ـ مهمة السرب ٢٥ قتال من اللواء الجوى الثانى

ضرب ميناء ايلات ضربة مركزة بقوة سرب

تاريخ التنفيذ

أ ـ تقوم أربعة طائرات بضرب المدار ومحطة توليد الكهرباء الموجودة بمنتصف المو وذلك أن تقوم طائرة القائد ورقم (٢) بضرب منتصف المو بالصوارين على رقم (٣) و (٤) ضرب المنطقة بالمدافع والصوارى شرعى دوران الى جهة اليسار بعد الخروج من الهجوم بالطيران الواطى لمدة نصف دقيقة (الوقت فوق الهدف من س + ٤ الى س + ٥) .

ب ـ تقوم أربعة طائرات بضرب مستودعات الوقود جنوب ايلات ومحطة تحويل المياه بضربة مركزة بالمدافع والصوارى ثم دوران لجهة اليمين والعودة الى القاعدة يحدد الهجوم على أن يقوم القائد ورقم (٢) بمهاجمة الوقود ويقوم رقم (٣) و (٤) بمهاجمة محطة تحويل المياه (الوقت فوق الهدف من س + ٥ الى س + ١) .

ج ـ تقوم أربعة طائرات بضرب محطة الرادار على أن تكون الميناء الجديدة ومخازن البوتاسيوم والفوسفات تبادل لــى . على أن يقوم رقم (١) و (٢) بمهاجمة موقع الرادار ٨ (٢٠ ...) ويقوم رقم (٣) و (٤) (بمهاجمة موقع الرادار (٢٠٠)

وموقى مايه صورة لموقع الرادار .

وفى حالة مهاجمة الغرض التبادلى يقوم رقم (١) و (٢) بمهاجمة أوناء الميناء التجارى الجديد رقم (٣) و (٤) بمهاجمة مخازن البوتاسيوم على أن يقوم بحمل دوران لليمين بعد الطيران الواطى لمدة نصف دقيقة والعودة للقاعدة (الوقت فوق الهدف من س + ٦ الى س + ٧) .

د ـ يتم تجميع التشكيلات الثلاث على ارتفاع ٢٠٠ متر والنزول الى ٥٠ متر أثناء الطيران للهدف والعودة وموقى طابع خطة الطيران للطلعات الثلاث .

٣ ـ الوحدات المعاونة

أ ـ سيقوم اللواء الجوى التاسع ـ ٤٠ بعمل مانعة بقوة ثمانية طائرات من ٢١ لحماية القوة الضاربة من وضع الدلالة الجوية رقم (١) . منطقة الدلالة المحدودة شمالا وجبل شمدون جنوبا وحتى ٣٠ كيلو جهة الغرب من خلالـ الجبلين . ارتفاع الدلالة من ٢ الى ٨ كيلو متر . مدة الدلالة من س + ٥ الى س + ٩ .

ب ـ اللواء الجوى الخامس من القاعدة ٢٣٢ س ٤٠ يكون مستعدا من وضع الاستعداد رقم ١ لتعزيز عملية الدلالة الجوية .

٤ ـ تدابير التعاون

.. التمارين بين قائد السرب ٢٥ واللواء الجوى الـ ٦١ .

17 Egypt: Operational Order No. 6/67 of the Second Air Brigade, eastern region air headquarters, regarding Wing 25's missions: the concentrated bombing of the Port of Eilat, state of alertness beginning at dawn, May 26, 1967.

(٢)

تأيـــــــــيد

الاشـــــارة

بتم الاتصال بطائرة الاتصال ل ١٤ على الموجة رقم (٤)٣٢و٣٣ الطلب المعاونة من
دائرة الحي ٢١ ويكون التردد رقم ١ ٧و١٢٥ ٥ احتياطى .
مركز قائد اللواء

يتم قيادة التشكيل من الجو وذلك بالطيران فوق طلعة الا ول ـــــــى المرتز ٣١٠
لاعطاء أى أوامر جديــــدة طارئة عن طريق الدائرة ل ١٤ .
وقت الاستعداد

يتم الاستعداد من أول ضوؤ يوم ٢٦ / ٥ / ١٩٦٧ .
تحدد ساعة س بواسطة قائد النوات الجوية والدفاع الجوى فى حينـــــه .

مقدم طيار / مدحى أحمد طلبة
قائد اللواء الجوى الثــــــانى
التوقيع /

٠ ٢٥١ ثد القاعدة الجويـــــة
٠ الا سراب الخامسة والعشـــرون
٠ ٢٦٠ القاعدة الجويـــة

287

(سري للغاية)

جمهورية العربية لمتحدة
قيادة منطقة لشرقية الجوية
تنظيم سرية الكابرة

أمر قتال رقم ٥/٦٧

أولاً: الموقف: قوات القوى والدفاع الجوى ؛

ثانياً: القرار المخصص لتنفيذ المهمة ؛

ثالثاً: مهام التشكيلات الجوية ؛

18 Operational Order No. 5/67 from the commander of the eastern air region regarding missions of the air force and air defense units, and including the bombing of the Port of Eilat and its vicinity. The timing of the operation will be determined by the commander of the air force. The operation's codename: "Asad."

— ٣ —

لد جمر ٦١ :

- يتقدم بمحور أرمنة المشيب بتعرف ٩ غازة —
- " " " المغاد يتقدم ٧ غازة
- " " " المعكرات بتقدم ٦ غازة —
- لمرفت تقدم الرتل من س + ٧ + ٠ الى س + ٠١
- التسليح قابل ... كم سدف ٠،٠٥ كم وقبل مرون

لد جمر ٦٥ :

- سيتقدم لمحور الميناء بتقدة ٤ ظوزائف لد سى س الرف ٩٥ وزمنه —
- " " من س + ٨١ م الى م سعت س + ٤٢ +

لد جمر ٩ :

- يتقدم بتقدة ٤ بعد تأمين قراتك المشتركة في لعملية لد جمر ٤ —
- لد جمر ٦١ ، لد جمر ٠٢ ، ورتبه هبه خلقة لمدلا الجوى —

رابعا : تنظيم التقادم :

سيتقدم قائد المنطقة لتزمية الجرمة بالإشراف عل تنظيم لتقادم بين قائر —
لد جمر ١١ ، ول جمر ٢ ، ول جمر ٩ فى هذه لعملية

خامسا : لقيادة والسيطرة :

- قيادة عمليات لمنحرات الجرية المركزية بواسفة قائد لمحرات لجرية والرتل لجوى —
من المركز ٢٠٢

- ستتار عمليات تهذيم لهذة المركز ٠٨٧ شبامى "المهنة" "خايز" —

سادسا : وقته المستعداد :

١ - يعود وقته المستعداد لتنفيذ الخطة أوامر خاصة لمحرات لجرية —
والرتل الجوى فى حينه

٢ - لغه سدى القسم أحدى "أسد" تنفذ الخطة —
٣ - ستتها من ستقود بواسفة قائد لمحرات لجرية والرتل الجوى فى مينه —

اللواء / مالك ابراهيم زيد
رئيس أركان المنطقة لترقية الجرمة
(امضاء)

(مخرى للغاية)

Notes

Preface

1   Elie Podeh, *Hachatira le-Hegimonya ba-'Ulam ha-'Aravi* (Tel Aviv, 1996), p. 239. The English version of the book *The Quest for Hegemony in the Arab World* (New York 1995) omits this sentence. According to the English version: "The struggle over the Baghdad Pact caused significant changes . . . These can be summarized as follows: (*inter alia*) the two major issues that had hitherto preoccupied the Arab world – the Palestinian problem and the Saudi–Hashimite conflict – were relegated to a secondary place . . . " p. 244.

2   For other evaluations and approaches to the background and causes of the war, see L. Carl Brown, "Nasser and the June 1967 War: Plan or Improvisation?" in, S. Sheikaly, R. Baalbaki & P. Dodd, eds., *Quest for Understanding: Arabic and Islam Studies in Memory of Malcolm H. Kerr* (American University of Beirut, 1991). For additional assessments, see Asher Susser, ed., *Shisha Yamim, Sheloshim Shana (Six Days, Thirty Years)*, (Tel Aviv, 1999) [Hebrew]; includes articles by: Itamar Rabinovich, Shimon Shamir, Asher Susser, Richard Parker, Shlomo Avineri and Hermann Eilts.

3   Malcolm H. Kerr, *The Arab Cold War: Jamal Abd Al-Nasser and his Rivals* (3rd edition, London, 1971), p. 115.

4   Avraham Sela, *The Decline of the Arab–Israeli Conflict* (New York, 1998), pp. 28–29, 52–53, 69.

5   Naji Alush, *al-Masira ila Filastin* (Beirut, 1964), p. 165.

6   Faysal Hourani, *al-'Amal al-'Arabi al-Mushtarak wa Isra'il, al-Rafd wa al-Qubul 1944–1967* (Nicosia, 1989), p. 110.

7   See Moshe Shemesh, *The Palestinian Entity 1959–1974, Arab Politics and the PLO* (2nd revised edition London, 1996).

1   The Arab–Israeli Conflict Escalates

1   Nasir, *Radio Cairo*, November 7, 1956.

2   Nasir, *Radio Cairo*, November 7, 1956, January 17, 1957, February 11, 1957, July 27, 1957, September 3, 1957, December 23 1957, March 20, 1958, and December 25, 1960.

3   *Al-Ahram*, October 23, 1960.

4   Muhammad Hasanayn Haykal, *al-Ahram*, December 20, 1958; *al-Ahram*, December 24, 1958.

5   Michel Aflaq (in a lecture at the meeting of Ba'th party members in Paris on June 21, 1964), *Nidhal Hizb al-Ba'th, Bayanat Qiyadatihi al-Qawmiya 1963–1966* (Beirut, October 1971), pp. 147–148.

6   The term "cold war" was employed by Butrus Ghali, who was then a lecturer and head of the Political Science Department at the College for Economy at Cairo University, in his book *Dirasat fi al-Diblomasiya al-'Arabiya* (Cairo, 1973), p. 237. See also: Malcolm Kerr, *The Arab Cold War* (London, 1971, 3rd edition).

7   Nasir, *Radio Cairo*, April 2, 1963, from an interview with Nasir in *al-Muharrir*, Beirut, April 2, 1963.

8   For the meaning of these terms see: Jamal Abd al-Nasir, *Filastin min Aqwal al*-Ra'is, 1953–1964 (Cairo, n.d.), pp. 39, 42, 145–147 [hereafter: Nasir, *Filastin min Aqwal*]; Nasir, *al-Ahram*, February 23, 1962; Haykal, *al-Ahram*, March 10, 1961, December 29, 1961, August 28, 1964.

9   Nasir, *Filastin min Aqwal*, pp. 59, 65, 79, 92.

10 Nasir, *Radio Cairo*, July 24, 1957, December 23, 1958, February 17, 1960, December 25, 1960.

11 On the UAR (Egyptian) policy see: UAR memo requesting that the chairman of the Arab League summon a meeting of the Arab League Council for a special debate on this issue, *al-Ahram*, January 5, 1960; Haykal, *al-Ahram*, May 18, 1962, January 4, 1963; editorial, *al-Ahram*, October 23, 1960; *al-Jarida*, Beirut, August 14, 1959.

12 On the development of the Egyptian army and its build-up between 1957 and 1967, see: Avi Shay, "Hayl Misrayim" ("The Egyptian Armed Forces") Part I, *Ma'rakhot*, 227 (January 1973) [Hebrew] ; ibid., Part II, *Ma'rakhot*, 228, (March 1973); see also: Muhammad Fawzi, *Harb al-Thalath Sanawat, Mudhakirat* (Beirut, 1983), pp. 58–68 [hereafter: Fawzi, *Harb al-Thalath*]; and also: Haykal, *al-Ahram*, September 25, 1964, for a review of the balance of forces between Egypt and Israel.

13 The need for the terms "Palestinian Entity" or "revival of the Palestinian Entity" stemmed from the political, social, and demographic conditions of the Palestinians after the 1948 War. In the wake of the war the term "Palestine" or "Filastin" disappeared from the geographical–political map of the Middle East. In April 1950 the eastern part of Palestine (that the Arab Legion had captured) was finally annexed to Jordan, and became the "West Bank of the Jordanian Hashemite Kingdom." The original inhabitants of the West Bank and the Palestinian refugees who fled to the kingdom became Jordanian citizens.

   The other part of Mandatory Palestine that the Egyptian army captured was not annexed, but remained a separate administrative unit under the new official name of "the region under the control of the Egyptian forces in Filastin" – commonly known as the Gaza Strip.

14 Adli Hashad, *sha' b Filastin fi Tariq al-'Awda* (Cairo, 1964) p. 104 [hereafter: Hashad, *sha'b Filastin*]; Muhammad Fawzi, 'Umar Rushdi, *al-Sahyoniya wa-Rabibatiha Isra' il* (Cairo, 1965) p. 402 [hereafter: Rushdi, *al-Sahyoniya*]; Ahmad al-Shuqayri, *Min al-Qima ila al-Hazima* (Beirut, 1971), p. 57 [hereafter: Shuqayri, *Min al-Qima*]; and also *al-Ahram*, April 6, 1959.

15 Fuad Matar, Bisaraha 'an *Abd al-Nasir, Hiwar ma' a Muhammad Hasanayn Haykal* (Beirut, 1975), pp. 98–99.

16 Ibid., p. 136.

17 *Al-Ahram*, June 24, 1959, July 9, 1959.

18 *Al-Masa'*, Cairo, July 17, 1959.

19 Haykal, *al-Ahram*, May 18, 1962, Haykal quoted from the protocol of the UAR government session. Akram al-Hourani's version (then the UAR vice-president) on this discussion appeared in the Syrian daily *al-Ayam*, June 13, 1962. Hourani quoted Nasir's statements as relayed by Haykal, but he omitted certain passages and completely ignored the sections that dealt with his dispute with Nasir. On the other hand, Salah al-Bitar's version that appeared in the newspaper al-Ba'th on August 18, 1962 was closed to the Haykal's version and was cited by the Egyptian ambassador to Lebanon during the debates in the Arab League Council, *al-Ahram*, August 26, 1962. The Lebanese ambassador in Cairo, Josef Abu-Khatir, discusses Nasir's position on this issue in a debate with Hourani. See Josef Abu-Khatir, *Liqa'at ma' a Jamal Abd al-Nasir* (Beirut, 1971), pp. 101–102, [hereafter: Abu Khatir, *Liqa'at ma' a Jamal*]; Haykal, went so far as to write in *al-Ahram* on September 7,

1962: "We do not want war as an adventure; the war must be carefully prepared for." Nasir reiterated his position in a speech on June 26, 1962 before the members of the Gaza Strip's legislative council: "At the time [November 1959], Hourani asked for military or limited operation, but talks about a limited operation are pure hogwash. If I carry out limited operations how can I be certain that Ben-Gurion will respond with limited moves, and not with an all-out military operation? If I decide to act, first of all I'll have to impose my opinion on my forces and afterwards my forces on Ben-Gurion himself and whoever stands behind Ben-Gurion, and not play games with the fate of my country; otherwise I'll wind up with a second disaster like that of 1948," *al-Ahram*, June 27, 1962.

20 Nasir, *(Radio) Sawt al-Arab*, June 26, 1962; *al-Ahram*, June 27, 1962.
21 *Ruz al-Yusef*, weekly, Cairo (an article by Mamduh Rida), December 15, 1963; Nasir, *al-Ahram*, December 24, 1961, June 27, 1962, July 23, 1963, August 28, 1963.
22 See: Nasir, *al-Ahram*, April 18, 1959, February 21, 1960, March 4, 1961; Nasir, *Filastin min Aqwal*, pp. 65, 67, 70; Haykal, *al-Ahram*, March 10, 1961.
23 Nasir, *al-Ahram*, April 26, 1960, October 19, 1960, June 2, 1965; Nasir, *Filastin min Aqwal*, pp. 82–83 (March 21, 1960); *al-Ahram*, June 30, 1959.
  The decisions of the General Assembly of the National Union in the UAR (July 16, 1960) expressed the UAR position on this issue:
  "The assembly congratulates the sons of Filastin, their struggle, and the tenacity [they retain] for their rights and Arab nationalism. The assembly sees them as the main pillars around which the Palestinian problem will be solved; the assembly recommends continuing the organization of the Palestinian people with an emphasis on the Palestinians' existence on Filastin soil. [The assembly] deplores any attempt at resettling the Palestinians or transferring them to other countries or obliterating the Palestinian problem." *Radio Cairo*, July 16, 1960; on the refugee issue, see: *al-Akhbar*, June 23, 1961, an article by Melhem Ayash that analyzes the Palestinian and refugee problems.
24 *Al-Ahram*, February 15 to March 10, 1959; Nasir, *al-Ahram*, February 22, 1959; for the various positions expressed in the Arab media, see: Egypt – *al-Musawar*, February 20, 1959; *Ruz al-Yusef*, February 23, 1959; *al-Akhbar*, February 21, 1959; *al-Ahram*, May 20, 1959; *Akhir Sa'a*, March 11, 1959; Syria – *al-Nasr*, Damascus, March 5, 1959; Jordan – *al-Jihad*, February 16, 1959, February 22, 1959; *Filastin*, Amman, February 18, 21, 1959; *al-Difa'*, February 19, 1959, *al-Bilad*, Amman, February 18, 1959; Lebanon – *al-Jarida*, February 17, 19, 22, 1959; *al-Hayat*, February 24, 1959; Iraq –*Radio Baghdad* commentary, February 17 8, 1959. 1
25 See: Proposal for the Continuation of United Nations Assistance to Palestinian Refugees, documents submitted by the Secretary General, 14th session, A/4121, June 15, 1959.
26 See: *NYT*, June 26, 1961; *Middle East Record* [*MER*], Shiloah Research Center (Tel Aviv, 1961), pp. 197–198.
  The memo stated: "It is my desire to assist in solving the tragic problem of the Palestinian refugees either on the basis of the principle of return, or by reparations for their property, and also to assist them in finding a just answer to the question of developing the Jordan's water sources and helping advance [a solution] to the other aspects of these complex problems . . ."
  The Egyptian newspaper *al-Akhbar* responded to Kennedy's note in an article entitled: "Imperialism's Attempts to Eradicate the Palestinian problem."
  "It is no secret that a number of Western states are preparing to quash the Palestinian problem. The Western states intend to empty the Palestinian problem of its political, national and future contents, supposedly to transfer it to the status of a refugee [problem], and then its solution will be the settlement and absorption of the refugees in a number of Arab states or the return of a small number of them and compensation to others . . . We

Notes to pp. 9–13

believe that the refugee problem is only the humanitarian side of the Palestinian problem." *al-Akhbar*, June 23, 1961.

27 Nasir, *Filastin min Aqwal*, p. 97 (October 19, 1960).
28 Nasir's conversation with Haykal, *al-Ahram*, June 30, 1959.
29 *Sawt al-Arab* commentaries, December 1–15, 1959. The "Palestinian Corner" on *Sawt al-Arab* made a significant contribution to this issue. In December 1959 the director of the *Sawt al-Arab* radio station Ali Hisham Rashid, a Palestinian from the Gaza Strip, changed the term "refugees" to "returnees" (*'a' idwun*). All the programs ended with the catchphrase: "We shall return" (*inana 'a' idun*).
30 Nasir, *al-Ahram*, October 19, 1960.
31 Nasir, *al-Ahram*, October 19, 1960 (Nasir's statements before the members of the Palestinian National Union's Executive Council in Damascus), March 4, 1961, June 27, 1962, (speech before the members of the Gaza Legislative Council), December 24, 1962, July 23, 1963, December 14–24, 1963; Nasir, *Filastin min Aqwal*, p. 136; Haykal, *al-Ahram*, January 17, 1961 (quoted Nasir), November 16, 1962; Commentary *Radio Cairo*, November 15, 1962. In an article entitled "All are for Filastin" (November 16, 1962), Muhammad Hasanayn Haykal, the editor of *al-Ahram* and confidante of Nasir, wrote: "I say unhesitatingly that the victory of the revolution in Yemen is a step in the direction of solving the Palestinian problem . . . The victory of the revolution in Saudi Arabia and Jordan, and in any other Arab state . . . are steps in the direction of victory in Filastin . . . [Egyptian soldiers] are fighting in Yemen for Filastin and for the strengthening of the entire Arab nation . . ."
32 For examples of this preaching, two articles (March 1963) by the Palestinian journalist-writer Khayri Hammad may be noted, in which he wrote, *inter alia*: "To tell you the truth and nothing but the truth: The way to unity is the Filastin way, and the way to Filastin is the way of unity . . . Therefore, the undertaking to save Filastin has to be combined with the struggle for unity, or to be more exact, is another side of it. The first goal of the undertaking is to attain the unity needed for the liberation of Palestinian land. Thus, the great role of the Palestinian people, wherever they are, is to realize unity. Since the UAR is the only liberated Arab state bordering Filastin, then the preparations for saving Filastin must fall to it [Egypt] with deep faith." Khayri Hammad, *al-Ahram*, March 2–3, 1963; see also Haykal, *al-Ahram*, August 17, 1962.
33 Nasir, *al-Ahram*, June 27, 1962, July 3, 1962; Nasir, *Filastin min Aqwal*, p. 128; see also: the speech by the deputy foreign minister of the UAR at the Arab League Council, *al-Jihad*, Amman, September 14, 1959
34 Decisions made at the Syrian Region's (UAR) National Union Assembly, *Radio Damascus*, June 25, 1960; for the Egyptian view, see: *al-Musawar*, July 10, 1959; *Akhbar al-Yawm*, December 31, 1960; *al-Akhbar*, August 14, 1959; *al-Ahram*, August 13 and 27, 1959, February 14, 1960, December 15, 1960; *Ruz al-Yusef*, September 5, 1960; *al-Wahda*, Damascus, May 20, 1960; *al-Siyasa*, Beirut, April 17, 1972; *al-Sayad*, Beirut, April 27, 1961.
35 Al-Qanun al-Asasi lil-Mantiqa al-Waqi'a Tahta Raqabat al-Quwat al-Misriya, *al-Jarida al-Rasmiya*, Law No. 225, 1955; see also: *al-Ahram*, September 6, 1960.
36 For the wording of the constitution, see: al-Nizam al-Dusturi li-Qita' Ghaza, *al-Jarida al-Rasmiya*, 75, March 29, 1962; *al-Ahram*, March 10, 1962.
37 Preface to A Provisionary Constitution for Filastin, in Rushdi *al-Sahyoniya*, pp. 387-388; the book is a text used in the Egyptian Military College; see also: commentaries, *(Radio) Sawt al-Arab*, March 7–11, 1962; editorials in *al-Ahram* and *al-Jumhuriya*, March 10, 1962.
38 Abd al-Hamid al-Saraj (head of the Syrian region's UAR Executive Council), *Radio Damascus*, July 11, 1961.
39 Nasir, *al-Ahram*, April 26, 1960; decisions of the General Assembly of the National Union, *al-Ahram*, July 17, 1960; *al-Ahram*, January 24, 1962; as part of operations of

293

Jordanian subversion in late 1961 weapons and leaflets were smuggled into the Gaza Strip.

40 In May 1950 the Arab League's Political Committee convened to discuss the Jordanian step. The Egyptians demanded that Jordan refrain from annexing the West Bank and that it guarantee that the area it acquired would be a deposit until a final agreement was achieved. Jordan rejected both this proposal and the attempt at a compromise. In June 1950 the Arab League's Council held a meeting without Jordan's participation and decided to continue its attempts to get Jordan to agree to the compromise that the area of annexation would serve as a deposit in Jordan's hands until the liberation of all of Filastin and a final agreement was reached that would meet the League's decisions. The "Free Officers" regime (in Egypt), which adopted the Arab League's position, not only opposed the Jordanian regime's right to represent the Palestinians (including Palestinians living in Jordan) but also denied the Kingdom of Jordan its right to exist. See Asher Goren, *Ha-Liga Ha-'Aravit 1945–1954* (Tel Aviv, 1954), pp. 204–205 [Hebrew], [hereafter: Goren, *The Arab League*].

41 See: Haykal, *al-Ahram*, February 10, 1961, March 31, 1961 (the wording of Nasir's dispatch to King Husayn from March 13, 1961), September 27, 1963 (report on Haykal's meeting with Husayn in Paris); see also: *al-Ahram*, December 24, 1961; Husayn, *Radio Amman*, October 20, 1961.

42 Nasir, *al-Ahram*, August 5, 1959; Haykal, *al-Ahram*, August 14, 1960, May 3, 1961, May 3, 1963; see also: *al-Ahram*, December 17, 1962, cites official sources in Cairo; an article by Tewfiq al-Maqdisi who analyzes Nasir's speeches, *al-Jarida*, Beirut, October 18, 1960; commentary *Sawt al-Arab*, June 3, 1960; and article by Mustafa Amin that emphasizes "the belief that the road to Filastin will soon pass through Amman," *Akhbar al-Yawm*, April 27, 1963.

43 *Akhir Sa'a*, May 23, 1962; *al-Hayat*, June 7, 1962, published an article by "a veteran Arab statesman" that "in the discussion two years ago between senior Arab and international officials, a plan for [solving] the Palestinian problem was proposed." The idea was "to oust the Jordanian regime and establish [in its place] a Palestinian Arab republic on both banks."

44 See the wording of the secret agreement for military cooperation between the UAR and Iraqi military delegations, signed in Baghdad on November 10, 1958. The agreement discussed the dispatching of Iraqi forces to Syria if war broke out with Israel "following an Israeli attack on the UAR, Lebanon or the West Bank of Jordan" (nothing was mentioned about the West Bank being part of the Kingdom of Jordan), *al-Ahram*, April 4, 1959; letter dated December 1, 1958 classified as top secret, from the "commander of the First Camp" (Syrian army) to the general commander of the Iraqi army concerning "the possibility of an Israeli attack against the West Bank of Jordan or the Syrian region . . ." *al-Ahram*, April 4, 1959; the failure to mention Jordan in either of the documents was obviously not accidental; see also: *al-Ahram*, September 13, 1958.

45 See *al-Ahram*, March 10, 1960; *al-Difa'*, January 17, 1960; *al-Jihad*, January 18, 1960; *Hawla al-'Alam*, Amman, February 18, 1960. Majali, *Radio Amman*, March 9, 1966.

46 On January 2, 1962 the Iraqi daily *al-Zaman* quoted the details released from official sources in Iraq on the number of Palestinian refugees dwelling in the country. The article stated that there were 10,202 refugees in Iraq; 7,737 in Baghdad, of whom 4,274 received a government stipend. It also noted that 339 were living in Mosul, and 239 in Basra. The article went on to say that according to the Special Committee and the government decision, 1,887 refugees were considered homeless, received no aid, and had to produce documents attesting to their Palestinian origins and had arrived in Iraq prior to June 25, 1958.

47 Qasim, Radio Baghdad, December 10, 1962.

48 A report by Jozef Abu-Khatir on a meeting with Qasim on July 16, 1959, see Abu-Khatir, *Liqa'at Ma'a Jamal*, pp. 227–229.

49 Qasim, Radio Baghdad, December 18, 1959, July 14, 1960, October 15, 1960, November 2, 1961, March 20, 1962, June 27, 1962, Jawad, Foreign Minister, *al-Jarida*, January 23, 1962; Abu Khatir, Liqa'at *Ma' a* Jamal, p. 289. In his speech on December 15, 1959, Qasim asked, "What are reasons for the Palestinian people's exile? "The reasons are: [Arab] egoism, the presentation of false achievements, and aggression against an entire people [the Palestinians]. I always stated that only the people of Filastin would restore the country [to themselves]. It would have been better that the brokers in the name Filastin called for the establishment of a Palestinian state whose inhabitants controlled it. We will support them and help them with all our resources just as we are currently helping Algeria. The liars might claim that this is a wild idea. My reply is that the idea is realistic, and that we must base it on the condition that we distance ourselves from egotism and return to the path of truth." Qasim, *Radio Baghdad*, December 15, 1959.

50 Qasim, *al-Zaman*, Baghdad, December 16, 1959.

51 Qasim, *Radio Baghdad*, December 15, 1959.

52 Qasim, *Radio Baghdad*, December 21, 1959.

53 Qasim, *Radio Baghdad*, December 15, 1959, July 29, 1960, February 2, 1961; *al-Thawra*, May 7, 1962; Jawad, *al-Jarida*, Beirut, August 20, 1960.

54 Qasim's statements, *Radio Baghdad*, December 15, 18, and 21, 1959, January 7 and 13, 1960, April 5, 1969, May 16, 1960, May 16, 1962; *al-Thawra*, April 8, 1962; *al-Zaman*, May 20, 1962; Jawad, *al-Jarida*, August 20, 1960. Qasim also claimed that, "The name Filastin has practically been erased since Zionism plundered the largest part of it. Jordan stole the West Bank, and Nasir's Egypt expropriated the Gaza Strip. This has meant that darling Filastin was plundered by three thieves: one thief was the undisguised enemy of Arab nationalism, that is – Zionism, the two other thieves come from the Arabs who have stolen the Arab Palestinians' homeland, and they are Husayn's Jordan and Nasir's Egypt."

55 Qasim, *Radio Baghdad*, March 28, 1960.

56 *Al-Waqa'i' al-'Iraqiya*, August 29, 1960, pp. 14–15.

57 Qasim, *Radio Baghdad*, March 27, 1960.

58 *Al-Zaman*, April 4, 1960.

59 See: Qasim, *al-Ayam*, Khartoum, April 5, 1960; *Radio Baghdad*, May 16, 1960; 'Isam Sakhnini, "al-Filastiniyun fi al-'Iraq," *Shuun Filastiniya*, No. 13, September 1972, pp. 90–116; see also: *al-Zaman*, April 17, 1960, December 6, 1962; *al-Bilad*, April 17, 1960; *al-Akhbar*, Baghdad, April 6, 1960; *al-Thawra*, February 19, 1962.

60 Sakhnini, ibid.

61 Qasim, *Radio Baghdad*, October 28, 1959, December 21, 1959, January 2 and 7, 1960; *al-Akhbar*, December 17, 1960; Commentary, *Radio Baghdad*, January 29, 1960, March 2, 1960.

62 Qasim, *al-Zaman*, August 12, 1960.

63 Qasim, *Radio Baghdad*, January 2, 1960.

64 Husayn, at an army camp, *Radio Amman*, March 13, 1960; editorial, *Hawla al-'Alam*, Amman, February 25, 1960.

65 Haza' al-Majali, *Radio Amman*, August 23, 1959.

66 Husayn, *Radio Amman*, March 16, 1960; Majali, *Radio Amman*, August 23, 1959, January 12, 1960, March 10, 1960, January 12, 1961; *al-Jihad*, September 14 and 16, 1959; Wasfi al-Tal, *Radio Amman*, July 2, 1962; editorial, *Filastin*, January 14, 1960.

67 Husayn, *al-Difa'*, January 13, 1960, February 23, 1960, March 13 and 17, 1960; *Radio Amman*, January 19, 1960, March 1, 1960, October 21, 1960; Majali, *al-Jihad*, September 16, 1959; *Radio Amman*, December 22, 1959; *al-Sayad*, Beirut, March 3, 1960.

68 Husayn, *Radio Amman*, March 16, 1960, *al-Difa'*, March 17, 1960.

69 Majali, *Radio Amman*, December 22, 1959; see also Husayn, *Radio Amman*, January 20, 1960, February 17, 1960; Musa Nasir, Foreign Minister, *Radio Amman*, February 17, 1960.

70   Majali, *Radio Amman*, January 19, 1960.
71   On July 2, 1962, the Jordanian prime minister, Wasfi al-Tal, presented "The White Paper" (*al-Kitab al-Abyad*) to journalists, who published it in the Jordanian press in the following days. See: *al-Jihad*, July 3, 1962; Filastin, 4–5 July, 1962; *al-Manar*, July 6, 8, and 9, 1962; see also: Husayn's memo to the Arab Student Conference in the United States (August 25, 1963) that was published in an official Jordanian brochure.
72   Ibid.
73   *Al-Thawra*, Baghdad, *April 26*, 1962, July 3, 1962; *al-Jihad*, May 28, 1962, October 21, 1962; *al-Difa'*, April 29, 1962; *al-Manar*, April 29, 1962; *al-Hayat*, Beirut, May 29, 1962; *al-Jarida*, July 25, 1962.
74   On the Egyptian proposals see Part I of Chapter 2.
75   See: MER, 1960, pp. 204–209; MER, 1961, pp. 217–221.
76   This section is based on the Ba'th documents including internal secret leaflets. These documents were incorporated in three series of books:
      (A) The old series entitled *Nidal al-Ba'th*: I. vol. 4, *al-Qiyada al-Qawmiya*, 1955–1961 (Beirut, 1964), [hereafter *Nidal* 1]; II. vol. 7, *al-Qutr al-'Iraqi*, 1958–1963, 2nd edition (Beirut, March 1972), (*Nidal* 2); III. vol. 8, *al-Qutr al-Lubnani*, 1951–1961 (Beirut, March 1972), (*Nidal* 3).
      (B) The new series entitled *Nidal Hizb al-Ba'th al-'Arabi al-Ishtiraki*: IV. *'Abr Bayanat Qiyadatihi al-Qawmiya, 1955–1962* (Beirut, June 1971), (*Nidal* 4); V. *'Abr Mu'tamaratihi al-Qwamiya, 1947–1964* (Beirut, June 1971), (*Nidal* 5); VI. *'Abr Mu'tamaratihi al-Qwamiya, al-Mu'tamar al-Thamin* (Beirut, April 1972), (*Nidal* 6); VII. *'Abr Bayanat Qiyadatihi al-Qawmiya* 1963–1966 (Beirut, October 1971), (*Nidal* 7).
      (C) The series *al-Ba'th wa-Qadiyat Filastin*: VIII. vol. 3, 1955–1959 (Beirut, 1974), (*Ba'th–Filastin*, vol. 3); IX. vol. 4, 1959–1964 (Beirut, 1974), (*Ba'th–Filastin*, vol. 4); X. vol. 5, 1964–1969 (Beirut, May 1975), (*Ba'th–Filastin*, vol. 5).
77   Michel Aflaq's lecture to party members in Berlin, July 1, 1963; *Nidal* 7, pp. 50–51.
78   Although the Arab Nationalists Movement failed to come to power, it was a partner in the UAR government and its representatives were members of the UAR and Iraqi governments. See Walid Kazziha, *Revolutionary Transformation in the Arab World* (London, 1975).
79   A secret report entitled "Taqrir Hawla Qadiyat Filastin" that the Filastin branch of the Ba'th Party in Lebanon submitted to the Eighth National Congress, April 1965, *Nidal* 6, pp. 139–146. The congress approved the report; see also: "The Congress's Recommendations on the Filastin Problem," ibid., p. 148; also *Ba'th–Filastin* 5, pp. 62–80.
80   The editor's introduction to the Report on the Seventh National Congress, *Nidal* 5, p. 254.
81   Ibid., pp. 44–80.
82   *Nidal* 1, pp. 121–122; *al-Sahafa*, Ba'th party organ, Beirut, February 16–17, 1960.
83   *Ba'th–Filastin* 4, pp. 24–26; *al-Sahafa*, Beirut, December 18, 1959, January 9, 1960.
84   Internal secret leaflet entitled "The Report on the 4th Regional Congress," distributed by the party in Lebanon, December 1959, *Nidal* 3, pp. 199–211; see also *al-Sahafa*, May 15, 1959.
85   *Nidal* 1, pp. 259–263; *Nidal* 4, pp. 121–124; *al-Sahafa*, January 9, 1960.
86   See: Faysal Hourani, *al-Fikr al-Siyasi al-Filastini 1964–1974* (Beirut, 1980), p. 19 [hereafter: Hourani, *al-Fikr al-Siyasi*]; "Recommendations of the Fourth National Congress," internal secret publication for members' only, October 1960, *Nidal* 5, p. 97; announcement of the Ba'th party on the seventh anniversary of the Algerian Revolt, *Nidal* 4, pp. 128–130; *al-Sahafa*, October 1, 1960.
87   Political decisions made at the Fourth National Congress, September 1960, *Nidal* 1, pp. 192–194; "Ba'th party memo to the Arab Foreign Ministers' Conference on the Filastin Problems and Algeria," Baghdad, January 31, 1961, ibid., pp. 228–238; the memo included

a section entitled "The Filastin Problem, the Political Entity Problem for the Palestinian People"; see also *Nidal* 3, pp. 261–263; an article entitled "Jabhat Tahrir Filastin fi Tariq al-'Awda," *al-Ishtiraki*, a party organ in Lebanon, March 11, 1961.

88 An announcement of the Iraqi Regional Ba'th Party, Baghdad, September 20, 1960, *Nidal* 2, pp. 84–85.

89 The Sixth National Congress, section entitled "Jabhat Tahrir Filastin," October 1963, *Nidal* 5, p. 167; a publication of the Socialist Ba'th Party-National Command entitled "The Decisions of the Sixth National Congress," October 5–23, 1963; and an identical publication entitled "The Decisions of the Sixth National Congress," Damascus, October 27, 1963.

2 Formulation of the Arab Strategy in the Arab–Israeli Conflict, 1964–1965: Prelude to the Six Day War

Part I The Intensification of Arab Activity, 1959–1963

1 Hashad, *Sha' b Filastin*, p. 104; Rushdi, *al-Sahyoniya,* p. 402; Shuqayri, *Min al-Qima*, p. 57.

2 Hashad, *Sha' b Filastin*, p. 101.

3 Majali, *Radio Amman,* March 23, 1960. Egypt accompanied this debate with an acute propaganda campaign against Jordan; *al-Aharam*, March 10, 1960, claimed that "Husayn wants to annihilate the Palestinian Entity and annex the West Bank, which is part of Filastin, to Jordan."

4 Hashad, *Sha' b Filastin*, pp. 105–6. See also Shuqayri's Report entitled *al-Kiyan al-Filastini* Appendix No. 3, which he submitted to the second Arab summit, September 1964, p. 9 [hereafter: *Shuqayri's Report*] in Ben-Gurion Archives, Ben-Gurion Research Institute, Sde-Boker, in private collection of documents consisting of Jordanian government files on the West Bank that include documents from the Jordanian security and intelligence services; this material was captured by the IDF in the Six Day War [hereafter: JGD – for Jordanian Government Documents].

5 For the text of the resolutions see Hashad, *Sha'b Filastin.*, p. 106; Musa Nasir, Jordan's foreign minister stated that "this resolution suited the Jordanian point of view, that is to say, the integration of the Palestinian Entity issue in the general planning, and transferring all the subject to one experts committee, this is what we initially have asked for," *Filastin*, January 11, 1961; also Zurayqat, the head of the Jordanian delegation to the Arab League, *Radio Amman*, September 22, 1963.

6 Mechanisms for Filastin affairs were established in Arab countries according to the decision of the League in March 1959. The decision was approved again at the meeting of the Arab League Council in September 1959.

7 *Shuqayri's Report*, pp. 15–16; *al-Jamahir*, Baghdad, September 1, 1963; *al-Hayat*, September 11, 1963; Naji Alush, *al-Masira Ila Filastin*, p. 123, claims that Iraq proposal was an "improvisation of the Iraqi foreign minister Talib Shabib."

8 See Jamal al-Shuqayri, *al-Kiyan al-Filastini* (n.d., n.p.), pp. 48–59; *al-Aharam*, September 11, 1963, September 14, 1963.

9 *Shuqayri's Report*, pp. 10–11, 17.

10 On the debate in government and the UN Security Council, see Aryeh Shalev, *The Israel–Syria Armistice Regime 1949–1955* (Jerusalem,1993), pp. 169–176. For details on the Security Council debate, see Yemima Rosental, ed., *Documents on the Foreign Policy of Israel,*Israel State Archives (Jerusalem, 1996) vol. 8, Document 444, pp. 760–771 (editor's note) [Hebrew]; on the government's decision of October 25, 1953, see also Document 473, 812 (editor's note): "1. If the chairman or Security Council respectfully requests that Israel [comply with] a temporary work halt so that the Security Council can clarify the matter in

a quiet atmosphere, [Foreign Minister Abba] Eban is authorized to agree to this. 2. Eban will be given further instructions to act in two directions: A. to gain time for the work's continuation. B. to obtain a guarantee from the United States that it will take a basically similar stand to the one it took on issue of the drainage of the Huleh."

11   The diversion operations that began in September 1953 quickly became the main issue in American–Israeli diplomatic activity and led to tension between the two countries that reached its climax in Secretary of State Dulles's announcement on October 20, 1953 that his government had decided to withhold financial aid from Israel. He explained the decision by Israel's refusal to fulfill its commitment and respect the demand of the chief of the UN observers to halt work in the north. The State Department pressured Israel to give a positive answer to the Security Council's request that it cease work in the north while the council debated the issue, after which the State Department would announce the renewal of American aid. The Israeli government accepted the offer; see Yemima Rosental, ed., *Foreign Affairs Documents*, Document 389, Telegram from Abba Eban to Moshe Sharett, September 24, 1953, p. 693.

12   This was actually the "Main Plan" (from the Boston office of Chas. & T. Main that prepared it under the supervision of the Tennessee Valley Authority). The plan dealt with using the exposed water in the Jordan River's drainage basin for irrigation in the Jordan Valley, *inter alia*, in order to enable Arab refugees to settle in the Jordan Valley located in the Kingdom of Jordan. According to the plan, the Sea of Galilee would serve as a regulated lake with two artificial lakes added to it – one, on the Yarmuk River, and the other on the Hasbani. See Yemima Rosental, ed., *Foreign Affairs Documents*, Document 778, 31 (editor's note); Rosental quotes The United Development of the Water Resources of the Jordan River Valley, prepared at the request of the United Nations under the direction of the T.V.A. by Chas. & T. Main Inc. (Boston, 1953). I wish to thank Moshe Yizra'eli for his clarification on the Johnston Plan.

13   See: *Foreign Relations of the United States (FRUS), 1952–1954*, vol. 14, Part 1, pp. 1347–1353. On the presentation of the letter of appointment to Israel, see the president's message to the Israeli prime minister, October 16, 1953, Yemima Rosental, ed., *Foreign Affairs Documents*, vol. 8, p. 436.

14   According to the plan the water would be distributed: Jordan (63.5%), Israel (32.5%), and Syria (4%).

15   On Johnston's activity from the American point of view, see *FRUS, 1955–1957*, vol. 14, and *FRUS, 1961–1953*, vol. 17, Near East 1961–1962, pp. 15–17. In January 1964 Israel and the United States held diplomatic talks. The Americans wanted to resolve the incongruities between the Israeli version and American Arab version over the distribution of the Jordan's water. Despite the understanding between Israel and the United States, the Americans failed to convince Jordan to enter negotiations – apparently because the subject was on the agenda of the Arab summit conference where a decision would be made. During these talks it was agreed that Israel would free 100 million cubic meters of water a year to Jordan; of this amount fifteen million cubic meters would be brackish water and 85 million cubic meters fresh water from the Sea of Galilee. On the other hand, Israel demanded that Jordan supply it with 25 million cubic meters of fresh water a year from the Yarmuk that Israel vitally needed in the irrigation season. (In this way Israel basically accepted the American–Arab version of the Johnston Plan).

16   See the document prepared by the State Department on February 6, 1961, entitled: "Jordan River Development," *FRUS, 1961–1963*, vol. 17, Near East 1961–1962, pp. 15–17.

17   *MER 1* (1960) p. 207; and *al-Hayat*, Beirut, September 12, 1959 and December 27, 1959.

18   *Al-Hayat*, December 24 and 27, 1959; *MER*, 1 (1960), p. 207. See also the announcement of the UAR Foreign Ministry on the discussions and participants at the conference, *Radio Damascus*, December 15, 1959.

19 On Arab and Egyptian activity during December 1959, see *al-Hayat*, December 12, 1959. The article discusses the Arab response to the Johnston Plan and notes that "fear on the Arab street still overpowers our sense of reason," *Al-Hayat*, December 15, 1959 (the article quotes Lebanese sources on this issue); December 16, 1959 (a public statement of the Higher Arab Committee, the organization of the Mufti Haj Amin al-Husayni, on Israel's plan to divert the Jordan); *al-Jarida*, December 17, 1959 (quotes well-informed sources in Amman that the Ghor Canal Project runs counter to the Johnston Plan); *al-Ayam*, Damascus, December 9, 1959 (discusses Arab activity to thwart Israel's scheme to divert the Jordan's water), December 10, 1959 (discusses the Arab League's talks on Israel's plan to divert the Jordan River; *Filastin*, Amman, December 16, 1959 (cites King Husayn's statements at a London press conference on Israel's plan to divert part of the Jordan River: "This act creates a dangerous situation not only for Jordan but for the entire Arab world. The Arab states are about to discuss the issue.") See also, *Kul Shay'*, Beirut, December 12, 1959; *al-Jumhuriya*, Cairo, December 17, 1959; *al-Nasr*, Damascus, December 10, 1959.

20 See the broadcasts and commentary of *Radio Cairo* and *Radio Sawt al-Arab* between December 1 and 15, 1959; *al-Aharam*, between December 2 and 31, 1959; and especially December 2, 5–7, 12–13, 15–16, 18–19, 25, 30, and 31.

21 See Telegram from British Embassy in Washington to Foreign Office London, December 11, 1959, Public Records Office, FO 371/142383 VR 1421/18, [hereafter: PRO]. It turned out that the British Foreign Office did not understand the background to the Arab outburst against Israel's plans to develop the Jordan's water, therefore the British turned to the State Department and requested information explaining this. The Americans referred them to the Johntson–Fawzi talks which they depicted as "secret information"; see also, Telegram from Amman to Foreign Office in London, December 16, 1959, PRO, FO 371/142383 VR 2/1426/20.

22 *Haaretz*, October 2, 1959.

23 Moshe Dayan, *Haaretz*, October 5, 1959.

24 Moshe Dayan, *Haaretz*, October 18, 1959. In his letter to the newspaper, published the next day, Dayan denied this version and claimed that "I said that if the Arabs refused an agreed upon system of distributing the Jordan's water and tried to deny our portion, we would take the water by ourselves, even if we had to overcome their opposition with force," *Haaretz*, October 19, 1959; see also *al-Hayat*, December 19, 1959.

25 *Haaretz*, November 19, 1959. According to information appearing in the Israeli daily *Davar* on December 10, 1959, "Yesterday political circles in Jerusalem repeated that the implementation of the plan for utilizing the Jordan's water stands at the same level of importance for Israel's development as freedom of navigation to Eilat, and none of the Egyptian threats on this issue will influence in any way whatsoever the implementation of the plan." The paper also noted that according to the Mekorot Company that was building the water carrier from the Sea of Galilee to Beit Shan, the average annual volume of the Jordan is 500 million cubic meters. According to the plan, at the finish of the first stage of the National Water Carrier 100 million cubic meters of water will channeled to the Negev, and with the completion of the entire project 200 million cubic meters will be used for irrigating fields in the Negev and other parts of the country.

26 *Al-Aharam*, December 5, 1959; commentaries on *Radio Cairo*, December 5–6, 1959.

27 *Al-Aharam*, January 5, 1960.

28 *Al-Aharam*, December 5, 1959. In this spirit *Radio Cairo* reviewed the headlines of the Cairene press on December 5, 1959 and noted that "Nasir demanded an immediate report of the counter-measures being taken in connection with the Israeli scheme. Israel was about to finish the practical work on the Jordan's diversion and suddenly announce that it had become operational . . . Two important meetings were held in Cairo and Damascus today to discuss this question."

On December 6, *Radio Cairo* stated in another press review that "Last night Nasir discussed in a government session Israel's steps in expropriating the Jordan's water. Also discussed were all the possibilities and moves that Israel's rulers were likely to take in order to divert the flow [of the Jordan River], a diversion that goes against the decisions of the UN and infringes upon the rights of the Palestinian refugees . . . The Ministerial Committee presented important recommendations at yesterday's government meeting headed by Nasir . . . Plans were drawn up for preventing Israel's diversion of the Jordan. Yesterday the government discussed all the necessary steps to prevent Israel from expropriating the Jordan's water . . . Nasir is facing up to Israel's threats."

29 Salah Salim, *al-Jumhuriya*, December 12, 1959. Against this background there were many reports in the Arab media in October and November 1960 regarding the urgent need to thwart Israel's diversion of the Jordan River. Apparently the declaration of Israel's minister of agriculture, Moshe Dayan, regarding the conclusion of the project at an earlier date than planned was one of the reasons for these announcements. On November 12, 1960 the newspaper *al-Hayat* reported, for example: "Sources in the Lebanese Ministry of Foreign Affairs have disclosed that the Lebanese government and the UAR agreed to speed up the diversion of their common tributaries in order to meet any surprise by Israel that has set next spring as the date for the diversion of the Jordan's water."

30 Nasir, *Radio Cairo*, December 23, 1963. See also Part II of this chapter.

31 See Hasanayn Haykal, *al-Aharam*, May 18, 1962, who cites the protocol of UAR government discussion in late 1959. See also Akram al-Hourani on this discussion in an article printed in the Syrian newspaper *al-Ayam* on June 13, 1962 in which he cites the protocol of UAR government discussion of November 29, 1959.

32 *Al-Sahafa* (the organ of the Ba'th Party in Lebanon), Beirut, February 3, 1960, October 19, 1960; *Ba'th–Filastin*, vol. 4, pp. 28–29.

33 See *al-Sahafa*, February 16, 1960; *Ba'th–Filastin*, vol. 4, p. 30; *Nidal* 3, pp. 67.

34 *Al-Ishtiraki* (the organ of the Iraqi Ba'th Party), January 1961; see also *Nidal* 2, pp. 95–97, *Ba'th–Filastin*, vol. 4, pp. 61–62; *al-Ba'th*, January 21, 1964.

35 *Al-Sahafa*, October 19, 1960; *Ba'th–Filastin*, vol. 4, pp. 57–59; see also *al-Ishtiraki*, January 1961.

36 Ba'th Party announcement, Lebanese branch, February 28, 1962, *Ba'th–Filastin*, vol. 4, pp. 81–85.

37 Ibid. See also the Arab–Socialist Ba'th Party announcement, Lebanon branch, April 18, 1962, *Ba'th–Filastin*, vol. 4, p. 85.

38 See *al-Sahafa*, February 16, 1960; *Ba'th–Filastin*, Vol. 4, pp. 29–34; *al-Sahafa*, February 17, 1960; *Nidal* 3, pp. 67–68.

39 See *al-Hayat*, March 1, 1960; *MER*, 1960, p. 20; Nasir's speech at the opening of the first Arab summit conference in which he surveyed the inter-Arab decisions on the water issue up until this time, *Radio Cairo*, January 13, 1964.

40 Haytham al-Kaylani, *al-Istiratijiyat al-'Askariya lil-Hurub al-'Arabiya-al-Isra'iliya 1948–1988* (Beirut, November 1991), p. 261 [hereafter: Kaylani, *Istiratijiyat*]. The writer cites the resolutions of the Arab League Council, August 28, 1960. According to Article 5 of the "Collective Security Pact" that was approved by the Arab League in April 1950, "A Permanent Military Committee would be established, made up of representatives from the staffs of the armies of the undersigned Arab governments, and would plan for joint defense and prepare the means and methods for implementing [joint defense] . . . The Permanent Committee will present reports to the Joint Defense Council on activity in the areas of its [the committee's] jurisdiction." For the formula of the "Collective Security Pact" see, Goren, *The Arab League*, pp. 383–384.

41 Kaylani, *Istiratijiyat*, p. 261. The author cites the resolutions of the Permanent Military Committee.

42 Kaylani, *Istiratijiyat*, pp. 261–262; *al-Hayat*, February 3–5, 1961 (see especially the report of its senior journalist, Salim Habaqi, on the discussions in the Arab League Council); *al-Jumhuriya* and also *al-Aharam*, February 3–5, 1961; *al-Siyasa*, Beirut, February 18, 1961. The supplement to the Collective Security Pact stated: "A military advisory body would be established [made up of] the heads of the general staffs of the countries' armies [that are members of the League] in order to supervise the Permanent Military Committee that is to be established according to Article 5 of the pact [see note 40 above] and in order to direct it on all issues that it is authorized to deal with as detailed in Article 1 of the military supplement. This body will receive Permanent Military Committee's reports and recommendations for approval before submitting them to the Joint Defense Council that is to be set up according to Article 6 of the pact. The military advisory body will submit its reports and recommendations on all matters related to the roles of the Joint Defense Council, for the review and approval of matters requiring approval." See Goren, *The Arab League*, p. 358.

43 Nasir, *Radio Cairo*, January 13, 1964; *al-Aharam*, April 27, 1961; Kaylani, *Istiratijiyat*, p. 262.

44 According to Article 6 of the Collective Security Pact of April 1950: "Under the supervision of the Arab League Council a Joint Defense Council will be established for dealing with all matters related to the implementation of Articles 2, 3, 4, and 5 of this pact. The Joint Defense Council will be comprised of foreign ministers and defense ministers of the undersigned states, or their representatives. The council's decisions, that are passed by a two-thirds majority will be incumbent upon the undersigned states." See Goren, *The Arab League*, pp. 484–485.

45 Article 5 of the Collective Security Pact's military supplement stated that "If no decision is made to select a general commander in a way other than the general agreement of the undersigned state governments, [then] it will be the right of the state, the majority of whose forces participate in military operations, to provide the general staff for the combat troops. The Joint Military Command will assist the general commander in handling military operations. See Goren, *The Arab League*, p. 388.

46 Nasir, *Radio Cairo*, January 13, 1964. For more information on the discussion and decisions of the Joint Defense Council, see also *al-Jihad*; *Filastin, al-Manar* – Amman, June 13–15, 1961; *al-Hayat*, June 15, 1961; *al-Aharam*, June 16 and 19, 1961; Kaylani, *Istiratijiyat*, p. 262, where he cites Decision Number 15 of the Joint Defense Council's Third Session, June 18, 1961.

47 Radio *Sawt al-Arab*, October 23, 1961.

48 See Itamar Rabinovich, "Hama'avak 'al Mei Hayarden Kamarkiv Basikhsukh Ha'aravi-Yisra'eli," (The Struggle for the Jordan's Water as a Factor in the Arab–Israeli Conflict), in A. Shmueli, Arnon Sofer, Nurit Cliot (eds.), *Artzot Hagalil*, II (Tel Aviv, 1983), pp. 863–868 [Hebrew].

49 Kaylani, *Istiratijiyat*, p. 262, quotations from the recommendations of the Arab chiefs-of-staff conference. On the conference's discussions, see also *al-Usbu' al-'Arabi*, December 16, 1963; *al-Safa'*, Beirut, December 17, 1963; *al-Hawadith*, Beirut, December 13, 1963; *al-Anwar*, Beirut, December 17, 1963; and *Ruz al-Yusef*, Cairo, December 15, 1963.

Part II   The Crystallization of Arab Strategy: Decisions of the First and Second Arab Summit Conferences, 1964

1 See *al-Thawra*, Damascus, December 5–7; *Radio Damascus*, December 4, 1963.
2 *Radio Damascus,* December 4, 1963.
3 *Radio Damascus*, commentary, December 15, 1963 (14:15 Israeli local time). See also *al-Ba'th* Damascus, December 11, 1963; *Radio Damascus*, December 18, 1963.

4   Nasir al-Din al-Nashashibi, *al-Jumhuriya*, Cairo, December 18, 1963.

5   Ibid., December 5. See also, Ahmad Sa'id, *Ruz al-Yusef*, December 15, 1963.

6   *Akhbar al-Yawm*, December 9, 1963.

7   *Al-Ba'th*, December 17, 1963, see also December 18, 1963; *al-Thawra*, December 20, 1963.

8   *Al-Ba'th*, December 17, 20; also *al-Thawra*, December 20, 1963.

9   *Radio Damascus*, commentaries, December 18, 19, 1963.

10   Ibid.

11   *Radio Damascus*, commentaries, December 18, 19, 1963.

12   Nasir, *Radio Cairo*, December 23; *al-Aharam* December 24, 1963.

13   Nasir, in Hasanayn Haykal, *al-Aharam*, May 18, 1962, quoting from the UAR Government Protocol.

14   Nasir, *Radio Cairo*, December 23, 1963; see also Nasir, *al-Aharam*, March 12–13, 1965 and November 20, 1965; Hasanayn Haykal, *al-Aharam*, May 18, 1965.

15   See Mahmud Riyad, *Mudhakirat*, vol. II (Beirut, 1986), pp. 282–283 [hereafter: Riyad, *Mudhakirat*, II.]

16   Kaylani, *Istiratijiyat*, p. 263.

17   Nasir, *al-Aharam*, January 14, 1964; Riyad, *Mudhakirat*, II, p. 284.

18   See Riyad, *Mudhakirat*, II, p. 284.

19   Summit resolution no. 11, January 17, 1964, as quoted in Kaylani, *Istiratijiyat*, p. 260.

20   Summit resolutions nos. 12, 13, 14 of January 17, 1964, as quoted in Kaylani, *Istiratijiyat*, p. 263. See also Riyad, *Mudhakirat*, II, pp. 284, 286.

21   Summit resolution no. 12, January 17, 1964, as quoted in Kaylani, *Istiratijiyat*, p. 264. see also Riyad, *Mudhakirat*, II, p. 285.

22   Arab Defense Council, fifth session resolution nos. 2, 5, 7 of January 10, 1965, as quoted in Kaylani, *Istiratijiyat*, p. 264.

23   Shuqayri, *Min al-Qima*, p. 50; *al-Aharam*, January 18, 1964.

24   Haykal, *al-Aharam*, September 15, 1964.

25   See second Arab summit secret resolutions nos. 18, 19 of September 11, 1964, as quoted in Kaylani, *Istiratijiyat*, pp. 262, 263. See also, Riyad, *Mudhakirat*, II, pp. 293–294.

26   Second Arab summit resolution no. 18 of September 11, 1964, as quoted in Kaylani, *Istiratijiyat*, p. 260. See also Nasir, *Radio Cairo*, May 31, 1965; Shuqayri, *Min al-Qima*, pp. 144–146; UAC officer commander's reports to the second and third Arab summits, as quoted in Ahmad al-Shuqayri, *'Ala Tariq al Hazima* (Beirut, 1972), pp. 262–269; Haykal, *al-Aharam*, September 15, 1964. See also *al-Ahram*, June 5, 1965; *al-Hayat* and *al-Jarida*, Beirut, September 10, 1964.

27   Kaylani, *Istiratijiyat*, p. 260; Shuqayri, *Min al-Qima*, pp. 143–144; Riyad, *Mudhakirat*, II, pp. 294–295.

28   Nasir, *Filastin Min Aqwal*, pp. 139–142.

29   JGD, Arab League Secretariat, Filastin Department, "top secret" protocol of the meeting of the heads of the Arab Delegations to the Mixed Armistice Commissions with Israel that was held in Jerusalem (February 27, 1964–March 1964). For the official English version of the Israeli–Jordanian Armistice Agreement of March 3, 1949, see Yemima Rosenthal, ed., *Documents on the Foreign Policy of Israel,* Vol. III (Jerusalem, 1983), pp. 713, 716. For the Israeli–Syrian Armistice Agreement of July 26, 1949, see ibid., p. 72.

3   Failure of the Arab Plan for Diverting the River Jordan's Tributaries

1   Details of the plan were published in the newspaper *al-Jumhuriya*, Cairo, October 24, 1964.

2   *Al-Aharam*, September 7, 1964.

3   See, for example, an article in *al-Hawadith*, Beirut, December 11, 1964; entitled "Is Lebanon a Member of the Arab League or NATO?" states that "Within less than two weeks

several incidents have occurred that cast doubt on Lebanon's 'neutrality' and raise the question whether Lebanon is [an] independent [state] or a U.S. satellite . . . Is it true that Lebanese leaders are involved with Zionist infiltration in the country? Is it true that the Lebanese diaspora is cooperating with the Jews?" In another article in the same issue the author warns those who criticize Egypt's economic situation – especially the anti-Egyptian press: "Their paid-for logic is of no value whatsoever, and they should thank God [for this], because once the Arab revolution senses that they pose a genuine danger to it or are holding back its progress, it will crush them and eradicate them from the earth."

4   See an article in *al-Jumhuriya*, Cairo, December 26, 1964; the article depicts the social and economic chaos in Lebanon and warns of the danger that it could turn into a Hong-Kong, and that "democracy in Lebanon is a sham and the Lebanese are proud of it . . . while this is the natural imperialist way of buying agents and the press against the interests of the Lebanese nation itself."

5   On Lebanon's position and considerations, see Riyad, *Mudhakirat*, II, pp. 293–294. These fears were later proven to be well-founded – during the civil war in Lebanon large contingents of Syrian forces entered the country in 1976.

6   Shuqayri provides details of the debate in the CAPM (mini-summit), see Shuqayri, *'Ala Tariq al-Hazima*, pp. 12–18; *al-Hayat*, January 12, 1965.

7   *Al-Hayat*, January 12, 1965.

8   Haykal, *al-Aharam*, March 19, 1965.

9   A report in *al-Hayat* on March 21, 1965 testifies to Lebanon's fear of commencing diversion operations: "According to political and military circles, the Tel Dan incident of March 17, 1965 demonstrated Israel's intention to obstruct diversion operations and deter Lebanon from beginning ground work."

10 *Al-Hayat*, March 21, 1965.

11 See Riyad, *Mudhakirat*, II, p. 300.

12 Shuqayri, *'Ala Tariq al-Hazima*, pp. 40–43.

13 *Al-Hayat*, August 3, 1965.

14 From the mini-summit's protocol, Shuqayri, *'Ala Tariq al-Hazima*, pp. 150–151.

15 See *al-Ba'th*, January 16 and 21, 1964; *Ba'th–Filastin*, Vol. 4, pp. 143–147.

16 "An Announcement of the National Command (Leadership) of the Arab Socialist Ba'th Party on the Palestinian Problem," June 14, 1965, *Ba'th–Filastin*, Vol. 5, pp. 97–111, 120–121; see also Munif al-Razaz, Ba'th party chairman, *al-Ba'th*, September 22, 1965; Moshe Ma'oz, *Syria and Israel: From War to Peacemaking* (Oxford, 1995).

17 *Ba'th–Filastin*, Vol. 5, pp. 97–111, 120–121; Ma'oz, ibid.

18 Chief-of-Staff Yitzhak Rabin said that following the incident and "the Armor Corps' bankruptcy in tank shelling" he called the commander of the Operations Branch, the general of the Northern Command, and the Armor Corps commander (two of whom had been in charge of the Armor Corps for many years) and said to them: "What do you have tanks for? You stand 800 meters from a house and you miss it . . . Talik (the commander of the Armor Corps) said: 'Don't worry, within three to five months it will be a different Armor Corps – [one] that can hit targets,' and he accomplished this, he really did." Yitzhak Rabin in an interview with Avi Shlaim, August 22, 1982. The interview was published in *Iyunim Bitkumat Yisra'el*, 8, 1998 [Hebrew].

19 *Radio Damascus* commentator, November 14–15, 1964; *al-Thawra*, Damascus, November 14, 1964.

20 *Al-Jumhuriya*, November 16, 1964; *al-Aharam*, November 16, 1964.

21 Regarding Israel's reaction, General Rabin said " there was a debate over the way of halting the diversion; and Moshe Dayan said (in his published article) ' I'd say that it is impossible to do this without a war.' And we said we would do this without [going to] war. There was a discussion, I asked Talik [Tal]: 'Can the tanks hit the tractors at this range?' He answered:

'Yes.' We staged an incident and knocked the hell out of the diversion. Then they moved further [away from the border], and in the end we got to a range of 4.5–5 [kilometers]. Afterwards we used the artillery and air force to wipe it out." Yitzhak Rabin in an interview with Avi Shlaim, August 22, 1982, *Iyunim*, vol. 8, 1998.

22 JGD, The General Secretariat of the Arab League, top secret protocol of the Third Session of the Heads of the Arab Delegations to the Mixed Armistice Commissions that was held between March 24 and 27, 1965.

23 *Radio Damascus* broadcasts, May 20, 1965. For details of the incident, see Shimon Golan, "Hama'avak 'al Mei Hayarden" (The Struggle over Jordan's Water) in A. Shmueli, Arnon Sofer, Nurit Cliot, eds., *Artzot Hagalil*, vol. II (Tel Aviv, 1983), pp. 853–862.[Hebrew]

24 Riyad, *Mudhakirat*, II, 300–301.

25 Munif al-Razaz, *al-Ahrar*, Beirut, June 7, 1965; *Ba'th–Filastin,* vol. 5, pp. 94–97.

26 Riyad, *Mudhakirat*, II, pp. 300–303; Shuqayri, *'Ala Tariq al-Hazima*, pp. 46–47.

27 Ibid.

28 Riyad, *Mudhakira t*, II, p. 301.

29 *Al-Hayat*, May 30, 1965; Shuqayri, *'Ala Tariq al-Hazima*, p. 65.

30 Shuqayri, *'Ala Tariq al-Hazima*, pp. 39–40.

31 Nasir, *Radio Cairo*, May 31, 1965.

32 *Radio Damascus*, commentator, June 1, 1965 (8:15 p.m.).

33 *Al-Thawra*, June 2, 1965.

34 On the dilemma of the Arabs in general and Syria in particular in light of Israel's determination to prevent the diversion operations, Yitzhak Rabin said: "We confronted them with a dilemma, to work [on the diversion] you cannot, if you do you'll be at war; and they did not go to war then. Then from a practical point of view, things joined together here and there, but these are two different operas: the problem of the demilitarized zones and the problem of a war over the diversion, and the third thing . . . the rise in terrorist activity after the establishment of the Palestinian entity, [and] after Yaser Arafat's struggle against Shuqayri by urging acts of sabotage . . ." Yitzhak Rabin, interview with Avi Shlaim, August 22, 1982, *Iyunim*, vol. 8, 1998.

35 On the IDF initiative, and the chief-of-staff's explanation on the nature of the IDF's response, see Golan, "*Hama'avak 'al Mei Hayarden*," pp. 853–862.

36 Riyad, *Mudhakirat*, II, p. 309; Shuqayri, *'Ala Tariq al-Hazima*, p. 85.

37 Shuqayri, *'Ala Tariq al-Hazima*, pp. 268–269.

38 Riyad, *Mudhakirat*, II, p. 303.

39 Decision number 34 of the third Arab summit conference, September 17, 1965, Kaylani, *Istiratıjıyat*, p. 263.

40 JGD, The Department for Filastin Affairs, Arab League Secretariat, report on the emergency meeting of the Heads of the Arab Delegations to the Mixed Armistice Commissions, January 9–11, 1966.

41 Shuqayri, *'Ala Tariq al-Hazima*, p. 150.

42 For details on the operation, see *Haaretz*, July 15, 1966.

43 Syrian Military spokesman's announcement, *Radio Damascus*, July 14, 1966.

44 *Radio Damascus*, commentaries, July 14–15, 1966; *al-Thawra*, July 15, 1966.

45 *Radio Damascus*, July 14, 1966.

4   The Rise of the Palestinians as a Factor in the Arab–Iraeli Conflict

Part I   Establishment of the PLO – The Jerusalem Congress, May 1964

1 Shuqayri, *Min al-Qima*, pp. 105, 135–138, 216; *Shuqayri's R.*, p. 6.

2 See Shuqayri, *Min al-Qima*, pp. 19–23, 72–90, 94–95; *al-Hayat*, October 16, 1963.

3 Shuqayri, ibid., p. 127; on different versions regarding his appointment see Alush, *al-Masira ila Filastin*, p. 188; Isam Sakhnini, "al-Kiyan al-Filastini 1964–1974," *Shuun Filastiniya*, No. 41–42, February 1975, pp. 46–72.

4 See Shuqayri in Abu Khatir, *Liqa'at Ma'a Jamal*, P. 143; Shuqayri, *'Ala Tariq al-Hazima*, pp. 3, 76–7, 104; *Shuqayri's R.*, p. 2; see also *Filastin*, Amman, November 2, 1963; *al-Manar*, October 17, 1963; *al-Jihad*, October 15, 1963; *al-Hayat*, October 13, 1963; *al-Akhbar*, Cairo, October 9, 1963.

5 Shuqayri, *Min al-Qima*, p. 183.

6 Ibid., pp. 61–2; see also King Husayn's statement, "We [he and Shuqayri] discussed all the surveys on the Palestinian Entity," *al-Jihad*, February 13, 1964.

7 *Shuqayri's R.*

8 *Al-Waqai' al-Filastiniya*, special edition, Gaza, May 30, 1962, pp. 737–741.

9 Shuqayri and Jordan found the composition of this delegation problematic. It consisted of three representatives from the PLF – *Jabhat al-Tahrir al Filastiniya* – two from *Harakat Tahrir Filastin*, one from *al-Shabab al-'Arabi*, one from *the Palestine Arab Office* in Washington, and four women.

10 See *al-Hayat*, August 11, 1964; *al-Usbu' al-'Arabi*, August 17, 1964; *al-Hawadith*, June 12, 1964; *al-Ahram*, September 7, 1964; *Akhbar al-Yawm*, July 25, 1964; *al-Jihad*, September 17, 1964; JGD, documents from files July–August 1964; Shuqayri, *Min al-Qima*, pp. 110–113.

11 Shuqayri, *Min al-Qima*, pp. 104, 116, 128–9; *Shuqayri's R.*, p. 5; JGD, documents from files August, October 1964; *al-Jumhuriya*, September 16, 1964.

12 Shuqayri, *Min al-Qima*, pp. 37–8, 44–7; *al-Jumhuriya*, January 10–21, 1964, May 29, 1964, September 16, 1964; see also Abd al-Rahman Yusef, *Mu'tamar al-Qima al-'Arabi*, brochure No. 8 in the series *Nidaluna*, Egyptian Armed Forces HQ, Cairo, March 1964; *Cairo Radio*, Commentaries, January 17, 21, 23, 25, 1964, May 28–30, 1964.

13 Sources close to King Husayn leaked to the Jordanian press Nasir's compliments to Husayn to improve his nationalist image among the Palestinians in the West Bank, see *al-Jihad*, January 15, 1965; *al-Manar*, January 15, 1964,

14 See Husayn, *al-Jihad*, February 13, 1964; Shuqayri, *Min al-Qima*, pp. 46, 50; Wasfi al-Tal, *al-Jihad*, July 5, 1966; *al-Difa'*, July 17, 1966.

15 Shuqayri, ibid., p. 94; Shafiq al-Hut's report on the PNC, *al-Hawadith*, June 5, 1964; *Kul Shay'*, May 23, 1964; JGD, ANM, *Adwa' 'Ala al-Mu'tamar al-Qawmi al-Filastini*, Jordan, June 1964; the ANM claimed that as a result of adding the members of the House of Deputies and of the Senate the numbers of the PNC increased from 200, as originally planned, to 381; PLO, *al-Nizam al-Asasi*, articles 13, 30, 31; PLO, *al-Mu'tamar al-Filastini al-Awal*, June 1964.

16 See Shuqayri, ibid., p. 95; *Shuqayri's R.*, pp. 60–61, 92–93; *al-Manar*, May 29, 1964; *Filastin*. Amman, May 30, 1964; Hut's reports, *al-Hawadith*, June 5, 1964; *al-Jarida*, May 30, 1964; JGD, ANM, *Adwa'*.

17 JGD, "*Security Order*", No. 2, May 24, 1964, "*Operation Order*" May 27, 1964, and documents dated May 28–30, 1964; *al-Hawadith*, June 5, 1964; *al-Jarida*, May 30, 1964.

18 See *Nidal 7*, pp. 63–6, 127–9; *Ba'th–Filastin*, Vol. 5 pp. 8–9, 70–73, 149–162; Abd al-Wahab al-Kayali, *al-Qadiya al-Filastiniya, Ara' wa-Mawaqif 1964–1966* (Beirut, December 1973), pp. 21–27, 222; Amin al-Hafiz, *Radio Damascus*, March 8, 1964; *Radio Damascus*, commentaries, February 27, 1964, March 30, 1964, May 28, 1964, June 16–18, 1964; *al-Ba'th*, May 8, 29, 1964, June 2, 1964; *al-Jarida*, June 7, 1964, statement by Syrian minister of information; *al-Difa'*, March 31, 1964.

19 *Nidal 7*, pp. 145–166, Aflaq's lecture in Paris June 21, 1964; *al-Ba'th*, May 24, 25, 29, 1964.

20 Salah Khalaf (Abu Iyyad), "*Mudhakirat*", *al-Watan*, Kuwait, October 9, 1978, *Filastini*, pp. 77–9; Shuqayri's version of these talks see Shuqayri, *Min al-Qima*, p. 9.

21 See Abu Iyyad, ibid.; Fatah, *al-Milad wa al-Masira*, pp. 32–3; Fatah, *Mafahim Asasiya*, for members only August 1972, p. 2; *al-Thawra*, Fatah Lebanon branch organ for members only No. 21, October 1976; Kamal Udwan (one of the founders of Fatah), *Lecture* in the first Cadres Course of Fatah, August 16, 1972, brochure for members only; *al-Ahram*, September 7, 1964.

22 *Filastinuna, Beirut*, No. 36, April 1964, p. 5; on the call for an "armed Palestinian revolution" see No. 38, July 1964, p. 5, No. 39, September 1974, pp. 28–31.

23 *Al-Ahrar*, March 15, 1964; *al-Muharrir*, March 16, 1964; *al-Hayat*, May 23, 1964; *al-Hawadith*, May 29, 1964; *Filastinuna*, No. 36, April 1964, p. 4.

24 Ghassan Kanafani, *Filastin, al-Muharrir* supplement, December 30, 1965.

25 JGD, documents from the years 1962, 1963, 1964 entitled "Jabhat Tahrir Filastin"; Subhi Muhammad Yasin, *Nazariyat al-'Amal li-Istirdad Filastin* (Cairo, 1964); also *al-Hawadith*, February 17, 1961, August 10, 1962; *al-Sayad*, May 3, 1962; *Kul Shay'*, November 10, 1961; *al-Anwar*, Beirut, May 20, 1962; *al-Hayat*, December 18, 1962, September 5, 1963; *al-Nahar,* August 21 1963.

26 *Filastinuna*, Beirut No. 11, November 1960, p. 3.

Part II Jordan's Confrontation with the PLO – National Awakening in the West Bank

1 Sa'id al-Tal, *al-Urdun wa Filastin, Wajhat Nazar 'Arabiya* (Amman, 1984) pp. 37–38.

2 On the development of the idea of "the revival of the Palestinian entity" and its impact on the Palestinians and Jordan, see Moshe Shemesh, *The Palestinian Entity 1959–1974, Arab Politics, and the PLO*, 2nd revised edition (London, 1996).

3 See Shuqayri, *Min al-Qima*, pp. 69, 104, 282–282, *'Ala Tariq al-Hazima*, pp. 102, 105, 163, 201–202; *al-Ahram*, February 12, 1967; *Ruz al-Yusef*, July 4, 1966, *Radio PLO*, July 1, 1965, July 18, 1966, September 10, 1966; Shafiq al-Hut, *al-Hawadith*, December 2, 196; Ben-Gurion Archives, Ben-Gurion Research Institute, Sde Boker, private collection of PLO documents from files captured by the IDF in the Six Day War in the PLO's Gaza offices (hereafter: GD – for Gaza Documents), Documents dated November–December 1966, circular from the PLO director of Moral Guidance Department, December 1966.

4 On Shuqayri's demands see Shuqayri, *'Ala Tariq al-Hazima*, pp. 90–92, *Min al-Qima*, p. 281; Shuqayri, *Radio PLO*, December 8, 1965, December 12, 1965, February 21, 1966 (PLO memorandum defining the PLO spheres of activities in Jordan); *al-Ahram*, October 9, 1965; *al-Jumhuriya*, December 13, 1965; *Akhir Sa'a*, January 5, 1966; *al-Muharrir*, December 16, 1965; see also *al-Jarida*, January 25, 1966; *Filastin*, Beirut, December 26, 1965; May 5, 1966; *al-Hawadith*, July 1, 1966; Jordan Foreign Ministry Proclamation, official brochure, *Mawqif al-Urdun Min Matalib Ra' is Munazamat al-Tahrir al-Filastiniya*, December 6, 1965 (hereafter: *J. Mawqif*).

5 Wasfi al-Tal, *al-Difa'*, July 17, 1966.

6 JGD, Wasfi al-Tal's top-secret memorandum to the ministers, the c-in-c and the c-o-s armed forces, governors, the head of General Intelligence and General Security, dated March 5, 1966, entitled "PLO" (hereafter, Tal's memorandum). On Jordan's conception, see also Tal, *al-Difa'*, July 17, 1966; *Filastin*, Amman, February 21, 1965; Husayn, *Ruz al-Yusef*, September 21, 1964; *Radio Amman*, March 29, 1966, in Shuqayri, *Min al-Qima*, p. 282; Husayn's letter to Nasir dated July 14, 1966, in Shuqayri, *'Ala Tariq al-Hazima*, p. 314; *J. Mawqif*; *al-Urdun wa Qadiyat Filastin*, Husayn's speech on January 5, 1966, official brochure.

7 Indeed, the dismantling of the National Guard allowed Husayn in 1965 to initiate his plan for the doubling of the Jordanian army, as approved by the UAC, through the plan for the formation within five years of five infantry-brigade groups and a number of armored

battalions. As a result, personnel strength of the army in 1967 was (according to Husayn) more than 55,000 soldiers. Husayn, *Radio Amman*, October 4, 1965, January 5, 1966, June 14, 1966 (speech in Ajlun), January 5, 1967; *al-Jihad*, July 28, 1966; *al-Nahar*, September 17, 1965; *J. Mawqif*; Tal, *al-Jihad*, July 5, 1966; *al-Ahad*, November 28, 1965; also *al-Hayat*, September 8, 1965.

8   Training of the residents of the front-line villages was done on a voluntary basis. But the villagers' response was very low, and the "operation" failed, just as the authorities had predicted and hoped. However, Jordan could claim to Shuqayri that it had distributed arms to the villages and so no longer needed the arms Shuqayri was offering for this purpose. See Tal, *Radio Amman*, June 6, 1965; *J. Mawqif*; JGD, documents from the files dated June 1965, October 1965, June 1966, and also Hittin Brigade, file entitled "Defense of the Front-line Cities and Villages," June 11, 1965; and 'Alia Brigade, file entitled "Jordanian Defense Plan," December 12, 1965.

9   *J. Mawqif*; Shuqayri, *Radio PLO*, December 8, 1965.

10 See Tal, *al-Difa'*, July 17, 1966; Shuqayri, *Min al-Qima*, p. 140; *PLO, GD*, Political Department file, the third Arab summit decisions concerning the Palestinian Entity and the PLA, Filastin Department, UAR Foreign Ministry.

11 See *al-Jihad*, June 20, 1965; *Filastin*, Amman, June 19, 1965, July 30, 1965; *al-Manar*, July 7, 1965; *al-Difa'*, July 7, 1965; *Akhbar al-Usbu'*, July 10, 1956; *al-Huriya*, August 16, 1965; Shuqayri, *Radio PLO*, August 6, 1965; on the PLA attitudes see *al-Huriya*, August 30, 1965; *al-Manar*, December 1, 1966,

12 See Shuqayri, *'Ala Tariq al-Hazima*, pp. 98–108, 114; *al-Jihad*, October 26, 27, 31, 1965; *al-Manar*, October 26, 1965, *al-Hayat*, October 27, 1965; on Jordanian propaganda attacks see *Filastin*, December 26,1965; *al-Manar*, December 26, 1965, *al-Jihad*, December 26, 1965; *al-Difa'*, December 28, 1965; see also Ahmad al-Shuqayri, *Kalimat 'Ala Tariq al-Tahrir 1965* (Gaza, January 11, 1966), pp. 100–141.

13 For text of the agreement see *Radio PLO*, January 8, 1966; *al-Hayat*, January 5, 1966; see also *al-Ahram*, January 31, 1966; *al-Akhbar*, January 4, 1966.

14 For text of the agreement see *Radio PLO*, January 10, 1966; see also *Radio Amman*, January 10, 1966; *J. Mawqif*.

15 *Filastin*, Amman, April 22, 1966; on the law of the Liberation Tax, July 14, 1965, Ben-Gurion Archives, Ben-Gurion Research Institute, Sde-Boker, private collection of documents from Egyptian directorate of General Investigation of the Internal Security Department in the Gaza Strip, that were captured by the IDF in the Six Day War, [hereafter: EGD, for Egyptian Government Documents]; see also PLO GD, report of the PLO EC to the third PNC.

16 JGD, Tal's memorandum, March 5, 1966.

17 See *al-Hayat*, April 14, 15, 1965; *al-Difa'*, May 8, 1966, July 6-8, 1966; *al-Manar*, July 10, 12, 14,15 1966; *al-Muharrir*, April 14, 1966, June 25, 28, 1966; *al-Nida'*, Beirut, June 28, 1966; *Sawt al-'Uruba*, October 23, 1966.

18 Husayn, *Radio Amman*, June 14, 1966; Husayn's letter to Nasir (July 14, 1966) in Shuqayri, *'Ala Tariq al-Hazima*, pp. 213–214.

19 Husayn, *Radio Amman*, June 14, 1966; first attack on Nasir published in *al-Manar*, May 1–2, 1966; Nasir, *Radio Cairo*, February 22, 1966, May 1, 1966; on February 23, 1967 Jordan announced that it recalled its ambassador in Cairo after Nasir's virulent attack on Jordan in his speech on February 22, 1967.

20 Fatah, internal circular, *op. cit.*; JGD, intelligence report on the PLO expected increased activities, May 17, 1966, also the report on the 3rd PNC, March 19, 1966; see also PLO, *al-Dawra al-Thalitha lil-Majlis al-Watani al-Filastini*, May 20–24, 1966; *al-Muharrir*, May 14, 16–17, 20, 1966.

21 On the IDF raid and its repercussions, see Moshe Shemesh, "The IDF Raid on Samu': The

Turning-Point in Jordan's Relations with Israel and the West Bank Palestinians," *Israel Studies*, Vol. 7 (1), Spring 2002.

22 EGD, Documents dated November–December 1966.
23 *Radio Amman*, November 13, 1966.
24 Wasfi al-Tal, *Radio Amman*, November 21, 1966; *al-Manar* (Jordanian daily, Amman), November 22, 1966.
25 JGD, documents dated November–December 1966.
26 Ibid.
27 Ibid.
28 Shemesh, *The Palestinian Entity*, pp. 67–80
29 Samir A. Mutawi, *Jordan in the 1967 War* (Cambridge, UK, 1987), p. 81, notes 63–64.
30 Sa' id al-Tal, *al-Urdun wa Filastin*, pp. 128–130
31 Husayn, *The Observer*, London, December 15, 1968.
32 On the announcement of the United Arab Kingdom Plan, its backgroudn, and repercussions, see Shemesh, *The Palestinian Entity*, pp. 222–226

5 The Fida'iyyun Organizations' Contribution to the Descent to the Six Day War

1 Fatah, Nabdha Ta'rikhiya, '*An-Harakat Fatah wa Zurouf Nash'atiha*, a brochure for cadres distributed by Lajnat al-Ta'bi'a wa al-Tanzim (no place of publication, 1968) [hereafter: *Fatah*]; Abu Iyyad (Salah Khalaf) *al-Tali'a* (Cairo, June 1969); Abu Iyyad, *Filastini bila Hawiya* (Kuwait, n.d.), pp. 57–58 [hereafter: *Filastini*].
2 Abu Iyyad, *Filastini*, pp. 61, 70.
3 Ghassan Kanafani, *Filastin* (a biweekly supplement to the Beirut daily *al-Muharrir*) December 30, 1965.
4 On the Fatah organization and its early development, see: Nabdha Ta'rikhiya, *Fatah*; *Fatah*, Internal Publication 106, al-Thawra al-Filastiniya al-Musalaha wa Marahil Tatawuriha, December 31, 1971; Limadha 'Ana Fatah, The Second Program, "al-Tala'i' al-Thawriya," 5; The Third Program, "Harb al-Tahrir al-Sha'biya"; see also Brochure 9, "Limadha Hiya Harb Tawilat al-Amad;" Brochure 10, "Kifahuna al-Musallah," p. 5.
5 Abu Iyyad, *Filastini*, pp. 79–81; Fatah, *Watha'iq 'Askariya*, vol. I (Beirut, 1968), p. 9 [hereafter: *Watha'iq*]. On the Fatah and its ideology, see: Yezid Sayigh, *The Armed Struggle and the Search for State* (Oxford, 1997).
6 Husam al-Khahtib, *Fi al-Tajriba al-Thawriya al-Filastiniya* (Damascus, 1972), p. 25. Khatib was a member of the PLO Executive Committee from September 1, 1969 to July 13, 1971. JGD, "Information on the West Bank Palestinians' Support of Fatah," District Governors' Weekly Reports, January, July, and September 1965.
7 The information on Fatah operations comes from the IDF spokesman and Israel Police monthly reports.
8 Fatah, *Watha'iq*, p. 67; see also: Sayigh, *The Armed Struggle and the Search for State.*
9 On Nasir's strategy, see Riyad, *Mudhakirat*, II, p. 293; on Nasir's policy in the conflict, see Shemesh, *The Palestinian Entity*, pp. 2–8, 55–62.
10 EGD, file entitled "Fatah 1965–1967."
11 On December 31, 1964, "Lebanese special security services discovered that the Fatah organization had decided to hatch the imperialist-Zionist plot as previously agreed upon by circles acting in the enemy's interest," *al-Anwar*, (a pro-Egyptian Lebanese daily), January 3, 1965; see also *al-Anwar*, January 11, 1965; *al-Jarida*, Beirut, May 19, 1965.
12 PLO announcement, *al-Hayat*, January 3, 1965.
13 *Al-Muharrir*, February 6, 1965; and *al-Anwar*, November 6, 1965.
14 *Filastin*, a biweekly supplement to *al-Muharrir*, December 30, 1965. The Egyptian media (as opposed to the Syrian media) refrained from publicizing Fatah announcements. It

sufficed in citing IDF reports of the organization's activities, and referring specifically to the "fida'iyyun" as the perpetrators of the sabotage. Nevertheless, the Egyptian press occasionally published articles by Palestinians– such as Amid al-Imam in *al-Jumhuriya* that sympathized with Fatah activity but avoided expressing open support of it.

15　See letter from the UAC C-in-C to the secretary general of the Arab League, cited by the chief-of-staff of the Jordanian army in his letter to the secretary general of the Arab League dated November 26, 1966, *Radio Amman*, November 27, 1966; see also, Wasfi al-Tal, *al-Hawadith*, June 18 1966; *al-Nahar*, June 19, 1965; JGD, letter from the commander-in-chief of the Jordanian army to the Jordanian chief-of-staff, May 24, 1965, that repeats the UAC's orders on this matter. See also, *Radio Amman*, Commentary, November 20 1966; *Radio Amman*, November 21, 1966.

16　JGD, documents from the file entitled "Meetings of the Heads of Arab Delegations to the Armistice Commissions, 1950–1967."

17　Ibid.

18　*Al-Hayat*, January 13, 1966.

19　*Al-Ba'th*, Damascus, September 12, 1965.

20　EGD, Fatah File; *Filastini*, p. 81; on Fatah activity in the Gaza Strip, see also: Hasan Khalil Husayn, *Safahat Majhula fi Hayat Abu Iyyad* (Amman, 1991), pp. 66–77.

21　On the change in the Egyptian position, see: *al-Jumhuryya*, June 23, 1966; *al-Ahram*, November 21, 1966; *Akhbar al-Yawm*, November 19, 1966; *al-Hawadith*, August 19, 1966, November 11, 18, 1966; December 2, 1966; *al-Muharrir*, November 21, 1966. On reservations about the timing of the Fida'iyyun operations, see: Kamal Rif'at (one of the revolutionary officers and a minister in the Egyptian government), *al-Ahram*, August 4, 1966; Salah al-Shibil, *al-Muharrir*, July 12, 17, 1966; *al-Hawadith*, December 2, 1966.

22　For expressions of Egyptian sympathy, see: The Egyptian press – "Israel is definitely suffering from fida'iyyun operations, and no one can deny the Palestinian people's right [to carry them out] . . ." *al-Ahram*, November 21, 1966; see also *Akhbar al-Yawm*, November 19, 1966. The pro-Egyptian Lebanese press – "Today al-'Asifa's *modus operandi* is presented as an example of all types of Palestinian operations, and all the areas of activity in the liberation [of Filastin] should become a large-scale version for activity [being carried out] by al-'Asifa's vanguard," *al-Hawadith*, August 19, 1966; see also *al-Hawadith*, November 11, 18, 1966.

23　Kamal Rif'at, *al-Ahram*, August 4, 1966; *al-Jumhuriya*, August 4, 1966.

24　Abu Iyyad, *Filastini*, pp. 87–88.

25　Salah al-Shibil (an activist in the Arab Nationalists Movement who generally expressed Egypt's position), *al-Muharrir*, February 6, 1967. The change in Egypt's position was highlighted when *Radio Sawt al-Arab* was the first station to broadcast Fatah communiqués on February 22, 1967 and one week later on March 1.

26　At a press conference held in Cairo on February 4, 1967, Nasir stated: "Regarding the Fida'iyyun, if the Palestinian people and the Palestinian entity organize themselves, then they have the right to defend their homeland . . . The Palestinian people is determined to demand its rights and not surrender its interests," Nasir, *Radio Cairo*, February 4, 1967; on the other hand, Nasir's personal representative, Hasan Sabri al-Khuli, declared on February 20: "We heartily congratulate every act designed to destroy Israel [that is carried out] by the Fida'iyyun or any other [group] . . ." *Ruz al-Yusef*, February 20, 1967.

27　*Sawt al-Arab* was the first station to broadcast Fatah communiqués of its January–February 1967 sabotage operations in the north and center of Israel. This was also the first station to transmit Fatah's March 1 bulletin about the killing of four al-'Asifa members who "were fulfilling their duty inside Israel."

28　For example, both *Radio Cairo* and *Radio PLO* broadcasts on February 20, 1967 gave an announcement of the "Abtal al-'Awda" organization about two explosions at water facilities in the north of Israel on February 15, 1967. The Cairo communiqué noted that "the fida'iyyun of the Abtal al-'Awda organization [linked to the PLO] struck at a number of Israeli targets on February 15, 1967 . . ."

29 Salah al-Shibil, *al-Muharrir*, February 6, 1967.

30 EGD, Fatah File; see also *al-Nahar*, January 10, 1967, containing a complaint by a Palestinian from the Gaza Strip over the arrest of al-'Asifa activists who had been caught circulating information about the organization.

31 Shuqayri "soared" in his September 1966 declarations: "We believe in a popular war for the liberation of Filastin . . . "

"The fida'iyyun are the elite of the Palestinian people and are our heroes . . . Our path is the armed struggle,." *al-Huriya*, November 21, 1966. He described the PLO as a fida'iyyun organization, claiming that, "The PLO should be regarded as a fighting fida'iyyun organization," *al-Muharrir*, November 21, 1966.

32 *Radio PLO*, February 2, 1967. Shuqayri linked fida'iyyun acts in Israel and Jordan, claiming that, "fida'iyyun activity faces two campaigns on two fronts: Jordan and Israel. This doubles Fida'iyyun heroism and adds honor and resolve to the Palestinian struggle." Shuqayri, *The Voice of Germany*, Cologne, July 10, 1967. For details on Abtal al-'Awda, see Yerid Saigh, *The Armed Struggle and the Search for a State*, pp. 134–135.

33 In a political communiqué on December 10, 1966, Fatah warmly congratulated "the PLO's initiative to extend immediate support to Palestinian fida'iyyun activity, discard its previous reservations, for the PLO's demand to assist the fida'iyyun's current activity both materially and morally, and urge the fida'iyyun commando forces to join the battlefield immediately." See Fatah, *Dirasat wa Tajarib Thawriya* (place and date missing), pp. 210–217; see also, *Sawt al-'Uruba*, Beirut, December 23, 1966.

34 "Taqrir 'an Qadiyat Filastin" presented to the "8th National Congress of the Ba'th," by the Ba'th's Filastin Branch in Lebanon, April 1965, Ba'th Filastin, Vol. 5, pp. 62–77.

35 Ibid., p. 76.

36 Ibid., pp. 77–79.

37 *Radio Damascus,* January 21, 1965; *Radio Damascus*, May 5, 30, 1965, September 6, 1965; *al-Ba'th*, August 27, 1965, September 17, 26, 1965, November 1, 1965; Abd al-Wahab al-Kayali, *al-Qadiya al-Filastiniya*, pp. 174–180, 194–197; *al-Ahrar*, Beirut, June 20, 1965, September 22, 1985.

38 The following excerpts illustrate the Syrian press's support of Fatah operations: An article entitled "al-'Asifa – the Fulfillment of our Dreams" appeared in the Damascene daily *al-Ba'th* on August 27, 1965. It claimed that al-'Asifa "is the fulfillment of Arab aspirations just as Algeria had been. The organization must be given tangible material assistance . . ." According to *al-Ba'th* on September 8, 1965: "[fida'iyyun] operations have put the Palestinian problem in a new light and on solid ground." The editorials of two Syrian dailies *al-Thawra* and *al-Ba'th* proclaimed on November 1, 1965 that, "The Arab states must encourage the fida'iyyun and help carry the struggle onto enemy's territory."

39 While the official Syrian position was distrustful of Fatah, a group of young officers was providing it with assistance. The dominant figures in the group were Hafiz al-Asad, commander of the Syrian air force, and Ahmad al-Suwaydani, the head of military intelligence. They helped Fatah run two training bases in Syria, one of them in al-Hama. Asad was instrumental in unloading Chinese weapons for Fatah at the port of Latakia despite the authorities' refusal. This alliance illustrates the degree of cooperation between Syrian intelligence officers and Fatah in this period in all areas of reconnaissance and intelligence gathering inside Israel. By the end of the period, Fatah was permitted to carry out sabotage acts in Israel across the Syrian border, or from the Lebanese and Jordanian borders when fida'iyyun saboteurs had penetrated these countries from Syria. See Abu Iyyad, *Filastini*, pp. 84–86; *al-'Awda*, No. 3, October 1965 (a Fatah-controlled bulletin of the

Palestinian Students' Union in West Germany, therefore it expressed the Fatah position); *Fatah* (an internal bulletin circulated among Fatah members in West-Germany), June 1966.

40 In April 1967, the Syrian chief-of-staff, Liwa (Maj. Gen.) Ahmad al-Suwaydani, accurately defined the goal of the "popular war of liberation"; "Israel is not a state, [it is] a military base for the imperialist camp. Therefore we must not wage a conventional war . . . The fida'iyyun form a basic element in a popular war . . ." Suwaydani, *al-Musawar*, Cairo, April 28, 1967. The regime added a new dimension to the doctrine of a "popular war of libera-tion." It termed it the "new strategy," or "offensive strategy" designed "to strike the enemy on his own territory, including civilian targets" in response to "Israeli aggression." See Rafiq al-Khuri, "What after the New Strategy in Damascus?" *al-Ahad*, Beirut, August 21, 1966. See also, *Radio Damascus*, August 22, 23, 1966; Dr. Zu'ayein, *Radio Damascus*, September 14, 1966; *Radio Damascus*, October 17, 1966 and January 9, 18, 1967; the Syrian minister of the interior, *Radio Damascus*, January 15, 1967.

41 Zu'ayein, the Syrian prime minister, *Radio Damascus*, April 18, 1966, 11 October 1966; the official Syrian spokesman, *Radio Damascus*, October 13, 1966; Atasi, *Radio Damascus*, December 7, 1966.

42 Hafiz al-Asad, on a visit to an airbase, *Radio Damascus*, May 12, 1966.

43 The official spokesman of the Syrian Foreign Ministry, *Radio Damascus*, August 14, 1966.

44 Dr. Yusef Zu'ayein, *Radio Damascus*, January 11, 1966; see also, the communiqué from the Syrian Foreign Ministry to foreign delegations in Damascus, *Radio Damascus*, October 13, 1966; in a conversation between the British military attaché in Damascus and the Syrian representative to the Israeli–Syrian Mixed Armistice Commission (MAC), Captain Adnan Abdallah, on November 20, 1965, the latter stated that "The Syrian government has no knowledge of al-'Asifa . . ." The British attaché also noted that Abdallah undoubtedly presented the official Ba'th position and that his statement should be taken with a grain of salt, see, PRO, FO 371/180658 E 10711/7G.

45 On sabotage operations on the Syrian border and Israel's response in 1967, see: *MER*, 1967, pp. 167–181.

46 For a survey of Fatah – Syrian relations from Fatah's point of view, see: *Fatah*, an internal publication, June 1966; *al-'Awda* (a bulletin of the Palestinian Students' Union in West Germany), No. 3, October 1965; see also, Abu Iyyad, *Filastini*, pp. 84–86; *al-Ba'th*, May 13, 1966; *Kifah al-'Ummal al-Ishtiraki,* July 17, 1966.

47 *Fatah, "al-Thawra al-Filastiniya wa Marahil Tatawuriha,"* internal publication, No. 106, December 31, 1969. A number of months before the Six Day War, the Syrian regime estab-lished the "Jabhat al-Tahrir al-Sha'biya al-Filastiniya," whose members were recruited from Palestinians members of the Ba'th. Their leader was Tahir Dablan, and they numbered close to a hundred members. This organization was designed to be the "military arm" of the "Palestinian section" of the Syrian Ba'th, headed by Lutfi Ghantus, and its goal was to carry out fida'iyyun operations in Israel. The Syrians also had charge of the "68th Palestinian Commando Battalion" (or "Jalal Ka'ush Unit") that took part in fida'iyyun operations. At the end of 1967 these organizations amalgamated into a new fida'yyun organization called "Talai' Harb al-Tahrir al-Sha'biya – Quwat al-Sa'iqa."

48 David Ben-Gurion, *Ma'rekhet Sinai* (*The Sinai Campaign*), (Tel Aviv, 1959), pp. 207–208 [Hebrew].

49 *Ben-Gurion Diary*, September 10, 1958, Ben-Gurion Archives, Ben-Gurion Research Institute, Sde Boker, Israel [Hebrew].

50 Mutawi, *Jordan in the 1967 War*, pp. 39–40.

51 Details on the crisis, including demonstrations, Jordanian police, and army directives are from JGD, documents dated April–May 1963.

52 Husayn, *Radio Amman*, April 23, 1963. In a speech before friendly, supportive delegations on April 28, he declared: "The loyal citizens [of the kingdom] will not surrender an inch of

Jordanian soil to enemies who wish to expand at the expense of this country," *Radio Amman*, April 28, 1963.
53   PRO, FO to Washington, FO371/170268 E 10741/1, April 28, 1963.
54   PRO, Tel Aviv to FO, FO371/170529 E 10819, April 11, 1963.
55   PRO, Cairo to FO, FO371/170274 E 103116/1, April 25, 1963.
56   PRO, FO memorandum, FO371/170182 E 1074/13, April 29, 1963; also, FO memorandum, FO371/170182 E 11265, April 29, 1963.
57   PRO, Cairo to FO, FO371/170274, E103116/1/a, April 30,1963; also, PRO, Cairo to London, FO371/17027, E103116/1/a, April 30, 1963.
58   Nasir's interview to the Lebanese newspaper *al-Muharrir*, *Radio Cairo*, April 2, 1963; see also, Hasanayn Haykal, in *al-Ahram*, May 3, 1963; and Nasir, in *al-Ahram*, July 23, 1963. But Nasir believed it unlikely that Israel would take military action according to the way the crisis was breaking. By late April he was assured that "the king would be able to control and overcome the crisis," National Archives, London to State Department, NND 939537, Box 3961, April 25, 1963; also, State Department memorandum, NND 39537, Box3961, April 24, 1963.
59   PRO, Tel Aviv to FO, FO371/170519, ER 1022/8/11, April 13, 1963; also, FO 371/170519, ER 1022/170, July 1, 1963 .
60   This section is based on various JGD files between 1965 and 1967 unless otherwise noted.
61   Attention was given to these instructions in a letter that circulated among unit commanders in late February 1965 regarding "evidence of a secret armed organization calling itself 'al-'Asifa' that is carrying out acts of sabotage in the occupied territory . . . we must make a maximum effort and [take] decisive measures to hunt down every member of this organization [Fatah] in order to uncover [its identity] and who is directing it. The arrest of members of this organization calls for tight surveillance along the armistice lines and close supervision in areas adjacent to the armistice lines that [the group] may use for setting up forward bases."
62   An expression of the regime's caution appears in Wasfi al-Tal's reply to a journalist from the Lebanese weekly *al-Ahad* (November 1965) regarding fida'iyyun operations in Israel: "In my opinion, the Palestinian campaign is not a campaign of individuals, heroic deeds, and personal sacrifice . . . I consider any organization whose Filastin activity deviates from the joint Arab plan as misdirected. I have great respect for these young men, and some of them are my friends. I admire their acts of bravery . . . but these acts [alone] are insufficient to liberate Filastin" (*al-Ahad*, Beirut, November 28, 1965).
       The Jordanian papers that published the interview with Wasfi al-Tal omitted, however, the section relating to the fida'iyyun lest it embolden Fatah members and Palestinians in Jordan who supported the organization. In this way, the vaguely defined policy encouraged troops in the lower ranks to help Fatah saboteurs infiltrate into Israel, and even the military and police were occasionally lax in obeying orders to ferret out Fatah activity.
63   Husayn, *Radio Amman*, October 4, 1965.
64   Moshe Zak, *Husayn 'Ose Shalom* (Husayn Makes Peace), (Jerusalem, 1996), pp. 80–82 [Hebrew].
65   Husayn, *Radio Amman*, May 25, 1966.
66   Tal, *Radio Amman*, November 21, 1966, following the IDF raid on the village of Samu'.
67   Husayn, *Radio Amman*, November 28, 1966. In this spirit, see: the Amman daily *al-Manar*, December 15, 1966. On Jordan's policy and its steps toward Fatah, see also: Husayn, *Amman Radio*, December 2, 1966; Wasfi al-Tal, *al-Muharrir*, October 24, 1966 and November 7, 1966, *al-Hawadith*, 18 November 1966 and January 6, 1967, *Sawt al-Arab*, January 19, 1967, and *al-Huriya*, January 23, 1967.
68   Husayn, *al-Manar*, February 10, 1967.

69   Statements made by King Husayn and prime minister Tal correspond with Jordan's propa-
      ganda line as opposed to that of Egypt, Syria, and the PLO. This can be seen in Tal's press
      conference on November 21, 1966, and in the communiqué by the chief of staff of the
      Jordanian army to the secretary-general of the Arab League in response to charges made
      by the commander of the UAC.
70   *Filastin*, November 27, 1966.
71   Husayn, *Filastin*, November 30, 1966.
72   Jordanian foreign ministry memorandum to the Secretary General of the Arab League
      (November 26, 1963) which included the Jordanian chief-of-staff reply to the United Arab
      Command and arguments pertaining Jordan's complaints against the United Arab
      Command's inability to assist Jordan during and after the IDF raid, *Radio Amman*,
      November 27, 1966.
73   Zak, *Husayn*, p. 91.
74   On the deterioration of relations between Jordan and the PLO–Shuqayri, see Shemesh, *The
      Palestinian Entity*, pp. 67–80.
75   Mutawi, *Jordan in the 1967 War*, pp. 77–78.
76   Ibid., p. 79.
77   Ibid., p. 74.

6   The Arab Military Build-Up

1   Section 5 of the "Collective Security Pact," see: Goren, *The Arab League*, p. 388. Decision
      Number 12 of the first summit, January 17, 1964, and the decision for Amer's appointment
      and the allocation of forces, see: Kaylani, *Istiratijiyat*, p. 164; Riyad, *Mudhakirat*, II, pp.
      284–285.
2   Riyad, *Mudhakirat*, II, pp. 284–285.
3   ADC decisions, numbers 2, 5, and 7, fifth session, January 10, 1965, see: Kaylani,
      Istiratijiyat, p. 264.
4   Riyad, *Mudhakirat*, II, p. 293.
5   Details on Ali Amer's report in the Lebanese press, see: *al-Jarida*, September 8–10, 1964;
      al-Hayat, September 8–10, 1964; *al-Nahar*, September 8–9, 1964; *al-Kifah*, September 9,
      1964.
6   Riyad, *Mudhakirat*, II, pp. 293–294; *al-Jarida*, September 13, 1964; decision number 19,
      second Arab summit, September 11, 1964, see: Kaylani, *Istiratijiyat*, p. 263; a section from
      the UAC commander's report to the Arab mini-summit, January 1965, see: Shuqayri, 'Ala
      Tariq al-Hazima, p. 266.
7   Ali Amer's report to the mini-summit, January 9, 1965; Amer's secret report was published
      in its entirety in *al-Nahar*, January 9–10, 1965.
8   Details of the discussion in the ADC and mini-summit, see: *al-Hayat*, January 12–13, 1965;
      al-Nahar, January 12, 1965; *al-Anwar*, January 12, 1965. On January 26, 1965 the ADC
      secretariat began to organize a committee that would prepare a proposal for a regulation
      to arrange the legal aspects of the entry of Arab forces into Arab states. UAC representa-
      tives and military, political, and legal representatives of all the Arab League states sat on
      the committee, but the problem clearly was not a legal one, but a political one, and without
      a basic change in the position of the Arab states involved in the matter (Lebanon, Jordan,
      and Syria) the committee's conclusions were meaningless.
9   *Radio Beirut*, January 22, 1965; According to Section 2 of the "Collective Security Pact":
      "The undersigned governments will view an armed attack on one of them, or a number of
      them, or on its forces as an attack on all of them; therefore they are obligated to extend
      assistance to the state or states being attacked, to immediately take all the necessary steps,
      either individually or collectively, and employ all the means at the their disposal including

the use of armed force in order to repulse the attack and restore security and peace," see Goren, *The Arab League*, pp. 383–384.

10 Shuqayri, 'Ala *Tariq al-Hazima*, p. 267; *al-Nahar*, May 28–29, 1965; *al-Jarida*, May 28–29, 1965; *al-Hayat*, May 29, 1965.

11 See: Mutawi, *Jordan in the 1967 War*, p. 59, the author's interview with Liwa (Major General) Amer Khamash.

12 Mutawi, *Jordan in the 1967 War*, p. 61, cites Husayn's speeches.

13 Mutawi, *Jordan in the 1967 War*, p. 62.

14 Husayn in an interview with the author, Mutawi, *Jordan in the 1967 War*, p. 61; in his January 25, 1967 speech, Husayn summed up Jordan's opposition to the entry of Arab forces into Jordan:
(A) The forces supposed to enter were small and aimed at closing the temporary gap in Jordan's defenses – a gap that Jordan has now filled with its own forces. (During the speech Husayn unprecedentedly reviewed the Jordanian army build-up since 1948).
(B) The entry of forces was liable to drag Jordan into a war with Israel that it was not ready for, and at a time when Egypt's troops were tied down in Yemen and the rest of the Arab armies – unlike Jordan – had not made war preparations according to the UAC's decisions.
(C) Jordanian authorities learned that the entry of these forces into Jordan was intended for subversive measures against the regime.
Husayn, *Radio Amman*, January 25, 1967.

15 Shuqayri, 'Ala *Tariq al-Hazima*, p. 269, quoting from Ali Amer's report to the third Arab summit, September 1965.

16 Shuqayri, 'Ala *Tariq al-Hazima*, p. 266; see also the article by Hasanayn Haykal in *al-Ahram*, that was broadcast on *Radio Cairo*, November 25, 1966.

17 For the decision's exact wording, see: Shuqayri, 'Ala *Tariq al-Hazima*, p. 17.

18 Details on the ADC discussions and the Prime Ministers Conference, see: *al-Hayat*, May 12–13, 1965; *al-Nahar*, January 12, 1965; *al-Anwar*, January 12, 1965; Shuqayri, *'Ala Tariq al-Hazima*, pp. 16–18.

19 Shuqayri, *'Ala Tariq al-Hazima*, pp. 47–49; *al-Nahar*, May 28, 1965; *al-Jarida*, May 28, 1965.

20 Shuqayri, 'Ala *Tariq al-Hazima*, p. 47, Riyad, *Mudhakirat*, II, p. 301.

21 *Al-Hayat*, May 309, 1965, June 1, 1965; *al-Nahar*, May 30, 1965, June 1, 1965; *al-Kifah*, May 30, 1965, June 1, 1965.

22 Shuqayri, 'Ala *Tariq al-Hazima*, pp. 88, 269; Riyad, *Mudhakirat*, II, p. 309; *al-Ahram*, September 12, 1965, quotes Ali Amer's report to the summit; *al-Hayat*, September 17, 1965; an article by Hasanayn Haykal in *al-Ahram*, broadcast on *Radio Cairo*, November 25, 1966.

23 See: Riyad, *Mudhakirat*, II, p. 314; Shuqayri, 'Ala *Tariq al-Hazima*, p. 209; *Radio Cairo*, November 25, 1966; Mutawi, *Jordan in the 1967 War*, p. 82; *al-Ahram*, December 8, 1966.

24 Details on Ali Amer's report, see: *al-Ahram*, December 8, 1966; *Radio PLO*, December 8, 1966; Shuqayri, *'Ala Tariq al-Hazima*, p. 259; Riyad, *Mudhakirat*, II, p. 314; an article by Hasanayn Haykal, in *al-Ahram*, broadcast on *Radio Cairo*, November 25, 1966; see also Fariq Awal (General) Ali Amer's letter to the heads of the Arab states and the secretary-general of the Arab League on August 19, 1968, at the conclusion of his role. Amer concentrated on the UAC's failure to fulfill its missions, Amin Huwaydi, *al-Furass al-Da'i'a* (Beirut, 1992), 3rd edition, pp. 545–549 [hereafter: Huwaydi, *al-Furass*].

25 For the decisions' exact wording, see: *al-Ahram*, December 11, 1966; *Radio Baghdad*, December 11, 1966; *Radio PLO*, December 11, 1966; Riyad, *Mudhakirat*, II, p. 314; the decisions and results of the ADC meeting, see: Shuqayri, *Radio PLO*, December 11, 1966; Akram Zu'aytar, *Radio Amman*, December 11, 1966; Syrian Foreign Minister Makhus, *Radio Baghdad*, December 11, 1966.

26 Husayn, *Radio Amman*, January 25, 1967.

27 As for the Iraqi initiative, the acting chief-of-staff of the Iraqi forces, Liwa (Major General) Mahdi Hamudi, stated on December 7, 1966: "The Iraqi units have crossed the border and halted, and are waiting for UAC instructions to engage Israel in combat." *Al-Jumhuriya*, Cairo, December 7, 1966.

28 Fawzi, *Harb al-Thalath*, p. 73.

29 Tal, *Radio Amman*, November 22, 1966.

30 Tal, *Radio Amman*, January 7, 1967.

31 Husayn, *Radio Amman*, January 25, 1967.

32 See: Shams Badran in his testimony in court after the Six Day War, *al-Ahram*, February 25, 1968; Fawzi, *Harb al-Thalath*, p. 73.

33 Mahmud Riyad, *Radio PLO*, December 8, 1966; *al-Ahram*, December 8, 1966; Riyad, *Mudhakirat*, II, p. 314; Shuqayri, *'Ala Tariq al-Hazima*, pp. 259–260; Haykal, *al-Ahram* that was broadcast on *Radio Cairo*, November 25, 1966.

34 Shuqayri, *'Ala Tariq al-Hazima*, p. 260.

35 See: *al-Ahram*, March 12, 1967; *MER, 1967*, p. 117; Shuqayri, *'Ala Tariq al-Hazima*, p. 274; see also, Ali Amer's letter at the conclusion of his role, Huwaydi, *al-Furass*, pp. 545–549.

36 Details on the ADC discussion, see: *al-Ahram*, March 13–14, 21, 1967; *al-Jumhuriya*, Cairo, March 24, 1967; *al-Hayat*, March 14–15, 1967; *al-Difa'*, Amman, March 14, 16, 1967; *Radio PLO*, March 12, 15, 1967; Shuqayri, *'Ala Tariq al-Hazima*, pp. 274–275; *MER, 1967*, p. 118.

37 *Al-Ahram*, March 15, 1967.

38 *Al-Muharir*, Beirut, March 18, 1967. In response to the ADC's decisions regarding the cessation of allotments to Jordan, Sa'ad Jum'a, the head of the Jordanian delegation to the Arab League Council that met in Cairo on March 17, 1967, said: "It is amazing that the state that refuses any Arab army to cross its borders in accordance with the UAC's decisions [the reference is to Syria] on the one hand is not considered having violated the decision, and on the other hand it receives money; a state that does not agree to the establishment of PLO units and the entry of Arab armies [into its territory] also receives money [the reference is to Lebanon]. This is taking place at a time when Jordan's only request of the UAC and the ADC is that the Arab states, without exception, comply with the ADC's decisions . . . Jordan is the first line of defense in the Arab world and for this reason it attributes no importance to the removal of Jordan and Saudi Arabia from any plan or the freezing of Arab commitments to it. The Filastin problem is Jordan's problem." *al-Hayat*, March 19, 1967.

39 See: Riyad, *Mudhakirat*, II, p. 283; JGD, documentation from the file "United Arab Command."

40 For the monetary aspect in the report of the Arab League's secretary-general to the mini-summit, see: *al-Nahar*, January 9–10, 1965; Ali Amer's report to the second summit, *al-Jarida*, September 8, 1964; Ali Amer's report to the mini-summit, January 1965, *al-Nahar*, January 9–10, 1965.

41 Husayn in an interview with Mutawi, see, Mutawi, *Jordan in the 1967 War*, p. 62; Husayn, *al-Ray al-'Am*, February 3, 1967; *al-Jarida*, September 8, 10, 1964.

42 *Al-Nahar*, September 8, 1964; *al-Jarida*, September 8, 10, 1964.

43 This section is based on JGD (which includes documentation from the operational file of the Western Front's headquarters); Operation Order 1/67 "Operation Husayn," May 25, 1967 (unless otherwise noted).

44 Husayn, *Radio Amman*, January 25, 1967.

45 In early 1967 the Syrian army numbered seven infantry brigades (three were mechanized or motorized), two brigades of medium tanks, two armored reconnaissance battalions, three commando battalions, and one Palestinian battalion that was "transferred" to the PLA.

46 Details on Lebanon's build-up plan were also published in *al-Jarida*, September 10, 1964 (the UAC commander's report to the second summit).

47 JGD, documents from the UAC file on the strengthening of Jordan, Syria, and Lebanon.

48 In January 1965, the Arab League secretary-general informed the mini-summit of the UAC's moves and read the UAC commander's letter (dated November 1, 1964):

"In light of the decision of the second Arab Kings and Presidents Conference in September 1964 to immediately begin the implementation of the technical operations for diverting the Jordan River's channel, the UAC has ordered the Arab forces to concentrate in areas close to the Israeli border. Furthermore, the military command has drawn up a plan for defending the countries bordering Israel if the latter attacks them during their implementation of these plans. The plan has determined the missions of each country's forces, and they have been ordered to present the general staff with detailed plans of their missions according to the UAC's instructions. The participating countries announced that they have amassed their forces. The Lebanese army headquarters has brought its operational plan, that is based on the UAC's instructions, before the ADC and has also demanded the UAC plan to be brought before the ADC according to Section A, on the basis of the authority of the general commander, as stated in the regulations of the UAC organization that was approved in the ADC meeting of June 1961. Therefore, the commander of the Lebanese army has requested that we bring this matter before you for discussion." The UAC commander's report to the Arab Prime Ministers meeting, January 1965, *al-Nahar*, January 9–10, 1965; Shuqayri, *'Ala Tariq al-Hazima*, pp. 268–269.

49 Ibid.; JGD, documents from the UAC file; Kaylani, *Istiratijiyat*, p. 265.

50 Kaylani, *Istiratijiyat*, p. 265; *al-Hayat*, May 30–31, June 1, 1965; *al-Nahar*, May 30–31, June 1, 1965.

51 Decision number 2 of the ADC from September 11, 1965, see: Kaylani, *Istiratijiyat*, p. 264.

52 Nasir, *Radio Cairo*, December 23, 1960.

53 The political announcement at the end of the second Arab summit, see: *Radio Cairo*, September 11, 1964.

54 The Arab League secretary general's report to the second summit, *al-Nahar*, January 9–10, 1965.

55 *Al-Jumhuriya*, May 31, 1965.

56 JGD, documents from the UAC file, ADC; Shuqayri, *'Ala Tariq al-Hazima*, p. 81.

57 Nasir, *Radio Baghdad*, February 20, 1966; *Radio Cairo*, February 22, 1966.

58 Hasanayn Haykal, *Radio Cairo*, October 15, 1966.

59 *Radio Beirut*, March 15, 1965.

60 *News Agencies*, March 16, 1967.

61 Nasir, *Radio Cairo*, February 6, 1967, quoted in an interview in the *Observer* (London).

62 *Radio PLO*, December 8, 1966, looks at sections from Ali Amer's report in the ADC; *al-Ahram*, December 8, 1966, also published sections from Ali Amer's report.

63 *Radio PLO*, December 10, 1966, quotes the council's decisions.

64 The sources that the section is based on: Mutawi, *Jordan in the 1967 War*, pp. 104–107; Zayd Rifa'i's statements in Efraim Kam, ed., *Husayn Poteyah be-Milhama* (Husayn Launches a War), (Tel Aviv, 1974) [Hebrew], [hereafter: Kam, *Husayn Launches a War*], pp. 46–48; King Husayn's statements, ibid., pp. 49–56; Sa'ad Jum'a's statements, ibid., pp. 279–286.

65 On Arab support forces to Jordan, their movement and participation in the war, see King Husayn's statements, in: Kam, *Husayn Launches a War*, pp. 87–90.

66 Fawzi, *Harb al-Thalath*, pp. 47–48.

67 Kam, *Husayn Launches a War*, p. 304; see also, Ali Amer's letter at the conclusion of his role, in Huwaydi, *al-Furass*, pp. 545–549.

68 Mutawi, *Jordan in the 1967 War*, p. 129; although this was the author's estimate, it reflects the Jordanian headquarter's position.

69 Riyad, *Mudhakirat*, II, p. 294.

70 Abu Khati, *Liqa'at Ma'a Jamal*, p. 141.

71 Riyad, *Mudhakirat*, II, p. 309.

7   Nasir's Steps toward the Six Day War: May 13 to June 5, 1967

1 Mushir (Field Marshal) Muhammad Abd al-Ghani al-Jamasi, *Mudhakirat Harb October 1973* (Paris, 1990), p. 37 [hereafter: Jamasi, *Mudhakirat*]. This information corresponds with what the Russians relayed to the Egyptians and to Anwar al-Sadat during his visit to the Soviet Union. See: Anwar el-Sadat, *In Search of Identity* (London 1978), pp.171–722. See also: Muhamed Hasanayn Heikal, *The Sphinx and the Commissar* (NewYork, 1978), pp. 174–755, in which he writes that " Semyonov the Soviet Deputy foreign Affairs, gave Sadat a confidential warning that . . . the Israelis were massing their forces on the Syrian frontier and that an attack was planned for some time between May 18 and 22. The Syrian had already relayed similar information to Cairo, their estimate being that eleven Israeli brigades were confronting them. On his return (14 May) to Cairo (Sadat) went to Nasir's house and described in fuller the warnings which he had received."

2 Fawzi, *Harb al-Thalath*, pp. 72–73.

3 Amin Huwaydi, Adwa' *'ala Asbab Naksat 1967 wa'ala Harb al-Istinzaf* (Beirut, 1975), p. 20 [hereafter: Huwaydi, Adwa'].

4 For a summary of different approaches that explain Nasir's moves from May 15, 1967 until the outbreak of war, see, Carl Brown, "Nasir and the June 1967 War: Plan or Improvisation." See also: Asher Susser, ed., *Shishah Yamim–Sheloshim Shanah*; Michael B. Oren, *Six Days of War: June 1967 and the Making of the Modern Middle East* (Oxford, 2002).

5 Riyad, *Mudhakirat*, II, p. 300.

Part I   Basic Factors in Syria's Estimation

1 See: Chapter 3.

2 Yitzhak Rabin, *Haaretz*, July 15, 1966.

3 Yitzhak Rabin, *Haaretz*, August 12, 1966.

4 In another interview Eshkol emphasized: "Against Syria's past campaign of provocation, Israel has restrained itself to the greatest extent, acting only when there was no other way to end these attacks. The recent events of last week indicate an increase in Syrian aggression. At any rate, we hope that the rulers in Damascus will consider the seriousness of the situation and avoid further provocations," *Yediot Aharonot*, September 14, 1966.

5 Eshkol, *Yediot Aharonot*, September 19, 1966.

6 Eshkol, *'Al-Hamishmar*, November 14, 1966.

7 Eshkol, *Davar*, January 6, 1967.

8 Abba Eban, *Jerusalem Post*, January 17, 1967.

9 Eshkol, *Haaretz*, January 18, 1967.

10 For details on the demilitarized zones along the Syrian border and the dispute with Syria over their status, see: Shalev, *The Israeli–Syrian Armistice Regime*.

11 *JGD*, Arab League Secretariat, Filastin Department, protocol of the meeting of the Heads of the Arab Delegations to the Mixed Armistice Commissions with Israel that took place March 24–27, 1965; also: Protocol of the Emergency Meeting of the Heads of the Arab Delegations to the Mixed Armistice Commissions with Israel that was held in Cairo January 9–11, 1966.

12 *Radio Damascus*, January 16, 1967.

13 Abba Eban, *Haaretz*, January 17, 1967.
14 See: *MER 1967*, pp. 172–173; *al-Hayat*, Beirut, January 26, 1967.
15 *Radio Damascus*, January 24, 1967. President Atasi explained Syria's participation in the talks: "From the beginning we were careful to point out that our agreement to participate in the meeting would not detract from our position on the Palestinian problem and our view that the correct path to liberation is through a popular war of liberation." *Radio Damascus*, February 8, 1967.
16 Muhammad al-Zu'bi, Syrian Minister of Information, *Radio Damascus*, January 27, 1967.
17 *Radio Damascus*, January 29, 1967.
18 *Haaretz*, February 3, 1967.
19 *Haaretz*, April 3 and 4, 1967; *MER*, 1967, pp. 174.
20 *Radio Damascus*, April 8, 1967.
21 Ben-Gurion Archives, Ben-Gurion Research Institute, private collection of Syrian government documents captured by the IDF on the Golan Heights in the Six Day War, [hereafter: *SGD*, for Syrian Government Documents].
22 *JGD*, documents from the UAC file and operations file of the Jordanian Army's western front headquarters.
23 Ibid.
24 *Radio Damascus*, May 5, 1966.
25 See: above, note 22.
26 Ibid.
27 On October 13, 1966, the Syrian defense ministry made the following announcement to the diplomatic representatives in Damascus: "On the pretext of fidai'yyun operations, Israel is preparing a wide-scale aggressive move against Syria. The plan is based on the collusion between Israel, colonialism, and Arab reactionaries. Israel uses the fidai'yyun operations and 'Asifa (Fatah) and the acts of the Palestinian people as a pretext, like it did in 1956 when it used fida'iyyun operations [as the reason for invading Sinai]. Its intention, as implied in the declarations of Israeli leaders, is to overthrow the [Syrian Ba'th] regime." *Radio Damascus*, October 13, 1966.
28 *JGD*, ibid.
29 Muhammad Ashawi, *Radio Damascus*, October 19, 1966.
30 Ibrahim Makhus, *Radio Damascus*, October 24, 1966.
31 See: above, note 22.
32 Ibid.
33 *Radio Damascus*, January 18, 1967; *al-Thawra*, Damascus, January 19, 1967, Syria petitioned the UN with a warning note, asking it "to use its influence on the United States, Britain, and Israel [to get them] to thrust aside their aggressive plans – if [the UN] wants to avoid setting off an international crisis."
34 *Haaretz*, May 27, 1967. For the wording of the message and the announcement to the *TASS News Agency*, see, Yosef Govrin, *Israel–Soviet Relations, 1953–1967: From Confrontation to Disruption* (London, 1998), pp. 292–294 [hereafter: Govrin, *Israel–Soviet Relations*].
35 *Pravda*, October 3, 1966; see also: Govrin, *Israel–Soviet Relations*, pp. 294–295.
36 Commentary of *Radio Moscow in Arabic*, October 8, 1966,
37 On the meeting of the Russian ambassador with Eshkol, see: Govrin, *Israeli–Soviet Relations*, p. 246.
38 The following entries illustrate typical Soviet propaganda statements as mentioned above:
On October 3, 1966 *Pravda*, the Soviet Communist Party newspaper, published an anti-Israeli article entitled "Rabin is Saber-Rattling" and stated: "Again Syria's southern border is restless. According to the foreign press, *military [forces] are concentrating on the Israeli side of the border* [my emphasis – M.S.]. A partial mobilization is underway in Israel. According to the Lebanese [newspaper] *al-Muharrir*, the decision was made to strike a

sudden and powerful blow at the Syrian border. The Israeli chief of staff is busy making operational plans for this strike. The chief of staff revealed in a newspaper interview in *Bamahaneh* that the real goal of the new schemes in Israeli army circles is [to undermine] independent Syria. Israel's aggressive preparations are taking place against the background of the rising pressure that the Imperialist superpowers and Arab reactionary forces are exerting on Syria. The Soviet Union is carefully following developments in the Middle East and Near East region that are taking place close to its borders."

On October 8, 1966 *Radio Moscow in Arabic* broadcast a program entitled "The Colonialist and Reactionary Scheming Against Syria Is Bound to Fail." The commentator stated: "Syria is not alone. The UAC backs it and so do the Arabs of all countries. [We recognize] the Imperialist conspiracy that the United States, Britain, and the reactionary Arab states have made against Syria."

On October 13, 1966 the following appeared in *Pravda*: "It seems that they wanted to get the Israeli steamroller moving. On the eve of a real plot, the chief of staff of the Israeli army announced that Tel Aviv's objective is to oust the present regime in Syria. *As of today several Israeli army brigades have been concentrated on the Syrian border*" [my emphasis – M.S.]. (In the same issue an editorial was published dealing with the same subject and written in the same style.)

On October 25 1966, the commentator of *Radio Moscow in Arabic* made a sharp and venomous anti-Israeli attack: "Israel, with the encouragement of the Imperialists, is waging a militant policy against Syria and openly threatening it with war. Its pretext is that groups of Palestinian refugees are infiltrating Israel from Syria in order to carry out acts of sabotage. After comparing this situation with that of 1956, and considering the excuse that Israel has chosen, other independent Arab states have expressed their willingness to come to Syria's aid. The Soviet Union has declared on more than one occasion that it will continue to support the Arab states, assist them in establishing their political and economic independence, and will defend the peace in the Middle East. Naturally the Soviet Union cannot remain indifferent to the attempts of the Imperialists and their allies to violate the peace in a region that borders directly on the Soviet Union."

On November 6, 1966 *Izvestia* published an article entitled: "Isn't it Time to Take Warning?": "All indications show that aggressive reactionary forces in Israel are preparing to attack Syria. Is the thinking of the Israeli politicians and military people so atrophied that they are grinding out the same old phonograph record of Suez a second time? Israel has no need to goad Syria, but the Imperialist superpowers and owners of oil monopolies have."

39 Govrin, *Israel–Soviet Relations*, pp. 303–305.
40 Foreign Minister Pachachi visited Moscow between April 17 and 22, 1967. A joint announcement published on April 26 after Pachachi returned to Iraq condemned "Israel's persistent acts of aggression against the Arab states" and expressed support "of the legitimate and inalienable rights of the Palestinian Arabs." *Tass*, April 26, 1967; see also *MER*, 1967, p. 29.
41 Zu'ayein and Suwaydani, *Akhir Sa'a*, November 9, 1966 discussed the agreement's significance:
(1) Suwaydani (the chief of staff): "The true value of the agreement is that it has an entirely different meaning from the UAC agreement. [The previous agreement] was a purely military one whereas the new one is primarily a political step, even in its military aspect."
(2) Zu'ayein (the prime minister): "The agreement opens up new horizons for us that can be measured in the hour of battle. For example, if Israel launches a large offensive against the sources of the Jordan [River] or Sinai, then we will learn the true meaning of the agreement." The agreement will be implemented against "any form of aggression by any side even if it turns out to be coming from a number of reactionary Arab forces."

42   The Egyptian chief of staff, Muhammad Fawzi, writes about this issue: "Despite the existence since 1966 of a bilateral agreement for joint defense against Israeli expansionism, actual coordination did not advance beyond the theoretical planning stage. Several alternative plans were drawn up, most of them defensive and preventive plans [*wiqa'iya*] that I personally designed along with the Syrian chief of staff, Ahmad Suwaydani. For example, an air strike against the enemy's airfields would be carried out by either of the two countries if Israel attacked one of them. But when the time came to implement these plans, none of them were put into practice." Fawzi, *Harb al-Thalath*, p. 48.

43   For details on the development of the April 7, 1967 incident, see: *MER*, 1967, pp. 176–177; see also: Eitan Haber, Hayom Tifross Milhamah (*Today War Breaks Out: The Reminiscenses of Brigadier General Israel Li'or* (Tel Aviv, 1987), pp. 142–144 [Hebrew], [hereafter: Haber, *Today War Breaks Out*].

44   *SGD*, documents from April 1967.

45   *Radio Damascus*, April 8, 1967. The same day, the Syrian minister of information outlined Syria's position on Radio Damascus in the following manner:

(1) This aggression has not at all surprised us. Since 1948 Israel has adopted a military, political, and propaganda line designed to strengthen the Israelis' morale, encourage Jews to immigrate to Israel, sow doubt in the heart of the Arab nation, and prove that Israel is so powerful that it would be difficult to wipe it off from the face of the earth.

(2) The March 8 Revolution by the Ba'th Party's leadership has raised new ideas for Palestinian activity and the problem of liberating Filastin . . . The problem of liberating Filastin is an inseparable part of the problem of liberating the Arab homeland and Arab people because the Zionist entity is first and foremost an Imperialist entity. From the national pan-Arab and logical point of view, the realization of the goals of the Arab nation – unity, freedom, and socialism – is inescapably tied to the destruction of the Zionist entity. The liberation of Filastin has to be done through a popular war of liberation. This is also how the third concept emerged – the conspiracy between [Arab] reactionaries, Zionism, and Imperialism.

(3) During the Sea of Galilee incident our planes penetrated [Israeli air space] and bombed the aggressor's bases for the first time since 1948. We announced that from now on we would respond to every act of aggression and hit the aggressor's bases.

(4) Israel has begun to focus its activity on the diplomatic level in order to twist public opinion to its favor; it is preparing for [additional] acts of aggression and a military operation. We ask friendly nations to take note of Israel's aggressive intentions on our border. Because of the ineffectiveness of its responses, Israel attacked Samu' in the attempt to restore the credibility that has been undermined among the Israelis themselves.

(5) Later, the Mixed Armistice Commission held talks, and as you know Israel tried to exploit these meetings in order to broach issues that were totally outside the jurisdiction of the meetings or the Armistice Commission. We demanded that Israel recognize the Mixed Armistice Commission's authority in the demilitarized zone; and we stipulated discussion of the cultivation issue on the evacuation of the military installations from the area.

(6) Once we realized that Israel was planning an offensive, we took all the necessary steps to prepare for it. Israel's aggression yesterday confirms our expectations and political and military assessments.

(7) We believe that yesterday's battle was neither the first nor last confrontation. Future battles will be harder and more brutal. Our goal has been stated: the liberation of Palestine and annihilation of the Zionist entity.

   The same day, President Atasi made the following statements about the incident: "The struggle between us and the reactionaries, Imperialists, and Zionists will not end in [one] battle, nor will victory [be attained] in [one] battle. All of us realize that our struggle will be lengthy. Our unbending method is the war of popular liberation that will purge all Arab

lands of the Zionists, Imperialists, and their henchmen among the [Arab] reactionaries."
Radio Damascus, April 7, 1967.

46 For details on sabotage activity in the period between April 7, 1967 and the outbreak of
the Six Day War, see: *MER*, 1967, pp. 177–178.

47 On the visit to Damascus of the delegation of the Egyptian prime minister, see: *MER*, 1967,
pp. 132–133.

48 Eshkol, *Haaretz*, May 12, 1967.

49 Eshkol, *Jerusalem Post*, May 14, 1967; *Kol Yisra'el* (voice of Israel), May 13, 1967.

50 Yitzhak Rabin, *Lamerhav*, May 14, 1967; *Hayom*, May 14, 1967; see also: *MER*, 1967, p.
179; Haber, *Today War Breaks Out*, p. 146, Yitzhak Li'or notes: "Rabin's statements
created a tempest. It had been accepted until then that we did not intervene in the regimes
of Arab states."

51 Additional statements that should be noted:
(1) Foreign Minister Abba Eban, speaking to students at the Hebrew University in
Jerusalem, warned Syria not to believe that it could send murderers to Israel without risking
an Israeli response; Israel would not agree to Syria's ongoing aggression, *Jerusalem Post*,
May 10, 1967.
(2) Eshkol, in a radio interview, declared: "It is clear that the terrorists' main staging area
is Syria, but we have determined the principle that we decide the time, place, and means for
responding to the aggressor." Eshkol added that Syria "had assumed the role of the
vanguard in the Arab campaign [struggle] against Israel." *Kol Yisra'el*, May 13, 1967.

52 On the report and its nature, see: *MER*, 1967, p. 187.

53 *Radio Damascus*, May 13, 1967, 13:15.

54 *Radio Damascus*, May 11, 1967; the following points were emphasized in the message:
(1) The Imperialists' support – Americans, British, and others – of the belligerent Zionist
entity, and their use of it to carry out their plots against the liberated Arab states as they
did in 1956, led to the April 7, 1967 flare-up.
(2) The Arab reactionary states' support of Israel and its aggressive intentions against Syria
stems from their common interest to overthrow the revolutionary regime in Syria. Thus
Israel was allowed to use Jordanian air space, in order to penetrate Syria and try to hit it
from the rear.

55 *Haaretz*, May 14, 1967; *MER*, 1967, p. 180.

56 *Radio Damascus*, May 13, 1967.

57 *Radio Damascus*, May 15, 1967; *MER*, 1967, p. 180

Part II Nasir and the Arab World March toward War

1 *Al-Anwar*, April 10, 1967.

2 *Al-Ahram*, May 13, 1967; on the visit, see also: *al-Aharam*, May 11–13, 1967; on the issues
discussed, see also: *al-Jarida*, Beirut, April 12, 1967; *al-Musawar*, April 14 and 21, 1967.

3 Nasir, *Radio Cairo*, May 1, 1967.

4 On the visit and its results, see: *al-Aharam*, April 18–23, 1967; *al-Hayat*, April 19, 1967;
MER, 1967, p. 132.

5 *Radio Damascus*, April 22, 1967.

6 Nasir, *Radio Cairo*, May 22, 1967.

7 Nasir, *Radio Cairo*, July 23, 1967: "We received information on an invasion of Syria from
different sources. We had information from our Syrian brothers that Israel had deployed
eighteen brigades opposite them. We checked this information and it turned out that Israel
had concentrated no less than thirteen brigades across from Syria."

8 Nasir, *Radio Cairo*, June 9, 1967. Dayan writes in his memoirs: "On May 12 an intelligence
officer from the Soviet Embassy in Cairo gave to Egyptian intelligence a confirmation of

the Syrians' report on Israeli military concentrations on the Syrian border." Moshe Dayan, *Story of My Life* (New York, 1976), p. 291.

9   Sadat, *In Search of Identity,* pp. 171–722 . Sadat adds, "When I arrived back in Cairo I realized that the Soviet Union had informed Nasir of this." See also: Amin Huwaydi, *al-Furass,* p. 74, and also the protocol of talks between Kosygin and Shams Badran, May 26, 1967, pp. 553–569.

10 Nasir, *Radio Cairo,* May 22, 1967. Nasir described the situation in his speech of the same day: "On May 13 reliable reports came in that Israel was concentrating a large force on the border estimated at between eleven and thirteen brigades and had decided to launch an attack on May 17, 1967. On May 14 Egypt took all the [necessary] steps and reviewed the matter with Syria. This was the aim of Fariq Awal (General) Fawzi's trip to Syria. He informed the Syrians that if Syria is attacked, Egypt would enter the battle from the first minute."

11 Nasir, *Radio Cairo,* May 23, 1967; Nasir, *Radio Cairo,* May 22, 1967.

12 Nasir, *Radio Cairo,* May 28, 1967. Eshkol did not make this announcement on May 12. Nasir apparently quotes a false version of the reports, also from the *UP News Agency* on May 12 and ties them to Eshkol's declarations from May 11 or 13.

13 Huwaydi, *Adwa',* p. 43.

14 Fawzi, *Harb al-Thalath,* p. 119; he added a note to this report: "This was a mistake. This number of Israeli brigades was not deployed on the Syrian front."

15 For the Hebrew wording of the order, see: Appendix 1 to the article by Major Yona, "Hareqa' le-Milhemet Sheshet Hayamim Be'ene ha-'Aravim: Misrayim ve-Knisatah la-Milhamah" ("The Background to the Six-Day War in the Eyes of the Arabs: Egypt and its Entry into the War") *Ma'rakhot,* 191–192 (July, 1968) [hereafter: Major Yona, "The Background to the Six-Day War"].

16 Fawzi, *Harb al-Thalath,* pp. 102–103.

17 *JGD,* documents from the operational file of the Western Front Headquarters.

18 Fawzi, *Harb al-Thalath,* p. 119; Fawzi points out that both comments are incorrect and proves that this was "a false estimate about the Israelis that created the wrong impression in the armed forces."

19 See: Cairo newspapers and broadcasts from May 15, 1967; see also the broad coverage in the Egyptian media, radio and press between May 16 and 17.

20 Ahmad Sa'id, radio commentary on *Sawt al-Arab,* May 17, 1967.

21 According to Husayn al-Shafi'i, the vice president, who was the president of the court during the trial of Shams Badran, the minister of war during the crisis and the war: "In the meeting that was convened by the president, and in which all his deputies took part, he presented the issue of the withdrawal of the UN Emergency Forces before the decision was made to demand their ouster: this act raises the likelihood of a military confrontation from 50% to 80%. The president turned his glance toward Mushir Amer who expressed full agreement with the president and agreed to carry out the plan since he believed that the army was able to deal with the expected upswing in the prospects of a military clash to 80%," *al-Ahram,* February 20, 1968.

22 Huwaydi, *Adwa',* p. 45.

23 For the wording of the letter to Rikhye, see: Fawzi, *Harb al-Thalath,* p. 73; *al-Aharam,* May 17, 1967; see also: Jamasi, *Mudhakirat,* p. 41; Mahmud Riyad, *Mudhakirat 1948–1978,* part 1, 2nd edition (Beirut, 1987) [hereafter: *Mudhakirat,* I].

24 Maj. Gen. Indar Jit Rikhye, *The Sinai Blunder* (London, 1980), pp. 19, 160–161.

25 On the chain of events, see: *MER,* 1967, p. 193.

26 See, for example: *MER,* 1967, p. 193; Muhammad Hasanayn Haykal, *Li-Misr . . . la li-Abd al-Nasir* (Cairo, 1976), pp. 77–79; Jamasi, *Mudhakirat,* p. 42; Riyad, *Mudhakirat* I, p. 37. Riyad tries to blame Mushir Amer for the decision as though Nasir was not partner to it.

27 Fawzi discusses the connection between the two issues: "When the UN Emergency Forces withdrew from the eastern border of Egypt with Israel the traces of the 1956 aggression were completely obliterated, and the conditions were set in the Sharm al-Sheikh and Ras Nasrani area to return to Egypt its lawful right to carry our searches in [its] territorial waters and take control of the Straits of Tiran," Fawzi, *Harb al-Thalath*, p. 76; see also the meeting between Kosygin and Shams Badran, above, note 9.

28 Fawzi, ibid., p. 71.

29 In another broadcast the same day (May 16, 1967) he said: "If Britain's participation in 1956 destroyed its ability to exist in the Arab East, then an American–Israeli scheme in 1967 will destroy any American presence [in the Middle East]. We ask you, Eshkol, to test our weapons. Put them to a test and it will mean the death and annihilation of Israel."

30 *Radio Cairo* repeated this charge on May 17, 1967: "Cairo perceives that the aim of the Israeli concentrations is not only to threaten Syria, but also Egypt." And he added: "Beginning today there is no longer any room for threats against an Arab country or an emerging Arab nation."

31 The Committee for Arab Affairs of the People's Council (The Egyptian Parliament) came out in support of the regime's position and discussed the inter-Arab situation in the presence of the foreign minister, Mahmud Riyad. An announcement published at the end of the meeting stated that the Egyptian people fully support the Syrian people in implementing the Joint Defense Agreement, and that the Egyptian people believe that the two revolutionary nations are dealing forcefully with Arab problems in general and the Filastin problem in particular, and that any aggression against an Arab state will be considered as aggression against the entire Arab homeland. *Sawt al-Arab*, May 16, 1967.

32 *Radio Cairo*, May 17, 1967.

33 On May 16, 1967 *Radio Cairo* announced: "Thanks to Egypt's declarations the Arab people feels that the Egyptian cannon muzzles are aimed at the Zionist conspirators, [Egyptian] planes are dealing with the enemy, and [Egyptian] tanks and soldiers are united in defending Arab interests." Another radio commentator noted that day: "Israel's special preparations and its aggressive posturing toward Syria is a new stratagem that recalls the tripartite aggression of 1956. The United States is playing the role of Britain and France. Nasir has made it clear that Israel is by itself incapable of carrying out these steps against the Arabs. If the tripartite conspiracy of 1956 failed, [then] the Israeli–American aggression will meet with failure even before it is launched."

34 *Al-Akhbar*, May 18, 1967.

35 *Radio Cairo*, May 17, 1967 quotes from the Israeli daily *Davar*.

36 *Radio Cairo* quotes *Yediot Aharonot*, May 17, 1967.

37 Commentary on *Radio Cairo*, May 17, 1967.

38 Fawzi wrote about the first steps taken at this stage: "In my opinion, I was already convinced at this same time that the steps toward mobilization were more of a feint [*harakiya*] than an actual threat against Israel, as in January 1960 when the Egyptian armed forces went on heightened alert and deployed their forces in Sinai [to prevent] Israel from attacking Syria. At that time the plan for an actual threat succeeded," Fawzi, *Harb al-Thalath*, p. 71.

39 *Reuters News Agency*, May 20, 1967; *Radio Cairo* reported this only on May 21, 1967 at 19:00.

40 *Al-Ahram*, May 18, 1967.

41 *Radio Cairo*, May 19, 1967.

42 *Al-Hayat*, Beirut, May 20, 1967.

43 Haber, *Today War Breaks Out*, pp. 153–154; Eshkol informed Rabin, Eban, Amit, Dinstein, Herzog, Levavi, and other figures that the call-up of 10,000 reservists had been approved, and that now, in light of Rabin's request, he was asking for an additional 2000.

In further consultation with Eshkol that day, it was agreed that the reserve call-up would reach 17,000.

44 Fawzi, *Harb al-Thalath*, p. 119. Fawzi notes that this report elicited disparagement in the enemy.

45 See: Eshkol's report to the Ministers Committee [for security affairs], May 21, 1967, in Haber, *Today War Breaks Out*, p. 161; on May 18, 1967 Israel expressed its opposition to Egypt's request to evacuate the UN Force and warned the superpowers about the consequences of this step.

46 *Al-Ahram*, May 18, 1967.

47 *Radio Cairo*, May 29, 1967 reported: "Israel fears that the defensive positions that Egypt seized will become offensive positions . . . The enemy has begun to transfer his forces from the north to the south, and is rapidly strengthening his positions with the help of helicopters."

48 *Radio Cairo*, May 19, 1967; *Akhbar al-Yawm*, May 10, 1967.

49 *Radio Cairo* commentary, May 19, 1967, 13:45.

50 Ahmad Sa'id, *Sawt al-Arab*, May 18, 1967.

51 *Al-Ahram*, May 21, 1967.

52 DSG.

53 On May 21 *Radio Damascus* broadcast an interview with the Syrian minister of information, Muhammad al-Zu'bi: "Eshkol's announcement refers not only to Syria, but to the entire Arab nation, therefore the masses must respond." We note that in the 10:30 broadcast on the same day [that is, before Egypt's official announcement that it was closing the straits] *Radio Damascus* reviewed the question of the straits: "The truth of the matter is that their closure has already been achieved and the question now is whether Israel and the colonialist powers will try to reopen them."

54 *Radio Baghdad*, May 20, 1967.

55 *Al-Hayat*, May 19, 1967.

56 Press announcement of the Saudi Embassy in Amman on May 27, 1967; the chief editor of the Saudi newspaper *al-Bilad*, Abd al-Majid Shabakshi, wrote a leading article on the Saudi dilemma whether to support Syria or Egypt: "We most definitely condemn the infidel regime in Syria, but this does not prevent us from standing on Syria's right hand side, we are obligated to do so from a religious standpoint and because of our common Arab identity. Our country's position on Zionism is unequivocal and reflects our belief in the Arab and Islamic need for solidarity in dealing with the threat stemming from the continued occupation of the usurped section of our great homeland . . . All of the Arabs' strength must be reunited in working together against Israel's existence in our region," *al-Bilad*, May 19, 1967.

57 *Al-Dustur*, Amman, May 31, 1967; the lead article in the Jedda newspaper *al-Madina* called for unity of the ranks, and observed that all the Arab powers are working together to fight for the common destiny. "On this occasion we must forget differences of opinion that [only] benefit the enemy."

58 *Al-Hayat*, June 1, 1967, the spokesman of the Saudi delegation in Brussels that accompanied King Faisal in his visit in Belgium, praised the rapprochement between Nasir and Husayn. The spokesman saw in the rapprochement the need for unity in the Arab ranks required for the coming war with Israel. He noted that this was King Faisal's message since the outbreak of the crisis in the region. The king himself stated in a press conference in Belgium: "No matter what the differences of opinion among the Arabs are, under no circumstances will they serve as an obstacle in the way of Arab solidarity and self-defense against the Israeli–Zionist brigand. Whoever supports Israel, Zionism, and its shameless aggression against the Arabs is against us", *al-Dustur*, June 4, 1967.

59 *Radio Amman* commentary, May 19, 1967.

60   *Radio PLO* commentaries, May 18, 19, 20, 1967.

61   Shams Badran, minister of war during the crisis, in his trial, *al-Ahram*, February 25, 1968.

62   Fawzi, *Harb al-Thalath*, pp. 78–80. Fawzi cites Nasir from a talk he held with him in 1968 on a discussion that took place on May 17, 1967. Fawzi also admits that a number of senior officers privately told him of the separation between the two moves, that is, between the takeover of Sharm al-Sheikh and closure of the straits. It is interesting to note that Baghdadi, who was member of the Revolutionary Council and vice president, relates in his memoirs that he believed that Nasir had to send the troops to Sharm al-Sheikh without taking steps against Israeli shipping so as not to push Israel into war, see: Abd al-Latif al-Baghdadi, *Mudhakirat* II (Cairo, 1977), p. 267; see also Jamasi, *Mudhakirat*, p. 46.

63   Fawzi, *Harb al-Thalath*, p. 70. See also: Jamasi, *Mudhakirat*, pp. 46–47.

64   Nasir, *Radio Cairo*, May 23, 1967. See also, Huwaydi, *al-Furass*, protocol of the Kosygin – Badran meeting, May 26, 1967, p. 555.

65   Fawzi, *Harb al-Thalath*, pp. 82–83. On May 24, 1967, the commander at Sharm al-Sheikh received a clarification to paragraph 5: "Ships escorting Israeli warships should be seen as enemy ships and be challenged." Thus, doubt was removed over the question whether escort ships should be stopped as foreign ships.

66   Nasir, *Radio Cairo*, May 26, 1967.

67   See: Fawzi, *Harb al-Thalath*, pp. 100–102; Yona Bandman, "Chatzi Ha'i Sinay Batfisa ha-Estrategit shel Mitzrayim 1949- 1967" ("The Sinai Peninsula in Egypt's Strategic Concept 1949-1962"), in Gedalia Gvirtzman, Avshalom Shmueli, Yehuda Gradus, Yitzhak Beit Aryeh, Menashe Harel, eds., *Sinai* (Tel Aviv, 1987), pp. 941–960 [hereafter: Bandman, "The Sinai Peninsula"], [Hebrew].

68   Fawzi, *Harb al-Thalath*, pp. 104–109, Fawzi adds that "This belief crystallized against the background of the enemy's psychological war. Thus, troop deployment was changed and the missions altered."

69   At 10:00 on May 26, the Mushir approved the "Fajr" offensive plan against the southern Negev and the "Ghasq" offensive plan against the northern Negev. He also instructed the air forces to prepare the "Asad" Plan to assist the "Fajr" Plan aimed at the southern Negev and Eilat. He ordered the 14th Armored Brigade to launch an offensive in the al-Haleisa region (northern Negev). The Field Marshal also took an interest in the preparations of the naval forces for carrying out a naval operation in the Gulf of Aqaba against Eilat, Fawzi, *Harb al-Thalath*, p. 112.

70   Bandman, "The Sinai Peninsula," see note 67 (above).

71   Fawzi, *Harb al-Thalath*, pp. 107–108.

72   Ibid., pp. 108–109.

73   Following Egyptian air reconnaissance and deep penetrations in the Negev and over Dimona, the IDF estimated that the Dimona reactor would become a target. This possibility was raised in the Ministers' Committee for Security Affairs on May 21. During the meeting Eshkol said: "I believe the Egyptians will try to stop Israeli passage through the straits and bomb the nuclear reactor in Dimona. This might be followed by an all-out attack." The committee decided, *inter alia*, that "if a certain security facility was bombed, [Israeli would retaliate] by bombing Egyptian airfields in Sinai and three or four additional airfields across the canal", Haber, *Today War Breaks Out*, pp. 162–163.

    According to Fawzi, Egypt carried out another air reconnaissance on May 26 "over the Negev at a depth of fifteen kilometers into Israel." Fawzi, *Harb al-Thalath*, p. 122.

    Mahmud Riyad notes in his memoirs: "At lunchtime on May 28 Amer told Nasir and me . . . laughing that Israel was in a panic just before noon because he had ordered two MiGs on a reconnaissance mission over Beer Sheva, and the planes had picked up Israeli transmissions that testified to the panic that had infected [the Israelis] from two Egyptian jets." Riyad, *Mudhakirat*, I, p. 44.

74   Haykal, *al-Ahram*, May 26, 1967.
75   Fawzi, *Harb al-Thalath*, pp. 123–124.
76   *EGD*, May 1967.
77   Riyad, *Mudhakirat*, I, p. 43; see also: Fawzi, *Harb al-Thalath*, p. 79.
78   Haykal, *al-Ahram*, May 26, 1967.
79   Ibid.
80   Amin Huwaydi, *Hurub Abd al-Nasir* (Beirut, 1979), p. 163 [hereafter: Huwaydi, *Hurub*].
81   Fawzi, *Harb al-Thalath*, pp. 120–121.
82   Nasir, *Radio Cairo*, May 26, 1967; Riyad, *Mudhakirat*, I, p. 44; see also the protocol of Badran's talk with Kosygin on May 26, Huwaydi, *al-Furass*, p. 588.
83   Nasir, *Radio Cairo*, June 4, 1967.
84   *Al-Jumhuriya*, May 25, 1967. Ahmad Baha' al-Din wrote in *al-Musawar*, May 26, 1967: "We realized a number of things from our experience in the Suez War: (1). Israel will not dare to enter an all-out war with Egypt by itself out of fear that Egypt's powerful air force will destroy it, and also because of its weakness, small population, loss of life on the battlefield, and Egypt's military superiority. (2). For these reasons Israel cannot carry out a large military action unless the atmosphere suits it. This means an atmosphere in which Egypt was in bitter conflict with the West so as to guarantee Western and American military and political support to Israel."
85   Huwaydi, *Hurub*, pp. 164–165.
86   Fawzi, *Harb al-Thalath*, pp. 106–110.
87   On the Soviet political activity toward Egypt during the crisis see: *MER 1967*, pp. 14–15, 188–190, 202–203; see also the Badran–Kosygin talk, note 82 (above).
88   *TASS*, May 23, 1967.
89   *Radio Cairo*, May 23, 1967.
90   Fawzi, *Harb al-Thalath*, pp. 93–94; Haber, *Today War Breaks Out*, pp. 83, 190–191; *MER 1967*, pp. 196, 197, 199.
91   Fawzi, *Harb al-Thalath*, pp. 95–100.
92   Huwaydi, *Hurub*, p. 162; see also the Badran–Kosygin talk, note 82 (above).
93   The following are selections from Soviet broadcasts:
     (1) "The situation in the Middle East remains tense because Israel continues to concentrate troops on the Syrian and Egyptian borders and the Sixth Fleet is still stationed in the Eastern Mediterranean." *Radio Moscow in Arabic*, May 28, 1967; "The Sixth Fleet is proceeding to Arab shores because of the situation created by radical circles in Israel." *Radio Moscow in Arabic*, May 28, 1967; Radio Moscow in Arabic bitterly attacked Imperialism calling it "the principle cause of tension in the region." *Radio Moscow in Arabic*, June 1, 1967; "The Western superpowers, first and foremost the United States, are inciting Israel to threaten the Arab states, especially Syria, with aggression," *Radio Moscow*, May 26, 1967.
     (2) "The tension on the border of the Arab–Israeli armistice lines is the result of American intelligence activity which is financed by the money of oil companies. American intelligence has initiated the war and is trying to topple the Syrian regime." ibid.
     (3) "Israel continues to threaten the peace of Syria, Egypt, and other Arab regions." *Radio Moscow Commentator*, May 30, 1967.
     (4) The broadcasts extolled "Arab unity in the face of Imperialist aggression;" "The stronger the unity, the greater the success in the struggle against the common enemy – Imperialism." Commentator on *Radio Moscow in Arabic*, June 1, 1967. The broadcasts also praised the "the Arab countries support of Syria's struggle to defend its independence and sovereign rights, as well as the aid that Syria and Egypt have received from Arab states, including Iraq which sent troops to Syria, and Algeria that has also decided to send a mili-

tary unit to the Middle East", ibid.; "The Arab states stand united as they never have before," *Radio Moscow in Arabic*, May 27, 1967.

94 Nasir, *Radio Cairo*, May 29, 1967.

95 Huwaydi, *al-Furass*, p. 565; for the precise wording of the message, see: Govrin, *Israeli–Soviet Relations*, p. 318; see also the Badran–Kosygin talk, note 82 (above).

96 See Badran's statements at his trial, *al-Ahram*, February 25, 1968. Mahmud Riyad recalls his meeting with the American ambassador on May 26, 1967 in which he handed him Nasir's message to President Johnson, and asked, "What are the chances of an Israeli attack against us?" and the ambassador replied, "Fifty percent," *Mudhakirat* I, p. 56; see also the Badran – Kosygin talk, note 82 (above).

97 Haber, *Today War Breaks Out*, pp. 187–188; and also Moshe Dayan, *Story of My Life* (New York 1976), pp.332–3; on June 4 Israeli intelligence informed the Ministers Committee for Security Affairs of Egyptian offensive plans in the southern and central fronts. The head of intelligence pointed out that the possibility is increasing hourly of an Egyptian–Jordanian–Syrian initiated attack. On the likelihood of an Egyptian air attack on the night of May 25/26 or 26/27, see the Israeli air force commander's report to Rabin on May 25, Yitzhak Rabin, *Pinkas Shirut (Service Notebook)* vol. I (Tel Aviv 1979), p. 163 [Hebrew].

98 Fawzi, *Harb al-Thalath*, p. 93, notes that "a short time after the meeting, it was publicized that the United States wanted to invite Vice President Zakariya Muhi al-Din for a visit [to Washington] to work out a political solution to the conflict in the region. In my humble opinion, the American invitation was designed to lengthen the time for preparations and alert the Israelis, especially after both the United States and Israel realized the Egyptians' determination to challenge Israel militarily by blocking the Gulf of Aqaba to Israeli shipping *and after reports were leaked regarding [plans for] an Egyptian air strike at daybreak on May 27, 1967, and detailed orders that had already reached advanced airbases in el-Arish and el-Sir whose forces were supposed to take part in the strike"* [my emphasis – M.S.]. The memo of the Egyptian ambassador in Washington undoubtedly relates to his meeting with Secretary of State Dean Rusk on May 26 in which Rusk expressed American apprehension over an Egyptian surprise attack and called for restraint on the part of Cairo while Washington used its influence to restrain Tel Aviv.

99 *MER, 1967*, p. 197.

100 Nasir, *Radio Cairo*, May 26, 1967.

101 Nasir, *Radio Cairo*, May 28, 1967.

102 Nasir, *Radio Cairo*, May 29, 1967.

103 This position was identical to Egypt's on Israeli shipping in the Suez Canal, a position that Nasir expressed in 1959.

104 The following anti-American broadcasts were transmitted on *Radio Cairo* and *Sawt al-Arab*:

    Radio Cairo, May 20, 1967: "An Israeli–American–Western plot has been hatched against Syria. The essence of the American scheme is the shift from an Israeli attack against Syria to the American defense of Israel's existence. All of America's plots in the region are intended to assault the region's progressive forces in the hope of striking them one after the other."

    Ahmad Sa'id, *Sawt al-Arab*, May 25, 1967: "It has been shown beyond all doubt that the United States supports Israel in all of its recent steps. The United States plan in the region has been adapted to Israel's fears by concocting a scheme between the two countries against the revolutionary Arab states."

    Radio Cairo, May 26, 1967: "We say to the United States, your Imperialist-Israeli bases will be destroyed and your interests [in the region] will come to an end. Everyone knows this except you." *Sawt al-Arab*, May 27, 1967: "The United States initiates everything that happens; it is the same as Israel."

105 Nasir, *Radio Cairo*, July 23, 1967. The following is the complete version of the passage:

"By our decision to move troops [into Sinai] and take the initiative in removing the danger from Syria, we were fully aware, from an international point of view that if we launched a first strike in a military campaign, we would be exposing ourselves to intolerable consequences. First, we would have to deal with direct American military involvement against us on the pretext that we fired the first shot. I would like to call your attention to several points regarding this factor.

First, there were the American warnings. You may have read about them. President Johnson's advisor summoned our ambassador in Washington at a late hour and told him that Israel obtained information that you are about to launch an attack that will put us in a very difficult situation. He asked us to restrain ourselves and mentioned that he had asked the same of Israel. I too received messages from the American president about the UN, requesting that we show restraint.

The second point . . . is that the next day the Russian ambassador handed me a message from the Soviet prime minister asking us to show restraint and alluding to his message to the Israeli prime minister. The Soviet prime minister noted that an Egyptian [military] operation would endanger the world.

The third point is that the whole world was against war. President De Gaulle's statements were clear: France will determine its position according to whoever fires the first shot.

Later the American presidential envoy [Yost] arrived. He said that an [Egyptian] vice-president should go to the United States. I agreed, on assumption that he meet with Johnson and inform him of our position. Afterwards I sent a message to the American president stating that we would welcome a visit of the American vice president, and at the same time I was ready to send Vice President Muhi al-Din to Washington for a meeting with him in order to clarify the Arab position. The next day I received a positive answer regarding Muhi al-Din's trip to Washington to meet with Johnson, requesting that the visit take place on Tuesday, June 6, 1967. We all know that [Israeli] hostilities began on June 5, 1967. We were in the midst of extensive political and diplomatic activity and were justified in not thinking that the explosion would come so quickly"; see also Huwaydi, *Hurub*, pp. 156–157.

106 On the Israelis' deliberations that were almost identical to Nasir's but whose conclusions were different, see Dayan, *Story of My Life*, pp. 338–349.

107 Fawzi, *Harb al-Thalath*, p. 107.

108 Ibid., pp. 124–127.

109 Ibid., pp. 126–127.

110 Ibid., pp. 109–110.

111 For the exact wording of the order, see: Major Yona, "The Background to the Six-Day War," Appendix 2.

112 The following are some of Amer's operational orders that were based on his assessments:

Directive No. 20/67, May 30: "An enemy surprise attack can be expected with its maximum armored strength in Sinai's southern axis." For this reason Amer ordered a realignment of his forces.

Directive No. 24/67, May 31, ordered a light mechanized force [Force Shazali] that had been waiting six days on the northern axis [May 22–28] to move in the direction of the southern axis for defensive purposes.

A directive from June 2, stated that the eastern region's assignment was to defend the Kuntilla– Qusseima–Umm Qataf–Rafah–el-Arish region in order to push the enemy back, destroy his forces, and prevent them from reaching the Suez Canal. According to the directive, the main defensive effort would be concentrated at Kuntilla, Qusseima, Umm Qataf, Hasne, and el-Mitle.

The Egyptians expected an IDF airborne operation either to the north or south of Ras Nasrani on the morning of May 29, and wanted close air cover over the region. After the region commander examined the plan, he concluded that a parachute drop was impractical since it required control of the Sharm al-Sheikh coast and the guarantee that an advanced force would be attached to the airborne forces.

113 Fawzi, *Harb al-Thalath*, p. 95; Jamasi, *Mudhakirat*, pp. 70–71.

114 Nasir, *Radio Cairo*, May 29, 1967.

115 *Al-Ahram*, May 30, 1967. Nasir sent a message to President Johnson on May 2 mentioning, *inter alia*, the Palestinian problem and "the basic fact that has been completely ignored [that] we view the rights of the Palestinian people as the most important issue to be recognized; the aggressor's armed forces have expelled a nation from its homeland and converted them into refugees on the border of their homeland." Riyad, *Mudhakirat* I, p. 48.

116 Mutawi, *Jordan in the Six-Day War*, p. 104.

117 Ibid., p. 106.

118 Sa'ad Jum'a, *Radio Amman*, May 24, 1967.

119 According to Mutawi, in *Jordan in the Six-Day War*, p. 119, "The agreement between Nasir and Husayn stipulated that in the first stages of the war on the Egyptian front Jordan's role would be to maintain a defensive profile and commence a limited offensive aimed at tying down the Israeli forces – otherwise the Israelis would concentrate their forces on the Egyptian and Syrian fronts. Jordan would expand its limited mission only after the fulfillment of two conditions: [one] that Iraqi and other [Arab] forces arrived at the front, and [two] solid information that developments on the Egyptian front were going as planned [in Egypt's favor]. Only after these two conditions were met would the Jordanians expand their operations on the front and enter the attack stage." On Husayn's request from Nasir and the latter's reply, and on Husayn's trip to Cairo, see also: Al-Husayn, *Mihnati ka-Malik* (Amman, 1978), (French version, 1975).

120 Husayn, *al-Hayat*, June 2, 1967.

121 Husayn said: "[We] are meeting the challenge of aggression as one nation, one hand, and one heart. This is a formative stage for our nation. [Under] these precarious circumstances there is great hope that we will attain our goals and retrieve our rights . . ." Nasir expressed his gratitude and appreciation to Husayn for this step and the [king's] initiative in coming to Cairo:

"We have had our differences but the present situation of the Arab nation compels us to take this step . . . We are dealing with a challenge not only from Israel, but also from its supporters . . . the United States and Britain, as everyone in the Arab nation knows. Today we have signed an agreement. Since this morning we have been holding military and political talks, and have agreed on everything. This has great meaning for the entire Arab nation. The Egyptian, Jordanian, Syrian, and Lebanese armies are stationed on Israel's borders in order to deal with the challenge, and backing us are the armies of Iraq, Algeria, Kuwait, Sudan, and the entire Arab nation. This act [of solidarity] will astound the world. Today the Arabs are in battle array, at an hour most needed. Israel, the United States, and Britain must realize that our decision is unswerving. This is not a question of the Gulf of Aqaba; this is a matter of the rights of Filastin." *Radio Cairo*, May 30, 1967.

122 The following are selected responses to the agreement and its ramifications:

The commentator on *Radio Cairo*, May 30, 1967: "The Arab armies have completely encircled Israel. In the past Israel has occasionally smitten Jordan, like in the Samu' attack, and other times Syria. But today it will do nothing, and if it does, it will be pulverized from all directions." According to the agreement: "If military operations commence and either of the two states is attacked, the enemy will face an army that includes both Egyptian and Jordanian forces. If we take into account the joint Egyptian–Syrian defense pact, then we can begin to fathom the dimension of Israel's encirclement." The commentator concluded:

"The Arab nation has arrived at the most important stage in its history. All of the Arab people will march in unison toward the realization of this goal."

On the same day the commentator Ahmad Sa'id emphasized "the tremendous importance" of the pact, and regarded it as a giant leap forward toward attaining the goals of the Arab nation. He pointed to the political and military benefits of the agreement and continued discussing the following day: "We are entering a campaign from which we must emerge the victors, not the losers as the Imperialists forced on us in 1948. Beginning yesterday, the Arabs' frontlines with Israel have greatly increased. The Jordanian border is 642 kilometers long, and the length of all the Arab countries' borders with Israel totals 950 kilometers." In contrast, on May 31 *Radio PLO* emphasized the Palestinian aspect [the West Bank and Palestinian population in Jordan] of the pact: "This agreement guarantees peace on the Jordanian border, serves the common struggle, and offers the Palestinian people a venue for their groundbreaking participation in the struggle. Today the battle for Filastin will determine Arab history."

On May 31 *Sawt al-Arab* spoke of "the brilliant historic victory" that the Arabs have won with the signing of the joint defense pact with Jordan that has created a united front against Israel. "The joint defense pact immediately bonded the military forces of Jordan and Egypt, and now the Jordanian–Israeli front is like the Sinai front in strength, concentration of forces, and preparations for the assault on the enemy in order to destroy and annihilate him . . ."

One hour after this broadcast *Radio Cairo* called attention to "the great shock that has overtaken the Israeli Imperialist circles after the signing of the joint agreement with Jordan. The agreement has forced the Israelis to open their eyes to the fact that they are surrounded on all sides by Arab forces . . . and that the agreement has rendered their situation extremely precarious."

123 Radio Damascus broadcast this assessment on May 28 at 13:30 (Israeli time):

"The whole world is asking: What will happen in the war that is on the verge of erupting in the Middle East? Has a turning point been reached? Has the struggle shifted from the military to the diplomatic sphere? And the most important question: What kind of diplomatic activity is taking place in the Arab camp?

124 Asad, *al-Thawra*, May 20, 1967.

125 Atasi, *Radio Damascus*, May 22, 1967.

126 *Al-Ba'th*, June 2, 1967 published a front-page article entitled "The List of the Kings' Betrayals in Filastin," that described how "King Abdullah handed over the Gulf of Aqaba to the Zionists." *Radio Damascus* announced on June 4 that, "The Arab masses cannot be duped or led to uncertainty because of their long-standing experience in the struggle. Unlike in the past, they are now fully aware that their enemies are the Zionists, Imperialists, and traitorous Arab reactionary regimes."

127 *Radio Damascus*, June 2, 1967.

128 *Radio Damascus*, June 3, 1967. On the Russians' position on Atasi's request to visit Moscow, see the conversation between the Egyptian ambassador in Moscow, Murad Ghalib, with Marshal Grechko on May 24, in Huwaydi, *al-Furass*, pp. 581–582.

129 *Radio Damascus*, May 23, 1967.

130 Fawzi, *Harb al-Thalath*, pp. 144–145.

131 On June 4 Iraq announced that it was joining the Egyptian–Jordanian joint defense pact. The Iraqi government convened a special meeting and resolved to prevent the export of oil to any country involved in aggressive acts against any Arab country. It also decided to summon a meeting of the Arab oil producing states in order to coordinate this policy.

Part III   The Arab Propaganda Campaign

1   *Sawt al-Arab*, May 31, 1967.
2   *Radio Cairo*, May 29, 1967.
3   *Radio Damascus*, May 23, 1967.
4   *Radio Cairo*, May 27, 1967.
5   *Sawt al-Arab*, June 4, 1967.
6   Haykal, *al-Ahram*, May 26, 1967.
7   *Radio Damascus*, May 23, 1967, intensified its incitement of the masses, exhorting them "to excise the Zionist cancer. Fight, O Arabs! Fight because victory is yours! Follow the example of the Algerian and the Vietnamese people!"
8   *Sawt al-Arab*, June 3, 1967.
9   *Al-Hayat*, May 30, 1967.
10 *Al-Quds*, East Jerusalem, June 2, 1967.

Part IV   Conclusion and Evaluation

1   Shafi'i [the chief justice in the trial of Shams Badran], *al-Ahram*, February 25, 1968.
2   Abd al-Karim Abu al-Nasr, *al-Nahar*, Weekly Supplement, December 31, 1967; see also: Nasir's message to Husayn, March 13, 1961, in Haykal, *al-Ahram*, May 11, 1961; see also, *al-Ahram*, March 3, 1961.
3   Nasir, *Radio Cairo*, May 26, 1967.
4   Nasir, *Radio Cairo*, May 29, 1967; Nasir continued to repeat this version until the war.
5   Nasir, *Radio Cairo*, April 2, 1963.
6   Bandman, "The Sinai Peninsula"; *MER, 1967*, p. 204.
7   Nasir, *Radio Cairo*, July 23, 1967; Nasir accurately described his plight after he received information and realized that Israel was planning to attack Syria:
    "What could we have done? We could have waited and satisfied ourselves with publishing a verbal declaration and sending telegrams of support. But if this country had acted like this, it would have given up its mission, purpose, and even its identity. The Syrians and we were committed to a joint defense pact. We do not regard our agreements with fellow Arab states or other nations as merely ink on paper. We honor [them] and see them as binding commitments. There was something between the Syrians and us, as there was between any other Arab country and us, stronger and more lasting than agreements and pacts. There was and will always be the belief in the common struggle and common destiny. Therefore we had to take definite practical steps to deal with the danger overshadowing Syria, especially since the threats of Israeli leaders, politicians, and military figures against Syria had been made publicly in the press and UN, and left no doubt in anyone's mind [of Israel's real intentions], therefore there was no time to weigh and mull over matters or procrastinate."
    During a May 28 press conference Nasir stated: "We could not allow Israel's threat against Syria to pass in silence. We could not accept [a threat] like this against Syria or any other Arab country. Therefore the Egyptian armed forces had to be deployed in forward positions so they could intervene effectively to counter any aggression. After this, most of the events proceeded according to plan without any surprises." *Radio Cairo*, May 28, 1967.
8   Nasir, *Radio Cairo*, December 23, 1958.
9   See: discussions of the Arab Defense Council, December 1966 and March 1967, *MER*, pp. 185–189.
10 Nasir, *Radio Cairo*, May 26, 1967.
11 Haykal, *al-Ahram*, May 26, 1967.
12 Nasir, *Radio Cairo*, May 26, 1967.
13 *Sawt al-Arab*, May 26, 1967.

14 Nasir, *Radio Cairo*, May 29, 1967.
15 Nasir, *Radio Cairo*, May 30, 1967.
16 Nasir, *Radio Cairo*, May 26, 1967.
17 Nasir, *Radio Cairo*, May 28, 1967.
18 Nasir, *Radio Cairo*, May 26, 1967.
19 Huwaydi, *Adwa'*, pp. 25–26; Fawzi, *Harb al-Thalath*, pp. 31–45.
20 Fawzi, *Harb al-Thalath*, pp. 3–4.
21 Ibid., p. 57; Jamasi, *Mudhakirat*, pp. 68–69.

8 In the Wake of the Six Day War

1   For the resolutions of the Khartoum summit see, Hut, *'Ishrun 'Aman*, pp. 252–253; Shafiq al-Hut, "Nahwa Istiratijiya 'Arabiya Jadida," *Shuun Filastiniya*, 109, December 1980, p. 20; Kaylani, Istiratijiyat, pp. 228– 229, quoting the resolutions of the fourth Arab summit, nos. 39, 40, 43, of September 1, 1967; see also, *al-Ahram*, September 2, 1967.
2   For the summit's announcement see, *al-Jumhuriya, al-Ahram*, September 2, 1967.
3   Haykal, *al-Ahram*, December 29, 1967.
4   See Haykal, *al-Ahram*, February 26, 1971, quoting Nasir in his meeting with Fatah's leaders; see also, Nasir in his meeting with king Husayn August 21, 1970, in Abd al-Majid Farid, *Min Mahadir Ijtima'at Abd al-Nasir al-'Arabiya wa al-Duwaliya 1967–1970* (Beirut 1979), p. 249.
5   Farid, *Min Mahadir*, pp. 92–93; Hut, *'Ishrun 'Aman*, pp. 160–161.
6   Huwaydi, *Hurub*, p. 249.
7   For Nasir's and Husayn's speeches in the summit, see Farid, *Min Mahadir*, pp. 90– 94, 102; Hut, *'Ishrun 'Aman*, protocol of the summit's debates, pp.160–163; see also Ahmad al-Shuqayri, *al-Hazima al-Kubra 2* (Beirut, 1973), pp. 214–216.
8   Farid, *Min Mahadir,* pp. 95–96; Hut, *'Ishrun 'Aman*, pp.167–169.
9   Shafiq al-Hut, *al-Filastini Bayna al-Tih wa al-Dawla* (Beirut, May 1977), pp. 70–71.
10 Shuqayri, *al-Hazima al-Kubra 2*, pp. 190–197; Hut, *'Ishrun 'Aman*, pp. 142–148.
11 Hut, *'Ishrun 'Aman*, p. 148.
12 Hut, *'Ishrun 'Aman*, pp. 156–157; Shuqayri, *al-Hazima al-Kubra 2*, pp. 212–213.
13 Hut, *'Ishrun 'Aman*, pp. 158–159.
14 Hut, *'Ishrun 'Aman*, pp. 159–162.
15 Farid, *Min Mahadir*, pp. 94–95.
16 Farid, *Min Mahadir,* pp. 98–103; also Shuqayri, *al-Hazima al-Kubra 2*, pp. 226–227.
17 Hut, *'Ishrun 'Aman*, pp. 175–176; Shuqayri, *al-Hazima al-Kubra 2*, pp. 226–227.
18 Shuqayri, *al-Hazima al-Kubra 2*, pp. 228–229; Shuqayri, *Radio PLO*, September 2, 1967; *al-Hayat,* September 3, 1967; Ahmad al-Shuqayri, "Dhikrayat 'an Mu'tamar al-Qima", *Shuun Filastiniya*, 4, September 1971.
19 Shuqayri, *al-Hazima al-Kubra 2*, pp. 190, 209, 297.

Conclusion: The Arab–Israeli Conflict between the *Nakba* and the *Naksa* – The Emergence of the New Palestinian National Movement

1   For a bibligraphy in Arabic of books and other publications on the Arab–Israeli conflict published during the 1950s, see, Naim Shahrabani, ed., *The Arab Israeli Conflict: A Bibliography of Arabic Books and Publications*, Truman Institute (Jerusalem, 1973); see also, Y. Harkabi, *Arab Attitudes to Israel* (London, 1972), appendix, Bibliography, Arabic sources, pp. 504–514.
2   Ibid.; on literature written in the wake of the Suez Campaign–Sinai War, see, Sasson Somekh, "The Suez War in Arabic Literature," in, S. Ilan Troen, Moshe Shemesh, eds.,

The Suez–Sinai Crisis 1956: Retrospective and Reappraisal (London, 1990), pp. 172–179; see also, Nasir's speeches during the years 1955–1959, in, *al-Majmu'a al-Kamila li-Khutab wa Ahadith wa Tasarih Jamal Abd al-Nasir*, vol. 2, 1955–1957 (Beirut, 1996), vol. 3, 1958–1959 (Beirut, 1999); also, *Filastin Min Aqwal al-Ra'is Jamal Abd al-Nasir* (Cairo, 1963).

3   See, Taqi al-Din al-Nabhani, *Inqadh Filastin* (Damascus, 1950), p. 5; also, Colonel Muhammad Safwat, *Isra'il al-'Aduw al-Mushtarak* (Cairo, 1952); Fakhri al-Baroudi, *Karithat Filastin al-'Uzma*, (Damascus, 1950); Muhammad Fadil al-Jamali, *al-Khatar al-Sihyoni* (Cairo, 1949).

4   See, Hasanayn Haykal, ed., Jamal Abd al-Nasir, Mudhakirat 'An Harb Filastin (Paris 1978); Fuad Matar, *Bisaraha 'An Abd al-Nasir* (Beirut, 1975); Jamal Abd al-Nasir, *Falsafat al-Thawra*, n.d., n.p.

5   See for example: Qustantin Zurayq, *Ma'na al-Nakba Mujaddadan* (Beirut, 1967).

6   Huwaydi, *al-Furass*, p. 299.

7   For reliable and documented analysis of the War of Attrition and its negative repercussions for Egypt, and for the background for Egypt's acceptance of Roger's initiative of June 1970, see, Huwaydi, *al-Furass*, pp. 169–244.

8   Khalid al-Hasan, a Fatah leader, *Shuun Filastiniya*, 4, September 1971, pp. 279–290.

Bibliography

The Bibliography lists only those sources which are directly cited in the text. State media are included under Media, even where generally regarded as expressing only government policies. Official organs or publications of Fatah and the PLO are classified under Palestinian Organizations.

Primary Sources

Archives

Ben-Gurion Archives, Ben-Gurion Research Institute, Sede Boker, Israel:

> Private Collection of Documents consisting of Jordanian government files on the West Bank that include documents from the Jordanian Security and Intelligence Services, captured by the IDF in the Six Day War.
> Private Collection of Documents from Egyptian Directorate of General Investigation of the Internal Security Department files in the Gaza Strip, captured by the IDF in the Six Day War.
> Private collection of PLO documents from files of the PLO offices in Gaza, captured by the IDF in the Six Day War.
> Private collection from files of Syrian government documents captured by the IDF on the Golan Heights in the Six Day War.
> Ben-Gurion's Diary (Hebrew).

Foreign Relations of the United States (FRUS).
IDF Archives.
Israel State Archives.
Yemima Rosental, ed., *Documents on the Foreign Policy of Israel,* vol. 3, 1983, vol. 8, 1996.
Public Record Office (PRO) [now the National Archives of the United Kingdom]

Memoirs (Books) and Articles

Abu Khatir, Josef, *Liqa'at Ma Jamal Abd al-Nasir* (Beirut, 1971).
Al-Baghdadi, Abd al-Latif, *Mudhakirat II* (Cairo, 1977).
Fawzi, Muhammad, *Harb al-Thalath Sanawat-Mudhakirat* (Beirut, 1983).
Farid, Abd al-Majid, *Min Mahadir Ijtima'at Abd al-Nasir al-Arabiya wa al-Duwaliya* (Beirut, 1979).
Haber, Eitan, *Hayom Tifross Milhama* (Tel Aviv, 1987), (Hebrew).
Haykal, Muhammad Hasanayn, *Li-Misr la li-Abd al-Nasir* (Cairo, 1976).

——— ,"*Bisaraha*", weekly articles in *al-Ahram*, 1959–1967.

——— , *The Sphinx and the Commissar* (New York, 1978).

al-Husayn, King, *Mihnati ka-Malik* (Amman, 1978).

al-Husayni, Muhammad Amin, *Haqa'iq an Qadiyat Filastin*, 3rd edition (Cairo, 1977).

al-Hut, Shafiq, *al-Filastini Bayna al-Tih wa al-Dawla* (Beirut, 1977).

——— , *'Ishrun 'Aman fi Munzamat al-Tahrir al-Filastiniya 1964–1984* (Beirut, 1986).

Huwaydi, Amin, *Adwa' 'Ala Asbab Naksat 1967 wa'Ala Harb al-Istinzaf* (Beirut, December 1975).

——— , *al-Furass al-Da'i'a* (Beirut, 3rd edition, 1992).

——— , *Hurub Abd al-Nasir* (Beirut, 1979).

al-Jamasi, Muhammad Abd al-Ghani (Mushir), *Mudhakirat Harb October 1973* (Paris, 1990).

Khalaf, Salah (Abu Iyyad), *Filastini Bila Hawiya* (Kuwait, n.d.).

Matar, Fuad, *Bisaraha 'an Abd al-Nasir, Hiwar Ma'a Muhammad Hasanayn Haykal* (Beirut, 1975).

Middle East Record, Shiloah Research Center, vol. 1 1960, vol. 2 1961, vol. 3 1967, vol. 4 1968 (Tel Aviv University).

Rabin, Yitzhak, *Pinkas Shirut* I, (Tel Aviv, 1979), (Hebrew).

Rikhye, Indar Jit, *The Sinai Blunder* (London, 1980).

Riyad, Mahmud, *Mudhakirat I, 1948–1978*, 3rd edition (Beirut, 1987).

——— , *Mudhakirat II* (Beirut, 1986).

al-Sadat, Anwar, *In Search of Identity* (London, 1978).

Shlaim, Avi, Interview with Yitzhak Rabin, *Iyyunim Bitkumat Yisra'el*, vol. 8, 1998 (Hebrew).

al-Shuqayri, Ahmad, *'Ala Tariq al-Hazima 2* (Beirut, 1972).

——— , Dhikrayat 'An Mu'tamar al-Qima fi al-Khartoum, *Shuun Filastiniya*, September 4, 1971.

——— , *Kalimat 'Ala Tariq al-Tahrir 1965* (Gaza, n.d.).

——— , *al-Kiyan al-Filastini*, Appendix no. 3, submitted to the second Arab summit (September, 1964).

——— , *Min al-Qima ila al-Hazima* (Beirut, 1971).

Official Documents

ARAB STATES

1. Egypt

Abd al-Nasir, Jamal, *Filastin Min Aqwal al-Ra'is 1953–1964* (Cairo, n.d.).

——— , *Falsafat al-Thawra* (Cairo, n.d.).

al-Nizam al-Dusturi li-Qita' Ghaza, *al-Jarida al-Rasmiya*, no. 75, March 29, 1962.

al-Qanun al-Asasi lil-Mantiqa al-Waqi'a Tahta Raqabat al-Quwat al-Misriya, *al-Jarida al-Rasmiya*, Law no. 255 1955.

al-Waqa'i' al-Filastiniya (Gaza).

2. Iraq

al-Waqa'i' al-'Iraqiya

3. Jordan

al-Urdun wa Qadiyat Filastin, Husayn's speech on January 5, 1966, official brochure, Ministry of Information (Amman).

al-Urdun wa al-Qadiya al-Filastiniya wa al-'Ulaqat al-'Arabiya (Amman, 1964).

Mawqif al-Urdun Min Matalib Ra'is Munazamat al-Tahrir al Filastiniya, Ministry of Foreign Affairs (December 6, 1965).

Mu'tamar al-Qima al-'Arabi, Ministry of Information (September 1967).

4. Syria (Ba'th)

al-Ba'th wa Qadiyat Filastin, vol. 3, 1955–1959 (Beirut, 1974).

——, vol. 4, 1959–1964 (Beirut, 1974).

——, vol. 5, 1964–1967 (Beirut, 1975).

al-Manhaj al-Marhali li-Thawrat al-Thamin 'Ashar, approved by the Extraordinary Regional Congress, June 1965, Ministry of Information (Damascus, July 22, 1965).

Nidal al-Ba'th, old series, vol. 4, *al-Qiyada al-Qawmiya 1955–1961* (Beirut, 1964).

——, vol. 7, *al-Qutr al-'Iraqi 1958*, 2nd edition (Beirut, February 1972).

——, vol. 8, *al-Qutr al-Lubnani 1951–1961* (Beirut, March 1972).

Nidal Hizb al-Ba'th al-Arabi al-Ishtiraki, new series, *'Abr Bayanat Qiyadatihi al-Qawmiya 1955–1962* (Beirut, 1971).

——, *'Abr Bayanat Qiyadatihi al-Qawmiya 1963–1966* (Beirut, October 1971).

——, *'Abr Mu'tamaratihi al-Qawmiya 1947–1964* (Beirut, June 1971).

——, *'Abr Mu'tamaratihi al-Qawmiya, al-Mu'tamar al Thamin* (Beirut, April 1972).

5. Israel

Ben-Gurion, David, *Ma'rekhet Sinay* (Tel Aviv, 1959), (Hebrew).

PALESTINIAN ORGANIZATIONS

1. Fatah

al-'Awda (West Germany).

Dirasat wa Tajarib Thawriya (n.d., n.p.).

Filastinuna (Beirut, monthly 1959–1965) .

Kamal 'Udwan, *Lecture*, in the first Cader's Course of Fatah, Brochure for members only (August 1972).

Limadha Ana Fatah, The Second Program, *"al-Tala'i' al-Thawriya"*; The Third Program, *"Harb al-Tahrir al-Sha'biya"* (n.d.).

Limadha Hiya Harb Tawilat al-Amad, Brochure no. 9 (n.d.).

Kifahuna al-Musalah, Brochure no. 10 (n.d.).

Mafahim Asasiya, for members only (August 1972).

al-Milad wa al-Masira (n.d.).

Nabdha Tarikhiya 'An Harakat Fatah (n.p. 1968).

al-Thawra al-Filastiniya al-Musalaha wa Marahil Tatawuriha, internal publication 106 (December 31, 1971).

al-Thawra.

2. PLO

al-Dawra al-Thalitha lil-Majlis al-Watani al-Filastini, Gaza, May 20–24, 1966.

al-Majlis al-Watani- al-Dawra al-Thaniya, Cairo, May 31–June 4, 1965.

al-Mu'tamar al-Filastini al-Awal, Cairo, May 28–June 2, 1964.

al-Mithaq al-Qawmi al-Filastini, al-Nizam al-Asasi (n.d.).

Media

1. News Agencies

Egypt: Middle East News Agency (MENA).

Iraq: Iraqi News Agency.

Jordan: Jordanian News Agency.

Syria: Syrian Arab News Agency (SANA).

USSR: Tass News Agency.

2. Radio

Egypt: Cairo, Sawt al-Arab.
Germany: The Voice of Germany, Cologne.
Iraq: Baghdad.
Israel: Kol Yisra'el-Jerusalem.
Jordan: Amman.
Lebanon: Beirut.
PLO: Sawt Filastin.
Syria: Damascus, Sawt Filastin.
USSR: Moscow, Moscow in Arabic.

3. The Press

EGYPT

al-Ahram.
al-Akhbar.
Akhbar al-Yawm
Akhir Sa'a al
al-Jumhuriya.

al-Masa'.
al-Musawar.
Ruz al-Yusef.
Tali'a.

IRAQ

al-Akhbar
al-Bilad
al-Ishtiraki
al-Jamahir.

al-Jumhuriya.
al-Thawra.
al-Zaman.

JORDAN

Akhbar al-Usbu'.
al-Bilad.
al-Difa'.
al-Dustur.

Filastin.
Hawla al-'Alam.
al-Jihad.
al-Manar.

KUWAIT

al-Watan.

LEBANON

al-Ahad.
al-Ahrar.
al-'Amal.
al-Anwar.
al-Safir.
Filastin (AHC).
Filastin (al-Muharrir).
al-Hawadith.
al-Hayat.
al-Huriya.

al-Jarida.
al-Jumhur.
Kul Shay'.
al-Muharrir.
al-Nahar.
al-Nida'.
al-Sahafa.
al-Sayad.
al-Siyasa.
al-Usbu' al-'Arabi.

337

SAUDI ARABIA
al-Bilad.
al-Madina.

SUDAN
al-Ayam.

SYRIA
al-Ayam.
al-Ba'th.
al-Nasr.
al-Thawra.
al-Wahda.

ISRAEL
'Al Hamishmar.
Davar.
Haaretz.
Jerusalem Post.
Lamirhav.
Yediot Aharonot.

ISRAEL DEFENCE FORCES: Announcements and Communiques, 1959–1967.

UNITED KINGDOM
The Observer

USA
New York Times.

USSR
Izvevstia.

Secondary Sources

Books
Alush, Naji, al-*Masira lla Filastin* (Beirut, 1964).
Ghali, Butrus, *Dirasat fi al-Diblomasiya al-'Arabiya* (Cairo, 1973).
Goren, Asher, *ha-Liga ha-'Aravit 1945–1954* (Tel Aviv, 1954), (Hebrew).
Govrin, Yosef, *Israel–Soviet Relations 1953–1967: From Confrontation to Disruption* (London, 1998).
Hashad, Adli, *Sha'b Filastin fi Tariq al-'Awda* (Cairo, 1964).
Hourani, Faysal, *al-'Amal al-'Arabi al-Mushtarak wa Isra'il, al-Rafd wa al-Qubul 1944–1967* (Niqosiya, 1989).
——, *al-Fikr al-Siyasi al-Filastini 1964–1974* (Beirut, 1980).
Husayn, Hasan Khalil, *Safahat Majhula fi Hayat Abu Iyyad (Salah Khalaf),* (Amman, 1991).
al-Kayali, Abd al-Wahab, *al-Qadiya al-Filastiniya Ara' wa Mawaqif 1964–1966* (Beirut, December 1973).

al-Kaylani, Haytham, *al-Istiratijiyat al-'Askariya lil Hurub al-'Arabiya – al-Isra'iliya 1948–1988* (Beirut, November 1991).

Kaziha, Walid, *Revolutionary Transformation in the Arab World* (London, 1975).

Kerr, H. Malcolm, *The Arab Cold War*, 3rd edition (London, 1971).

al-Khatib, Husam, *Fi al-Tajriba al-Thawriya al-Filastiniya* (Damascus, 1972).

Ma'oz, Moshe, *Syria and Israel: From War to Peacemaking* (Oxford, 1995).

Mutawi, Samir, *Jordan in the 1967 War* (Cambridge, 1987).

Oren, Michael, *Six Days of War: June 1967 and the Making of the Modern Middle East* (Oxford, 2002).

Podeh, Elie, *Hachatira le-Hegimonia ba-'Ulam ha-'Aravi* (Tel Aviv, 1996), (Hebrew); English version, *The Quest for Hegemony in the Arab World* (New York, 1995).

Rushdi, 'Umar, and Fawzi, Muhammad, *al-Sahyoniya wa Rabibatiha Isra'il* (Cairo, 1965).

Sayigh, Yezid, *Armed Struggle and the Search for State, the Palestinian National Movement, 1949–1993* (Oxford, 1997).

Sela, Avraham, *The Decline of the Arab–Israeli Conflict* (New York, 1998).

Shalev, Aryeh, *Israel–Syria Armistice Regime 1949–1955* (Jerusalem, 1993).

Shemesh, Moshe, *The Palestinian Entity 1959–1974: Arab Politics and the PLO,* 2nd revised edition (London, 1993, 1996).

al-Shu'aybi, 'Isa, *al-Kiyaniya al-Filastiniya 1947–1977* (Beirut, 1979).

al-Shuqayri, Jamal, *al-Kiyan al-Filastini* (n.p., n.d.).

Susser, Asher, ed., *Shisha Yamim, Sheloshim Shana* (Tel Aviv, 1999), (Hebrew); articles by: Itamar Rabinovich, Shimon Shamir, Asher Susser, Richard Parker, Shlomo Avineri and Herman Ielets .

al-Tal, Sa'id, *al-Urdun wa Filastin, Wajhat Nazar 'Arabiya* (Amman, 1984).

Yasin, Subhi Muhammad, *Nazariyat al-'Amal li-Istirdad Filastin* (Cairo, 1964).

Yusef, Abd al-Rahman, *Mu'tamar al-Qima al-'Arabi*, Brochure No. 8 in the series *Nidaluna*, (Egyptian) Armed Forces HQ (Cairo, March 1964).

Zak, Moshe, *Husayn 'Ose Shalom* (Jerusalem, 1996), (Hebrew).

Articles

Bandman, Yona, "Chatzi Ha'i Sinay Batfisa ha-Estrategit shel Mitzrayim 1949–1962," in, G. Gvirtzman, A. Shmueli, Y. Gradus, Y. Beit Aryeh, M. Harel, eds., *Sinai* (Tel Aviv, 1987), (Hebrew).

Brown, L. Carl, "Nasser and the June 1967 War: Plan or Improvisation?" in, S. Sheikaly, R. Baalbaki & P. Dodd ,eds., *Quest for Understanding: Arabic and Islam Studies in Memory of Malcolm H. Kerr* (American University of Beirut, 1991).

Golan, Shimon, "Ha-Ma'avak 'Al Mei Hayarden," in, A. Shmueli, Arnon Sofer, Nurit Cliot, eds., *Artzot Hagalil*, vol. 2 (Tel Aviv, 1983), (Hebrew).

Rabinovich, Itamar, "Ha-Ma'avak 'Al Mei Hayarden Kamarkiv Basikhsukh Ha'aravi–Yisra'eli," in, A. Shmueli, Arnon Sofer, Nurit Cliot (eds.), *Artzot Hagalil*, vol. 2 (Tel Aviv, 1983), (Hebrew).

Sakhnini, Isam, "Al-Filastiniyun fi al-'Iraq, " *Shuun Filastiniya*, 13, September, 1972.

——, "Al-Kiyan al-Filastini 1964–1974", *Shuun Filastiniya*, 41–42, February 1975.

Shay, Avi, "Hayl Misrayim," Part 1, *Ma'rakhot*, 227 (January, 1973), Part 2, *Ma'rakhot*, 228, (March, 1973). *See* also Yona, below (Hebrew).

Shemesh, Moshe, "The IDF Raid on Samu': "The Turning Point in Jordanian Relations With Israel and the West Bank Palestinians," *Israel Studies*, vol. 7, 1, Spring 2002.

Yona (Bandman), Major, "Hareqa' le-Milhemet Sheshet ha-Yamim Be'ene ha-'Aravim: Misrayim ve-Knisatah la-Milhama," *Ma'rakhot*, 191–192, July 1968 (Hebrew).

Index

Abd al-Nasir, Gamal, x–xii, xiv–xvi, 1–3, 5, 7, 11, 12, 14, 19, 36, 61, 62, 68, 95, 101, 108, 135, 136, 147, 155, 177, 190, 204–206, 227, 229, 258; and Arab summit conference, 27, 41–45, death of, 253; pan-Arab policy, 39; and Arab world, 46, 47, 107, 121, 124, 187,189, 191, 192, 195, 196, 213–215, 218, 236, 237, 254, 255; and Lebanon, 53, 54, 122, 193; and Arab–Israeli conflict, 69, 94, 131, 241–245, 250–252, 259; and Shuqayri, 70, 71, 75, 76, 80, 83, 85, 246; and Husayn, 74–76, 84, 118, 151, 222; and Filastin liberation, viii, 78; and Arab solidarity, 82; speech at Port Sa'id on December 23, 1963, 5, 43; and Israel, 8, 94, 96, 148–150, 153, 170, 197, 202, 216, 217, 220, 249; and Fatah, 99; and United States, 109, 209–212; and Jordan, xvii, 13, 194, 219, 221; and Syrian Ba'th regime, ix, 120, 127, 171, 178, 235, 257; and UN, 132, 243; and Amer, Abd al-Hakim, 238–240; and the Soviet Union, 206–208, 210; and Iraq (Qasim), 14, 15, 17, 226; and Palestinian problem, 4, 6, 9, 10, 230, 233, 234, 260; and UAR government, 35, 37, 38; and Six Day War, xviii, 158, 159, 161, 180, 184, 186, 200–203, 231, 232, 262

Abd al-Qudus, Ihsan, 42

Abdulla, King, 106

Abtal al-'Awda, 100 102 115

Abu Ammar, *see* Yasir Arafat

Abu Gharbiya, Bahjat, 73

Abu Iyyad, *see* Salah Khalaf

Abu Jihad (Khalil al-Wazir), 92

Abu Khatir, Jozef, xiv

Abu Lutuf, *see* Faruq al-Qadumi

Abu Odeh, Adnan, 117

Aflaq, Michel, 22

al-Ahram, xiv, 2, 9, 52, 187, 189, 190, 217, 226

Algeria, 11, 20, 24, 25, 72, 93–95, 104, 128, 153, 194, 218, 223, 235, 258

Ali, Musa, 99

Allon, Yigal, 255

Alush, Naji (Palestinian writer), xi

Amer, Mushir Abd al-Hakim (Field Marshal, deputy supreme commander of the Egyptian armed forces), ix, x, xviii, 7, 158, 238, 239

Amer, Fariq Awal Ali Ali (General, chief-of-staff of the Egyptian army and commander of UAC), 46, 51, 52, 62, 63, 97, 119, 121–136, 138, 140, 141, 146, 148–150, 153–155, 158, 180, 181, 184, 186, 190, 194–202, 204, 214–216, 232, 235, 238, 239

Arab Collective Security Pact, 61, 62

Arab Defense Council (ADC), *see* Joint Arab Defense Council (JADC)

Arab diversion plan, 8, 33–39, 41, 43, 49–53, 55, 61, 63–68, 92, 119, 141, 164

Arab foreign ministers conference, 24, 25, 27, 30, 35, 38, 149

Arab League, xi, 11, 19, 30, 36, 37, 40, 44, 63, 65, 80, 147, 148, 218, 256; decisions of the, xiv

Arab League Council (ALC), 25, 27–32, 34–36, 38, 40, 123, 130, 254; first session of, 6; and Jordan, 21, 29; Filastin representatives in, 30, 31, 46, 70, 75; technical committee, 34, secretary general of the, 54, 58, 97, 119

Arab League Political Committee, xiv, 28

Arab National Command, 22, 24, 76, Ba'th, 23

Arab national goal, 2, 47, 155

Arab Nationalism, viii, xv, 1, 2, 3, 4, 9, 15, 230, 232, 235, 241, 249, 254, 259

Arab Nationalists Movement (ANM), 72, 75, 85, 102, 254

Arab Nationalist view, 2, 3, 24, 170, 254

Arab Socialist Union, 100, 195, 197

Arab solidarity, 1, 82, 142, 153, 155, 171, 229, 230

Arab summits, xii, xiv, xvi, 22, 43, 44, 47, 65, 85, 92, 95, 120, 121, 133, 142, 159, 171, 233, 235, 254, 257; (December 23, 1963), 3, 37; first conference (Cairo, January 1964), ix, 6, 7, 27, 28, 32, 41, 67, 71, 79, 94, 97, 191, 256; second conference (Alexandria, September 1964), ix, 27, 28, 49–51, 55, 59, 70, 121, 123, 136, 147; third conference (Casablanca, September 1965), 63, 98, 140, 146, 159; fourth conference (Khartoum, August 1967), vii, xii, xiv, xviii, 241, 242, 243, 244, 246, 248, 252, 254, 257, 259, 260, 261; seventh conference (Rabat, October 1974), 253; decisions, 54, 55, 112, 114, 119, 126, 243, 247, 249

Arab Youth, 80, 82–84

Arab–Israeli Conflict, viii, ix, xi, xii, xv, xvi, xviii, 1, 4, 5, 6, 26–28, 46, 69, 85, 91, 104, 107, 226,

340

235, 251, 252, 261–264; Egyptian Strategy in, 7, 9–11, 170, 250, 253, 254; Qasim's strategy in, 13, 14; Jordan strategy in, 19, 21, 255; Syrian strategy in, 22, 25, 37, 106, 257; water struggle, 32–34, 36, 41, 43, 68, 147; Israel's nuclear weapon, 150; Six Day War, 241, 249, 259

Arafat, Yasir (Abu Ammar), 92, 100, 104, 262, 264

Arif, Abd al-Rahman (president of Iraq), 128, 151, 220, 226, 230, 264

Armistice Agreement, 13, 33, 47, 107, 163; Israeli–Jordanian, 47, 48, 111; Israeli–Syrian Armistice Agreement, 66, 161

Armistice Commissions, see Mixed Armistice Commissions

al-Asad, Hafiz, 104, 164, 222, 224, 257, 258, 262–264

al-Atasi, Nur al-Din (president of Syria), 61, 146, 158, 171, 222, 223, 264

Awad, Lewis, 105

'Awda (The right to return), 258, 264

Ba'th party, Syria, 22, 24, 25, 44, 72, 159, 164, 223, 254; sixth congress, 23; and Israel, 37, 176, 263; and Nasir, 38, 120, 127, 154, 177, 191, 221, 222, 224, 233, 256, 257; in Iraq, 40, 108, 179; and the liberation of Filastin, 53; and PLO, 75, 76, 84, 86; activists, 89; and Fatah, 102–106; and Palestinian organizations, 258, 262

Badran, Shams, 100, 186, 194, 201, 206–209, 214, 215

Baghdad Pact, viii, 233

al-Baghdadi, Abd al-Latif, xiv

Baghdadi, Ibrahim, 7, 228

Bamahaneh, 160, 165, 176

Barbour, Walworth (American ambassador to Israel), 210

Ben-Gurion, David, xix, 107, 132

Black September (September 1970 in Jordan), 254, 255, 260, 262; see also Fatah

Bull, Odd (head of the UN Observers), 162, 163

Cairo Agreement, see Egyptian–Syrian Agreement

Central Treaty Organization (CENTO), 96

Churchill, Winston, 13

Dayan, Moshe, 35

De Gaulle, Charles, 149, 207, 212, 223

Demilitarized Zone, 32, 33, 35–37, 40, 48, 57–59, 61, 64, 161, 152, 163, 164, 166, 172, 174, 234

al-Dustur, 194, 228

Eastern Front, 111, 152, 153, 198, 199, 228

Eban, Abba, 161, 162, 177, 209, 210, 255

Ede, Michel (Lebanese minister of science), 230

Egyptian–Israeli agreement, 253, 263

Egyptian nationalism, 13, 233

Egyptian–Jordanian Agreement, 153, 208, 219, 220

Egyptian–Jordanian military pact, 151, 219, 220, 221, 222, 223, 226, 230, 237

Egyptian–Syrian Agreement (The Cairo Agreement), 177, 179, 181, 187, 219

Eilat, xviii, 14, 143,196, 198, 199, 223

Eisenhower, Dwight D, 33, 35

Executive Committee of PLO (EC), 72–75, 77, 80, 84, 88, 101

Farid, Abd al-Majid, xiv, 246

Fatah (Palestinian Liberation Movement), 25, 86, 98, 99, 103, 107, 110, 181, 193, 201; establishment of, vii, xvii, 78, 95; operations against Israel, ix, 65, 91, 94, 97, 105, 166, 176, 253; fida'iyyun, xii, xiv, 76, 102; in Jordan, xiii; and Syria, 68, 72, 92, 100, 104, 106, 115, 160, 164, 165; and PLO, 77, 85, 87, 88, 96, 101, 250, 255, 258, 259, 261; in Algeria, 93; and Jordan, 110–114, 116

Fawzi Mahmud (Egyptian foreign minister), 35

Fawzi, Muhammad (Egyptian chief-of-staff and minister of war), xiv, 131, 153, 157, 158, 181, 182, 184–187, 198–202, 206, 207, 210, 213–215, 225, 238

Faysal, King (of Saudi Arabia), xi, 193

Fida'iyyun, ix, xii, xiv, xvii, xviii, 12, 22, 75, 78, 83, 85–88, 91–94, 96, 97, 99–106, 110–117, 165, 174, 190, 191, 194, 201, 216, 219, 249–251, 255, 256, 258–260, 262

Filastinuna, xiv, 77, 78, 92, 93, 95

Gaza Strip, ix, 7, 16, 72, 131, 258; and Egyptian administration, xiii, 12, 13; Egyptian army in, 61, 140, 158, 171, 181, 182, 185, 186, 201; withdrawal of the IDF from, 1, 243, 245, 246; establishment of the Palestinian state in, 6, 15, 17, 76, 85, 216, 255, 264; legislative council of, 7; and Egyptian view, 11, 207, 217; government, 19; and Husayn (Jordan), 21, 114, 129; and PLO, 31, 74, 256, 263; Palestinian organizations in, 78, 93, 94; Israel's occupation of, 92, 260, 261; Fatah in the, 95, 96, 99, 100, 101, 103, 106; UN in, 188, 198; Israeli threat, 199; IDF attack on, 200

General Union of the Palestinian Students, 78

Ghalib, Murad (Egyptian ambassador to Moscow), 180

Golan Heights, xiii, 105, 165, 166, 174, 179, 225, 245

Government of All-Filastin, 30

Great Britain, 6, 33, 95, 107, 109, 136, 168, 196, 201, 205, 210, 217, 228, 236, 237, 245

Habash, George, xiv, 102

al-Hafiz Amin (president of Syria), 40, 45

Hakim, George (Lebanese minister), 54

al-Hamma (Syria), 65, 74, 76

Hammarskjöld, Dag, 9, 132, 191

al-Hasan, Khalid (a Fatah leader), 77

Hatim, Abd al-Qadir, 7

al-Hawadith, xiv, 22

Hawatma, Nayif, xiv
al-Hayat, 52, 54, 226, 228, 230
Haykal, Muhammad Hasanayn, xiv, 52, 148, 186, 226, 229, 236, 242
Hebron, 85, 86, 95, 128, 182
Helou, Charles (Lebanese president), 51, 52, 68
Herzog, Ya'akov, 116
Hijazi, Muhammad Bakir, 99
Hilmi Abd al-Baqi, Ahmad, 30
al-Hourani, Akram, 8, 37
Hourani, Faysal, xi
House of Deputies, *see* Jordanian House of Representatives
Humphrey, Hubert (American vice president), 212
al-Huriya, 227
Husayn, Hasan Khalil, 99
Husayn, King (of Jordan), xiv, 3, 18, 256; and Israel, xii, xii,i 106, 107, 108, 128, 260, 263; and the PLO, xvi; and Shuqayri, xvii, xviii, 75, 82, 84, 245, 247, 248; and Nasir, 13, 32, 71, 73, 74, 76, 83, 101, 109, 110, 113, 114, 115, 118, 131, 159, 193, 204, 208, 218, 219, 220, 222, 226, 230, 242, 243, 246, 255; and Syria, 178; and the UAC, 124, 132, 136, 144; and Iraq, 151; and the Jordanian army, 137, 138, 191; and the raid on Samu', 116; and the Six Day War, 17, 127, 138, 221, 244, 257; and Palestinian entity, 17, 79, 80, 81, 85, 90; and Gaza Strip, 21, 261; and Mubarak, 252
al-Husayni, Mufti Haj Amin, 72, 78, 110
al-Hut, Shafiq, xiv, 96, 102, 115, 244, 247
Huwaydi, Amin (Egyptian minister of war), xiv, 158, 177, 181, 202–204, 207, 238, 243, 253
al-Ifranji, Muhammad, 99
International Atomic Energy Committee, 149
Iraq, xiv, 2, 3, 29, 46, 119, 128, 135, 148, 150, 170, 205, 219; Qasim, 13, 14, 17, 25; Ba'th revolution in, 40; and Palestinian Entity, 15, 16, 24, 31; and Egypt, viii, 6, 28, 78, 118, 188; position on the Arab–Israeli conflict, xiii, 7; and Jordan, 21, 50, 72, 151, 158; forces in Jordan, 106, 107, 108, 120, 124, 125, 126, 127, 129, 130, 131, 134, 138, 152, 154, 215, 216, 218, 220; and Syria, 22, 26; Syrian defense pact, 153; and UAR, 30; and PLA (Palestinian Liberation Army), 140, 143; UAC's plan for defense, 142, 143, 144, 146, 166; and Israel, 168, 169, 179, 192, 212; and Six Day War, 226, 227, 230, 233, 234, 235, 258; and Shuqayri, 247,
Israel, xi, 11, 20, 31, 100, 228, 229, 230, 250, 252, 253, 257, 258; and Nasir, viii, x, 3, 7, 8, 9, 29, 41, 45, 220, 226, 227, 231–233, 237, 239, 251; and Palestinians, 241, withdrawal of, xii, xviii, 1, 133, 241, 243, 245, 255, 261, 264; and Egypt, 184–209, 217, 218, 222, 224, 225, 234–236, 263; Arab strategy towards, ix, xii, xv, 5, 15, 23, 24, 25, 43; and Husayn, xii, xiii, 106, 107, 108, 128, 221, 260, 263; and fida'iyyun, ix, xvii, 110, 115, 117, 174; military confrontation with, xvi, xviii, 94,

200, 213; borders, 4, 12, 52, 62, 91, 98, 99, 122, 131, 262; Straits of Tiran, xviii, 132, 151, 187, 188, 201, 235, 236; and Qasim, 14; water struggle, 21, 27, 32–34, 36–40, 42, 44, 50, 55, 57, 58, 61, 66, 67, 121; aggression (attack), 22, 35, 46, 47, 53, 54, 59, 60, 68, 119, 126, 127, 134, 135, 136, 138, 141, 142, 143, 144, 145, 146, 170, 208, 210, 214, 215, 242, 249; and Jordan, 30, 92, 111, 113, 115, 124, 125, 128, 129, 130, 219; in the West Bank,106, 107, 108, 109, 110, 118, 243, 244, 246; and Shuqayri, 247; Fatah operations against, 65, 85, 93, 95, 96, 97, 102, 103, 104, 112; and PLO, 80, 101; and Samu' raid, 86, 89, 90, 114, 116, 117; and Syria, 105, 133, 158, 159, 160, 161, 162, 163, 164, 165, 166, 167, 168, 169, 171, 172, 173, 174, 175, 176, 177, 178, 179, 180, 181, 182, 183, 197; 223; nuclear project, xvii, 39, 129, 147–151, 184; UAC,152, 153, 154, 155, 194; Six Day War, 157; and Gaza Strip, 199, 201; and the US, 211, 212, 255; occupation, 259, 260, 261
Israel Air Force (IAF), 57, 62–65, 68, 141, 152, 172, 173
Israel's National Water Carrier (NWC), ix, xv, xvi, 4, 5, 8, 10, 32, 33, 39–44, 50, 55, 67, 92, 154
Israeli–Jordanian Armistice Agreement, 47, 48
Israeli–Syrian Armistice Agreement, 48, 161–163
Israeli Defense Forces (IDF), xvi, 40, 94, 121, 129, 136, 145, 146, 152, 165, 175, 183, 232, 239; raid in Jordan, 112, 116; Samu' raid, ix, xi, xvii, 79, 85, 86, 91, 128, 130, 166; in the Six Day War, xiii; on the Syrian border, xviii, 57, 58, 60, 61, 63–66, 68, 167, 168, 171–174, 180, 225, 234, 235; and Syrian diversion operation, 159, 160, 164; withdrawal from Sinai, 1; Syrian fire on, 55; and the Egyptian front, 184, 197, 198, 199, 201, 213; in Gaza Strip, 200,
Israeli military government, 7

al-Jamasi, Fariq Awal Abd al-Ghani (General, Egyptian chief-of-staff), xiv, 186
Jarring mission, xii, 243, 253
Jawhar, Salah, 7
Jericho, 152
Jerusalem, 13, 19, 20, 47, 86–88, 106–109, 117, 145, 176, 223, 242–245, 255, 264; and Husayn, xii; Palestinian National Council in (May 1964), xvi, 70, 71, 73–77; capital of Filastin, 80
Jerusalem Congress, 70, 71, 73, 74, 76, 77
Jewish Agency, 77
Jibril, Ahmad, 92, 102
Johnson, Lyndon B, 149, 206, 209, 211–213, 246
Johnston, Eric and Johnston plan, 33–36, 49, 50, 53, 67
Joint Arab Command (JAC), xi, 5, 22, 39, 40, 45, 50, 55, 58, 95
Joint Arab Defense Council (JADC) (later ADC),

32, 39, 52, 119, 121, 122, 126–134, 136, 141,
143, 144, 146–150, 154, 171
Joint Defense Agreement, 178, 179, 181; *see also*
Joint Arab Defense Council (JADC)
Jordan, ix, xi, xii, xiii, xvi, xvii, 2, 7, 13, 40, 58, 71,
73, 92, 110, 116, 150, 153, 154, 168, 184, 187,
225, 233–236, 247; Palestinians in, 11, 12,
252, 257, 258; Palestinian land, 15, 17, 243,
245, 260; and Qasim's strategy, 17, 31; stand
on the Palestinian problem, 18–22, 29,
30–35, 244, 256, 263; and Israel, 33, 34, 54,
63, 65, 66, 67, 93, 107–109, 117, 151, 152,
175, 215, 216, 218, 219, 221, 249, 262, 264;
water problem, 46, 50; and Egypt, 55, 60, 71,
118, 120, 159, 193, 194, 220, 222, 226, 251,
255; and PLO, 74, 75, 79–89; and Fatah, 77,
91, 94–97, 102, 110–115, 261; and Syrian
Ba'th, 104–106, 160, 161; and UAC,
119–121, 124–136, 138, 141–148, 165, 166
Jordan National Guard, 12, 18, 113, 137, 138, 145
Jordan River, 4, 9, 13, 15, 20, 33, 40, 46, 47, 48,
64, 66, 76, 87, 95, 181, 225; diverting the, ix,
xvi, 5, 8, 9, 21–25, 32, 34–39, 41–45, 49, 50,
53, 54, 57, 62, 63, 65, 67, 91, 112, 155, 254
Jordanian–Israeli Peace Agreement, 263
Jordanian Arab Army (JAA), xiii, 13, 75, 81, 82,
85–89, 106, 108, 111, 114–117, 120, 136, 137,
138, 141–143, 151, 152, 154, 159, 219
Jordanian Entity, 73, 81
Jordanian front, 124, 125, 129, 143, 145, 154, 159,
215, 219, 220
Jordanian government, 13, 18, 20, 21, 29, 72, 80,
83, 116, 218, 219
Jordanian House of Representatives (House of
Deputies), 19, 72, 74, 82
Jum'a, Sa'ad (Jordanian prime minister), xiv, 151,
218
al-Jumhuriya, 42, 243
al-Jundi, Abd al-Karim (head of the Syrian military intelligence), 158

Ka'ush, Jalal, 99
Kanafani, Ghassan (writer and a leader of the
ANM), 75
Kennedy, John F., 9
Kerr, Malcolm, xi
Khalaf, Salah (Abu Iyyad, a Fatah leader), xiv,
77, 93, 100
Khalid Ben-al-Walid Dam (Mukheiba), 50, 56,
67, 112, 143
Khamash, Amer, 82, 111, 117, 124
Khartoum summit (August 1967), 241, 242, 243,
244, 246, 248, 252, 254, 257, 259, 260, 261;
see also Arab summits
al-Khatib, Anwar (Jordanian ambassador to
Cairo), 83
al-Khawaja, Muhammad, 99
al-Kaylani, Haytham, xiv
Kuwait, 72, 78, 93–95, 102, 104, 119, 194, 227

Lausanne Agreement, 17
Lebanon, xiii, xiv, 11, 24, 29, 32, 34, 38, 40,

46–56, 58, 63–66, 68, 72, 75, 78, 91–99,
101–104, 106, 115, 119, 120–128, 134–136,
140–143, 146–148, 160, 175, 193, 218, 226,
258, 262
Libya, 72

al-Madani, Wajih (PLA commander), 102
al-Majali, Abd al-Wahab (Jordanian prime
minister), 18, 19, 29
Makhus, Ibrahim (Syrian foreign minister), 165,
166, 223, 224
Malik, Ya'akov (Soviet deputy foreign minister),
169
Mar'i, Sayid, xiv
al-Masri, Hikmat, 73
Mixed Armistice Commissions, xiii, 47, 98, 110,
192, 174, 182; Arab heads of, 64, 97, 111; *see
also* Armistice Agreement
Morocco, 148 218
Mubarak, Husni, 252, 254
Muhi al-Din, Zakariya, 53, 61, 158, 212, 213, 222
Mukheiba Dam, *see* Khalid Ben al-Walid Dam
Murtaja, Fariq Awal Abd al-Muhsin Kamil
(General, commander of the Egyptian
front), 182, 190, 199

Nablus, 73, 86, 87, 88, 108, 110, 111, 220
Nasir, Musa (Jordanian foreign minister), 29
Nasir-Husayn pact, *see* Egyptian–Jordanian military pact
Nasr, Salah (head of Egyptian general intelligence), 100
National Ba'th Congress (NC), 102, 103, 223; 3rd,
23; 4th, 24, 25; 6th, 25; 8th, 23
New Palestinian National Movement, x, xi, xviii,
6, 93, 233, 241, 249–251, 253, 255, 259–263;
see also Palestinian National Movement
Nussaibah, Hazem (Jordanian foreign minister),
89, 117

Operation Husayn, 144, 145
Oslo Agreement, 258, 263, 264

Palestinian Liberation Front, 25, 26, 95, 102
Palestine Experts Committee (PEC), 29, 30
Palestinian army, 12, 16, 17, 18, 30, 78; *see also*
Palestinian Liberation Army (PLA)
Palestinian Entity, viii, xi, xv, xvi, xvii, 6, 8, 9,
11–13, 15, 17, 18, 19, 21–24, 26, 27–32, 46,
70, 71, 73–81, 85, 95, 99, 110, 156, 216,
253–256, 258, 259
Palestinian government, 6, 11, 12, 18, 24, 31, 78,
216, 243
Palestinian Liberation Army (PLA), 16, 17, 31,
70, 72, 73, 75, 79, 80, 82, 83, 101, 102, 134,
135, 140; *see also* Palestinian Army (PA)
Palestinian Liberation Movement, *see* Fatah
Palestinian Liberation Organization, *see* PLO
Palestinian National awakening, xi, xiii, xvii, 6,
78, 79, 85, 90, 118, 221, 257–261
Palestinian National Council (PNC), 71–76, 79,
80, 82, 83, 85, 31; 1st (May 1964), xvi, 70; 2nd

Palestinian National Council (PNC) (*continued*)
(May 1965), 62, 111; 3rd (May 1966), 85
Palestinian National Movement, x, xi, 77, 93, 221,
233, 241, 250, 251, 253, 255, 258–263, *see
also* New Palestinian National Movement
Palestinian National Union (PNU), 12, 72
Palestinian problem (question), x–xiii, xv–xviii,
28–30, 32, 36, 37, 69, 81, 91, 147, 163, 182,
197, 212, 213, 229, 230, 232–235, 237, 238,
249–252, 254, 256, 257, 259–261, 263 264;
Egyptian strategy, 1, 4–7, 9–13, 216, 217;
Qasim's strategy, 14–16; Jordan's strategy,
17–21; Syrian Ba'th's strategy, 22–27, 104;
new Arab strategy, 241, 243–248
Palestinization, xviii, 13, 88, 262
Pan-Arab nationalism (qawmiya), 3, 4, 10, 22, 24,
257
PLO (Palestinian Liberation Organization),
xi–xvii, 6, 17, 46, 54, 70, 87, 88, 141, 156,
244, 246, 248, 250, 262, 263; recognition of,
253, 254, 256; 260; and Shuqayri, 71, 72, 73,
88, 242, 259; and Husayn (Jordan), 74,
78–86, 89, 100, 110, 112, 116, 155, 247; and
Egypt, 92, 99, 101, 102, 111, 194, 216; and
the Syrian Ba'th party, 75, 76; and Fatah,
77, 85, 86, 93, 95, 96, 104, 114, 255, 258,
261
Pravda, 168

al-Qadumi, Faruq (Abu Lutuf), 100
al-Qadumi, Hani, 77
al-Qamhawi, Walid, 73
Qasim, Abd al-Karim (leader of Iraq's July 1958
revolution), ix, xi, xv, 3, 36, 233; strategy,
13–17; and Nasir, 19; position on the
Palestinian problem, 23; and UAR, 24; plan
for the establishment of a Palestinian
republic, 25, 76
al-Qishawi, Awni (Abu Mu'in), 99
al-Qudwa, Musa Arafat, 99

Rabin, Yitzhak (chief-of-staff), 57, 160, 167, 168,
174, 175, 177, 187
Radio Amman, 214, 219, 220
Radio Baghdad, 228
Radio Beirut, 149
Radio Cairo, 178, 183, 185–191, 196, 219, 227, 231
Radio Damascus, 41, 58, 60, 62, 103, 166, 174,
176, 192, 223, 225, 227, 228, 231
Radio Moscow in Arabic, 168, 169, 205
Radio PLO, 83, 194
al-Razaz, Munif, 61
Rif'at, Kamal, 7, 100
Rikhye, Indir Jit (commander of the UNEF), 185,
186
Riyad, Fariq Abd al-Mun'im (Lieutenant
General, chief-of-staff UAC), 115, 119, 126,
151, 152–154, 219, 225
Riyad, Mahmud (Egyptian foreign minister), xiv,
62, 122, 132, 133, 134, 155, 186, 202, 211
Ruz al-Yusef, 42, 43

Sabri, Ali (Egyptian minister for the republican
presidential affairs), 7
Sabri, Husayn Dhu al-Fiqar (Egyptian deputy
foreign minister), 7
al-Sadat, Anwar, xiv, 180, 240, 243, 253, 254, 255,
263
Salim, Mahmud Ahmad (commander of the
Western Front – Jordan), 45, 112, 117, 144
Sawt al-Arab, 42, 109, 159, 183, 187, 226–229,
231, 236
Sekik, Umar, 99
Sela, Avraham, xi
al-Sha'ir, Fahd (Syrian chief-of-staff), 61–63, 127,
147, 148
al-Shak'a, Walid, 73
Sharaf, Sami (Egyptian minister of information),
109
Shmayit, Yusef (Lebanese chief-of-staff), 122
Shukur, Yusef (the Syrian chief-of-staff), 44, 45
Shuqayri, Ahmad (head of the PLO), xi, xii, xvi,
xvi–xviii, 31, 32, 46, 53, 54, 62, 140, 156, 194,
220, 242, 244–248, 256, 259, 260; and the
PLO foundation, 6, 70–77, 79–89; and
Egypt's initiative, 30; and Fatah, 93, 96, 101,
112
Sidqi, Fariq Awal Mahmud (General,
commander of the Egyptian air force), 177,
178, 199, 214
Sidqi, Sulayman (Egyptian prime-minister), 179,
195
Soviet Union, xviii, 3, 33, 116, 149, 151, 155, 158,
167–170, 180, 204–208, 210– 212, 215, 223
Straits of Tiran, x, xviii, 118, 131, 132, 151, 184,
187, 188, 194, 198, 201, 217, 223, 234, 235,
236
Suez Canal Company, 1, 9, 14, 131, 165, 195, 197,
234; nationalization of, 1, 196, 227
Supreme Executive Committee, 76, 195, 197
al-Suwaydani, Ahmad (Syrian chief-of-staff),
153, 187, 222, 223, 225
Syria, viii, ix, xii, xiii, xvi–xviii, 7, 13, 22, 25, 40,
46, 76, 84, 107, 108, 110, 119, 134, 350, 257,
264; and Egypt, 1–3, 39, 56, 127, 131, 133,
157–159, 179, 180, 187, 188, 191–194, 212,
219, 220, 222–224, 226, 227, 231, 234–236,
239, 249, 251, 255, 258; and Iraq, 25, 26; and
water problem, 32–34, 37, 41, 42, 44, 49–69;
and Palestinian problem, 43; and Israel, 57,
58, 60, 91, 159–166, 171, 174–184, 189–191,
196, 197, 201, 202, 234, 235; and Jordan,
117, 151, 153; and PLO, 72, 85, 86, 89, 100,
102, 114, 262; and Fatah, 92–95, 98,
103–106, 112, 115, 116; and UAC, 97, 120,
121, 124–128, 130, 135, 139, 142, 145–148,
154; and ADC, 134, 146; and PLA, 140, 141,
245; and UN, 162, 163; and Soviet Union,
167–170, 204–208

Tal, Isra'el, 55
Taqla, Philip (Lebanese foreign minister), 53, 122
Tass News Agency, 167–169
Tel Dan, 50, 57, 58

Thant, U (UN Secretary General), 157, 176, 185, 195, 201, 222
al-Thawra, 62, 166, 169

UN (United Nations), 7, 13, 130, 162, 165, 172, 174, 176, 188, 189, 191, 211; observers, 162; and the refugees, 29; and partition resolution, 15, 212, 216
UN General Assembly, 4, 9, 31, 35
UNEF (UN Emergency Forces), on the Egyptian border, ix, xii, xiii, 14, 43, 61, 129, 131, 132, 134, 158, 166, 171, 190, 194, 195, 198, 203, 231, 234–237, 239
United Arab Command (UAC), xvi, xvii, 5, 41, 45, 92, 119
UNSC (UN Security Council), 33, 36, 177, 207, 222, 243
West Bank, xi–xiii, xvii, 14, 31, 72, 194, 218, 220, 243, 244, 252, 258, 263; Palestinian state, 6, 15, 17, 76, 78, 104, 216, 245, 246, 255, 261, 264; Jordan's annexation of, 13, 18; and Jordan, 19, 20, 106–112, 124, 126, 131, 142, 151, 242, 245, 254, 256, 259, 260; and PLO, 73–75, 79, 80, 82, 84–90, 94; and Israel, 116–118, 144, 145, 218, 221, 234, 257

al-Yamani, Ahmad (a leader of the ANM), 75
Yariv, Aharon, 176

Zionism, 4, 9, 10, 11, 15, 19, 25, 29, 155, 223, 257
Zionist congress, 73
Zu'ayein Yusef (Syrian prime minister), 171, 223